OBJECT-RELATIONAL DATABASE DEVELOPMENT

A Plumber's Guide

ISBN 0-13-019460-3

9 780130 194602

Inform*i*x® Press

For a complete list of Informix Press titles, please visit
www.phptr.com or www.informix.com/ipress

Object-Relational Database Development

A Plumber's Guide

Paul Brown

Prentice Hall PTR
Upper Saddle River, New Jersey 07458
www.phptr.com

Library of Congress Cataloging-in-Publication Data

Brown, Paul Geoffrey, 1968-
    Object-relational database development : a plumber's guide / Paul G. Brown
        p. cm. -- (Prentice Hall PTR Informix series)
    Includes bibliographical references and index.
    ISBN 0-13-019460-3
      1. Database design. 2. Object-oriented databases. 3. Relational databases. I. Title. II. Series.

QA76.9.D26 B77 2001
005.75'6--dc21   00-049165

Editorial/Production Supervision: *Vincent Janoski*
Acquisitions Editor: *Miles Williams*
Editorial Assistant: *Richard Winkler*
Manufacturin Manager: *Alexis Heydt*
Cover Design Direction: *Jerry Votta*
Manager, Informix Press: *Judy Bowman*

Informix® Press

© 2001 by Prentice-Hall
Published by Prentice Hall PTR
Prentice-Hall, Inc.
Upper Saddle River, NJ 07458

Informix Press
Informix Software, Inc.
4100 Bohannon Drive
Menlo Park, CA 94025
http://www.informix.com/ipress
ipress@informix.com

Prentice Hall books are widely used by corporations and government agencies for training, marketing, and resale.

The publisher offers discounts on this book when ordered in bulk quantities. For more information, contact: Corporate Sales Department, Phone: 800-382-3419; Fax: 201-236-7141; E-mail: corpsales@prenhall.com; or write: Prentice Hall PTR, Corp. Sales Dept., One Lake Street, Upper Saddle River, NJ 07458.

The following are trademarks of Informix Corporation or its affliates, one or more of which may be registered in the U.S. or other jurisdications: INFORMIX®, Informix® DataBlade® Module, Informix's Dynamic Scalable Architecture, Informix® Illustra™ Server, InformixLink®, INFORMIX-4GL, INFORMIX-4GL Compiler, INFORMIX®-CLI, INFORMIX®-Connect, INFORMIX®-ESQL/C, INFORMIX®-MetaCube™, INFORMIX®-Mobile, INFORMIX®-NET, INFORMIX®-NewEra™, INFORMIX®-NewEra™ Viewpoint®, INFORMIX®-NewEra™ Viewpoint® Pro, INFORMIX®-OnLine, INFORMIX®-OnLine Dynamic Server™, INFORMIX®-OnLine Workgroup Server, INFORMIX®-OnLine Workstation, INFORMIX®-SE, INFORMIX®-SQL, Superview™, INFORMIX®-Universal Server

All products or services mentioned in this book are the trademarks or service marks of their respective companies or organizations.

Printed in the United States of America
10 9 8 7 6 5 4 3 2

ISBN 0-13-019460-3

Prentice-Hall International (UK) Limited, *London*
Prentice-Hall of Australia Pty. Limited, *Sydney*
Prentice-Hall Canada Inc., *Toronto*
Prentice-Hall Hispanoamericana, S.A., *Mexico*
Prentice-Hall of India Private Limited, *New Delhi*
Prentice-Hall of Japan, Inc., *Tokyo*
Prentice-Hall Asia Pte. Ltd.
Editora Prentice-Hall do Brasil, Ltda., *Rio de Janeiro*

For my Mother and Father

Contents

Foreword

Understanding how to use a new technology is as important as knowing what the new technology is. This book should help readers bridge that gap with object-relational databases.

It has been almost six years since extensible database engines left the lab and began to receive commercial attention. Just as it took relational database technology a number of years to become mainstream, object-relational databases are just today beginning to demonstrate their potential. But today, almost all mainstream DBMS vendors describe their products as being object-relational. Of course, there are huge differences in how well they implement the ideas.

Perhaps the chief difficulty with the technology has been a "forest-verses-trees" problem. Most developers understand that geographic data, and digital media, are becoming increasingly important. Hand-held, "gizmo" consumer devices are already capable of telling people where they are, anywhere on the globe, at any point in time, and Internet entrepreneurs can use this information to create an entire new class of personal information services.

Putting latitude/longitude points into database columns is therefore an obvious requirement. Similar demand for organizing digital content is driving the growth of a number of media asset management companies. But each of these examples is only a tree.

What has been less clear is how database extensibility solves all of these apparently unrelated problems. Extensibility, in our forest-and-trees analogy, is the forest. It is an abstract, software engineering idea about how to build a DBMS product that can contain lots of trees. To someone who has never seen a tree, or someone who has never seen a single extension, the idea of a forest—or an extensible database—is difficult to fathom.

This book describes the forest by showing readers lots and lots of trees, and explaining how they can add their own. Along the way, they will get a feeling for what the forest is all about.

And by the end of the book they will be able to add their own extensions to the database, and will have learned enough about object-relational technology to go about the task of building the next great wave of database applications.

—Michael Stonebraker

Preface

New technologies are useful to the extent that they enhance some human ability. Simple machines like levers, pulleys, and inclined planes are useful because they make us stronger: that is, they increase the amount of mass that an individual can lift. Information technology—computer hardware and the software running on it—makes us smarter by enhancing our abilities to remember, reason, and communicate.

Computer hardware and software enhances mental abilities because they do the following things extremely well.

- Store information. Computers can record enormous amounts of data, far more than a single person can remember. And a computer's powers of recall are quicker and more accurate than our own.
- Process information. Computers can make a tremendous number of simple deductions quickly and without mistakes. This allows them to process large amounts of raw data to create new knowledge: to produce an analytic summary or to extract a subset of information from it.
- Communicate. Computer networks are very efficient at making information available to widely distributed community of user. And computers can be used to create flexible, intuitive interfaces, helping users comprehend and manipulate information.

These properties account for the way computer systems, and particularly information management systems, have become an indispensable part of modern corporate life. In today's knowledge-based economy, companies are organized into networks of cooperating employees. Each interconnected employee's work assignment is a subtask of what the company as a whole is trying to accomplish. What ties employees together is the information they share. So coordinating employee efforts requires an effective and efficient information management system.

Taking this idea one step further, it is becoming increasingly common to consider your customers and partners as part of the network too. Over the next few years economic transactions between businesses will increasingly be handed electronically. Achieving this requires that businesses make internal information systems available to outside agencies.

The intent of this book is to describe a new information management technology, Object-Relational Database Management Systems software, and explain how to use it. Although most DBMS vendors lay claim to selling object-relational databases, Informix's Dynamic Server product possesses the most complete set of features combined with exceptional performance, scalability, and reliability.

Most readers will come to this book with a familiarity with Informix's earlier products. Some may be anxious about the changes the new technology brings, but hopefully, this book will convince them that everything they know is still valid and useful. For other readers, this will be their first exposure to both INFORMIX and to extensible DBMS technology. Many of these readers will be building information systems that make specific use of the new features.

At this time, most of the features and functionality described in this book are scheduled for inclusion in all mainstream DBMS products. Implementation details vary, but the idea that a database's data model can include more semantic information than is captured with a VARCHAR() has become mainstream. It is enshrined in the SQL-3 standard, and as we shall see it is supported by several open language standards.

Acknowledgments

This book is the product of four years of writing and rewriting. It began life as a handbook for Illustra consultants. As it evolved it has taken on considerably more heft and has benefited from the interest of many colleagues, customers, and friends.

I would first like to acknowledge the influence of Mike Stonebraker. The greatest insights are often those that appear most obvious in hindsight. The principles of extensible databases were implicit in the theoretical framework used to construct earlier relational DBMS products, but the software engineering involved was far from obvious. I am similarly indebted to the many writers on database topics whose insights I have benefited from: Ted Codd, Chris Date, Hugh Darwen, Joe Chelko, Tobey Teorey, and Jeffrey Ullman.

I am tremendously grateful for the interest and the efforts of many colleagues: most particularly, Jonathan Leffler, Jean Anderson, Don Payne, Jacques Roy, Billy "Spokey" Wheeler, and Bill White, all of whom read more than one chapter and provided valuable feedback. Many other colleagues, Charlie Bowen, Linas Cepele, Akmal Chaudhri, Dave Fafarman, Mark Mears, Elein Mustain, Chuck O'Neil, Mike Segel, Paul Taylor, all read sections and improved the book by their suggestions.

Miles Williams, Vincent Janoski, and all of the team at Prentice Hall have shown more patience than any author has a right to expect. They have contributed enormously and persevered with this project through my inconsistency.

If anything useful is present in these pages, it is thanks largely to these people. Errors that remain—and there are errors—are entirely my own.

Finally, I would like to acknowledge and thank my wife, Michele Fabrega. Writing a book on this scale has involved time management decisions that have been painful. But it would not have been possible without her patience, support, and understanding.

Introduction to Object-Relational Database Development

Overview

This book describes the *Object-Relational Database Management Systems (ORDBMS)* technology implemented in the *INFORMIX Dynamic Server (IDS)* product, and explains how to use it. This first chapter introduces the basic ideas behind object-relational, or extensible, DBMSs. It is intended as a road map to guide readers in their own exploration of the material.

We begin with a little historical background explaining the motivation behind an ORDBMS product such as IDS. At this early stage of the book, it is enough to say that ORDBMS technology significantly changes the way you should think about using a database. In contrast with the more byte-oriented *Relational DataBase Management System (RDBMS)* technology, an object-relational database organizes *the data and behavior of business objects* within an *abstract data model*. Object-Relational query statements deal with objects personal name, part, code, polygon and video, instead of `INTEGER`, `VARCHAR` or `DECIMAL` data values.

The chapter continues with a high-level description of the features and functionality of IDS. We introduce the *Object-Relational (OR)* data model, type and function extensibility, storage manager extensibility, and active database features. Later chapters of the book address each topic in more detail.

Moving along, we take a little time to examine how an ORDBMS is implemented internally. This digression is important because it provides a framework for understanding the best way to use the technology. An ORDBMS is a lot like an operating system. It manages resources such as memory, I/O, thread scheduling, and interprocess communications. Developers can acquire these resources from the ORDBMS for their own programs, which run under the control of the ORDBMS (instead of the operating system). Where the ORDBMS differs from a traditional operating system is in how it reorganizes its programs. Instead of running business logic, an ORDBMS executes it as part of a declarative query expression

We conclude this chapter with a brief description of the Movies-R-Us website—a sample database application—which provides many of this book's examples.

Evolution of Database Management Systems

The history of *DataBase Management Systems (DBMS)* is an evolutionary history. Each successive wave of innovation can be seen as a response either to some limiting aspect of the technology preceding it or to demands from new application domains. In economic terms, successful information technology lowers the costs incurred when implementing a solution to a particular problem. Lowering development costs increases the range of information management problems that can be dealt with in a cost-effective way, leading to new waves of systems development.

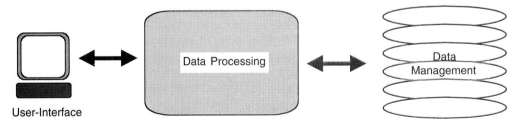

Figure 1–1. *Functional Decomposition of an Information System*

As an example of changing development costs, consider that early mainframe information systems became popular because they could make numerical calculations with unprecedented speed and accuracy (by the standards of the time). This had a major impact on how businesses managed financial assets and how engineering projects were undertaken.

It took another evolutionary step—the invention of higher level languages such as COBOL—to get to the point that the economic return from a production management system justified the development cost. It took still another innovation—the adoption of relational DBMSs—before customer management and human resource systems could be automated.

Today it is difficult to imagine how you could use COBOL and ISAM to build the number and variety of e-commerce Web sites that have sprung up over the last three years. And looking ahead, as we move into an era of ubiquitous, mobile computers and the growing importance of digital media, it is difficult to see how RDBMS technology can cope.

Early Information Systems

Pioneering information systems of the late 1960s and early 1970s were constrained by the capacity of the computers on which they ran. Hardware was relatively expensive, and by today's standards, quite limited. Consequently, considerable human effort was devoted to optimizing programming code. Diverting effort from functionality to efficiency constrained the ambition of early developers, but the diversion of effort was necessary because it was the only way to develop an information system that ran with adequate performance.

Information systems of this era were implemented as monolithic programs combining user-interface, data processing logic, and data management operations into a single executable on a single machine. Such programs intermingled low-level descriptions of data structure details— how records were laid out on disk, how records were interrelated—with user-interface management code. User-interface management code would dictate, for example, where an element from a disk record went on the screen. Maintaining and evolving these systems, even to perform tasks as simple as adding new data fields and indexes, required programmers to make changes involving most aspects of the system.

Experience has shown that development is the least expensive stage of an information system's life cycle. Programming and debugging take time and money, but by far the largest percentage of the total cost of an information system is incurred after it goes into production. As the business environment changes, there is considerable pressure to change systems with it. Changing a pre-relational information system, either to fix bugs or to make enhancements, is extremely difficult. Yet, there is always considerable pressure to do so. In addition, hardware constantly gets faster and cheaper.

A second problem with these early systems is that as their complexity increased, it became increasingly important to detect errors in the design stage. The most pervasive design problem was redundancy, which occurs when storage structure designs record an item of information twice.

Relational DataBase Management Systems

In 1970 an IBM researcher named Ted Codd wrote a paper that described a new approach to the management of "large shared data banks." In his paper Codd identifies two objectives for managing shared data. The first of these is *data independence*, which dictates that applications using a database be maintained independent of the physical details by which the database organizes itself. Second, he describes a series of rules to ensure that the shared data is *consistent* by eliminating any redundancy in the database's design.

Codd's paper deliberately ignores any consideration of how his model might be implemented. He was attempting to define an *abstraction* of the problem of information management: a general framework for thinking about and working with information.

The Relational Model Codd described had three parts: a data model, a means of expressing operations in a high-level language, and a set of design principles that ensured the elimination of certain kinds of redundant data problems. Codd's relational model views data as being stored in *tables* containing a variable number of *rows* (or records), each of which has a fixed number of *columns*. Something like a telephone directory or a registry of births, deaths, and marriages, is a good analogy for a table. Each entry contains different information but is identical in its form to all other entries of the same kind.

The relational model also describes a number of logical operations that could be performed over the data. These operations included a means of getting a subset of rows (all names in the telephone directory with the surname "Brown"), a subset of columns (just the name and number), or data from a combination of tables (a person who is married to a person with a particular phone number).

By borrowing mathematical techniques from predicate logic, Codd was able to derive a series of design principles that could be used to guarantee that the database's structure was free of the kinds of redundancy so problematic in other systems. Greatly expanded by later writers, these ideas formed the basis of the theory of normal forms. Properly applied, the system of normal form rules can ensure that the database's logical design is free of redundancy and, therefore, any possibility of anomalies in the data.

Relational Database Implementation

During the early 1970s, several parallel research projects set out to implement a working RDBMS. This turned out to be very hard. It wasn't until the late 1980s that RDBMS products worked acceptably in the kinds of high-end, online transactions processing applications served so well by earlier technologies.

Despite the technical shortcomings RDBMS technology exploded in popularity because even the earliest products made it cheaper, quicker, and easier to build information systems. For an increasing number of applications, economics favored spending more on hardware and less on people. RDBMS technology made it possible to develop information systems that, while desirable from a business management point of view, had been deemed too expensive.

To emphasize the difference between the relational and pre-relational approaches, a four hundred line C program can be replaced by the SQL-92 expression in Listing 1–1.

```
CREATE TABLE Employees (
    Name            VARCHAR(128),
    DOB             DATE,
    Salary          DECIMAL(10,2),
    Address         VARCHAR(128)
);
```

Listing 1–1. *Simple SQL-92 Translation of the Previous C Code*

The code in Listing 1–1 implements considerably more functionality than a C program because RDBMSs provide transactional guarantees for data changes. They automatically employ locking, logging, and backup and recovery facilities to guarantee the integrity of the data they store. Also, RDBMSs provide elaborate security features. Different tables in the same database can be made accessible only by different groups of users. All of this built-in functionality means that developers focus more of their effort on their system's functionality and less on complex technical details.

With today's RDBMSs, the simple Employees table we introduced in Listing 1–1 is more usually defined as shown in Listing 1–2.

```
CREATE TABLE Employees (
        FirstName       VARCHAR(32)     NOT NULL,
        Surname         VARCHAR(64)     NOT NULL,
        DOB             DATE            NOT NULL,
        Salary          DECIMAL(10,2)   NOT NULL
                              CHECK ( Salary > 0.0 ),
        Address_1       VARCHAR(64)     NOT NULL,
        Address_2       VARCHAR(64)     NOT NULL,
        City            VARCHAR(48)     NOT NULL,
        State           CHAR(2)         NOT NULL,
        ZipCode         INTEGER         NOT NULL,
              PRIMARY KEY ( Surname, FirstName, DOB )
);
```

Listing 1–2. *Regular SQL-92 Version of the Employees Table*

Today the global market for RDBMS software, services, and applications that use relational databases exceeds $50 billion annually. SQL-92 databases remain a simple, familiar, and flexible model for managing most kinds of business data. The engineering inside modern relational database systems enables them to achieve acceptable performance levels in terms of both data throughput and query response times over very large amounts of information.

Problems with RDBMSs

Starting in the late 1980s, several deficiencies in relational DBMS products began receiving a lot of attention. The first deficiency is that the dominant relational language, SQL-92, is limiting in several important respects. For instance, SQL-92 supports a restricted set of built-in types that accommodate only numbers and strings, but many database applications began to include deal with complex objects such as geographic points, text, and digital signal data. A related problem concerns how this data is used. Conceptually simple questions involving complex data structures turn into lengthy SQL-92 queries.

The second deficiency is that the relational model suffers from certain structural shortcomings. Relational tables are flat and do not provide good support for nested structures, such as sets and arrays. Also, certain kinds of relationships, such as subtyping, between database objects are hard to represent in the model. (Subtyping occurs when we say that one kind of thing, such as a SalesPerson, is a subtype of another kid of thing, such as an Employee.) SQL-92 supports only independent tables of rows and columns.

The third deficiency is that RDBMS technology did not take advantage of object-oriented (OO) approaches to software engineering which have gained widespread acceptance in industry. OO techniques reduce development costs and improve information system quality by adopting an object-centric view of software development. This involves integrating the data and behavior of a real-world entity into a single software module or *component*. A complex data structure or algorithmically sophisticated operation can be hidden behind a set of interfaces. This allows another programmer to make use of the complex functionality without having to understand how it is implemented.

The relational model did a pretty good job handling most information management problems. But for an emerging class of problems RDBMS technology could be improved upon.

Object-Oriented DBMS

Object-Oriented Database Management Systems (OODBMS) are an extension of OO programming language techniques into the field of persistent data management. For many applications, the performance, flexibility, and development cost of OODBMSs are significantly better than RDBMSs or ORDBMSs. The chief advantage of OODBMSs lies in the way they can achieve a tighter integration between OO languages and the DBMS. Indeed, the main standards body for OODBMSs, the Object Database Management Group (ODMG) defines an OODBMS as a system that integrates database capabilities with object-oriented programming language capabilities.

The idea behind this is that so far as an application developer is concerned, it would be useful to ignore not only questions of how an object is implemented behind its interface, but also how it is stored and retrieved. All developers have to do is implement their application using their favorite OO programming language, such as C++, Smalltalk, or Java, and the OODBMS takes care of data caching, concurrency control, and disk storage.

In addition to this seamless integration, OODBMSs possess a number of interesting and useful features derived mainly from the object model. In order to solve the finite type system problem that constrains SQL-92, most OODBMSs feature an *extensible* type system. Using this technique, an OODBMS can take the complex objects that are part of the application and store them directly. An OODBMS can be used to invoke methods on these objects, either through a direct call to the object or through a query interface. And finally, many of the structural deficiencies in SQL-92 are overcome by the use of OO ideas such as inheritance and allowing sets and arrays.

OODBMS products saw a surge of academic and commercial interest in the early 1990s, and today the annual global market for OODBMS products runs at about $50 million per year. In many application domains, most notably computer-aided design or manufacturing (CAD/CAM), the expense of building a monolithic system to manage both database and application is balanced by the kinds of performance such systems deliver.

Problems with OODBMS

Regrettably, much of the considerable energy of the OODBMS community has been expended relearning the lessons of twenty years ago. First, OODBMS vendors have rediscovered the difficulties of tying database design too closely to application design. Maintaining and evolving an OODBMS-based information system is an arduous undertaking. Second, they relearned that declarative languages such as SQL-92 bring such tremendous productivity gains that organizations will pay for the additional computational resources they require. You can always buy hardware, but not time. Third, they re-discovered the fact that a lack of a standard data model leads to design errors and inconsistencies.

In spite of these shortcomings OODBMS technology provides effective solutions to a range of data management problems. Many ideas pioneered by OODBMSs have proven themselves to be very useful and are also found in ORDBMSs. Object-relational systems include features such as complex object extensibility, encapsulation, inheritance, and better interfaces to OO languages.

Object-Relational DBMS

ORDBMSs synthesize the features of RDBMSs with the best ideas of OODBMSs.

- Although ORDBMSs reuse the relational model as SQL interprets it, the OR data model is opened up in novel ways. New data types and functions can be implemented using general-purpose languages such as C and Java. In other words, ORDBMSs allow developers to embed new classes of data objects into the relational data model abstraction.

- ORDBMS schema have additional features not present in RDBMS schema. Several OO structural features such as inheritance and polymorphism are part of the OR data model.
- ORDBMSs adopt the RDBMS query-centric approach to data management. All data access in an ORDBMS is handled with declarative SQL statements. There is no procedural, or object-at-a-time, navigational interface. ORDBMSs persist with the idea of a data language that is fundamentally declarative, and therefore mismatched with procedural OO host languages. This significantly affects the internal design of the ORDBMS engine, and it has profound implications for the interfaces developers use to access the database.
- From a systems architecture point of view, ORDBMSs are implemented as a central server program rather than as a distributed data architectures typical in OODBMS products. However, ORDBMSs extend the functionality of DBMS products significantly, and an information system using an ORDBMS can be deployed over multiple machines.

To see what this looks such as, consider again the Employees example. Using an ORDBMS, you would represent this data as shown in Listing 1–3.

```
CREATE TABLE Employees (
            Name            PersonName       NOT NULL,
            DOB             DATE             NOT NULL,
            Salary          Currency         NOT NULL,
            Address         StreetAddress    NOT NULL
                            PRIMARY KEY ( Name, DOB )
);
```

Listing 1–3. *Object-Relational Version of Employees Table*

For readers familiar with relational databases, this CREATE TABLE statement should be reassuringly familiar. An object-relational table is structurally very similar to its relational counterpart and the same data integrity and physical organization rules can be enforced over it. The difference between object-relational and relational tables can be seen in the section stipulating column types. In the object-relational table, readers familiar with RDBMSs should recognize the DATE type, but the other column types are completely new. From an object-oriented point of view, these types correspond to class names, which are software modules that encapsulate state and (as we shall see) behavior.

As another example of the ORDBMS data model's new functionality, consider a company supplying skilled temporary workers at short notice. Such a company would need to record each employee's resumes, the geographic location where they live, and a set of Periods (fixed intervals in the time line) during which they are available, in addition to the regular employee information. Listing 1–4 illustrates how this is done.

```
CREATE TABLE Temporary_Employees (
        Resume          DOCUMENT              NOT NULL,
        LivesAt         GEOPOINT              NOT NULL,
        Booked          SET( Period NOT NULL )
) UNDER Employees;
```

Listing 1–4. *Object-Relational Version of the Temporary_Employees Table* [1]

Readers familiar with earlier RDBMS releases of Informix Dynamic Server (IDS) will also be struck by the use of the UNDER keyword. UNDER signifies that the Temporary_Employees table inherits from the Employees table. All the columns in the Employee table are also in the Temporary_Employees table, and the rows in the Temporary_Employees table can be accessed through the Employee table.

Answering business questions about temporary employees requires that the information system be able to support concepts such as "Is Point in Circle," "Is Word in Document," and "Is some Period Available given some set of Booked Periods." In the IDS product such behaviors are added to the query language. In Listing 1–5, we present a query demonstrating OR-SQL.

"Show me the names of Temporary Employees living within 60 miles of the coordinates (-122.514, 37.221), whose resumes include references to both INFORMIX and 'database administrator,' and who are not booked for the period between today and seven days ahead."

```
SELECT Print(E.Name)
   FROM Temporary_Employees E
   WHERE Contains (GeoCircle('(-122.514, 37.221)',
                              '60 miles')),
                   E.LivesAt )
       AND DocContains ( E.Resume,
                         'INFORMIX and Database Administrator')
       AND NOT IsBooked ( Period(TODAY, TODAY + 7), E.Booked );
```

Listing 1–5. *Object-Relational Query against the Employees Table*

---

[1] Note that this is illegal syntax. This figure is intended to illustrate a data modeling principle, rather than to demonstrate a use of OR-SQL. Refer to Chapter 2 for more details.

Again, many readers will be familiar with the general form of this SELECT statement. But this query contains no expressions that are defined in the SQL-92 language standard. In addition to accommodating new data structures, an ORDBMS can integrate logic implementing the behavior associated with the objects. Each expression, or *function name*, in this query corresponds to a behaviorial interface defined for one of the object classes mentioned in the table's creation. Developing an object-relational database means integrating whatever the application needs into the ORDBMS.

The examples in Listings 1–5 and 1–6 are both obvious extensions of SQL. But an ORDBMS is extensible in other ways too. Tables in an object-relational database can be more than data storage structures. They can be active interfaces to external data or functionality. This allows you, for example, to integrate software that interfaces with a paging system directly into the ORDBMS, and use it as shown in Listing 1–6.

"Send a page to all Temporary_Employees living within 60 miles of the coordinates (-122.514, 37.221), whose resumes includes references to both INFORMIX and 'database administrator,' and who are not booked for the period between today and seven days ahead."

```
INSERT INTO SendPage
( Pager_Number, Pass_Code, Message )
 SELECT E.Pager_Number,
        E.Pass_Code,
        Print(E.Name) ||
    ': Call 1-800-TEMPS-R-US for immediate INFORMIX DBA job'
   FROM Temporary_Employees E
  WHERE Contains (GeoCircle('(-122.514, 37.221)',
                            '60 miles')),
        E.LivesAt )
    AND DocContains ( E.Resume,
                      'INFORMIX and Database Administrator')
    AND NOT IsBooked ( Period(TODAY, TODAY + 7), E.Booked );
```

Listing 1–6. *Object-Relational Query Illustrating External Systems Integration*

In a SQL-92 DBMS, SendPage could be only a table. The effect of this query would then be to insert some rows into the SendPage table. However, in an ORDBMS, SendPage might actually be an active table, which is an interface to the communications system used to send electronic messages. The effect of this query would then be to communicate with the matching temporary workers!

Object-Relational DBMS Applications

Extensible databases provide a significant boost for developers building traditional business data processing applications. By implementing a database that constitutes a better model of the application's problem domain the information system can be made to provide more flexibility and functionality at lower development cost. Business questions such as the one in Listing 1–6 might be answered in systems using an SQL-92 and C. Doing so, however, involves a more complex implementation and requires considerably more effort.

The more important effect of the technology is that it makes it possible to build information systems to address data management problems usually considered to be too difficult. In Table 1–1, we present a list of applications that early adopters of ORDBMS technology have built successfully. Other technology changes are accelerating demand for these kinds of systems.

One way to characterize applications in which an object-relational DBMS is the best platform is to focus on the kind of data involved. For thirty years, software engineers have used the term "data entry" to describe the process by which information enters the system. Human users *enter* data using a keyboard. Today many information systems employ electronics to capture information. Video cameras, environmental sensors, and specialized monitoring equipment record data in rich media systems, industrial routing applications, and medical imaging systems. Object-relational DBMS technology excels at this kind of application.

It would be a mistake to say that ORDBMSs are only good for digital content applications. As we shall see in this book OR techniques provide considerable advantages over more low-level RDBMS approaches even in traditional business data processing applications. But as other technology changes move us towards applications in which data is *recorded* rather than *entered*, ORDBMSs will become increasingly necessary.

ORDBMS Concepts and Terminology

In this section, we introduce some of the terminology used to describe extensible database technology. For reference purposes, this book also includes a glossary that defines much of the language you will encounter. Subject areas corresponding to each heading in this section are covered in much more detail in later chapters. Note that this book goes beyond merely describing ORDBMS technology. It also contains

Table 1–1. Extensible Database Problem Domains

Application Domain	Description
Complex data analysis	You can integrate sophisticated statistical and special purpose analytic algorithms into the ORDBMS and use them in knowledge discovery or data mining applications. For example, it is possible to answer questions such as "Which attribute of my potential customers indicates most strongly that they will spend money with me?"
Text and documents	Simple cases, such as Listing 1–5, permit you to find all documents that include some word or phrase. More complex uses would include creating a network that reflected similarity between documents.
Digital asset management	The ORDBMS can manage digital media such as video, audio, and still images. In this context, manage means more than store and retrieve. It also means "convert format," "detect scene changes in video and extract first frame from new scene," and even "What MP3 audio tracks do I have that include this sound?"
Geographic data	For traditional applications, this might involve "Show me the lat/long coordinates corresponding to this street address." This might be extended to answer requests such as "Show me all house and contents policy holders within a quarter mile of a tidal water body." For next-generation applications, with a GPS device integrated with a cellular phone, it might even be able to answer the perpetual puzzler "Car 54, where are you?"
Bio-medical	Modern medicine gathers lots of digital signal data such as CAT scans and ultrasound imagery. In the simplest case, you can use these images to filter out "all cell cultures with probable abnormality." In the more advanced uses, you can also answer questions such as "show me all the cardiograms which are 'like' this cardiogram."

chapters dealing with subjects such as OR database analysis and schema design, as well as the detailed ins and outs of writing your own user-defined extensions.

Data Model

A data model is a way of thinking about data, and the object-relational data model amounts to *objects in a relational framework*. An ORDBMS's chief task is to provide a flexible framework for organizing and manipulating software objects corresponding to real-world phenomenon.

The object-relational data model can be broken into three areas:

- Structural Features. This aspect of the data model deals with how a database's data can be structured or organized.
- Manipulation. Because a single data set often needs to support multiple user views, and because data values need to be continually updated to reflect the state of the world, the data model provides a means to manipulate data.
- Integrity and Security. A DBMS's data model allows the developers to declare rules that ensure the correctness of the data values in the database.

In the first two chapters of this book, we introduce and describe the features of an ORDBMS that developers use to build information systems. We then spend two chapters describing the second important aspect of the ORDBMS data model: user-defined type and function extensibility.

Enhanced Table Structures

An OR database consists of group a of tables made up of rows. All rows in a table are structurally identical in that they all consist of a fixed number of values of specific *data types* stored in columns that are named as part of the table's definition. The most important distinction between SQL-92 tables and object-relational database tables is the way that ORDBMS columns are not limited to a standardized set of data types. Figure 1–2 illustrates what an object-relational table looks like.

The first thing to note about this table is the way that its column headings consist of both a name and a data type. Second, note how several columns have internal structure. In a SQL-92 DBMS, such structure would be broken up into several separate columns, and operations over a data value such as Employee's Name would need to list every component column. Third, this table contains several instances of unconventional data types. LivesAt is a geographic point, which is a latitude/longitude pair that describes a position on the globe. Resume contains documents, which is a kind of Binary Large Object (BLOB).

Employees

Name::PersonName	DOB::date	Address::MailAddress	LivesAt::Point	Resume::Document
('Einstein','Albert')	03-14-1879	('12 Gehrenstrasse . .)	'(-127.4, 45.1)'	'Physics, theoretical
('Curie','Marie')	11-07-1867	('19a Rue de Seine . .)	'(-115.3, 27.5)'	'Physics, experimental
('Planck','Max')	04-23-1858	('153 Volkenstrasse .)	'(-121.8, 31.1)'	'Physics, experimental
('Hilbert','David')	01-23-1862	('10 Geneva Avenue .)	'(-119.2,37.81)'	'Mathematics, politics

Figure 1–2. *Structure and Data for an Object-Relational Table*

In addition to defining the structure of a table, you can include integrity constraints in its definition. Tables should all have a *key*, which is a subset of attributes whose data values can never be repeated in the table. Keys are not absolutely required as part of the table's definition, but they are a very good idea. A table can have several keys, but only one of these is granted the title of *primary key*. In our example table, the combination of the Name and DOB columns contains data values that are unique within the table. On balance, it is far more likely that an end user made a data entry mistake than two employees share names and dates of birth.

Object-Oriented Schema Features

Another difference between relational DBMSs and ORDBMSs is the way in which object-relational database schema supports features co-opted from object-oriented approaches to software engineering. We have already seen that an object-relational table can contain exotic data types. In addition, object-relational tables can be organized into new kinds of relationships, and a table's columns can contain sets of data objects.

In an ORDBMS, tables can be *typed*; that is, developers can create a table with a record structure that corresponds to the definition of a data type. The type system includes a notion of *inheritance* in which data types can be organized into hierarchies. This naturally supplies a mechanism whereby tables can be arranged into hierarchies too. Figure 1–3 illustrates how the Employees table in Figure 1–2 might look as part of such a hierarchy.

In most object-oriented development environments, the concept of inheritance is limited to the structure and behavior of object classes.

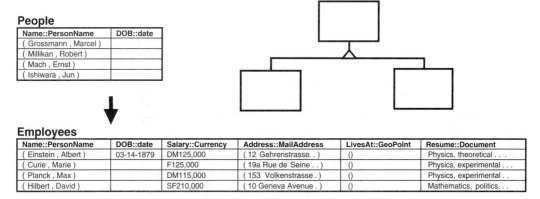

People

Name::PersonName	DOB::date
(Grossmann , Marcel)	
(Millikan , Robert)	
(Mach , Ernst)	
(Ishiwara , Jun)	

Employees

Name::PersonName	DOB::date	Salary::Currency	Address::MailAddress	LivesAt::GeoPoint	Resume::Document
(Einstein , Albert)	03-14-1879	DM125,000	(12 Gehrenstrasse. .)	()	Physics, theoretical . . .
(Curie , Marie)		F125,000	(19a Rue de Seine . .)	()	Physics, experimental . . .
(Planck , Max)		DM115,000	(153 Volkenstrasse .)	()	Physics, experimental . .
(Hilbert , David)		SF210,000	(10 Geneva Avenue .)	()	Mathematics, politics. . .

Figure 1–3. *Inheritance in an Object-Relational Database*

However, in an object-relational database, queries can address data values through the hierarchy. When you write an OR-SQL statement that addresses a table, all the records in its subtables become involved in the query too.

Another difference between ORDBMSs and traditional relational DBMSs can be seen in the Booked column of the Temporary_Employees table. The table in Figure 1–4 illustrates how this might look.

SQL-92 DBMS columns can contain at most one data value. This is called the *first normal form* constraint. In a traditional RDBMS, situations in which a group of values are combined into a single data object, are handled by creating an entirely separate table to store the group. In an ORDBMS this group of values can be carried in rows using a *COLLECTION*, which can contain multiple data values.

In Chapter 2 we explain how to create table hierarchies and tables with COLLECTION columns. In Chapter 3 we explain how they are integrated into the query language, and in Chapter 4, we explain the part they play in the extensible type system.

The ORDBMS data model is considerably richer than the RDBMS data model. Unfortunately, this new richness complicates database design. There are more alternative designs that can be used to represent a particular situation, and it is not always obvious which to pick. Unthinkingly applying some of these features, such as the COLLECTION columns, creates problems. However there are data modeling problems for which a COLLECTION is an elegant solution. An important objective of this book is to provide some guidance on the subject of object-relational database design. Chapters 8 and 9 are devoted to questions of analysis and design.

Extensibility: User-Defined Types and User-Defined Functions

The concept of *extensibility* is a principal innovation of ORDBMS technology. One of the problems you encounter developing information systems using SQL-92 is that modeling complex data structures and implementing

Temporary_Employees

Name::PersonName	DOB::date	Booked::SET(Period NOT NULL)
('Szilard','Leo')	'2/11/1898'	{ '[6/15/1943 – 6/21/1943]','[8/21/1943 – 9/22/1943]'}
('Fermi','Enrico')	'9/29/1901'	{ '[6/10/1938 – 10/10/1939]','[6/15/1943 – 12/1/1945]', '[9/15/1951 – 9/21/1951]' }

Figure 1–4. *Non-First Normal Form (nested Relational) Table Structure*

complex functions can be difficult. One way to deal with this problem is for the DBMS vendor to build more data types and functions into their products. Because the number of interesting new data types is very large, however, this is not a reasonable solution. A better approach is to build the DBMS engine so that it can accept the addition of new, application-specific functionality.

Developers can specialize or extend many of the features of an ORDBMS: the data types, OR-SQL expressions, the aggregates, and so on. In fact, it is useful to think of the core ORDBMS as being a kind of software backplane, which is a framework into which specialized software modules are embedded.

Data Types

SQL-92 specifies the syntax and behavior for about ten data types. SQL-3, the next revision of the language, standardizes perhaps a hundred more, including geographic, temporal, text types, and so on. Support for these common extensions is provided in the form of commercial DataBlade™ products. A separate tutorial in this book described the range of currently shipping DataBlade™ products.

However, relying on the DBMS vendor to supply all of the innovation does not address the fundamental problem. Reality is indifferent to programming language standards. With an object-relational DBMS developers can implement their own application specific data types and the behavior that goes with them. Table 1–2 lists some of the expressions added to the OR-SQL language to handle a geographic quadrilateral data type (an object with four corner points and parallel opposite edges).

Table 1–2. Data Type Extensibility: Partial List of Functions for Geographic Quadrilateral Data Type

Data Type: GeoQuad

Expression:	Explanation:	Example Query:
GeoQuad(GeoPoint, GeoPoint)	Constructor function. Takes two corner points and produces a new Quadrilateral data type instance.	`INSERT INTO QuadTable VALUES ( GeoQuad ( '(0,0)', '(10,10)' ) );`

(continued)

Data Type: GeoQuad

Expression:	Explanation:	Example Query:

GeoQuad (double, double, double, double)	Constructor function. Takes four doubles that correspond to the X and Y values of the lower left and upper right corner.	`SELECT GeoQuad (MIN(X),`
		`                 MIN(Y),`
		`                 MAX(X),`
		`                 MAX(Y)  )`
		`  FROM Locations;`

Contains (GeoPoint, GeoQuad)	Operator function. Returns true if the first point falls within the geographic extent of the quadrilateral.	`SELECT COUNT(*)`
		`  FROM QuadTable T`
		` WHERE Contains(`
		`          '(5,5)',`
		
		`          T.Quad);`

Union (GeoQuad, GeoQuad)	Support function that computes a new quadrilateral based on the furthest corners of the two quadrilaterals inputs.	Used internally by the ORDBMS as part of R-Tree indexing.
GeoQuad (String)	Constructor function. Creates new GeoQuad using the string. A symmetric function implements the reverse.	Used to convert literal strings in queries into the internal format for the type.
GeoQuad (String)	Constructor function. Creates new GeoQuad using the string. A symmetric function implements the reverse.	Used to convert literal strings in queries into the internal format for the type.

To extend the ORDBMS with the GeoQuad type introduced in Table 1–2, a programmer would:

1. Implement each function in one of the supported procedural languages: C, Java, or SPL.
2. Compile those programs into runnable modules (shared executable libraries or Java JAR files) and place the files somewhere that the ORDBMS can read them.
3. Declare them to the database using the kind of syntax shown in Listing 1–7.

```
CREATE OPAQUE TYPE GeoQuad (
     internallength = 32
);
--
CREATE FUNCTION GeoQuad ( lvarchar )
RETURNING GeoQuad
WITH ( NOT VARIANT,
       PARALLELIZABLE )
EXTERNAL NAME
"$INFORMIXDIR/extend/2DSpat/2DSpat.bld(GeoQuadInput)"
LANGUAGE C;
--
CREATE CAST ( lvarchar AS GeoQuad WITH GeoQuad );
--
CREATE FUNCTION GeoQuad ( double precision,
     double precision,
     double precision,
     double precision )
RETURNING GeoQuad
WITH ( NOT VARIANT,
       PARALLELIZABLE )
EXTERNAL NAME
"$INFORMIXDIR/extend/2DSpat/2DSpat.bld(GeoQuadFromDoubles)"
LANGUAGE C;
```

Listing 1–7. *Data Type Extensibility: Partial SQL Declaration of User-Defined Data Type with External Implementation in C*

In Chapters 4 and 5, we describe the extent of this functionality, and in Chapter 10, we spend considerable time on the question of how to use C to implement the fastest possible data type extensions. A special Java tutorial explores how to achieve the same thing using the Java™ language, and the SQL-J standard.

SQL-92 includes some general-purpose analytic features through its aggregates (MIN, MAX, COUNT, AVG, and so on). Aggregate functions can be used in conjunction with other aspects of SQL-92 to answer questions about groups of data. For example, the query in Listing 1–8 uses the SQL-92 table to find out what is the mean salary of each group of Employees in different cities.

"What is the average salary of Employees for each of the cities where they live?"

```
SELECT E.City,
       AVG(E.Salary)
  FROM Employees E
 GROUP BY E.City;
```

Listing 1–8. *Simple Analysis Query Using a SQL-92 Aggregate Function*

The range of aggregates in SQL-92 is limited. In data mining, and in the larger field of statistical analysis, researchers have described a tremendous number of useful analytic algorithms. For example, it might make more sense to calculate the median salary, rather than the mean salary, in the query above. Or it might be more useful to create a histogram showing how many employees fall into certain ranges of salaries. SQL-92 does not provide the means to answer such analytic questions directly. With the ORDBMS, however, these algorithms can be integrated into the server and used in the same way as built-in aggregates.

The OR-SQL query in Listing 1–9 uses the Employees table defined in Listing 1–4. It calculates the correlation between the number of words in an Employees resume and his or her salary.

"What is the correlation coefficient between Employee salaries and the number of words in their resumes?"

```
SELECT Correlation ( E.Salary,  WordCount( E.Resume ) )
  FROM Employees E;
```

Listing 1–9. *Analysis Query with a User-Defined Aggregate (Correlation)*

In this book we take the view that an aggregate is a special kind of function, so we introduce the idea in Chapter 6. However, much of the detailed material external C description in Chapter 10 is also relevant to user-defined aggregates.

Database Stored Procedures

Almost all RDBMSs allow you to create database procedures that implement business processes. This allows developers to move considerable portions of an information system's total functionality into the DBMS. Although centralizing CPU and memory requirements on a single machine can limit scalability, in many situations it can improve the system's overall throughput and simplify its management.

By implementing application objects within the server, using Java, for examples, it becomes possible, though not always desirable, to push code implementing one of an application-level object's behaviors into the ORDBMS. The interface in the external program simply passes the work back into the IDS engine. Figure 1–5 represents the contrasting approaches. An important point to remember is that with Java, the same logic can be deployed either within the ORDBMS or within an external program without changing the code in any way, or even recompiling it.

In Chapter 6, we introduce the novel idea that the ORDBMS can be used to implement many of the operational features of certain kinds of middleware. Routine extensibility, and particularly the way it can provide the kind of functionality illustrated in Figure 1–5, is a practical application of these ideas. But making such system scalable requires using other features of the ORDBMS: the distributed database functionality, commercially available gateways, and the open storage manager (introduced below). Combining these facilities provides the kind of *location transparency* necessary for the development of distributed information systems.

Storage Management

Traditionally the main purpose of a DBMS was to centralize and organize data storage. A DBMS program ran on a single, large machine. It would take blocks of that machine's disk space under its control and store data in them. Over time, RDBMS products came to include ever more sophisticated data structures and ever more efficient techniques for memory caching, data scanning, and storage of large data objects.

In spite of these improvements, only a fraction of an organization's data can ever be brought together into one physical location. Data is often distributed among many systems, which is the consequence of autonomous information systems development using a variety of technologies, or through organizational mergers, or because the data is simply not suitable for storage in any DBMS. To address this, the IDS product adds a new extensible storage management facility. In Figure 1–6, we illustrate this *Virtual Table Interface* concept.

ORDBMSs possess storage manager facilities similar to RDBMSs. Disk space is taken under the control of the ORDBMS, and data is written into it according to whatever administrative rules are specified. All the indexing, query processing, and cache management techniques that are part of an RDBMS are also used in an ORDBMS. Further, distributed database techniques can be adapted to incorporate user-defined types and functions. However, all of these mechanisms must be re-implemented to generalize them so that they can work for user-defined types. For example, page management is generalized to cope with variable length OPAQUE type objects.

You can also integrate code into the engine to implement an entirely new storage manager. Developers still use OR-SQL as the primary interface to this data, but instead of relying on internal storage, the ORDBMS can use the external file system to store data. Any data set that can be represented as a table can be accessed using this technique.

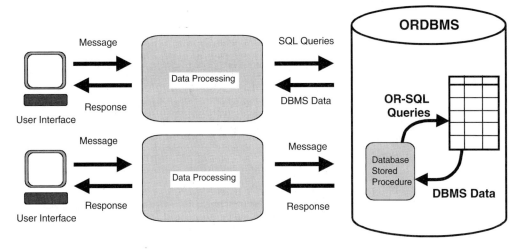

Figure 1–5. *Routine Extensibility and the ORDBMS as the Object-Server Architecture*

Developers can also use this technique to get a snapshot of the current state of live information. It is possible to represent the current state of the operating system's processes or the current state of the file system as a table. You can imagine, for example, an application intended to help manage a fleet of trucks and employees servicing air conditioners or elevators. Each truck has a device combining a Global Positioning System (GPS) with a cellular phone that allows a central service to poll all trucks and to have them "phone in" their current location. With the ORDBMS, you can embed Java code that activates the paging and response service to implement a virtual table, and then write queries over this new table, as shown in Listing 1–10.

"Find repair trucks and drivers within '50 miles' of 'Alan Turing' who are qualified to repair the 'T-20' air conditioning unit."

```
SELECT T.Location, T.DriversName
  FROM Trucks T, Customers C
 WHERE Distance (T.Location, C.Location) < '50 miles'
   AND C.Name = 'Alan Turing'
   AND DocContains ( T.DriverQualifications,
                     'Repair for T-20');
```

Listing 1–10. *Query Reaching to Data Outside the ORDBMS*

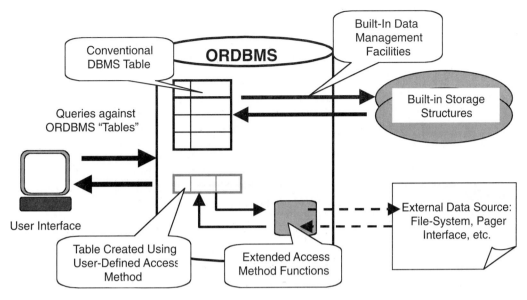

Figure 1–6. *Extensible Storage Manager*

This functionality should fundamentally change the way you think about a DBMS. In an object-relational DBMS, SQL becomes the medium used to combine components to perform operations on data. Most data will be stored on a local disk under the control of the DBMS, but that is not necessarily the case.

The Virtual Table Interface tutorial describes these features in more detail.

Distributed Deployment

Often the volume of data in a single information system, or the workload imposed by its users, is too much for any one computer. Storing shared data, and providing efficient access to it, requires that the system be *partitioned* or *distributed* across several machines. Combining extensibility with distributed database features makes new system architectures possible. This concept is illustrated in Figure 1–7.

This figure illustrates a Web site configuration. A large central machine contains canonical copies of all data. Surrounding it is a cloud of other, smaller installations. These might cache replicated (read only) copies of a sub-set of the total data. All this data and all the modules of logic implementing the various extended types and functions can be queried from everywhere. The effect of this kind of architecture is to distribute the load across several machines, without compromising from data integrity.

In Chapter 6, we discuss the distributed query and replication features that make this kind of deployment possible.

Ad-Hoc Query Language

You manipulate data stored in an ORDBMS using an extended version of the SQL declarative data language that we call OR-SQL. OR-SQL is a reasonably complete implementation of a *declarative relational language.* We say it is *declarative* because OR-SQL expressions describe *what* it is that is wanted, rather than a procedural, step-by-step algorithm defining *how* the task is to be accomplished. OR-SQL expressions are strings that the ORDBMS can parse, optimize, and execute at runtime.

We say OR-SQL is *relational* because it expresses operations over relational schema objects such as tables and views. OR-SQL statements are *value-oriented.* Queries make no reference to physical data management details, such as pointers, or to memory management. In fact, the same OR-SQL statement can be processed internally by the ORDBMS in many different ways. The actual operational schedule depends on factors such as the physical configuration of the database, the presence of indices on certain columns, the number of rows the ORDBMS needs to manage at various stages of the query processing, and so on.

Using declarative, value-oriented interfaces to database data distinguishes ORDBMSs from most OODBMSs. OODBMSs traditionally rejected query-centric interfaces as being too cumbersome. Recently, the OODBMS community has moved to embrace the Object Query Language (OQL) as a standard declarative interface to their systems.[2] But OR-SQL is such likely to be the dominant language because SQL is "inter-galactic database speak."

The OR-SQL implemented in IDS is a very different language from what is described in the SQL-92 language standard. The SQL-92 standard provides a definition for an entire language: a grammar, keywords, a set of data types, and a list of language expressions that can be used with these types. The OR-SQL philosophy is somewhat different. Although the

---

[2] It is worth noting that whether this turns them into object-relational systems is still an open question. The internal design of an ORDBMS is greatly influenced by the need to support declarative operations in a transactional system. Retrofitting either of these functions to a system that was not designed primarily to support them has been shown to be extremely difficult.

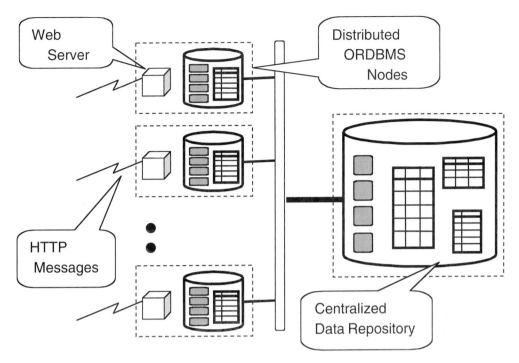

Figure 1–7. *Distributed Information System Deployment*

same four basic data operations present in SQL-92—INSERT, DELETE, UPDATE and SELECT—form the basis of OR-SQL, the rest of the language is left "as an exercise for the implementor."

Listings 1–5 and 1–10 show examples of ORDBMS SELECT queries. In Listing 1–11, we introduce several queries that manipulate data.

"Delete the record associated with Employee Marie Curie."

```
DELETE FROM Employees
  WHERE Name = PersonName('Curie','Marie')
    AND DOB  = '11-07-1866';
```

"Update Albert Einstein's Employee record with a new resume taken from the supplied file."

```
UPDATE Employees
    SET Resume = GetDocument('C:\temp\Albert.doc',
                             'client')
  WHERE Name = PersonName('Einstein','Albert')
    AND DOB  = '03-14-1879';
```

"Insert an Employee record for 'Ernst Mach'."

```
INSERT INTO Employees
( Name, DOB, Salary, Address, Resume, LivesAt, Booked )
VALUES
( PersonName('Mach','Ernst'),
  '03-18-1838',
  Currency(120000.00,'DM'),
  Address('123 Gehrenstrasse',
          'Berlin','GERMANY', 8485),
  GetDocument('C:\temp\Albert.doc','client'),
  '(11.54, 47.6722 )'::GeoPoint,
  SET()
);
```

Listing 1–11. *SQL Write Queries*

Chapter 2 and Chapter 3 describe OR-SQL in detail. Numerous examples throughout this book illustrate different kinds of query expressions. Readers wanting more information on how to write OR-SQL are advised to consult the many books on SQL-92. Obviously, these books overlook OR-SQL specific issues, but the way they generally talk about using SQL remains valid.

Application Programming Interfaces

There is always more to an information system than a database. Other, external programs are responsible for communication and for managing user interfaces. An information system will use a variety of languages to implement the non-DBMS parts of the final system. Consequently, there are several mechanisms for handling *applications programming interfaces (API)*.

OR-SQL queries can be embedded into external programs and then passed into the ORDBMS at runtime. In return, the ORDBMS sends result data to the external program. Another, very powerful way to use SQL is to write logic that actually creates SQL queries based on end-user input. Tools such as Microsoft Access, although they do not take advantage of many of the innovative features described in this book, epitomize this approach.

The most traditional API approach involves embedding OR-SQL statements directly into C programs and using a pre-parser to turn embedded OR-SQL into a procedural program. More recent approaches involve functional interfaces such as ODBC and the JDBC standard for Java programs. For Web applications, you can use mark-up tags that convey to the Web server that a OR-SQL query needs to be executed and its results formatted according to a set of mark-up rules.

We describe three of these interfaces, ESQL/C, JDBC and the Web Blade, in detail in Chapter 7. Another interface—the Server API, or SAPI—is used by C logic executing within the ORDBMS. We do not cover the SAPI OR-SQL facilities in this book.

ORDBMS Advantages

Why is all of this useful? What advantages does this give you? ORDBMS technology improves upon what came before it in three ways.

The first improvement is that can enhance a system's overall *performance*. The IDS product can achieve higher levels of data throughput or better response times than is possible using RDBMS technology and external logic because ORDBMS extensibility makes it possible to move logic to where the data resides, instead of always moving data to where the logic is running. This effect is particularly pronounced for data-intensive applications such as decision support systems and in situations in which the objects in your application are large, such as digital signal or time series data. But in general, any application can benefit.

The second improvement relates to the way that integrating functional aspects of the information system within the framework provided by the ORDBMS improves the *flexibility* of the overall system. Multiple unrelated object definitions can be combined within a single ORDBMS database. At runtime, they can be mingled within a query expression created to answer some high-level question. Such flexibility is very important because it reduces the costs associated with information system development and ongoing maintenance.

The third benefit of an ORDBMS relates to the way information systems are built and managed. An ORDBMS's system catalogs become a metadata repository that records information about the modules of programming logic integrated into the ORDBMS. Over time, as new functionality is added to the application and as the programming staff changes, the system's catalogs can be used to determine the extent of the current system's functionality and how it all fits together.

The fourth benefit is that the IDS product's features makes it possible to incorporate into the database data sets that are stored outside it. This allows you to build federated databases. From within single servers, you can access data distributed over multiple places.

In this section of the chapter, we explain each advantage in detail and in turn.

Performance

It is important to understand that in a well-implemented extensible DBMS, the code you embed within it does not run on a client machine or in a middle-ware layer wrapped around the database core. Rather, the code runs inside the ORDBMS engine, as close as possible to where the data is stored. Figure 1–8 illustrates the difference.

The diagram on the left illustrates how procedural logic and relational databases are deployed today. Consider what happens when you need to apply some kind of complex logic to distinguish interesting rows in a table from uninteresting ones. Achieving this with SQL-92 requires that each row retrieved from the DBMS be filtered using logic in the middle-ware. On the right, the OR approach is presented. Here, the filtering logic is embedded within the ORDBMS and invoked as part of query processing.

Moving logic into the ORDBMS can have significant performance benefits. To explain why, we first need to introduce some of the basic performance properties of computer systems. Table 1–3 lists the approximate latencies of several common, low-level operations. Each row of this table corresponds to a data movement operation, and each latency time reflects the average amount of time taken to perform the operation on 1 K of data. You can think of these as per-operation taxes paid to the operating environment and computer hardware.

Some of these numbers are fairly obvious and are included as references. Their relative sizes are due to the fundamental physics involved.

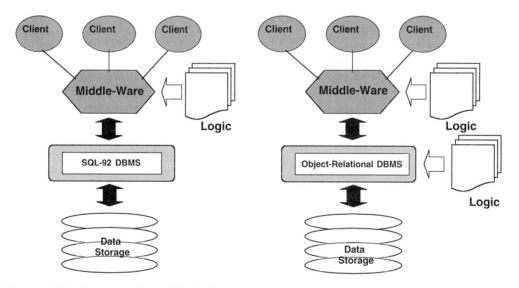

Figure 1–8. *Alternative Extensible Architectures*

Table 1–3. Latency Timings for Low-Level Data Movement Operations

Operation	Typical Mechanism Involved	~Latency (secs)
Random disk read or write	fopen(), read(), write(), seek(), and so on	0.01
Local area network (LAN)	Sockets	0.000 1
Interprocess communication	pipes and shared memory	0.000 001
Block memory copy	Memcpy	0.000 000 01

The reason that it takes such an enormous amount of time (relatively speaking) to move data from magnetic disk into physical memory is because this is the only stage in the data management food chain that involves mechanical movement. At the other extreme, mempy() compiles down to a handful of low-level instructions that are executed very quickly.[3]

Between these extremes, moving data across a local-area network requires that you involve your computer's operating system, which in turn needs to interact with the networking hardware, and then the remote computer's operating system, often many times. Similarly, the time taken even to move data between two processes running on the same computer is significantly longer than the memcpy(). This is due to the operating system's mediation of the exchange. Such a transfer involves many more instructions and necessitates several process context switches.

The implication of this is obvious: the less you move data, the less overhead you incur, and the better your overall system performs. Of course, some data movement is unavoidable. Data must travel from its disk storage to where the user's eyeballs can see it. A good design principle to adopt, however, is to position the functional modules of your system in such a way that you minimize the volume of data being moved about by the information system's workload.

By providing the ability to host more procedural logic adjacent to the data, the ORDBMS opens up new possibilities, especially in the newer kinds of applications.

---

[3] Register caching on modern CPUs is adding another level of performance difference. In general it can be 10 to 100 times as expensive to read data from RAM than from a register.

Working an Example

A major financial customer saw the performance possibilities of
ORDBMSs early. Their problem was in calculating the value of certain
complex financial instruments. Slightly simplified, the data they were
dealing with was stored as shown in Listing 1–12.

```
CREATE TABLE Instruments (
                ID            INTEGER        NOT NULL PRIMARY KEY,
                Portfolio     INTEGER        NOT NULL,
                Issuer        VARCHAR(32)    NOT NULL,
                Issuer_Class  CHAR(4)        NOT NULL,
                Principal     MONEY          NOT NULL,
                Issue_Date    DATE           NOT NULL,
                Rate          FLOAT          NOT NULL
);
```

Listing 1–12. *Table for Financial Instrument Data*

The primary purpose of the application was to how much a particular portfolio (a set of instruments) was worth. Calculating this value
required figuring out the value of each instrument in the portfolio on
some date, and then adding up all the values. To solve this problem,
they wrote the program in Listing 1–13.

```
dec_t *
CalculatePortfolioValue (
EXEC SQL BEGIN DECLARE SECTION;
PARAMATER integer Portfolio_Argument;

EXEC SQL END DECLARE SECTION;
{
    EXEC SQL BEGIN DECLARE SECTION;
            dec_t  * decTotal;
    EXEC SQL BEGIN DECLARE SECTION;
    DecTotal = malloc( sizeof(dec_t) );

EXEC SQL DECLARE Curs1 CURSOR FOR
    SELECT Issuer_Class,
           Principal,
           Issue_Date,
           Rate
      FROM Instruments
     WHERE Portfolio = :Portfolio_Argument;

    EXEC SQL OPEN UpdCurs1 Curs;
    while(1)
```

```
        {
                EXEC SQL FETCH Upd_Curs INTO
                :chIssuer,:decPrincipal, :nIssueDate, :fRate;
                if ((ret = exp_chk("fetch", 1)) == 100)
                        break;
                decTotal = decadd ( decTotal,
                                CalcValue (chIssuer, decPrincipal,
                        nIssueDate, fRate ));
        }
        EXEC SQL Close Curs1;
        return decTotal;
        }
```

Listing 1–13. *External Code for Portfolio Calculation*

Figuring out how much something is worth is never simple. The most valuable part of this program was the CalcValue() function, which we do not show here. CalcValue() was quite complex (and secret) because the firm had figured out how to incorporates the risk of the issuer defaulting into its calculations of an instrument's value. Government instruments, having no risk of default, generate predictable income. On the other hand, debt issued by riskier organizations tends to have higher nominal returns, but sometimes the lender may go broke. Intuitively, you consider money deposited in a bank account quite differently from money lent to an unreliable relative.

Internally, CalcValue() used a number of rather sophisticated mathematical procedures. These made it extremely difficult to implement the calculation using the stored procedure language.[4]

The financial firm's idea was to take that CalcValue() function and to integrate it into IDS. This reduced the whole code fragment in Listing 1–13 to what is shown in Listing 1–14.

"What is the total value of Instruments in portfolio X?"
```
        SELECT SUM ( CalcValue (Issuer_Class,
                                        Principal,
                                        Issue_Date,
                                        Rate
                                ))
        FROM Instruments
        WHERE Portfolio =:Portfolio_Argument;
```

Listing 1–14. *Object-Relational SQL for Portfolio Calculation*

---

[4] For the record, these were linear algebra operations: find the dot product of a matrix of correlation coefficients and a vector of values supplied with the instrument.

The performance improvement was spectacular. Calculating a portfolio's value was reduced from about two hours to about ten minutes. The difference was entirely due to the reduction in data movement, and also to the way that the ORDBMS could take advantage of parallelism while processing this query. Instead of moving all the matching rows from the Instruments table out of the DBMS, the calculation was instead performed "in place."

Flexibility and Functionality

Explaining flexibility is more difficult because the advantages of flexibility are harder to quantify. But it is probably more valuable than performance over the long run. To understand why, let's continue with the financial company example.

As it turned out, the more profound result of the integration effort undertaken by our financial firm was that the CalcValue() operation was liberated from its procedural setting. Before, developers had to write and compile (and debug) a procedural C program every time they wanted to use CalcValue() to answer a business question. With the ORDBMS, they found that they could simply write a new OR-SQL query instead. For example, the query in Listing 1–15 is a join involving a table that, while in the database, was beyond the scope of the original (portfolio) problem.

"What is the SUM() of the values of instruments in our portfolio grouped by region and sector?"

```
SELECT IS.Country,
       IS.Region,
       SUM( CalcValue ( I.Issuer_Class,
                        I.Principal,
                        I.Issue_Date,
                        I.Rate
            ))
  FROM Instruments I, Issuers IS
 WHERE I.Portfolio = :Portfolio_Argument
   AND I.Issuer    =  IS.Name
 GROUP BY IS.Country, IS.Region;
```

Listing 1–15. *Object-Relational SQL for Portfolio Calculation*

With the addition of a small Web front end, end users could use the database to find out which was the most valuable instrument in their portfolio or which issuer's instruments performed most poorly, and so on. It was known that the system had the data necessary to answer all these questions before. The problem was that the cost of answering them using C and SQL-92 was simply too high.

Maintainability

After some investigation, the developers discovered that, over time, there had been several versions of the CalcValue() function. Also, once the CalcValue() algorithm was explained to end users, they had suggestions that might improve it. With the previous system, such speculative changes were extremely difficult to implement. They required a recode-recompile-relink-redistribute cycle. But with the ORDBMS, the alternative algorithms could be integrated with ease. In fact, none of the components of the overall information system had to be brought down. The developers simply wrote the alternative function in C, compiled it into a shared library, and dynamically linked it into the engine with another name.

What all of this demonstrates is that the ORDBMS permitted the financial services company to react to changing business requirements far more rapidly than it could before. By embedding the most valuable modules of logic into a declarative language, they reduced the amount of code they had to write and the amount of time required to implement new system functionality. None of this was interesting when viewed through the narrow perspective of system performance. But is made a tremendous difference to the business's operational efficiency.

Systems Architecture Possibilities

Having implemented several such functions, the next problem confronting the development team was that although their system worked fine, it would be more useful to include data that was stored in another database. In fact, because their operations were international, they needed to transfer data across significant distances and convert data along the way. Bulk copy and load was considered unfeasible, because the remote data was volatile, and although intersite queries were rare, accurate answers were critical.

None of the other groups wanted to migrate off their efficient and stable production systems. The basic problem was that the data lived "out there" in flat files, in another information system, or in another DBMS. Nonetheless, the local business users still wanted to access it.

As an experiment, the developers decided to use the external data access features of the ORDBMS to turn it into a federated database system. Achieving this required a mix of technologies. First, simply getting to the data was a problem. In one case, the data lived in an RDBMS. Fortunately the ORDBMS product possessed a *gateway* to the other RDBMS. However, the more difficult problem was currency conversion, which was achieved by including routines to perform the translation in the ORDBMS.

Another data set was stored in a text file and manipulated by a set of Perl programs. Incorporating this into the database was harder. You might move the flat-file implementation entirely into the ORDBMS, but that would require a rewrite of the Perl scripts. In the end, the developers wrote a very simple interface that created a new storage manager to understand the external file's format and to make its data available through OR-SQL within the ORDBMS. Once this development was complete, the final system looked something like Figure 1–5.

ORDBMS Engineering

Another way to answer the question "What is an ORDBMS?" is to describe how an OR engine is constructed. An ORDBMS is an example of what is known as a *component-centric software system*. It works by allowing developers to combine many different extensions within the framework it provides. In this section, we explain how an ORDBMS works by describing how it processes a query. Along the way, we show you how integrated extensions are managed.

Processing an Object-Relational Query

When it receives an OR-SQL query, the ORDBMS breaks it up into a series of smaller, simpler operations. Each simple operation corresponds to an algorithm that manipulates a set of row data in some way. An important part of what the ORDBMS does is optimizing these operations. Optimization involves ordering the sequence to minimize the total amount of computer resources needed to resolve the query. Consider the query in Listing 1–16.

"Show me the names of Employees born on January 1st, 1967, and print the list in name order."

```
SELECT E.Name
   FROM Employees E
   WHERE E.DOB    = '01-01-1967'
   ORDER BY E.Name;
```

Listing 1–16. *SQL Example*

A ORDBMS query processor parses this query and converts it internally into a series of steps, as shown in Listing 1–17.

```
1.    TABLESCAN( Employees,
                      (DOB = '01-01-1967) )
2.    PROJECT(1., Name)
3.    SORT(2., Name)
```

Listing 1–17. *Query Plan*

In Step 1 of the series, the ORDBMS scans all records in the Employees table. If the record satisfies the predicate that is supplied as the second argument to the TABLESCAN operation (DOB = '01-01-1967'), the matching record is passed into Step 2. In Step 2 the Name column is stripped out of the record and a list consisting of just the names of matching employees is passed into Step 3. In this final step, the names are sorted. The ordered result, the consequence of three separate operations, is returned to the user who submitted the query in the first place.

Clearly, there are many opportunities for optimizations here. For example, if an index existed on the Employees.DOB column, the database may elect to use an INDEXSCAN rather than the TABLESCAN. Also, it might be advantageous to use a slightly different plan that strips out Name and DOB query processing *before* checking if the date-of-birth matches.

The complete list of operations—TABLESCAN, INDEXSCAN, PROJECT, JOIN, SORT, UNION, and so on—is quite extensive, and the IDS product includes several different algorithms for performing the same logical operation. Consider the sorting operation, for example. In Don Knuth's *The Art of Computer Programming Vol. 3: Sorting and Searching*, the author describes over a dozen sorting algorithms, each with slightly different properties. Some work better when the data fits into main memory and others are more efficient when the data must be written to disk. One of the query planner's tasks is to figure out which of the alternate algorithms is the best one in any given circumstance.

ORDBMS Evolution from RDBMS

Let's look at sorting in more detail. One of the most popular sort algorithms is a called *insertion sort*. Insertion sort is an O (N^2) algorithm. Roughly speaking, the time it takes to sort an array of records increases with the square of the number of records involved, so it should only be used for record sets containing less than about 25 rows. But insertion sort is extremely efficient when the input is almost in sorted order, such as when you are sorting the result of an index scan.

Listing 1–18 presents an implementation of the basic insertion sort algorithm for an array of integers.

```
InsertSort( integer arTypeInput[] )
{
    integer      nTypeTemp;
    integer      InSizeArray, nOuter, nInner;

    nSizeArray = arTypeInput[].getSize();

    for ( nOuter = 2; nOuter <= nSizeArray; nOuter ++)   {
            vTypeTemp = arTypeInput[nOuter];
            nInner = nOuter - 1;

            while (( nInner > 0 ) &&
                    (arTypeInput[nInner] > vTypeTemp)) {
                    arTypeInput[nInner+1] = arTypeInput[nInner];
                    nInner--;
            }

            arTypeInput[nInner+1] = vTypeTemp;
    }
}
```

Listing 1–18. *Straight Insertion Sort Algorithm*

Sorting algorithms such as this can be generalized to make them work with any data type. A generalized version of this insert sort algorithm appears in Listing 1–19. All this algorithm requires is logic to compare two type instances. If one value is greater, the algorithm swaps the two values.

In the generalized version of the algorithm, a *function pointer* is passed into the sort as an argument. A function pointer is simply a reference to a memory address where the Compare() function's actual implementation can be found. At the critical point, when the algorithm decides whether to swap two values, it passes the data to this function and makes its decision based on the function's return result.

```
InsertSort( Type arTypeInput[],
            (int) Compare( Type, Type) )
{
    Type            vTypeTemp;
    integer InSizeArray, nOuter, nInner;

    nSizeArray = arTypeInput[].getSize();

    for ( nOuter = 2; nOuter <= nSizeArray; nOuter ++)
      {
```

```
            vTypeTemp = arTypeInput[nOuter];
            nInner = nOuter - 1;
            while (( nInner > 0 ) &&
                Compare(arTypeInput[nInner],vTypeTemp) > 0 )
            {
              Swap(arTypeInput[nInner+1],arTypeInput[nInner]);
              nInner--;
            }
            Swap(arTypeInput[nInner+1], vTypeTemp);
            }
    }
```

Listing 1–19. *Generalized Sort Algorithm*

Note how the functionality of the Swap() operation is something that
can be handled by IDS without requiring a type specific routine. The
ORDBMS knows how big the object being swapped is, and whether the
object is in memory or is written out to disk. To use the generalized
algorithm in Listing 1–19, all that IDS needs is the Compare() logic.
The ORDBMS handles the looping, branching, and exception handling.

Almost all sorting algorithms involve looping and branching
around a Compare(), as does B-Tree indexing and aggregate algorithms such as MIN() and MAX(). Part of the process of extending the
ORDBMS framework with new data types involves creating functions
such as Compare() that IDS can use to manage instances of the type.

All data management operations implemented in the ORDBMS are
generalized in this way. In an RDBMS, the number of data types was
small so that the Compare() routines for each could be hard-coded
within the engine. When a query such as the one in Listing 1–16 was
received, Step 3 of the query execution plan would involve a call to a
function that looked like that which is contained in Listing 1–20.

The first two arguments to this function are a pointer to the records
to be sorted and a pointer to a structure that specifies that part of the
records should be sorted. Within this function, the engine calls the
InsertSort routine introduced above, and passes in the same array of
records it received. In addition, however, it passes a pointer to the
appropriate compare function for the built-in type.

```
Sort( void ** parRecords, IFX_TYPE * pRecKey ... )
{
switch(pRecKey->typenum)
    {
        case IFX_INT_TYPE:
        case IFX_CHAR_TYPE:
          InsertSort(parRecords, IntCompare);
        break;
```

```
    case IFX_FLOAT_TYPE:
        InsertSort(parRecords, DoubleCompare);
    break;
        // etc for each SQL-92 type
    default:
        ifx_internal_raiseerror('No Such Type');
    break;
    }
}
```

Listing 1–20. *SQL-92 Sort Utility*

How does an ORDBMS know what to pass into the InsertSort() routine? To turn an RDBMS into an ORDBMS, you need to modify the code shown in Listing 1–20 to allow the engine to access `Compare()` routines other than the ones it has built-in. If the data type passed as the second argument is one of the SQL-92 types, the sorting function proceeds as it did before. But if the data type is not one of the SQL-92 types, the ORDBMS assumes it is being asked to sort an extended type.

Every user-defined function embedded within the ORDBMS is recorded in its *system catalogs*, which are tables that the DBMS uses to store information about databases. When asked to sort a pile of records using a user-defined type, the ORDBMS looks in these system catalogs to find a user-defined function called `compare` that takes two instances of the type and returns an `INTEGER`. If such a function exists, the ORDBMS uses it in place of a built-in logic. If the function is not found, IDS generates an exception. Listing 1–21 shows the modified sorting facility.

```
Sort( void ** parRecords, IFX_TYPE * pRecKey . . . )
{
    switch(pRecKey->typenum)
  {
    case IFX_INT_TYPE:
    case IFX_CHAR_TYPE:
      InsertSort(parRecords, IntCompare);
    break;
    case IFX_FLOAT_TYPE:
     InsertSort (parRecords, DoubleCompare);
     break;
    // etc for each SQL-92 type
     . .
    default: // ah! Not SQL-92. Must be user-defined.
      if( (pUDRCompare=udr_lookup(pRecKey->typenum,
```

```
                                        "Compare")) ==NULL)
            ifx_internal_error("No Such Function.');
        else
            InsertSort (parRecords, pUDRCompare );
        break;
    }
}
```

Listing 1–21. *ORDBMS Generalization of the Sort Utility*

Using the ORDBMS generalization of the sort utility has several
implications:

* When you take a database application developed to use the previous generation of RDBMS technology and upgrade to an ORDBMS,
  you should see no changes at all. The size of the ORDBMS executable is slightly increased, and there are some new directories and
  install options, but if all you do is to run the RDBMS application on
  the ORDBMS, the new code and facilities are never invoked.
* This scheme implies extensive modifications to the RDBMS code. You
  not only need to find every place in the engine that such modifications are necessary, but also need to provide the infrastructure in the
  engine to allow the extensions to execute within it. In Chapter 10,
  we go into considerable detail about this execution environment.
* Finally, you should note how general such an extensibility mechanism is. As long as you can specify the structure of your data type,
  and define an algorithm to compare one instance of the type with
  another, you can use the engine's facilities to sort or index
  instances of the type, and you can use OR-SQL to specify how you
  want this done.

In practice, renovating an RDBMS in this manner is an incredibly
complex and demanding undertaking.

Data Storage in an ORDBMS

Data storage in an ORDBMS is more or less unchanged from what it
was in the RDBMS. Data is organized into pages. A set of pages (possibly very many) holds all data for a particular table. Blocks of memory
are reserved by the ORDBMS for caching frequently accessed pages to
avoid the cost of going to disk each time the page is touched. As data
is accessed through queries, pages are read from disk and ejected from
the memory cache.

Figure 1–9 illustrates how IDS combines data and logic at run-time. Whenever the ORDBMS invokes some user-defined logic (Foo() in this example) as part of query execution it first reads relevant data pages from disk into the memory cache. Changed pages, or infrequently accessed pages, may be written back to disk if the cache is full. As it invokes the logic, the ORDBMS passes pointers to the memory resident data as arguments.[5] The ORDBMS doesn't care what the function does, or how it does it. All it cares about is the logic's return value.

Each time a single execution of the embedded logic is completed, the ORDBMS is free to read more data from pages in memory and to invoke the logic again with different arguments. The important point is that the ORDBMS does not store the logic with the object data. It binds them together at run-time.

Later in this book we investigate certain aspects of data storage in considerable detail. Chapter 3, for instance, explains how new data types can be created, in Chapter 10, we describe the low-level facilities provided by the ORDBMS for 'C', and Tutorial 1 describes a number of details about IDS physical storage.

Large Object Data Storage

Large object data presents a particular set of challenges. Because extensible database applications tend to involve a lot of large data

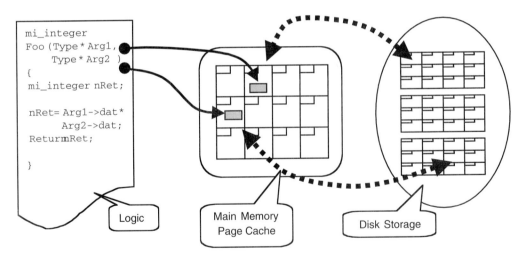

Figure 1–9. Overview of ORDBMS Table Data Store Management

---

[5] Actually, the ORDBMS first copies the data from the page to another memory location. This is done for performance and reliability reasons. User-defined logic is unable to affect what is on pages directly, and the ORDBMS would like to minimize the amount of time a page must be kept resident in the cache.

objects, dealing with them efficiently is particularly important. Data pages used for table records are relatively small: traditionally only a few kilobytes in size. Requiring that new types fit within these pages would be an unacceptable constraint, so IDS provides special mechanisms for supporting data objects of any size.

Storing large object data, such as the polygon corresponding to a state boundary, with table data, such as the state's name and current population, would result in a massive increase in the size of the table. Assuming that fewer queries access the large object data, such a strategy would dramatically increase the time taken to complete the majority of queries. Therefore, the ORDBMS separates the storage of large object data from table data. When a data object's value is stored as a large object only, a *handle for the large object* data is stored with the row. User-defined functions implementing behavior for large objects use this handle to open the large object and access its contents.

Figure 1–10 illustrates how the mechanism works. First, the table's data page is read from its storage location. If one of the table's columns contains a large data object, space in the record is reserved to hold a string that uniquely identifies a large object stored elsewhere on the local disk. Interface functions within the ORDBMS allow logic components to use this handle like a file name and to access bytes within the large object. This strategy makes it possible to combine large objects

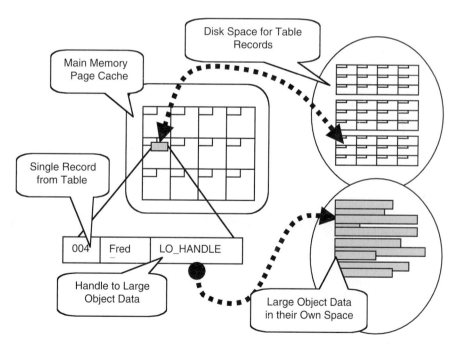

Figure 1–10. ORDBMS Management of Large Object Data

with more conventional data within a table's row and to embed logic that manipulates large object data into OR-SQL.

Development Example

This book is intended to be a practical manual of ORDBMS development, so throughout, we provide a great many examples. For consistency, almost all are drawn from a single application: a Web site providing information services about movies. The idea is to provide realistic demonstrations of how to use an ORDBMS and a body of working code to read and draw upon.

Movies-R-Us Web Site Description

This example system depicts a fairly typical electronic commerce (e-commerce) Web site. The primary purpose of the hypothetical site is promotional. The site contains information about the movies produced by various studios for release around the world. Site employees collect and organize marketing material, stills from the movie production process, off-cuts from editing, interviews with stars and movie makers, industry gossip, and so on. The site also sells promotional merchandise: t-shirts, mugs, compact discs, posters, and so on.

The mission of the Web site is to become a single point of reference for movie-going consumers. They can review new releases, find out about screening times and locations, and order merchandise. For example, a visitor to the site might begin by browsing new releases, plot synopses, ratings, and reviews. The visitor may elect to purchase some of the movie merchandise or ask the site for information about where and when the movie is playing. The user may offer reviews of the movies he or she has or join a cinema club through which the movie studio offers discounts.

Site Architecture

The Movies-R-Us Web site is split between a back-of-shop operation and front-of-shop operation. The only component shared by both halves of the system is the ORDBMS. The database mostly stores data used to service the demand of people visiting the site. These public users run a commercial *browser* that sends messages to the site and accepts marked-up pages to display in return. These pages contain content, such as digital image data and text, and sophisticated layout instructions. The browser formats the content according to the layout instructions. In addition, WWW technology includes support for features that allow the public users to upload information to the site. This data can then be inserted into the database.

Employees of the movie studio, on the other hand, use a broader variety of interfaces. They access the public site to review and test it, but they are heavier users of specialist tools for tasks such as multimedia content editing, inserting and updating material in the site, processing merchandising orders, and analyzing usage patterns.

The way that this single database supports multiple user views is consistent with our earlier observation of how database technology is used. Different employees of Movies-R-Us have different tasks relating to the site's data. Public users, depending on their status (whether they are members of the cinema club or have purchased merchandise in the past, for example) get different views of the site.

This set of requirements yields a site architecture that looks like Figure 1–11.

Included with this book is the complete set of source code used in the example. This source code includes the following:

- About a dozen complete database extensions, which are user-defined types and associated functions that implement various aspects of the overall system
- A set of scripts that create the schema within the ORDBMS
- A few rows of legitimate sample data for the Web Site schema, together with a body of reference data that populates other tables

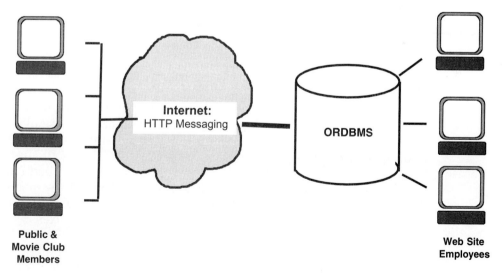

Figure 1–11. *Architecture of Movies-R-Us Web Site*

- Scripts to create bulk data to perform scalability tests on the database implementation
- A set of client-side examples that illustrate how to use the various APIs to interact with the ORDBMS

Structure of this Book

This book is divided into two sections. In the first section, consisting of Chapters 2 through 7, we describe the features and functionality of the ORDBMS in some detail. We explain the ORDBMS data model, query language, the basics of extensibility, certain ideas concerning middleware and the ORDBMS, and the APIs used to integrate the ORDBMS with other components of the overall information system.

Beginning in Chapter 8, we describe how to use these features to build a complete system. This second section describes a semi-formal approach or methodological road map to follow during development and digresses into several important subject areas that are meant for the consumption of programmers working with specialized aspects of the technology.

Along the way there are several tutorials. These are separated from the main body of the text because they are subjects that can stand alone and read at any time. They are included in the book because they cover topics of interest to both the beginning and advanced programmer. They may be skipped on a first reading.

Note on Development Philosophy

In addition to being a book about a specific software technology, this is a book that describes a unique, interesting and hopefully useful way of looking at the whole problem of information systems development. In his great 1905 paper that introduced the idea that light could be thought of as a particle, rather than a wave phenomenon, Albert Einstein referred to his insight as a heuristic viewpoint. By this, he meant that it was simply a different way of looking at the entire problem and useful to the extent that it helped resolve certain inconsistencies.

The design of this book is also guided by a heuristic viewpoint. We refer to the new idea as *organic* information system development. Historically, software engineers cycled through code-compile-deploy iterations when building information systems. Once deployed, an information system went into "maintenance." The problem with looking at development this way is that "maintenance" seems to consume the majority of development effort.

Organically developed information systems have no maintenance mode, and they are not monolithic systems that must be shut down when the time comes to upgrade them. Instead the approach calls for rapid response to changing end-user requirements by either combining pre-existing components in new ways (through OR-SQL) or adding new components to the system (using extensibility). In general, this can be accomplished without affecting other components or dependent programs. The result is an information system that *grows*, rather than one that is *developed* in the conventional sense.

Some readers will think, perhaps rightly, that this whole idea is just full of it. It is hoped that such readers can nevertheless learn something of interest in these pages.

Chapter Summary

In this chapter we have introduced object-relational DBMS technology, illustrated something of the role ORDBMSs will play in developing information systems to support the modern enterprise, and briefly described the major components of the technology. An ORDBMS

- is a data repository that can be extended to manage any kind of data and to organize any kind of data processing,
- represents the next logical step in the evolution of DBMS technology. It both preserves those aspects of relational DBMS technology that proved so successful (abstraction, parallelism, and transaction management) and augments the features with ideas, such as extensibility and advanced data modeling, derived from object-oriented approaches to software engineering,
- can be thought of as a *software back plane*, which is a general framework within which new pieces can be integrated as occasion demands.

We began this book by explaining the importance of information systems to modern organizations. Information systems use database technology for storing, communicating and analyzing information. In fact, database technology is so useful that it has become essential for running large, modern enterprises.

We then reviewed the history of DBMS technology and noted the way that information systems have had to become both increasingly flexible (because of their support for abstracted interfaces and declarative queries) and increasingly capable of coping with complexity in modern times through component based development. In a sense, Object-Relational DBMS (ORDBMS) represents the next logical step in this continuing evolution. An ORDBMS combines the RDBMS capabilities for flexibility with an object-oriented DBMS's capacity for extensibility into a single system.

We then moved on to describe the main technological features of an ORDBMS. First, we described the ORDBMS data model. We introduced inheritance and polymorphism, which are two features derived from object-oriented approaches to software engineering. Then we introduced the most important object-oriented concept, extensibility, which allows you to extend the basic framework of the ORDBMS with your own problematic domain-specific objects. Finally, we examined the dynamic query language interface that lets you combine the data stored in the database schema with the extension code.

Looked at as a whole, these technical innovations provide two key advantages. First, by moving code to data rather than data to code, you get significant performance advantages. Second, because the software modules comprising your information system are available through a declarative interface, the result is a far more flexible system. Instead of being obliged to write large amounts of procedural C, C++, or Java code, you can use the declarative query language to answer business questions.

We continued this chapter with a brief examination of the software engineering required to turn an RDBMS style of engine into an ORDBMS. An RDBMS implements a large number of data processing algorithms such as sorting, indexing, and so on. These algorithms consist of some looping, branching, and exception handling code built around a handful of lower level operations such as `Compare()` and `Swap()`. To generalize an RDBMS, you need to make the engine capable of using the `Compare()`-style routines that developers implement instead of only the built-in semantics of the language. Not only does this make complete extensibility possible, but also it makes the problem of upgrading to the new technology less of an issue. If you already have a SQL-92 engine, your existing database application should not need to execute any of the new code!

Finally, we gave a brief overview of the contents and structure of this book, which now awaits your further exploration.

Facts, Tables, and Schema: The Object-Relational Data Model

Introduction: Data Models

The primary function of any database is to supply developers and end users with a logical view of a body of information that represents their *problem domain*. All DBMS products provide facilities to structure such information and make it available for external access, and collectively these features constitute the DBMS's *data model*.

In practical terms, an ORDBMS is a tool that developers use to create central *databases* of the kind required by Movies-R-Us. A single database may be used by a number of *applications*, each of which reflects the set of tasks undertaken by employees, to answer questions about

- the *state of the world*, such as "When is John Wayne's birthday?" , "What Cinemas within '30 Miles' of a movie club member's location are showing a 'Classic Western'?" and "How has the average inventory value of a particular item of Merchandise changed over time?"
- the *structure of the problem domain*, such as "What information describes a Movie?", "How are Merchandise items related to MovieClubMembers?" and "How do I add a new Order?"

Databases are *abstractions*. Loosely speaking, abstraction involves ignoring less-important aspects of some phenomenon in order to focus on other, more important aspects. Abstraction is helpful for coming to grips with the complexities of the real world that information systems are built to help manage, and abstraction is used by software developers in that they can encapsulate sophisticated algorithmic details behind a single entry point.

The ORDBMS makes use of abstraction in many ways. In this chapter we introduce the logical, schema-level structural features of the ORDBMS data model as implemented in the IDS product. In later chapters we explain how information in an IDS database is accessed and manipulated, and we explore the lower-level features that provide support for embedding new objects within a logical schema.

Object-Relational Databases and Data Models

The OR model, which is closely derived from the relational model, enables developers to do the following:

- Define or construct database *schema* corresponding to the structure of the data in the Universe of Discourse (UoD). A schema consists of a set of tables and views that store information and rules that govern relationships among them.
- Answer questions about the database structure. In other words, the ORDBMS needs to store *metadata*, or data about the data structure, in a useful format. Metadata is recorded in system catalogs.
- Provide for multiple, overlapping user views of the data that change over time. Relational and Object-Relational DBMS products support an *ad hoc* query mechanism for retrieving and manipulating data stored in the database.
- Tune the structures for performance. In theory, developers should not have to pay any attention to physical details. A perfect DBMS would perform all storage related tasks efficiently and automatically. In practice, physical data management is very important, and requires human intervention.

Readers should be familiar with host or schema features. In the IDS ORDBMS, object instances are stored in *tables*. Each table contains a number of *rows* (or records). Every row in a table has the same structure, that is, a set of named, typed *attributes* (or columns). As with SQL-92 DBMSs, tables possess *keys* that are used to uniquely identify rows within a table and to manage relationships between tables.

However, the ORDBMS data model extends SQL-92 considerably. It incorporates many features from object-oriented data models, including COLLECTIONs, inheritance, and polymorphism. The most important object-oriented concept implemented in the ORDBMS is the idea of an extensible type system. Although we defer discussion of this topic to Chapters 4 and 5, readers should be aware that the mechanism by which new object classes are introduced into the ORDBMS is almost completely orthogonal to the logical schema features. Traditional, SQL-92 tables are perfectly acceptable OR-SQL tables, and you can incorporate user-defined types and functions into your ORDBMS not found anywhere in the database schema.

In Chapters 2 and 3, we focus on how the ORDBMS dynamic query language OR-SQL is used to organize and manipulate information.

Chapter Overview

In the first, short section of this chapter, we introduce the theoretical concepts underlying data model features such as tables, rows, and attributes. You will learn that an object-relational data model implements some of the original relational model ideas better than RDBMSs supporting SQL-92. The bulk of the material here consists of an extensive examination of those portions of the extended SQL language used to define object-relational schema. The portions include how to create tables, define integrity rules, administer and maintain schema, provide security, and so on.

In the next chapter, we move on to show how to manipulate the data stored in an ORDBMS database. Even though SQL-92 possesses a relatively small set of core features, in practice it is a very large and powerful language, even when applied to SQL-92 databases. Because of its extensibility, OR-SQL is even more powerful.

The Object-Relational Data Model

Understanding a little of the theory underpinning object-relational technology is very useful when working with the ORDBMS. Readers familiar with relational theory will realize what a small step it is from the relational to the object-relational data model. Those with a background in object-oriented software development learn how OO techniques fit into the relational approach.

Further, we noted earlier that the data model provided with the ORDBMS is closer to the spirit of the original relational theory than SQL-92 DBMSs. Implementing the relational model more completely influences how we think about database management. Far from being a dull-witted but efficient storage manager for bits and bytes, an ORDBMS is a venue for structuring complex objects and reasoning around them with a declarative language.

Structural Features of the Relational Model

Dr. Edward Codd, an IBM Mathematician, introduced the relational model in his 1970 paper, "A Relational Model of Data for Large Shared Data Banks," which was published in the *Communications of the ACM*. In this paper, Codd describes certain problems that plagued the information systems being developed at the time. He then proposed his novel solution: the relational model. Fundamentally, the relational model is *a way of thinking about data*. For Codd, implementation questions were an afterthought.

The first problem that his model addressed was data and application interdependence. Pre-relational information systems were characterized by a tight coupling between all of the various functional components of the system, which included the user interface, data processing logic, and data storage. In extreme cases this resulted in the entire system being implemented as a single, monolithic program, which made it difficult and expensive to modify or extend.

Codd's relational model attempted to provide a degree of *data independence*. Rather than having the screen management logic knowing that the eight-byte field, which was at byte offset 36 in file IM_ACCOUNT, contained the address of the record containing the customer's details, he thought it better to adopt an abstracted logical view or data.

The second issue that his model addressed was *data consistency*. Before the relational model, developers had no formal methods for ensuring the correctness and consistency of data in their systems. There was no way to check that any one piece of information was recorded just once. If an item of information is recorded more than once and someone tries to modify, there is no guarantee it will be modified everywhere. This inevitably leads to errors in the data that in turn causes mistakes in the real world.

Codd envisioned a centralized database system in which rules guaranteeing data correctness could be enforced as part of the database's design. The relational model provides a set of principles for analyzing database structures to discover when the possibility for error exists in the system, and it provides formal remedies to eliminate such problems.

Since 1971 the relational model has undergone considerable evolution in response to the changing demands placed on DBMSs by developers. Modern versions of the relational model include concepts such as inheritance, three-value logic, and, of course, domain extensibility. Even today, however, the greatest strength of the relational model lies in the way it provides developers with a framework for addressing the problems of correctness and flexibility.

Mathematical Basis of the Relational Model

As its name suggests, the relational model is based on the logical/mathematical idea of a *relation*. A mathematical relation is literally a "relationship among instances of groups." For example, mathematicians say that the relation "less than" exists for certain pairs of integers ({1, 2}, { 2, 3 } . . . {*N, N+M* }). One way to represent the concept of the *LessThan* relation formally is

LessThan < **a** , **b** > | a, b ∈ Integer
:=   {   . . .
               (0, 1),
               (0, 2),
               (0, 3),
               . . .
               (1, 2),
               . . .
               (99, 113),
               etc   }

Translated into English, these symbols say that there is a relation named *LessThan* which holds for a pair of values **a** and **b** such that **a** and **b** are both integers and that what follows is a list of all valid entries in this relation. Written out in its entirety, *LessThan* would be very long indeed.

There are several non-obvious but profound aspects to the relation concept:

- The set of pairs of integers belonging in this relation is a subset of the group of all possible pairs of integers. A relation is like a list of true statements, which is a subset of all possible statements implied by the relation's definition (pair of integers, in our example). For instance, it is true that four (4) is less than five (5), so *LessThan* < 4, 5 >, is part of the relation.
- Any statement about whether one of a pair of integers is less than the other is guaranteed to be *false* if the pair is not present in the

relation. If we had before us the complete list of all pairs in this *LessThan* < **a** , **b** > relation, it would simply be a matter of looking in this list to see if a candidate expression (say *LessThan* < 3, 5 >) is in fact true. (Sometimes you will see the term "closed universe assumption" used when referring to this idea.)

- We can arrive at new true statements, which are not explicitly represented in any relation, by combining truths from several different relations. For example, suppose I had another relation

GreaterThan < **c** , **d** > | c, d ∈ Integer, c > d

Combining *LessThan* < a, b > with *GreaterThan* < c, d > produces a third relation, which we can call *ProductofLTandGT* < a, b, c, d > (for want of a better name). And by limiting *ProductofLTandGT* < > to only those elements in which a = d, you arrive at a new relation:

Between < **c, b, e** > | c, b, e ∈ Integer, e > c and e < b

Although mathematicians generally limit themselves to relations involving numbers, the principles that apply to mathematical relations also work for almost any kind of object.[1] Consider two groups that we will define as the group of "all women" and the group of "all men." Several kinds of relationships exist between instances of these groups (between people). One such relationship is suggested by the existence of three separate facts: "Geoff *fathered_a_son* Paul," "Cecil *fathered_a_son* Geoff," and "Robert *fathered_a_son* Cecil," where Cecil, Geoff, and Paul are members of the group "all men." This produces

fathered_a_son < **a, b** > | a, b ∈ 'all men'
:=   { ('Geoff', 'Paul'),
         ('Cecil', 'Geoff'),
         ('Robert', 'Cecil'),
         etc }

We call concepts such as the group of "all men" or "Integers" *domains*. We say that logical *relations* hold between certain elements or instances of given domains.

The fact that a relation such as *fathered_a_son* < **a, b** > exists where **a** and **b** are elements of the domain "all men" does not at all imply that *all* elements of that domain must participate in the relation. Among our example elements from the group of "all men," Paul has not fathered anyone and therefore his participation in the relation is limited to being in the second column. Another way of explaining the

---

[1] Generalizing to relations over relations is fraught with hazard.

idea is to say that the relation *fathered_a_son* < **a, b** > exists only to the extent that there are pairs of elements satisfying the relation. These are pairs for whom the corresponding fact is true.

Now consider a second relation:

mothered_a_son < **c, b** > | c ∈ 'all women', b ∈ 'all men'
:=   { ('Elaine', 'Paul'),
            ('May', 'Geoff'),
            ('Mary', 'Cecil'),
            etc }

Here, another domain comes into play (the group of "all women"). We say that **c** is a variable that stands for a member of the group/domain of "all women," and **b** is a variable standing for a member of the group/domain of "all men." *mothered_a_son* relation represents another set of true statements, and what it illustrates is that relations can involve members of different domains. In any given UoD there are probably a very large number of domains and a number of relationships among them. Also, domains can be as complex as you need them to be, but regardless of the complexity of a domain, it can still participate in a relation.

Most of the relations we have shown so far have only two domains (these are called binary relations). In general, relations may have any number of elements. This is what is meant by the term "*n*-ary relation"; there may be some *n* variables in the relation, as shown in the following:

parented < **a, c, d, e**^{2} > | a ∈ 'all men', c ∈ 'all women',
                                    d ∈ 'all women' ∪ 'all men', e ∈ 'dates'
:=   { ('Geoff', 'Elaine', 'Paul', 'May 24th, 1968'),
            ('Norman', 'Mavis', 'Elaine', 'April 14th, 1941'),
            ('Cecil', 'May',' Geoff', 'December 13th, 1936'),
            ('Robert', 'Mary', 'Cecil', 'June 21st, 1897'),
            etc   }

In this logical relation, **a** is an instance of the group "all men," **c** is an instance of the group "all women," and **d** can be an element of either set, or more formerly, of the *union* between the two domains. **e** is an element of a new domain, which is the domain of dates. In *parented*, **e** indicates the date on which the child **d** was born to parents **a** and **c**.

---

[2] This example is not so far removed from reality as it might first appear. This is precisely the relation being recorded and used in genetics research.

This example illustrates the first of several differences between mathematical/logical relations and the relations of the relational database model. Element order defines a mathematical relation. By convention, variables in mathematical relations are identified by their position within the *tuple* (a tuple is simply one instance of the set of values that makes up the relation's body). Instead, in a database relation, each component, whether column or attribute, has a *name*. Columns in ORDBMS tables are generally referred to by name, rather than by position.

In our example, if we substitute the labels Mother, Father, Person, and BirthDate for the positions of **a**, **c**, **d**, and **e**, respectively, we get closer to the flavor of the relations of the relational database model. The OR-SQL statement in Listing 2–1 defines the *parented* relation.

```
CREATE TABLE Parented (
        Father              All_Men,
        Mother              All_Women,
        Child               All_People,
        DateOfBirth         date
);
```

Listing 2–1. *Simple SQL-like Table Definition*

A second difference is less obvious. Theoretical relations have set properties. You cannot have duplicate tuples in theoretical relation. However, by default, duplicate records are permitted in relational databases. Figure 2–1 illustrates a valid instance of the table defined in Listing 2–1, but would be an illegal example of a relation.

Father	Mother	Child	DateOfBirth
Geoff	Elaine	Paul	May 24th, 1968
Norman	Mavis	Elaine	April 14th, 1941
Cecil	May	Geoff	December 13th, 1936
Geoff	Elaine	Paul	May 24th, 1968
Robert	Mary	Cecil	June 21st, 1897
Robert	Mary	Cecil	June 21st, 1897

Figure 2–1. *Data for Table Defined in Listing 2–1*

One more important feature of mathematical relations deserves attention. The observant reader will have picked up on the fact that certain operations exist to combine and transform relations. For example, if you take the *parented* <**a**, **c**, **d**, **e**> relation, and eliminate the **a** and **e** part of it, you have *mothered*<**c, d**> | c ∈ 'all women', d ∈ 'all women' ∪ 'all men'

:=   { ('Elaine', 'Paul'),
             ('Mavis', 'Elaine'),
             ('May',' Geoff'),
             ('Mary', 'Cecil'),
             etc }

Further, if you restrict the values of the **c** part to include only members of the set "all men" (or to look only at members of the set "all men"), you have

mothered_a_son <**c, a**> | c ∈ 'all women', a ∈ 'all men'

:=   { ('Elaine', 'Paul'),
             ('May',' Geoff'),
             ('Mary', 'Cecil'),
             etc   }

As we shall see in the next chapter, these kinds of transformations are a powerful part of the relational model. From a computer programming point of view, they can be automated using efficient algorithms and combined into ever more complex operations.

Allowing domains to be whatever developers want them to be is what object-relational databases are all about. Early DBMS implementations of the relational model standardized a group of domains based on the COBOL type system. Such an assumption was clearly appropriate when the primary purpose of DBMS products was supporting business information systems that were characterized by the way they managed names and numbers.

In contrast, in the object-relational data model, domains can be literally anything. They can be as simple as numbers, such as INTEGER, DECIMAL, rational, or complex numbers. However, a domain can also be a complex object, such as movie titles, points in space, names, addresses, part numbers, and even encoded descriptions of parts. Within this interpretation of the relational model, objects as complex as video data or animated medical imagery can be considered as just another logical domain, albeit a very complex one.

For example, you can easily imagine the following relation:

mothered_a_brown-eyed_daughter <**c, f**> | c, f ∈ 'all women'
:=   { ('Mavis', 'Elaine'),
             etc }

mothered_a_brown-eyed_daughter (a subset of *mothered* <**c, d**>) represents facts about brown-eyed woman and their mothers. Real-world concepts such as "having brown eyes" can be defined as domain properties. In practical terms, you could write code that would examine a photographic image and determine eye color. Then you could apply this function in a query statement in place of more conventional ones, such as <, <=, =, and so on.

By now, you should see how object-oriented ideas fit into the relational model. The analysis of domains, of what constitutes a domain instance, and how instances can be compared or manipulated, is outside the scope of the relational model. At this point we are speaking of *objects*: data structures that are defined in terms of their state and behavior. The OR data model permits developers to model objects, organize these objects into schema, and to reason about them afterwards. In other words, the OR data model represents "objects to-the-power-of relations" (or vice versa).

Tuples and Records

Object-relational databases structure data into *records* (or *tuples* or *rows*). A record is a grouping of one or more named *columns* (or *attributes*). The idea is that each record corresponds to a *fact* about the problem domain being modeled. For example, every movie release can be described by a convoluted sentence of the following form:

> *"There exists a film, titled* The Maltese Falcon, *released on July 7, 1944, produced by Warner Brothers, which is a crime drama that cost $15,000 to make, has taken in $2,590,000 since release, is available on video, and is described as 'private eye and cast of mysterious and beautiful strangers pursue a falcon across San Francisco.'"*

The structure of such sentences is identical for every movie, but the information in each sentence varies. With today's electronic media, we can also store pieces of information that are difficult to represent in a written sentence. For example, a promotional video clip could be included within this tuple. Values at each placeholder of the sentence must comply with the rules defining what is expected there. For example, it would make the sentence meaningless if we were to replace the dollar values in the sentence above with the names of people or video clips.

The ORDBMS data model represents each sentence with a record. The previous movie sentence can be represented in the tuple/record shown in Figure 2–2.

All data values in each column conform to the rules of the column's data type or domain. For example, a column that is to hold instances of a State_Name data type, which is designed to model the domain of data values corresponding to U.S. state names, cannot be made to contain a Movie_Title (except for the coincidental exceptions, such as Oklahoma). If you should attempt to insert something such as *The Maltese Falcon* into a column that expected a state name, the code implementing the State_Enum data type would generate an error and reject the insert. If you attempt to compare States and MovieTitles, you will also receive an error (no such comparison exists). To find Movies that use the name of a state as their title, the query needs to explicitly convert one object, or the other, or both, into a comparable form.

The ORDBMS implementation DBMS implementations of real-world domains such as movie titles can cater to their specific peculiarities. For example, two people might write down the title of their favorite film differently. One might write *The Maltese Falcon*, while the other, who is a librarian, might write "Maltese Falcon, The." The implementation of the type, however, knows that these are both legal, and moreover, equivalent.

As part of the schema definition, developers can impose additional constraints over the values a particular column can have. For example, you can constrain a column in one place to ensure that the only legal State_Enum values the column can contain are California, Oregon, or Washington and do so while using the same data type in another column without the constraint.

Relations: Tables and Views

As in a relational DBMS, groups of records all possessing the same structure are stored in *tables*. Tables are the basic data container in

Title	Released	Produced	Genres	Cost	Revenue	OnVideo	Description	VideoClip
Maltese Falcon, The	7/7/1944	Warner	{ 'Crime', 'Drama' }	$150000	$2590000	TRUE	Private eye and cast of mysterious . . .	

Figure 2–2. Tuple Data

an ORDBMS. For example, in our movie database, there is a table recording facts about Movie Club members, who are people who pay a subscription fee to gain access to areas of the site that are off-limits to the casual visitor. As shown in Figure 2–3, our movie database stores the following information about Movie Club members: name, address, date of birth, credit card number, and so on.

The only way to access data in an ORDBMS is by using OR-SQL to query tables. Several OR-SQL statements can be bundled into a database stored procedure and then invoked like a subroutine in a more conventional programming language. However, there is nothing in the IDS product that corresponds to something like the POSIX file-system interface. Programs cannot open a table's on-disk storage, loop through it one record at a time, and then close the table: doing so requires a SELECT query and a CURSOR. The smallest unit of data that you can insert into a table or delete from a table is a single row, although you can address individual columns while selecting and updating.

With relational DBMSs, the table is the basic container for data storage, and the table is the target of query expressions. But in an ORDBMS, other data sources can be treated like a table in an OR-SQL statement. These include user-defined functions that return a set of values, another query, a COLLECTION that acts as a variable table, and data reached through a user-defined interface to an external data source.

MovieClubMembers

Id	Name	DOB	Address	Phone	Location	Preferences	Photo	Credit Card
10020	('Freyen-bauger', 'Mira')	3/2/1964	('100 Heart St', PALO ALTO', "CA', 94714)	(650) 394 0596	(-131.126, 35.12)	{'History', Drama', "Art'}		('MCD', '123427 623445', '03/ 1999')
10111	('Hume', 'David')	1/12/1961	('1113 Grand', 'ALAMEDA', ' CA', 94726)	(510) 769 8732	(-131.51, 37.23)	{'Documentary', 'History', 'Drama'}		
10101	('Eliot', 'George')	3/2/1964	('23B West Av', 'PREORIA', 'IL', 32654)	(234) 934 5677	(-119.94, 42.721)	{'Romance', 'Comedy', 'Drama' }		(AMEX, '2345 9854 2', '05/99')

Figure 2–3. *Sample Table Data from Movies-R-Us Web Site Database*

The Object Data Model

Critics of the basic relational data model point out many useful data modeling ideas. In this section we introduce several features that the OR model has incorporated from object-oriented data models, and one that it has not. In each case we first explain what the feature is in object terms and then explain how IDS supports it.

Each of these changes represents an extension of the original relational data model that complicates it. Hopefully, these new ideas are not over-complications. Incorporating these features greatly increases the range of design possibilities but on balance, it is possible that the additional design effort may exceed the benefits to be had from a superior final design. Useful innovations make life easier.

Objects: Data and Behavior

The essence of the object data model, and the model's most significant contribution to software design and development, is the concept of the object. Software objects represent the *state* and *behavior* of real-world phenomenon as a single, indivisible software module. An earlier section of this chapter outlined the theoretical foundations of the relational model. In doing so, it described the correspondence between relational domains and objects.

In the ORDBMS, objects are represented using the *user-defined type (UDT)* and *user-defined function (UDF)* features. The only way to address or manipulate an object is through the set of methods making up the object's *interface*. The only way to work with ORDBMS data is by applying UDFs to type instances in OR-SQL queries, a kind of operational *encapsulation*.

We devote Chapters 4 and 5 to more detailed coverage of these topics.

COLLECTION Data

Data values in relational database tables were *atomic* or *scalar* values. This means that data in a column was always a single instance of a particular type. Grouping data into sets and arrays was forbidden by what is known in relational theory as the First Normal Form rule. In some circumstances this restriction forced developers into awkward data models and complex queries.

No such limitation exists in object data models, where elements or attributes can be sets or arrays of other object instances. Allowing a similar kind of flexibility is one goal of the ORDBMS data model.

Figure 2–4 illustrates the two approaches.

For example, each movie is associated with a set of genres (Action, Romance, History, Documentary, and so on). There are not all that many different movie genres, perhaps twenty in all, but movies mixing genres are quite common. In a relational DBMS the only way that a Movie's genres can be modeled is by using a second table to hold all genres for all movies. When that is in place, a single Movie's information can be retrieved using a join query to recombine the two tables. Consider, however, the common task of finding movies with a particular mix of genres. Doing this using the relational approach is quite hard.

For some problems, however, the relational solution is adequate and can have some advantages. When an application calls for a query that finds all records where a COLLECTION within the record includes a certain element, the relational approach has the advantage because the server can decide whether it is more efficient to scan R_SET_TABLE or R_TABLE first. With object-relational style COLLECTION columns, the engine's only alternative is to scan the entire table.

ORDBMSs can support other kinds of collections. One of the most lucrative problems in database management involves the management of *timeseries* data. A timeseries COLLECTION is similar to an array, except the array index is a timestamp rather than an integer. Because the ORDBMS provides support for extensible data types, you

OR_TABLE

Key	Title	Genres
1	Casablanca	{ 'Drama', 'Romance', 'World War II' }
2	Maltese Falcon	{ 'Crime', 'Noir'}

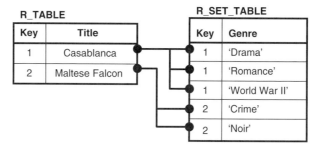

Figure 2–4. *Alternatives for Storing COLLECTION Data*

can create extensions that manage other kinds of collections, such as stacks, frames, queues, and so on.

Identity and Reference

Any two objects in the world are somehow distinct from each other, even when they are identical in every measurable way.[3] They each possess an identity that is something more than simply being the sum of different parts. This intuitively appealing notion, that every object has a distinct identity, is represented in the object data model by assigning every object a unique identifier: an object-id, or OID. Throughout the life of the object, even if all of its attributes change, its OID remains unaffected.

In object-oriented program languages, the most important use for the OID is as a reference for the object. An OID value can be stored some distance away from the location where the actual object is stored. This identifying value can then be used to reference back to the object it identifies without knowing things such as the name of the table in which the object is stored.

Relational systems deal with this issue by providing system-generated data values that are guaranteed to be unique for each table. This is not, however, even a remote approximation of object identity. Relational primary and foreign key constraints are limited to table relationships, rather than relationships between objects. In addition, values in a relational table's foreign key column can refer only to rows in one other table. Object-identity, permits references between multiple tables, as shown in Figure 2–5.

Object identity is more flexible than foreign key constraints, and a small number of straightforward extensions to SQL allow developers to "chase the pointers." Identity used in this way has its critics, however. It tends to lead to a "navigational" style of data manipulation which can complicate certain queries, and make it difficult for the query processor to arrive at efficient plans. For example, a query that wanted to join data in Table A with related data in Table B could do so directly using the foreign key approach but is required to go through Table C when identity based relationship management is employed.

Strong support for identity is missing from the IDS product. The difficulties are practical, rather than theoretical, in nature. It is very difficult to create a scaleable OID-generating facility, particularly when you

---

3 Philosophically, this is a highly controversial thesis. Is an ax with a new head and a new handle the same ax? Can we swim in the same river twice?

consider the way in which ORDBMSs work in distributed environments. Simply wrapping physical row addresses in new syntax does not constitute object identity.

Inheritance

Inheritance is used for representing situations in which one kind of data is related to another kind of data in a particular way. It is represented in several aspects of the ORDBMS data model.

Traditionally, the relational model only catered to one kind of relationship: an association between two tables that is defined using a primary key/foreign key reference. However, you cannot represent all relationships this way. Second, the extensible type system can permit the introduction of a huge number of new objects into the database. One way to simplify this task, and to make the myriad types more

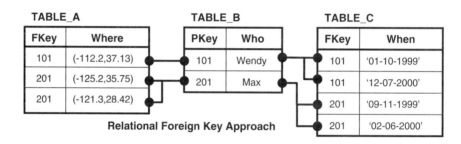

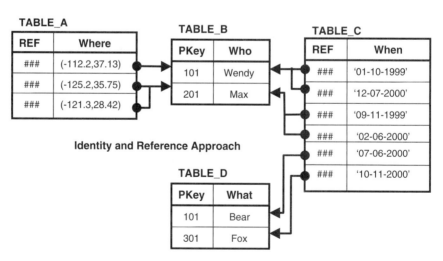

Figure 2–5. *Representations of Identity and Foreign Key Integrity*

manageable, is to reuse the implementation of one data type in the implementation of another.

In the general case, there are at least two kinds of relationships: *has_a* for peer-to-peer associations between dissimilar things and *is_a* for similar things. It is generally better to represent *is_a* relationships inheritance. Inheritance is used in the IDS product to support

- the reuse of a previously declared type and its methods in the declaration of other types,
- the implicit inclusion of data from one table in another, even if the definition of the two tables is not identical.

To simplify the explanation, we refer to the first as *type* inheritance and the second as *table* inheritance. In this chapter we focus on table inheritance. In Chapter 4, where we cover the ORDBMS type system, we explain type inheritance.

Figure 2–6 illustrates several styles of inheritance. All three figures present some root entity labeled "A" from which other entities ("B" and "C") inherit structural properties.

In our Movies database, for example, we need to store information about a group of entities collectively referred to as Merchandise. At times, it is useful to write queries against the entire group. The query might be "List all Merchandise related to *Casablanca* and suitable for a 5 year-old." At times it is useful to direct queries against a single set of objects. In this case, the query might look like "How many different

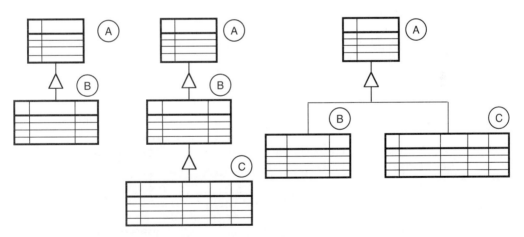

Figure 2–6. *Modeling Inheritance: Either Tables or Data Types*

T-Shirts do we sell?" In this situation, the rows in the Apparel and Toys tables are also in the Merchandise table.

There is no limit to how deep, or how wide, an inheritance hierarchy can be. Multiple-inheritance, where a single new type or table inherits from multiple parents, is, however, not supported.

Object-Relational Structured Query Language (OR-SQL)

The IDS product uses a version of SQL, which we call OR-SQL, to perform all database operations. Developers use OR-SQL both to create the database structure (or *schema*), and to write *queries*, which are OR-SQL language statements that retrieve or update data stored in the database. SQL has its roots in SEQUEL (Structured English QUEry Language), a language created as part of the IBM System Relational DBMS prototype during the late 1970s. The SQL language has undergone several revisions, with each iteration adding new functionality. The latest revision, called SQL-99 or SQL-3, includes support for most of the features described in this chapter.

We divide the description of OR-SQL into descriptions of its two sublanguages: Data Definition Language (DDL) and Data Manipulation Language (DML):

- DDL is used to define or modify the structure of schema features such as tables, views, indices, functions, procedures, data types, operator classes, and so on. The principle DDL language statements are CREATE, ALTER, and DROP.
- DML is used to read and modify data values accessed through the database. The four main DML operations are SELECT, INSERT, UPDATE, and DELETE. In addition, there are two similar commands to invoke procedural logic embedded within the engine: EXECUTE FUNCTION and EXECUTE PROCEDURE.

Because of its relationship with traditional SQL, OR-SQL includes a third set of facilities to perform tasks involving items such as external connections, security and control permissions, and transactions. These statements affect the behavior of the ORDBMS and modify the ways it handles other OR-SQL statements. These miscellaneous language elements are covered within the body of this book's text.

Data Definition Language (DDL)

DDL statements define and modify schema objects. In OR-SQL, all schema objects, such as types, functions, tables, views, and indices, are created using the variations on the `CREATE` command, and removed from the database using the `DROP` command. Most schema objects can be modified using the `ALTER` command. However, inter-dependencies between different schema objects can make it difficult to modify them. For example, you may be prevented from dropping a type if there is a table or routine that uses the type.

Database design tools give developers an even more abstracted interface to the data model. These tools can generate entire scripts from diagrams representing an even more abstracted view of the database. DDL statements are run through an interactive database query tool, or they can be embedded in a host language program. Most often a specially empowered user of the ORDBMS, who is known as the database administrator or DBA, creates the schema objects to ensure that nonprivileged users cannot drop or change them. In addition, the DBA can limit the access privileges different users have with respect to these schema objects.

The bulk of this chapter is devoted to describing the features of OR-SQL DDL.

Data Manipulation Language (DML)

The `SELECT`, `INSERT`, `UPDATE`, and `DELETE` DML commands perform data retrieval, input, update, and deletion, respectively. The body of any OR-SQL query statement specifies the schema objects that are to be operated on (tables or views) and the operations that are to be applied to the data stored in them. DML statements almost always include some literal variable values too.

OR-SQL DML statements, which are more commonly called *query statements*, can get very complicated. They can cover many tables and combine them in complex ways. OR-SQL is also the means by which user-defined logic is bound to data in tables. Expressions in a query that specify the objects in the table the query is interested in and what operations to perform on those objects. For example, Listing 2–2 combines the transformations described earlier to find all mothers of all brown-eyed daughters.

```
SELECT Name(P.Mother), Name(P.Child)
  FROM Parented P
 WHERE IsFemale(P.Child)
   AND HairColor(P.Child, 'Brown');
```

Listing 2–2. *Object-Relational SQL Query*

We devote Chapter 3 to a more detailed examination of the DML portion of the ORDBMS query language.

Object-Relational Schema Definition

A large number of DDL statements collectively define a database schema, which is a logical description of the database's structure. The ORDBMS stores these definitions in its *system catalogs*, which are a set of tables that the ORDBMS itself uses to manage metadata about your database schema. System catalogs are consulted by the ORDBMS as it processes queries, and developers can also use them to get information about the tables, types, and functions in the database.

There are three principal kinds of structural features in a database schema:

- Tables. Tables contain data. OR-SQL DML statements are used to retrieve data from them and to change the data they contain.
- Views. Views are a kind of virtual table. Like tables, data in views can be retrieved and sometimes updated using SQL queries. Unlike tables, views don't physically exist. Instead, a view is defined in terms of a SQL SELECT query involving one or more tables.
- Indices. Indices are used to accelerate query processing. Indices store data in a way that makes finding a specific value (or range of values) very efficient. A database's indices are not explicitly referenced in OR-SQL queries. The ORDBMS automatically figures out, based on the query expression, when it is appropriate to use an index.

Usually all of the DDL commands used to create a database schema are combined into a set of script files, and IDS product includes tools to help administrators export a schema definition to be reused in another database. DDL rarely represents more than a tiny percentage of the total code written to implement an information system, but it is the most important code of all.

Creating Tables

Tables are the basic unit of data storage in an object-relational database, just as they are in relational databases. In an ORDBMS, tables are created using the CREATE TABLE command. As part of the CREATE TABLE command, you provide the following:

- Table Name. This must uniquely identify the table within the database. (Note that in the IDS product, if the database is created in ANSI mode then the name of the table's owner is part of its unique name.)
- Table Structure. A table's structure is its set of columns or attributes. The table's column names and column types need to be specified in the table creation.
- Integrity rules and relationships that apply to the table. An ORDBMS schema consists of an interrelated set of tables and rules designed to ensure data correctness.
- Physical storage management details. As a practical matter the CREATE TABLE statement is a convenient place to specify the table's physical storage.

There are two ways to specify a table's structure. In exactly the same way that was supported in RDBMS products, developers can simply specify a list of named, typed columns as part of the CREATE TABLE statement. Alternatively, they can use the definition of a ROW TYPE to define the table's structure. We discuss each approach in turn.

Creating Table of Columns (Untyped Table)

Tables without a corresponding ROW TYPE are called *untyped tables*, because in contrast with typed tables, the table's structure does not correspond to the structure of a ROW TYPE. Instead, you can use any of the types defined in your database. Listing 2–3 shows the general form of the CREATE TABLE statement when used to create an untyped table.

```
CREATE TABLE Table_Name (
      Column_Name_1        Data_Type       [COLUMN CONSTRAINT],
      Column_Name_2        Data_Type       [COLUMN CONSTRAINT],
      .

      .

      Column_Name_N        Data_Type       [COLUMN CONSTRAINT],
      { [TABLE CONSTRAINT] , }
);
```

Listing 2–3. *Basic Structure for ORDBMS CREATE TABLE Statement*

For example, Listing 2–4 illustrates how to create tables to store information about cinemas showing the movies that the Movies-R-Us web site promotes, and about members of the site's movie club.

```
CREATE TABLE Cinemas (
        Id           INTEGER        NOT NULL       PRIMARY KEY,
        Name         VARCHAR(32)    NOT NULL,
        Address      AddressType    NOT NULL,
        Phone        PhoneNumber    NOT NULL,
        Location     Point          NOT NULL,
        Photo        Image
);
CREATE TABLE MovieClubMembers (
        Id           Membership_Num NOT NULL       PRIMARY KEY,
        Name         PersonName     NOT NULL,
        DOB          DATE,
        Address      AddressType    NOT NULL,
        HomePhone    PhoneNumber    NOT NULL,
        Location     Point          NOT NULL,
        Preferences  SET(Genre_Enum NOT NULL),
        Photo        Image,
        CreditCard   CCDetails
);
```

Listing 2–4. *CREATE TABLE Statements from Movies Database*

The first thing you need to specify in a CREATE TABLE statement is the name of the table and the names of all of the columns in it. Table and column names, as well as the names of types and functions, are *database identifiers*, which are character strings composed of ASCII characters ("a" to "Z"), digits ("0" to "9"), or the underscore character ("_"). Identifiers are used to name database objects such as types, functions, tables, columns, indices, databases, and so on. Note that an identifier cannot begin with a digit. In prior releases of the ORDBMS, identifiers had to be eighteen characters or less. In more recent releases, this restriction is removed and identifiers can be 128 characters.

Our examples use a variety of data types in each table. INTEGER, VARCHAR(32), and DATE are built-in data types that the core SQL language defines. Other types in Listing 2–4 are user-defined types corresponding to various complex objects. AddressType, PhoneNumber, and PersonName could be implemented as a ROW TYPE or using Java, while Image and Point could be OPAQUE TYPES or a DISTINCT TYPE of some kind.

The MovieClubMembers table also contains an example of a COLLECTION column. Each member has a set of Genre preferences that are stored in a single column. Genre_Type itself is another user-defined type.

You can re-use a data type as many times as you need to in an
ORDBMS table (and of course, you can use the same data type in several
tables). However, each column's name is unique within a single table.

Creating Tables Using Named ROW TYPEs (Typed Tables)

A second way to create a table is to specify that the table uses the same
structure as a named ROW TYPE. We call these *typed* tables. Created in
this way, the columns of the new table correspond to the elements of the
ROW TYPE. The table's column names match the element names of the
ROW TYPE and each element's data type corresponds to the table column's type. In addition, if the elements of the ROW TYPE are constrained
by modifiers such as NOT NULL, the table's columns are similarly constrained. Table rules, such as primary key and foreign key constraints,
must be declared with the table. Listing 2–5 shows the general pattern of
the CREATE TABLE statements that use a ROW TYPE.

```
CREATE TABLE Table_Name
OF TYPE Type_Name
  ( [CONSTRAINTS] );
```

Listing 2–5. *Structure for CREATE TABLE OF TYPE Declaration*

The Listing 2–6 illustrates a script that is (almost) equivalent to the
ones you've just viewed.

```
CREATE ROW TYPE Cinema_Type (
      Id          INTEGER        NOT NULL,
      Name        VARCHAR(32)    NOT NULL,
      Address     AddressType    NOT NULL,
      Phone       PhoneNumber    NOT NULL,
      Location    Point          NOT NULL
      Photo       Image
);
CREATE TABLE Cinemas
OF TYPE Cinema_Type
( Primary Key ( Id )
);
CREATE ROW TYPE MovieClub_Member_T (
      Id             Membership_Num    NOT NULL,
      Name           PersonName        NOT NULL,
```

```
      DOB            DATE,
      Address        AddressType    NOT NULL,
      HomePhone      PhoneNumber    NOT NULL,
      Location       Point          NOT NULL,
      Preferences    SET(Genre_Enum NOT NULL),
      Photo          Image,
      CreditCard     CCDetails
);
CREATE TABLE MovieClub
OF TYPE MovieClub_Member_T
( Primary Key ( Id ) );
```

Listing 2–6. *Examples of CREATE TABLE OF TYPE From the Movies Database*

The advantage of untyped tables lies in their simplicity. Creating a typed table requires that you create a ROW TYPE first. A second advantage of untyped tables is their flexibility. You can alter untyped tables directly, whereas modifying a typed table is a much more complex undertaking. The type's existence makes altering the table directly impossible, and the presence of subtypes and subtables can complicate matters further.

Typed tables, however, provide additional functionality. You can implement user-defined functions taking an instance of the entire ROW TYPE as an argument and returning a computed value. This allows you to create virtual columns that extend typed tables. Also, when you implement a table hierarchy, you must have a corresponding type hierarchy, and therefore you must use a ROW TYPES in these cases.

Addressing a Table Columns in Queries

As far as the DML aspects of the query language are concerned, there is no difference between tables created using either technique. In queries you use the identifiers that name tables and columns to specify data involved in the query. For example, table names appear in the FROM clause of SELECT queries, and elsewhere the query uses the names of columns from these tables. The syntax used to specify tables and their column names is called *cascading dot notation*. Cascading dot notation looks like this:

```
Table_Name.Column_Name {.Attribute_Name }
```

In the case of a ROW TYPE column queries can address the attributes within that column using in the same style of notation, and for ROW

TYPE elements themselves created using a ROW TYPE cascading dot notation can be applied recursively. For example, suppose the Address-Type data type has the following internal structure shown in Listing 2–7.

```
AddressType (
            First_Line,
            Second_Line,
            City,
            State,
            ZipCode
             );
```

Listing 2–7. *Structure of a Complex Data Type (ROW TYPE Implementation)*

Listing 2–8 shows how to address columns within the tables defined above, regardless of which of the two declaration alternates is used.

```
MovieClubMembers.Id                    Cinemas.Id
MovieClubMembers.Address.City          Cinemas.Name
```

Listing 2–8. *Cascading Dot Notation for Addressing Row Data*

Listing 2–9 illustrates how cascading dot notation is used in an OR-SQL query involving the MovieClubMembers table.

```
SELECT MovieClubMembers.Address.ZipCode.Major,
       Print(M.Name)
  FROM MovieClubMembers M
 WHERE MovieClubMembers.Address.City = 'PALO ALTO'
    AND M.Address.State = 'CA';
```

Listing 2–9. *Query Illustrating Use of Cascading Dot Notation*

Note how this last query substitutes a *table alias* , M for the entire table name. Table aliases simplify query expressions and cater to the case where a table is joined with itself. Cascading dot notation does not discriminate between a table or view name, of a table alias in a query.

Temporary Tables

All of the previous listings demonstrate how to create what are known as base tables. Once created, base tables remain within the database until the table is dropped explicitly, and all users with appropriate permissions can access data in a base table.

Sometimes, developers want to create a private table that is visible only within a single session and that the ORDBMS removes automatically when the session ends. Such tables are known as temporary tables, and you signify them by use of the TEMP keyword in the CREATE TABLE statement, as shown in Listing 2–10.

```
CREATE TEMP TABLE MyPrivateMovieClub
(
      Id            Membership_Num  NOT NULL PRIMARY KEY,
      Name          PersonName      NOT NULL,
      DOB           date,
      Address       AddressType     NOT NULL,
      HomePhone     PhoneNumber     NOT NULL,
      Location      Point           NOT NULL,
      Preferences   SET(Genre_Enum  NOT NULL),
      Photo         Image,
      CreditCard    CCDetails
);⁴
```

Listing 2–10. *CREATE Temporary Table Example*

Temporary tables are identical to base tables in almost all respects. You can create indices and integrity constraints on them. Typically, you populate a temporary table by using an OR-SQL SELECT statement. Unlike views, data in a temporary table is actually stored on disk. Temporary tables can be dropped like a base table, or the ORDBMS removes them at the end of the user session. They are typically used to store intermediate results as part of a more complex data management operation: in a database stored procedure, for example.

Constraining Table Data

Tables can be created with rules to constrain the data values its columns contain. For instance, you might want to limit the range of data values in a column, enforce a rule that involves several data elements within each record, or create a rule that limits a column's values based on a relationship with a column in another table.

---

4   Note that in practice temporary tables are almost always created WITH NO LOG, and often assigned to a special on-disk table space. Refer to the Administration Guide for more details.

Such constraints are useful because they improve the quality of the information in the database by excluding illegal data. In other words, they are useful for ensuring the correctness of the database's data. If an application programmer writes an incorrect query, or an end user enters invalid data, the ORDBMS can recognize that the action violates some constraint and then preempt it Typically, IDS returns an error status to the external program.

Declarative constraints such as the ones in the following section are also called *integrity constraints*. Integrity constraints can be classified into two types: column integrity constraints and table integrity constraints. Constraints are one way that semantic information can be introduced into the database schema.

Column Constraints

Column constraints, which are also known as *role* constraints, affect the data values in a single column of a single row. They restrict the values that an attribute or attributes of a row may have. In this section, we explore the range of column constraints that the IDS product supports.

The first is NOT NULL, which instructs the ORDBMS to ensure that the column contains a value of the right data type. "NULL-able" columns, which are the default in all SQL tables, are intended to address the problem of missing information. Information may be missing when, for example, movie club members choose not to provide a credit card number or a digital photograph of themselves. To accommodate missing information an attribute value may assume a NULL value.

Unfortunately NULL values have some drawbacks. Most notably, they complicate query processing. By default, expressions over NULL data values always return a NULL result, which is a behavior consistent with three-valued logic (3VL). Consequently, queries involving nullable columns in the WHERE clause can return strange results. For example, suppose the movie site's management sells a mailing list to a credit card company that is interested in people who do not already have their card. If you were to ask for all the records from the movie club member's table WHERE CreditCard.CardType != 'MASTERCARD', you would miss out on all the members with NULL values in that column.

It is, therefore, generally a good idea to provide columns with default values (see below) wherever possible, to enforce the NOT NULL constraint wherever using a default value is not feasible, and to allow NULL-able column only as a last resort. Most of the columns in our example tables are declared to be NOT NULL.

This is why most columns in the examples in this book preclude NULL values. In Listings 2–4 and 2–6, the NOT NULL extension to the Address column definition and to the Id and Location columns in the Cinemas table ensures that these columns contain data values. Any attempt to accidentally insert an unidentified cinema, a cinema without a location, or set the cinema's Id or Location to unknown with an UPDATE statement is prevented by the ORDBMS.

The second column constraint is the DEFAULT [EXPRESSION | VALUE] modifier, which tells the ORDBMS that the column must contain some data value (that it cannot hold a NULL) and provides a default value for the column.

When an OR-SQL INSERT statement fails to mention the column name, the ORDBMS substitutes the specified default value. Of course, the supplied default must be a legitimate instance of the column's data type. If the column is declared as an OPAQUE TYPE, the default value must be supplied as a legal literal (a string or number) instance of the OPAQUE TYPE.

When the column uses certain SQL-92 data types, you can also use an expression to generate a default value. For example, it is often useful to automatically record the date and time that a new row was inserted or the name of the user performing the insert. To do so, you need only use the system-supported CURRENT and USER keywords for default values.

Listing 2–11 shows all examples of column declarations that include a default constraint.

```
CREATE TABLE Constraint_Examples (
When        DATE              DEFAULT TODAY,
What        DISTINCT_INTEGER  DEFAULT 1,
Proportion  Rational          DEFAULT '( 1 / 2 )'
);
```

Listing 2–11. *DEFAULT Constraints on Column Values*

DEFAULT constraints are very useful. They lift the burden of providing data values from the application programmer while avoiding the pitfalls of allowing columns to accept NULL values (see above).

The third constraint is CHECK (< boolean EXPRESSION >). Sometimes it's desirable to enforce a more complicated constraint, one that limits the values in a column with an expression or that ensures that some rule applies over the entire row. With a CHECK constraint you can specify a condition that is evaluated whenever a row is inserted into the table or an update statement modifies one of the columns affected by the constraint. If the condition evaluates to false, the ORDBMS rejects the change. Listing 2–12 illustrates the uses of CHECK constraints over various built-in data types.

```
CREATE TABLE Check_Constraint_Test (
    When      DATE      NOT NULL CHECK (When > '01\01\1930'),
    What_1    INTEGER   NOT NULL CHECK ( What_1 IN
                                         ( 1, 2, 3, 4, 5, 6) ),
    After     DATE      NOT NULL,
              CHECK ( After > When )
);
```

Listing 2–12. *CHECK Constraints on Column Values*

Note that the DEFAULT and CHECK constraints can be declared only as part of the CREATE TABLE statement, but cannot be specified as part of a ROW TYPE. A single table can contain several CHECK constraints. CHECK constraints over a single column can be included with the column's definition, while CHECK constraints involving more than one column are declared as a body after the last column is declared.

Each of the constraint mechanisms we have seen so far works independent of the others. Columns with DEFAULT and CHECK constraints can still be made to except a NULL if one is specified explicitly in a query statement. Combinations of column constraints are encouraged, as we see in Listing 2–13.

```
CREATE TABLE Constraint_Example (
        Id      INTEGER DEFAULT 1 NOT NULL CHECK ( Id > 1 )
        Name    Opaque_Type DEFAULT 'public_form' NOT NULL
);
```

Listing 2–13. *Combinations of Column Constraints*

Table Constraints

A relation or table constraint is a rule that applies to a table as a whole. For example, it is fairly common to have a column (or a set of columns) where the data values in the column(s) are unique within the table. We call columns with such a property a *candidate key*. In contrast with the column constraints described earlier in this chapter, when it verifies that some new data values comply with this rule, the ORDBMS must search the entire table rather than examine a single row.

Table constraints are very important in both the relational and object-relational data models. Like column constraints, table constraints help to ensure the correctness of the information in the database by ensuring the following:

- No duplicate records exist in the table. If an attempt is made to insert information about the same real-world entity into a table twice, the ORDBMS can identify the first instance and preempt the second insert.
- Key values identify a single row in a table. Any data values in a well-designed ORDBMS database can be addressed with the combination of a table's name, a key value for that table, and the name of the attribute being addressed.
- Unique values provide a means of managing relationships between tables. Columns used to uniquely identify rows in one table (called the parent table) can be stored in another tables (called child tables). Then you can reconstruct the relationship with joins.

For example, consider the table used to contain information about Movies, in Listing 2–14.

```
--
--      ROW TYPE
--
CREATE ROW TYPE Movie_Type (
          Id              Movie_Id            NOT NULL,
          Title           Title               NOT NULL,
          Release_Date    DATE                NOT NULL,
          Produced_By     Prod_Company        NOT NULL,
          Genre           SET (Genre_Enum     NOT NULL ),
          Budget          US_Dollars          NOT NULL,
          Takings         US_Dollars          NOT NULL,
          Plot_Summary    Doc_Type            NOT NULL,
          OnVideo    BOOLEAN                   NOT NULL
);
--
-- Table
--
CREATE TABLE Movies
OF TYPE Movie_Type
( PRIMARY KEY ( Id ) CONSTRAINT Movie_Id_Primary_Key,
  UNIQUE ( Title, Release_Date )
          CONSTRAINT Movie_Title_and_Release_Unique
);
```

Listing 2–14. *Implementing Column Constraints for a ROW TYPE Table*

These statements create a table storing information about movies, such as the movie's title, a release date, the genre, and so on. It also includes two constraints that apply rules to movies' data as it is added or modified by OR-SQL queries:

- The Id column is specified as the table's *primary key*.
- The column pair Title and Release_Date is *unique* within the table.

The Id column uniquely identifies each row in the table, and its data values can be stored in other tables to represent relationships between movies and other aspects of the problem domain. The unique constraint on Title and Release_Date prevent data entry errors. Both of these constitute alternate candidate keys. In theory, the decision about which of them to make the primary key is fairly arbitrary. In practice, it is usually fairly obvious which one to choose. The simple axiom applied here is that smaller keys are better.

Table constraints, as their name suggests, are usually specified as part of the table creation. However, you can add them to a table after it has already been created. Modifying a table to include additional rules is achieved using the ALTER TABLE statement.

Primary Key Constraint

One column, or a set of columns, can be declared as the table's PRI-MARY KEY. In practice it is an excellent idea to ensure that every table has a primary key. Columns defined using a built-in type, OPAQUE TYPE, or DISTINCT TYPE can be part of a PRIMARY KEY. COLLECTION columns, ROW TYPE columns, and NULL-able columns cannot. When you use a ROW TYPE to create a new table, you must include the PRI-MARY KEY declaration with the table rather than the ROW TYPE.

Listing 2–15 shows the first alternative, which is to create the row type first, and then create the table. The primary key is declared as part of CREATE TABLE.

```
CREATE ROW TYPE PK_Test_Type (
    Id          Type_One    NOT NULL,
    Value       Type_Two    NOT NULL
);
CREATE TABLE PK_Test_Table
OF TYPE PK_Test_Type
PRIMARY KEY ( Id ) CONSTRAINT PK_Test_Primary_Key;
```

Listing 2–15. *Implementing Primary Key Constraints for ROW TYPEd Table*

Alternatively you might create the table directly, as shown in Listing 2–16. In this case, because the primary key has a single column, it is declared with that column.

```
CREATE TABLE PK_Test_Table (
    Id          Type_One    NOT NULL    PRIMARY KEY
                                        CONSTRAINT   PK_Test_Primary_Key,
    Value       Type_Two    NOT NULL
);
```

Listing 2–16. *Implementing Primary Key Constraints for an Untyped Table*

When the primary key involves more than one column, it must be declared separately from the columns, as is the case for CHECK constraints of more than one column, as shown in Listing 2–17.

```
--
CREATE TABLE PK_Test_Table (
            PK_First_Col            Type_One        NOT NULL,
            PK_Second_Col           Type_Two        NOT NULL,
            Value                   Type_Three      NOT NULL,
            PRIMARY KEY ( PK_First_Col, PK_Second_Col )
                        CONSTRAINT PK_Test_Primary_Key
);
```

Listing 2–17. *Implementing Multi-Column Primary Key Constraints*

Because the primary key constraint is checked for each new row inserted into the table, the IDS product automatically creates an index on primary key columns.

Unique Constraints

When a column (or combination of columns) is declared to be UNIQUE, the ORDBMS ensures that no two rows in the table have the same values in those columns. In other words, you cannot insert a new row into a table if a data value in a unique column already exists elsewhere in the table.

Tables can have several UNIQUE constraints. As with other constraints, you can declare them when you create the table, or add them later with an ALTER TABLE statement. Listing 2–18 illustrates how to declare a uniqueness constraint over a single column and over a pair of columns in the table.

```
CREATE TABLE Unique_Example (

        .
    Value    INTEGER        NOT NULL        UNIQUE,

        .
    Column_1    UDT_1      NOT NULL,
    Column_2    UDT_2      NOT NULL,

        .,
            UNIQUE ( Column_1, Column_2 )
);
```

Listing 2–18. *Implementing UNIQUE Constraints*

Primary key values on the other hand are often used in more than one table as part of a foreign key. Consequently, when a primary key value changes in one table, the change must be propagated to tables. Therefore, a useful rule is to avoid using keys that change as primary keys. Use the unique constraint instead.

Table Constraints and User-Defined Data Types

In the CREATE TABLE statement in Listing 2–14, the Id column is declared to be the table's *primary key*. Notice how the data type of this column is user-defined; it is a Movie_Id type. Regardless of what it actually looks like (it might be a system generated identifier or a text string assigned by some industry body), the table constraint rule instructs the ORDBMS to ensure that Id values are not repeated in the table.

The example in the previous paragraph illustrates something important about developing user-defined types in an ORDBMS. When we say that a data value is unique within a column, we are saying (more formally) that there exists no data value in the column that is *equal* to any other. Relational integrity constraints discussed in this chapter are all variations of such uniqueness constraints. So, to enforce these rules, IDS must at the very least be able to detect when two type instances are equal.

In SQL-92 databases this is quite straightforward. All data types come with equality built-in, and the DBMS can create indices for these types to make enforcing uniqueness rules efficient. However, in a database that includes user-defined types, the ORDBMS needs an Equal() user-defined function to detect violations of the rule. This explains why, when creating a new data type, it is important to create a set of support functions for it.

Thus our Movie_Id data type needs to have a set of supported user-defined functions, such as Equal (Movie_Id, Movie_Id). Further, to enforce any of these uniqueness constraints efficiently, the ORDBMS needs to build a b-tree index on the unique column, which requires a `Compare ( Movie_Id, Movie_Id )`. Before you can use an `OPAQUE` or `DISTINCT` type column in a key, you need to ensure that you have created an appropriate operator class for that type.

Naming Constraints

Constraints are named. This allows you to drop or suspend them without dropping or modifying the entire table. Also, whenever a constraint is violated, the ORDBMS provides the name of the constraint within the error message it returns to the client. If you do not specify a name for your table constraint, the ORDBMS will assign one for you, and the names it picks aren't particularly intelligible.

To name a constraint, append the word `CONSTRAINT` to your declaration and provide an identifier name. Constraint names must follow rules applying to identifiers. Listings 2–14 through 2–17, and 2–19 and 2–20, illustrate how to name table constraints.

Suspending Constraints

If for some reason we wanted to suspend these constrains, which may be useful when bulk loading data into the table, you use the syntax in Listing 2–19.

```
    SET CONSTRAINTS
            Movie_Id_Primary_Key, Movie_Title_and_Release
    DISABLED;
    --
-- Perform the bulk load into Movies
    --
    SET CONSTRAINTS
            Movie_Id_Primary_Key, Movie_Title_and_Release
    ENABLED;
```

Listing 2–19. *Disabling and Enabling Named Constraints*

As we mentioned earlier, the default behavior when an integrity constraint is violated is to reject the change and to generate an error message. But you can instruct the ORDBMS to take one of a range of other actions. In addition to turning them off and on, you can get the ORDBMS to filter changes instead of rejecting them, silently reject the row rather than generating an error or maintain a violations table. Consult the IDS product documentation for more details.

Referential Integrity Constraints

We have already seen how a table's primary key can be used to uniquely identify a row of data within it. If an end user or developer has a valid Movie_Id, he or she can retrieve information about that movie from the `Movies` table. In addition, the Id primary key can be used to refer to rows in the `Movies` table from rows in other database tables. Rules governing these inter-table references can be used to improve the quality of data in a database.

In our Movies-R-Us Web site database, for example, every item of Merchandise must be associated with a Movie. So we carry the Movie_Id column in the `Merchandise` table and all of its subtables to hold a value that refers back to the `Movies` table's primary key. This arrangement is called a *foreign key* relationship, and it is an example of what is known as a *referential integrity constraint*. Defined like this, any attempt to insert an item of `Merchandise` without a valid Movie_Id will be rejected by the ORDBMS.

The situation is illustrated in Figure 2–7, where we show the relationship between the `Movies` and `Merchandise` tables.

Foreign key constraints from multiple tables can all reference the primary key of a single table. For example, the table in our schema that contains details about when and where movies are being shown also has a foreign key relationship to the `Movies` table. You can even have foreign keys that reference the primary key of their own table!

Creating Foreign Key Constraints

The SQL statement in Listing 2–19 demonstrates how to declare a foreign key as part of a `CREATE TABLE` statement. In this example, we first create the `ROW TYPE` that defines the structure of the `Merchandise` table. Then the `CREATE TABLE` statement specifies that the Id column is the table's primary key and that the Movie column is a foreign key that refers back to the Movies table (from Listing 2–14). Note how we also name this referential integrity constraint.

```
CREATE ROW TYPE Merchandise_T (
    Id              Part_Code       NOT NULL,
    Name            ProductName     NOT NULL,
    Movie           Movie_Id        NOT NULL,
    Description     lvarchar        NOT NULL,
```

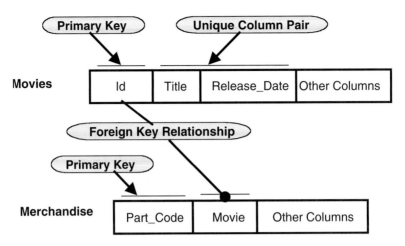

Figure 2-7. *Foreign Key Relationships*

```
        Price             Currency        NOT NULL,
        ShippingCost      Currency        NOT NULL,
        NumberAvailable   Quantity        NOT NULL
);
--
CREATE TABLE Merchandise
OF TYPE Merchandise_T
( PRIMARY KEY ( Id ) CONSTRAINT Merchandise_PK,
   FOREIGN KEY ( Movie )
   REFERENCES Movies ( Id ) CONSTRAINT Merch_Movies_FK
);
```

Listing 2-20. *Declaring a Named Foreign Key Constraint*

Whenever an INSERT statement adds a new row to the Merchandise table (or any of its subtables), the ORDBMS checks to ensure that the value in the new row's foreign key column (Merchandise.Movie in this case) exists in the Movies table's primary key column (Movie.Id). If no matching value is found, the ORDBMS generates an error and rejects the INSERT. Note that the data type for both columns must be the same. The strongly typed ORDBMS data model requires that columns participating in a foreign key/primary key relationship take values from the same domain.

Foreign Key CASCADING DELETE

What happens when you delete a row from the table that holds the primary key? For example, what happens to the rows in the Merchandise table when you delete a row from the `Movies` table? This might leave the database in an inconsistent state, and a query, such as one that counts currently available products, would return a wrong answer. To deal with the problem, you can specify additional behavior with the `FOREIGN KEY` constraint to tell the ORDBMS what to do under these circumstances.

Automating the way that the ORDBMS reacts when data in related tables is modified helps because it minimizes the amount of OR-SQL that must be written as part of table maintenance. Also, it centralizes the implementation of the rule making maintenance easier. Alternative approaches require that every external program that modifies data be aware of all of the information system's rules. Listing 2–21 illustrates how delete rules are declared.

```
CREATE TABLE Orders (
        Id              Order_Num        NOT NULL PRIMARY KEY
                        CONSTRAINT Order_Primary_Key,
        Customer        Membership_Num   NOT NULL,
        DeliverTo       DeliveryAddress  NOT NULL,
        OrderedOn       DATE             NOT NULL,
        ShippedOn       DATE
);
GRANT ALL ON Orders  TO PUBLIC;
--
CREATE TABLE Order_Line_Items  (
        Order           Order_Num        NOT NULL
                        REFERENCES Orders ( Id )
                        ON DELETE CASCADE
                        CONSTRAINT Orders_to_Line_Numbers_Key,
        Merchandise     Part_Code        NOT NULL,
        NumberBought    Quantity         NOT NULL
);
GRANT ALL ON Order_Line_Items  TO PUBLIC;
```

Listing 2–21. *Declaring a Named Foreign Key Constraint with DELETE CASCADE*

When a row in the parent table is deleted, the ORDBMS ensures that any dependent rows in the child table are deleted too. This kind of constraint can be applied over a sequence of parent-child foreign key relationships. For example, the `Order_Line_Items` table in the Listing 2–21 includes a reference to the `Merchandise` table. Deleting a movie would delete all related rows in the `Merchandise` table and cascade to delete all related rows in the `Order_Line_Items` table too.

Identity, Primary Keys, and Foreign Keys

Earlier we introduced the idea of object *identity.*, which refers to the way that real-world entities possess a certain property (called identity) that somehow distinguishes each from all other entities, even those that have identical properties. Another way to explain the idea is to say that object-oriented models make a distinction between objects and values. Although an object's data may change, its identity remains the same.

In object-oriented systems, it is common to use object-identifiers to manage whatever relationships an object has. References to other objects, which are included as part of an object's definition, may be followed (or de-referenced) to navigate to another, related object. There are a number of differences between the object-oriented model of identity and the relational primary key/foreign key approach.

- Object relationships are negotiated navigationally, while the key relationship is handled using a join in a query.
- Key constraints are limited to relationships between rows of tables, while an object in an ORDBMS can be a row in a table, a value in a column, or an element of a COLLECTION in a column.
- In object systems it is unusual to support ideas such as referential integrity between an object and the other objects containing references to it. In fact, one of the criticisms of object-oriented DBMSs is that they place the responsibility for maintaining referential integrity on the developer.

The idea of a unique, invariant identifier is very useful. Therefore the ORDBMS includes a special facility, the *system generated* data values, that can be used as primary keys for a table. This is the SERIAL data type.

In the `MovieClubMembers` table, you can declare that the Membership_Num data type that re-use the SERIAL facility. Columns that are unique can be declared as such, but because these columns are not used to reflect relationships between tables (see the foreign key discussion in the following section), there are no problems when the value changes. The ORDBMS can still enforce the semantic rule without limiting the flexibility of the database schema.

Data Inheritance

Data, or table, inheritance is a feature that distinguishes the ORDBMS data model from relational DBMS products. It is useful for modeling a special kind of relationship that occasionally exists between a subtable and a supertable. Table inheritance means that each record in the subtable *is_a* record in the supertable too. In other words, rows in the subtable can be accessed with queries against the supertable.

Data inheritance is useful when it simplifies schema modeling and writing query expressions. Rather than creating a number of tables containing similar kinds of information, and addressing them separately in query statements, table inheritance creates a single hierarchy to address them all at once. For example, in Figure 2–8, we illustrate the `Merchandise` table inheritance hierarchy from the Movie-R-Us database.

Figure 2–8 illustrates several tables arranged in a hierarchy. The Merchandise table in this example, which is referred to as the root table of the hierarchy, is empty. All actual items of merchandise are found in one of the subtables in the hierarchy. Each subtable extends the columns of the `Merchandise` table with its own specialised columns. An important point to note is that although all rows in the subtables can be seen from the root table, each additional column in each subtable cannot; that is, you cannot address the `Sizes` column of the `Apparel` table in queries against the `Merchandise` table.

Queries over table hierarchies, including the important concept of polymorphism, are covered in Chapter 3.

Merchandise

id	name	movie	description	price	shipping	num		

Tickets

id	name	movie	description	price	shipping	num	showing	
200	Full Price Movie Tickets	100303	Full price ticket	ROW (USD, 7.50)	ROW (USD, 1.50)	10000	30101	
201	Full Price Movie Tickets	100101	Full price ticket	ROW(USD, 7.50)	ROW(USD, 1.50)	10000	30101	

Apparel

id	name	movie	description	price	shipping	num	kind	sizes
101	Rick T-Shirt	100303	T-Shirt with . . .	ROW (USD, 12.50)	ROW (USD, 1.50)	200	T-Shirt	{ 'P', 'S', 'M', 'X' }

***Figure 2–8.** Data in a Table Hierarchy*

Creating Tables in a Hierarchy

Tables involved an inheritance hierarchy must be typed tables, that is, a table inheritance hierarchy must have a corresponding ROW TYPE hierarchy. The ROW TYPE hierarchy is necessary because IDS uses the types associated with a table hierarchy to resolve *polymorphic* queries. In Listing 2–22, we present the code used to create the table hierarchy shown in Figure 2–8. All of these tables inherit from the Merchandise table introduced in Listing 2–21.

```
CREATE ROW TYPE Apparel_Type (
      Maker       Manufacturer   NOT NULL,
      Sizes       SET(Size_Enum NOT NULL),
      Photo       Image
) UNDER Merchandise_T;

CREATE TABLE Apparel
OF TYPE Apparel_Type
UNDER Merchandise;

CREATE ROW TYPE Ticket_Type (
         Showing    Showing_Id     NOT NULL
)
UNDER Merchandise_T;

CREATE TABLE Tickets
OF TYPE Ticket_Type
( FOREIGN KEY ( Showing ) REFERENCES Showings ( Id )   )
UNDER Merchandise;
```

Listing 2–22. *Implementation of Table Hierarchy*

In Listing 2–22, note how the Merchandise table itself has no rows in it. In RDBMS systems, empty tables are rare. In an ORDBMS, however, empty tables can still be queried upon and contain rows, because they might be the root table of a hierarchy.

Table Inheritance and Table Behavior

Subtables inherit all behaviors (constraints, physical storage organization, and triggers) defined for the tables above them. For example, when the root table of an inheritance hierarchy is declared to have a primary key constraint, all tables under that root table share it. In the Merchandise hierarchy example, values in the Id column are unique up and down the set of tables; that is, you cannot have a row in the

`Apparel` subtable with the same `Id` column value as a row in the Tickets table, even though they represent different branches of the hierarchy structure.

Further, column constraints applied in a super table are also applied in any subtables. A `CHECK` constraint defined for the Merchandise table is also checked whenever you modify data in the subtables of the hierarchy. While you cannot remove behaviors inherited from supertables, it is possible to define additional behaviors on subtables. `ALTER TABLE` can add a constraint or create new triggers. Remember that constraints are additive, that is, if you add a constraint (say a `CHECK` constraint) to a subtable, the ORDBMS validates both constraints on supertables and the new constraint.

How Table Inheritance is Implemented

How are table inheritance hierarchies implemented? How is the data actually stored, and how do queries over a table turn into queries over a hierarchy? In this section, however, we describe how the ORDBMS manages rows of data in a table hierarchy.

Rows from the different tables of a hierarchy are stored in different data spaces. When it receives a query for a table in a hierarchy, the ORDBMS uses its system catalogs to create a query plan that includes all subtables. Whenever an OR-SQL statement scans rows in a table hierarchy, the ORDBMS organizes the scanning of each subtable separately. Figure 2–9 illustrates what this mapping looks like.

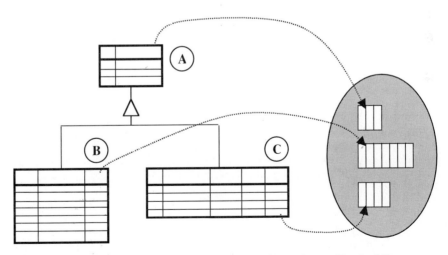

Figure 2–9. *Table Partitioning for Distributing Rows Across Physical Storage Spaces*

This approach has its advantages. It implies excellent performance for queries that only consider rows in a single table of the hierarchy. Also, it offers the greatest range of physical tuning opportunities. By default, the tables in a hierarchy inherit their physical storage properties (their partitioning strategy) from their supertable. When you create subtables, however, you can override the supertable's physical storage rules. This means that each table in a hierarchy can use different storage strategies (different partitioning schemes, different data spaces, and so on).

Indices are handled somewhat differently. If you create an index over the Merchandise table, the index entries from all of its subtables are collected into a single structure. Pointers from within this index structure tie back to rows in the hierarchy, regardless of which table the row is stored. This improves the performance of index scans over the entire hierarchy, at some cost to index scans over single tables.

Non-Traditional Table Storage

An important difference between the ORDBMS and traditional RDBMSs is that data accessed through an ORDBMS table might not be stored within the DBMS at all!

In an RDBMS the database administrator allocates disk resources that the DBMS uses to store data. This facility is called the *storage manager*. A special interface within the ORDBMS, which is called the Virtual Table Interface, or VTI, allows developers to implement their own storage manager. This means that the data accessed through a table might be stored somewhere outside the database (in a file system, for example).

We call this new kind of storage manager a *user-defined access method*. Tutorial 7 in this book describes how to use the interface to create a user-defined storage manager. In this chapter, however, we illustrate how to use a user-defined access method to create a table. Instead of allowing the default table spaces to store the table's data, we indicate that the data is read and written using an alternative as part of the CREATE TABLE statement. To do this, we create the table using the syntax in Listing 2–23.

```
CREATE TABLE PWD (
        dir_name        direct          NOT NULL,
        file_name       lvarchar        NOT NULL,
        perms           lvarchar        NOT NULL,
```

```
link_cnt          integer      NOT NULL,
owner             lvarchar     NOT NULL,
group             lvarchar     NOT NULL,
access            datetime year to second NOT NULL,
modified          datetime year to second NOT NULL,
stat_changed      datetime year to second NOT NULL,
eof_size          integer      NOT NULL,
block_cnt         integer      NOT NULL
) USING File_System_AM (root="/tmp");
```

Listing 2–23. *CREATE TABLE with User-Defined Access Method*

So far as the rest of the ORDBMS is concerned, PWD looks like just another table. The data it contains, however, is information about the contents of the "/tmp" directory in the file system of the computer on which the IDS server is installed. When you write a query against tables such as PWD, the ORDBMS calls a set of user-defined functions that implement the user-defined access method, instead of the built-in functions.

Modifying Tables

This section describes the facilities provided by the ORDBMS for working with tables after they have been created. Frequently, developers need to evolve a database schema over time. Using the facilities described in this section, you can drop tables, alter them by adding constraints or rules to their definition, and for untyped tables, add or remove columns.

The kinds of table modifications described in this section are usually the final step in building a database. By default, the ORDBMS checks all rules as it loads data, and any errors will cause the entire load to fail. Therefore, a useful technique is to create the table schema initially without any integrity rules. Once the data is loaded and cleaned, the schema's integrity rules are added by altering each table.

Altering Database Tables

The ORDBMS provides support for database schema evolution through the ALTER TABLE command, which allows developers to change a table's structure and any of its integrity rules without affecting the data in the table. Interdependencies between the table schema and the database's type system complicates the procedure. For *untyped* tables, the ALTER TABLE command can be used to

- ADD, DROP, or MODIFY table columns
- ADD, DROP, or MODIFY constraints on the table
- associate an untyped table with a ROW TYPE
- MODIFY the physical organization of the table

The ALTER TABLE statement is quite complex. Listing 2–24 illustrates the various ways it can be used. Beginning with the following example table.

```
CREATE TABLE Alter_Example (
    Id          INTEGER      NOT NULL,
    Value_1     String       NOT NULL
);
```

Listing 2–24. *Initial CREATE TABLE for ALTER TABLE*

You can add a new column to this table with the statement in Listing 2–25.

```
ALTER TABLE Alter_Example
ADD (Value_2 String DEFAULT 'Value_1 Default');
```

Listing 2–25. *Adding Column with ALTER TABLE*

As a consequence of the statement in Listing 2–25, the Alter_Example table is changed so that it appears as if it was created with the statement in Listing 2–26.

```
CREATE TABLE Alter_Example (
    Id          INTEGER      NOT NULL,
    Value_1     String       NOT NULL,
    Value_2     String       DEFAULT 'Value_1 Default'
);
```

Listing 2–26. *Resulting Table Structure from ALTER TABLE*

In Listing 2–25, the new column is added to the end of the row. As an alternative, the ALTER TABLE variation in Listing 2–27 might be used to place the new column between other columns of the table.

```
ALTER TABLE Alter_Example
ADD (Value_2 String DEFAULT 'Value_1 Default' BEFORE
Value_1);
```

Listing 2–27. Inserting New Column into Table Structure with ALTER TABLE

This would yield a table that resemble Listing 2–28. Note the different column order.

```
CREATE TABLE Alter_Example (
      Id          INTEGER     NOT NULL,
      Value_2     String      DEFAULT 'Value_1 Default',
      Value_1     String      NOT NULL
);
```

Listing 2–28. Result of Inserting New Column into Table Structure

Columns can be removed from tables using the syntax in Listing 2–29. After this statement completes, the named columns cannot be addressed by OR-SQL statements (queries that do generate errors) or any related indices. In addition, triggers and constraints are removed.

```
ALTER TABLE Alter_Example DROP ( Value_2 );
```

Listing 2–29. Removing a Column from a Table with ALTER TABLE

Other variations on the ALTER TABLE statement affect the way that the IDS stores the data in the table, and how it handles queries over the data. Such actions are usually undertaken by database administrators, rather than developers. Consult the product documentation for more details.

Adding CONSTRAINTS

ALTER TABLE can be used also to add constraints to tables and the CHECK, UNIQUE, PRIMARY, and FOREIGN KEY data integrity rules. The ALTER TABLE statement in Listing 2–30 illustrates how to add a PRIMARY KEY constraint.

```
ALTER TABLE Alter_Example ADD CONSTRAINT (PRIMARY KEY (Id));
```

Listing 2–30. Adding a CONSTRAINT Using ALTER TABLE

You should note that the ORDBMS checks that data in the modified table complies with the new constraint at the time the ALTER TABLE is issued. The presence of any illegal records in the table will cause the command to fail. Therefore, it is a very good idea to use a query to first identify any potential problem rows and fix them before adding the new constraint.

Altering Columns in Database Tables

You can use the ALTER TABLE statement to modify columns by changing their names, their data types (within certain limits), the default values, and whether the column is NULL-able. The range of column changes that are possible in the ORDBMS is limited. ROW TYPE and COLLECTION columns cannot be modified. In addition, it is important to keep in mind that whenever a table's column is altered, all constraints involving that column are removed.

The OR-SQL example in Listing 2–31 demonstrates how to modify a column.

```
ALTER TABLE Alter_Example MODIFY ( Id Movie_Id NOT NULL );
ALTER TABLE Alter_Example

        ADD CONSTRAINT ( PRIMARY KEY ( Id ));
```

Listing 2–31. *Changing Column Definitions with ALTER TABLE*

With the ORDBMS, you change an untyped table into a typed table. The intention is to make it possible to use Object-Relational features such as inheritance and polymorphism with an existing relational schema. Before a table can be modified in this way, you must have a ROW TYPE with a structure that corresponds to the table's column structure. Then you can use the ALTER TABLE statement as shown in Listing 2–32.

```
CREATE ROW TYPE Alter_Example_Type (
     Id          INTEGER      NOT NULL,
     Value_1     String       NOT NULL
);
ALTER TABLE Alter_Example ADD TYPE Alter_Example_Type;
```

Listing 2–32. *Assigning an Untyped Table to a ROW TYPE with ALTER TABLE*

By associating a ROW TYPE with a table, you can write queries that include user-defined functions defined for that type.

ALTER TABLE Implementation

The IDS product documentation notes that the performance implications of ALTER TABLE statements are extremely variable. Some ALTER TABLE statements, such as making columns NULL-able or adding constraints, merely change system catalog entries. Such changes are called *fast alters* because they can be completed quickly. For other kinds of modifications, however, the only way to make the change is to touch every row in the table. For large tables this can consume significant computational resources.

For changes that affect row structures, the ORDBMS uses two algorithms. The first of these effectively scans the entire table being modified and creates a copy of each row in some new location. This approach, which is called the *slow alter*, renders the table unavailable for queries while the change is being made. But once completed, the new table appears as though it always had the new structure.

The second approach is called the *in-place alter*. In-place alters do not modify the entire table in one operation. Rather, as the set of workload queries is applied to the database after the ALTER TABLE command is issued, the ORDBMS changes rows in the table as it processes them. This amortizes the cost of the table change over time and does not render the table unavailable.

Predicting the performance impact of an ALTER TABLE is difficult because the rules governing which approach IDS chooses are quite complex. Before altering a table in a production database, developers and administrators are well advised to consult the product documentation.

Dropping Tables

Tables are dropped with the DROP TABLE command. Because you can create tables in an inheritance hierarchy, it may be impossible to DROP a single table without scrambling the table relationships (removing a table with both a supertable and subtables). If you try to drop a table between two other tables, the ORDBMS generates an error. If you DROP the root of a table hierarchy, the ORDBMS will remove all tables in the hierarchy. Listing 2–33 shows a DROP TABLE.

```
DROP TABLE Cinemas;
```

Listing 2–33. *DROP TABLE Example*

Dropping a table deletes all data in the table, removes any indices created with the table, drops any TRIGGER rules defined for the table, and removes the table's definition from the schema. If the table is created using a ROW TYPE, dropping the table does not drop the type, because a type may be used in several other tables and in user-defined functions.

Views

Views are a powerful feature of the relational model. They permit database developers to

- present a subset of data in a table and thereby hide information and enforce security
- simplify complex or often repeated OR-SQL query operations by moving them within a view definition
- present certain users with a customized view of data by changing table name and column names without having to store data more than once

A view is a kind of *virtual* table. Views are created by writing a SELECT query and giving it a name. Once created, views look just like a real table as far as the other SELECT queries are concerned. View names are identifiers that can be used in queries instead of table names, and columns in a view can be addressed just such as columns in a table. Some simple view definitions also permit data values in their underlying base tables to be modified.

Creating Views

Listing 2–34 illustrates how to use the CREATE VIEW statement. It illustrates both the OR-SQL SELECT query (called the *defining query*) and the way it is assigned an identifying name. When the defining query produces two columns with the same default name or when it calculates some additional result columns, the view definition must supply names to disambiguate the columns of the view.

```
CREATE VIEW MovieClubByCounty
( ID, Name, County )
AS SELECT  M.Id,
           M.Name,
           C.Name AS County
```

```
        FROM MovieClub M, Counties C
        WHERE Contained(M.LivesAt, C.Boundary);


    CREATE VIEW SeniorMovieClub
        ( ID, Name, Age )
        AS SELECT M.Id,
                  M.Name,
                  Age(M)
            FROM MovieClubMembers M
            WHERE M.DOB < '01/01/1938';
```

Listing 2–34. *CREATE VIEW Example*

Rules concerning table and column identifiers apply to views too; column names must be unique, and views cannot have the same name as another table or view.

Views enable developers to present different perspectives of the database without having to store data more than once. Views can even represent a vast amount of data, so much in fact, that you would never want to select all of it at once. Queries on such a view include predicates that limit the return result to a manageable number of rows. For example, we can create a view that contains all products ever bought by members of the movie club; a conceptual view of the data that might be useful to Web site employees using reporting tools. Examine Listing 2–35.

```
CREATE VIEW MerchandisePurchased
( Member_Id, Member_Name, Product_Name,
  NumberBought, Price, OrderedOn, ShippedOn)
AS
SELECT C.Id,
       C.Name,
       M.Name,
       I.NumberBought,
       M.Price,
       O.OrderedOn,
       O.ShippedOn
  FROM Merchandise M, MovieClubMembers C, Order_Line_Items I,
       Orders O
 WHERE O.Customer    = C.Id
   AND O.Id          = I.Order
   AND I.Merchandise = M.Id;
```

Listing 2–35. *Hypothetical Relation View*

The total number of rows in MerchandisePurchased would be very large. However, for end users interested in outstanding orders, orders for a particular merchandise item, or orders by a particular customer, this view provides a logical place to answer their questions. Complex inter-relationships between base tables are hidden within the view definition, simplifying the queries they would write. Typical queries against this view will return a small subset of the rows it theoretically contains.

Views are particularly useful because they allow for *dynamic columns*. Such columns are the result of a calculation performed for each row. Somewhat simplistically, in the SeniorMovieClub view, the third column is actually the result of running the Age() function over the movie club member. By employing user-defined functions and built-in expressions in view definitions it is possible to create views where column values vary over time without updates to the underlying tables.

A more sophisticated use of the technology would be to call out to the ORDBMS in the function. For example, consider a function, CreditCardLimit(), that took as an argument a credit card object and called out to a service to establish the available limit on purchases NOT NULL using the card. You could then create the view in Listing 2–36. Each time you select from the view, the ORDBMS invokes the function once for each row in the result set. Such a function is easily created using Java.

```
CREATE VIEW MovieClubLimits
( ID, Name, CreditCard, CreditLimit )
AS
SELECT M.Id,
       M.Name,
       M.CreditCard,
       CreditCardLimit(M.CreditCard)
  FROM MovieClubMembers M;
```

Listing 2–36. *Using VIEWS to Implement Virtual or Calculated Columns*

Later, when we introduce physical storage techniques such as functional indices, we revisit the topic of dynamic columns.

Updateable Views

Some views are read-only and therefore can be used only in SELECT queries. Other views are *updateable*, and they can be used in both read and write queries. In general, a view is updateable if each row in the view can be traced back to a single row in an underlying base table, and if that base table contains no mandatory columns (columns with constraints) absent from the view. In other words, views where the view query eliminates rows or mandatory columns through one of the following query constructs are not updateable:

- views leaving out non NULL-able columns in base table
- aggregation (a GROUP BY) query
- a join or correlated subquery
- an attribute of the view that is produced by running a function

The views previously created in this chapter are not updateable. By contrast, the view definition in Listing 2–37 is updateable. When you modify its data values, IDS actually updates the corresponding rows in the MovieClubMembers table.

```
CREATE VIEW MemberMailingList
SELECT Id,
       Name,
       Address,
       HomePhone,
       GeoLocation,
       Preferences
  FROM MovieClubMembers;
```

Listing 2–37. *Updateable View Definition*

Note that what we are describing here is not a *materialized view*. At this time, the ORDBMS does not possess materialized view functionality.

Implementing Views

The ORDBMS stores view names and definitions in system catalogs. At runtime, when it detects the view's name in a query, the ORDBMS grafts the view's definition into the query plan. It literally adds all of the view's table names to the FROM clause and then adds predicates to the WHERE clause. Column names from tables in the underlying SELECT query substitute for the names of columns in view. Once this grafting is complete, the rewritten query proceeds through standard query processing. As such, ORDBMS can use its optimizer to produce different query plans depending on what the query over the view is interested in.

Sometimes grafting is not possible. In such circumstances, the ORDBMS will materialize the data in the view as part of query processing; that is, the ORDBMS executes the view query and stores the result in a temporary table. Then it grafts the name of the temporary table into the original query specification and processes the query over the materialized data. Finally, it cleans up the temporary table.

Physical Database Design

DBMS products adopt the relational model to gain data independence. Developers and end users interact with the database using declarative OR-SQL expressions that specify *what* is wanted, rather than blow-by-blow descriptions of *how* to proceed. The task of responding efficiently to user queries falls to automatically query processing facilities within the ORDBMS: parser, optimizer, executor, and storage manager.

The IDS product takes each OR-SQL expression and examines it to see what tables, columns, and functions are involved. Then it evaluates a large number of alternative ways to do the work implied by the query expression and selects the most efficient plan it can. The DBMS engine's capacity to respond efficiently to OR-SQL queries is enhanced by good physical design. Physical database design involves

- the creation of appropriate indexing structures
- distributing table data among the available physical storage units
- distributing large object data among available resources

The point of data independence is that changes to a database's physical design rarely require that other changes be made to OR-SQL queries to gain the advantage of the new layout. In this section we review the syntax used to perform physical design.

Indices

Indices speed up data retrieval. In an index, data from the table is stored in a special structure, called an *access method*. Access methods allow the ORDBMS to quickly retrieve the list of records that satisfy some predicate expression. For example, a common problem is to find the record in a table in which the table's primary key value is equal to a value supplied by an end user. Scanning the table and checking each row individually is clearly the slowest (and surest) way to find it, but indices make such scans unnecessary.

Instead of examining every row, the ORDBMS passes the key value into the index access method, and it returns the physical location of the matching record. Then the engine can use this physical location to quickly access the row.

All DBMS systems provide a set of built-in access methods that can be used with built-in data types. The most common of these is the B-Tree, which is useful for finding records in which a column value is in a particular range. Because IDS manages a variety of data types, it needs to support a variety of access methods. Non-standard indexes may be used to find all documents containing a certain word (text indices), all spatial objects within a certain distance of a given location, or all time intervals that overlap a given interval (both of which can be addressed using the R-Tree access method).

CREATE INDEX Statement

Indices are created using the CREATE INDEX statement. This specifies, at a minimum, the name of the new index, the name of the table to be indexed, and the columns in the table that will be included in the index. Listing 2–38 shows both the general form of the CREATE INDEX DDL statement and an example.

```
CREATE INDEX Index_Name
ON Table_Name( Column_Name [{ ,Column_Name}] [ op_class ])
[ USING Acess_Method ]


CREATE INDEX MovieClub_ndx1
ON MovieClub(DOB);
```

Listing 2–38. *CREATE INDEX Statement*

By default, the ORDBMS will try to build a B-Tree index. If you want to create an index using another access method, you need to specify it with the CREATE INDEX statement. For example, to create an index using the R-Tree, you would use the syntax in Listing 2–39.

```
CREATE INDEX MovieClub_ndx2
ON MovieClub( Location spatial_ops )
USING RTREE;
```

Listing 2–39. *CREATE INDEX Statement for the R-TREE Access Method*

Sometimes, you might want to build an index on columns defined with a user-defined type. For example, in our movies database, it would be very useful to have an index on the `Movie.Title` column. An ORDBMS can index user-defined types because all access methods that it ships with have been generalized in the way we described in Chapter 1. As long as you can define a function to *compare* two Movie_Title instances (to determine if the first is less than, equal to, or greater than the second), you can use the B-Tree access method.

When you create an index for a user-defined type, it is a good idea to specify the *operator class* that includes the compare logic. In Listing 2–40 we illustrate how an operator class for a B-Tree specified in a `CREATE INDEX`. This instructs the ORDBMS which `Compare()` function to use and which expressions, such as Equal and GreaterThan, that can be accelerated by using the new index.

```
CREATE INDEX Movies_Title_ndx
ON MOVIES ( Title Title_Btree_Ops );
```

Listing 2–40. *CREATE INDEX for User-Defined Type with Operator Class*

In Chapter 4, in which we examine user-defined types such as Movie_Title in more detail, we explain what an operator class is and how to create one.

Columns that are regularly used in query predicates are good candidates for indices. Primary key, foreign key and uniquely constrained columns have indices created for them automatically. Indexes can be physically partitioned like tables (see the next section of this chapter). Subtables inherit any indices created on tables above them in a hierarchy; that is, if you were to create an index on the Price column of the `Merchandise` table, all subtables in that hierarchy would share that index. Queries over the hierarchy involving the indexed column perform a single index scan, rather than multiple scans at the rate of one per subtable.

Functional Indices

One consequence of the way it adopts object-oriented approaches to software development is that the IDS product makes no distinction between the columns that make up a table's structure and the functions that compute values based on the data in a row. In practical terms, function results can be indexed, just like columns. Developers can create an index that uses as its key, instead of a column name, the results of a function run over elements of that table. Such indexes are called *functional indices*.

The CREATE INDEX statement in Listing 2–41 creates an index that stores, for each row, the result of the Soundex() function (which returns a string that represents the pronunciation of the name).

```
CREATE INDEX MovieClubMembers_ndx3
ON  MovieClubMembers(Soundex(Name.Surname));
```

***Listing 2–41.** A CREATE INDEX for Functional Index*

When the ORDBMS receives a query such as the one in Listing 2–42, it has the option to use the MovieClub_ndx3 index to look up the movie club members where the names sound alike. As is the case with conventional indices, the ORDBMS stores the key value for each row and a physical pointer back to a table location in the functional index. In such cases it first executes the Soundex("Brown") function, and uses the results to navigate through the index to identify matching rows in the table.

```
SELECT M.Name
    FROM MovieClubMembers M
    WHERE Soundex(M.Name.Surname) = Soundex("Brown");
```

***Listing 2–42.** A Query That Would Use the Functional Index*

Functional indices are useful in several ways. First, they reduce the amount of disk space you need. If a function can be used to compute the value, it may make sense to store the computed value only in an index rather than add a column to the base table. Second, when it takes a long time to compute the result that is stored in the index, the ORDBMS can use pre-computed results from UDF computed values rather than invoking the function again over each result row. This means that the functional index can dramatically reduce overall query time in situations in which the query involves "expensive" functions, particularly those dealing with documents.

One final note about indices in general. The ORDBMS keeps indices synchronized with the data in base tables. Inserts, updates, and deletes cause the ORDBMS to visit each index on the base table if it needs to,and adjust each accordingly. In the case of functional indices, the ORDBMS will run the function before modifying the index. Synchronizing indexes slows down write transactions. Deciding on an indexing scheme that balances the performance needs of the read and write operations in the database is therefore a challenge. If you have too many indices, the write transactions run unacceptably slowly, because they spend lots of time modifying indexes. If you have too few indices, the read queries don't perform.

Data Partitioning

Databases can grow very large, frequently much larger than a single disk's capacity. Therefore, the ORDBMS can distribute data tables across multiple disks. This data management technique, called *partitioning*, was developed for RDBMSs, and it works equally well with the ORDBMS data model. In addition, partitioning turns out to be the key to providing parallel data management.

Several schemes can be used to partition data. Each scheme is a procedure that the ORDBMS uses to allocate rows to different disk areas (called *table spaces*). Figure 2–10 illustrates the general idea of data partitioning.

The three schemes that the DBMS can use are as follows:

- Round robin. New records are allocated to data spaces in a cyclical fashion. The advantage of this approach is its simplicity and the way that it ensures good load balancing. It is the scheme with the best worst-case distribution.
- Hash. Hash partitioning divides the data according to a hash-based scheme. This is an essentially pseudo-random distribution, but a poorly chosen hash column, such as one with a small range of data values, can result in poor load balancing properties.
- Range partitioning. Tables can be partitioned in a way that rows are distributed among data spaces according to some expression. A well-chosen range expression can be a tremendous boon to query performance because the ORDBMS can sometimes ignore all rows in a physical storage area. A poor choice of partitioning expression can result in extremely bad load balancing.

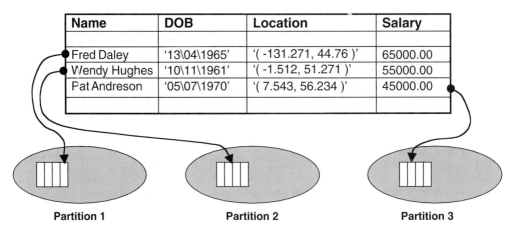

Name	DOB	Location	Salary
Fred Daley	'13\04\1965'	'(-131.271, 44.76)'	65000.00
Wendy Hughes	'10\11\1961'	'(-1.512, 51.271)'	55000.00
Pat Andreson	'05\07\1970'	'(7.543, 56.234)'	45000.00

Partition 1   Partition 2   Partition 3

Figure 2–10. *Table Partitioning for Distributing Rows Across Physical Storage Spaces*

Partitioning directives are included as part of the CREATE TABLE statement. Physical organization rules consist of the set of table spaces to be used to hold the table data and the algorithm to be used to allocate rows to table spaces. For example, the statement in Listing 2–43 creates the MovieClubMembers table from the MovieClub_Type ROW TYPE and instructs the ORDBMS to distribute rows in the table over several table spaces using a round robin algorithm.

```
CREATE TABLE MovieClubMember (
        Id          Membership_Num   NOT NULL PRIMARY KEY,
        Name        PersonName       NOT NULL,
        DOB         date,
        Address     AddressType      NOT NULL,
        HomePhone   PhoneNumber      NOT NULL,
        Location    Point            NOT NULL,
        Preferences SET(Genre_Enum   NOT NULL),
        Photo       Image,
        CreditCard  CCDetails
)
FRAGMENT BY ROUND ROBIN IN
        Table_Space_1, Table_Space_2, Table_Space_3;
```

Listing 2–43. *A Physical Partitioning Scheme Specified with CREATE TABLE*

You also can alter the partitioning scheme, or add a partitioning scheme to a table, by using the ALTER FRAGMENT command.

The choice of appropriate partitioning strategy depends on the specifics of the table's data, the query workload, and the performance objectives. In addition, the effectiveness of query parallelism is highly dependent on the partitioning scheme. When the ORDBMS uses parallel processing techniques to execute a query, it creates several query segments, one per partition. Ideally, you would like all of these query segments to take about the same time to complete, so the distribution of data among partitions is a critical issue.

Fortunately, these important issues relating to data partitioning and query parallelism, in particular data skew, apply just as much to ORDBMSs as to RDBMSs. Principles and techniques developed for RDBMS parallelism apply also with ORDBMSs.

Large Object Data Management

Efficient management of large object data is more important in an ORDBMS than it was in RDBMSs. Object-relational database applications manage more digital signal data, documents, and time series information than relational DBMSs. In addition, ORDBMS databases move the logic that operates on such data into the query engine.

Certain aspects of the problem can be dealt with as part of the internal design of the large object data interfaces and storage management facilities. Instead of pulling an entire BLOB out of the RDBMS and into an external program in order to extract a few bytes, the ORDBMS provides interface functions that can go into a large object's data and read only relevant segments of it into memory.

Disk storage for large objects is reserved by the ORDBMS as smart large object spaces (*sbspace*). As part of the CREATE TABLE DDL statement, database administrators inform the DBMS about how large object data in a table is allocated into sbspaces. In Listing 2–44 we illustrate how to associate the large objects in a particular column with a particular large object data space.

```
CREATE TABLE Personalities (
        Id          Personality_Id   NOT NULL PRIMARY KEY
        Name        PersonName       NOT NULL,
        DOB         date             NOT NULL,
        Died        date,
        LivesIn     State_Enum,
        Biography   Doc_Type         NOT NULL,
        Photo       Image            NOT NULL
) PUT Biography IN (sbspace_01),
   PUT  Photo IN (sbspace_02);
```

Listing 2–44. *Physical Data Management for Large Object Data Types*

The techniques used to manage large object storage will undergo substantial evolution over the next few versions of the ORDBMS product. Consult the product documentation for detail.

Hierarchical Storage Managers

In modern multimedia databases, the volume of large object data is often so great that magnetic disks are an expensive storage solution. In these circumstances, tertiary storage devices such as WORM CD jukeboxes or tape robots are common. This kind of storage technology is a poor choice for table data, where most access is random, but they perform very well for streaming large volumes of continuous data, such as images, video, large time series, and so on.

The ORDBMS relies on the operating system for *file system* services. Hierarchical storage managers (HSMs) typically plug into the operating system at a low level. They allow programs such as the ORDBMS to store data in the HSM as though they were storing data on magnetic disks. Database administrators can create subspace partitions in areas of their computer's file system that are in fact implemented by the HSM.

Database Security and Access Privileges

A database is a resource shared by a number of users, so security is an issue that database developers DBMS need to address, and for databases containing sensitive information security issues can be complex. For example, access to personal information about movie club members may be restricted to a few employees working on the Movies-R-Us Web site. Meanwhile, the site's management may decide to prevent most employees from altering merchandise prices while all users need to read that information.

The IDS product includes a variety of access rules that define the privileges users need to perform operations over various schema objects. These rules differ depending on whether the database was created to conform to the ANSI security rules, or the IDS product's historical approach. In general, ANSI defines very restrictive security rules while the IDS product's own rules were somewhat looser. In this section we provide a general overview of database security facilities.

DBMS Security Model

ANSI mode security begins by assuming that users (except DBA) have no access privileges at all. Before they can execute queries involving a database object, users must be granted the appropriate privileges. With ANSI databases only the user who created the table or view can access it by default. By contrast, IDS default security permits all objects to be accessed by anyone in the PUBLIC role, essentially anyone who can connect, unless permission is revoked by the DBA or owner.

At runtime the ORDBMS checks each action to ensure that the user initiating the action has the appropriate privileges. If the user does not, the ORDBMS will raise an error.

Access privileges are granted over all kinds of database objects, including entire databases, tables, views, and columns within tables, as well as the user-defined types and routines introduced in Chapters 4 and 5. For simplicity, an administrator can group users into *roles* and control access by granting privileges to roles instead of individual users. There is also a special role known as *public*, to which all users automatically belong. Granting privileges over a database object to public therefore implies that all users share that privilege.

For an entire database, the DBA or the database's creator can grant the privileges shown in Table 2–1:

Table 2–1. Database-Level Privileges

Privilege	Explanation
CONNECT	Named users or roles can connect to the database. Once connected, they can issue DML queries (SELECT, INSERT, UPDATE, and DELETE), and the legality of these operations then depends on the table-level privileges the user has. The only DDL permitted to users with this basic level of privilege is the creating of temporary tables. Once in production, this is the most typical level of privilege granted to users. You want them to use your database, but not to change any elements of the schema.
RESOURCE	Granting this privilege to a user allows them to connect to a database and then extend the database's schema with their own tables, indices, routines, and types, and grant schema level access privileges over these types.
DBA	This is the highest level of privilege to grant to a user because it lets him or her grant privileges to other users, create and drop permanent schema objects, and perform administrative tasks.

Table 2–2. Database Object-Level (Table) Privileges

Privilege	Explanation
ALL	Grants all privileges described in this table to the named user.
INSERT	Insert rows into the table.
DELETE	Delete rows from the table.
UPDATE	Allows the user to change data values in a table. As part of the UPDATE privilege, you can also specify which *columns* in the table the user can UPDATE.
SELECT	Allows a user to read data from the table. As with the UPDATE privilege, you also can specify which columns the user can SELECT.
REFERENCES	Allowing this privilege means that the grantee, who is the user mentioned in the GRANT statement, can define referential integrity constraints over the table.
ALTER	Grants the user the privilege to change the table's definition with the ALTER TABLE statement.
INDEX	User is allowed to create and modify indices for the table.

For a specified database table, a user can be granted the privileges in Table 2–2.

GRANT Command

User privileges are controlled with the GRANT command. In this section we focus on how the GRANT command is used to control privileges over schema objects. In subsequent chapters we show how the GRANT command is used to control privileges for other objects, such as types and functions. The basic form of the GRANT command is shown in Listing 2–45.

```
GRANT [ DATABASE PRIVILEGE ] TO [ USER_LIST | ROLE ];
```

Listing 2–45. *General Form of GRANT Command for Database-Level Privileges*

For example, it would probably be a good idea to grant RESOURCE privileges to all users for the Movie-R-Us Web site database. To do this, you would connect to the database as the administrative user and issue the command in Listing 2–46. This command applies to the database you are connected to at the time you issue it.

```
GRANT RESOURCE TO PUBLIC;
```

Listing 2–46. *GRANT Command for Database-Level Privileges*

For tables and views, you use the general form of the GRANT command, as shown in Listing 2–47.

```
GRANT [ TABLE PRIVILEGE ]
ON [TABLE or VIEW ]
TO [ USER_LIST | ROLE ];
```

Listing 2–47. *General Form of GRANT Command for Table-Level Privileges*

In Listing 2–48, the statements GRANT SELECT privileges on the Merchandise table hierarchy to everyone, but restrict the privilege to make changes to the Merchandise data to users who are part of the accounting role.

```
GRANT SELECT ON Merchandise TO PUBLIC;
GRANT ALL ON Merchandise TO accounting;
```

Listing 2–48. *GRANT Command for Table Level Privileges*

You also use the GRANT command to group users into roles. The pair of SQL statements in Listing 2–49 creates a role called accounting and places three users into that group.

```
CREATE ROLE accounting;
GRANT accounting TO eeverage, bwayne;
```

Listing 2–49. *Creating ROLES and Adding Users to Roles*

REVOKE Command

The REVOKE command is the complement to the GRANT command. It removes a privilege from a user or group. For example, the SQL statement in Listing 2–50 removes the SELECT privilege from the PUBLIC role.

```
REVOKE SELECT ON Merchandise FROM public;
```

Listing 2–50. *A REVOKE Command to Revoke a Privilege from User or Role*

ROLES and Users

Managing users individually is difficult when there are a great many of them. The IDS product allows database administrators to group individual into a ROLE. A set of CREATE, DROP, GRANT and REVOKE commands are provided to manage roles and organize users according to the established roles. Roles can be defined recursively: all of the users in role B are assigned into role A when role B is assigned into role A.

Note that upon connecting, users need to establish with the ORDBMS the role in which they are operating. This is achieved using the SET ROLE command. Readers are advised to consult the IDS product documentation for more details on this topic.

Chapter Summary

In this chapter we introduced the principle structural ideas behind the object-relational data model, and the syntax that the OR-SQL language provides to support these features. The ORDBMS data model provides high-level, flexible data management services. A central principle of these features can be seen in the way that developers using SQL can specify what it is they want to achieve. While the details of how queries are actually executed are worked out at runtime by the ORDBMS. The resulting flexibility enhances programmer productivity and improves the quality of the overall information system.

The ORDBMS data model is a synthesis of the best ideas from the relational and object data modeling approaches. It is an extension of the relational model with certain object-oriented features such as inheritance, collections, and polymorphism. Objects in an ORDBMS database are stored in tables, which you can think of as a variable number of identically structured records. Developers use the SQL DDL facilities to create tables and to endow those tables with rules that ensure the correctness of the data they contain.

Object-relational tables are very similar to SQL-92 tables, except for the following facts:

- The range of data types used to define their columns is greatly expanded.
- Columns can be groups of data in a COLLECTION, in addition to single, atomic values.
- Developers also can create tables in hierarchies. Hierarchies are sets of tables containing a common set of columns and constraint rules.

The ORDBMS supports a wide range of table and schema management functionality. Once a table has been created, developers can modify it by adding and removing columns and constraints. Developers can specify the physical storage rules for their tables, partitioning the data in tables across data spaces according to several algorithms. They can also create various kinds of indices that the ORDBMS can use to accelerate queries by quickly finding matching values for certain kinds of query expressions. Finally, the ORDBMS supports a sophisticated security model that permits a privileged user to grant and revoke certain kinds of query privileges to different groups of users.

In this chapter we have seen how to create and manage ORDBMS database schema objects, such as tables, views, and indices. In the next chapter we examine how to write queries against these schema objects. Then we move on to explain how to create the user-defined data types and functions that are arranged within the framework provided by the relational features of the ORDBMS.

Physical Data Organization

In this tutorial, we provide a brief overview of the how the IDS product performs physical data management. This tutorial is intended mainly for readers new to the product, although some of the information here is useful for developers wanting a clearer understanding of low-level data management issues. The details described here also help to explain certain performance characteristics in large, production environments.

Table Data: Pages, Heaps and Table Spaces

Table data is stored on *pages*. Pages are the smallest unit of I/O: the IDS product does not read or write in increments of less than a page, which has a fixed size on each platform. In most cases this is either 2 KB (2048 bytes) bytes or 4 KB (4096 bytes). Page-based data organization is used for storing table data, index data, logging information, and for describing the physical condition of the database's disk storage structure.

Data values in each row, regardless of the value's data type, are arranged into a sequential byte array. In Figure 1–1 we present the basic layout of row data within a single table page. The other kinds of pages are all quite similar. Every page contains a header describing what kind of page it is, its physical address within the storage system, how full the page is, and whereabouts on the page space is available. Rather than sequentially searching a page to find a row of data the page's data layout is indexed in the *slot table*, which grows from the end of the table towards the header. Timestamps in the header and the footer of the page indicate whether the page's contents could be corrupted.

Let us first focus on how row data and table pages are arranged. Unless a row's size exceeds the page size, several pages are used to hold the row and a single row is not divided across pages. Consequently, if a row's width exceeds one half of a page's size, IDS will dedicate an entire page to hold it, and excess space on the page is not used. Large tables with row widths exceeding one half of page size will waste considerable amounts of space.

2 KB is not a lot of data. Most disks and disk controllers can read far larger blocks for the cost of a single head movement, and in large table scans issuing many small read instructions is inefficient. So groups of pages from a table are arranged into *extents*, which are contiguous

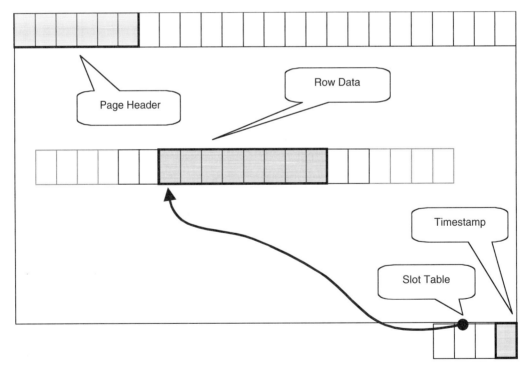

Figure 1–1. *Page Layout for Table Data Pages*

areas of disk space. As it scans a table, the ORDBMS reads data extent at a time, rather than page at a time, as shown in Figure 1–2.

Index scans adopt a different strategy. Navigating an index involves reading a series of single pages containing references to other index pages, or to pages holding table data. We discuss index structures later in this tutorial.

Extents are allocated out of storage spaces called *table spaces*, which are logical rather than physical structures. A table space is made up of a set of chunks, and it is at the chunk level that disk storage is mapped to physical resources such as files or raw devices. When a database or a table is created any data within it is mapped to a set of table spaces which IDS in turn maps into disk reads and writes at the chunk level.

One chunk can hold many extents. Each extent holds data for a single table, and a single table can have multiple extents. In Figure 1–2, we illustrate this idea by assigning each extent its own coloration pattern. In addition to extents containing data pages, chunks include a small set of

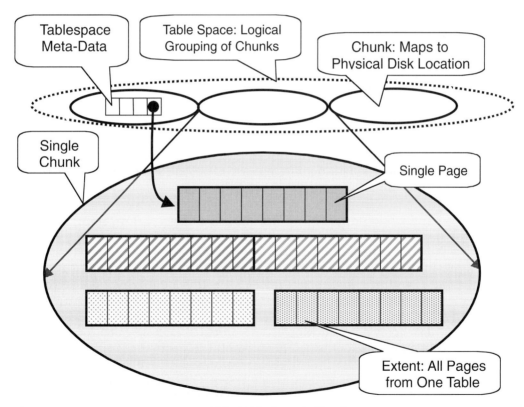

Figure 1–2. *Extent Management Within Table Space's Chunk*

pages that manages information about the chunk, including the chunk's identity, extent locations, free space, and so on.

Pages are also used in the *logging* system. Whenever table data is changed—by INSERT, UPDATE, or DELETE statements or a bulk-load operation—the ORDBMS uses logging facilities to record what the data looked like before the change, and a description of the changes made to that data. Logging data is used for several purposes. If the IDS or the computer it is running on crashes, logging data is used to recover the database to a consistent state. Replication services also use logging information as a means of capturing every data change with minimal computational overhead.

Large Object Management

The way IDS handles large object data is one of the most obvious differences between it and other DBMS products. The ORDBMS provides transactional guarantees for all changes to large object data; that is, developers can create code that modifies the bytes within a large object. It also includes the following:

- The ORDBMS guarantees that it can recover the object to the state it was in before any change was initiated if the modifying operation is rolled back or the system crashes.
- No two users can conflict with each other, although they can be reading and writing different aspects of the same large object at the same time.

Individual large objects are stored in *sbspaces* (for "Smart Blob Spaces"). These are analogous in many ways to table spaces because they are logical units of storage consisting of multiple physical chunks of disk space. The address of each large object is encapsulated within a *large object handle*. It is this identifying address label that is stored within the columns of a table or inside an OPAQUE TYPE structure.

Like table data, large objects are stored in *extents*, which consist of a contiguous block of pages. If you know the size of the large object, use the mi_lo_specset_estbytes() DataBlade API call to get the ORDBMS to pre-allocate space for it as one extent. Otherwise it is probably best to let the ORDBMS deal with managing extent allocation.

There are advantages and disadvantages to handling large objects internally to the ORDBMS. Because all changes are made with transactional guarantees, the read and write performance of large objects stored in smart blob spaces may not be as good as large object data stored in a file system. But for certain kinds of operations, the ORDBMS can take advantage of techniques like pre-fetch—where larger blocks of data consisting of an entire extent can be read in a single operation.

Memory Caching

Reading data from disk into memory is enormously computationally expensive. And in many databases, a small subset of data is subjected to a disproportionate amount of user access. Optimizing the use of memory, particularly with respect to large queries, is a high-priority goal of any DBMS.

About all that an administrator can do to affect memory usage is to obtain more of it, and to allocate more of it to the ORDBMS's data buffers. Monitoring the amount of data being exchanged between the buffer cache and disk can indicate when the problem has become critical. This done using the `onstat` utility.

What complicates the process is the way that IDS exploits certain features of its physical data management to achieve other objectives, notably locking and recovery. As data on cached pages changes, the ORDBMS does not write the changed page back to disk immediately. Instead, it waits until what it considers to be a convenient period of time before synchronizing cached data with data on disk; a technique called *checkpointing*.

Indices: B-Trees and R-Trees

Indices accelerate individual queries and reduce the total amount of computer resources necessary to support a query workload. IDS provides two index access methods: B-Tree and R-Tree (or Region Tree). An important innovation in the ORDBMS is that all of the access methods are *generalized*, that is, rather than simply allowing developers to build indices out of complex objects by specifying the precedence of elements (element has highest precedence, which one next, and so on), the ORDBMS provides an interface-based mechanism instead.

B-Trees and R-Trees are structurally quite similar. Both index structures are *dynamic,* which means that the structure changes as new data is added into it, and *height balanced,* which means that the number of levels of internal pages is the same throughout. In Figure 1–3, we illustrate what such tree structures look like, and how they tie back to table data.

What is the difference between the two access methods? Basically, each is suitable for a different kind of data.

B-Tree Indices

B-Trees are among the oldest and best known indexing technique. They are useful for indexing data that can be sorted into some meaningful order; that is, data where some algorithm exists that determines if one instance of the object class is less than, equal to, or greater than, another. This includes all of the built-in SQL-92 types and the majority of user-defined object classes. In this book, almost all of the User-defined Type (UDT) examples have operator classes associated with them that can use the B-Tree.

In Figure 1–4 below we illustrate what a B-Tree index looks like. Note that this is simplified to a considerable degree. B-Tree pages

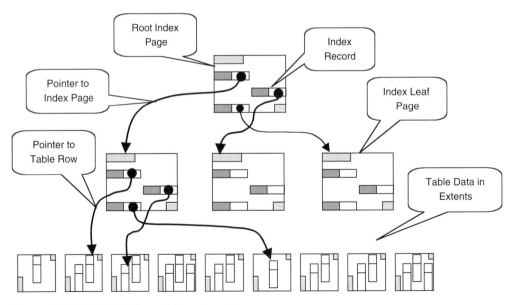

Figure 1–3. *Height Balanced Tree Overview*

Root Page

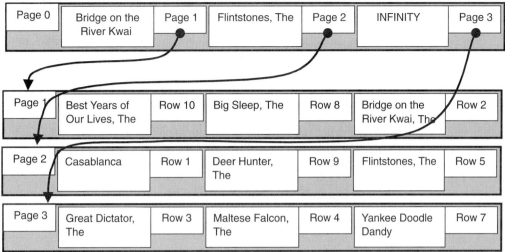

Figure 1–4. *B-Tree Logical Structure*

almost always contain more than three entries. And the algorithms used to manage B-Tree pages efficiently—particularly when it is desirable to have more than a single write transaction modifying the tree at the same time—are quite complex.

Note how, in this figure, we show how space on B-Tree pages is preallocated in much the same way it is on table pages. Also, note how important it is to pack as many index entries onto each internal node of the tree as possible. Consequently, the ORDBMS imposes a limit on how large key data can be. Types with a MAXLEN in excess of 256 bytes cannot be stored in a B-Tree. But when an OR-SQL query's WHERE clause includes one of the *ordinal operators* { '<', '<=', '=', '=>', '>' and '<>'), it is a pretty good bet that a B-Tree index would help the query's performance.

R-Tree Indices

R-Trees are a more recent innovation. Originally intended to solve the problem of indexing spatial data types such as Polygons, Boxes and Points, R-Trees also have proven themselves effective indexing concepts such as temporal periods (intervals of time fixed in the timeline) and ranges of other types. In this book, the Period data type provides an example of the kind of object that can benefit from using an R-Tree.

The best way to explain R-Trees is with a diagram. In Figure 1–5 we present a set of polygons. These might represent the geographic range of an animal or the customers who shop at a particular store, for example.

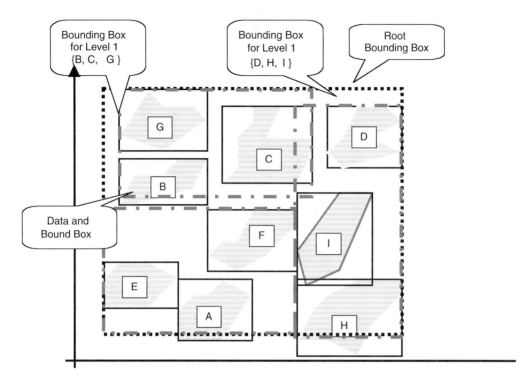

Figure 1–5. *Distribution of Spatial Data Objects (Polygons)*

The operations that the R-Tree index is useful for are spatial in nature and include Overlap, Within, Contains, and Equal. In an R-Tree, index nodes store rectangles. In the leaf page nodes of the index, these rectangles correspond to the *minimum bounding rectangle* for the data being indexed (polygons on our example). Higher up in the index the rectangles correspond to the minimum bounding rectangle for *all rectangles in the index nodes below*. In Figure 1–6 we present the logical internal structure of an R-Tree.

So how does this work? Regardless of the predicate in the query (Overlap, Within, Contains or Equal) the ORDBMS can use the R-Tree to identify a small set of candidate data values quickly. Or, stating it another way, the ORDBMS figures out what pages it can ignore as soon as possible.

It begins with the *target* shape, and the root page of the index. Any of the next level pages whose bounding box entries do not *overlap* the target are left out of the scan. Only subpages with overlapping bound boxes get investigated. But at the level of the leaf nodes, the ORDBMS checks the bound box against the actual predicate and target value.

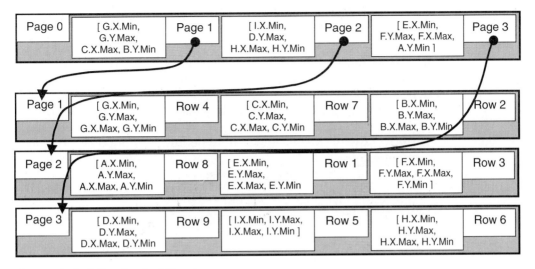

Figure 1–6. *R-Tree Logical Structure*

So, if we wanted to find all polygons that Overlap the polygon labeled "I", then according to Figure 1–6, the scan would ignore Page 2, checking only Pages 1 and 3. And on these pages, it could quickly eliminate all bounding boxes on Page 1 and only match for "I" on Page 3. As with B-Trees, index pages in R-Trees carry a great many more entries than can be shown in our example (about 50). Overall, the R-Tree combines excellent performance with simple OR-SQL syntax.

Tools, Utilities, and Techniques

For the most part, the IDS product tries to keep developers implementing user-defined extensions, and those writing OR-SQL queries, from needing to know too much about physical data management details. Instead, the task of ensuring that the logical database makes the most effective use of hardware falls to the *database administrator* or DBA. This role straddles the worlds of the DBMS hardware and operating system. But DBAs are frequently called upon to help resolving application level issues such as poorly performing queries or conflicting transactions.

Every effort is made to allow the DBA to alter a database's physical configuration without making its table contents unavailable for queries. Tasks such as adding disk space, creating indices, and altering table structures do not require shutting down the DBMS. More work in this direction is necessary. Creating an index, for example, while it does not shut down the database, has the unfortunate side effect of rendering the table unavailable while the index is being built. For large tables in busy systems, this can be a problem.

DBAs work with the ORDBMS's data definition language, to create schema objects such as types, tables, views and indices, and with non-SQL utilities to add and manage disk space.

Data Definition Language and Physical Organization

In Chapter 2, we introduced the optional syntax in OR-SQL's CREATE TABLE and CREATE INDEX DDL statements that specifies how data in the table or view is to be *fragmented* across a set of *table spaces*. Fragmentation is essential to high performance data management for the following reasons:

- Fragmentation balances I/O load across available disk resources. By dividing a table across several disks in such a way that the number of rows modified on each disk is the same, an administrator minimizes the likelihood of "hot-spots" which are frequently accessed pages or extents.
- Internally, the ORDBMS can break a single query expression into one *query per fragment* or *table space.* The result of this division is that all of the available disk bandwidth can be used concurrently, which is the key to query parallelism. Thus, fragmentation reduces response time for large queries.

Fragmentation is a technique that administrators can use to overcome either a throughput or a response time problem. But it is not a magic wand. Taking advantage of query parallelism will improve the performance of a single query. But it does not reduce the overall computational workload: it simply permits the ORDBMS to devote more hardware resources to the query in question. So parallelism will not improve throughput (time taken to complete a given workload of many queries). In fact, it will probably make matters worse!

But fragmenting does achieve a degree of I/O load balancing. This improves overall throughput by minimizing the potential for resource conflicts between transactions. The more disk arms the ORDBMS can keep busy, the mote data it can read and write in a given time, although this does not affect the performance of any one query. In fact, it might slow it down.

Administrative Tools and Utilities

IDS includes a suite of administrative tools for monitoring the performance of the instance and for managing it. The most useful of these tools are summarized in Table 1–1.

Interested readers are advised to consult the product documentation for more details. Readers familiar with how the previous SQL-92-based versions of the DBMS worked can rest assured that the utility of their skill set is unaffected by any of the innovative features to be found in the ORDBMS. DBAs everywhere will still have a job.

Table 1-1. Overview of DBS Tools and Utilities

Tool Name	Description
oncheck	Used to monitor the internal structure of a disk space. Provides options to check the consistency of its physical layout, meta data describing its contents, the structure of tables, indices and large objects in the space, and a means of dumping raw data.
onmode	Used to instruct the ORDBMS to change its operational configuration at runtime. For example, this utility provides the means to shutdown an instance, add or reduce memory, and modify physical aspects of the run-time environment such as the degree of query parallelism.
onspaces	Used to add or drop table spaces, smart blob spaces, and the chunks within them.
oninit	Used initially to install the ORDBMS, and thereafter to start the installation after a shutdown. This is also the name of the primary ORDBMS executable.
onstat	Used to monitor the run-time state of the instance. This utility connects to the ORDBMS's resident memory portion and reports the data held there. Similar information can be retrieved using the System Management Interfaces (SMI), which are a set of system catalog "tables" that work in the same way.

Chapter 3

Object-Relational Queries

Manipulating Object-Relational Data

Developers use the *Data Manipulation Language (DML)* features of OR-SQL to work with the data in an ORDBMS database. DML statements are usually called *queries*. Different kinds of queries insert, update, delete, and retrieve data, or invoke a module of procedural logic embedded within the ORDBMS. A query is a string that contains a mix SQL's *keywords* (or reserved words), *identifiers* that name the schema objects involved in the query (tables, columns, and elements within a ROW TYPE), and *expressions* (or functions) to manipulate individual data objects. Almost all OR-SQL statements also include some constant data type values.

With each kind of query certain keywords are required to appear in certain places. For example, the first word of any query indicates the action it performs (INSERT, UPDATE, DELETE, SELECT, or EXECUTE). SQL keywords are fixed by the language's specification, user-defined functions expressions that are part of a DataBlade Product can be re-used in several different databases, while table and column names are typically specific to a particular database schema.

Table 3–1 presents the more common keywords used in OR-SQL. Words in bold are the ones most frequently used in queries. Other keywords are used in the data definition language to create schema objects, or are reserved by the language standard.

Table 3–1. ANSI SQL Reserved Works. Query Keywords in Bold

ADA	ALL	AND	ANY
AS	ASC	AUTHORIZATION	AVG
BEGIN	**BETWEEN**	**BY**	**CAST**
CHAR	CHARACTER	CHECK	CLOSE
COBOL	**COMMIT**	CONTINUE	**COUNT**
CREATE	**CURRENT**	CURSOR	DEC
DECIMAL	DECLARE	**DELETE**	**DESC**
DISTINCT	END	ESCAPE	**EXECUTE**
EXISTS	**FETCH**	FLOAT	FOR
FORTRAN	FOUND	**FROM**	GO
GOTO	**GROUP**	**HAVING**	IN
INDICATOR	**INSERT**	INT	INTEGER
INTO	IS	LANGUAGE	**LIKE**
LIST	**MAX**	**MIN**	MODULE
MULTISET	**NOT**	**NULL**	NUMERIC
OF	ON	OPEN	OPTION
OR	**ORDER**	PASCAL	PLI
PRECISION	PRIMARY	PROCEDURE	PRIVILEGES
PUBLIC	REAL	**ROLLBACK**	SCHEMA
SECTION	**SELECT**	**SET**	SMALLINT
SOME	SQL	SQLCODE	SQLERROR
SUM	**TABLE**	TO	**UNION**
UNIQUE	**UPDATE**	USER	**VALUES**
VIEW	WHENEVER	**WHERE**	WITH
WORK			

Keyword lists only grow, and DBMS products vary with respect to the restrictions placed on their use as schema object identifiers (table and column names, for example). The IDS product is quite lenient, allowing for tables named "INDEX" and columns named "NULL." It is, however, considered bad database programming practice to use keywords to name schema objects because it leads to confusing queries and makes porting difficult.

OR-SQL as a Query Framework Language

By convention, descriptions of SQL begin with an overview of the data types and expressions that the language supports. But while OR-SQL shares many features with more conventional SQL, it is useful to describe it somewhat differently. In this book we treat OR-SQL as a syntactic framework, rather than a complete language. Developers who install the ORDBMS for the first time will find that almost none of the example queries in this book will work. Contrast this with traditional SQL-92, where all SQL-92 DBMS products support a nearly identical language.

All queries in this chapter include some user-defined extensions, and what is important about each example is its syntactical structure. Developers building their own database applications will reuse the query patterns introduced here but they will involve extensions that reflect their business problem. The meaning of an object-relational query is determined by the way that it combines database table and column identifiers with user-defined functions. Another way to say this is that the ORDBMS is an example of a software framework. It accepts user-defined components—user-defined types and user-defined functions—and makes it possible to use them within a set of algorithmic patterns—represented by the object-relational data model and its query language.

Overview of Chapter

This chapter introduces the query language aspects of object-relational SQL and describes how they are used. We proceed by first explaining the theoretical foundations of the relational model's data manipulation operations. Understanding how the model works is helpful when formulating more complex queries. Then we move on to describe OR-SQL syntax in detail, explaining how to use each of the basic statements. As you progress through this chapter the examples get increasingly complex. For each kind of query, we introduce it with a simple example explain its various parts in some detail. Then we explore its more sophisticated forms.

Relational Manipulation Operations

In the previous chapter we saw how the relational model organizes data into *relations,* which are sets of identically structured records. The relational model also includes a set of relational *operators.* These describe how the data in relations can be combined and manipulated. Relational operators are algorithmic patterns, each of which is a procedure that takes one or two relations as input and produces a single relation as output. OR-SQL statements—even relatively simple ones—combine a number of relational operators into a single, higher-level expression.

In this section we introduce several of the simpler relational operators in order to illustrate the general idea. Each description includes a simple OR-SQL example that performs an equivalent operation. The idea is to introduce you to the flavor of what OR-SQL looks like and to demonstrate how user-defined extensions and query syntax interrelate. Also, note that throughout this section, the functionality of each relational operator is described in terms of *relations*, rather than tables. This is because the operators apply to the intermediate results of queries and COLLECTION data as well as to base tables storing persistent data.

Projection

When you *project* a relation, you produce as output a new relation with the same number of rows as the input, but with a different number of columns. We saw an example of projection in Chapter 2, where the *Parented* relation was transformed to produce the *Fathered* relation we. The MovieClubMembers table introduced in the previous chapter could be projected to a result consisting of only the Name and DOB columns. Such an operation, and its result, would look like Listing 3–1.

```
SELECT Name, DOB
   FROM MovieClubMembers;
```

Name::PersonName	DOB::DATE
('Freyenbauger','Mira')	3/2/1964
('Hume', 'David')	1/12/1961
('Eliot', 'George')	3/2/1964

Listing 3–1. Simple PROJECTION Relational Operator and SQL Equivalent

Listing 3–1 illustrates query results in terms both column names and each column's data type. Including type information with query results emphasizes the fact that in an extensible database, information about a column's contents must include its data type. Whereever space permits we adopt this style throughout this chapter.

In our sample data, "George Eliot" and "Mira Freyenbauger" share a birthday. According to the strict letter of the theoretical relational model, query results should never contain duplicate rows. But eliminating duplicates is computationally expensive, and application operations that are required not to return unique rows are the exceptions, so by default the IDS product does not do so. When duplicate rows in the result are not acceptable, the query can use the DIS-TINCT keyword to eliminate them. The pair of queries in Listing 3–2 demonstrates how this is achieved.

```
SELECT DOB
    FROM MovieClubMembers;
```

DOB::DATE

```
1/12/1961
3/2/1964
1/12/1961
```

```
SELECT DISTINCT DOB
    FROM MovieClubMembers;
```

DOB::DATE

```
3/2/1964
1/12/1961
```

Listing 3–2. *Using DISTINCT Keyword in SQL Query*

For the more visually oriented, Figure 3–1 is a diagrammatic representation of the projection operation. Note how this figure and all of the other diagrams in this section adopt the practice of using exotic characters and symbols to emphasize the way that an object-relational DBMS columns can contain user-defined objects. Data type and function extensibility features do not limit the relational operators in any way.

Some books explain the concept of projection by saying that the columns making up the output relation are a subset of the columns in the input. However, with OR-SQL, it is important to emphasize the way

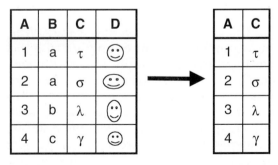

Figure 3–1. *Diagrammatic Presentation of PROJECTION*

that data values in the result can be calculated in the query, which is another kind of projection. For example, the query in Listing 3–3 returns the name and age of each movie club member. It includes a user-defined function called `Print()`, which that formats a person's name for presentation, and another called `Age()`, which calculates the interval in years between the member's date of birth and the current date.

```
SELECT Print(M.Name) AS Name,
       Age(M) AS Age
  FROM MovieClubMembers M;
```

Name::IVARCHAR	Age::INTEGER
Mira Freyenbauger	34
Joe Blogs	30
Van Quoc	47
Paul Brown	30

Listing 3–3. *PROJECTION of Calculated Result*

Of course, calculating new results in a query expression is not new to OR-SQL. In an object-relational database however, the way that a query can incorporate new user-defined functions makes this style of query very useful.

Listing 3–3 also illustrates how a user-defined function can be applied to an entire table row. In this case the `Age()` UDF takes a single argument—a `ROW TYPE` called MovieClubMember_Type that is also used to define the table's structure—and calculates its result based on elements contained within the `ROW TYPE`. Listing 3–3 demonstrates how to use a table alias to represent a `ROW TYPE`. Later in this chapter this syntax appears again, when we investigate the mechanics of polymorphic queries.

Restriction

Projection involves columns. *Restriction* affects rows. When the ORDBMS restricts a relation it produces another with the same number of columns as the input, but usually with a different number of rows. As the operator is working, it checks each row from the input and executes some boolean expression over it. Rows where the expression is true are passed through to the output, while the others are discarded. We say that all of the rows in the result *satisfy* the *predicate*. In OR-SQL queries, predicates are found in the query's WHERE clause as shown in Listing 3–4.

"Show me movie personalities whose family name is Wyler."

```
SELECT *
  FROM MoviePersonalities M
  WHERE M.Name.Family_Name = 'Wyler'::ShortString;
```

Id:: Person_Id	Name:: PersonName	DOB:: Date	DIED:: Date	Lives_at:: Geo_Point	Biography:: Document	etc
101	('Wyler, 'William')	07/01/ 1902	07/27/ 1981	NULL	Born in Meuhl-hausen, Germany	etc.

Listing 3–4. *RESTRICTION Relational Operator and Equivalent OR-SQL Example*

Figure 3–2 illustrates the effect of a restriction operation.

Note the use of the asterisk (*) character in the query in Figure 3–1. An asterisk in the SELECT clause indicates that the query returns all of the table's columns. In other words, this query performs no projection.

Earlier we mentioned that OR-SQL queries combine several relational operations into a single expression. The query in Listing 3–5 combines projection and restriction.

"What are the names and dates of birth of the movie club members whose surname is 'Eliot'?"

```
SELECT Print(M.Name) AS Name, M.DOB
  FROM MovieClubMembers M
  WHERE M.Name.Family_Name = 'Eliot'::ShortString;
```

Name::LVARCHAR	Dob::DATE
George Eliot	03/02/1964

Listing 3–5. *SQL Query Combining Projection and Restriction*

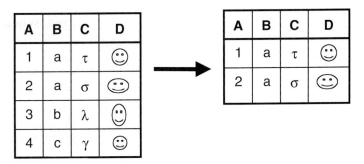

Figure 3–2. *Diagrammatic Presentation of RESTRICTION*

Relational operations are all examples of *closed* algorithms, that is, their output is the same type—a relation—as their input. Further, an important property of relational operations is that they are, subject to certain rules, *commutative*. This means that the order in which the ORDBMS engine performs each relational operation does not affect the final result. As it processes the query in Listing 3–5, the ORDBMS can project the table first and then restrict it, or vice versa.

Predicate expressions—functions appearing in a WHERE clause—can be very complex. Any built-in expression or user-defined function returning a boolean result can be used as a predicate, and a query can combine several boolean expressions using logical AND, OR, and NOT keywords. Also, you can nest functions to compute some intermediate value and then use it in a predicate expression, as shown in Listing 3–6.

"What are the names of movie club members between 35 and 45, who either have red hair or whose family name sounds like 'Eliot'?"

```
SELECT M.Name
  FROM MovieClubMembers M
 WHERE Age(M) BETWEEN 35 AND 45
   AND ( HasRedHair(M.Photo)
    OR   Soundex( GetFamilyName(M.Name) ) =
                Soundex('Eliot')
         );
```

Name::PersonName

('Eliot','George')

Listing 3–6. *SQL Query Combining Expressions to Form a Complex Predicate*

In addition to using constant values in boolean predicates the OR-SQL query language allows the nesting of query statements. An inner query can compute a value used in an outer query.

Join

The third common relational operation is the *join*. Strictly speaking, there are several kinds of join, but they all begin with the basic *cartesian product*. This is an algorithm that takes two inputs and produces a single output. The result of a cartesian product is a new relation containing the set of rows produced by concatenating each row of the first input with each row from the second. Figure 3–3 illustrates the idea.

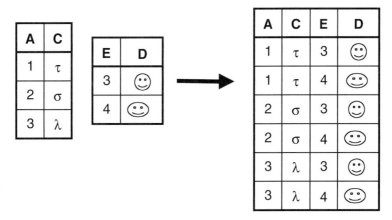

Figure 3–3. *Diagrammatic Representation of the CARTESIAN PRODUCT Operation*

Listing 3–7 is a query that computes a cartesian product of the `Name` and `DOB` columns for the sample rows from the `MovieClub-Members` table.

"Show me the cartesian product of all names and dates of birth from the MovieClubMembers table."

```
SELECT M1.Name, M1.DOB, M2.Name, M2.DOB
    FROM MovieClubMembers M1, MovieClubMembers M2;
```

Name::PersonName	Dob::DATE	Name::PersonName	Dob::DATE
('Eliot', 'George')	3/2/1964	('Eliot', 'George')	3/2/1964
('Eliot', 'George')	3/2/1964	('Freyenbauger','Mira')	3/2/1964
('Eliot', 'George')	3/2/1964	('Hume', 'David')	1/12/1961
('Freyenbauger','Mira')	3/2/1964	('Eliot', 'George')	3/2/1964
('Freyenbauger','Mira')	3/2/1964	('Freyenbauger','Mira')	3/2/1964
('Freyenbauger','Mira')	3/2/1964	('Hume', 'David')	1/12/1961
('Hume', 'David')	1/12/1961	('Eliot', 'George')	3/2/1964
('Hume', 'David')	1/12/1961	('Freyenbauger','Mira')	3/2/1964
('Hume', 'David')	1/12/1961	('Hume', 'David')	1/12/1961

Listing 3–7. *Example of CARTESIAN PRODUCT Query*

The number of rows in the result of a cartesian product is equal to the number of rows in the first input times the number of rows in the second. The query in Listing 3–7 is limited to three rows in each of the inputs. Therefore, the result has nine rows. Also, there is a column in the output for each column in the input relations; that is, the number of columns in the output is equal to the sum of the number of columns in each input.

Basic cartesian products aren't all that useful. In practice, join operations apply additional filters to the rows resulting from a cartesian product. We make such a big deal about joins because the IDS engine typically combines the cartesian product and subsequent filtering step into a single algorithm that is more computationally efficient than performing each operation separately.

Perhaps the most common kind of join is the *equi-join*. An equi-join filters (restricts) the rows returned from the cartesian product, only passing on those rows that have a value from one input table's column equal to the value in a column from the second. Listing 3–8 is an example of an equi-join. It limits the rows from the cartesian product to only those cases where the two movie club members were born on the same day.

"Show me the names and dates of birth of movie club members born on the same day."

```
SELECT M1.Name, M1.DOB, M2.Name, M2.DOB
   FROM MovieClubMembers M1, MovieClubMembers M2
   WHERE M1.DOB = M2.DOB;
```

Name::PersonName	Dob::DATE	Name::PersonName	Dob::DATE
('Eliot', 'George')	3/2/1964	('Eliot', 'George')	3/2/1964
('Eliot', 'George')	3/2/1964	('Freyenbauger','Mira')	3/2/1964
('Freyenbauger','Mira')	3/2/1964	('Eliot', 'George')	3/2/1964
('Freyenbauger','Mira')	3/2/1964	('Freyenbauger','Mira')	3/2/1964
('Hume', 'David')	1/12/1961	('Hume', 'David')	1/12/1961

Listing 3–8. *Example of an equi-join Query*

The most common use for the equi-join is to connect data in one table with data in another along a foreign key. For example, Listing 3–9 demonstrates an equi-join between the `MovieClubMembers` and `Orders` tables, using the `Orders.Customer` and `MovieClubMembers.Id` columns for the equi-join predicate.

"For each movie club member who has ever placed an order, show me the date on which the order was placed and a printout of the Invoice statement."

```
SELECT M.Name,
         O.OrderedOn
   FROM MovieClubMembers M, Orders O
   WHERE O.Customer = M.Id;
```

Name::PersonName	Orderedon::DATE
('Eliot', 'George')	9/11/1998

Listing 3–9. *Example of an equi-join Query Joining Two Related Tables*

By substituting other boolean functions for "=," developers using RDBMSs could employ a limited number of other join predicates. Non–equi-joins are sometimes called *theta-joins*. For example, it was relatively common to write a join query to find all records with date column values occurring before a date column in another table (i.e., all dates prior to another date).

One of the most powerful innovations in an ORDBMS is that it makes an enormous number of additional joins predicates possible. Any user-defined function producing a boolean (true or false) result can be used in a join query. For example, Listing 3–10 expresses a join between the `MovieClubMembers` table and a table storing the names and boundaries of U.S. states. The join predicate in this case is spatial (`Contained()`). This kind of operation is usually called a *spatial join*.

"Show me the name of the movie club member and the name of the state in which the movie club member lives."

```
SELECT M.Name, S.Name AS State_Name
  FROM MovieClubMembers M, States S
  WHERE Contained(M.LivesAt, S.Boundary);
```

Name::PersonName	State_Name::String
('Freyenbauger','Mira')	'CALIFORNIA'
('Hume', 'David')	'MARYLAND'
('Eliot', 'George')	'UTAH'

Listing 3–10. *Example of a theta-join Query Joining Two Related Tables*

User-defined join functions make it possible to compute new relationships within an ORDBMS schema. For example, many databases are used to store demographic information—age, gender, income, household size, etc.—about customers, employees, or movie club members. Sometimes, it is desirable to find all records that are similar to one another and where a column value is *like* a value in another table. Algorithms that compute this kind of similarity can be very complex; they can use fuzzy-logic techniques or schemes that weight the various features being compared according to their distribution. But once you have created a boolean *like* UDF, it can be used to compute new interrelationships in your database.

The Movies-R-Us Web site schema includes images of the faces of movie personalities and movie club members. A standard image processing technique is to extract a set of features from each face image, including hair color, distance between pupils, width of mouth, and length of ears. You can use this approach to write functions for comparing faces to determine how similar the faces are and makes querie like "Show me the members of my movie club who *LookLike* some movie star." As shown in Listing 3–11.

"Show me movie club members who look like Ingrid Bergman."

```
SELECT M.Name, P.Name
   FROM MovieClubMembers M, MoviePersonalities P
  WHERE M.Photo LIKE P.Photo
     AND P.Name = PersonName( 'Bergman','Ingrid');
```

Listing 3–11. *A Fantasy Query*

Project-restrict-join queries are very common. The relational operations introduced in the remainder of this section are useful in specific circumstances.

Outer-Join

What happens in a join query when there are no rows in the cartesian product that satisfy the join predicate? For example, what happens if no movie club members live in the United States or no one who looks like Ingrid Bergman? Joins eliminate all rows where no match exists, so such queries would return no rows at all. Sometimes you would rather have at least one row in the result for each row in one of the inputs, which is behavior that is achieved with an *outer join* operation.

When there is a matching row an *outer join* behaves exactly like an ordinary join. But when no matching row exists in the second table, the outer join substitutes NULL values for all missing columns. Listing 3–12 illustrates the outer join in practice. Rows in this query's results are a superset of the rows produced by the query in Listing 3–10.

"Show me the name of the movie club member and the name of the state in which the movie club member lives, if the member lives in one."

```
SELECT M.Name, S.Name AS State_Name
   FROM MovieClubMembers M, OUTER States S
  WHERE Contained(M.LivesAt, S.Boundary);
```

Name::PersonName	State_Name::String
('Freyenbauger','Mira')	'CALIFORNIA'
('Hume', 'David')	'MARYLAND'
('Yamamoto', 'Yoshi')	NULL
('Eliot', 'George')	'UTAH'

Listing 3–12. *Example of an outer-join Query*

For a long time, theoreticians about the relational model resisted including the OUTER JOIN because of problems relating to NULL values and three-value logic. The reluctance was due also to the observation that an OUTER JOIN frequently indicates a database design problem. With ORDBMSs, because of their enhanced set of join predicates, the OUTER JOIN is frequently very useful.

Union

Two relations that have identical column structures in their SELECT list can be combined into a single relation with the *union* operation. Unions take two inputs and produce a single output, just like joins. Unlike joins, however, unions append all of the rows from one input onto the end of the other. The number of rows in the result of a join is equal to the sum of distinct rows in the two inputs, as shown in Listing 3–13.

"Show me names of movie club members and the country they live in if they do not live in the U.S."

```
SELECT M.Name, N.Name AS Country_Name
   FROM MovieClubMembers M, Nations N
  WHERE Contained(M.Location, N.Boundary)
    AND N.Name != 'United States';
```

Name::PersonName	Name::String
('Yamamoto', 'Yoshi')	'JAPAN'

"Show me union names of movie club members and the country they live in if they do not live in the 'United States' with the names of movie club members and the US state they live in (where they live in a US state.)."

```
SELECT M.Name, N.Name AS Home_Name
   FROM MovieClub M, Nations N
  WHERE Contained(M.Location, N.Boundary)
    AND N.Name != 'United States'
  UNION
SELECT M.Name, S.Name
   FROM MovieClub M, State S
  WHERE Contained(M.Location, S.Boundary);
```

Name::PersonName	HomeName::String
('Freyenbauger','Mira')	'CALIFORNIA'
('Hume', 'David')	'MARYLAND'
('Yamamoto', 'Yoshi')	'JAPAN'
('Eliot', 'George')	'UTAH'

Listing 3–13. *Example of a UNION Query*

Summarize or Aggregate

The summarize or aggregate operation is not strictly part of relational theory, but in practice it is very useful. Summarizing an input relation involves picking a set of columns that we call the grouping columns, and for each of the remaining columns in the input relation (which are called the aggregated columns), choosing a function that summarizes the data in it. The result of the summarize operation is a relation that contains one row for each distinct value in the grouping columns and the result of some aggregate function run over a set of values in the aggregate columns.

Aggregate functions are different from other expressions. They each take a set of data values—one for each row in the input relation—and produces a single result value. SQL-92 includes a set of aggregate functions such as COUNT, AVG, SUM, MIN and MAX. The aggregate operator is difficult to represent in a diagram, but we give it a shot in Figure 3–4.

```
SELECT A, MAX(B), SUM(D), COUNT(*)
    FROM Table
    GROUP BY A;
```

Listing 3–14. *Aggregate Queries in SQL-92*

In this example, the "A" column is the grouping column, while the "B" and "D" columns are both used in aggregate functions. Note the additional column that counts the number of rows in each grouping.

A	B	C	D
1	a	τ	12.0
2	a	σ	13.0
3	b	λ	11.0
3	c	λ	12.5
1	e	τ	11.5
2	c	σ	13.0
3	c	τ	13.5

A	MAX(B)	SUM(D)	COUNT(*)
1	e	23.5	2
2	c	26.0	2
3	c	37.0	3

Figure 3–4. *Summarize or Aggregate Operation*

Aggregation can be performed using computed columns, too. In Listing 2-25 of the previous chapter, we saw how to create a view called `MerchandisePurchased`. A subset of the columns in this view might contain rows like the ones in Listing 3–15.

MerchandiseOrdered

Id::Member_Id	Qty::Quantity	Price::Curency
10020	1	ROW(15.50, 'USD')
10020	1	ROW(5.50,'USD')
10111	1	ROW(35.00, 'USD')
10111	3	ROW(1.50, 'USD')
10111	1	ROW(7.50, 'USD')
10101	2	ROW(1.50, 'USD')

Listing 3–15. *Rows in the MerchandiseOrdered View*

You would use an aggregate query like the one in Listing 3–16 if you wanted to answer a question such as "What was the value of all orders for each movie club member?"

"What is the total value (Qty * Price) of all merchandise ordered by each member of the movie club?"

```
SELECT M.Member_Id,
       SUM(M.NumberOrdered * M.Price) AS Value
  FROM MerchandisePurchased M
 GROUP BY M.Member_Id;
```

Id::Member_Id	Value::Currency
10020	ROW(21.00, 'USD')
10111	ROW(47.00, 'USD')
10101	ROW(3.00, 'USD')

Listing 3–16. *Aggregate Query over MerchandiseOrdered View*

This example also illustrates why it is important to describe relational operators in terms of relations, rather than in terms of tables. The `MerchandisePurchased` defined using view is a complex query.

As you might expect, the ORDBMS allows you to create your own user-defined aggregate functions. Just like the built-in aggregates, user-defined aggregates take a set of data type instances and compute a single result. In simple cases, this is usually an instance of the same type. For example, it is frequently useful to compute the *n*th largest of a set of values rather than just the largest or smallest. A query that uses this kind of aggregate might look like Listing 3–17.

"What was the second biggest budget ever spent on a film?"

```
SELECT SecondBiggest ( M.Budget )
  FROM Movies M;
```

Secondbiggest::Currency

ROW(USD,15000.0000)

Listing 3–17. *Aggregate Query Using User-Defined Aggregate*

You can also use aggregates as constructors for other data types. For example, consider the `Cinemas` table and the column of latitude/ longitude points recording theater locations. Often, a cluster of closely theater franchises in an area may have a single owner, and it might be interesting to see how many people live in a particular owner's area. This requires that you calculate the "convex hull" of the theater locations.[1] Such a query might look like Listing 3–18.

"Show me the polygon formed from the set of theater locations owned by Mr Burns."

```
SELECT ConvexHull( C.Location )
  FROM Cinemas C, Owners O
 WHERE C.MovieTheater = O.Id
   AND O.Name  = 'Mr Burns';
```

Listing 3–18. *ConvexHull User-Defined Aggregate*

We cover the implementation of user-defined aggregates in more detail in Chapter 5. In Tutorial 6, were we describe some useful extensions to the ORDBMS, we introduce a user-defined aggregate that performs operating similar to the one in Listing 3–17.

Using SQL Data Manipulation Language (DML)

A powerful characteristic of dynamic query languages such as OR-SQL is the way they can be used in ad hoc (for the task) situations. Databases are implemented as a centralized service to which multiple external programs can connect. These external programs can be written in a

---

[1]   A convex hull is the polygon that would be formed if you enclosed the points in a rubber band.

variety of languages (called *host languages*) but regardless of what language is chosen, they all use OR-SQL for data access. The ORDBMS accepts an OR-SQL query string at runtime, processes it, and returns result data to wherever the query was submitted from.

Most information systems include a large set of static queries whose structure and purpose is known at development time, but are written to accept variables supplied at runtime. The most powerful kinds of client programs are those that construct queries dynamically in response to user input, rather than those that simply execute precompiled ones. The IDS product, like most DBMS engines, excels at both types of interaction. In Figure 3–5 we illustrate how you use OR-SQL within the process architecture of an information system.

In addition to ad hoc OR-SQL queries, the ORDBMS lets you invoke user-defined functions directly, using the EXECUTE FUNCTION or EXE-CUTE PROCEDURE statement. This allows developers to invoke user-defined functions implemented on the server using the same protocol and interface provided for ad hoc queries. You can use one of a variety of languages to implement server side extensions that embed several OR-SQL statements into a business process.

Consequently, there is no absolute necessity to include any INSERT, UPDATE, DELETE, or SELECT queries at all in external programs. Instead, it can all be encapsulated within database-stored procedures running within the ORDBMS server. This shared logic can be invoked from a multitude of client programs using the interfaces designed for queries, as shown in Figure 3–6.

This style of interaction between an external program and a DBMS is useful because it can reduce the amount of data being exchanged between external programs and the DBMS, and because centralizing the business processing logic makes it simpler to manage the evolution of the information system. Whatever actions the database procedure undertakes are invisible to the external program, so one group of developers can modify them without requiring changes to the external program.

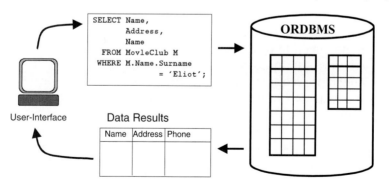

Figure 3–5. *Using OR-SQL Queries Within an Information Systems Architecture*

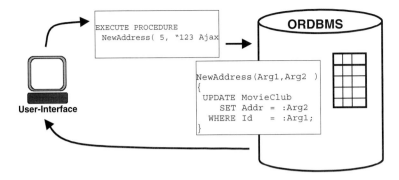

```
  EXECUTE PROCEDURE
    NewAddress( 5, "123 Ajax
```

```
NewAddress(Arg1,Arg2 )
{
  UPDATE MovieClub
    SET Addr = :Arg2
    WHERE Id   = :Arg1;
}
```

ORDBMS

User-Interface

Figure 3–6. *Embedding OR-SQL into Database Procedures*

On the other hand, centralizing logic in this way creates a scalability bottleneck. The IDS product's architecture is designed to work best on a single, large server computer. But the Internet makes it feasible to support much larger communities of users than were supported within traditional architectures. In Chapter 7 we explore how developers can exploit distributed DBMS models to overcome some of these scalability problems. But, in general, the advice is to be flexible about how you elect to map an information system's data processing logic to hardware and software frameworks.

Basic SELECT Queries

OR-SQL has a single, general-purpose, read operation: the SELECT statement. A SELECT query's results can be thought of as a transient table, which is a set (or more properly, a multi-set) of identically structured rows. Result rows only exist for as long as the query is active. Once the client interrupts the query, closes the client-side CURSOR (the name given to a control structure for handling query results), or the external API indicates that there are no more rows to return, the ORDBMS cleans up the result set.

The general form of simple OR-SQL SELECT queries is shown in Listing 3–19.

```
SELECT [DISTINCT] * | [ Column | Expression [ AS Name ]]
        { , Column | Expression [ AS Name ] }
  FROM data_source [ alias name ]
```

```
                  {, data_source [ alias name ] }
    [  WHERE [ NOT ] condition {[ AND | OR | NOT ] condition }
    [  GROUP BY [ column {, column } |
                 column_number ]
       [ HAVING condition ] ]
    [  ORDER BY [ column | column_number  [ ASC | DESC ]
                {, [ column | column_number ][ ASC | DESC ] } ];
```

Listing 3–19. *General Form of Simple ORDBMS SELECT Query*

SELECT statements have four subparts:

- Target list. This is the set of columns that the query produces between the SELECT keyword and the FROM keyword. Target lists can include constant values, column names, and expressions or functions over column data. Any of the user-defined functions or aggregates embedded within the server can be used in a target list. And target list syntax also allows developers to give names to the result columns.
- Data sources. This specifies where the data operated on by the query comes from. Individual data sources are spelled out in a comma delimited list after the FROM and before the WHERE. In the IDS product the list of database objects that can act as data sources is greatly increased over what was possible with RDBMSs. Data sources in an ORDBMS query can be a table, view, COLLECTION, another SELECT query expression, or a virtual table whose data is stored externally to the ORDBMS.
- Query predicates. The expressions after the WHERE keyword that specify how data from the sources is combined and filtered to produce the result in the target list make up the predicate list. As in the target list, any of the functions defined to the server can be used as predicate functions. However they are combined, the functions in the predicates must evaluate to a boolean (true or false result).
- Summarize and order by clauses. These are (optional) aspects of a query expression that comes at the end of the query. They can be used to order the results of a query or to modify the basic query result in some way.

OR-SQL statements tend to have a simpler form than SQL-92. In many cases, SQL-92 queries were required to be structurally complex because the language's simplicity forced developers into complicated data models and exotic, compound expressions in order to represent higher-level concepts. By contrast, in an ORDBMS database, such ideas can be more directly implemented as user-defined extensions.

Single Table SELECT Statements

The SQL query in Listing 3–20 illustrates the kind of `SELECT` typical in SQL-92 RDBMS development. It retrieves records from the `MovieClub-Members` table where the member's birthday is "today." Note that this question is more complex than it appears. Naively checking for equivalent months and days means that anyone born in a leap-year will only get a birthday card once every four years (except on the century, except every four hundredth year when they would receive a card).[2] In fact, even this query doesn't do quite the right thing. It allocates members born on a leap day two birthdays during a leap year.

"Show me names and addresses of each Movie Club members whose birthday is today."

```
SELECT  Name,
        Address
   FROM MovieClubMembers M
  WHERE (
          (
            ((MONTH(M.DOB) = 2) AND (MONTH(TODAY) = 2))
           AND
            ((DAY(M.DOB)  IN (28,29)) AND
             (DAY(TODAY)  IN (28,29)))
          )
          OR
          (
            (MONTH(M.DOB) = MONTH(TODAY)) AND
            (DAY(M.DOB)   = DAY(TODAY))
          )
        );
```

Listing 3–20. *Simple SQL-92 Style Query*

Now suppose the information system was using XML to manage data exchange with another system. When using an RDBMS, the

---

[2] Introducing stopwatches into the delivery room would complicate matters even more. Every year or so—22 times between 1972 and 1999—because the earth's rotation is slowing, all clocks are jiggled by a second. Anyone born in the first second of the first day of April, therefore, ought to pay attention.

results of this query would need to be formatted by external, procedural logic before it could be sent on its way. Over the next few pages we contrast this with the OR-SQL approach to the same problem in an effort to illustrate what is unchanged between SQL-92 and OR-SQL and also how OR-SQL query expressions and user-defined extensions interact.

User-Defined Types, Functions, and Expressions in OR-SQL

Any SQL-92 expression can be used in an OR-SQL query, and you can also any of the user-defined functions implemented as part of the database's object extensions. The query in Listing 3–21 accomplishes the same result that the query in Listing 3–20, in combination with modules of external logic, achieves. It includes several user-defined functions performing various tasks. The peculiar behavior of birthdays is encapsulated within a user-defined type and its associated functions, while other functions format the address label into an XML character string.

"What is the formatted name and address of the movie club members whose birthday is today?"

```
SELECT Salutation(M.Name) AS Header,
       M.Address.City AS City,
       XML(M.Address) AS Label
  FROM MovieClubMembers M
 WHERE Birthdate(M.DOB) = Birthdate(TODAY);
```

Listing 3–21. *ORDBMS SQL Equivalent of Birthday Query*

The result of this query might look like Table 3–2:

Table 3–2. Result of Query in Listing 3–19. Note HTML Mark-up of Address Label

Header::String	City::String	Label::XML
Dear Lou Gomez,	Palo Alto	\<ADDRESS\> \<LINE_1\>12-A Euclid Avenue\</LINE_1\> \<LINE_2\>PALO ALTO CA 94714\</LINE_2\> \</ADDRESS\>

The first user-defined function in the target list is `Salutation`
(`PersonName`). It extracts information from the `PersonName`
data type and presents it as a salutation to appear on letterhead,
for example. UDFs like `Salutation()` can appear anywhere in
the query: in the `SELECT` list, the `WHERE` clause, or in the `GROUP BY`
and `HAVING` blocks.

The query renames result column `Salutation( PersonName )` as
`Header`. Recall that in an ORDBMS, we can treat a query result like a
transient table. The IDS will assign default names to the columns of
this result table, but you can specify the names you want the result
column to have. By default, the computed columns are all named
something generic such as "expression." Later when we investigate the
topic of closure in OR-SQL and client interfaces, naming results
becomes more important.

The only other function explicitly mentioned in Listing 3–21 is
`Birthdate(DATE)`, and the only operator expression in our simple
query's predicate list—another name for a `WHERE` clause—is the '='
symbol. In cases where the data types being compared for equality are
built-in types—say, `INTEGER`—this symbol tells the ORDBMSe to use its
built-in comparison logic. In this case the type being compared is an
extended type that is the result of the `Birthdate(DATE)` UDF. For the
purposes of the query expression there is no need to know anything
about how it works.

When it parses the '=' symbol the ORDBMS tries to find a UDF
called `Equal(Birthdate, Birthdate)` returning a boolean result.
In fact, the '=' expression is equivalent to the alternative predicate in
Listing 3–22.

```
WHERE Equal(Birthdate(M.DOB), Birthdate(TODAY));
```

Listing 3–22. *Alternative Form of the = Operator with User-Defined Function*

Other query language symbols such as < and >= use the same technique. By implementing the corresponding functions—`LessThan()`
and `GreaterThanorEqual()`—a developer can make these operator
symbols mean precisely what the type's behavior requires.

One advantage of this alternative form is that it makes life easier
when dealing with the SGML-based mark-up languages, XML and
HTML. The mathematical symbols conventionally used as query operators have other, special meanings: "<" and ">" correspond to the
opening and closing of a mark-up tag. Some mark-up language
parsers can find it difficult to distinguish a close tag symbol from the
">"operator in an embedded OR-SQL query. This problem can be

overcome by using the function names, rather than the symbols for queries embedded in HTML pages.

The purpose of this example was to illustrate the way that even a relatively simple OR-SQL query can accomplish a great deal. In a single `SELECT` statement the ORDBMS brings together a significant amount of application level functionality.

Table Aliases in SQL Statements

Listing 3–21 includes an example of a table alias in the line, `FROM MovieClubMembers M`. Two tables in a single query can have columns with the same name and the table alias is necessary to disambiguate them. The most obvious case occurs in queries joining a table with itself (called self-join queries) of the type shown in Listing 3–23.

"List names and cities of Movie Club members whose surnames sound like the surname of the Movie Club member with identifier 10111."

```
SELECT Print(M2.Name) AS Name,
       M2.Address.City
  FROM MovieClubMembers M1, MovieClubMembers M2
 WHERE M1.Id = '10111'
   AND Soundex(M1.Name.Family_Name) =
       Soundex(M2.Name.Family_Name);
```

Listing 3–23. *Join Query Illustrating the Need for Table Aliases*

It would be perfectly legal to include the table's entire name instead of the alias. However, table names in modern databases can be quite long. With a schema of tables named using 128-byte identifiers, you can tell how tedious this might be.

Logical Operators and OR-SQL Queries

The combination of user-defined functions and built-in expressions in a `WHERE` clause must yield a boolean result. In fact, `boolean` itself is a valid data type in an ORDBMS. You can create tables with `boolean` columns and you can drop such a column name into a `WHERE` clause anywhere that a UDF returning a boolean result might appear, as shown in Listing 3–24.

"List all movies released on Video."

```
SELECT M.Title
  FROM Movies M
  WHERE M.OnVideo;
```

Listing 3–24. *Object-Relational SQL Query Using a Column Defined as Boolean*

Listing 3–25 illustrates how several predicate functions can be combined using AND, OR, and NOT keywords. Also, note the use of parenthesis to indicate the precedence of operations. Using parenthesis like this is encouraged as a matter of OR-SQL style because it helps to make query statements more readable.

"List all movie not available on video that, in addition either cost less than $1 million to make or where the film's plot summary indicates that it dealt with 'war veterans'."

```
SELECT M.Title
  FROM Movies M
 WHERE NOT M.OnVideo
   AND ( M.Budget  < Currency(1000000, 'USD')
     OR  DocContains('war veterans', M.Plot_Summary)
        );
```

Listing 3–25. *Query Combining Predicates with AND, OR, and NOT*

While the search conditions in a WHERE clause always reduce to true or false, other functions can be used to transform data into types that another function can use. This sounds obvious, but it has implications for the way extensions should be designed. For example, the WHERE clause in Listing 3–26 below includes an Age() function to compute the age of movie club members. This computed result is then used as input to a search condition that restricts the query to members older than 30. The second predicate constructs a circle based on two constant values (which may be supplied from a user interface) and then finds all those living within that circle.

"Give me a list of all Movie Club members who are older than 30, and who live within a 30-mile circle around a particular latitude/longitude point."

```
SELECT Print(M.Name)
  FROM MovieClubMembers M
 WHERE Age(M) > 30
   AND Contains( Circle( Point (-122.2654,37.8783),
                         DegreesFromMiles(30.0)),
                 M.LivesAt );
```

Listing 3–26. *Building Intermediate Values Using User-Defined Functions*

Combining functions in this way allows developers to create very complex queries. This is similar in style to what is known as functional programming, which simply means that OR-SQL expressions do not include any assignment of a value to variables. In functional programming, functions can be thought of as possessing value. One function can be used as an argument to another.

The important concept to keep in mind when designing extensions is that there is no need to create a function for every purpose. Instead, you should strive to create user-defined functions that implement some indivisible computation, such as creating a circle from a center point and a radius. Many atomic functions can be combined into complex expressions.

As an example of what not to do, consider Listing 3–27.

"Give me a list of all Movie Club members who are older than 30, and who live within a 30-mile circle around a particular latitude/longitude point."

```
SELECT Print(M.Name)
  FROM MovieClubMembers M
 WHERE IsOlderThan(M, 30)
   AND IsWithinThirtyMiles( M.Location,
                            Point(-122.617,27.175));
```

Listing 3–27. *The Perils of One Function for Every Purpose*

While this kind of approach is attractive in some ways, in practice it is rarely a good idea. The problem with these routines is they are very task specific. A function per task implies a lot of functions to write and maintain. Ideally, you should be able to reuse your routines in many different queries. Functions such as `IsWithin-FiveMiles()` or `IsOlderThan()`, while fulfilling the requirements of this query, are unlikely to be widely useful. A multipurpose function such as `Age(DATE)` on the other hand might be used to refer to the longevity of a movie or a movie personality.

Functionally complex UDF extensions can also cause problems for the query processor and optimizer. The IDS product currently does not "flatten out" the UDF logic and graft it into the query, so the optimizer cannot "see" the function's internal operation. Within the `IsOlderThan()` UDF, for example, there is likely to be a call to the built-in `LessThan (DATE, DATE)` logic. The ORDBMS could, under other circumstances, use a B-Tree index for this predicate, but because the indexable predicate in Listing 3–27 is buried within the UDF logic, it cannot.

`Age()` in Listing 3–26 exhibits similar weaknesses. The ORDBMS cannot use an index on the `DOB` column with the `Age(M) > 30` predicate. A faster approach might be to use a function that calculates a date based on a number of years of age as an argument and then looks for all prior birth dates. The ORDBMS only considers indexes over the columns listed in the query expression. For optimal performance make your queries as transparent as possible, and keep the UDFs as simple as possible.

DISTINCT Keyword

In Listing 3–2 we saw how the DISTINCT keyword eliminate duplicate rows a query's results. The manner in which the ORDBMS computes a DISTINCT list of data type values results is another example of how tightly object-relational extensibility and OR-SQL are integrated. The DISTINCT keyword can be used in a query, as shown in Listing 3–28.

"Give me a list of all cities in which Movie Club members live."

```
SELECT DISTINCT M.Address.City
    FROM MovieClubMembers M;
```

Listing 3–28. *Using the DISTINCT Keyword*

Filtering a list of data values to reduce it to a list of distinct values requires that the ORDBMS determine when two data values are equal and eliminate duplicates. For large data sets the most efficient way to perform this filtering is to sort the entire list, which, as we saw in Chapter 1, requires a Compare() function. Without a Compare() function for the type the ORDBMS will generate an exception.

This means that it is a very good idea to implement Compare() for any new data type you create, even if the order it stipulates isn't very sensible. For example, sorting temporal data types such as Period, or spatial types such as GeoPoint, is semantically meaningless. Providing OR-SQL developers with the ability to discard duplicate values from a set of results, however, is very useful.

CASE Expression

To overcome some of the limitations of SQL-92 the language's standards committee—following the lead of some RDBMS vendors—considerably complicated the language by adding a procedural "back door": the CASE expression. The basic idea is to allow developers to put some simple IF-THEN-ELSE logic into a query's target list or WHERE clause. A query using the CASE expression is illustrated in Listing 3–29.

"For each Movie Club Member, categorize them according to the geographic region in which they live."

```
SELECT Print(M.Name) AS Name,
       CASE
           WHEN M.Address.State IN ('TX','CA','AZ','NV','UT')
               THEN 'South West'
           WHEN M.Address.State IN ('OR','WA','ID')
               THEN 'North West'
           WHEN M.Address.State IN ('CO','WY','NM','MT')
               THEN 'Mountain'
           WHEN M.Address.State IN ('ND','SD','NE','KS','OK')
               THEN 'Central'
           WHEN M.Address.State IN ('IL','IN','IA','MI','MN',
                                     'MS','OH','WI')
               THEN 'Mid West'
           WHEN M.Address.State IN ('AL','AR','FL','GA','KY',
                                     'LA','NC','SC','TN')
               THEN 'South East'
           WHEN M.Address.State IN ('CT','ME','MA','NH','RI',
                                     'VT','DE')
               THEN 'New England'
           WHEN M.Address.State IN ('VA','WV','PA','MD','NY',
                                     'NJ','DC')
               THEN 'North East'
           ELSE 'Non-US'
       END CASE
   FROM MovieClubMembers M;
```

Listing 3–29. *Example of Using the CASE Keyword*

Although this syntax is clearly useful in a SQL-92 context, adding user-defined functions to the ORDBMS query language solves many of the problems that the CASE expression was intended to address. For example, the CASE statement in the query may be replaced by a user-defined function that maps states to regions. Then Listing 3–29 could be rewritten as shown in Listing 3–30.

"For each Movie Club Member, categorize them according to the geographic region in which they live."

```
SELECT Print(M.Name),
       Region(M.Address.State)
   FROM MovieClubMembers M;
```

Listing 3–30. *Alternatives to Using CASE*

User-defined functions have several advantages over a CASE expression. Functions are more modular; changing the mapping of states to regions requires modifying a single function rather than every query the mapping appears in. There is also the option of creating a functional index over the Region() UDR to improve the query performance. In general, if you find that you have a CASE expression that is being repeated in multiple queries, it is probably better off implemented as a user-defined function.

Data Sources

Data sources—the list of identifiers coming between the FROM and the WHERE keyword—specify from where the query's data comes. In SQL-92 databases the only possible data sources were tables and views. These are still the most common data sources in ORDBMS queries because, even though the physical storage mechanisms have been generalized and the nature of database data is quite different, OR databases still organize data into tables. Data sources in applications upgraded from SQL-92 operate in an identical fashion in the ORDBMS.

As part of query processing, the ORDBMS uses tables and view names in the data sources to figure out things such as the data types of columns identified in the query. From the type names it can further establish what UDFs are indicated by the query expression. For example, in the query in Listing 3–30, the ORDBMS looks at the MovieClubMembers table and sees that the data type of the Address column is MailAddress, so the type of the State element is State_Enum. From this, it can infer that the query is invoking a UDF declared as Region(State_Enum).

The IDS product considerably extends the list of things that can be used as data sources. A query's data sources can be a COLLECTION instance, an iterator function, and even an entire SELECT query specification. We return to this topic later in this chapter.

Ordering Result Rows

By default, rows are returned from a SELECT statement in no particular order. As a side effect of the way the query was executed the result might be ordered, but it is a very bad idea to rely on it because query plans change as data volumes increase or new indices are added. Therefore, OR-SQL provides a means to order query results explicitly. To specify the order for a query's result rows, append an ORDER BY clause to the SELECT statement as shown in Listing 3–31.

"List all Movie Club members whose membership period ends before today, ordered by membership Id."

```
SELECT M.Id,
       M.Name
  FROM MovieClubMembers M
 WHERE Before(M.Membership_Period, Period(TODAY))
 ORDER BY M.Id;
```

Listing 3–31. *Ordering Query Results with ORDER BY*

The ORDER BY clause can specify table column or target list result name, or simply the rank number of the column from the target list. You can include as many columns in the ORDER BY clause as there are in the query's target list. And they can be ordered in either ascending (the default) or descending order, as shown in Listing 3–32.

"Give me a list of all Movie Club members who are older than 30, and who live within a 30-mile circle around a particular latitude/longitude point ordered by their distance from that point in descending order."

```
SELECT M.Id,
       Print(M.Name) AS Name,
       MilesFromDegrees( Distance(M.LivesAt,
                             Point(-122.2654, 37.8783))
                       ) AS Miles_Distance
  FROM MovieClubMembers M
 WHERE Age(M) > 30
   AND Contains(Circle(Point (-122.2654,37.8783),
                       DegreesFromMiles(30.0)),
                M.LivesAt)
 ORDER BY 3 DESC;
```

Id::Member_Id	Name::String	miles_distance::Physical_Quantity
10030	Joe Blogs	23.899 MILES
10041	Van Quoc	0.007924 MILES

Listing 3–32. *More Complex Ordering of Query Results*

Recall in Chapter 1 where we explained how an ORDBMS differs internally from an RDBMS by using the ORDBMS's sorting facilities as an example. When it receives a query like the ones in the previous listings, the ORDBMS uses these facilities to order result rows. To sort them, the ORDBMS must be able to compare two instances of the data type it is being asked to sort. In other words, if a query specifies that its result is to be ordered, then the ORDBMS must have a `Compare()` function defined for the sorted data type.

For example, consider the query in Listing 3–33.

"List all movies made for less than $10,000 that made money, ordered by Movie Title."

```
SELECT  M.Title,
        M.Budget,
        M.Takings,
        M.Takings - M.Budget
  FROM Movies M
 WHERE M.Budget  < Currency(10000.00, 'USD')
   AND M.Takings > M.Budget
 ORDER BY M.Title;
```

Listing 3–33. *Query Sorting its Result Using User-Defined Types*

In the Movies-R-Us, the `Movie.Title` column is an `OPAQUE TYPE` called Title. For the ORDBMS to order this result correctly, it needs a `Compare()` routine such as `Compare(Title, Title)`.

Aggregation

Earlier in this chapter we introduced the related query language concepts of grouping and aggregation. These operations are not part of the original relational model, but at the time SQL was being standardized, it was decided that the language needed to include some reporting and analysis functionality. So SQL-92 has come to include a set of built-in aggregates for summarizing columns of data values. Conceptually, an aggregate steps through a list of data values of the same type and produces as its result some analysis of the entire list. For example, aggregates perform tasks such as finding the total sum of a set of numerical values, finding the largest or the smallest value in a list, and so on.

Listing 3–34 illustrates one such aggregate. It calculates the total value of all stocked merchandise and illustrates one way that the built-in aggregates can be combined with user-defined extensions to the query language.

"What is the total value of Merchandise we have in stock (what is the sum of values arrived at by multiplying the Qty by the Price for all Merchandise Items)?"

```
SELECT SUM(M.Price * M.NumberAvailable::INTEGER) AS Sum
  FROM Merchandise M;
```

Sum::Currency

ROW(USD,515075.00)

Listing 3–34. *Aggregate Query Using SUM Aggregate*

The complete set of built-in aggregates that ship with the IDS product are reproduced in Table 3–3.

Table 3–3. Aggregate Query Using SUM Aggregate

Aggregate	Explanation
MIN()	Returns the smallest values from a set.
MAX()	Returns the largest value from a set.
COUNT()	Returns the number of rows passed in. This should be distinguished from CARDINALITY, a quasi-aggregator that performs the same function for COLLECTION instances. The COUNT() aggregate can be used in several ways: COUNT(*), COUNT(col_name), and COUNT(DISTINCT col_name).
AVG()	Returns the arithmetic mean of a set of (numeric) values.
SUM()	Returns the sum of a set of (numeric) values.
RANGE()	Returns the (numeric) value of (MAX() – MIN()) for the values supplied.
VARIANCE()	Returns this statistical variance: $(SUM(X_I{}^2) - (SUM(X_I{}^2)/N))/(N-1)$.
STDEV()	Returns the standard deviation, which is the square root of the VARIANCE.

Aggregate queries are used to analyze the state of the problem domain by identifying relevant sub-sets of the database's data and applying some analytic algorithm over each sub-set. As with other aspects of the language, the aggregate functions provided by SQL-92 represent a minority of the techniques developed over time to analyze data. Spreadsheet software typically implements hundreds of analytic functions, and a thriving community of data mining companies sell tools that are much more sophisticated than SQL-92.

As you might expect, the ORDBMS lets developers create *user-defined aggregates* (UDA) in much the same way it supports user-defined functions. For example, it might be useful to have an aggregate for performing statistical analysis over some data. Among the most useful kinds of analysis performed by business users is something called *linear regression*. This term describes a set of techniques that help quantify relationships between two measurable observations; say, the age of the stars in a movie and the age of movie club members who buy tickets. Such considerations influence marketing decisions.

Linear regression is a complex subject, but the basic idea is that given a set of paired the calculation arrives at a model for predicting what the value of one variable—say age of ticket buyers—will be given the value of another—age of stars.[3] Statistically rigorous aggregates of this kind must also compute factors like error estimators and values that describe the significance of the result. The query in Listing 3–35 illustrates how this kind of analysis might look like in an OR-SQL statement.

> *"What are the coefficients of linear regression between the age of a movie goer and the age of the movie's star in movies for movies released in the last 10 years?"*

```
SELECT LinearRegression( P.Cust_Age, P.Movie_Star_Age )
  FROM MovieTicketPurchases P, Movies M
 WHERE P.Movie = M.Id
   AND M.Release_Date > TODAY - (10) UNITS YEAR;
```

Listing 3–35. *Aggregate Query with User-Defined Aggregate*

Creating user-defined aggregates involves combining several user-defined functions in a particular way. We describe how this is achieved in more detail in Chapters 5 and 10.

GROUP BY and HAVING

All aggregate query examples so far return a single row. However, the problem being solved often calls for a set of aggregate calculations over different subsets of the input data. Of course, the query must specify how rows are to be grouped into subsets, and this is done using the GROUP BY syntax.

---

[3] This is a crude example. In the first place linear regression is really only applicable to continuous variables, while age is discrete. In practice, a range of factors like gender of movie stars and genre of film may also be relevant. Establishing the joint and independent impacts of a set of factors on some outcome is known as *multivariant analysis*.

For instance, you may want to divide `MovieClubMembers` into separate groups, one group for each city, and then find the number of members in each group. The query in Listing 3–36 illustrates how to use the GROUP BY syntax to achieve this. When the ORDBMS sees the GROUP BY, it classifies rows returned by the rest of the query (data sources and WHERE clause) into disjoint sets based on the columns in the GROUP BY. As it performs this grouping the ORDBMS computes the aggregate separately for each subset.

For example, consider the following subset of data values from the `MovieClubMembers` table, which is Table 3–4.

Table 3–4. Sample Data for GROUP BY Query

Name	DOB	Address.city
Paul Brown	5/24/1968	BERKELEY
Mira Freyenbauger	2/2/1964	PALO ALTO
Lou Gomez	11/12/1959	BERKELEY
Mary Meyers	6/10/1971	PALO ALTO
Joe Blogs	3/2/1968	REDWOOD SHORES

Listing 3–36 illustrates how to use GROUP BY to determine how many movie club members live in each city.

"How many Movie Club members live in each city in which we have members?"

```
SELECT M.Address.City,
       COUNT(*)
  FROM MovieClubMembers M
 GROUP BY 1;
```

Address.City	COUNT(*)
BERKELEY	2
PALO ALTO	2
REDWOOD SHORES	1

Listing 3–36. *Sample GROUP BY Query and Result*

Sometimes you want to apply an additional restriction over the results of the aggregate. For example, suppose you wanted to modify the query above to return cities with more than one movie club member. SQL provides an optional extension to the GROUP BY clause in the form of the HAVING keyword. HAVING provides a means of expressing restrictions over the results computed in the aggregate columns. Listing–37 provides an example of how the HAVING clause is used

"How many Movie Club members live in each city in which we have more than one member living?"

```
SELECT M.Address.City, COUNT(*)
  FROM MovieClubMembers M
 GROUP BY 1 HAVING COUNT(*) > 1;
```

Address.City	COUNT(*)
BERKELEY	2
PALO ALTO	2

Listing 3–37. *More Complex GROUP BY Query and Result*

Extensible DBMS technology makes entirely new kinds of analytic queries possible. The query in Listing 3–37 uses built-in functions in the HAVING clause (COUNT(*) and GreaterThan()), but user-defined functions and user-defined aggregates are also perfectly legal. For example, the query in Listing 3–38 checks to see if the convex hull polygon produced by the aggregate contains a particular point.

"Show me all of the area codes and their geographic range, where their geographic range includes a particular point."

```
SELECT M.HomePhone.AreaCode,
       ConvexHull( M.LivesAt )
  FROM MovieClubMembers M
 GROUP BY M.HomePhone.AreaCode
      HAVING Contains( ConvexHull(M.LivesAt),
                    '(-122.517, 27.3311 )'::sp2Pnt
            );
```

Listing 3–38. *User-Defined Aggregate and HAVING Query Example*

Executing this kind of query in an ORDBMS also require that the types involved have the necessary functions defined for them. When it performs a GROUP BY operation, the ORDBMS might sort all rows by the grouping column and then scans the ordered rows. Alternatively, IDS might use a hash table. This means that, as with an ORDER BY, you need to supply a Compare() function or indicate that the type involved in the query can be hashed.

So far as OR-SQL is concerned, there is no difference between built-in aggregates and user-defined aggregates. This makes user-defined aggregates a particularly powerful feature of ORDBMS technology. Traditionally developers faced with sophisticated analytic problems have been obliged to employ two different software tools: a scalable data manager and an external statistical analysis package. Such division of labor has discouraged the development of information systems that integrated sophisticated decision support with online transaction processing.

Clearly, there are benefits in being able to take into consideration an analysis of very recent events when making operational decisions. In general, the more information buyers and sellers have about market conditions, the more flexible pricing needs to be. Comparison-shopping once required sturdy shoes and a good street map. Today it requires a good Web search engine and a few mouse clicks. In such an environment flexible pricing, the ability to adjust prices up or down based on recent events becomes a competitive weapon. But this requires an information management infrastructure that goes beyond traditional *data warehousing*.

Object-Relational Structural Features and SELECT Queries

In Chapter 3 we saw some of the ways that the object-relational data model extends the structures features of the SQL-92 data model. We saw how an ORDBMS schema can include user-defined types, table inheritance, polymorphism, and COLLECTION attributes. Also, we noted earlier that in an ORDBMS the kinds of things you can use as data sources in queries—in addition to RDBMS tables and views—is significantly extended. Over the next few pages we explain how these new features impact the query language.

Strongly Typed Queries

An important property of object-relational queries is that they are *strongly typed*. In practice, strong typing means that as the ORDBMS parses query expressions it maps each of them to a single user-defined function. If no matching function exists, or if there is some ambiguity about which function to use, the parser generates an error and does not execute the query.

This is very different behavior from what developers got from an RDBMS. With SQL-92, database designers had to use the same types repeatedly throughout a schema definition. For example, in a SQL-92 database the `Merchandise` and `MovieClubMembers` tables would both be likely to both include `INTEGER` columns as identifiers. This made it possible to express semantically meaningless queries like "Show me all merchandise items where the item Id is the same as Fred's membership Id." Also, SQL-92 allowed comparisons between different data types—between say `INTEGER` and the various character data types—without generating errors, though such queries would sometimes generate a runtime exception. An SQL-92 query could relate the movie title "7" with `INTEGER` columns in other tables.

In the ORDBMS the SQL-92 behavior is retained for all of the built-in types, but queries involving user-defined types or user-defined functions are checked by the parser. To give you some idea what this means, consider the query fragment in Listing 3–39.

```
WHERE Movie.Title = MoviePersonality.Family_Name
```

Listing 3–39. *Query Fragment Syntactically Correct in ORDBMS and SQL-92*

If Listing 3–39 were part of a query in a SQL-92 database then the DBMS would have no objection. Both columns are character strings—they would probably be represented as `VARCHAR`—and SQL-92 knows how to compare them. However, in our movies Web site database queries with this kind of predicate will fail. There is no way to directly compare surnames and movie titles. If such a comparison is required both types can be converted into a third type—a character string—where character string comparison logic applies. From a theoretical point of view, these two types belong to different *domains*.

Strong typing is a good idea because it allows developers to build more accurate models of their information system's problem domain and because it reduces system development costs by making it easier to maintain. Coding errors and conceptual mistakes that would go undetected until late in development are picked up early, as the code is written. And over time, as the information system grows larger and more complex—some SQL-92 database schema have thousands of tables—strong typing makes it possible to answer questions about the database's structure and simplifies the task of turning semantic questions into OR-SQL queries.

At first glance strongly typed schema may seem problematic because they imply a lot of development effort. It seems to imply that developers must create a unique function for *every* operation. Fortunately there is not as much extra work as it you might think. Other features of the object-relational type system, which we discuss in the next chapter, allow you to reuse code in a systematic way. The ORDBMS parser goes to considerable lengths to find a matching function. It searches the list of user-defined functions for any types above the apparent types in an inheritance hierarchy, types the apparent type is a distinct type of and for which implicit casts exist.

Strong typing does have its drawbacks. Overemphasizing strongly typed schema semantics can cause you to clutter your query with *casts*. Sometimes, an `INTEGER` is just an `INTEGER`.

Queries and Table Hierarchies

Recall from the previous chapter that in an ORDBMS database a number of tables can be structured into an inheritance hierarchy. When a table that is part of such a hierarchy is accessed by a query, the ORDBMS processes rows from the named table and also all of the rows in tables created under it. For example the query in Listing 3–40 will return a count of rows from all of the tables below the `Merchandise` table (which is empty).

> *"What is the total number of items of Merchandise we sell through the site?"*

```
SELECT COUNT(*) AS Merchandise_Count
    FROM Merchandise;
```

Listing 3–40. *Query to Count Row in Merchandise Table and All Tables UNDER It*

When a query accesses a table in the hierarchy, it can only address columns defined in that table. Additional columns in a subtable are invisible from the super table: they cannot appear in the `SELECT` list or `WHERE` clause. For example, queries that address the `Merchandise` table will return rows from all of the tables in this hierarchy, but only their Id, Name, Movie, Description, Price, CosttoShip, and Qty columns. Listing 3–41 illustrates the return results for queries over different tables in this hierarchy.

> *"Show me all currently available items of Merchandise priced at less than 15 British Pounds."*

```
SELECT M.Name,
       M.Description,
       M.Price + M.ShippingCost AS NetPrice,
       M.NumberAvailable
  FROM Merchandise M
 WHERE M.Price            < Currency(15, 'GBP')
   AND M.NumberAvailable > 0;
```

Name:: String	Description:: String	Netprice:: Currency	Numberavailable:: Quantity
Full Price Movie Tickets	Full price movie tickets, valid for any showing	ROW(USD, 9.00)	10000
Full Price Movie Tickets	Full price movie tickets, valid for any showing	ROW(USD, 9.00)	10000
Full Price Movie Tickets	Full price movie tickets, valid for any showing	ROW(USD, 9.00)	10000
Full Price Movie Tickets	Full price movie tickets, valid for any showing	ROW(USD, 9.00)	10000
Full Price Movie Tickets	Full price movie tickets, valid for any showing	ROW(USD, 9.00)	10000
Full Price Movie Tickets	Full price movie tickets, valid for any showing	ROW(USD, 9.00)	10000
Half Price Matinee Movie Tickets	Half price movie tickets, valid for matinee showings	ROW(USD, 5.00)	10000
Rick T-Shirt	T-shirt with Rick, proprietor of Rick's Cafe American, played by Humphrey Bogart; black and white image.	ROW(USD, 14.00)	200
Rick and Elsa Monogram Shirt	Black and white image of Rick and Elsa, in the climactic airport scene.	ROW(USD, 16.50)	300

Listing 3–41. *Query Addressing Columns in a Hierarchy of Tables*

Note the way that conversion between currency denominations is handled entirely within the `Currency` type's definition. As exchange rates vary, the query in Listing 3–41 may return different results without any change to the contents of the table!

If the query addresses a table that is midway down the hierarchy, then the rows it returns come from the named table and all the tables below it. Rows from sibling tables, and tables above the named table, are ignored. For example, the query in Listing 3–42 returns rows from the `Apparel` table. The results of this query differ from the one in Listing 3–41 in that it returns a column called Sizes defined as part of the `Apparel` table and present in all tables below it.

> *"Show me all currently available items of Apparel Merchandise items priced at less than 15 British Pounds."*

```
SELECT A.Name,
       A.Description,
       A.Price + A.ShippingCost AS NetPrice,
```

```
            A.NumberAvailable AS Qty,
            A.Sizes
       FROM Apparel A
       WHERE A.Price < Currency(15, 'GBP');
```

Name::String	Description::String	Netprice:: Currency	Qty:: Quantity	Sizes:: SET (Size NOT NULL)
Rick T-Shirt	T-shirt with Rick, proprieter of Rick's Cafe American, played by Humphrey Bogart; black and white image.	ROW (USD, 14.00)	200	SET{'P','S',','M', 'L', 'XL', 'XXL'},
Rick and Elsa Monogram Shirt	Black and white image of Rick and Elsa, in the climactic airport scene.	ROW (USD, 16.50)	300	SET{'P','S','M','L', 'XL '}

Listing 3–42. *Query Addressing Columns in a Hierarchy of Tables*

At this time so-called "jagged-row" queries are only supported through the ORDBMS's server API (SAPI). This is because none of the standard client APIs provides a mechanism to handle a set of return rows that have varying structure. Listing 3–43 illustrates what a jagged row query looks like. For each result row, the ORDBMS needs to return to the interface not only the row data, but also a description of its structure.

"Show me details of currently available items of Merchandise priced at less than 10 British Pounds."

```
SELECT *
    FROM Merchandise M
    WHERE M.Price < Currency(10.0, 'USD');
```

Id	Name	Movie	Description	Price	CostToShip	Qty	Maker	Sizes	Photo
10	Shirt	102	Denim Shirt	22.50	5.50	225	Merves	{S, M, L}	DATA

Id	Name	Movie	Description	Price	CostToShip	Qty	Copyright
31	Poster	422	Promotional	12.50	1.50	75	TRUE

Id	Name	Movie	Description	Price	CostToShip	Qty	Copyright	Sample	Length
99	Video	1013	Cassette	35.00	5.50	20	TRUE	DATA	135 M
73	Video	1013	DVD	65.00	3.50	31	TRUE	DATA	135 M

Listing 3–43. *"Jagged-Row" Query Addressing a Hierarchy of Tables*

OR-SQL queries can address rows in a single table of a hierarchy. For example it is quite reasonable to query for only media items priced at less than $10. To do this, you would use the query in Listing 3–44.

"Show me all currently available items of only Media priced at less than 10 US Dollars."

```
SELECT *
  FROM ONLY(Media) M
 WHERE M.Price < Currency(10.0, 'USD');
```

Id	Name	Movie	Description	Prive	Shipping_cost	Num.	Kind
402	The Maltese Falcon Book	100404	Published by Classic Crime Inc. . .	ROW(USD, 9.50)	ROW(USD, 1.20)	25	Book
403	Casablanca Script	100404	Copy of the script for the film.	ROW(USD, 7.50)	ROW(USD, 1.20)	25	Book

Listing 3–44. *Query over Single Table in a Table Hierarchy*

To query only the rows in the specified table, you need to wrap the table name in parenthesis and prepend the ONLY keyword to the data source. The query in the Listing 3–45 considers Media table rows only.

UPDATE and DELETE queries adhere to the same rules. They can only address visible columns in the tables specified as data sources. UPDATE queries modify rows in the table named in the query and in any tables under it, and DELETE removes rows from any table in the hierarchy below the one you specify. Only columns that exist in the table named in the query, however, can be used in the SET or WHERE clauses of these queries.

INSERT queries and bulk load operations can only be applied to a single table. There is no notion of an INSERT statement that "figures out" which table in the hierarchy a row belongs to.

Polymorphism

Polymorphism describes a particular aspect of query behavior where table hierarchies and overloaded user-defined functions are involved. In an OR-SQL query, different functions with the same name can be applied over different tables in a hierarchy. Although they all have the same name these function can have different implementations and where one is actually invoked by the ORDBMS depends on the table involved.

Figure 3–7 represents the Merchandise table hierarchy introduced above in diagrammatic form. This figure illustrates how a set of *over-loaded* functions—all called BriefDescription()—can be defined for tables at different levels in the hierarchy. Actually, the multiple

`BriefDescription()` function definitions correspond to the different user-defined types making up a `ROW TYPE` hierarchy, and the `ROW TYPES` are used to define the table hierarchy.

When you run a query as shown in Listing 3–45 over the `Merchandise` table, the query accesses rows from all the tables in the hierarchy. While processing `Apparel` rows, the ORDBMS will apply the `BriefDescription()` function defined for the `Apparel` table's data type, and when processing rows from the `Media` table, it calls the `BriefDescription()` function defined for the `Media` table's type.

"Give me a description of all items of available merchandise."

```
SELECT BriefDescription(M) AS Description
  FROM Merchandise M
 WHERE M.Price < Currency(10, 'USD');
```

Description ::String

Media: Book: The Maltese Falcon Book
Media: Book: Casablanca Script
Merchandise: Full Price Movie Tickets
Merchandise: Full Price Movie Tickets
Merchandise: Full Price Movie Tickets
Merchandise: Full Price Movie Tickets
Merchandise: Full Price Movie Tickets
Merchandise: Full Price Movie Tickets
Merchandise: Half Price Matinee Movie Tickets
Apparel: Sam Cap Cap available in sizes {S, M, L }
Apparel: Sam Spade Sox Sox available in sizes {P, S, M, L, XL }
Apparel: Falcon T-Shirt T-Shirt available in sizes {S, M , L , XL}

Listing 3–45. *SELECT Query over Table Hierarchy with Polymorphic Function*

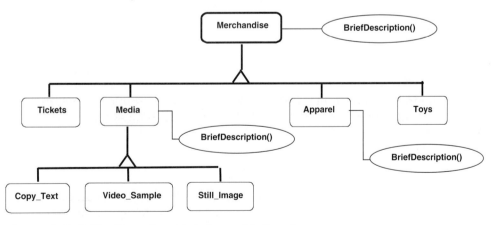

Figure 3–7. *Table Hierarchy with Polymorphic Functions*

Notice the "gaps" in Figure 3–7, where the function used in List-ing 3–45 is not defined explicitly at some level in the hierarchy. For instance, `BriefDescription()` is not defined over the `Toys` table. In situations where the query processor determines that a function does not have a perfect match, it tries to substitute the closest one it can find by looking upwards in the table hierarchy. Thus, in Listing 3–45 first two rows result from calling the `BriefDescription()` defined for `Media`. Each of the next several rows should come from the `Tickets` table, but as there is no `BriefDescription()` defined for `Tickets` the ORDBMS defaults to the function defined over its super-table, which in this case is `Merchandise`. The final rows use the `BriefDescription()` defined for `Apparel`.

Chapters 4 and 5 describe how type hierarchies and overloaded functions are created and go into more detail concerning the way the ORDBMS figures out which function it invokes.

Data Sources in OR-SQL

Recall how the theoretical relational model defines relational operators such as project, restrict, and join as algorithms that apply to *relations*. In RDBMS products this meant tables, views, and (with come products) `SELECT` queries. But the ORDBMS data model is closer to the theoretical relational model in how it define data sources. You can create OR-SQL `SELECT` queries over many other things that look like relations. This innovation simplifies certain queries, and it makes it possible to use the database in new ways.

In practical terms, developers can use combination of the following new types of data source in a `FROM` clause.

COLLECTION Data Structures

Columns in a table and the variables and arguments in database pro-cedures can consist of a `COLLECTION` of data values. Each `COLLECTION` is a group of identically structured data values, conceptually very simi-lar to a relation. OR-SQL queries can treat a `COLLECTION` as if it were a kind of small table. In effect, a `COLLECTION` dropped into a query acts like a kind of *variable table*. For example, the OR-SQL `SELECT` query in Listing 3–46 retrieves the contents of a `COLLECTION`.

```
SELECT G
   FROM TABLE (
            SET{'Romance','History','Action','Western',
                'Comedy'}::SET(Genre_Enum NOT NULL)
           ) G;
```

g ::ROW(Genre)

ROW('Romance')
ROW('History')
ROW('Action')
ROW('Western')
ROW('Comedy')

Listing 3–46. *Query with COLLECTION as Data Source*

In Listing 3–47, we assign the COLLECTION an alias name. Each data value from the COLLECTION can be addressed using this alias. The query in Listing 3–47 is a more practical example of what can be achieved with a variable table. In data sources taken from a COLLECTION, there will be as many rows in the data source as there are elements in the COLLECTION, and with sets of ROW TYPE instances the elements within the row type appear as columns from a table would appear.

"Select all movie personalities who are Pisces, Aries or Leo."

```
SELECT Print(P.Name) AS Name,
       S.Sign
  FROM MoviePersonalities P,
       TABLE(
             SET{
                  ROW('Pisces'),ROW('Aries'),ROW('Leo')
                }::SET(ROW(Sign lvarchar) NOT NULL)
            ) S
 WHERE BornUnder (P.DOB, Star_Sign(S.Sign));
```

Name::String	Sign::LVARCHAR
Sherwood Sherwood	Pisces
David Lean	Aries
William Holden	Aries
Alec Guinness	Aries
Myrna Loy	Leo
Julius Epstein	Leo
Philip Epstein	Leo
John Houston	Leo

Listing 3–47. *Join Query with COLLECTION as Data Source*

This query uses a SET of lvarchar values as a data source. Star_Sign is an enumerated data type modeling the twelve signs of the zodiac.[4] About the only thing that can be done with a `Star_Sign` is to determine if someone—a movie personality in this case—born under that sign, based on birth date. Note how in this query data from the `COLLECTION` data source is used in both the `WHERE` predicates and in the `SELECT` list.

All of the examples so far have demonstrated variable tables containing single, atomic data values. But queries can address a `COLLECTION` of `ROW TYPE` instances where—much like a table—each element contains subelements. Further, user-defined functions that return a `COLLECTION` are also eligible for the same kind of treatment.

The following slightly contrived example combines several of these ideas. In financial analysis, it is common to compute results by quarter. But different companies structure their quarters differently. Listing 3–48 creates a user-defined data type to represent a financial quarter and a user-defined function that returns a set of these objects that correspond to the quarters for a particular year.

```
CREATE ROW TYPE Quarter (
    Year          INTEGER NOT NULL,
    Quarter       INTEGER NOT NULL,
    Range         Period  NOT NULL
);

CREATE FUNCTION Quarters ( Year INTEGER )
RETURNING SET(Quarter NOT NULL)
    DEFINE  rtQuart SET(Quarter NOT NULL);

    INSERT INTO TABLE(rtQuart)
    SELECT ROW( Year,
                S.Num,
                Period( (S.Start || '/' || Year)::DATE,
                        (S.End || '/' || Year)::DATE)
              )::Quarter
      FROM TABLE( SET{ROW( 1, '01/01', '03/31'),
                      ROW( 2, '04/01', '06/30'),
                      ROW( 3, '07/01', '09/30'),
                      ROW( 4, '10/01', '12/31')
                    }::SET(ROW(Num     INTEGER,
                               Start LVARCHAR,
                               End     LVARCHAR) NOT NULL) ) S;
    RETURN rtQuart;
END FUNCTION;

SELECT Q.*
  FROM TABLE(Quarters(1998)) Q;
```

---

[4] By no means does this imply any belief on the author's part in astrology. But as it seems to be something many ardent star-watchers are interested in, doubtless the Web site would provide the service.

Year::INTEGER	Quarter::INTEGER	Range::Period
1998	1	01/01/1998 to 03/31/1998
1998	2	04/01/1998 to 06/30/1998
1998	3	07/01/1998 to 09/30/1998
1998	4	10/01/1998 to 12/31/1998

Listing 3–48. *Implementing a Functional COLLECTION*

The final query in this example illustrates how the function return-ing a set can be included in an OR-SQL SELECT query. Quarters() is an example of an iterator function, which is a UDF that returns a series of values rather than a single result.

Other SELECT Queries

In the IDS product a developer can treat an entire SELECT query as a data source for another query. This is called "query nesting," or more formally, *query closure*. When it encounters a nested query expression, the ORDBMS executes the inner query and materializes its results in a temporary table. Then the ORDBMS runs the outer query over the rows in the temporary table. The basic pattern is illustrated in Listing 3–49.

```
SELECT F.A,
       B.Col_One
  FROM Foo F,
       TABLE(MULTISET( SELECT T.B, T.C
                         FROM Table T
                        WHERE Some_Predicate(T.D)
                     )
            ) B (Col_One, Col_Two)
 WHERE F.C = B.Col_Two;
```

Listing 3–49. *General Form of Query Closure or SELECTs as a Data Source*

In Listing 3–49 the outer query is a join between two data sources. The first of these is simply a table, called Foo. But the second data source is actually another independent SELECT query. To indicate that a query should be treated as if it were a table, you first cast its results into a MULTISET and second convert this MULTISET to a table using the same TABLE keyword we saw in the previous section.

In practice, query closure is most immediately useful when nesting aggregate queries, as shown in Listing 3–50.

"Find the number of items of merchandise where we have sold more than 100 units in the last week."

```
SELECT COUNT(*)
   FROM TABLE(MULTISET(SELECT O.Merchandise,
                              SUM(O.NumberBought)
                  FROM Order_Line_Items O, Orders D
                  WHERE D.OrderedOn > TODAY - 7
                    AND D.Id = O.Order
                  GROUP BY O.Merchandise
                  HAVING SUM(O.NumberBought) > 100
                  )
         ) B ( M, S );
```

Listing 3–50. *Example of SELECT Query as a Data Source*

Query closure allows you to answer certain business questions—such as the one in Listing 3–50—with a single query, replacing several queries involving temporary tables. There are limitations, however, on the kinds of SELECT queries that can be nested. These constraints, and the rather convoluted syntax of Listing 3–49, will be removed over time, but temporary tables look likely to become less common rather than disappear completely.

Statement Local Variables

Statement local variables are another IDS product innovation that allows you to return more than one result from a user-defined function. This additional result can be used in other parts of the query. Statement local variables (SLVs) are best explained with an example.

Consider a Document data type. One of the more common queries involving documents finds all documents in a table that are similar to some given document. For example, we might say that for two documents to be similar, the total number of distinct words in both documents is only 10% more than the number of words in the bigger of the two. Such a query might look like Listing 3–51.

```
SELECT M.Title
   FROM Movies M
   WHERE DocLike ( M.PlotSummary,
                   "Cowboy saves town and gets girl.");
```

Listing 3–51. *Example of SELECT Query for Document Similarity*

Of course, such queries frequently return multiple rows. Most applications would want to present these results in such a way that the most similarly plotted movies appear first. In other words, they would like the results of this query to be ordered by their degree of similarity. But the `DocLike()` function—even though it likely computes a measure of similarity internally—only returns a boolean. Statement local variables are intended to overcome this difficulty.

In the ORDBMS, functions such as `DocLike()` can also return what is known as an out parameter. In our example, this out parameter would be a measure of similarity, but you can also use the out parameter to return the extent of overlap between two polygons, or a measure of similarity between a particular customer's demographics and a target market's demographics. OR-SQL uses statement local variables to hold the value of the out parameter so that it can be used by other parts of the query.

For example, Listing 3–52 illustrates how an augmented `DocLike()` function would be used to solve the problem introduced above.

"What are some Movies whose plot is something like 'Cowboy saves town gets girl,' ordered by the closeness of the document to this description?"

```
SELECT M.Title,
       Similarity
  FROM Movies M
 WHERE DocLike ( M.PlotSummary,
                 "Cowboy saves town and gets girl.",
                 Similarity # INTEGER )
 ORDER BY Similarity, Title;
```

Listing 3–52. *Example of SELECT Query Using Statement Local Variable*

In Listing 3–52 the out parameter returned as the third argument to `DocLike()` is assigned to an SLV using the '#' symbol. SLVs are typed—meaning that the OR-SQL statement needs to know what data type they are to take—and they must be given an unambiguous name within the query expressions. A UDF can return multiple out parameters, and a single query can contain multiple statement local variables.

We explain how to implement functions returning out parameters in Chapter 5.

Changing Data Using OR-SQL

So far we have focused on explaining how to use OR-SQL to retrieve data from the database. But to service the full set of information system requirements OR-SQL can change data in the database to reflect changes in the real world. Three general-purpose query statements insert new data, delete unwanted data, and update data. The next section of this chapter is devoted to describing these statements and explaining how they work.

Write queries are handled in the same way that the ORDBMS handles SELECT statements. At runtime, it parses each query to determine what tables, columns, and functions are involved. For UPDATE and DELETE queries with WHERE clauses, or correlated queries where the data change is affected by SELECT statements embedded within the write query, the ORDBMS will perform an optimization step to minimize the hardware resources that the query consumes. Write queries can be issued from external programs using the same interfaces that support SELECT query, albeit using different aspects of those interfaces. Write queries are often embedded within database stored procedures that run within the ORDBMS.

Transactions

An important topic whenever an information system's functionality calls for incremental data changes of the kind handled using write queries is the subject of *transactions*. The ORDBMS provides certain quality of service guarantees whenever an end user or an external program issues a query that changes data. Collectively, these assurances mean that each data change

- either succeeds entirely or has no effect whatsoever on the database
- always leaves the database in a correct state with respect to both its internal data structures and any integrity rules defined at the logical schema level
- is performed in such a way that several different—but concurrently executed—data operations (read, write, or a mixture) all proceed without interfering with each other
- once made, is irrevocable, and enduring.

We explore the transaction concept and its implications in Tutorial 2. All information system developers are highly advised to have a thorough understanding of the transaction concept. It is among the most profound in all of computer science.

INSERT Queries

An INSERT statement appends new data values to one of the following data sources:

- Tables. An INSERT statement can add a row either by addressing the table directly or through an updateable view. OR-SQL makes no distinction between base and temporary tables.
- COLLECTION variables. Because they are similar in many ways to tables, OR-SQL uses the INSERT statement to add new data values to a COLLECTION. The user-defined function in Listing 3–48 illustrates how this is done.
- User-defined access methods. Tables created using a user-defined access method can also be the target of an INSERT query. In this case, the ORDBMS will call the appropriate method from the virtual table interface to complete the operation.

In its simplest form the INSERT statement must provide a target table name and a list of constant data values of the appropriate type or values computed by user-defined functions for each of its columns. More sophisticated INSERT statements can append the row values from a SELECT query to the target table.

If the target table is a base table or a temporary table—that is, if the data in the data source is managed by the ORDBMS internally—the engine appends the new row(s) to the table's data on disk. As it does so it ensures that the new row(s) do not violate any of the table's integrity rules. Also, it changes all indices associated with the table. The ORDBMS query processor turns INSERT queries that add rows into updateable views into INSERT queries against the underlying base table, and check the integrity rules there.

COLLECTION objects behave like small, entirely in-memory tables. New values are added to the COLLECTION by the INSERT statement, and any rules about membership of the COLLECTION are checked. Unlike tables, COLLECTION instances are not subject to transactional integrity because their content is not shared among many users. COLLECTION data is not locked or logged until it finds its way into a table.

In this section we describe OR-SQL INSERT syntax and illustrate how it works with tables, views, and external data sources. We review how to use the INSERT statement with COLLECTION structures in Chapter 4, where we describe the ORDBMS type system.

INSERT a Single Row of Values

The simplest version of the INSERT statement inserts a single row into a table. It appends the new row to whatever rows already exist in the table. Listing 3–53 shows the most basic structure of an INSERT query.

```
INSERT INTO Table
[ ( Column_Name {, Column_Name }) ]
VALUES
( Constant | Expression { , Constant | Expression } );
```

Listing 3–53. *General Form of Simple, Single Row INSERT Query*

When a row is added to a table using this kind of statement, the INSERT query must supply a value for every column in the table that needs one. Columns that take NULL, or columns that have a DEFAULT value, can be left out. The target list—the list of column names between the target table name and the VALUES keyword—is optional but very useful. Without it, the set of values in the constant list must be presented in the same order that columns are present in the table. By providing a target list a query can address columns in a different order than they appear in the table, and it can step over columns that have DEFAULT values. Many ORDBMS databases will be adding and occasionally removing columns from tables, so including the target list is often a good idea.

Listing 3–54 illustrates two INSERT queries: a simple and then a more advanced example. The first adds a new row to the table recording when movies are shown at various cinemas. In this first example, because of the data integrity constraints that relate Showings to Cinemas and Movies, the constant values supplied with the query must be present in the other tables. Later, when we review correlated INSERT statements, we will see another way to handle such relationships. The second query adds a new row to the MovieClubMembers table. Unlike the first INSERT, the second has only that table's constraints to check.

```
INSERT INTO Showings
( Id, Cinema, Movie, Duration, Discount )
VALUES
( 110104, 10005, 100500,
  Period(TODAY - 31, TODAY + 93), 'f' );

INSERT INTO MovieClubMembers
(
  Id, Name,
  DOB,
  Address,
  HomePhone,
  Location,   Preferences,
  Photo, CreditCard
  ) VALUES (
```

```
    10071, PersonName( "Brown", "Paul"),
    "5/24/1968",
    Address ("123 Main Street",
            "", "BERKELEY", "CA", ZipCode(94704)),
    PhoneNumber(332, 3948753),
    "(-130.109, 34.917)", "SET{'Art','Foreign'}",
    FileToBLOB('C:\tmp\Me.pcx', 'client')::Image,
    CCDetails("VISA", "989873459864", "07/1998")
  );
```

Listing 3–54. *Example of SELECT Query Using Statement Local Variable*

There are several things to note in these statements. Many of the data values being inserted in these queries are actually constructed from literal values with user-defined functions. Because object-relational tables contain more complex data structures, this kind of pattern is fairly common. Finally, note the use of the `FileToBLOB()` function. This takes the contents of a file and moves it into the database, but casts the large object handle into an `Image` type instance.

INSERT AS SELECT

Recall how earlier we described the structure of an OR-SQL `SELECT` statement's results as looking a lot like a table. This makes it possible to redirect the rows produced by a `SELECT` statement into a table that has the same structure. This kind of query is often called a correlated `INSERT`. Listing 3–55 shows its general form.

```
INSERT INTO Table
Select_Statement;
```

Listing 3–55. *General Form of INSERT-AS-SELECT Query*

The `Select_Statement` in Listing 3–55 can be any legal `SELECT` query of the kind described earlier in this chapter. Obviously, the structure of a query's result rows must match the structure of the target table. The query producing the input data can include subqueries, or retrieve data from views or virtual tables. You can even inserted values from a `COLLECTION`, making it possible to reduce a series of separate `INSERT VALUES` queries into a single `INSERT-AS-SELECT-FROM-MULTISET` query.

For example, when a new movie is added to the site, it's likely that most of the people who worked on the film are already stored in the database. To associate the person with the new movie, a row is inserted into one of the hierarchy of tables managing the relationship between `Movies` and `MoviePersonalities`, as shown in Listing 3–56.

"Record the fact that John Houston Directed 'The Maltese Falcon.'"

```
INSERT INTO Directed
SELECT M.Id,
       P.Id
  FROM Movies M,
       MoviePersonalities P
 WHERE M.Title = 'The Maltese Falcon'
   AND P.Name  = PersonName('Houston', 'John');
```

Listing 3–56. *Example of INSERT AS SELECT Style of INSERT Query*

To process this statement, the ORDBMS first runs the `SELECT` statement—which is a join in this case—to produce a row result. Then it will `INSERT` the rows of result data into the target table. Regardless of how many rows are produced by the `SELECT`, the ORDBMS checks that each of them complies with all of the target table's integrity rules.

Bulk Data Load and INSERT

Faced with the task of getting a large amount of data into a table, doing it one row-at-a-time gets tedious. So the ORDBMS provides the means to bulk-load data from an external file into a table. Data in the file must have an appropriate format for the table, and the data in the file must comply with its rules. Errors in the data cause the load to fail.

The following figure illustrates the simplest of these bulk load techniques. Unfortunately, this command can only be issued from a SQL interface tool such as `dbaccess`. In practice, this means that using this involves writing a server-side script and invoking it using the `SYSTEM` feature of the stored procedure language. In Listing 3–57 we present the basics syntax. Note that the `DELIMITER` keyword is optional: By default the IDS product uses a tab character as a field separator.

```
LOAD FROM "/tmp/zip1.dat"
DELIMITER "|"  INSERT INTO ZipCodes;
```

Listing 3–57. *Example of Bulk Load Using INSERT*

The IDS product ships are several other *loader* tools. Unlike the LOAD/UNLOAD syntax, these tools involve more administrative effort. For very large data sets these tools parallelize the load operation, splitting it up into several concurrently running operations, and are capable of much higher load rates.

Similar functionality can be implemented by creating a user-defined access method using the virtual table interfaces (VTI). With such a virtual table, you can use an INSERT-SELECT kind of query to do much the same thing. In Tutorial 7, where we describe the virtual table interface, we describe how to develop just such a loader interface.

UPDATE Statement

An UPDATE statement modifies data values in a table. Each UPDATE needs to identify the table whose rows are being changed, how the affected columns are to be changed, and it uses a WHERE clause to identify the row(s) to be modified. The change the UPDATE statement makes, which columns are affected and the new values they are to have, is specified in the SET clause. UPDATE statements typically include literal constant values. Listing 3–58 shows the general form of the UPDATE statement:

```
UPDATE table_name
    SET ( column_name { , column_name } ) =
            [ ( expression {, expression } ) |
              ( select query ) ]
    [ WHERE [NOT] condition { [ AND | OR | NOT ] condition } ];
```

Listing 3–58. *Structure of UPDATE Query statement*

Each UPDATE can change a single row, a set of rows, a single column, a set of columns, or a set of columns in a set of rows. If the table's data is stored in the DBMS's internal storage then the data pages containing the records are overwritten with the new values. As it makes these changes the ORDBMS checks all integrity rules and modifies any indices. As with all OR-SQL queries, UPDATE statements can be issued from an external program through the various ORDBMS APIs, or they can be embedded within a database procedure.

Single Row UPDATE

The simplest way to use the UPDATE statement is to change a column value in a single row. This requires that the expressions in the WHERE clause are sufficient to uniquely identify a row, which usually means that the WHERE clause includes a primary key column, and the SET clause modifies one column, as shown in Listing 3–59.

> *"Stock-taking has indicated that for Part_Code 103, we actually have 200 items available."*

```
UPDATE Apparel
   SET NumberAvailable = 200
   WHERE Id = 103::Part_Code;
```

Listing 3–59. *Example of Singleton UPDATE Query*

Rather than simply replacing an old value with a new one, it can be useful to modify it to a new value created by invoking a user-defined function. The examples in Listing 3–60 illustrate what this kind of query looks like.

> *"We just bought another 100 of Part_Code 103."*

```
UPDATE Apparel
   SET NumberAvailable = NumberAvailable + 100::Quantity
   WHERE Id = 102::Part_Code;
```

> *"Movie Club Member 'Mira Freyenbauger' informs us that we have misspelled her name."*

```
UPDATE MovieClubMembers
   SET Name = PersonName(Name.Family_Name::lvarchar,'Myra' )
   WHERE Name = PersonName ( 'Freyenbauger','Mira')
      AND DOB  = '03/02/1964';
```

Listing 3–60. *Computed Singleton UPDATE Queries*

Any of the functions embedded in OR-SQL can be used to construct new data values in an UPDATE. Modifying a data value, however, involves creating a new instance of the correct data type possibly using a copy of the original value as a starting point. Replacing one data value with another is the approach taken instead of altering the data structure in place because it simplifies query processing. Listing 3–60 might be replaced with the query in Listing 3–61.

```
UPDATE MovieClubMembers
    SET Name = SetFirstName( Name,'Myra' )
  WHERE Name = PersonName ( 'Freyenbauger','Mira')
    AND DOB  = '03/02/1964';
```

Listing 3–61. *Computed Singleton UPDATE Queries*

Either approach is reasonable, although the latter is slightly more object-oriented in its flavor and therefore results in a more straight-forward data type design.

Multiple Row UPDATE

As with all OR-SQL statements, an UPDATE can affect many rows. In practice this simply means that the WHERE predicates match more than one row. For example, an update statement that reduces by 10% the prices of all merchandise items valued at more than $20 would look like Listing 3–62.

> *"Discount all merchandise priced above $20 by 10%."*

```
UPDATE Merchandise
   SET Price = Price * 0.9
 WHERE Price > Currency (20, 'USD');
```

Listing 3–62. *Example of Multi-Row Query*

To update every row in a table, leave out the WHERE clause altogether.

Multiple Column UPDATE

A single UPDATE statement can change multiple columns. Queries that do this need to list all the columns to be modified and then supply a list of expressions computing their new values in the same order. In SQL-92 systems, where complex objects were represented as multiple columns, this was more common than it is in ORDBMS systems.

Listing 3–63 demonstrates what such a query looks like.

> *"Discount all merchandise priced above $20 by 5% and make the shipping of these items free."*

```
UPDATE Merchandise
SET (Price, Shipping ) =
    ( Currency((GetQuantity(Price)*0.9),GetUnits(Price)),
      Currency ( 0.0, 'USD' ))
  WHERE Price > Currency ( 20, 'USD');
```

Listing 3–63. *Example UPDATE Query Modifying more than One Column*

In fact, the query in Listing 3–63 modifies multiple columns in multiple rows.

Correlated UPDATE

We have already introduced the concept of a correlated INSERT, where the results of a SELECT query are used in an INSERT. SELECT query results can also be used to determine what rows to change and the new values that the modified columns are to have. We call this a *correlated* update. In Listing 3–64, we present one simple and one more complex example of this kind of query.

```
UPDATE Target_Table
    SET Column = (SELECT Value()
                    FROM Other_Tables O
                    WHERE Join_Predicates(Target_Table.Column,
                                          Other_Tables.Column)
                 )
    WHERE EXISTS ( SELECT 1
                    FROM Other_Tables O
                    WHERE
                      Join_Predicates(Target_Table.Column,
                                      Other_Tables.Column)
                 );
```

"Restocking. Increase the quantities of each item of Apparel merchandise by the number we sold over the last week."

```
UPDATE Apparel
    SET NumberAvailable = NumberAvailable +
                ( SELECT SUM(L1.NumberBought)
                    FROM Orders O1, Order_Line_Items L1
                    WHERE L1.Merchandise = Apparel.Id
                      AND O1.Id          = L1.Order
                      AND O1.OrderedOn    > TODAY - 7
                )
    WHERE Apparel.Id IN (
                SELECT L2.Merchandise
                    FROM Order_Line_Items L2, Orders O2
                    WHERE O2.Id           = L2.Order
                      AND L2.Merchandise = Apparel.Id
                      AND O2.OrderedOn    > TODAY - 7
            );
```

Listing 3–64. *Example of Correlated UPDATE Query*

These examples include a query structure we describe in detail later: the *sub-query*. Here, we use an IN subquery to limit the rows affected by the UPDATE to those Apparel rows where the Id columns is one of the Id values returned from a query that joins two other tables.

Without the subquery in the WHERE clause an UPDATE statement such as the one in Listing 3–64 will change *every* row in the table. In this case, the WHERE clause minimizes the number of rows the query processes thereby improving its overall performance. Note the way that the structures of the subqueries in the SET and WHERE clauses of each statement are very similar. In correlated queries like this it is very important that the right values be applied to the right rows.

DELETE Statement

The DELETE statement removes records from a database table and reclaims the row's storage space for new data. Note that space allocated to any large objects that are referred to from a deleted row are not marked for reuse immediately. Instead the ORDBMS decrements the large object's reference count (a count of the number of rows referring to the object). Other space management logic reuses the large object's space only when its reference count is zero. The DELETE statement takes the general form in Listing 3–65.

```
DELETE FROM Table Name
[ WHERE [NOT] condition { [ AND | OR | NOT ] condition } ];
```

Listing 3–65. *General Form of DELETE Query*

Tables that contain a PRIMARY KEY used to define a relationship to another table can cascade a DELETE operation to the related tables. Automating deletes of related rows is achieved by using the ON DELETE CASCADE syntax with the foreign key declaration. UPDATE changes to PRIMARY KEY columns, however, cannot be cascaded.

Single Row DELETE

To delete a single row from a table requires that the predicates in the WHERE clause identifies one row in the table. For example, to delete a row from our movie club members table, you would use the query in Listing 3–66.

```
DELETE FROM MovieClubMembers
  WHERE Id = 10111::Membership_Num;
```

Listing 3–66. *Simple Example of DELETE Query*

Candidate key columns, which identify rows uniquely, are the best mechanism for indicating which row is to go.

DELETE Multiple Rows

Frequently a single query is called upon to delete multiple rows. To do this, the statement's WHERE clause predicates identify the set of rows to be removed. For example, it might be useful to DELETE all future showings for a turkey of a movie while leaving the currently scheduled runs alone. Developers can delete multiple rows using a query like the one in Listing 3–67.

```
DELETE FROM Showings
  WHERE Movie = 1030402::Movie_Id
    AND AFTER( Duration , Period ( TODAY, TODAY ) );
```

Listing 3–67. *Simple Example of DELETE Query*

As with all write queries touching multiple rows, it is possible that this WHERE clause might not find any rows to change. A write query that affects no rows will not cause an error, but it will not have any effect on the database, either. All of the client interfaces used to submit queries include facilities to find out how many rows the last query changed. This can be useful to check the correctness of a write operation.

Correlated DELETE

As with INSERT and UPDATE queries, a DELETE can use a sub-query to determine which rows to remove. In the query in Listing 3–68, we illustrate a correlated DELETE query.

"George Eliot phoned us to say that her six-year-old son placed a set of Orders, and asked for them to be deleted, please."

```
DELETE FROM Orders
   WHERE Customer = ( SELECT M.Id
                         FROM MovieClubMembers M
                         WHERE M.Name =
                               PersonName('Eliot','George')
                   );
```

Listing 3–68. *Example of Correlated DELETE Query*

This query deletes rows from the `Orders` table. Because of the cascading constraint, this query has the effect of also removing rows from the `Order_Line_Items` table too.

General Note on Correlated Queries

A common problem when writing information systems using RDBMS is that developers cannot take advantage of the performance and flexibility of correlated queries. SQL-92 is limited in the range of expressions it supports, so developers are often obliged to use a client language to write complex computational functions. Then they would iterate over data streamed out of the DBMS using a `SELECT` query and within each loop use a write query to change data in the database.

As we pointed out in Chapter 1, relying on the client code to perform these tasks leads to situations where data is moved out of the DBMS process and into an external program and then back again. In fact, even when the looping is implemented in a stored procedure, passing data between the ORDBMS's query executor and stored procedure language interpreter incurs overhead.

For example, supposing that the site's management decides they want to offer variable discounts on all merchandising items for movies that have been in release more than six months old. The discounting procedure might apply a couple of rules to the merchandise item in order to calculate the discount. For instance, if there are less than ten items in stock or if the item (plus shipping) is less than $10, don't discount them at all. Otherwise, for each $10 of value more than $10, discount by 5% up until $30. For merchandise worth more than $30, apply a flat 25% discount. With an RDBMS developers have little choice but to implement this function in a host language or a database stored procedure.

Developers can attain the best possible performance by implementing such data processing operations as external user-defined functions and then employing them within an OR-SQL query. If nothing else, this gives the ORDBMS the option of parallelizing the query so as to minimize the total time it takes to complete. Analysis and design in ORDBMS database development involves identifying the set of these operations and describing them. In fact, the way that such operations can be added into a running information system without stopping it is a property of ORDBMS technology that differentiates it from other approaches to information system development.

That said, correlated queries suffer from an irksome limitation. The target of a correlated query cannot be used in the subquery. Getting around this requires the use of temporary tables.

Advanced SQL

The SQL syntactical framework is not very big: just four data manipulation operations. OR-SQL's usefulness lies in the way each of its parts can be combined into more involved operations, for example, in the correlated queries introduced above. In this section we focus on some of the other, more sophisticated combinations that can be performed in an OR-SQL query.

There are a number of excellent books that go into considerably more detail about SQL than space allows here. Although the kinds of programming problems discussed in these books often arise in the first place because SQL-92 provided such limited support for user-defined extensions, many of these book's observations on declarative programming style and on SQL structural tricks remain useful.

Joins-Multiple Data Source Queries

Earlier we explained what is meant by the relational join, we have seen several examples of joining two tables. But queries can join data from any number of data sources. The most common reason for multi-table joins is to navigate relationships among a set of tables interconnected by foreign keys

For example, answering the business question in Listing 3–69 requires data from the `MovieClubMembers`, `Movies`, `Tickets`, `Orders`, and `Order_Line_Items` tables. This query also includes a view called `OrdersPlaced`, which is itself a join between the `Orders` and `Order_Line_Items` physical tables.

"Who has bought tickets to Casablanca over the last week?"

```
SELECT  Print(C.Name)
  FROM  MovieClubMembers C,
        OrdersPlaced P,
        Tickets T,
        Movies M
 WHERE  M.Title       = 'Casablanca'
   AND  P.OrderedOn   > TODAY - 7
   AND  T.Movie       = M.Id
   AND  P.Merchandise = T.Id
   AND  P.Customer    = C.Id;
```

Listing 3–69. *Example of Multi-Data Source Join Query*

In this query the last three expressions in the WHERE clause specify the navigational join conditions between the data sources (three tables and a view). The other two expressions in the WHERE clause specify what rows to take from their respective data sources. If the base tables in this query were very large and lacked appropriate indices, this query may run very slowly. Therefore, an important goal of physical database design involves creating indices to make this kind of query complete quickly.

Function Joins

Function joins are a very powerful innovation in the ORDBMS. Function joins allow you to create queries where a *semantic* relationship is computed in the join. All that is required for a function-join is a user-defined function that returns a boolean result from two arguments. Earlier in this chapter, Listing 3–10 introduced the concept of a spatial join, which is a join between two tables based on a spatial relationship, such as Contains().

Several functions can be used in conjunction to compute a join. For example, the query in Listing 3–70 uses two unconventional predicates in a join.

"Show me everyone living in Boulder County who looks like Ingrid Bergman."

```
SELECT  Print(M.Name)
  FROM  MoviePersonalities P,
        MovieClubMembers M,
        Counties C
 WHERE  P.Name      = PersonName('Bergman','Ingrid')
   AND  C.Name      = 'Boulder'
   AND  Contained ( M.LivesAt, C.Boundary )
   AND  LooksLike ( M.Photo,   P.Photo );
```

Listing 3–70. *Example of Multi-Data Source Function-Join Query*

This is a slightly silly example, but it introduces a powerful idea. Joins that use equality are often useful, but many other kinds of relationship can exist between objects of the same class, and often between objects of different classes. Two time periods can overlap, one SET can be a subset of another SET, or a video can contain an individual's voice or face. Applications managing these kinds of data are becoming increasingly common. And the usefulness of ORDBMS technology becomes clearer when you consider that solving real problems involves mixing new kinds of data with the old.

Nontraditional data poses multiple challenges to query processing. The objects tend to be large and extremely variable in size, which complicates resource allocation for the ORDBMS. UDFs tend to be very expensive, making it very important to execute them as few times as possible. Indexing is a difficult issue, but for many of these types—spatial data and ranges of information—it is possible to exploit the IDS product's advanced indexing features.

As complex as these issues are, the alternative is worse. The evidence is that it is simply not feasible from either a performance or system flexibility point of view, to implement such algorithms in external programs and try to balance query processing between it and the DBMS.

UNION

Earlier we introduced the UNION relational operation, which is similar to a union in set theory. To find the UNION of two (or more) sets of like objects, you create a new set that contains one instance of every value from the sets being merged. This requires more than simply putting all of the objects from both inputs into an output set. Duplicate values in the result must be eliminated, too.

UNION in OR-SQL combines the results of several distinct OR-SQL SELECT queries into a single result. All of the SELECT queries being unioned must have identical column lists. If one of the inputs has an extra column, or if it contains a column of a different type, then the union is impossible. Listing 3–71 illustrates how three query results may be combined into a single set of rows with UNION.

```
SELECT  PRINT(M.Name) AS Name,
        Age(M.DOB) AS Age
   FROM MovieClubMembers M
  WHERE Age(M.DOB) = 35
  UNION
SELECT  Print(M.Name) AS Name,
        Age(M.DOB) AS Age
   FROM MovieClubMembers M
```

```
  WHERE M.Name.Family_Name = 'Eliot'
  UNION
SELECT Print(M.Name) AS Name,
       Age(M.DOB) AS Age
  FROM MoviePersonalities M
 WHERE Age(M.DOB) > 90
   AND M.Died IS NULL;
```

Name ::lvarchar	Age ::INTEGER
George Eliot	35
MacKinlay Kantor	95
Mira Freyenbauger	35

Listing 3–71. Example of Multi-Part UNION Query

UNION queries eliminate duplicate rows. In the example, the single row returned by the second leg of the query is also present in the rows returned by the first half of the query. When it computes a UNION, the ORDBMS combines the results of each leg of the UNION (there may be more than two) and in doing so eliminates duplicate rows. For large query results this elimination step is expensive (you need to sort each input list before you can merge them) and often it's not needed (the WHERE clauses in each leg of the union guarantees that the inputs are mutually exclusive, that is, there cannot be any common rows).

Therefore SQL provides an alternative syntax that lets you tell the engine to ignore duplicates. In Listing 3–72 we repeat the query in Listing 3–71, only we use a UNION ALL, rather than the duplicate eliminating UNION.

```
SELECT PRINT(M.Name) AS Name,
       Age(M.DOB) AS Age
  FROM MovieClubMembers M
 WHERE Age(M.DOB) = 35
 UNION ALL
SELECT Print(M.Name) AS Name,
       Age(M.DOB) AS Age
  FROM MovieClubMembers M
 WHERE M.Name.Family_Name = 'Eliot'
 UNION ALL
SELECT Print(M.Name) AS Name,
       Age(M.DOB) AS Age
  FROM MoviePersonalities M
 WHERE Age(M.DOB) > 90
       AND M.Died IS NULL;
```

name ::lvarchar	age ::INTEGER
Mira Freyenbauger	35
George Eliot	35
George Eliot	35
MacKinlay Kantor	95

Listing 3–72. *Example of Multi-Part UNION ALL Query*

As with other operations (sorting and indexing), the ORDBMS must make use of user-defined functions to perform the "sort and discard duplicate values" step in a union. This means that you can only write UNION queries where all of the data types in the result set have Compare functions. In Listing 3–69, therefore, you need to use the Print() function to convert the PersonName to a data type that can be sorted. But for the query in Listing 3–72, we could leave out the Print() function because sorting to discard duplicates is unnecessary.

Subqueries

In this section we describe what a subquery is and illustrate how it are used. A subquery is a SELECT statement embedded within another query that produces a value—or a table of temporary values—that is used by an expression in the "outer" query. A SELECT in a subquery can be as complex as a regular SELECT: it can be a join, and it can even contain another subquery. The only restriction is that a subquery can return only a single column result. It can produce zero, one, or many rows, however.

You can think of a subquery as returning a table of interim results that is used in the outer query. If the table has a single row, the result of the query can be treated as if it were a single, atomic value. This is most typical when the subquery includes an aggregate operation, as shown in Listing 3–73.

"Show me Movies with above average budgets."

```
SELECT M.Title
  FROM Movies M
 WHERE M.Budget > ( SELECT AVG(M2.Budget)
                      FROM Movies M2 );
```

Title ::Title

Best Years of Our Lives, The
Casablanca
Maltese Falcon, The

Listing 3–73. *Subquery with Aggregate, Producing Atomic Value Result*

Of course, a subquery can return either no rows, or many rows. The most common way that subqueries with this kind of result are used is to check that some condition is false, or more precisely, to check that no data exists that satisfies the condition. Such queries are usually correlated subqueries. That is, the subquery includes a value or expression from a table in the outer query, as shown in Listing 3–74.

"Show me MovieClubMembers who have not placed orders"

```
SELECT Print(M.Name)
  FROM MovieClubMembers M
 WHERE NOT EXISTS ( SELECT 1
                      FROM Orders O
                     WHERE O.Customer = M.Id);
```

Listing 3–74. *Example of NOT EXISTS Subquery, Checking that Condition is FALSE*

As with join queries, the ORDBMS's extensibility significantly enhances the power of subqueries. The UDFs can be used either in the subquery to perform the condition check, or in the outer query's expression that uses the subquery's atomic result. For example, one regular use for subqueries is to perform a limit kind of analysis to identify "interesting" data that the outer query returns in detail. The query in Listing 3–75 follows just such a pattern.

```
SELECT *
  FROM Merchandise M
 WHERE M.Id IN ( SELECT Top_K( O.Merchandise, 10,
                               O.NumberOrdered * O.Price )
                   FROM MerchandiseOrdered O
                  WHERE O.SaleDate  >  TODAY - 30 );
```

Listing 3–75. *User-Defined Aggregate in Subquery*

This query also illustrates the `Top_K` user-defined aggregate, which deserves a moment of explanation. This aggregate works over a set of triples. The first argument is an `INTEGER` Id. The second is an integer count that is a constant: This is the "K." The third is a value—in this case, a `DECIMAL` type. What the aggregate does is to return a `SET ( INTEGER )` of Ids where the value of the corresponding third argument is ranked in the top "K" of all third argument values.

In other words, this query returns details about the items of Merchandise responsible for the ten largest sales over the last 30 days. The equivalent SQL-92 query is a challenge to create and will perform poorly for large data sets with a large number of different kinds of merchandise.

In Tutorial 6 we describe how this aggregate is built.

NULL and Three-Value Logic

The SQL language standard complicates query processing by adopting a three-value logic. As its name suggests, a three-value logic (3VL) system considers three logical values: TRUE, FALSE, and UNKNOWN. This technique is a response to the problem of missing information. As we saw in the previous chapter, a table's column values can be NULL in situations where the column's data may not be known.

But it has important implications for query processing too. According to the rules defining three-value logic, a boolean operator function can be true if and only if it returns a TRUE result. FALSE and NULL are both taken to mean "not true" (so the row does not qualify). Where FALSE and NULL differ is in terms of how they are combined using the logical operators AND, OR, and NOT. NOT FALSE is TRUE, but NOT NULL is still NULL, and therefore does not satisfy the predicate. The same rule applies for the other logical operators.

Strictly speaking, functions receiving NULLs as an argument should return a NULL result. In the next chapter, we explain how to override this behavior.

The tables in Listing 3–76 below explain the behavior of three-value logic.

AND

	TRUE	NULL	FALSE
TRUE	TRUE	NULL	FALSE
NULL	NULL	NULL	FALSE
FALSE	FALSE	FALSE	FALSE

OR

	TRUE	NULL	FALSE
TRUE	TRUE	TRUE	TRUE
NULL	TRUE	NULL	NULL
FALSE	TRUE	NULL	FALSE

NOT

TRUE	FALSE
FALSE	TRUE
NULL	NULL

Listing 3–76. *Three-Valued Logic Truth Tables*

So far as the query processor is concerned a NULL data value and a boolean FALSE are very hard to distinguish. Therefore, OR-SQL includes special facilities to determine whether a value is NULL or not. The NULL status of any data value can be determined with the IS NULL expression, as we see in Listing 3–77.

"Give me a list of Movie Club members names where the member has no recorded middle name."

```
SELECT Print(M.Name)
  FROM MovieClub M
  WHERE M.Name.OtherNames IS NULL;
```

Listing 3–77. *Three-Valued Logic Truth Tables*

This query returns the names of movie club members where no middle name is recorded for them. For example, this information might not be known or it might not be available.

Three-value logic has the potential to complicate query processing tremendously. For this reason, you should use it sparingly. There are circumstances where 3VL is appropriate, for example, to handle genuinely missing or not applicable information, but in general it's prudent to minimize its use. Sometimes the presence of a NULL column can be an indication that something is not quite right in the schema design; for instance, you might be able to make a column NOT NULL by moving it into a subtable. In the next two chapters, when we review how to extend the ORDBMS with new data types and functions, we will need to consider NULL values again.

Chapter Summary

Data in an ORDBMS database is retrieved and manipulated using a dynamic programming language called OR-SQL (Object-Relational Structured Query Language). Internally to the ORDBMS, each OR-SQL statement—called a query—is transformed by the IDS server into a series of lower level operations that read data from disk and manipulate it in memory. A useful way to think about object-relational query languages is that it is a *framework* or *software back-plane* into which developers embed extensions that reflect the details of their application's problem domain.

OR-SQL includes four basic commands for manipulating data: INSERT, UPDATE, DELETE, and SELECT. Each of these four basic query statements has a structure that is delineated by the language's SQL keywords. Basically, each manipulation statement specifies what data sources are being addressed, what data within these sources, and how the data is to be manipulated.

The strength of OR-SQL lies in the way different kinds of statements can be combined and nested, one inside the other. For example, you can use a SELECT query within the WHERE clause of another SELECT query (called a subquery), or in the target list (to select data out of a COLLEC-TION column), or even in the FROM clause of a SELECT (called query nesting or closure). This flexibility combined with ORDBMS extensibility makes OR-SQL a very powerful data manipulation interface.

The Transaction Concept and its Applications

In this tutorial we explain the importance of the *transaction* concept, and describe how the ORDBMS supports it. A transactional system makes a set of *quality of service* guarantees over the operations it performs. An understanding of what transactions are and how they are implemented helps explain certain ORDBMS behaviors and helps developers avoid certain performance and reliability problems.

Transactions

Object-relational technology adds nothing to the basic principles of transaction processing. Well-engineered ORDBMS engines re-use techniques developed for RDBMS products. On the other hand, object-relational technology does not diminish the importance of transactional data processing. Multi-user systems must mediate access to shared resources to achieve consistent outcomes.

Transactions Concept

The kinds of problems that transactions are intended to solve are best explained by telling some "what if" stories about how data in the Movie-R-Us database might be accessed. For the purpose of this exercise, we are interested in only one item of `Merchandise`, and only the NumberAvailable column value for that item, for example, the number of "Rick Fedora Hats" in stock.

Suppose there are two database users: Pat, who is the inventory manager, and Robin, a clerk who handles phone orders the old fashioned way. In Listing 2–1 we present a schedule of database operations that Pat and Robin undertake.

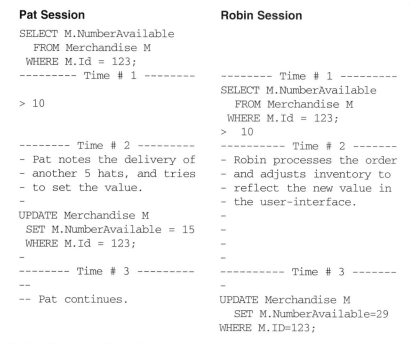

```
Pat Session                        Robin Session

SELECT M.NumberAvailable
  FROM Merchandise M
 WHERE M.Id = 123;
--------- Time # 1 --------        -------- Time # 1 ---------
                                   SELECT M.NumberAvailable
> 10                                  FROM Merchandise M
                                    WHERE M.Id = 123;
                                   >  10
-------- Time # 2 ---------        ---------- Time # 2 -------
- Pat notes the delivery of        - Robin processes the order
- another 5 hats, and tries        - and adjusts inventory to
- to set the value.                - reflect the new value in
-                                  - the user-interface.
UPDATE Merchandise M               -
  SET M.NumberAvailable = 15       -
 WHERE M.Id = 123;                 -
-                                  -
-------- Time # 3 ---------        ---------- Time # 3 -------
--                                 -
-- Pat continues.                  UPDATE Merchandise M
                                     SET M.NumberAvailable=29
                                   WHERE M.ID=123;
```

Listing 2–1. *Schedule of Read and Write Operations in Two Transactions*

The problem, of course, is that the final state of the database depends on the precise order in which these actions occur. No such ambiguity arises in the real world; there will always be 14 hats left on the shelf. However, what happens if the software fails in the process at some point, for example, at Time # 3? Without transactions the database might come back up in a state that is logically inconsistent with respect to the schema definition, with in-flight operations only partially completed, or worst of all, physically corrupted.

Providing transactional guarantees will safeguard database data against these calamities. It also adds a few commands to OR-SQL because, as you can tell from the example in Listing 2–1, operations that change data can span multiple queries. The transaction concept also determines how the system behaves if a query is terminated because it violates some schema rule, or when the DBMS or operating system software crashes.

ACID Properties of Transactions

We say that a data management system is *transactional* if it guarantees that all operations it performs exhibit what are known as the *ACID* properties:

- Atomic. The atomicity property states that every transactional operation either completes successfully, or it has no affect on the data at all. In the case of an error, a transactional system restores the database state to the condition is was in at the start of the transaction.
- Consistent. The consistency property ensures that every transactional operation complies with the rules constraining the database. That is, at the end of the transaction and once all triggered operations have completed, the database is correct with respect to the schema's integrity rules.
- Isolated. The isolation property ensures that every transactional operation proceeds in complete isolation from all other concurrently executing operations. Expressed differently, all write operations are applied to the data as if they were *serialized*, that is, executed one after the other rather than all at the same time.
- Durable. The durability property means that once a change has been made (once a transaction is completed), the change is forever. This means that if the DBMS software, the operating system, or even the hardware on which the DBMS is running fails, the database can be recovered to a consistent state.

The software engineering that goes into a DBMS to support the ACID properties is extremely sophisticated. To give you some idea of the complexity, consider that these algorithms must not only be able to roll back a transaction and recover a database in the case of failure, but also must know what to do if something crashes *during* a rollback or recovery. Indeed, were it not for the need to meet ACID requirements, DBMS engines would probably look different than they do today.

Isolation Levels

Within this transaction framework the ORDBMS's facilities provide several degrees of flexibility. Sometimes in an application, a developer might want the ORDBMS to prevent users from reading data that another user is in the act of modifying, or data that has been read by a user before they subsequently update it. At other times, however, it is reasonable to allow a set of users to read whatever data they want, including data being changed by another transaction, to ensure that they can finish their tasks in a timely fashion.

The degree to which in-flight transactions are permitted to interact is referred to as the transaction's *isolation level*. Isolation levels determine the rules governing read operations. Interactions between write operations are completely inflexible: two writers never can modify the same data at the same time. In practical terms, the ORDBMS provides three ANSI isolation levels, and a fourth, proprietary isolation level.

READ UNCOMMITTED, or *dirty read*, is the lowest isolation level. It provides minimal guarantees as to the correctness of the data being returned at any time. When an OR-SQL retrieves data from the ORDBMS at this level of isolation, it simply grabs whatever data it finds in the table's pages. It ignores other transactions and does nothing to interfere with them. Consequently, the data being read may change at any time. In fact, if another transaction is currently modifying the data, the dirty read query will return its in-flight state; sometimes, this is referred to as *phantom* data.

Clearly, developers should be cautious in using READ UNCOMMITTED, but in many applications it is completely acceptable. For example, the result of queries that perform some kind of analytical operation rarely changes by much when a few rows change. Preventing changes to the underlying data, however, in order to ensure the aggregate's fidelity obstructs other users of the system, or customers of the Web site in our example.

Pat and Robin's operations cannot be performed at the READ UNCOMMITTED isolation level. When the ORDBMS receives the UPDATE, it raises an exception because READ UNCOMMITTED transactions are only for read operations.

By contrast, the result of any READ COMMITTED query is guaranteed to be correct and consistent *at the time the query executes.* That is, if there is an in-flight transaction modifying the object being read, a READ COMMITTED transaction will be blocked until the in-flight transaction completes. Consequently, unlike READ UNCOMMITTED queries, READ COMMITTED is guaranteed to be free of *phantom* data.

However, this isolation level does not guarantee that the data will be the same if it is retrieved again within the same transactional context. Other transactions can modify the data between reads. READ

COMMITTED makes a good isolation level for external programs reading data for display. However, as the example in Listing 2–1 illustrates, it is inadequate when the query result is used in the external program to compute a value to be written back to the database. Performing Pat and Robin's operations at READ COMMITTED will not generate a system error, but the last writer wins.

Although ANSI defines the REPEATABLE READ and SERIALIZABLE isolation levels differently, their implementation within IDS is identical. The idea is to ensure that, between reads (and between reads and a write), the data value in the database cannot be changed by another transaction. In fact, what happens is that the ORDBMS supports ANSI SERIALIZABLE behavior for both REPEATABLE READ and SERIALIZABLE isolation levels.

Using this isolation level instructs the ORDBMS to prevent other transactions from overwriting any data objects it touches by *locking* them. Thus, although both Pat and Robin would be able to read the number of fedora's available, each would be blocked when it tried to UPDATE the value.

Although this addresses the issues of data correctness, it creates problems of its own. If, at Time # 2, Pat steps out for a coffee, Robin waits, and angry phone calls may ensue. Designing efficient and effective transaction processing systems involves trading off between data correctness and user convenience.

Isolation levels are controlled using the ANSI SET TRANSACTION ISOLATION LEVEL statement. Listing 2–2 illustrates the syntax.

Non-ANSI mode IDS databases can employ the CURSOR STABILITY isolation level. As its name suggests, it refers to the behavior of data in the current row of a CURSOR. When an external program is processing cursor rows at this isolation level, the IDS product treats the current row at the REPEATABLE READ isolation level and all other rows at the READ COMMITTED isolation level. The idea is to ensure that a row's value do not change while the external program is handling it, and at the same time, to allow changes to other data in the database.

Lock Mode

So far, whenever we have discussed conflict between transactions, we have used the generic term "blocked." In addition to specifying a transaction's isolation level, it is useful to specify how the ORDBMS is to behave when a transaction blocks. By default, the ORDBMS immediately raises an exception when it determines that two transactions are in conflict. It does this by raising an error when it fails to acquire a lock.

Using the SET LOCK MODE statement, a developer can adjust how the ORDBMS behaves when it encounters a locked object. Two possibilities exist. The ORDBMS can either raise an exception immediately without waiting, or it can wait for the other (blocking) transaction to complete. Of course, waiting forever is rarely a good strategy, so the SET LOCK MODE command allows developers to specify a number of seconds to wait before raising an exception.

In production systems it is a good idea to set the ORDBMS to wait for a reasonable number of second before generating an error. Listing 2–2 illustrates how this is done.

BEGIN WORK and COMMIT WORK

By default, each OR-SQL statement is a separate transaction.[1] Several separate OR-SQL statements can be grouped into a single transaction by placing them between transaction delimiters, the BEGIN WORK and COMMIT WORK statements. For example, in Listing 2–2, we reprise Pat's work from Listing 2–1, adding statements to control its transactional behavior.

```
BEGIN WORK;
--
-- NOTE: In ANSI databases, or when you use the ANSI SET
--       TRANSACTION syntax, the isolation level can
--       be set only once, at the start of a transaction.
--
SET TRANSACTION ISOLATION LEVEL REPEATABLE READ;
SET LOCK MODE TO WAIT 20;

  SELECT M.NumberAvailable
    FROM Merchandise M
   WHERE M.Id = 123;

  UPDATE Merchandise M
     SET M.NumberAvailable = 15
   WHERE M.Id = 123;

COMMIT WORK;
```

Listing 2–2. *Multi-Query Transaction*

---

[1] Different assumptions are made about transactions in default databases and in databases created using ANSI semantics. This tutorial adopts ANSI syntax. Consult the product documentation for more details.

BEGIN WORK and END WORK tell the ORDBMS that the database operations between them must comply with the transaction rules described earlier; that is, both statements complete entirely or fail utterly. If the client program crashed in the middle of the UPDATE, the database will be left as if the transaction was never begun.

In implementation terms, this means that the IDS product will continue to acquire locks and logging resources until the end of the transaction. A set of OR-SQL queries embedded in a stored procedure are subject to similar transactional guarantees by default, but developers have some control over transactions within SPL code.

ROLLBACK WORK

An in-flight transaction may be halted and rolled back at any time for any number of reasons. Most often, as it is performing the transaction, IDS will detect that a schema integrity rule has been violated. When integrity violations are detected the query processor automatically undoes all data changes that the transaction has made so far and returns an error message to the client.

Sometimes, the application code performing the transaction may want to halt the transaction and reverse all changes made so far. This intention is communicated to the ORDBMS using the ROLLBACK WORK OR-SQL statement. Listing 2–3 illustrates how this statement can be used within an ESQL/C program.

```
EXEC SQL BEGIN DECLARE SECTION;
    string szResult[RES_LENGTH], szArgString[RES_LENGTH];
EXEC SQL END DECLARE SECTION;
.
.
.
EXEC SQL EXECUTE FUNCTION UpdateEntity( :szArgString )
                    INTO :szResult;

if (strcmp( szResult, "repeat" ) == 0 )
{
    printf("Error: Repeated Entity Value \n");
    EXEC SQL ROLLBACK WORK;
    return 0;
}
```

Listing 2–3. *ESQL/C External Program Illustrating ROLLBACK WORK*

To help readers acquire a richer understanding of transactions, the CD examples that accompany this book include a simple ESQL/C program and a set of small OR-SQL scripts. The ESQL/C program inserts records into a table and can be instructed to begin and commit transactions. By using another interface, such as the `dbaccess` tool, for example, readers can see how isolation levels affect transactional interactions for both reads and writes.

Deadlocks

Deadlocks are the snakes at the bottom of the transactional garden. A deadlock is a condition that arises when the schedule of data operations leads to a conflict that cannot be resolved automatically. This usually happens when one transaction wants to access an object another transaction has already accessed, but the second transaction is blocked and waiting for an object that the first one has accessed. This is also known as the *deadly embrace*.

The possibility for a deadly embrace exists in Listing 2–1 if Pat and Robin are operating at REPEATABLE READ isolation level. If Pat reads the NumberAvailable but has not yet issued the UPDATE query, Robin also can read it. When, however, Pat does issue the UPDATE, it will be blocked by Robin's read. (At REPEATABLE READ, once an object is read, IDS blocks all data changes until the end of the transaction.) Thus, when Robin goes to perform the second UPDATE, Pat's lock blocks it. Pat and Robin are now in a deadly embrace with respect to the data object in question.

It is impossible to avoid deadlocks completely. They occur as a consequence of the way the transaction concept is defined. Applications in which different users can UPDATE the same objects are especially vulnerable, but for the most part, good application design minimizes and can even eliminate them. The following list presents some tricks and techniques to improve concurrency and to minimize deadlocking problems.

- Avoid transactions that require end users to make decisions while shared data is locked. For multiscreen operations, use temporary tables and apply changes to shared data as a last step.
- Use correlated queries wherever possible. Chunk-at-a-time queries beat row-at-a-time queries every time.
- Where possible, address tables in alphabetical order. Often, business processes will involve modifying rows in several tables. If every transaction modified tables in the same order, the possibility of deadlocks is removed.
- Update queries should be written around the change being made, rather than the new value. For example, if the new values in Listing 2–1 were calculated based on the old values, the possibility of error is reduced. Again, this is not always possible.

- It is good defensive programming practice to surround any code in external programs that performs a database transaction with appropriate error handling and retry looping.

When they do occur, deadlocks are fairly easy to detect and diagnose. Modifying the data base table's lock granularity from PAGE (the default) to ROW, or rewriting the logic of the transactions participating in the deadlock, almost always resolves the problem.

Implementing Transactions

The first papers on the transaction concept were published in the late 1970s. Since then, an enormous amount of effort has been expended researching low-level software engineering techniques to support them efficiently. In this section we briefly describe how transactional properties are supported by IDS.

Logging and Recovery

Durability and atomicity are supported with a technique known as *write ahead logging*. Recall that all data in IDS is allocated into fixed size pages and that the only way to change data in the ORDBMS is through the OR-SQL query language. Logging techniques exploit these features in two ways:

- The ORDBMS stores a copy of all pages before they are modified in a *physical log*. Initially, this copy is written in memory, but as the operation progresses, the physical log is written to disk.
- The effect of all OR-SQL queries that modify data are tracked in the *logical log*. These, too, are written out to disk.

Information in the logs is used for both transaction rollback and failure recovery. Transaction rollback uses the physical log records to restore the database pages to the condition they were in before the transaction began. Logical log records are used in conjunction with physical log records to roll forward the state of the physical database pages at the time IDS is restarted after a crash.

This helps developers estimate how much log resource they require. Databases with large transactional workloads require more log space. In addition, it is possible to suspend logging operations or modify the way logging is conducted by the server. Management of logging is generally a database administrator (DBA) task.

Locking

The ORDBMS uses a facility called the *lock manager* to mediate access to database data IDS allocates a section of memory that holds a list of all locks currently held by all transactions in the database. Whenever an OR-SQL operation touches a data object the IDS engine determines the object's transactional status by looking in the lock manager's memory. If the object is not currently locked, IDS creates an entry identifying the object, the transaction, and the lock status.

Large queries touch lots of data, and in systems with a great many concurrent users the lock manager itself has the potential to become a bottleneck. The amount of time the ORDBMS spends managing locks is determined by the *locking granularity* it is observing. At one end of the scale, locking larger granularity objects, an entire TABLE or DATABASE for instance, minimizes both the size of the in-memory lock register and the number of messages to the lock manager. Large granularity locking has a serious drawback, however: it can restrict the number of concurrently executing query operations. This happens when, for example, one query needs access to a row in a table being modified by another. Locking at the smallest, ROW granularity practically eliminates the chance of incidental conflict between transactions, at the expense of more CPU overhead and memory resources.

By default, the IDS product opts for the middle path. It locks data at the PAGE level. Experiments have shown that under a broad range of conditions page locking provides an optimal trade-off between the two objectives: maximizing concurrency while minimizing computational overhead. Of course there are, however, circumstances where either granularity extreme is necessary and developers should not hesitate to employ them.

Locking granularity can be configured in several ways. In Listing 2–4 we illustrate how to set the granularity for a table to row level instead of to the default page level. The Orders table likely is to be among the more volatile tables in the movies database, so it makes sense to configure its locking granularity in this way.

```
CREATE TABLE Orders (
        Id              SERIAL          PRIMARY KEY
                        CONSTRAINT Order_Primary_Key,
        Customer        Membership_Id   NOT NULL,
```

```
                DeliverTo       DeliveryAddress  NOT NULL,
                OrderedOn       DATE             NOT NULL,
                ShippedOn       DATE
      ) LOCK MODE ROW;
```

Listing 2–4. *CREATE TABLE with Row-Level Locking Granularity*

In general, use page-level locking where you can and row where you must. Locking at larger granularity levels is typically used to exclude users from accessing a table or a database.

ORDBMSs and Transaction

For the most part, OR-SQL queries accessing table data are handled by the lock manager and the logging facilities in exactly the same way as they were in the RDBMS. Features such as user-defined functions, which may contain write queries of their own, and smart large object storage, which can be locked and logged, require further explanation.

Transactions on Large Objects

Modules of user-defined logic embedded within the ORDBMS can modify large object data. For example, a UDF can splice a scene into video data. But if the operation fails (the function can enforce a rule on how long a video can be, for example), it would be ideal if the ORDBMS could reset the state of the large object. In addition, if two users are working on the same video, it would be ideal to prevent the same scene simultaneously.

Internally, IDS implements a sophisticated byte-range locking scheme that keeps track of the large objects being accessed at any point in time. This same scheme keeps track of the ranges of bytes within these large objects that are being manipulated by each user. This means that the ORDBMS can detect conflicting user actions in a large object. For example, when two users concurrently try to over-write the byte range within the same large object, the ORDBMS handles this like any other resource conflict.

In addition, changes to the large object's pages are logged in much the same way that a table's pages are logged. Consequently, it is a very good idea to disable logging when loading even a small number of large objects to prevent the logical logs from filling up.

Transactions and User-Defined Functions

User-defined functions (UDFs) can contain OR-SQL statements, and these OR-SQL statements can perform writes in the database. However, in a conventional RDBMS, a SELECT will only acquire read locks on data. To achieve very high levels of performance, the RDBMS query processor made assumptions about how SELECT queries and the lock manager interact; it assumed that it would never need to acquire write locks.

To support transactions, however, IDS always places write locks on modified objects. Consequently, a SELECT query with a UDF that contains a write query would need to acquire write locks. From a traditional query processing perspective, this is very counterintuitive and would require substantial renovations to the ORDBMS engine.

If it detects write queries in a UDF used in a SELECT statement, IDS generates an error. As a result, it is not quite true that any UDF can be used anywhere in a SELECT query. In addition, UDFs should be data-type specific, rather than database specific, and therefore should avoid including OR-SQL wherever possible. This behavior is yet another reason to stay away from the practice.

Chapter

4

Data Type and Function Extensibility

Introduction to ORDBMS Data Type Extensibility

Over the next two chapters, we describe the facilities provided by the ORDBMS for *extending* the database with user-defined object classes. In theoretical terms, these classes correspond to the relational model's concept of a *domain*; self-contained, indivisible units of meaning. In practical terms, they are represented using *user-defined types* (UDT) to specify each object's structure and size and *user-defined functions* (UDF) that implement its behavior. The ORDBMS allows developers to create a very larger number of extensions and combine them within a single database. For example, the query in Listing 4–1 illustrates how a database can mix business objects and geographic data.

"Show me the name and a rotated image of movie club members living in California who have indicated that they like Crime Mysteries."

```
SELECT Print ( M.Name ),
       RotateImage ( M.Photo )
  FROM MovieClubMembers M, States S
```

```
AND Within ( M.LivesAt, S.Boundary )
AND S.Name = 'California'
AND GenreMatches ( M.Preferences,
                          SET { 'Crime','Mystery' } );
```

Listing 4–1. *Query Illustrating Mix of Extended Objects*

This approach is to be contrasted with using specialized software to manage each different kind of data. *Geographic Information Systems (GIS)* software and document management systems have been commercially available for some time. While specialist software packages are likely to outperform the ORDBMS within their area of specialty, such products are much less flexible: they lack features such as a general-purpose query language, transactional storage, distributed capabilities, and standardized APIs.

But the real value of the ORDBMS can be seen when you consider applications that involve several, very different kinds of information. Information systems developed using the ORDBMS will inevitably involve the extensibility features to some degree: either through a commercial DataBlade™ product or building customized types and functions to implement business objects. Object-relational technology allows business problems involving a variety of arbitrarily complex software modules to be combined within a declarative OR-SQL query's WHERE clause.

In this chapter, and in Chapter 5, we focus on the topic of database *extensibility* and how to implement new object classes within an object-relational database. We first introduce the terminology used to describe the *Object-Oriented (OO)* concepts underlying database extensibility, explain the ideas behind each term, and briefly illustrate how the ORDBMS supports them. Then we describe the user-defined type and user-defined function features in detail.

Overview of Object-Oriented Software Development Concepts

The important insight of OO approaches to software engineering is that the challenge of developing complex software is made easier by thinking about entities in the application's problem domain as "objects." In OO software projects—and in OR databases—real world phenomena like phone numbers (or part numbers, or longitude/latitude points, or video data, or text documents, or people's names) are implemented as autonomous, indivisible software modules. These software *components* specify both the state and behavior of the object. That is, each software object reflects not only what the real-world entity consists of, but also how it works.

The object-oriented viewpoint is useful, first because it is a very intuitive way of thinking about the world, and second, because these intuitions can drive software design and engineering. OO approaches help meet the complexity challenges of modern information systems in the following ways:

- OO approaches promote a clean decomposition of the overall development task into sub-tasks. Development teams working on different object implementations can proceed with only minimal need for communication with other groups. In ORDBMS development projects, you frequently see the project staff divided into teams responsible for developing the extended types and the database schema design. The schema design team is driven by questions relating to the general structure of the business problem, while the extensibility teams focuses on questions about how the smallest atomic aspects of the problem are best provided for.
- OO architectures are ideally suited to writing re-useable software components. An expert in a particular area of data management, say GIS, can create a set of code that performs all of the calculations specific to their area. Developers using these spatial objects in applications do not need to know how, for example, distance over the geode (the lumpy surface of the earth) is calculated. They can re-use the expertise of the anonymous specialist.
- Using OO techniques results in simplified information system deployment and maintenance. You can upgrade or extend certain components within an OR database without re-writing other components. There is no need to change the OR-SQL queries or even recompile the external logic that embeds them, for example, if you fix a bug in an extension.

Through its extensibility mechanisms, the ORDBMS allows developers to take advantage of OO techniques. The ORDBMS becomes the framework for both component developers, who write type extensions, and application developers, who deploy these types in the database schema, to interact.

Objects, Classes and Interfaces

When we find a phone number written on a piece of paper, we can identify it as a phone number based on its properties such as how many numerals it has, how these numerals are grouped, and so on. We can distinguish a phone number from a vehicle's license plate number based on their differences. And we can also compare phone numbers using some learnt procedure to determine if they are the same or not. We understand how to manipulate phone numbers to extract area codes or apply a number to make a call.

In other words, we instinctively to create *classifications* of objects and *distinguish* among object classes based on their properties and their behavior. A primary motivation for using OO software development techniques is to co-opt these psychological habits when developing information systems.

An important concept in object-oriented software engineering is the separation of an object's *interface*—the means by which other software interacts with it—from its *implementation*—the logic and data structures that actually do the work. Again, we are familiar with this idea from our experiences of the world. An alarm clock has a limited number of *interface* components: a face, a screw to adjust time, and a button. Internally, the alarm clock's mechanism stores information about the current time, and provides the means to read it and adjust it. But the intricate mesh of gears and springs within it are hidden. Alarm clock users do not need to understand how their clock is constructed (or *implemented*) in order to use it.

An *object* is any single instance of something. The term *class* is reserved for the definition of something—all alarm clocks. We use the terms *data type* and *object class* synonymously in this book. We illustrate the concept of an object class and its internal behavior in Figure 4–1.

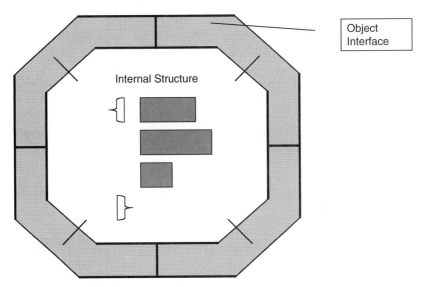

Figure 4–1. *Diagrammatic Representation of Object Encapsulation*

Object-oriented software engineering concepts were developed and refined in programming languages such as Smalltalk, C++, and Java. Such languages typically implement each class as a separate software module. One module might use another by addressing its interface in the code implementing the first object. Ultimately the object definitions are compiled into a single program that can be run. Part of the OO language compiler's task is to resolve the linkages between different modules in the overall system. Changing an object's implementation therefore requires a recompile to produce a new program that can be run.

ORDBMS databases, on the other hand, are more dynamic. Database users have high expectations for reliability, and the ORDBMS acts as an integrating framework for multiple different extensions. Therefore, developers must frequently modify object extensions without stopping the running DBMS. To achieve this goal, object definition is broken into two related tasks: the definition of the object class's size and structure (called its *type*) and the definition of the object's behavior (through *functions*). This allows developers to add to the behavior of a pre-existing object by defining a new function. At runtime (rather than at compile time), the ORDBMS ensures that the appropriate function is run in response to a query invoking an interface to an object.[1]

Elements, Methods and Encapsulation

We call the set of data values making up an object's state *elements*. The object's behavior is implemented in code that runs in *methods*. Methods are algorithms that use the state information represented in the object's elements to compute some result. The only way to interact with an instance of an ORDBMS object is by using the built-in facilities for handling it, or one of the methods defined for it, which is a concept known as *encapsulation*.

In the ORDBMS, an object class's structure is declared using the CREATE TYPE statement. Methods that manipulate these objects are created using CREATE FUNCTION and CREATE PROCEDURE commands. For example, in our Movies-R-Us database, part of the development process involves defining what a "MailAddress" object looks like. The structure of a MailAddress might look something like Table 4–1.

Using the ORDBMS's ROW TYPE mechanism, the MailAddress object can be represented as shown in Listing 4–2. An alternative technique, called an OPAQUE TYPE, could be used instead. An OPAQUE TYPE, as its name suggests, are simply opaque arrays of byte values and do not

---

[1] The alternative language approach is to have a CREATE CLASS, which incorporates both type and functions, and a separate MODIFY CLASS statement for alterations. The superiority of one syntactic style over the other is a religious question.

Table 4-1. Definition of the MailAddress Object's Data Elements

MailAddress

Element	Element Type
Line_1	String
Line_2	String
City	String
State	State
PostCode	PostCode
Country	String

have any structure at all so far as the ORDBMS is concerned. All that can be recorded about the internal structure of an OPAQUE TYPE is its length. We describe the ROW TYPE and OPAQUE TYPE in detail later in this chapter.

```
CREATE ROW TYPE MailAddress (
    First_Line   ShortString       NOT NULL,
    Second_Line  ShortString,
    City         ShortString       NOT NULL,
    State        State_Enum,
    PostCode     PostCode          NOT NULL,
    Country      ShortString       NOT NULL
);
```

Listing 4-2. *Implementing Structure of MailAddress Object as a ROW TYPE*

Methods (user-defined functions) that operate on this type can be implemented in a variety of languages in 3GLs such as C or Java, or in database procedural languages such as the stored procedure language (SPL). The functions that perform operations on the MailAddress object are included in Table 4-2.

A reasonable algorithm to use in the Equal function might first check that both MailAddress objects have the same Country, Postcode, State, City, and FirstLine. Using SPL, the implementation of such a function would look like Listing 4-3.

Name	Arguments	Return Value	Comment
GetPostCode	MailAddress	PostCode	Returns the address's PostCode element.
FormatMailLabel	MailAddress	StickyLabel	Formats address and return label string for printing or for a web page.
Equal	MailAddress, MailAddress	Boolean	Returns boolean true if both MailAddresses are "equal".
Similar	MailAddress, MailAddress	Float	Returns an indicator of the similarity of two addresses.
MailAddress	String, String, String, State, PostCode, String	MailAddress	Creates a new MailAddress and sets initial values for its elements and is a Constructor method.

```
CREATE FUNCTION Equal ( Arg1 MailAddress, Arg2 MailAddress )
RETURNS boolean
    IF (( Arg1.Country     = Arg2.Country    ) AND
        ( Arg1.PostCode    = Arg2.PostCode   ) AND
        ( Arg1.State       = Arg2.State      ) AND
        ( Arg1.City        = Arg2.City       ) AND
        ( Arg1.First_Line  = Arg2.First_Line )) THEN
            RETURN 't';
    END IF;
    RETURN 'f';
END FUNCTION;
```

Listing 4–3. *SPL Implementation of Method to Determine Equality of Mailing Addresses*

When an application developer writes an OR-SQL query that retrieves the address of a movie club member with a particular name, they need not know in detail how the result of their query is computed. If the development team decides that another algorithm should be used to determine MailAddress equality a DBA can make the change by replacing a single function. The OR-SQL queries do not need to change. All applications that use the database will behave consistently.

Inheritance, Overloading, and Polymorphism

In object-oriented systems, classes of objects can be defined in such a way that they possess a special kind of relationship with respect to each other. We say that one class *inherits* its elements and behavior from another. When creating the second class (called the subclass or *subtype*), you can *specialize* it by adding elements or behaviors to those inherited from its parent (called the superclass or *supertype*).

For example, there may be another class called DeliveryAddress that inherits from MailAddress, and adds several extra elements or new methods. It might, for example, include another string element that can be used to record special delivery instructions such as "Beware of the dog." The complete structure of the DeliveryAddress class appears in Figure 4–2.

By default, all user-defined functions defined over a supertype also work when they are invoked on an instance of any of its subtypes. For example, what a query invokes the `Equal()` function and passes it two DeliveryAddress instances, the ORDBMS would call the `Equal()` function defined for the MailAddress type. This works, of course, because the logic implementing the inherited behavior must use super-type elements, which will always be part of the subtype.

The ORDBMS manages functions in a somewhat different style from other programming systems. In an ORDBMS, it is possible to have two different functions with the same name. For instance, the ORDBMS recognizes a difference between functions "Equal `(MailAddress, MailAddress)`," "Equal `(ZipCode, ZipCode)`," and "Equal `(PersonName, PersonName)`." These functions have the same name, and would appear as identical in query statements, but IDS distinguishes among them because their arguments are different. This technique, called *function overloading*, permits developers to create functions with the same name that have different behaviors when operating over different data types.

When overloading is combined with inheritance, the result is called *polymorphism*. If the data types in a function's argument vector are

DeliveryAddress

Element	Element Type
Line_1	String
Line_2	String
City	String
State	State
PostCode	PostCode
Country	String
Instructions	String

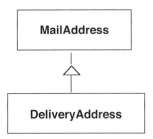

Figure 4–2. Definition of the DeliveryAddress Object's Data Elements

part of an *inheritance hierarchy*, IDS can use a function with a matching name that takes data type arguments *above* the given type. In other words, if you can implement a function once for the root type in a hierarchy, then any subtypes within the hierarchy can also use it. Consider the code sample in Listing 4–4 (which continues the hierarchy started in Listing 4–2).

```
CREATE FUNCTION FormalMailLabel ( Arg1 MailAddress )
RETURNS lvarchar
--
--    Details omitted for brevity.
--
END FUNCTION;
--
CREATE ROW TYPE DeliveryAddress   (
     Instructions     ShortString
) UNDER MailAddress;
--
--    The MailAddress type is used in the MovieClubMembers
--    table, and the DeliveryAddress type is used in the
--    Orders table.
--
SELECT FormatMailLabel ( M.Address )
   FROM MovieClubMembers M;
SELECT FormatMailLabel ( O.DeliverTo )
   FROM Orders O;
```

Listing 4–4. *Query Illustrating Data Type Polymorphism*

In Listing 4–4 we first illustrate a user-defined function FormalMail-Label (MailAddress) over the root type of the hierarchy. Then, with a second `CREATE ROW TYPE` statement we extend the hierarchy with a new type under MailAddress. In both of the queries, it is the Formal-MailLabel (MailAddress) function that is actually executed. DeliveryAddress is said to inherit this function from its super type.

Suppose we now extend this code with a second user-defined function definition, as shown in Listing 4–5.

```
CREATE FUNCTION FormalMailLabel ( Arg1 DeliveryAddress )
RETURNS lvarchar
--
--    Details omitted for brevity.
--
END FUNCTION;
```

Listing 4–5. *Addition of a New Polymorphic Function to Type Hierarchy*

Now, when the last two queries in Listing 4–4 are rerun, the result of the first query is unchanged. However, the second query now invokes the newly created FormalMailLabel function. In Figure 4–3, we present in diagrammatic form the "before" and "after" pictures representing the situation before and after we created the function in Listing 4–5.

The advantage of this kind of functionality—overloading, inheritance, and polymorphism— is that it minimizes the amount of code you need to write and helps to maintain consistency among similar schema objects. But inheritance in IDS has its limitations. For example, you cannot insert a MailAddress value to a column defined using the Delivery-Address type for example.

Identity and Reference

Another OO idea is the notion of *identity* and *reference*. The idea is that every object instance possesses an intangible property called *identity* that distinguishes it from all other object instances. In OO systems, this invisible and immutable identity property— called an OID—can be used as a reference or handle to the object. Other objects can store an OID as one of their data elements, and this is the favored technique for indicating that a relationship of some kind exists between two objects.

The question of what constitutes identity generates heated debate. Some theorists (such as C. J. Date) argue that identity can be achieved by a combining a sufficient set of an object's properties. In other words, if you can't distinguish between objects based on the properties you use to describe them, then your analysis is incomplete. Nothing in the real world has a unique number perpetually attached to it. On the other hand it is pointed out that the values of an object's identifying properties may change occasionally, and coping with these changes is a difficult problem in practice.

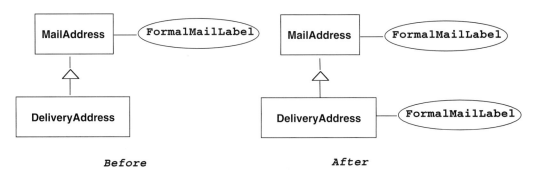

Before   *After*

Figure 4–3. *Polymorphic Type Hierarchy Diagram*

Identity, in the sense most object-oriented software understands it, is not supported as part of the ORDBMS type extensibility. Instead, it is the values and behavior of the objects themselves that are modeled. Relationships between objects are represented as schema structures. One type instance cannot directly reference another.

DataBlade Products

Datablade, or more properly *DataBlade™ Product*, is a term many readers will have heard before. But what exactly is a DataBlade™ product?

The term has a dual meaning. In its most common usage it refers to a commercial product that is a library of extensions created and marketed by a software company who are experts in a specialist field. For example, the structures and algorithms used to store and manipulate GIS data are very complex. Writing algorithms to calculate distance over the surface of the globe or whether two polygons overlap requires an understanding of arcane topics such as geodal coordinate systems and non-Euclidean geometry.

By creating a set of extensions for the IDS product these companies can bring their expertise to a much broader market. Information system developers can use the DataBlade™ Product to build applications where the focus is on solving a business problem that involves GIS, rather than on a specialist mapping or land management problem where GIS is the focus.

DataBlade™ product, in this sense is more a marketing term than a technical definition. A DataBlade™ product is *not* a complete application solution. It is a bundle of building blocks. In addition to the code to implement the extensions, datablades require extensive testing, documentation, marketing, and technical support infrastructure.

Marketing aside, there is a second meaning. When any developer creates a library of type and function extensions implementing some specialized functionality, they have in fact created a DataBlade™ module. There is no technical difference between the software customers write and the software that they bought as a datablade. Third-party vendors use the same set of API calls and facilities as other developers.

The only difference relates to the market for the extensions. While GIS or document data management is a fairly common problem, managing a particular company's part codes is not. In fact, the software developers create to manage this kind of business object can come to represent the company's competitive advantage. So the term "DataBlade" also has a strictly technical definition. A DataBlade extension is simply a set of semantically related, and user-defined, data types and functions.

Tutorial 3 presents a list of DataBlade™ products available with the ORDBMS. Chapter 10 goes into considerable detail about the facilities IDS provides to third party companies to complete this kind of work.

ORDBMS Data Types

In this section we explore the implementation alternatives available to developers creating new object classes. The ORDBMS supports a variety of mechanisms for creating data type extensions, as shown in Figure 4–4.

Data types fall into one of three major categories: built-in data types, COLLECTION data types, and user-defined types (UDTs).[2] You will also note that there are multiple kinds of user-defined types. Each kind of UDT represented in Figure 4–4 is implemented in a different way. When you are creating a new object class, your choice of extension mechanism is determined by the properties of the object you are adding to the database. What are its desired performance characteristics? How big is it? How much time do you have to develop it?

The intention in this chapter is to give developers enough information to choose the appropriate implementation strategy. In Chapter 9 we review these properties in the light of a development methodology.

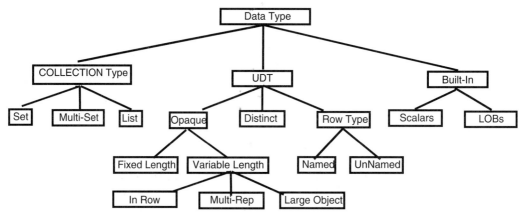

Figure 4–4. *Hierarchy of Different Kinds of Data Type*

---

[2] The product documentation classifies the types somewhat differently. COLLECTION and ROW TYPES are described as *complex data types*. This is done because it is a useful way to describe these concepts in terms of their syntax and functionality. Here, we let COLLECTION types have their own category and avoid the term complex data type. We choose this classification scheme because this is more useful from an analysis and design point of view.

Built-In Data Types

SQL-92 defines a small set of data types that we call the *built-in* types. We present a list of them in Table 4–3. Readers experienced with SQL-92 should already be familiar with each built-in type, its behavior, and how to use it. For the most part, the composition of this list reflects the type systems of common host languages from two decades ago—C, COBOL, and 4GLs—and the business data processing problems early DBMSs addressed.

Table 4–3. List of ORDBMS Built-In Data Types

Type Name	Description
CHAR(N) or NCHAR(N)	Fixed length string of N characters up to 32767. NCHAR permits a locale specific sort order for the characters, while CHAR is sorted in codeset (standardized) order.
VARCHAR(N) or NVARCHAR(N)	Variable length string of up to N characters in length. NVARCHAR permits locale specific sort order for the characters, while VARCHAR is sorted in codeset (standardized) order. These types can be up to 255 characters in length.
LVARCHAR	Large, variable length string up to 2048 bytes in length when used in a table, and 32K when used for an SPL variable. LVARCHAR is not the same thing as mi_lvarchar, which is a C type that can hold objects up to 2 Gigabytes in size, although LVARCHAR data is turned into mi_lvarchar when it is passed into an EXTERNAL UDF.
SMALLINT	Integer between $-(2^{15} - 1)$ and $(2^{15} - 1)$ (-32765 to 32765).
INTEGER	Integer between $-(2^{31} - 1)$ and $(2^{31} - 1)$ (about -2.1 billion to 2.1 billion).
INT8	Integer between $-(2^{64} - 1)$ and $(2^{64} - 1)$.
DECIMAL(N,M)	Decimal number, with N numerals in total and M to the right of the decimal place.
MONEY(N,M)	Money amount, with N numerals in total and M to the right of the decimal place. No denomination is recorded.
SMALLFLOAT	Floating point number, up to 8 significant digits.
REAL	Synonym for SMALLFLOAT.
FLOAT	Floating point number, up to 16 significant digits.
DOUBLE PRECISION	Synonym for FLOAT.
DATE	Calendar Date (Gregorian Calendar)
DATETIME	Point in time, fixed by DATE, and then timed within the 24-hour period. Depending on the operating system platform can reflect precision down to fractions of a second.

(continued)

Table 4-3. List of ORDBMS Built-In Data Types (continued)

Type Name	Description
INTERVAL	Interval between two DATE or DATETIME values.
BOOLEAN	True or False value that has "t" or "f" literal values.
BYTE	Large-object data where the object's internal data cannot be addressed.
TEXT	Large-character data where the object's internal data cannot be addressed.
BLOB	Other, non-character large-object data that is internally addressable.
CLOB	Other, character large-object data that is internally addressable.

Built-in types fall into one of two categories: elementary *scalar* types such as numbers, characters and dates, and *large-object types* or BLOBS that the DBMS can store and retrieve but not directly operate on. Built-in large-object data types are typically used to store big (>32K) binary data objects on behalf of some external program. Scalar types contain single instances of smaller values.

The most significant difference between scalar and large-object types is that OR-SQL includes an extensive set of expressions for doing interesting things with scalar types such as sorting them and performing mathematical operations or string manipulation with them. About all you can do with large-object types is insert them into the database and then export them again. You cannot, for example, apply the built-in operators over the contents of large objects, or use them in aggregates, GROUP BY clauses, or ORDER BY clauses.

The CREATE TABLE example in Listing 4–6 is typical of what you would expect in SQL-92 database. We use this table over the next few pages to illustrate how the built-in types and expressions work.

```
CREATE TABLE Movies
(    Id              INTEGER          PRIMARY KEY,
     Name            VARCHAR(32)      NOT NULL,
     Producer        VARCHAR(32)      NOT NULL,
     Studio          VARCHAR(32)      NOT NULL,
     Director        VARCHAR(32)      NOT NULL,
     Writer          VARCHAR(32)      NOT NULL,
     ReleaseDate     DATE             NOT NULL,
     ProductionCost  DECIMAL(10,2)    NOT NULL,
     Poster          BLOB             NOT NULL,
     PublicityBlurb  CLOB             NOT NULL
) PUT Poster IN (sbspace1),
     PublicityBlurb IN (cbspace1);
```

Listing 4–6. *Example of SQL-92 Version of Database Table*

Even handling these built-in types is data is a surprisingly complex technical problem. DBMS software needs to cope with a multitude of challenges related to the fact that the real world is a very diverse place:

- Information systems are often required to work across a variety of hardware platforms. Data types are represented rather differently on Intel™ and SPARC™ machines and on 32-bit and 64-bit hardware.
- Information systems are deployed in different countries, so they must cater to a variety of local languages.
- In addition to run-time usage, the DBMS also needs to provide backup, recovery, and bulk data load/unload functionality.

But at the same time, for competitive reasons, a DBMS cannot afford to sacrifice performance or reliability. The way that RDBMS products handle data types provides the model for how the developers creating OPAQUE type extentions proceed. Each built-in type has an *internal binary* storage format, which is used on disk, and two external representations: *literal ASCII strings* and an *external binary*. Both are used when data is moved between the DBMS and external code.

Literal ASCII Strings

Literal ASCII strings are the form the ORDBMS expects to see representing constant values for a type in query strings. It is also the format returned from the DBMS when the client code handling the query performs an ASCII fetch. As it processes a dynamic query statement, the ORDBMS converts literal representations of built-in types into the internal binary storage format before it stores the data type instance on disk or uses the data in a calculation.

The basic rule of thumb for literal formats is that numerical values can be represented directly while other scalar values are enclosed in single quotes. For example, an INTEGER type can be represented simply as a number—such as 5 or 123—but the literal representation of date and datetime types is rather complicated—"1999–02–11 12:01:00," for example. Whenever it returns a literal ASCII value, the ORDBMS's client/server communication code ensure that it conforms to the client's language locale.

External Binary

External binary format is used for client-side variables passed into prepared queries or returned by default from the IDS product as query results. Because the data is in a binary format, the client's language locale is not an issue. This is also the format used when the DBMS is backed up, and sometimes when data is moved between nodes of a distributed database.

Internal Binary

Internal binary is the format used when an instance of the type is stored in a table, or when it is passed into a UDF running within the ORDBMS. It might, or might not, be different from the external binary format. For instance, the maximum size of the internal binary format for any user-defined type is 32 Kilobytes. This limit is a consequence of the fact that the type must fit within data pages. As we shall see, larger objects are stored outside the table's rows with a reference to their location stored within the row. When moving data back to the client, however, it is often necessary to create a single contiguous array of bytes that the client's host language understands.

Built-in types provide a good model for thinking about how to implement user-defined types. When you design a new data type, the important questions include:

- What is the type's internal (binary) storage structure?
- What do the type's external (ASCII and binary) formats look like?
- How should the external, literal value be parsed and converted into the internal storage format?

Operations and Expressions on Scalar Built-In Data Types

All built-in scalar types can be manipulated using a set of pre-defined SQL-92 expressions and operators. For instance, all built-in data types can be compared using the ordinal mathematical operators: <, <=, =, >=, and >.In information systems built using SQL-92, these were the predicates that could be used in a WHERE clause.

In addition, each of the built-in types possesses a reasonably extensive set of expressions for modifying instances of the built-in types. For example, character data types can be compared using operators such as LIKE, and the query language includes expressions to extract substrings. An extensive body of mathematical functions such as LOG(), SIN(), and SQRT() and calculations such as +, *, and - can be used with any of the numbers types. The complete list of these manipulator expressions is quite large. The query in Listing 4–7 shows how several built-in functions can be used.

"How many weeks have each of Warner's summer movies been released?"

```
SELECT  M.Name,
        INTERVAL (TODAY - M.ReleaseDate) WEEKS
  FROM  Movies M
 WHERE  M.Studio LIKE '%Warner%'
   AND  M.ReleaseDate > '03/01/2000'
 ORDER  BY 2;
```

Listing 4–7. *Query Example using SQL-92 Built-In Expressions*

Because of its SQL-92 RDBMS roots, all of this built-in functionality is hard coded within the ORDBMS. IDS handles operations such as sorting, indexing, backing up and recovering, and copying instances of the built-in types between the ORDBMS and external programs, and does so automatically. These physical data management facilities are largely invisible to users, but understanding how they work is instructive because the built-in types are a model for how user-defined types, and most particularly OPAQUE TYPE, behave. Designing a new OPAQUE TYPE instances requires thinking through how to support comparison operators, sorting, and mathematical or manipulation functionality with a set of user-defined functions.

Operations Over Large-Object Data Types

Far fewer query language operations apply to large-object data types (or binary large objects, BLOBS). Indeed, one of the objectives of ORDBMS technology is to allow developers to do more with large data objects.

Developers using SQL-92 are limited to inserting and retrieving entire instances of large-object data types. Accessing the internals of BLOB data is possible only from a client program either by retrieving the entire BLOB to a client-side file or by using a low-level API provided by the IDS product. While it is possible to use the ORDBMS's internal *Server API (SAPI)* to access large-object data from within a user-defined function, it is still a good idea to provide facilities for handling instances of user-defined large-object types in the same way BLOBs are handled by the SQL-92.

Traditionally, the most convenient place to store individual large objects has been as files in an operating system's filesystem. The following functions take the entire contents of a named *file* and insert it into the database as a BLOB. These functions both return a *handle* that identifies the newly created BLOB, and the bytes that make up this handle's data is what is stored in the table's column.

```
FILETOBLOB (Filename, Location)

FILETOCLOB (Filename, Location)
```

The source file's path (Filename) is supplied as the first argument, and the machine on which the file resides—either the client or the server—is supplied as the second argument. For example, the Movies table defined in the query in Listing 4–8 inserts a new row. It takes the binary file from a client file in "C:\tmp\EP.gif" a large character object from a server file "\tmp\EPBlurb.txt" and combines them with more standard data types in a single query.

"Add the new movie details."

```
INSERT INTO Movies
(    Id, Name, Producer,
     Studio, Director,
     Writer, ReleaseDate,
     ProductionCost,
     Poster,
     PublicityBlurb )
VALUES
(    123456,  'The English Patient',  'Saul Zaentz',
     'Mirimax', 'Anthony Minghella',
     'Anthony Minghella', '05/06/96',
     25000000.00,
     FILETOBLOB('C:\tmp\EP.gif','client'),
     FILETOCLOB('\tmp\EPBlurb.txt','server')
);
```

Listing 4–8. *SQL INSERT Including Large-Object Functions*

Understanding the relationship between large-object handles, which are stored in the table's rows or in memory as variables, and large-object data, which is stored in specially assigned storage spaces, is very important. OR-SQL queries that INSERT data into one table using rows selected from another do not create new copies of the underlying large-object data. Rather, they only copy the handle (and increase the reference count on the large object to ensure that the ORDBMS does not re-use the disk space assigned to it if the original row is deleted.). We illustrate the way this is organized in Figure 4–5.

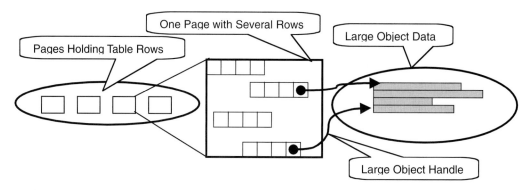

Figure 4–5. *Diagrammatic Representation of Large Object Data Management*

This is the same model used with user-defined large-object data types and the logic that implements their behavior. Functions working with large-object data receive a large-object handle stored in the row as an argument. SAPI includes facilities like those traditionally found on the client-side supporting random access to the corresponding large object's data. This means that significant portions of functionality that in the past had to reside outside the database—such as image format converters and faster processing functionality—can be integrated within it. We return to this topic in Chapter 10.

Duplication of large objects must be done explicitly. This is achieved with the LOCOPY() function:

```
LOCOPY(SourceColumn, SourceTable, Column)
```

The query in Listing 4–9 illustrates how to use this function.

"Update the publicity blurb for the movie 'Home Alone 8,' setting it to the same one we used for 'Home Alone 7.'"

```
UPDATE Movies M1
    SET PublicityBlurb = (
     SELECT LOCOPY(PublicityBlurb,
                        Movies,
                        PublicityBlurb )
        FROM Movies M2
      WHERE M2.Name = 'Home Alone 7')
   WHERE M.Name = 'Home Alone 8';
```

Listing 4–9. *UPDATE Query Illustrating the Use of the LOCOPY Built-in Function*

The first argument to the LOCOPY() function is the name of the column containing the source data. The second and third arguments are a table identifier and column combination specifying the physical location where the new copy of the large object is to be stored. Recall in Chapter 2 that we saw how the mapping of a large-object column to a physical storage space is specified as part of the CREATE TABLE statement. Therefore, this combination tells the IDS product where to *physically* store the new large object copy. The query that calls LOCOPY() specifies the table and column where the new copy is to be placed *logically*. That is, this is where the large object handle referring to the new large object data is saved.

For example, in Listing 4–9, the new copy of the large object will be located in the same partition as its original. You can use this to specify a new physical location for your copy: a new physical storage space. You could use the LOCOPY() function in the following way:

```
LOCOPY( PublicityBlurb,
        AnotherTable,
        ColumnInOtherTable  )
```

There is a symmetric operation to FILETOBLOB that moves large objects into the file-system, either on the client-side of a connection or onto the server. The general form of this SQL-92 function is in Listing 4–10.

```
LOTOFILE(Column, Filename, Location)
```

"Get me the posters for John Houston's movies."

```
SELECT LOTOFILE(DISTINCT M.Poster,
                        'C:\tmp\Fin', 'client'),
        M.Title
   FROM Movies M, WorkedOn W, MoviePersonalities P
  WHERE W.Movie  = M.Id
    AND W.Person = P.Id
    AND P.Name   = PersonName('Houston','John');
```

Listing 4–10. *Query Illustrating the LOTOFile() Function for Extracting Large Objects*

LOTOFILE() takes three arguments: a column name, the name of a directory or a directory and file stub, and finally the location ("client" or "server") where the data is to be placed. The function returns a string containing name of the file where the large-object data has been placed. Mostly this function will be used to copy one LO at a time out of the database, but a single query can be used to copy a number of them. LOTOFILE() ensures that the filenames it creates for each LO is unique within the directory.

lvarchar Data Type

The lvarchar data type is a new built-in data type that was not part of the RDBMS. lvarchar is used to hold variable length string data. When used in a table the type can store strings of ASCII characters up to 32K in length. But the lvarchar type has another, important use.

lvarchar is used within the IDS product as a general-purpose technique to pass variable length data values around. When it encounters a literal string in a query—character data bounded by quotation marks— the query parser's first action is to create an lvarchar instance and copy the string into it. IDS does not know the type that this lvarchar will be turned into, but by examining the other aspects of the query plan, it can figure this out. Ultimately, IDS may have to call a C function, in which case it copies the literal string into an ml_lvarchar structure. Figure 4-6 illustrates what the memory map of an ml_lvarchar looks like.

Note that this is not an accurate memory map for the type. The SAPI provides a set of routines for accessing the contents of an lvarchar instance within a C UDF which we describe in detail in Chapter 10. Developers are strongly advised to use the SAPI facilities rather than accessing ml_lvarchar directly.

Once it has parsed the rest of the query, the ORDBMS will know which data type each literal string needs to be converted to. In Figure 4–6 the literal string needs probably to be converted into a Movie_Title instance. An important task when implementing new user-defined types—particularly an OPAQUE TYPE—involves creating functions to convert data between lvarchar and the type's internal representation, and symmetric functions to complete the inverse transformation.

Converting between lvarchar and your UDT is just a special case of more general *constructor* functionality. Sometimes you want to use one of the numeric types as your literal; for example, a Quantity user-defined type might be best off using an INTEGER as its literal representation. We return to this topic later in this chapter when we look at casting between data type values.

Using Built-In Types

The biggest advantage of the built-in types is their maturity. They are built into the IDS core and INFORMIX's engineers have optimized their functionality over many years. Application development languages such as C or a 4GL have data types that correspond to the SQL-92 built-in types so working with them on the client side is relatively easy. The standards community, who create specifications for interfaces such as ODBC and JDBC, have developed considerable client-side infrastructure to support these types.

However, the built-in data types are subject to many limitations. For example, there is always disagreement about the semantics of any standard. SQL-92's handling of all things temporal—dates, times and

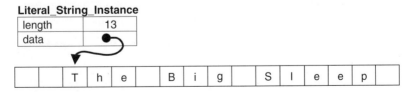

Figure 4–6. Representation of the Internal Structure of the Invarchar Data Type Instance

intervals—is, to put it mildly, cumbersome. Often, database developers want slightly different behavior than the standard mandates and are obliged to jump through hoops to get it. And finally, there are certain things such as spatial data, large text that the built-in types simply cannot support with even halfway reasonable efficiency.

Many ORDBMS developers reading this book will be adapting existing RDBMS databases to make use of extensibility. One way to make immediate use of ORDBMS extensibility is to implement user-defined functions that operate over the built-in types. But another effective way to use built-in data types is in conjunction with other extended type mechanisms: ROW TYPE and DISTINCT TYPE. These can leverage the strengths of the built-in types—their behavior, server nativity, and so on—while achieving the desirable data modeling goal of strong typing. For example, business objects such as names, addresses, and so on can be composed from a combination of built-in types.

Sometimes the kind of data you're dealing with is difficult to accommodate using built-in types. Objects like Polygons, video data and bitmap fall into this category. When confronted with such a problem it may be necessary to create a new OPAQUE TYPE . An OPAQUE TYPE mimics the built-in types in every way. But instead of the ORDBMS knowing how to parse, communicate, and store instances of the type, all of this must be explained to it by a developer through a series of user-defined *support functions*.

COLLECTION Data Types

COLLECTION type instances are a group of instances of another type, such as a set of clothing sizes, movie genres, or even another COLLECTION. Formally, a collection type T_c is a named *group* of instances of another type T_b. The value of COLLECTIONS lies in the way that they permit a number of data values to be contained within a single data element and therefore within a single row/column cell within a table. The alternative is to normalize the COLLECTION and model it in a separate table. With this approach, the group of values must be reconstructed with a query that joins the two tables.

COLLECTION types come in three built-in flavors: SET, MULTISET and LIST. Internally, the ORDBMS's implementation of each kind of COLLECTION uses the multi-representational functionality, so there is no limit to how large a COLLECTION can grow. However, large COLLECTION sinatces are discouraged (see Table 4–4).

The several kinds of COLLECTION differ in the rules that are applied over their contents. Each declaration of a COLLECTION type consists of a constructor that defines the kind of COLLECTION and an element type that defines what this is a COLLECTION of. The rules that each kind of COLLECTION imposes on the data elements it contains are summarized in Table 4–4.

Table 4–4. COLLECTION Data Types and their Semantics	
SET	SETs obey the rules that define mathematical sets. This means that any set can contain at most one instance of a given value.
LIST	Elements in a LIST are numbered. LIST is like an array.
MULTISET	MULTISET is a bag or simply generalized group of values. An element value can be present many times in a set.

COLLECTION data types are quite different from the other data types. Indeed, it's unclear whether they are data types at all. You might classify them among the structural features of the OR data model as something that distinguishes an ORDBMS from the SQL-92 style relational table structure. In this book, we include this description in the chapter dedicated to data types because of the way that COLLECTION data can be passed around as arguments to functions.

Defining COLLECTION Data Types

COLLECTION types can be used to define a table's column type, arguments to a function, or variables within a function's body. The general form and use for creating a COLLECTION type in any of these situations is shown in Listing 4–11:

```
COLLECTION_CONSTRUCTOR( Element_Type NOT NULL )
```

Note that the NOT NULL syntax here is syntactic sugar. If it is not present, however, the ORDBMS will generate a syntax error.

```
SET ( INTEGER NOT NULL )
LIST ( VARCHAR(40) NOT NULL )
MULTISET ( PersonName NOT NULL )
LIST ( LIST ( Revenue NOT NULL ) NOT NULL )
SET ( ROW ( Name PersonName NOT NULL,
          DOB  DATE NOT NULL ) NOT NULL )
```

Listing 4–11. *SQL Examples of Declaring a COLLECTION Type Instance*

The OR-SQL fragment in Listing 4–12 illustrates how to define a table that includes several COLLECTION columns. The examples that follow in this section use this table definition to illustrate various aspects of COLLECTION handling in OR-SQL.

```
CREATE TABLE Collection_Examples (
     Id               INTEGER      NOT NULL      PRIMARY KEY,
     List_Example     LIST( VARCHAR(16)    NOT NULL ),
     Set_Example      SET( INTEGER NOT NULL ),
     MSet_Example     MULTISET( Name_Value_Pair NOT NULL )
);
```

Listing 4–12. *COLLECTION as Table Column*

Creating Instances of COLLECTIONs

Each COLLECTION type has a corresponding constructor: SET{}, MULTISET{}, or LIST{}. Constructors enforce the rules of their respective kind of COLLECTION. If you were to try to insert a SET that contained duplicate instances into this table, the IDS parser would raise an exception. This means that the ORDBMS must be able to determine when two data type values in a SET are equal. To insert a new record into the table fragment in Listing 4–12, you would use the OR-SQL in Listing 4–13.

```
INSERT INTO Collection_Examples
VALUES
( 1,
  LIST{'Fred','Barney','Wilma','Betty'},
  SET{1,2,3,4,5,6,7,8,9,10},
  MULTISET{ ROW('Stars',3)::Name_Value_Pair,
            ROW('Forks',4)::Name_Value_Pair,
            ROW('Stars',3)::Name_Value_Pair}
);
```

Listing 4–13. *INSERT Query Illustrating the use of a COLLECTION Constructor*

You might also use a constructor to initialize the value of a COLLECTION variable in a database procedure, as shown in Listing 4–14.

```
DEFINE   stRetVal     SET(INTEGER NOT NULL );
     .
     .
     .
LET stRetVal = SET{1,2,3,4,5};
```

Listing 4–14. *SPL Example Illustrating Use of COLLECTION Constructor*

The internal DataBlade API SAPI includes a set of functions that allow developers implementing external user-defined function to work with COLLECTION instances. These low-level calls perform operations like creating an empty COLLECTION, inserting values into a COLLECTION, and iteratively retrieving the elements stored within a COLLECTION. Manipulating COLLECTION data structures in C requires complex code, however, and the resulting EXTERNAL UDF is not noticeably faster than an SPL implementation.

Operations Involving COLLECTIONS

Entire COLLECTION instances can be retrieved to an external program or passed as arguments to user-defined functions. For example, the following query selects all rows from the table created in Listing 4–2. COLLECTION data is represented differently depending on the best language used. The data format shown in Listing 4–15 is the default representation of a COLLECTION type converted into a default string literal.

```
SELECT *
  FROM Collection_Examples;
```

Id	list_example	set_example	mset_example
1	LIST{'Fred','Barney', 'Wilma', 'Betty'}	SET {5,6,7,8,9,10}	MULTISET{ ROW('Stars',3), ROW('Forks',4), ROW('Stars',3) }
2	LIST{'Willie', 'Road'}	SET {1,2,3,4,5,6}	MULTISET{ ROW('Stars',3), ROW('Forks',1) }
3	LIST{'Sylvester', 'Tweetie'}	SET {1,2,3,4,5,6}	MULTISET{ ROW('Stars',2), ROW('Forks',2), ROW('Birdcage', 7) }

Listing 4–15. *Query Retrieving COLLECTION Instances from Table*

A few functions operate over entire instances of COLLECTION types. The CARDINALITY function returns the number of members of a single COLLECTION instance. It can be used in queries as shown in Listing 4–16.

```
SELECT C.Id,
       CARDINALITY ( C.List_Example ) AS Num_in_List,
       CARDINALITY ( C.Set_Example ) AS Num_in_Set,
       CARDINALITY ( C.MSet_Example ) AS Num_in_MSet
  FROM Collection_Examples C;
```

id	num_in_list	num_in_set	num_in_mset
1	4	10	3
2	2	6	2
3	2	6	3

Listing 4–16. *SQL Query Using CARDINALITY Function over COLLECTIONs*

Developers can create user-defined functions in SPL that use OR-SQL expressions to manipulate the contents of a COLLECTION object. In the next section of this chapter, we illustrate how to create a function that determines whether two COLLECTION arguments intersect, and one that modify the contents of a COLLECTION.

OR-SQL to Access COLLECTION Elements

OR-SQL queries can access the contents of a COLLECTION instance. The query in Listing 4–17 illustrates the first approach to accessing data within a COLLECTION. This query uses the SQL IN keyword, which was used in earlier versions of SQL to check for a particular data values within a list of constant values.

```
SELECT Id
  FROM Collection_Examples
 WHERE 'Betty' IN List_Example;

id
1
```

Listing 4–17. *Using the IN Keywords to Examine Contents of COLLECTION*

In Chapter 3 we saw how you can turn a COLLECTION into a kind of table, and use it as a data source in the FROM clause of a query. The following example illustrates how to exploit this kind of functionality to implement other set operations as a user-defined function. This UDF—implemented in the INFORMIX SPL for simplicity—returns true if there is at least one data element shared by both COLLECTION arguments, as shown in Listing 4–18.

```
CREATE FUNCTION Intersects ( Arg1 SET(lvarchar NOT NULL),
                             Arg2 SET(lvarchar NOT NULL))
RETURNING boolean
   DEFINE nQuery    INTEGER;

   LET nQuery = ( SELECT COUNT(*)
                    FROM TABLE(Arg1) F,
                         TABLE(Arg2) S
```

```
                        WHERE  F = S
                    );
    IF  (nQuery > 0)  THEN
        RETURN  't'::boolean;
    END IF;


    RETURN  'f'::boolean;
END FUNCTION;
```

Listing 4–18. *User-Defined Function Implementing SET Intersection*

This function can be used in the kind of query found in Listing 4–19.

"Show me Movies that share a genre with Casablanca."

```
SELECT M1.Title, M1.Genre,
       M2.Title, M2.Genre
  FROM Movies M1, Movies M2
 WHERE M1.Title  = 'Casablanca'
   AND M2.Title != 'Casablanca'
   AND Intersects ( M1.Genre, M2.Genre );
```

Listing 4–19. *Using the Intersects UDR to Compare COLLECTION Instances*

In a similar fashion other OR-SQL statements can be used to modify the contents of a COLLECTION. The user-defined function in Listing 4–20 illustrates several aspects of how to work with COLLECTION data. First, it loops over the data in the COLLECTION argument, checking to see if the element is to be removed from the result. Then inside the loop, valid elements are inserted into the functions return result. Note that, in keeping with the rules governing all user-defined functions, this one must compute a new result value rather than modify its argument.

```
CREATE FUNCTION RemoveElement ( Arg1 SET(LVARCHAR NOT NULL),
                                Arg2 LVARCHAR )
RETURNS SET(LVARCHAR NOT NULL)
    DEFINE   setRetVal    SET(LVARCHAR NOT NULL);
    DEFINE   lvCurrent    LVARCHAR;

    FOREACH Cursor FOR SELECT *

                       INTO lvCurrent
                       FROM TABLE( Arg1 )
        IF ( lvCurrent != Arg2 ) THEN
            INSERT INTO TABLE(setRetVal)
            VALUES ( lvCurrent);
        END IF;
    END FOREACH;
```

```
            RETURN setRetVal;
    END FUNCTION;

    EXECUTE FUNCTION RemoveElement (
                    SET{'Hello', 'Good-Bye', 'So Long' },
                    'Hello');

    (expression):: SET{ LVARCHAR NOT NULL }
    SET{'Good-Bye', 'So Long'}
```

Listing 4–20. *Use of SQL's Write Operations to Access COLLECTION Elements*

SPL embeds OR-SQL statements like these that INSERT, UPDATE and DELETE from a COLLECTION variable, and as this example shows UDFs can also return entire COLLECTION instances.

Using COLLECTIONs

COLLECTION types are potentially very powerful, but they have significant limitations in IDS. In fact it is probably best to use them in tables only in a fairly limited set of circumstance. At this time, the ORDBMS provides fairly poor indexing support for "IN" queries. Consequently, in situations where a query tries to retrieve data from a large table using "IN" over a COLLECTION column, the ORDBMS is obliged to scan every row in the table. Also, the query language does not support directly modifying a COLLECTION value from within an OR-SQL statement. Changing a COLLECTION requires that the COLLECTION instance first be taken out of the table and placed into a variable, then modified, before being replaced in the table.

COLLECTION objects are most useful in query language statements, and as a mechanism for passing variable arguments into user-defined functions. In circumstances where a client application needs to process an operation over a variable number of objects, there are advantages to using a single message exchange between the client and the ORDBMS instead of a number of separate invocations.

Other Kinds of COLLECTION Types

COLLECTION types are example of *non-first normal form* (NFNF) data values. The examples we include above show you how a COLLECTION, and by extension other NFNF types, are characterized by a kind of dualism. Some operations consider the COLLECTION as a whole (CARDINALITY, Intersects etc) while others address the elements within the COLLECTION.

Certain real-world phenomena lend themselves very well to being modeled in this way. Consider the progress over time of the price of a particular stock. Some business questions address the entire history of the price—for example, "What are the fifty and two hundred day moving averages of the stock price?"—while others address a particular element within it—"What was the price at the close of trade on October 27, 1987?"

ORDBMS extensibility lets developers embed the means to manage their own variations on COLLECTION types within the ORDBMS. In Chapter 10 we describe the techniques used to implement types like these, and in a tutorial section of this book we describe the functionality of the Timeseries DataBlade™ (See Tutorial 3) which applies these techniques.

CAST: Converting Between Data Types

Before embarking on a detailed description of the other UDTs, it's useful first to cover another important topic: *casting*. A CAST is a mechanism for automatically turning an instance of one data type into an instance of another as part of query execution. In fact, what a CAST does is to instruct the ORDBMS to invoke a particular UDF—one that actually takes an instance of one type and creates an instance of the other— before it processes data in a query.

Casts are useful for many reasons. They make is possible to apply functionality implemented for one data type—say a built-in type such as lvarchar—over instances of another data type such as OPAQUE TYPE or DISTINCT TYPE. In other words, CAST is a technique to reduce the total amount of code to write. In this section we explain how they work, and how to create them. We introduce this material here because CAST plays in important part over the next few sections of this chapter. User-defined types and particularly the OPAQUE TYPE employ the CAST mechanism extensively.

CAST Concept

Casting is best explained with an example. SQL-92 provides DECIMAL data type that can be used to store quantities of money, so long as the entire information system assumes a consistent denomination, say, U.S. dollars. But our Movies-R-Us Web site would (hopefully) encounter a variety of currencies. A useful service to non-U.S. visitors might be to quote all prices in local denominations. In a different problem domain, a multinational organization may coalesce account information from many countries into a single financial statement.

A user-defined CURRENCY type representing the state (quantity and denomination) and behavior (adding up, converting, and so on) of money could be implemented using any of the UDT mechanisms. Columns declared to use this type would, in fact, let the database store amounts of money using a variety of denominations, such as Japanese yen, U.S. dollars, and Zambian Kwacha, all in the same table. The obvious advantage of such a scheme is that external applications need not repeat the implementation of conversion logic.[3]

However, when working in the Web site database it is frequently convenient to express money quantities in queries as DECIMAL values, such as 10.20, or 5.20, rather than $10.20. The UDT's implementation can assume that a particular denomination—U.S. dollars, say—is the default. Now, developer might write a UDF that converts one data type—the SQL-92 DECIMAL—into another—our CURRENCY UDT. Such a UDF might look like the one we show in Listing 4–21.

```
CREATE FUNCTION DecimalToCurrency ( Arg1 DECIMAL ( 14, 4 ) )
RETURNING Currency
```

Listing 4–21. *Fragment of UDR Converting Between DECIMAL and Currency Types*

This function can be used in OR-SQL queries and SPL database procedures in the manner illustrated in Listing 4–22.

"Show me items of Merchandise worth less than 50.00 (the query assumes $US)."

```
SELECT M.Name
  FROM Merchandise M
  WHERE M.Price < DecimalToCurrency(50.00);
```

Listing 4–22. *Using UDR to Convert Types in a Query*

Recall from Chapter 3 that when the ORDBMS parses the < operator symbol in this query, it will look for a function named LessThan to perform the comparison. In fact, it must find a LessThan function for CURRENCY types specifically. Supporting the full range of OR-SQL's

---

[3] Also, there are some applications that need to preserve the original currency. For example, debt amounts and contractual prices expressed in overseas denominations.

built-in comparisons is a tedious task. Instead, it would be useful to convert all values back into DECIMAL by always using the default denomination. Then the built-in DECIMAL type's comparisons are available.

In Listing 4–23 we introduce a UDF called CurrencyToDecimal() that does exactly this, and illustrate how these two functions would be used in a query.

"Show me items of Merchandise worth less than $50 ."

```
CREATE FUNCTION CurrencyToDecimal ( Arg1 Currency )
RETURNING DECIMAL ( 14, 4 )

SELECT M.Name
  FROM Merchandise M
 WHERE CurrencyToDecimal(M.Price) <
               CurrencyToDecimal(
                      DecimalToCurrency(50.00));
```

Listing 4–25. *Using UDR in a WHERE Clause to Convert Data*

Using conversion functions in this way leads to long, confusing queries. Further, if you were to change the name of the conversion function, you would need to change every query that uses it. A better way is to tell the ORDBMS how an instance of the DECIMAL type can be turned into an instance of the Currency type (and vice versa). In other words, casts are a means whereby you can instruct the ORDBMS to invoke the conversion function automatically.

CREATE CAST

To create a new cast between two data types you use the CREATE CAST statement. CREATE CAST requires the names of the two types involved, and where necessary the name of the conversion function to use. In certain cases—such as when one type is a DISTINCT TYPE of the other, or when the types are the same, fixed size—the ORDBMS can cast between the types without using a transformation function. The general form of the CREATE CAST statement is shown in Listing 4–24.

```
CREATE [ IMPLICIT | EXPLICIT ] CAST
(    FirstType AS SecondType
     [ WITH ConversionFunctionName ]
);
```

Listing 4–24. *General Form and Example of the CREATE CAST DDL Statement*

The `ConversionFunctionName()` UDF needs to take as a single argument a value of the `FirstType`, and return as a result a value of the `SecondType`. In our example, we use the function defined in Listing 4–21. Note that casts defined like this work only one way. To cast the other way, from the `SecondType` to the `FirstType`, requires another casting function, and a second, symmetric CREATE CAST statement, as shown in Listing 4–25.

```
CREATE [ IMPLICIT | EXPLICIT ] CAST
(    SecondType AS FirstType
     [ WITH AnotherConversionFunction ]
);

CREATE IMPLICIT CAST
(    Currency AS DECIMAL
     WITH CurrencyToDecimal
);
```

Listing 4–25. *Symmetrical Cast to the One Created in Listing 4–16*

There are two casting modes: EXPLICIT and IMPLICIT. By default, the ORDBMS assumes a CAST is EXPLICIT. The CREATE CAST statement places in the ORDBMS's system catalogs a record of the existence of the CAST and the identity of the transformation function.

An EXPLICIT CAST tells the ORDBMS that the conversion is possible, but that the ORDBMS should not consider the cast as part of its automatic query processing. To use EXPLICIT casts in queries, you need to explicitly use the "double colon" notation or the CAST( ) keywords to invoke the casting function in OR-SQL statements.

Telling the ORDBMS that a cast is IMPLICIT makes it consider casting between the types automatically. These modes are mutually exclusive: your cast can be either EXPLICIT or IMPLICIT cast, but not both. Also, before a user can use a cast in a query they need to have permission to use the casting function.

You can drop casts with the corresponding DROP CAST statement. Because you cannot have both an implicit and an explicit cast defined between two types it's necessary to first drop the existing cast before creating the new one. The code in Listing 4–26 illustrates how to drop both casts that we just defined.

```
DROP CAST (Currency AS DECIMAL );
DROP CAST (DECIMAL AS Currency );
```

Listing 4–26. *DROP CAST Statement*

DROP CAST removes the record of its existence from the system catalogs.

Using CAST

There are two ways to invoke the EXPLICIT, or inline, cast. First, you can use the CAST ( ) OR-SQL keyword, as shown in Listing 4–27.

"Show me the names and prices Merchandise items worth less than $5"

```
SELECT M.Name,
       CAST( M.Price AS DECIMAL ) AS Price
  FROM Merchandise M
 WHERE M.Price < CAST( 5.00 AS CURRENCY );
```

Listing 4–27. *Long-winded Use of CAST in Query*

Alternatively, you can append a pair of colons and the target type's name or to the constant value or column to instruct IDS to perform the cast, as shown in Listing 4–28.

```
SELECT M.Name,
       M.Price::DECIMAL
  FROM Merchandise M
 WHERE M.Price < 5.00::Currency;
```

Listing 4–28. *Double-Colon Notation for Using CAST*

IMPLICIT casting is trickier. Implicit casting works by affecting how the ORDBMS figures out which function(s) to run based on what it sees in the query expression. This can lead to some interesting quirks. For example, suppose we created casts from DECIMAL to Currency and Currency to DECIMAL. Consider the Listing 4–29 version of the query in Listing 4–23.

```
SELECT M.Name
  FROM Merchandise M
 WHERE M.Price < 5.00;
```

Listing 4–29. *Queries Illustrating CASTing Trickiness*

With casts defined to convert both types into instances of each other this query might result in an ambiguity. Suppose there is a UDF Equal(Currency, Currency) in addition to the built-in Equal

(DECIMAL, DECIMAL) functionality? Does the ORDBMS cast both sides of the comparison to Currency and invoke this function, or does it cast both to DECIMAL and use the built-in Equal function? These might product different answers! Rather than imposing some arbitrary semantics on the query the ORDBMS will detect the ambiguity and requests that the developer resolve it explicitly by removing one of the casts.

IMPLICIT casting is really useful when you want to convert a literal data type—such as lvarchar—into an internal representation on an OPAQUE TYPE. But despite their usefulness, it is important to be careful applying CASTs. As each of the various UDTs is introduced, we explain how to use CAST to avoid these problems.

User Defined Types (UDT)

User-defined Types (UDT) are the third kind of type mechanism that can be used in an ORDBMS. UDTs model the *state* of the user-defined objects embedded within the database, including its size and whatever internal elements it has. There are three mechanisms that can be used to implement user-defined types: DISTINCT, ROW, and OPAQUE TYPE. Each of them uses a different set of techniques to achieve its OR-SQL functionality, and these differences impact the mechanism's performance and determine how simple or complex the mechanism is to use.

A single ORDBMS database can contain a large number of UDTs implemented using the full range of UDT mechanisms. In fact, so far as a developer using OR-SQL or an end-user is concerned, it is difficult to tell which mechanism is used for a particular type.

Data Types and Extension Languages

Any of the user-defined function extension languages—C, SPL, or Java—can be used with any of the different kinds of data type; for example, you can extract elements from a ROW TYPE and create a ROW TYPE return result within a C UDR. In fact, you can pass different kinds of UDT into a function, or write functions in all of the extension languages that take different kinds of types as arguments. You can implement a UDF in Java that takes a ROW TYPE and a DISTINCT TYPE argument (both UDTs) and returns a boolean result (a built-in).

That said, there are synergies between different languages and different kinds of UDT. The stored procedure language SPL is generally used with the ROW TYPE, while C UDFs are ideal for OPAQUE TYPE implementations. Java is a slightly special case. As at time of writing Java works well with both OPAQUE TYPE and DISTINCT TYPE extensions, but by the time you read this it may work just as well for a ROW TYPE.

It is also important to note that while UDTs are usually described in terms of how they are used in a database's schema, keep in mind that the ORDBMS's type system and its data storage are quite separate. Just as you can create a table that uses only built-in types, you can also implement a UDT and then not use it in any table.

CREATE TYPE Statement

UDTs are created using some variation of the CREATE TYPE statement. In the CREATE TYPE statement, you specify the following:

- The name of the new type (a valid OR-SQL *identifier*). Type identifiers must be unique with the database.
- Varying degrees of detail about the new type's internal structure (depending on the UDT mechanism).
- Where possible, constraints that apply to values the new type can have.
- What, if any, data types from which the new type inherits structure and behavior.
- Information about the type for the use of the ORDBMS query processor.

Different kinds of UDT are created using variations of this statement. We present the most common forms of CREATE TYPE in Listing 4–30.

```
CREATE DISTINCT TYPE New_DISTINCT_Type_Identifier
AS Original_Type_Identifier;

CREATE ROW TYPE New_ROW_Type_Identifier (
        Element_Name        Element_Data_Type       [ NOT NULL ]
    {, Element_Name        Element_Data_Type       [ NOT NULL ]
}
) [ UNDER Parent_ROW_Type_Identifier ];

CREATE OPAQUE TYPE New_OPAQUE_Type_Identifier
(
        INTERNALLENGTH = [integer | 'variable']
        {, TYPE_MODIFIER = value }
);
```

Listing 4–30. *General Forms of CREATE TYPE Statement*

Listing 4–31 provides several examples illustrating how to create different kinds of types.

```
CREATE DISTINCT TYPE ShortString AS LVARCHAR;

CREATE ROW TYPE BirthDate (
       MMonth            INTEGER NOT NULL,
       DDay              INTEGER NOT NULL,
       FromLeapYear      BOOLEAN NOT NULL
);

CREATE OPAQUE TYPE Period
(      INTERNALLENGTH = 8,
       ALIGNMENT = 8
);
```

Listing 4–31. *Various CREATE TYPE Statements*

The ORDBMS stores information about each type's kind and size (and
structure in the case of a ROW TYPE) in its system catalogs. Types must
be created before they can be used; that is, you cannot create a table
or a function and use a type identifier that has not yet been defined.

DROP TYPE Command

UDTs can be removed from the system with the DROP TYPE command. If the data type is being used somewhere in the schema then
the DROP TYPE will fail with an error. When removing an object
(data type and behavior functions) it is generally a good idea to
remove each component of the object in the reverse order they were
declared. DROP the user-defined functions before dropping the type
syntax, as shown in Listing 4–32.

```
DROP [ROW] TYPE Type_Name [RESTRICT];
```

Listing 4–32. *General Form of DROP TYPE Statement*

Dropping each kind of data type also requires a slightly variant syntax.
For example, when dropping a ROW TYPE, you need to tell the ORDBMS
that you are deleting a ROW TYPE. When dropping a DISTINCT TYPE
or a ROW TYPE the statement must include the RESTRICT modifier.
Dropping a type removes it from the system catalogs. Listing 4–33 illustrates several examples of DROP TYPE commands.

```
DROP TYPE ShortString RESTRICT;    - A DISTINCT Type.

DROP ROW TYPE BirthDay RESTRICT;   - A ROW Type.

DROP TYPE Period;                    - An OPAQUE Type.
```

Listing 4–33. *DROP TYPE Syntax*

In the next few sections, we review each of the several kinds of UDTs in more detail. We begin with the simplest kind of UDT—the DISTINCT TYPE. Later, we explain the ROW TYPE, and finally the OPAQUE TYPE mechanism.

DISTINCT TYPES

Formally, a DISTINCT TYPE is an existing data type T_1, with a new name, T_2. A DISTINCT TYPE is similar to SQL-92's domain. They are most useful where you want to re-use an existing type and its behavior for another purpose.

For example, the Movies-R-Us database needs to provide an artificial primary key column for some tables. Within the MoviePersonality table, we use a column called Id for this purpose. Each new row in the MoviePersonality table is assigned a new, unique value in its Id column. It would be useful if the type of this column were something more semantically interesting than a four byte INTEGER or SERIAL type. Using INTEGER everywhere results in a schema where it is difficult to answer questions such as "What tables contain data related to Movie-Personalities?"[4] Creating several DISTINCT TYPE variants of INTEGER—called Personality_Id and Movie_Id for example—solves this problem.

You can re-use any of the other data types when you create a DISTINCT TYPE: built-in type, ROW TYPE, OPAQUE TYPE, or even another DISTINCT TYPE. New DISTINCT TYPE instances "inherit" the properties of their "parent" type. They have the same storage space requirement; a DISTINCT TYPE of a built-in or OPAQUE TYPE take up the same number of bytes. When you create a DISTINCT TYPE of a ROW

---

[4] Referential integrity constraints enforce rules about relationships between tables, but it is possible for there to be another table containing movie personality Ids that are not present in the primary table.

TYPE, the new DISTINCT TYPE has the same elements and constraints as its parent. In contrast with the semantics of ROW TYPE inheritance (see below), a new DISTINCT TYPE cannot be specialized by adding new elements or increasing the type's length.

Creating DISTINCT TYPE

To create a new DISTINCT TYPE you must specify the parent type to re-use and the name that the new DISTINCT TYPE is to have. Listing 4–34 illustrates several examples of DISTINCT type creation.

```
CREATE DISTINCT TYPE Quantity
     AS INTEGER;

CREATE DISTINCT TYPE GeoPoint
AS st_point;

CREATE DISTINCT TYPE Anniversary
     AS BirthDay;
```

Listing 4–34. *CREATE DISTINCT Type*

Instances of the DISTINCT TYPE Quantity defined above are stored, compared, added, sorted, and presented externally in exactly the same way that the SQL-92 INTEGER is. When you create an index over the Quantity type, IDS uses the Compare() function defined for the INTE-GER, and when you backup or unload the table, IDS uses that type's built-in infrastructure. Likewise, all spatial indexing facilities defined over the st_point type can be used with the GeoPoint type.

CAST and DISTINCT TYPEs

As part of the DISTINCT TYPE creation, the ORDBMS automatically installs a pair of EXPLICIT *casts* between the new type and it's parent. This mechanism is what permits the DISTINCT TYPE to re-use functions defined for parent type. This casting arrangement is quite powerful. In this sub-section, we explore the implications of using CAST with DIS-TINCT TYPE instances. Note that all of the principles introduced here apply equally to the other kinds of extensible types, too.

The first problem with the default casting is it performs no conversion or data integrity checks. For example, consider the example introduced in Listing 4–35. Instances of the Currency type can have a range of denominations while the Yen objects should be restricted to containing only Yen amounts. Unfortunately, calling the new type "Yen" doesn't make it so. By creating a cast conversion function to check that the new type is valid, developers can achieve the desired behavior.

By dropping the existing cast, and creating a new cast using the new conversion function, you instruct the ORDBMS to use this function whenever it turns an instance of a Currency type into an instance of the Yen DISTINCT TYPE.

```
CREATE DISTINCT TYPE USDollars
          AS Currency;

CREATE DISTINCT TYPE Yen
          AS Currency;

CREATE FUNCTION CurrencyToYen ( Arg1 Currency )
          RETURNING Yen
     RETURN Convert(Arg1, 'JPY');
END FUNCTION;

DROP CAST ( Currency AS Yen );

CREATE CAST ( Currency AS Yen WITH CurrencyToYen );
```

Listing 4–35. *Using CASTs to Enforce Data Type Integrity Rules*

A second problem is that the use of EXPLICIT casting means that OR-SQL requires the explicit casting or double-dot notation. Adding "::" to every query quickly becomes a pain, particularly in situations involving a DISTINCT TYPE of one of the built-in types. For example, in our first DISTINCT TYPE example we were creating several different kinds of INTEGER to model different unique identifiers. But with the default casting behavior, whenever a query includes a literal constant value for the new type it must be explicitly cast.

The way to overcome this problem is to make the casting from the parent instance to the DISTINCT TYPE IMPLICIT. We illustrate how this would be achieved in Listing 4–36.

```
DROP CAST ( Currency AS Yen );

CREATE IMPLICIT CAST ( Currency AS Yen WITH CurrencyToYen );
```

Listing 4–36. *Using Non-Default IMPLICIT Casting*

Note, however, that you should leave the cast from an instance of the DISTINCT TYPE to the parent EXPLICIT (which is the default). IMPLICIT casts both ways leads to the kind of ambiguous situation illustrated in Listing 4–29.

By default, no provision is made for casting between sibling types (DISTINCT TYPE instances with the same parent, such as Yen and USDollar in Listing 4–35). But of course, developers can define their own CAST between the two. In practice this is frequently useful. In the conversion function in Listing 4–37, we first cast the argument, which is in Yen, back to the shared parent, Currency, before converting the data to U.S. dollars and casting the result back into the USDollars type. The final step illustrates creating an EXPLICIT cast from one DISTINCT TYPE to its sibling.

```
CREATE FUNCTION Yen2USDollars ( Arg1 Yen)
RETURNING USDollars
    RETURN Convert (Arg1::Currency,'USD')::USDollars;
END FUNCTION;

CREATE CAST (
    Yen AS USDollars
    USING Yen2USDollars
);
```

Listing 4–37. *CREATE CAST Between Different DISTINCT Types of Same Parent*

For visually oriented readers, Figure 4–7 summarizes the relationships between the various types we have seen in this section. We have used three types: Currency, Yen, and USDollars. For the two DISTINCT TYPE extensions we have illustrated several user-defined functions associated with them. We have created a new SalesTax() function for the Yen DISTINCT TYPE and a new Equal() for the USDollar type, as shown in Figure 4–7.

You can change DISTINCT TYPE behaviors by overloading any of its parent type's functions, even if the parent is a built-in type. For example, you might want to define a new Equal() function for a DISTINCT TYPE like Yen. This new function overloads whatever "Equal" is defined for the parent type, as shown in Listing 4–38.

```
CREATE FUNCTION Equal ( Arg1 Yen, Arg2 Yen )
RETURNING boolean
    .
```

Listing 4–38. *User-Defined Function Overloading Parent's Behavior for DISTINCT Type*

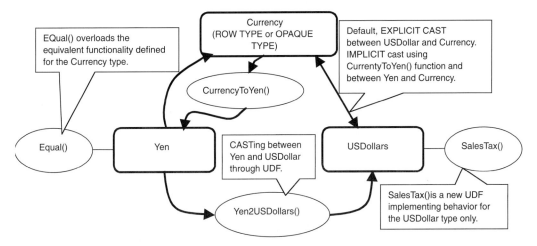

Figure 4–7. Diagrammatic Representation of ROW TYPE Hierarchy

Developers can extend DISTINCT TYPE behavior by writing new UDFs. For example, merchandise in different countries may be taxed differently. To model this, each DISTINCT TYPE of Currency can have a separate function to calculate its tax. In Listing 4–39 we use such a function to illustrate the idea.

```
CREATE FUNCTION SalesTax (Arg1 USDollars)
RETURNING USDollars
  RETURN Currency((GetQuantity(Arg1)*0.1),'USD')::USDollars;
END FUNCTION;
```

Listing 4–39. User-Defined SalesTax() Function for DISTINCT Type

The ORDBMS will generate an error if a developer tries to apply a function like this the one in Listing 4–40 on the Currency, or the Yen type. Providing the same behavior for the Yen type requires the addition of another UDF with the appropriate signature, SalesTax(Yen).

How does this look when used in OR-SQL? Because our Movies-R-Us Web site will have international appeal it might make sense to record loans or lines of credit extended to the Web site's managers by international merchandise manufacturers. One useful set of facts to record might concern the lines of credit extended by Japanese and U.S. companies. Two tables in Listing 4–40 record this information.

```
CREATE TABLE JapaneseLoans (
     Loan       Loan_Identifier        NOT NULL   PRIMARY KEY,
     Creditor   Company_Name           NOT NULL,
     Principal  Yen                    NOT NULL
);

CREATE TABLE USLoans (
     Loan       Loan_Identifier        NOT NULL   PRIMARY KEY,
     Creditor   Company_Name           NOT NULL,
     Principal  USDollars              NOT NULL
);
```

Listing 4–40. *Tables Using DISTINCT Type of Currency*

As values are inserted into these tables, the ORDBMS ensures that the types being inserted match the column types. Inserting a row therefore requires that you provide data of the appropriate types. Of the following two queries only the second will succeed. It explicitly casts the Currency instance created by the constructor function into an instance of the Yen DISTINCT TYPE, as shown in Listing 4–41.

```
INSERT INTO JapaneseLoans
VALUES
( '123456', 'Sony', Currency(100000.00,'JPY') );
--
--     This will succeed.
--

INSERT INTO JapaneseLoans
VALUES
( '123456', 'Sony', Currency(10000.00,'JPY')::Yen );
```

Listing 4–41. *INSERT Data into Tables with DISTINCT TYPE Column*

This kind of *strong typing* is applied in all queries. Although the DISTINCT TYPE inherits the behavior of the parent type, the same behaviors cannot be used when you mix a parent and a DISTINCT TYPE of it in a single expression. Consequently, of the two queries in Listing 4–42, only the second succeeds.

"Show me all Japanese loans greater than 50,000 yen."

```
--
--     This will fail.
--
SELECT J.Creditor,
       J.Principal
  FROM JapaneseLoans J
 WHERE J.Principal > Currency(10000.00,'JPY');
```

```
SELECT  J.Creditor,
        J.Principal
  FROM  JapaneseLoans J
 WHERE  J.Principal > Currency(10000.00,'JPY')::Yen;
```

creditor ::company_name Principal ::yen
Hitachi   ROW(JPY,100000.0000)

Listing 4–42. *Second Table and Query Illegally Comparing DISTINCT Type of Currency*

Relationships between extended data types, and the way the CAST mechanism works, seems quite complicated. In practice, however, the distinctions are usually fairly intuitive. The whole idea is to catch OR-SQL expressions that return insensible answers as soon as possible. Syntax errors indicate to the developer that their query made no semantic sense.

Using DISTINCT TYPEs

The DISTINCT TYPE approach is useful because it allows developers to create new data types with scarcely any effort. If a new type has very similar properties to something already implemented, then a DISTINCT TYPE is your best alternative. This type of situation motivated the Currency/Yen/USDollars example introduced in the previous section.

The disadvantage of DISTINCT TYPE is that you cannot add much semantic information to them. Developers cannot add extra elements to a new DISTINCT TYPE, and data integrity constraints—for example, if you wanted to ensure that Quantity was always a *positive* integer—must be implemented by changing the casting behavior between the parent and the new type.

ROW TYPE

A ROW TYPE combines a group of data elements under a single name. The resulting structure is similar in many ways to the structure of a row in a table. Each ROW TYPE attribute has a name, a data type, and may have a NOT NULL integrity constraint defined for it. In fact, one of the differences between the ROW TYPE mechanism and other extensible types is that a ROW TYPE can be used to define the new table's structures.

Any of the ORDBMS's variety of data type mechanisms can be used to define an element within a ROW TYPE. This means that, ultimately, every ROW TYPE is constructed out of a combination of built-in or OPAQUE TYPE. (Note that a DISTINCT TYPE is also composed ultimately out of either a built-in or OPAQUE TYPE.) So to facilitate communication, backup and recovery for a ROW TYPE the ORDBMS combines the low-level support routines implemented for these fundamental "encapsulated" types. For similar reasons, each ROW TYPE internal (on disk) size is equal to the sum of the sizes of its elements.

Several properties of a ROW TYPE distinguishes it from other UDT mechanisms. The most important of these relates to how the ORDBMS processes queries involving table columns that contain ROW TYPE data. Query operations requiring support functions— such as sorting, indexing, SELECT DISTINCT, UNION, and so on—cannot operate on a ROW TYPE. In other words, you cannot ORDER BY a ROW TYPE column, nor write a UNION query where one of the results columns is a ROW TYPE (although UNION ALL is acceptable). This is simply a deficiency in the current implementation. Over time, the limitation will be lifted.

Creating ROW TYPEs

Listing 4–43 illustrates both the general form of how a ROW TYPE is created and a simple example.

```
CREATE ROW TYPE Type_Name (
     Element_Name   Data_Type      [ NOT NULL ]
     {, Element_Name        Data_Type [ NOT NULL ] }

);


CREATE ROW TYPE PersonName (
     Family_Name      ShortString     NOT NULL,
     First_Name       ShortString     NOT NULL,
     Title            Title_Enum      NOT NULL,
     OtherNames       ShortString
);
```

Listing 4–43. *General Form of CREATE ROW TYPE and Example*

More formally, if you have any group of data types $T_{[1..n]}$, then the creation of a ROW TYPE involves the naming of a new type T_m that has as components the types $T_{[1..n]}$, named $N_{[1..n]}$. The type's name, and the names of its elements, must all be valid OR-SQL identifiers and element names in $N_{[1...n]}$ must be unique.

In Listing 4–44, ShortString is a DISTINCT TYPE, the Title _Enum attribute uses an OPAQUE TYPE. And, of course, a ROW TYPE can be used within another ROW TYPE as we demonstrate in Listing 4–44. Also in Listing 4–44 we illustrate the way that

NOT NULL constraints can be enforced over attributes of a ROW TYPE. The IDS product validates that ROW TYPE instances have appropriately typed data values in all NOT NULL elements. Other integrity rules need to be enforced in the UDF constructor functions for the type.

Deploying ROW TYPEs in an ORDBMS Schema

A ROW TYPE can be used like any other kind of user-defined data type. They can be used to define a table column's type, or an element in another ROW TYPE, or as an argument to a user-defined function, or as a variable in an SPL routine. In addition, a ROW TYPE can be used to define the column structure of a table, as we saw in Chapter 2. We illustrate the various uses for an ROW TYPE in Listing 4–44.

```
CREATE ROW TYPE MovieClub_Member_T (
      Id                  Membership_Num    NOT NULL,
      Name                PersonName        NOT NULL,
      DOB                 date,
      Address             Address_Type      NOT NULL,
      HomePhone           PhoneNumber       NOT NULL,
      Location            GeoPoint          NOT NULL,
      Preferences         SET(Genre_Enum    NOT NULL),
      Photo               Image,
      CreditCard          CCDetails
);

CREATE TABLE MovieClub
OF TYPE MovieClub_Member_T
( Primary Key ( Id ) );

CREATE FUNCTION Age ( Arg1 MovieClub_Member_T )
RETURNS INTEGER
      RETURN (( TODAY - Arg1.DOB ) / 365.241);
END FUNCTION;
```

Listing 4–44. *General Form of CREATE ROW TYPE and Examples of Use*

Attributes of a ROW TYPE are not encapsulated. They can be addressed using *cascading dot notation* in both OR-SQL statements and in SPL routines. For example, the query in Listing 4–45 illustrates how elements within a column of the `MovieClubMembers` table are addressed. The target list of the query illustrates how to use cascading dot notation to address the Surname element of the PersonName row type within the `MovieClubMembers` table.

"Show me family names of all Californians with American Express credit cards."

```
SELECT M.Name.Family_Name
  FROM MovieClubMembers M
 WHERE M.Address.State = 'California'
   AND M.CreditCard.Type = 'AMX'::CardType_Enum;
```

Listing 4–45. *Cascading-Dot Notation to Address ROW TYPE Elements*

Cascading dot notation is recursive. If an element within the column's ROW TYPE is itself a ROW TYPE then its sub-elements can also be accessed in this way. For example, the expression in Listing 4–46 addresses the Major ZipCode element within the Address column (MailAddress ROW TYPE) within the MovieClubMembers table.

```
MovieClubMembers.Address.ZipCode.Major
```

Listing 4–46. *SQL Fragment Illustrating Recursive Nature of Cascading-Dot Notation*

Cascading dot notation can also be used to separate sttributes within a ROW TYPE instance returned from a user-defined function. Recall that in the ORDBMS we adopt a more object oriented point of view; wherever possible, we smear over the differences between computational results and data values. For example, in the query in Listing 4–47, we re-use a UDF, `BirthDate()`, that is a constructor method for the BirthDate ROW TYPE created in Figure 4–31.

```
SELECT BirthDate(M.DOB).*,
       Print(M.Name) AS Name
  FROM MovieClubMembers M
 WHERE BirthDate(M.DOB).FromLeapYear;
```

Mmonth	Dday	fromleapyear	name
3	2	True	Mira Freyenbauger
3	2	True	Joe Blogs
5	24	True	Paul Brown
3	2	True	George Eliot

Listing 4–47. *Cascading-Dot Notation and User-Defined Function Example*

Note that there is a dark side to this syntax. Mention a UDF more than once in an OR-SQL statement, and the ORDBMS's query processor will execute it more than once.

ROW TYPE Constructors

OR-SQL includes a general mechanism for creating ROW TYPE instances on the fly. This syntax creates an instance of what is known as an *unnamed ROW TYPE*. Unnamed ROW TYPE data values have structure and data, but are not identified as being any an instance of any particular ROW TYPE recorded in the system catalogs.

Listing 4–48 provides four examples that use the ROW TYPE constructor syntax. Any NULL values in the unnamed ROW TYPE need to be listed explicitly, and each of them should be typed. Note that the second two examples CAST from an unnamed to a named ROW TYPE.

```
ROW ( 'Freyenbauger','Mira','Ms','')

ROW ( '1000 Heart St',NULL::ShortString,
      'PALO ALTO', 'CA',
      ROW(94304,NULL::INTEGER)::ZipCode,
      'USA' )
--
--   In the following examples the unnamed ROW TYPEs created
--   above are CAST into named ROW TYPEs. This use of the
--   CAST functionality is a bit different from what is
--   described earlier in this chapter. It is completely
--   automatic, and cannot be modified through a UDF.
--
ROW ( 'Freyenbauger','Mira','Ms','')::PersonName

ROW ( '1000 Heart St',NULL::ShortString,
  'PALO ALTO', 'CA',
  ROW(94304,NULL::INTEGER)::ZipCode,
      'USA' )::MailAddress
```

Listing 4–48. *General Purpose ROW TYPE Constructor Examples*

This technique creates instances of a ROW TYPE to server as a constant value in an OR-SQL query or in SPL code. Generalized ROW TYPE constructors are, however, limited in some ways. First, creating a ROW TYPE using this technique requires that the query provide a data value—or a NULL—for every element. Second, it is difficult to enforce data integrity rules on the elements within the ROW TYPE.

A useful approach to the problem of constructing ROW TYPE instances is to create specialized constructor functions that allow an OR-SQL programmer to leave out certain, assumed or calculated values. For example, the two in Listing 4–49 each illustrates an instance of a PersonName ROW TYPE constructor UDF.

```
CREATE FUNCTION PersonName ( argFamily_Name lvarchar,
                             argFirst_Name  lvarchar,
                             argTitle       lvarchar,
                             argOtherNames  lvarchar)
RETURNING PersonName;
    IF ((argTitle IS NOT NULL) AND
        (NOT validTitle_Enum ( argTitle ))) THEN
        RAISE EXCEPTION -746,0,
                "PersonName: Invalid Title";
    END IF;
    IF (( argFamily_Name IS NULL) OR
        ( argFirst_Name IS NULL )) THEN
        RAISE EXCEPTION -746,0,
        "PersonName: Family_Name,First_Name cannot be NULL";
    END IF;

    RETURN ROW(argFamily_Name,argFirst_Name,
               argTitle,argOtherNames)::PersonName;
END FUNCTION;

CREATE FUNCTION PersonName ( Arg1 lvarchar, Arg2 lvarchar )
RETURNING PersonName;
    RETURN ROW(Arg1,Arg2,"","")::PersonName;
END FUNCTION;
```

Listing 4–49. *Multiple Constructor Functions for ROW TYPE*

Constructor functions such as the one in Listing 4–49 are very useful. To a degree, they encapsulate the structure of the ROW TYPE, making it possible to evolve the type's definition without having to rewrite an OR-SQL that involves the type. Also, any integrity rules to be applied to the UDT can be enforced within them.

Inheritance and ROW TYPES

Multiple ROW TYPE instances can be created in an inheritance hierarchy. Using inheritance developers can create a new ROW TYPE that reuses the properties and behavior of the parent ROW TYPE. Unlike the

DISTINCT TYPE mechanism, the new type can be augmented with additional structural elements. When a new ROW TYPE is created under another, it inherits

- all elements making up the parent ROW TYPE
- constraints (NOT NULL) defined in the parent ROW TYPE
- the behaviors (user-defined functions) defined of the parent ROW TYPE

Formally, in a ROW TYPE inheritance hierarchy, a given ROW TYPE T_n with an attribute list $A_{[1..i]}$ can be re-used in the definition of a number of a number of new ROW TYPE instances $T_{[n+1...m]}$. Each of these new types has at least the same attribute set $A_{[1..i]}$, and they may each be extended with additional attributes $A_{[i+1..j]}$.

By convention, the parent ROW TYPE is known as the *supertype*, and types declared under others are known as *subtypes*. The subtype's declaration specifies any new attributes and uses the UNDER keyword to indicate its parent type. For example, Listing 4–50 illustrates how to create a ROW TYPE hierarchy.

```
CREATE ROW TYPE Merchandise_T (
        Id                 Part_Code      NOT NULL,
        Name               VARCHAR(32)    NOT NULL,
        Movie              Movie_Id       NOT NULL,
        Description        lvarchar       NOT NULL,
        Price              Currency       NOT NULL,
        Ship_Handling      Currency       NOT NULL,
        Qty_Avail          INTEGER        NOT NULL
);

CREATE ROW TYPE Apparel_Type (
        Kind               Clothing_Enum NOT NULL,
        Sizes              SET(Size_Enum NOT NULL),
        Photo              Image
) UNDER Merchandise_T;

CREATE ROW TYPE Toy_Type (
     Kind           ToyKind_Enum      NOT NULL,
     Age_Range      Age_Range         NOT NULL,
     Photo          Image             NOT NULL
) UNDER Merchandise_T;
```

Listing 4–50. *Creating a ROW TYPE Hierarchy*

Listing 4–51 illustrates what the entire structure of the Apparel_Type definition from our Movies-R-Us web site database looks like. This type gets it first seven elements from the `Merchandise_T` adding three more as part of its definition.

```
Id             Part_Code     NOT NULL,
Name           VARCHAR(32)   NOT NULL,
Movie          Movie_Id      NOT NULL,
Description    lvarchar      NOT NULL,
Price          Currency      NOT NULL,
Ship_Handling  Currency      NOT NULL,
Qty_Avail      INTEGER       NOT NULL,
Kind           Clothing_Enum NOT NULL,
Sizes          SET(Size_Enum NOT NULL),
Photo          Image
```

Listing 4–51. *Complete Structure of the Apparel_Type ROW TYPE*

The inheritance scheme implemented by the ORDBMS uses single inheritance (subtypes may only have a single supertype). There is no practical limit to the number of sub-types a ROW TYPE can have, nor to the depth of a hierarchy. ROW TYPE instances are, however, limited by the number of bytes a table row can contain.

User-Defined Functions and ROW TYPE Inheritance

Subtypes also inherit all behavior defined for their supertype. In other words, any functions defined for the supertype can also be used with the subtype. Developers can add new functions to the ones that a sub-type inherits from its supertype, and overload—change the functionality—of a supertype's function. In Listing 4–52 we create several UDFs that apply to types in the hierarchy defined in Listing 4–50.

```
CREATE FUNCTION BriefDescription ( Arg1 Merchandise_T )
RETURNING lvarchar;
    RETURN 'Merchandise: ' || Arg1.Name::lvarchar;
END FUNCTION;

CREATE FUNCTION BriefDescription ( Arg1 Apparel_Type )
RETURNING lvarchar;
DEFINE szRetString lvarchar;
    DEFINE seVar Size_Enum;
    DEFINE stSizes SET(Size_Enum NOT NULL);
    DEFINE blFirst boolean;
LET blFirst = 't';
```

```
        LET stSizes = Arg1.Sizes;
        FOREACH cursor1 FOR
            SELECT * INTO seVar FROM TABLE(stSizes)
                    IF ( blFirst = 't') THEN
                        LET szRetString = seVar;
                        LET blFirst = 'f';
                    ELSE
                        LET szRetString = szRetString || ', ' ||
                                          seVar::lvarchar;
                    END IF;
            END FOREACH;
            RETURN 'Apparel: ' || Arg1.Name::lvarchar || ' - ' ||
                    Arg1.Kind::lvarchar || ' available in sizes {'
                    || szRetString || '}';
        END FUNCTION;
```

Listing 4–52. *Polymorphic Functions and ROW TYPE Hierarchy*

If the `BriefDescription()` function is invoked and passed an instance of a `Merchandise_T` data type as its argument, then the behavior is explicitly defined. If you run it over the `Apparel_Type`, the ORDBMS knows to use the second function defined in Listing 4–52, because it too is explicitly defined over the type. But what if the `BriefDescription()` function is invoked and passed an instance of the `Toy_Type` data type?

When this happens, the type inheritance mechanism kicks in. Failing to find a perfect match for the UDF in its system catalogs the ORDBMS looks to see if a matching function exists for types *above* it in its inheritance hierarchy (assuming it is part of one). So in this case, the ORDBMS will invoke the `BriefDescription()` function defined to take `Merchandise_T` as a parameter, but it passes into it an instance of the `Toy_Type` instead. This works because while the subtype can extend its supertype's definition with extra elements it cannot remove any. Therefore, any function that uses elements of the supertype will have these elements available to it in the subtype.

As we saw in the earlier description of the DISTINCT TYPE mechanism, additional behaviors can be defined for subtypes. Listing 4–53 presents a user-defined function that checks if a toy is suitable for someone born on a particular date.

```
        CREATE FUNCTION SuitableFor ( argToy Toy_Type, argDOB DATE )
        RETURNS boolean
            DEFINE nYearsOld INTEGER;
            LET nYearsOld = ( TODAY - argDOB ) / 365.241;
```

```
              IF (( argToy.Suitable_For.Youngest <= nYearsOld ) AND
                  ( argToy.Suitable_For.Oldest   >= nYearsOld )) THEN
                  RETURN 't'::boolean;
              END IF;
              RETURN 't'::boolean;
          END FUNCTION;
```

Listing 4–53. *New Behavior and ROW TYPE Hierarchy*

For the more visually oriented, Figure 4–8 presents a diagrammatic overview of the complete hierarchy of the ROW TYPE examples in this section and the functions that implement their behavior.

In the next chapter we explore in detail how the ORDBMS decides which user-defined function to invoke as it processes an OR-SQL query. The algorithm allows for completely dynamic function invocation and it is quite complicated. What it makes possible, however, is for developers to invoke a function within the logic implementing another, and allow the ORDBMS to search the type hierarchy to find the appropriate function. This can lead to subtle complexities. For example, consider the type hierarchy illustrated in Figure 4–9.

First, consider what happens where only the functions drawn with solid lines exist. When you invoke the function F(Second_Sub), the ORDBMS actually uses F(First_Sub), because that is the closest function it can find to the one nominated. Within the implementation of the F(First_Sub) logic, the ORDBMS encounters a call to G(Second_Sub). Again, it examines the inheritance hierarchy and chooses G(First_Sub).

But consider the second case, where the hierarchy include a G(Second_Sub) function (the one with the dotted line) . As part of its execution of F(Second_Sub)—which again is resolved as F(First_Sub)—the ORDBMS will actually run G(Second_Sub)!

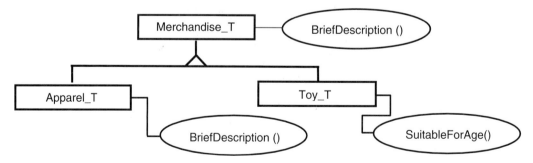

Figure 4–8. *Diagrammatic Representation of ROW TYPE Hierarchy*

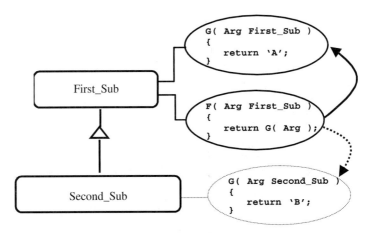

Figure 4–9. *Alternatives for Storing COLLECTION Data*

This seems like a fairly obvious result. But in situations where the inheritance hierarchy is many layers deep, determining exactly which function is being invoked becomes difficult.

While ROW TYPE hierarchies can be used to construct table hierarchies, and different ROW TYPE instances can be used in different tables, the schema declaration imposes a *strong typing* discipline on ROW TYPE usage. This means that a subtype cannot be substituted for a supertype in a table's column.

```
CREATE ROW TYPE CCDetails (
        Type     CardType_Enum    NOT NULL,
        Number   CardNumber       NOT NULL,
        Expiry   CardExpiry       NOT NULL
);


CREATE ROW TYPE CCWithLimit (
        Limit    Currency         NOT NULL
) UNDER CCDetails;
```

Listing 4–54. *Small ROW TYPE Inheritance Hierarchy*

The CCDetails type created in Listing 4–54 is used in the MovieClub_Member_T ROW TYPE and the MovieClubMembers table defined from it. The strong typing discipline means that an instance of the CCLimit type cannot be inserted into the CCDetails column of the MovieClubMembers table. Should a query attempt to do so, IDS will generate an exception.

Using ROW TYPEs

A ROW TYPE is necessary whenever tables are created in an inheritance hierarchy. When it is possible to compute a value from a group of column values within a table and it is desirable to encapsulate the calculation within a UDF—as we saw in Listing 4–53—using a ROW TYPE to define even a single table can be useful. But because it is impossible to apply ALTER TABLE commands over typed tables, it is difficult to modify them once they are in place.

Unfortunately, the limitations the ORDBMS places on operations like sorting and indexing ROW TYPE columns are crippling. At this time, it is best to avoid using the ROW TYPE mechanism for types that will be used in a table's columns. Many of the examples in this section—PersonName and CreditCard—are better off done as a DISTINCT TYPE or OPAQUE TYPE. In the Java tutorial (Tutorial 4), we give an example of how to implement the PersonName type using this approach.

The ROW TYPE mechanism is, however, effective for columns that do not need indexing, or for data types used in database stored procedures. Also, restrictions on the ROW TYPE are solely the result of IDS product engineering priorities. Over time expect that this mechanism will be brought into line with the other extended types. Consult your product documentation: perhaps by the time you read this they already have.

OPAQUE TYPE

OPAQUE TYPE is the final mechanism for integrating new object classes into the database. This UDT mechanism distinguishes INFORMIX's IDS from all other Object-Relational products. New OPAQUE TYPE instances are completely independent of any pre-existing type in the ORDBMS. The intention is to provide developers with the ability to embed completely new user-defined types of arbitrary size and complexity. In short, an OPAQUE TYPE is whatever you need it to be.

Unlike the ROW TYPE, an OPAQUE TYPE structure is fully encapsulated. So far as disk storage and caching is concerned, the ORDBMS treats an OPAQUE TYPE instance as an array of bytes, without caring as to what the bytes mean. To access its internal state or to manipulate it OR-SQL developers must invoke the user-defined functions defined for the OPAQUE TYPE. The most that you can say formally about the OPAQUE TYPE mechanism is that it represents the introduction of some new type ,T_v.

The OPAQUE TYPE represents the most fundamental kind of database extensibility, which makes them especially powerful. You can implement literally *any* kind of data object as an OPAQUE TYPE. When you buy a commercial DataBlade product providing geographic points and polygons, multiple image formats, video and audio digital recording, molecular chemistry and so on, you will be using this mechamism.

Creating OPAQUE Types

Developers specify the internal structure of a new OPAQUE TYPE using a C structure. The ORDBMS stores the bytes making up object instances, and passes this data into the user-defined functions implementing the type's behavior. However, this internal structure is not visible to end-users or even to the ORDBMS itself, hence the name opaque. You cannot use cascading dot notation to access an OPAQUE TYPE's elements. In fact, even the ORDBMS itself cannot pry the type apart during query processing.

Unlike other data types, the ORDBMS can infer very little about the innards of an OPAQUE TYPE. But to manage instances of the type, the server needs information like the number of bytes of space that the type uses—if it is of fixed length—or the maximum size of the type—if it is of variable length. Additional information, supplied with a series of optional modifiers, can be used by the ORDBMS to improve its storage and data processing efficiency. All of this information is specified as part of the CREATE OPAQUE TYPE command, the general form of which is shown in Listing 4–55.

```
CREATE OPAQUE TYPE Type_Name (
      Internallength = [ integer | 'variable' ]
                       [ { ,Modifier } ]
);
```

Listing 4–55. *General Form of the CREATEOPAQUE TYPE DDL Statement*

OPAQUE TYPE internal length depends on how it is defined in C. For example, if you define a new OPAQUE TYPE that has an internal C structure such as the one shown in Listing 4–56, you can tell that the structure will always be exactly eight bytes long. This is the number you give the ORDBMS for the internal length in the CREATE OPAQUE TYPE statement. For fixed length types, the value to use is the value returned from the standard C library function sizeof().

```
/*
**   'C' typedef defining the structure of an OPAQUE type to
**   implement the T-SQL 'Period' data type. Note that the
**   mi_date type's definition is handled by the ORDBMS. Each
**   mi_date takes up four bytes of storage. (They are
**   actually integer days since 1899-12-31.)
*/
typedef struct
{
    mi_date          start;
    mi_date          finish;
} Period;


--
--   This is the SQL DDL statement that tells the ORDBMS
--   about the new 'Period' OPAQUE TYPE. The ORDBMS will
--   always allocate eight bytes of memory or disk to store
--   instances of this type.
--
CREATE OPAQUE TYPE Period
(        internallength = 8   );
```

Listing 4–56. *OPAQUE TYPE Using C Typedef to Calculate internallength*

The length of some objects varies from instance to instance. Movie titles are an example of such an object. For a variable length OPAQUE TYPE you substitute a special `variable` keyword instead of the constant INTEGER value.

By default, the ORDBMS allocates 2048 bytes of space on disk pages to hold instances of a variable length OPAQUE TYPE. If the data object is larger than 2048 bytes—but less than 32474 bytes—IDS adjusts accordingly. But by default it never allocates less space to instances of the OPAQUE TYPE that are smaller than 2048 bytes. 2K is clearly excessive for objects like movie titles, so a variable length OPAQUE TYPE declaration can also provide a maximum length value. This value becomes the number of bytes of space that the ORDBMS reserves on data pages. An appropriate maximum length of an OPAQUE TYPE is an important design decision.

Variable length OPAQUE TYPE extensions are declared as we show in Listing 4–57. To ensure that no movie title object exceeds the maximum pre-allocated length any C code that constructs an instance of the type should check the length before returning it to the ORDBMS.

```
/*
**   The mi_lvarchar 'C' data type is also implemented
**   with the ORDBMS. We discuss how this type is used
**   at length in chapter ten.
**/
```

```
typedef title_type mi_lvarchar;

--
-- This is the SQL CREATE OPAQUE TYPE command that
-- specifies the length (variable), the maximum length
-- and the appropriate alignment of the Title data type.
--
CREATE OPAQUE TYPE Title(
        internallength = variable,
        maxlen     = 255,
        alignment = 1
);
```

Listing 4–57. *OPAQUE TYPE Example with Variable Length and One-Byte Alignment*

Variable length OPAQUE TYPES objects can be up to 32 kilobytes in length. This limit is imposed because OPAQUE TYPE instances will be stored in table rows. If an instance of the type will be larger than this—for example Video data, Polygons, etc—then the data must be stored in specialist large-object spaces. Only a *large-object handle*, which is a smaller fixed length value, is kept in the table as a reference to the actual data. This means that you might end up declaring a large, variable length data objects as fixed length OPAQUE TYPE instances.

OPAQUE TYPE Modifiers

There are four OPAQUE TYPE modifiers—in addition to internallength—used to give the ORDBMS additional information. These are listed in Table 4–5.

Table 4–5. OPAQUE TYPE Modifiers and Meanings

Modifier	Explanation
MAXLEN	For variable length types, this modifier tells the ORDBMS what the maximum length of the type is to be. This information is used by the ORDBMS's page management facilities to ensure that there is always enough room on a data page to UPDATE an OPAQUE TYPE instance.
CANNOTHASH	Most data types are bit-hashable. This means that a general hashing algorithm can be applied in GROUP BY operations or hash joins. For some types, however, this is not the case. For example, types where the result of functions such as Equal() varies with time. Also, the built-in hashing functions may not be the best ones to use with the new type. Use this modifier to tell the ORDBMS that the type cannot be hashed with the built-in algorithm and must instead use one supplied by the type developer.

(continued)

Table 4–5. OPAQUE TYPE Modifiers and Meanings (continued)

ALIGNMENT	Depending on the internal structure of the OPAQUE TYPE, it may be possible to pack data values onto pages a little tighter than simply aligning the objects on four byte boundaries. The value that is supplied with this modifier tells the ORDBMS how it can pack the object on the one-, two-, four- or eight-byte boundary.
PASSEDBYVALUE	Depending on the size of the object, it may be better to pass instances of the object into user-defined functions by reference or by value. By default, all objects are passed by reference (pointer). Objects are passed by value if they are up to four bytes of fixed length and this modifier is supplied with the type creation.

This information is kept in the system catalogs. As it processes OR-SQL queries the ORDBMS consults these tables to ensure the correctness of what it plans to do. Over time, as the ORDBMS adds new capabilities, this list will expand.

How OPAQUE TYPE Data is Managed

The individual bytes making up OPAQUE TYPE instances are stored on data pages just as built-in data type values were in a SQL-92 RDBMS. This leverages all of the data management facilities of the ORDBMS: data caching, locking, logging, and so on. We illustrate the basic idea in Figure 4–10. On the right is the detailed page layout of a single page. Overall, the figure represents the page as an array of single bytes. Thick lines separate individual records, and the columns within each record are labeled.

```
CREATE TABLE Disk_Page_Example (
     First_Column          VARCHAR(11)      NOT NULL,
     Second_Column         Period           NOT NULL
);
```

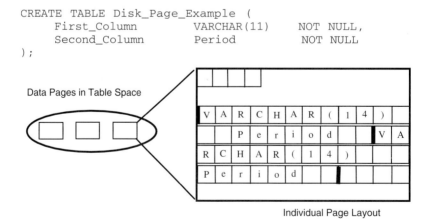

Individual Page Layout

Figure 4–10. *Management of OPAQUE TYPE Data in Table's Data Pages*

User-defined functions implementing behavior for the type are passed OPAQUE TYPE bytes—or pointers to arrays of bytes—as arguments. Handling data in this way encourages designs that are strongly encapsulated. Ideally, all of the host language logic—C or Java— that implements OPAQUE TYPE functionality ought to be contained within a single source code file.

Large-Object OPAQUE Types

When an OPAQUE TYPE is too large to be stored within a table's row the ORDBMS stores the data in *smart large-object* (SBLOB) data spaces. Only a large-object handle or reference to that data is placed in the row. When a user-defined function needs to deal with the actual large-object data—for example, to search inside a Video for a particular frame—the code within the function must employ a set of SAPI routines that know hot to use this handle.

Large-Object Handles (LO Handles) are a fixed length array of character data. The exact size of an LO Handle is platform specific, so programmers should use the C macro named MI_LO_SIZE or the MI_LO_HANDLE structure when allocating memory to hold one. In Listing 4–58, we present the C structure and declaration of an OPAQUE TYPE for Sun's Solaris™ platform that contains a large-object reference.

```
/*
**      This 'C' structure defines the layout of the large
**      object OPAQUE TYPE. Note how it has a single data
**      element - the handle. Large object handles are
**      generated by the ORDBMS at the time that the large
**      object is created.
*/
typedef struct
{
        MI_LO_HANDLE     data;
} Video_t;


--
-- This is the SQL CREATE OPAQUE TYPE DDL command for the
-- OPAQUE TYPE. Note that there is nothing about this
-- declaration to indicate that what is stored here is
-- actually a large object type.
--
CREATE OPAQUE TYPE Video
(    INTERNALLENGTH = 72       );
```

Listing 4–58. *OPAQUE TYPE Structure and Definition for Large-Object Type*

Handling large-object data in this way has several consequences. First, while all of the large object's raw data is stored separately from the row object's location, the row object can still contain a summary or characterization of the row. For example, most of the spatial DataBlades store a polygon's bounding box or central reference with the LO_Handle in the row. This allows the logic in the function to perform a quick, initial check before going to the trouble of accessing the entire array of bytes.

Second, the large object handle mechanism allows several different rows in the database to contain references to the same block of data stored in a SBLOB space. This is done to prevent an explosion of storage space requirements. If each row value corresponded to a single, unique large-object instance rather than having (possibly multiple) handles to each LO, the amount of storage space required would be considerably increased, as shown in Listing 4–59.

"Insert all the videos in the temporary load table into the Video_Samples table."

```
CREATE TABLE Video_Sample_Temp
OF TYPE Video_Sample_Type;

INSERT INTO Video_Samples
SELECT TV.Id,              TV.Name,
       TV.Movie,           TV.Description,
       TV.Price,           TV.ShippingCost,
       TV.NumberAvailable, TV.Kind,
       TV.Video
  FROM Video_Sample_Temp;
```

Listing 4–59. *Query Duplicating many Large Objects*

This `INSERT` query copies data rows from a temporary table into the `Video_Samples` table. As part of this operation, the LO Handles in the temporary table are duplicated in the `Video_Samples` table. However, the large video data itself is not copied, only the handle. Creating a second, different copy of the actual LO data requires a user-defined function, similar to the `LOCopy()` built-in expression, specifically created for the task.

In fact, several different type instances can refer to different sections of a single large object. For example, a single Video object might be referred to by multiple Scene objects. Each Scene stores the large object to which it refers, and the offset and duration within that data at which it is to be found.

Internally, IDS maintains a count of the rows referencing each LO instance. When you delete a row that includes a large-object data type, the ORDBMS checks that large-object reference count. If the reference count is greater than one, the ORDBMS decrements it. If the reference count is one, IDS increments it to zero and marks the space used by the LO data as eligible for re-use. We present the overall idea in Figure 4–11.

Multiple users can be changing data concurrently in different parts of a single large object. For example, several users can be working on different parts of the same Video object. These changes are made with the same transactional guarantees that apply over row data. Users are prevented from overwriting other's "in progress" changes with a *byte-range locking* mechanism. If a user terminate a set of changes unexpectedly, the large object's state reverts to what it was before the changes began.

Of course, allowing multiple rows to reference a single large object has a serious drawback. By invoking user-defined functions on what are apparently two different data objects two users can modify the same block of byes. For example, in the Video storage example we described earlier, if one user edits a single scene within a Video than another user who extracts the entire Video will find that it contains the modified scene! Developers should be aware of this behavior when designing applications. Large object copies must be explicit: SQL's INSERT as SELECT was only intended to work for COBOL types.

Multi-Representational OPAQUE Types

A multi-representational OPAQUE TYPE (multi-rep types) is the third and final OPAQUE TYPE pattern we describe. It is intended to solve the problem of data objects that are variable in size from a few bytes up to many gigabytes.

Consider again the polygon type, used to store national or state boundaries. At one extreme, it needs to cope with countries, such as Norway, that have intricate coastlines. On the other hand, land-locked nations such as Chad have boundaries following latitude/longitude lines. The number of points in the polygon describing Norway's outline is quite large while the number of points for Chad is relatively tiny. For this important class of data type the size of the object is extremely variable. Sometimes, it makes sense to store it in the row. Sometimes, you have no choice but to store it as a large object.

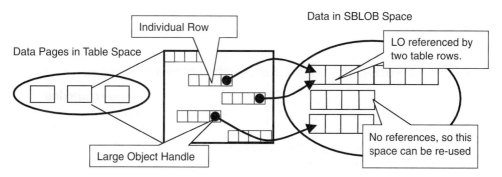

Figure 4–1. *Large-Object Handles and Large Object Management*

Multi-representational types are intended to overcome this problem. When the size of the data stored in this type is less than some thresh-hold size which is determined by the type's implementation, the data itself is stored in the table page. When the object's size exceeds the thresh-hold, it is stored in the smart blob space and the LO handle is stored with in the record. In Listing 4–60, we illustrate what a multi-rep type structure looks like in C.

```
/*
**    'C' structure for storing polygon data. The two
**    attributes 'flags' and 'data' are used to abstract
**    away how the data is stored. If the data is less
**    than some thresh-hold then it will be found in the
**    data. If it exceeds the thresh-hold then an LO_HANDLE
**    will be stored there instead. In the code that uses
**    this type, you need to use some ORDBMS facilities to
**    'pin' the large object data into the structure.
*/
typedef struct
{
mi_integer                Npnts; /*How many points?    */
     MI_MULTIREP_SIZE     Flag;  /*Is large object or not*/
     Box                  BBox;  /* bounding box        */
     MI_MULTIREP_DATA      data;
} Polygon;

-- And this is the SQL.Note that the type's internal length
-- is variable because the size of the object varies. This
-- is only fixed whenever the actual polygon data is stored
-- in the SBLOB spaces.
--
CREATE OPAQUE TYPE Polygon(
     internallength = variable,
     alignment = 8,
     maxlen    = 128
);
```

Listing 4–60. *Multi-Representational OPAQUE Data Type*

Multi-representational types are the most complicated OPAQUE TYPE to create. As you can see from this example, developing such types involves a couple of server facilities provided to cope with their unusual nature.

Using OPAQUE TYPEs

Taken by itself, an OPAQUE TYPE is pretty useless. Unlike the other kinds of user-defined type each OPAQUE TYPE comes into existence without any supporting utilities, and depends utterly on user-defined functions to implement its behavior. OR-SQL developers cannot create new instances of an OPAQUE TYPE or interrogate one about its contents (as they can with a COLLECTION or ROW TYPE), compare one of them with another instances of itself, index, modify, back up, or load and unload them (as they can with the built-in types). Every use for an OPAQUE TYPE requires an EXTERNAL UDF.

The OPAQUE TYPE mechanism is redeemed, however, because it is extreme flexibility and because it provided the very best performance. Because developers can control the structure of the type from a single bit level all the way up to giga-byte object, and because they can access these structures using logic written in low-level languages, an OPAQUE TYPE can be made to do whatever is required.

DataBlade products make extensive use of the OPAQUE TYPE mechanism. Often, the algorithms and data structures DataBlades use are highly complex and it has taken a software company with years of experience working in the subject area to perfect. Such vendors can use the OPAQUE TYPE mechanism to create their extensions, compile them into libraries, and ship the product without worrying about revealing their trade secrets. This makes the OPAQUE TYPE mechanism attractive to them.

Administration of User-Defined Types

In this final section of Chapter 4 we focus on how the various extensible type mechanisms interact with other aspects of the ORDBMS like security, bulk data management, backup, and recovery. With conventional RDBMSs, the server software, being aware of how all built-in types are structured, implements these automatically. But with an ORDBMS there are additional considerations.

Security Administration

User-defined types are schema objects that, like tables, can be shared by several users. Therefore the ORDBMS includes a set of security features to control the use of these types. The approach is very similar to the security scheme enforced for other schema objects. Depending on the mode in which the database is created, the ORDBMS makes an initial assumption about user privileges over a new type and only the type's creator or the database administrator can change user privileges. In Listing 4–61 we introduce the general syntax used to grant usage permissions on a new type and an example of its use.

```
GRANT USAGE ON TYPE [ Type_Identifier ] TO [ User or Role ];

GRANT USAGE ON TYPE Quantity TO PUBLIC;

GRANT USAGE ON TYPE Order_Line_Item_T TO PUBLIC;
```

Listing 4–61. *GRANTing Privileges on New Data Types*

Without appropriate permission, developers and end users are prevented from executing OR-SQL containing any reference to the new type. Such explicit granting of usage privileges on types is an important difference between RDBMSs and ORDBMSs. Permissions can be revoked with a symmetric REVOKE operation. We illustrate this in Listing 4–62.

```
REVOKE USAGE ON TYPE Quantity FROM PUBLIC;
```

Listing 4–62. *REVOKE Privileges on Data Type*

It is generally a good idea to GRANT USAGE on all the types you create. Traditionally all IDS users possessed full permissions on all data types because they were built-into the DBMS, although they couldn't do much with them. So for backward compatibility, GRANT and REVOKE privileges do not apply to the built-in types.

Bulk Loading and Unloading

All DBMSs possess utilities for loading and unloading large amounts of data from an external data source. Unloading data produces a file (or files) containing all data in the nominated database table, formatted in a standard way. SQL-92 databases use mechanisms as simple as a delimitered file where each row produced by a SELECT query corresponds to a line in the file, and each column's data is separated by a special character, often a tab. Developers moving data into the database have the ability to format load data according to the standard rules and simply employ the load utility to append the data to a table.

With the ORDBMS, the standard load format has been enhanced to cater to the extended type system. In Listing 4–63, we illustrate the contents of an unload file containing the data from the Cinemas table. For clarity, this example uses a pipe symbol ("|") for a delimiter.

```
10003|Moinahan Mall Theatre|ROW('2230 Middlefield Rd', '',
'OAKLAND', 'CALIFORNIA', ROW(94601, NULL), 'USA')|ROW(510,
21439825)|0, 593, blob7bc8.b16|t|t|8|(-122.217, 37.78)|
10004|Seven Oaks Theatre|ROW('30311-A College Avenue', '',
'BOGUE', 'KANSAS', ROW(67625, NULL), 'USA')|ROW(654 , 3948679
)|593, 593, blob7bc8.b16|t |f |4 |(-99.679, 39.378)|
10005|Mega-Movie Complex|ROW('30-A Dos Pesos', '', 'ARVADA',
'COLORADO', ROW(80003,NULL), 'USA')|ROW(313, 9116598)|b26,
593, blob7bc8.b16|t|f|28|(-123.5, 48.23)|
10001|Poignant Point Movie Theatre|ROW('1001 Boundary Rd',
'','ARLINGTON HEIGHT','ILLINOIS', ROW(60004,NULL),
'USA')|ROW(620,12039874)|10b9, 593, blob7bc8.b16|t|t|10|(-
87.979099, 42.111619)|
```

Listing 4–63. *Sample UNLOAD File*

Built-in types can be represented in an unload file by their literal string. User-defined types that re-use built-ins—ROW TYPE and COLLECTION— are identified delineated using special keywords. An OPAQUE TYPE can also be represented using its literal string, but for some it is possible to unload it to a more concise representation than the default. Consequently the ORDBMS provides an interface allowing other user-defined functions to be used in by the bulk load facilities. A sub-task when implementing a new OPAQUE TYPE is deciding on its unload format.

Large-object data also requires special handling. In addition to an unload file containing the data in Listing 4–63, unloading the Cinemas table produces a set of files containing each of the large objects in the table. Note that in this example, only one file called 'blob7bc8.b16' is created because our example data re-uses the same image for each cinema.

Backup and Recovery

Backups use each type's binary format to minimize the size of the backup data. Again, for the built-in types, the ORDBMS can use the same approach it always did for built-in types, although for user-defined types the ORDBMS can either combine other type formats or rely on the developer's support functions for OPAQUE TYPES. Regardless of how large the database is, the ORDBMS organizes backups and recovery of its data subject to a database administrator's control.

Chapter Summary

In this chapter we began our exploration of how the ORDBMS integrates new classes of objects into the data model. Types define a new object's structure and the element or elements used to record its state. These new types are used within the OR-SQL query language in exactly the same way that SQL-92 types were used in RDBMS products.

First, we introduced some basic object concepts for readers unfamiliar with the object-oriented approaches to software engineering. This list of concepts is not a complete description of object-oriented ideas. Extensibility within the ORDBMS might better be characterized as component centric, rather than object-centric. Properties such as object identity and reference, and certain aspects of other features such as multiple inheritance, are not supported within the ORDBMS data model. The importance of object-oriented approaches to software engineering with ORDBMS databases lies in the way they can be used to analyze and reason about an application's problem domain and incorporate this analysis into the database's detailed design.

Building as it does on relational DBMS foundations, the object-relational DBMS includes all data types that characterized SQL-92 databases. We presented an overview of these types and the facilities supported by the ORDBMS to manage them. The most important use of these types in object-relational databases is as building blocks for the other user-defined types we discuss next. User-defined types represent the structural aspects of the software objects corresponding to real-world entities. Converting between type instances, either between the built-in literal types like lvarchar and integer or among user-defined types, can be automated with casts.

The ORDBMS supports several user-defined type mechanisms. In Table 4–6, we list them and briefly summarize their properties.

We continue this examination in the next chapter where we review how user-defined functions that implement the useful behavior for these UDTs are embedded within the server.

Table 4-6. User-Defined Types and their Properties

Type Mechanism	Properties
Built-in Types	Standardized in SQL-92. Small set of text and number data types, and query language facilities. In an ORDBMS, their most valuable role is as building blocks for other UDTs.
COLLECTION	Non-first normal form type. COLLECTION types are a kind of meta-type. They represent a grouping of instances of the same type within a single data value. Useful when the data type within the COLLECTION has a small domain of values.
DISTINCT	Renaming of a pre-existing type. All properties and behaviors of the *parent* type are re-used by the DISTINCT TYPE. Useful for ensuring that the database schema is *strongly typed*.
ROW	Aggregation of several different types into a record-like structure. Useful for creating types to define table structures, particularly when the schema calls for several tables arranged into a hierarchy. Unfortunately, ROW TYPE instances are subject to several restrictions with respect to how they can be processed in queries. These limitations make them unsuitable for defining columns in tables.
OPAQUE	An OPAQUE TYPE is a completely new *abstract data types*. The ORDBMS stores OPAQUE TYPE instances as anonymous arrays of bytes. Small objects (< 32 K) to larger ones (multiple gigabytes) can be handled with the OPAQUE TYPE mechanism. Low-level languages such as C and Java are used to implement the behavior for each OPAQUE TYPE, which makes them the best mechanism for performance and scalability. Commercial DataBlade products make wide use of the OPAQUE TYPE mechanism.

A Tour of the Available DataBlade Products

For the most part, this book focuses in the functionality of the ORDBMS, and on explaining how to use it to develop object-relational database applications. In addition to the core functionality, however, readers using the ORDBMS will have at their disposal a number of precooked bundles of user-defined extensions. The marketing term used to refer to them is DataBlade™ products, or more commonly, just datablade. In this tutorial, we explore the range of DataBlade™ products that are available and give a brief overview of their use.

This list changes constantly. INFORMIX partners bring out new Data-Blade™ products regularly. In addition, some older datablades are bundled with a ORDBMS as part of a licensing agreement. Also, note that a range of free-ware BladeLets is available from various sources on the Web. In Tutorial 5 of this book, we introduce three of them and explain how they can be used.

Categories of DataBlade Products

DataBlade™ products are classified based on the kind of problem they are designed to solve. In all cases, a DataBlade™ extends the set of data types that can be used in database tables and the set of expressions that can be used in OR-SQL queries. Some DataBlade™ modules use the indexing facilities provided by the ORDBMS, for example, all spatial blades use the R-Tree. Others require specialist access methods. The text management DataBlade™ products all include an indexing access method of some kind, and the Timeseries datablade uses its own physical storage algorithms instead of the ones used for table data.

Over the next few pages we review several categories of DataBlade™ module. The idea is to describe what is possible in the ORDBMS and to give readers some idea of how these technologies work. All OR-SQL examples in this tutorial are deliberately generic. Different products tend to provide slightly different performance and functionality. Developers are advised to pick the right one for their product based on its specific goals.

Bio-Informatics and Chemical Modeling

Many branches of manufacturing, industrial research, environmental monitoring, and medicine require information systems that can store and reason about chemical reagents and reactions. Indeed, chemistry is sometimes called "the central science." Software engineers have developed methods to encode complex chemical formula a ways that allow chemists to answer questions, such as "Is this molecular form a *substructure* of another?" or "What is the atomic weight of this molecule?"

For example, consider the pair of molecular forms in Figure 3–1. A reasonable question to ask in a chemical database is whether either of these would react with free hydrogen (H^+) to produce water (H_2O) (plus a residual). Eligible reagents are those with an OH^- site.

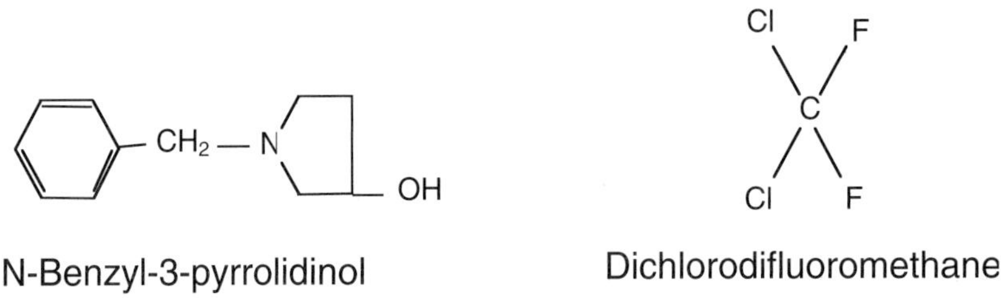

N-Benzyl-3-pyrrolidinol   Dichlorodifluoromethane

Figure 3–1. *Complex Molecular Structure Encapsulated in a UDT*

Using the DataBlade™ modules, such questions can be asked and answered in OR-SQL. Further, as the indexing permitted by the ORDBMS improves, it will be possible to answer such questions much more quickly than can be answered today.

DataBlade™ products are typically used in applications that address data management needs in specialized fields. In real-world chemical databases, the number of molecules is usually very large, and the chemistry is combined with other kinds of information. Production scheduling and safety management in chemical engineering, for example, employ SQL-92 types.

This kind of DataBlade™ product has other potential uses. For example, the author knows of one academic research project combines this functionality with geographic information system (GIS) types to monitor the impact of chemical pollutants on aquatic ecosystems.

Digital Media and Digital Asset Management

In Chapter 1, we noted the increasing numbers of new applications where the primary data entry method is digital recording devices like video cameras, instead of a keyboard. DataBlade™ products concerned with *digital media* address the kinds of requirements for these systems. For the most part, they are libraries of types and functions that perform operations on a specific kind of recorded media, such as still images, video, and audio.

As with other DataBlade™ products, it is rare to find an information system devoted exclusively to managing digital assets. Like all information, digital assets have value, so most applications use these types in a schema that manages rights tracking, terms of use and licensing, editorial workflow, publication scheduling, and so on.

Still Imagery

Almost all Web sites include GIFs and JPGs. In fact, despite the recent e-commerce hype, sites providing access to large galleries of glossy pictures remain the most lucrative businesses on the Web. In addition, in this age of the image, organizations are becoming increasingly reliant on digital media for external marketing and internal education. Even traditional business applications such as personnel management are beginning to use digital imagery to record employee's faces.

Working with digital imagery has traditionally been very labor intensive. Managing large libraries of images using a file system creates administrative problems because separating the storage of the large-object data in the file-system name space from the database makes it difficult to answer a question such as "Is this image (file) actually used anywhere?" Fortunately, DataBlade™ modules allow the large objects to be stored internally to the ORDBMS which tracks what images are being used and where. Asset security is another justification for storing images inside the ORDBMS.

On the other hand, getting objects into the ORDBMS and extracting them again is more computationally expensive than using a file system, and many popular software packages for working with image data expect file-system storage. Therefore, DataBlade™ products typically permit external storage of the individual assets in addition to internal storage. Regardless of whether the large object data is stored inside or outside of the IDS data storage facilities, Developers use OR-SQL, such as in Listing 3–1, to manage imagery in the database. The `Image` column of the `Banner_Images` table holds data which can only be accessed using the other functions that the image processing DataBlade adds to OR-SQL.

```
CREATE TABLE Banner_Images (
     Id              SERIAL            PRIMARY KEY,
     Licensee        Licensee_Id       NOT NULL FOREIGN KEY
                     REFERENCES Licensees ( Id )
                     CONSTRAINT Banner_Images_Licensee_FK,
     Image           imgDescriptor     NOT NULL,
     Features        imgFeatureVector
);
```

Listing 3–1. *CREATE TABLE with Digital Image Data Column*

Constructing an `imgDescriptor`, which encapsulates an image, can get quite complex. At its simplest, it involves reading a file from the file system into the ORDBMS. Logic embedded within the ORDBMS can then determine image properties such as format and size. .

Digital images come in a variety of sizes and employ a variety of low-level formats. In addition, in most information systems that deal with this kind of data, there is a requirement to convert between formats to allow for the combination of several images into one. Thus, image-handling DataBlade™ products include large libraries of UDFs that perform these kinds of operations. Table 3–1 presents a list of the common functionalities.

The `Banner_Images` table in Listing 3–1 includes a column called `Features` whose purpose we have not yet explained. Today, it is possible to use software to compare images for "similarity." Such techniques are called *query by image content searches*. The technique involves extracting a set of *features* from every image in the database, and then using these features to determine the similarity of two images.

Different DataBlade™ products use different sets of image features to determine similarity. In Table 3–2, we introduce some of the common techniques. For more details, consult each product's documentation.

Table 3–1. Common Image-Processing Functionality

Functionality	Description
Convert image format	Takes as arguments an instance of an `imgDescriptor` type and a string identifying a new *format* (GIF, JPG, TIF, etc). This UDF creates a new `imgDescriptor` instance that contains the same image as the first, but stored using a new format. Sometimes, these conversions degrade the quality of the image because the new format is less precise than the old.
Convert image type	These UDFs are similar to the format converters, except they create new images of a different *type* (gray scale, RGB, HSV, or bit maps). Image types are generally orthogonal to image formats.
Image compression	Different `imgDescriptor` instances can use different compression techniques, depending on their format and type. This UDF returns the algorithm used to compress the image data.
Pixel size (width and height of image)	Usually a pair of UDFs that returns the number of pixels along each side of the image.
Scaling and rotating	These UDFs take an `imgDescriptor` instance and scale it (make it larger or smaller by some factor) or rotate it (pivot it about its central point).
Combining and masking	It is often useful to combine digital images to apply a consistent block header or filter over the image to achieve a consistent look and feel through the site, for example, branding each image with a company logo or trademark, or invisibly watermarking an image to enforce licensing conditions.

Logic supplied as part of the DataBlade™ module can extract all of these features from each image. These feature values, which are recorded as an instance of the `imgFeatureVector` data type in Listing 3–1, are stored in the additional column, which is then used in similarity queries. The sensitivity of the similarity algorithm to each feature can be "tuned"; that is, each feature can be assigned a weight or importance as a similarity criterion. In Listing 3–2, we illustrate what all of this looks like in OR-SQL.

Table 3–2. Commonly Used Features in an Image-Similarity Search

Technique	Brief Description
Fourier transforms	Colors correspond to light frequencies. An image can be interpreted as a single, extremely complex waveform. Fourier transforms and, more strictly, Fast Fourier Transforms (FFT), compute the highest frequency wavelengths in the image. Based on the degree of similarity between the coefficients of two FFTs, a measure of the similarity between the underlying waveforms is possible.
Color histograms	This technique takes an image and counts the number of pixels falling into several color (or gray-scale) ranges. Two images can be compared on the basis of the degrees of similarity between the histograms. In addition, in certain, application-specific cases, an image can be categorized based on the presence (or absence) of a particular color (or colors).
Shapes	Images contain regions of different colors. Larger regions of consistent color constitute a shape in the image. The size and orientation of an image's shapes can be used to determine its similarity to other images.
Texture	Measures of the variation in gray scale or color in an image. For example, images of straw and vegetation have much more texture than images of houses.
Intensity	Intensity is related to color. By convention, most images represent pixel color using a triple of red/green/blue (RGB) intensity values. Roughly speaking, the brightness of an image corresponds to its intensity. However, as with color, it is more usual to represent image intensity using a histogram.

```
--
--   Insert a new image into the Banner_Images table using
--   a file in the server's file system. This large object
--   may also be inserted through the ESQL/C or JDBC APIs.
--
INSERT INTO Banner_Images
( Licensee, Image )
SELECT L.Id,
       imgDescriptorFromFile('/tmp/01.tif')
  FROM Licensees L
 WHERE L.Name = PersonName ( 'Avendon','Richard');
--
--   Use the constructor UDF for the imgFeatureVector UDT
--   to extract the features from the image.
--
```

```
UPDATE Banner_Images
    SET Features = imgFeatureVector ( Image )
  WHERE imgFeatureVector IS NULL;
--
--  Now, given a second image, find similar ones in the
--  Banner_Images table.
--
SELECT B.Id, Similarity
  FROM Banner_Images B
  WHERE Similar (
            B.Features,
            imgFeatureVector (
                    imgDescriptorFromFile('/tmp/target.tif')
            ),
            -- Set of values weighting features ,
            Similarity #REAL)
  ORDER BY rank;
```

Listing 3–2. *OR-SQL Queries Illustrating the use of Image-Similarity UDFs*

Note the use of the OUT PARAMETER and statement local variable in this example.

Unfortunately, it is not possible at this time to use any indexing techniques with this kind of query. Consequently, image similarity queries scan the entire table, checking imgFeatureVector instances one at a time. Also, many applications have requirements that are too specialized for the simple matching algorithms used in these products. Fingerprint, face, and voice identification methods employ domain-specific algorithms that these general similarity searches cannot duplicate.

The range of applications for this technology, however, is surprisingly extensive. Developers are using it to perform trademark and logo searches, detect flaws in manufactured goods using x-ray images, and limited product searches. The more adventurous use the image similarity functionality over so-called *false-color* images to estimate snow coverage, agricultural land use, and to make calculations in scientific disciplines such as astronomy. This last class of application frequently includes other DataBlade™ products, such as spatial extensions.

Video

Historically, the kind of equipment needed to manage video data, such as expensive cameras and sound recording gear, juke-boxes for tape storage, editing desks, and transmission and high-bandwidth communication infrastructure, created high barriers to entry. Today, however, professional quality video recording equipment is inexpensive, and commodity computers running widely available software are replacing the jukebox and mixing desk.

Video data has an image and an audio component. Although, as with still images, a variety of on-disk formats are used for video data, end users working with it share a consistent mental model. Each video is made up of a series of *segments*. A segment can be an audio segment, an image segment (a scene), or a segment that is more conceptually abstract. A single audio or conceptual segment can overlap several scenes. Think of a movie in which a scene has multiple shots and a large part of the illusion of continuity is created by the consistent sound effects. Figure 3–2 illustrates these ideas.

Segments are represented by their first and last frame offset within the video. Some segments, such as individual scenes in which the camera was turned on for an interval of time and then turned off again, can be identified automatically. The simplest algorithm counts the numbers of pixels that change between frames and reports a scene change whenever this value exceeds some threshold. Higher levels of abstraction, such as the brief descriptions in Figure 3–2, are produced by human users watching the tape. Ultimately, aesthetic judgments, such as "Good shot of Tiger

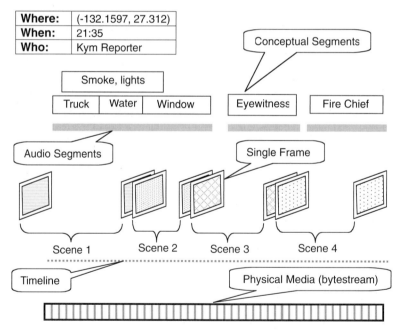

Figure 3–2. *Video Data Layers of Abstraction*

Woods' golf swing," will always defy attempts at automatic classification because these are subjective assessments.

Broadcast quality video involves extremely large data objects. Uncompressed video consumes between 25 and 125 K for each second of action, so it is usual to store the broadcast data separate from the ORDBMS (in a specially designed jukebox) and to use lower resolution video for editing and searching.

The overlapping, segmented nature of video data makes it useful to introduce another user-defined type that manages range concepts. Each segment has a beginning and an ending offset within the video. In practice, many queries look for video data that contains several properties. For example, a query such as "show all videos with a scene showing fire seen through a window" means finding all videos in which two abstract concepts, fire and window, *overlap* in a single scene. The presence of flames in a still image is detectable using the kinds of techniques we described for similarity search in still images, and the word match on "window" might be used in a text index.

Range data objects such as this are very similar to the Period OPAQUE TYPE we discuss in several places throughout this book.

Audio

Audio data shares many properties with video and still images. For the most part, audio is extracted from video data or recorded using microphones. And like most rich media, audio data can be stored in a variety of formats. At a minimum, audio DataBlade™ products provide types to store audio data and perform format conversions.

There are two other ways that it is used, however. First, the audio datablade embeds within OR-SQL a set of software tools used in digital signal processing. These allow developers to create OR-SQL queries that perform pitch shifting, time scaling, and gain adjustment, or to extract information about audio data such as sample rate, number of channels, sample size, and sound duration. This kind of extension is popular in applications that manage rich media for broadcast because creating video for broadcast involves manipulating sound as well as image.

Second, the products provide similarity searches on audio. As with still images, the idea is to extract a feature vector for each sound segment within an audio data object. Similarity algorithms can compare these features, which are properties such as a sound's pitch, loudness, or tone, to find matches. For example, it is possible to examine the audio track from a video and automatically detect the presence of sirens, shots, voices, or music. Just like similarity searches with still images, audio similarity does not extend to identifying individual speakers or performing audio-to-text transcription. Such operations require more specialized extension libraries.

Financial Data Management and Timeseries Analysis

Although the DataBlade™ products described in this section are almost always associated with financial data management, for example, managing portfolios of assets such as stocks, bonds, and options, they can be used in many other applications as well. In mathematical terms, these extensions facilitate what is known as *regression analysis*. Regression analysis concerns itself with modeling the relationship between two quantifiable, real-world phenomena.

Financial applications typically deal with market information, how many changed hands and for how much, and attempt to use history to predict what will happen in the future. The interesting relationship is between time and market events, such as price or volume.

Why does this kind of analysis require special treatment? The fact that many useful algorithms are most efficient when they can iterate over data in time order complicates query processing over this kind of data. In addition, the algorithms require that one day's values be compared to the previous day's. Providing a platform to execute these algorithms efficiently is, in a nutshell, what the timeseries Data-Blade™ product is all about.

In Figure 3–3 we illustrate how the DataBlade™ extensions manage time series information. The first part of the figure is an OR-SQL example showing how to define a time series *element* and then use it in a CREATE TABLE. The second part illustrates how, at a low level, the data is stored. It is important to understand that the elements within a time series are *not* stored in a table. Rather, they are arranged on disk as a contiguous array of bytes.

To illustrate why this is useful, consider *options pricing*. Options are contracts establishing *price* and *quantity* of an equity (for example, 100 shares of INFORMIX at $15) that the person who buys the option might choose to make the seller of the option make good on at some time in the future. For example, I may be prepared to bet that the price of INFORMIX will rise above $15 by January 2001, and I may back that bet up by buying from someone else the right to acquire from them 100 shares of INFORMIX for $15 each on January 1st. The tricky question is, how much should I pay for that right?

The math is complex, to say the least. But a fair price can be calculated using what is known as the Black-Scholes option formula. This

```
--
CREATE ROW TYPE Equity_Ticker (
      Open       Currency       NOT NULL,
      Close      Currency       NOT NULL,
      Volume     Quantity       NOT NULL
);
--
CREATE TABLE Stock_Exchange (
      Symbol     Stock_Symbol    PRIMARY KEY,
      Ticker     TIMESERIES( Equity_Ticker ) NOT NULL
);
```

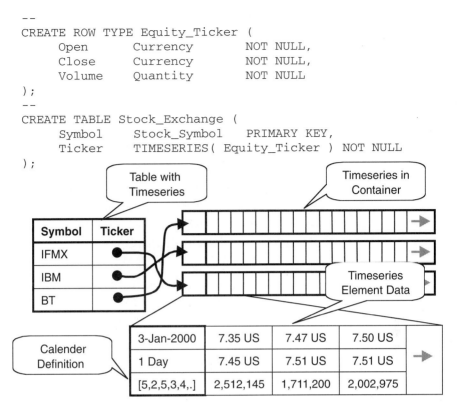

Figure 3–3. *Timeseries DataBlade™ Physical Layout*

equation uses the information in the following list: The last item is hard to calculate. The others are simple values.

- Current stock price ($5)
- Strike price ($15)
- Dividend yield (0.0 in this case)
- Current interest rate (5.236%)
- Time until the option expires
- Underlying equity's *volatility*.

Volatility refers to the up-and-down-ness of the underlying equity's price. Formally, it is the annualized standard deviation of the logarithm of *returns*, which is the difference between the closing price on any given day and the closing price on the previous *trading* day. Still with me? Now think about how to efficiently calculate the value in SQL-92. Then, figure out how to compute it for a very large number of options over a large number of equities.

Fortunately, by using the timeseries DataBlade™, this exercise can be reduced to the query in Listing 3–3. `Volatility()` operates over data elements that are already stored in time order and arranged sequentially on disk, so it can compute its results with a single pass over each symbol's history.

```
SELECT BlackScholes( getTSDatum(E.Timeseries,CURRENT).Close,
                     Currency (15, 'US'),
                     E.Yield,
                     5.236::Percentage,
                     TradeDays ( E.Expiry, CURRENT ),
                     Volatility ( E.Timeseries ) )
  FROM Equities E
 WHERE E.Symbol = 'IFMX';
```

Listing 3–3. *OR-SQL Query Using Timeseries Extensions*

Despite its mathematical complexity, this kind of analysis is intuitively straightforward. For example, it is standard practice to analyze time series data in terms of four component parts:

- Trend. This is the general, long-run central tendency of the data. Trend may be up or down, or it may change direction over time. For instance, the number of Web users is trending up over time.
- Cycle. Trend might be derived from several years of data, but within each year, there might be a long cycle. Crop yields around the Pacific fluctuate according to the seven-year El Niño ocean current cycle.
- Seasonality. Seasonality is a shorter-term pattern than cycle. For example, retail shops do almost half of their business in the last quarter of the year.
- Residual. In any time series, there will be small, random fluctuations. This is called the residual, and is generally assumed to be a random fluctuation.

Extracting each of these components from raw time series data requires a considerable degree of mathematical sophistication. However, by embedding this logic within the ORDBMS as a datablade, even the most tattooed HTML/OR-SQL developer can create Web pages that help a procurement manager make good pricing decisions on a B2B portal. Such numerical algorithms represent the second kind of financial analysis DataBlade™ product, and like the timeseries extensions, they have broad applications.

Spatial Data Management

Managing spatial data, such as geographic information locating objects of interest in the real world, was among the earliest motivating cases for extensible DBMS technology. It turns out that dealing with the complexities of geography is far from easy. A number of highly profitable companies focus exclusively on providing specialist GIS software. Embedding spatial data types in the ORDBMS, however, provides a mechanism whereby a more business-centric applications can incorporate spatial information.

Spatial geometry involves spectacularly complex algorithms. For example, determining whether two large, concave polygons represented as a sequence of floating point value pairs *overlap* or *touch* is best handled with an algorithm that is not exactly obvious.. Determining which of a large *set* of possibly overlapping polygons actually overlap a target is harder still. In addition, GISs use spatial algorithms in odd ways.

We all know that the world is round,[1] but its roundness is rather peculiar. It is neither a sphere, nor strictly an ellipsoid (flattened at the poles). Rather, it is a large number of ellipsoids superimposed on each other. The difference matters. The earth's equatorial diameter is 12,756 km (7,926.6 miles), and its polar diameter is 12,718 km (7,902 miles), about a 0.3% variance. This isn't much, until you run out of pipe sections ten feet short of completing an oil line between Houston and Dallas.

All spatial DataBlade™ products add a set of types for storing spatial objects and a set of for reasoning about them. Two tables in the Movies-R-Us database schema include spatial columns: `MovieClub-Members` and `Cinemas`. In Listing 3–4 we present a set of tables illustrating the range of spatial types.

```
CREATE TABLE Land_Parcels (
    Id              SERIAL          PRIMARY KEY,
    Boundary        ST_POLYGON      NOT NULL
);
--
CREATE TABLE Bridge (
    Label_Name      Short_String    PRIMARY KEY,
    Location        ST_POINT        NOT NULL,
    Bridge_Height   Length          NOT NULL
);
--
```

---

[1] This comment is made with apologies to the Flat-Earth Society. Sorry guys, you haven't convinced me yet. (http://www.flat-earth.org/)

```
CREATE TABLE Rivers (
       Name             Short_String    NOT NULL,
       Segment_Num      INTEGER         NOT NULL,
       Bed              ST_PATH         NOT NULL
);
--
```

Listing 3-4. *Spatial Data Types and Schemas*

Typically, a user-defined function is specific to a single data type. By contrast, the functions that are installed with the spatial DataBlade™ products tend to interrelate different spatial types with each other in addition to providing behavior for each spatial type. They permit developers to write OR-SQL queries that combine spatial concepts with other types. In Listing 3–5 we present one such query.

"If the San Jaochim river rises 15 feet, it will cut off some bridges. What area of land may be cut off if these bridges go out?"

```
SELECT ConvexHull ( L.Boundary )
  FROM Rivers R, Bridges B, Land_Parcels L
 WHERE R.Name = 'San Joachim'
   AND B.Height < '15 F'

   AND Point_on_Path ( B.Location, R.Bed )
   AND Overlaps ( R.Bed, Buffer( L.Boundary, '1 Mile'));
```

Listing 3-5. *Queries Employing Spatial Operators*

Supporting spatial operations requires efficient indexing. Search operations such as `Overlap`, `Within`, `Contains`, `Equal`, and `Nearest Neighbor` are made faster by the ORDBMS's built-in R-Tree. Further, the R-Tree indexing in the ORDBMS is a highly concurrent access method. Several read and write queries can be reading and modifying a single index at the same time. In future applications supporting large numbers of mobile users, this kind of functionality will become essential.

Acquiring spatial data can present a challenge. Fortunately, the same vendors who supply the spatial DataBlade™ modules also sell data. In addition, in most countries, government agencies have been established to act as libraries for this kind of data. For example, the U.S. Census Bureau, a division of the Department of Commerce, sells data sets describing the demographic distribution of people within the United States, and the United States Geological Survey provides data sets describing geographic features such as rivers and roads.

Text and Document Management

Document management is hard. First, there is the sheer volume of data. Many document management systems run to thousands of reports, meeting notes, and e-mails. Second, there is (again) the variety of data formats and languages involved. Some formats, such as Post-script™ and HTML, are relatively simple. Others, such as the propri-etary formats supported by word processing products, use binary storage in an effort to save disk space. In addition, written languages such as Hebrew, which is read right to left, and Kanji, which does not possess a strict "sort order," create additional complications.

Any effective document management application needs to support query by document content. This requires indexing techniques that can return matching documents fast *while* permitting other users to INSERT documents at the same time.

Managing Scale

Different text DataBlade™ modules take slightly different approaches to the problem of scale. For the most part, they permit the document data to be stored either internally to the ORDBMS or within large object storage spaces. However, because a document index is required to store every word for every document in a table's column, indices tend to grow very large (although rarely as large as the original docu-ments). Listing 3–6 illustrates how to use the document data type in a table.

```
CREATE TABLE Project_Reports (
Id          Report_Id          PRIMARY KEY,
Author      PersonName         NOT NULL,
Created     DATE               NOT NULL,
Document    Doc_Data_Type  NOT NULL
);
```

Listing 3–6. *Schema with Document Type*

Document types such as Doc_Data_Type in Listing 3–6 can be refer-ences to file-system locations, or document objects can be fragmented across several data storage spaces like other large objects. There is no difference between these strategies so far as searching is concerned; most searches will employ the index, which is stored internally.

Format and Filtering

Document datablades employ a technique known as *filtering* to cope with the multiplicity of formats. Filtering extracts the readable words from a document and passes the resulting word list to the indexing facilities. Thus a single column can contain documents stored in a variety of formats. Note that the different document DataBlade™ products support different, but overlapping, sets of document formats. Examine Listing 3–7.

```
INSERT INTO Project_Reports
VALUES
( 'CMU-12-A.7', PersonName('Juan','Guitierez','Dr'), TODAY,
  File_To_Doc ( "D:\Documents\Word\Report.doc", "client" )
);
```

Listing 3–7. *INSERT a New Document*

Filtering is handled automatically by the document DataBlade™ functions. Filter logic first checks the header information in each document. By default, if the filter does not recognize the format, it returns an error. Unsupported document formats usually must be converted to ASCII before they are inserted into the indexed column.

Format conversion is a more difficult challenge. Most document formats provide mechanisms to include figures and images. However, some document DataBlade™ products do include UDFs that can modify a document, to highlight certain keywords, for example, as shown in Listing 3–8.

```
SELECT Blade_MarkUp(R.Document,
                     "<b>","</b>","rubber chicken")
  FROM Project_Reports R
  WHERE Blade_Contains( R.Document, "rubber chicken");
```

Listing 3–8. *SELECT Query Retrieving Documents and Marking Them Up*

Such functions ensure that the appropriate change is made to the document depending on its file format.

Indexing Documents

Content searches require indexing if the searches are to be at all practical. In fact, some document DataBlade™ products can use only the index to perform searches. Listing 3–9 illustrates what it looks like to create a document index.

```
CREATE INDEX Report_Doc_Index
ON Project_Reports (Document Blade_Op_Class)
USING Blade_Access_Method
IN Smart_Blob_Space;
```

Listing 3–9. *CREATE INDEX over Documents*

Creating document indices can take a long time, and with earlier versions of these extension libraries, developers were obliged to do so fairly frequently. Document management solutions were traditionally used to cope with relatively static libraries. Adding a new document required procedural code that invoked an API and that was generally single-threaded. Today, Web sites routinely support a large community of users uploading their own content, so the more recent releases of the document DataBlades™ are a tremendous improvement over the initial implementations.

Searching by Content

Several search strategies are implemented in DataBlade™ products. The simplest of them is a *keyword* search that returns a list of all documents in which a supplied keyword, or keywords, is present. Listing 3–7 provides an OR-SQL query that performs a phrase search for documents containing an adjacent pair of words.

Keyword searches are quite flexible. Users can request documents containing a word, a phrase, a word or synonyms for that word, documents containing a pair of words that are close (though not necessarily adjacent), and a range of fuzzy searches for synonyms or related concepts. Different DataBlade™ products vary in the kinds of searches they perform and in their run-time performance for each kind of search.

Two important concepts in text searches are the notions of *stopwords* and *thesaurus*. Stopwords are word lists that the indexing mechanism can ignore. Each DataBlade™ module ships with its own stopword list. In many applications, however, it can be useful to extend this list with terms that are so common as to be useless for searches. For example, a text index over the sections of this book could afford to ignore the word "database."

A thesaurus lists related words. It is used to support concept-based searches. As with the stopword list, DataBlade™ products providing thesaurus functionality are shipped with general content. Domain specific document libraries, such as those managing information from a specific branch of knowledge, should extend this list to derive maximum benefit from the technology.

Other DataBlade Approaches

DataBlade™ products, either bundled with the product or supplied by third parties, are useful in many applications. In addition to the broad categories introduced in this tutorial, other commercial datablades are available to assist in tasks such as data cleansing, fuzzy logic queries, and security. Over time, this list is likely to grow.

Object Behavior and User-Defined Functions

Introduction to Extending the ORDBMS with User-Defined Routines

Developers using SQL-92 were constrained by the way the language provided only basic mathematical operations, simple string manipulation, and some special purpose expressions for built-in types such as DATE, DATETIME, and BLOB. Consequently, programmers had to combine many low-level operations into long, complex queries, or implement much of their information system's functionality outside the DBMS, in host language code. Developing this way is tedious, error prone, and results in inflexible information systems; all problem that are exacerbated when the same business processes must be reimplemented in several different front end programs.

To make life easier for database developers DBMS vendors modified their products by adding nonstandard functions to SQL, and the proliferation of proprietary extensions has led to the divergence you find in RDBMS products today. ORDBMS technology replaces such a piecemeal strategy with something more systematic. We have already seen how an ORDBMS may be extended with new data types. But perhaps a more profound kind of extensibility involves letting developers embed modules of procedural logic into the ORDBMS.

Embedded procedural logic can be implemented in a variety of languages, such as C, Java, or *Stored Procedure Language (SPL)*. Procedural extensions can either be invoked directly, just as database stored procedures were, or they can be included in OR-SQL queries alongside any of the built-in expressions defined in SQL-92. In a commercial relational DBMS, only the vendor's engineers were able to perform such surgery. The motivation for extensible DBMS technology is to eliminate the dependency on a few, overworked vendor engineers, and allow database developers to make the DBMS product behave exactly as they want it to.

The basic *User-defined Routine (UDR)* mechanism is used to support many powerful features:

- To extend OR-SQL. For example, regular expression matching routines are very useful tools for string manipulation, and adding them using the UDR techniques outlined in this chapter is relatively straightforward. Also, the problem of query language diversity among RDBMS products can be addressed by embedding logic to mimic the functionality different vendors provide.
- To provide SQL-92 functionality for new data types. For example, database extension logic can be used to overload the functionality of SQL's mathematical operations, +, -, *, /, and even aggregates like SUM(), AVG(), and so on, for new data types that model concepts such as Mass and Distance.
- Extension logic can implement UDT specific behaviors. OR-SQL expressions that construct new type instances, manipulate and modify them, or compare them with each other, are implemented as UDRs. For example, our Movies-R-Us Web site database includes a BirthDay data type. We need to be able to construct new instances of it using DATE data, compare two BirthDay objects to see if they are equal and use routines that modify attributes of a BirthDay.
- Support functions modules used by the data management facilities implemented within the ORDBMS to work with instances of user-defined types. Sorting new types, using a secondary access method for an index, or communicating type instances between a client program and the server, all require that the type's developer supply the ORDBMS with an appropriate extension to perform each task.
- Information systems consist of more than just a database. Many of the data processing aspects of an information system can be implemented using database stored procedures, which is one way to use the UDR features.

- Most programming systems include functionality supporting inter-process communication and interaction with file systems and file data. The ORDBMS provides interfaces by which several modules of embedded logic may be combined and used to present external data as if it were just another database table.

To developers using OR-SQL, these additions are integrated seamlessly. The design objective is that instead of writing queries that work with byte arrays and machine-level types like INTEGER, developers write object queries.

Chapter Overview

In this chapter, we explain what kinds of use-defined routines are possible and how to implement them. We begin by describing in general terms what a UDR is and how the ORDBMS handles them internally. Then we move on to describe in general terms how to write one and embed it into the ORDBMS. Our discussion focuses on describing the kinds of things that can be achieved with these database extensions, so our examples are for the most part quite simple. Chapter 10 and Tutorial 4 go into considerably more detail about how to use low-level languages such as C and Java to implement UDRs.

We move on in this chapter to describe several advanced UDR techniques: aggregators, iterators, and OUT parameters.

User-Defined Routines: Functions and Procedures

User-defined routines can be divided into two categories depending on whether or not it returns a value. We call a routine that returns value(s) a FUNCTION (user-defined function or UDFs) and routines that do not return values (but might encapsulate OR-SQL operations) a PROCEDURE[1] (or database stored procedure).

Of course, database stored procedures are nothing new. Most RDBMS products have allowed developers to embed procedural code encapsulating multiquery business operations into the DBMS for some time.

---

[1] Syntax confuses this distinction. Database procedures in prior version of INFORMIX's DBMS could return values. However, in the ORDBMS, only FUNCTIONS may be used in SQL queries. A PROCEDURE that returns a value may only be executed directly. One way to think about this is to consider PROCEDUREs in the IDS product as necessary for backwards compatibility.

Stored procedures are invoked from an external program in much the same way that such a program would invoke a local subroutine. The stored procedure technique replaces series of OR-SQL statements exchanged between the external program and the DBMS with a single message, thereby minimizing interprocess communication. Stored procedures became popular in client/server information systems.

Stored database procedures are not, however, the same thing as user-defined functions. UDFs are a mechanism for extending OR-SQL directly, rather than wrapping data management operations within looping-and-branching procedural logic. As we saw in Chapter 1, embedding extension logic within the declarative query language makes the database more flexible, and addresses certain performance-related problems that have limited the functionality developers could achieve. A runtime and end user can compose an OR-SQL query that includes many different UDF extensions, and the ORDBMS can parse and execute that query.

There are other, more technical differences as well:

- Procedural languages supported by RDBMSs were designed to work with the built-in SQL-92 data types. They are less powerful than are general purpose programming languages such as Java and C, which can work with data down to the bit level.
- UDFs can be invoked from within the stored procedure language, so they can also increase the range of things that are possible within stored procedures. For example, it is inconceivable that you would write digital signal processing routines in a database procedural language. Such things are best handled with C. But once such a routine is added to the ORDBMS, it can be deployed within a stored procedure.
- UDF execution can be parallelized (with certain restrictions); that is, the ORDBMS can invoke a single UDF in multiple, concurrent threads, as part of a single query's execution. This is necessary because of the way UDFs are used by the ORDBMS engine. With database procedures on the other hand, the queries embedded within them can be parallelized, but the procedure itself cannot.
- Database procedural languages are DBMS specific. Modern software development emphasizes *component* techniques that allow runnable modules of programming logic to be copied between computer systems. UDRs implemented using Java can be moved between a DBMS server computer and a client user-interface program without recompilation. A DBMS's procedural language code cannot.

Both varieties of UDR (functions and procedures) are declared within the ORDBMS and managed using OR-SQL's DDL sublanguage.

All information about embedded routines is stored in the ORDBMS's system catalogs. At runtime, when it encounters a UDF name in a query or when one is called from within a stored procedure, the ORDBMS figures out which routine is intended by consulting its catalogs. Then it invokes the logic implementing the routine, passing data into it as it does.

User-Defined Routine Architecture

It is important to emphasize that in a well-engineered ORDBMS, user-defined routine logic is managed entirely *within the DBMS engine*. Extensions are not, for example, implemented in a program that runs somewhere outside the DBMS run-time engine, perhaps on the same computer but possibly on another system accessed over a network. UDR logic is linked into the ORDBMS engine and invoked as a local subroutine call; the equivalent of a JMP machine code instruction.

In contrast, some DBMS vendors employ mechanisms such as a remote procedure call (RPC) or a message queue. These systems invoke the UDR logic by directing a message to a remote program each time. To achieve maximum performance the IDS products always executes UDR logic in the same process address space as the rest of the ORDBMS, regardless of whether it is implemented in C or Java.

Embedding procedural logic into a query processing framework like the IDS product has consequences for how user-defined functions are written. As you implement UDF logic, it is useful to think of the ORDBMS server as a kind of minioperating system. Facilities traditionally supplied to programs by environments such as UNIX® or NT®—memory management, data I/O, communication, and process scheduling—are supplied to the embedded logic by the ORDBMS.

However, because of the way it emphasizes query-centric operations, the ORDBMS is a very unusual operating system. Traditionally, programs that ran in an operating system embed within them operations to read and write data. By contrast, UDFs in an ORDBMS tend to be small, discrete blocks of code. They are more like subroutines than complete programs. I/O, execution scheduling, and so on are handled outside the UDF by the ORDBMS. To complete the analogy, instead of users 'running' the program, in an extensible database they use a query expression to specify what it is they want done and let the ORDBMS do the rest.

ORDBMS Process Architecture

In this section, we provide an overview of the architectural design of the ORDBMS. Understanding how the ORDBMS uses hardware resources is very helpful when it comes time to implement extensions in C. It also helps to explain some of the limitations that are imposed on UDFs. In Figure 5–1 we illustrate the process and memory architecture of the running ORDBMS.

From the operating system's point of view, a running ORDBMS instance consists of multiple, cooperating processes. Processes, which we illustrate with squared boxes in this figure, are known as *virtual processors*, or simply VPs. Different VPs have specialized functions. CPU-VPs are responsible for SQL operations; parsing, optimization, execution, and so on. Other VPs handle tasks such as network communication and I/O.

Some CPU-VPs can be marked as belonging to a certain *VP class*, which means that in addition to its OR-SQL processing responsibilities, such processes are the venue for some specialized user-defined processing. For

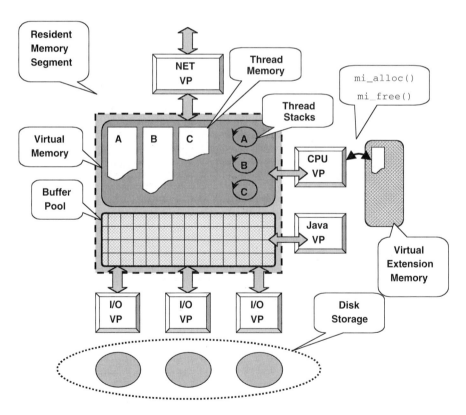

Figure 5–1. *IDS Instance Architecture*

example, the several virtual processes running Java all belong to a JVP class. New UDFs can be marked to ensure that they are always executed on a VP belonging to a particular class. UDFs that perform certain "unsafe" operations must be handled in this way.

From the OS's (UNIX® or NT®) process management perspective, the ORDBMS architecture consists of the following:

- On UNIX, a process group (a set of processes spawned from a single "master" process). These processes all share a large segment of shared memory that they use to manage database data, to use memory resources, and to communication with each other.
- On NT, a single, multi-threaded NT process. An NT process is roughly analogous to a UNIX process group, and NT threads within the process are like individual UNIX processes within the ORDBMS's process group.

You start the ORDBMS by running an initial program in the operating system. Once this is up and running, it replicates itself several times until all of its VPs are active. Shutdown reverses the process. Each VP terminates by first writing whatever data is still in its cache back to disk.

Shared Memory

When the first virtual process starts, it allocates several segments of core memory from the operating system.

- The *resident* portion, which is used to store all the ORDBMS server's run-time data structures. For example, this is where information about the number of participating VPs, connected users, and active threads is stored.
- The *buffer cache* is part of the resident portion. This is where the ORDBMS caches data. Rather than rely on operating system's disk caching algorithms, which are suboptimal from a query-processing perspective, the ORDBMS imposes its own priorities over what should and should not be kept in memory, rather than read from disk each time it is touched.
- The *extended virtual* portion. This is an area of memory that grows and shrinks depending on the queries currently being executed. When a UDF requests memory using the `mi_alloc()` or `mi_dalloc()` database API call, this is from where the data is allocated.

The ORDBMS manages this memory much as an operating system does. It tracks allocated (used) and free (unused) space. On operating systems that support it, the ORDBMS instructs the OS not to swap this memory out to disk. If the ORDBMS runs short of memory, it requests an additional allocation from the operating system. The size of the initial segments and the size of the chunks of memory allocated from the operating system are configurable.

These memory segments are shared by all concurrently connected users, so to minimize the total memory in use at any point in time, the ORDBMS aggressively reclaims whatever memory UDFs allocate as soon as it thinks it is safe to do so. How it tells when memory is eligible for reclaiming is a complex question.

Multi-threading

Each connected user has at least one corresponding *thread* in the ORDBMS. Threads are independent contexts within the ORDBMS where the various user tasks—OR-SQL queries, database procedures, and UDF invocations—execute. When user-level operations such as queries contend for the same object—the same row in a table, say —the ORDBMS mediates the conflict using the lock tables, which are kept in *virtual* memory.

A principle challenge for an ORDBMS is to make the best possible use of available hardware resources. To operate at maximum efficiency, a DBMS should be capable of performing as many simultaneous tasks as the computer it is running on has physical CPUs. If there is database work to be done, a means must be found to schedule it onto one of the physical CPUs. To achieve this, the ORDBMS allows user threads to move *between* ORDBMS virtual processors. Whenever the operating system schedules one of the ORDBMS's VPs onto a CPU, that VP looks to see what work needs to be done. The first thread it finds with work to do gets its attention. In other words, during the time that it is being used to process a query a single DBMS thread can migrate between several VP processes.

Passing threads around in this way accounts for most of the limitations imposed on developers writing UDFs. For example, one of the C language features forbidden to UDF developers is the use of 'static' variables. You should think of local variables in C routines declared to be `static` as having a memory location inside the *executable*. Other local variables are allocated out of the thread space in virtual resident memory, and `mi_alloc()` memory comes from the extended virtual portion, both of which can be accessed by all VPs.

When the ORDBMS invokes a UDF twice in one query execution pass—which happens very often—it can end up calling the embedded UDF logic from within two different processes, say VP-1 and VP-2. By the time it gets to VP-2, values in the static variable assigned in VP-1 might not be what the UDF code expects. Hence, `static` C variables, non-threadsafe code, and direct operating system calls that allocate resources to a process (not a thread), are all forbidden. We cover this topic in more detail in Chapter 10.

Function Manager and Language Manager

Recall that the physical details of how a UDF is implemented are not apparent at the OR-SQL level. A single query might include an internal UDF and external UDFs implemented in C or Java. Supporting all of these extensibility mechanisms simultaneously requires that the IDS product implement a *function manager* module.

When the ORDBMS invokes a UDF, it passes the function manager module a data structure that describes the function to be invoked, where to find any argument values, and where to put results. Depending on how the UDF is implemented, the function manager can do one of several things. It might call the internal interpreter for SPL functions. Or it might link in a C external function's runnable library and invoke the function's logic directly. Finally, for language environments such as Java, the ORDBMS might need to use an abstraction known as the *language manager* to invoke the logic.

We illustrate the basic design of this module in Figure 5–2.

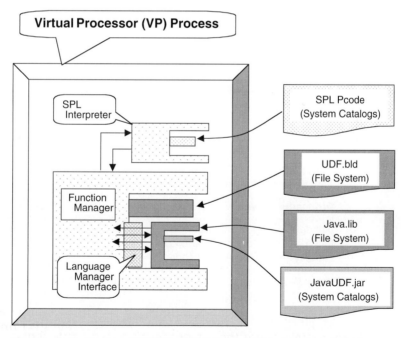

Figure 5–2. *Design of IDS Product's Extensibility Function Manager*

The Java-VP in Figure 5–1 is an example of a specialized virtual processor in which the language manager ensures that Java's executable environment—the *virtual machine*—is loaded into this ORDBMS VP. Runnable objects, either shared libraries of compiled C or Java archives "(jar files) are loaded into the appropriate ORDBMS process when a UDR implemented within them is invoked. That is, the details in Figure 5–2 relating to how the Java language environment is managed only apply inside a Java VP.

System Catalogs and User-Defined Functions

Information about every UDF in the database is stored in the SYSPRO-CEDURES system catalog table. System catalog data is especially useful in an ORDBMS because of the special challenge extensibility presents for OR-SQL developers.

Some object-relational databases have tens of user-defined types and thousands of user-defined functions. Writing valid OR-SQL queries requires that the spelling of function identifiers and the function's argument order be perfect. Because the ORDBMS's query processor uses the information in the system catalogs to interpret queries, developers can help to ensure their query's correctness by checking it against the same data.

In Listing 5–1 we present a query that extracts information from this table and some rows illustrating what its contents look like.

"How can I construct an instance of the Birthday data type?"

```
SELECT P.procname,
       P.owner,
       ifx_ret_types(P.procid) AS Return_Types,
       P.numargs,
       P.paramtypes
  FROM SYSPROCEDURES P
  WHERE ifx_ret_types(P.procid)::lvarchar = 'birthday';
```

Procname	Owner	Return_types	Numargs	Paramtypes
birthday	Informix	Birthday	3	Integer, Integer, Boolean
birthday	Informix	Birthday	2	Integer, Integer
birthday	Informix	Birthday	1	Date

Listing 5–1. *System Catalog Query Against SYSPROCEDURES*

This query returns three UDFs that construct a Birthday type instance. (Note that the catalogs adhere to the rule that all character data is in lower case, and like all tables system-catalog data is case sensitive.) Each has the same function name ("birthday") but they differ in their argument vectors. Once it has been declared within the database, a UDF's details are available in this table regardless of the language used to implement it.

Creating User-Defined Functions

User-defined functions should be considered part of the database's schema. New functions are added to the IDS product with data definition language (DDL) statements, and information about the new functions is stored in system catalogs. Removing a UDF from a database without first determining how it is used has similar effects to removing a table from a traditional SQL-92 database; queries may stop working and the entire information system may be rendered useless.

There are two mechanisms for embedding logic within the ORDBMS. First, you can use the database procedural language, SPL. We call UDFs that use SPL *internal* functions because they use facilities built into the ORDBMS. Regardless of platform or operating system or whatever development environments are installed, the IDS product's SPL compiler and interpreter are always available.

Alternatively, you can implement your UDF in a general purpose, non-DBMS language such as C or Java. We call these *external* functions because they are written and compiled using an external development environment before the CREATE FUNCTION DDL command declares them to the ORDBMS. The library object containing an external function's compiled code is linked into the ORDBMS when it is needed, whereupon the logic within it is executed.

So far as developers writing OR-SQL queries are concerned, there is no way for them to tell how a function is implemented. Most object-relational database applications mix internal and external UDFs. For simplicity, most of our examples in this chapter are internal UDFs that use SPL. But always keep in mind that any of these examples might just as easily be implemented using another language.

CREATE FUNCTION Statement

New UDFs are declared within the database using the CREATE FUNCTION DDL statement. As part of a CREATE FUNCTION statement, you need to supply the following:

- The function's name. As with other schema objects function names are OR-SQL identifiers, which are character strings up to 128 bytes in length.
- The function's argument list. Depending on whether the UDF is external or internal, the argument list specification takes a different form.
- The name of the function's return type.
- Modifiers and hints to the server. The ORDBMS uses these at runtime to optimize how it processes queries that include the UDF.
- The 'function body' or implementation of the function. As with the argument list, the specification of a function's body varies depending on whether the UDF is external or internal.
- Where necessary, additional information about the function.

Listing 5–2 illustrates the basic outline of a `CREATE FUNCTION` statement.

```
CREATE FUNCTION Function_Name ( [ Argument {, Argument } ] )
RETURNING Return_Type
[ WITH ( { Modifier = Value } ) ]
FUNCTION_BODY_DECLARATION
[ LANGUAGE [C | Java] ];
```

Listing 5–2. *Outline of CREATE FUNCTION Statement*

`CREATE FUNCTION` statements can be issued using the same techniques as other `CREATE` statements; either with a script that is run through a client tool such as `dbaccess` or `SQLEditor` or embedded into a client program. The IDS product also provides a utility intended to make working with large bundles of extensions easier. This tool, called BladeManager®, allows you to install and upgrade DataBlade™ products, which are shipped as a directory of install files and executable libraries. The BladeManager utility opens the install files, extracts the list of new UDFs and data types to add, and performs all of these operations for you. The *DataBlade Development Kit (DBDK)* automates the creation of these scripts.

In Listing 5–3 we present several examples illustrating how UDFs are declared. All of these `CREATE FUNCTION` statements are taken from the sample code used to create the Movies-R-Us Web site database.

```
--
--   Example 1. External C function for constructing a new
--   instance of a State_Enum type based on a String. This
--   UDF can be used directly in OR-SQL queries, but it is
--   more likely that it will be used to implement a cast.
--
```

```
CREATE FUNCTION State_EnumIn (lvarchar)
RETURNS State_Enum
WITH (  NOT VARIANT, PARALLELIZABLE )
EXTERNAL NAME
"$INFORMIXDIR/extend/State/bin/State.bld(State_EnumInput)"
LANGUAGE C;
--
--   Example 2. SPL internal function that computes an Age
--   (in years) from a PersonType. The PersonType includes
--   an attribute that records the date of birth, and all
--   function does is access that attribute to compute its
--   result.
--
CREATE FUNCTION Age( Person PersonType)
RETURNS integer
     RETURN (TODAY - Person.DOB) / 365.241;
END FUNCTION;
--
--   Example 3. External 'C' UDR implementing an operator
--   that overloads the functionality of the '<' symbol.
--   Note the modifiers, which assist query planning.
--
CREATE FUNCTION LessThan (State_Enum, State_Enum)
RETURNS boolean
WITH ( NOT VARIANT, NEGATOR     = GreaterThanOrEqual,
       COMMUTATOR = GreaterThan, PARALLELIZABLE
)
EXTERNAL NAME
"$INFORMIXDIR/extend/State/bin/State.bld(State_EnumLessThan)"
LANGUAGE c;
--
--   Example 4. External Java UDR implementing a function
--   that accesses a value within the type.
--
execute procedure install_jar (
"file:C:\informix\extend\PersonName.jar","PersonName");
--
CREATE FUNCTION GetFamilyName ( PersonName )
RETURNING lvarchar
WITH ( NOT VARIANT, PARALLELIZABLE )
EXTERNAL NAME
'PersonName:PersonName.getFamily_Name(PersonName)'
LANGUAGE Java;
```

Listing 5-3. *Examples of Several CREATE FUNCTION Statements*

Over the next few sections, we examine various aspects of user-defined function declarations in detail. We defer discussion of UDF *function bodies*, which covers the implementation of UDF logic, and how this logic is bound into the ORDBMS, to a later section.

User-Defined Function Names

Function names are the identifiers used to refer to UDFs in OR-SQL query statements. They are also used when creating other kinds of server extensions that combine multiple UDFs such as user-defined access methods, operator classes, aggregators, and so on.

For example, the identifier strings `State_EnumIn`, `Age`, `LessThan`, and `GetFamilyName` would be used in queries when referring to the functions declared in Listing 5–3. Notice that if the UDF is implemented in a compiled C library, or a Java "jar file," the ORDBMS does not use the name of the sub-routine as it appears in the source code (called the function's *external symbol name*). As a result, two UDFs with different OR-SQL function names can refer to the same logic in a shared library. We illustrate what this might looks like in Listing 5–4.

```
--
--   Example 5. External Java UDR that re-uses the Java
--   method implementing GetFamilyName() in Figure 5.
--
CREATE FUNCTION GetLastName ( PersonName )
RETURNING lvarchar
WITH ( NOT VARIANT )
EXTERNAL NAME
 'PersonName:PersonName.getFamily_Name(PersonName)'
LANGUAGE Java;
```

Listing 5–4. *Declaration of UDR Using a Java Implementation for a Second Time*

In this case, the two different OR-SQL functions `GetLastName()` and `GetFamilyName()` use the same Java implementation and would exhibit identical behavior.

Function names ought to reflect what the function does. It is generally not a good idea to include a reference to whatever types the function operates on because this leads to confusion when you create subtypes or overload a function. A function's name is the first component of its *signature*, which is the combination of the function's name and its' argument list. In the next section, where we describe the argument list in more detail, we explain how the practice of uniquely identifying functions by their full signature is the mechanism that makes function overloading possible.

Some function names are reserved for implementing specific behaviors. These identifiers are bound to particular operator symbols or expression names in the OR-SQL language. For example, the `Equal()` and `Times()` function names correspond to the "=" and "*"symbols, respectively. Whenever the ORDBMS sees a "= " character in a query comparing two type instances, it looks for a function named `Equal` with two arguments of the type being compared in the query. In Table 5–1 below we present a list of these special functions and the SQL language symbol or standard expression to which they correspond.

Table 5–1. SQL Operator Symbols and UDF Signatures

Function	Return Type	SQL Level Example
LessThan(Type,Type)	Boolean	Type < Type
LessThanOrEqual(Type,Type)	Boolean	Type <= Type
Equal(Type, Type)	Boolean	Type = Type
GreaterThanOrEqual(Type,Type)	Boolean	Type >= Type
GreaterThan(Type, Type)	Boolean	Type > Type
NotEqual(Type,Type)	Boolean	Type <> Type or Type != Type
Like(Type, Type)	Boolean	Type LIKE Type
Matches (Type, Type)	Boolean	Type MATCHES Type
Plus (Type, Type)	Type	Type + Type
Minus (Type, Type)	Type	Type – Type
Times (Type, Type)	Type	Type * Type
Divide (Type, Type)	Type	Type / Type
Concat (Type, Type)	Type	Type II Type

An extensive list of other built-in SQL expressions can be overloaded for new types with UDFs. All of the mathematical expressions such as `ABS()`, `POW()`, `SQRT()`, and so on can be made to work for user-defined types, as can character expressions such as `LENGTH()`. These special function names also apply to operators between different types. For example, it is useful to create a `DIVIDE()` UDF that divides a user-defined type value by an `INTEGER` and returns another instance of the same type, as we show in Listing 5–5.

```
--
--   The Mass UDT is an OPAQUE type that encapsulates both
--   a unit ('KILOGRAMS','POUNDS','OUNCES' etc) and a
--   quantity value. Functions implementing its behavior
--   perform all of the necessary conversions to compute
--   comparisons and other mathematical operations
--   automatically.
--
CREATE FUNCTION Divide (Mass, integer)
RETURNS Mass
WITH (
        NOT VARIANT, PARALLELIZABLE
)
EXTERNAL NAME
"$INFORMIXDIR/extend/Mass/bin/Mass.bld(MassIntDivide)"
LANGUAGE C;
```

Listing 5–5. *UDF Illustrating Built-in Function Overloading SQL Mathematical Operation*

Reserving specific function names for certain data type behaviors is a pervasive technique. Another example is the way the ORDBMS looks for a support function called `Compare()` when sorting or indexing user-defined types. Later, when we discuss the User-defined Aggregate (UDA) feature, we will see how this techniques is also applied to OR-SQL's built-in aggregates (`SUM()`, `MIN()`, `MAX()`, and so on).

Argument List

The argument list is the vector of data types supplied as parameters to the UDF. An argument list makes up the second part of the function's *signature*. Any data type can be used as an argument to a UDR. For example, you can pass a `ROW TYPE` or a `COLLECTION` into a C external function, or an `OPAQUE TYPE` to an SPL internal function. Each host language environments has facilities for handling the different kinds of data type.

Depending on how the UDF is implemented, there are differences in how the argument list is declared. External UDFs require only a list of data types, while internal UDFs require both data types and a *variable name* for each parameter. Arguments to internal functions are named because parameter values are addressed in the logic making up the function's body. With external functions, the inner workings of the UDF are invisible to the ORDBMS and the code implementing the external function's logic has its own method of handling parameters. It is the responsibility of the external language implementation to have appropriate C or Java data structures in place to receive argument data from the ORDBMS.

Several of our previous examples illustrate how an argument list is used for external functions. In Listing 5–6 we present a complete internal UDF implementation that shows how named parameters can be used in the function's body. This example uses a ROW TYPE defined in Chapter 4.

```
CREATE FUNCTION SetSurname( Arg1 PersonName,
                           Arg2 ShortString )
RETURNING PersonName;
    DEFINE rtRetVal PersonName;
    LET rtRetVal = Arg1;
    LET rtRetVal.Family_Name = Arg2;

    RETURN rtRetVal;
END FUNCTION;
```

Listing 5–6. *Sample UDF with a Mixture of Data Type Arguments*

Earlier, we mentioned that by using the entire signature to identify UDFs, the ORDBMS can *overload* functions. Overloaded functions have the same identifying name me but a different argument list. In Listing 5–7 we create several functions to illustrate various aspects of how overloading works.

The first of these UDF declarations is intended as a demonstration of what function overloading is not. The CREATE FUNCTION Age(Person-Type) in Listing 5–7 will fail, because although the behavior it implements is different from the function in Example 2 of Listing 5–2, the *signature* of the second function is identical to the *signature* of the first. Even though the first function is an external function, the ORDBMS determines that a row in the SYSPROCEDURES table already exists with the same function name and parameter list.

```
CREATE FUNCTION Age ( PersonType )
RETURNS INTEGER
WITH ( NOT VARIANT )
EXTERNAL NAME 'PersonType:PersonType.Age(PersonType)'
LANGUAGE Java;

CREATE FUNCTION Equal( Arg1 PersonName, Arg2 PersonName )
RETURNING boolean;
    IF  ((Arg1.Family_Name = Arg2.Family_Name) AND
         (Arg1.First_Name  = Arg2.First_Name) AND
         (Arg1.Title        = Arg2.Title)) THEN
            RETURN 't'::boolean;
    END IF;
```

```
        RETURN 'f'::boolean;
END FUNCTION;

CREATE FUNCTION Equal ( Movie_Title, Movie_Title )
RETURNING boolean
WITH ( NOT VARIANT, PARALLELIZABLE,
       NEGATOR = NotEqual, COMMUTATOR = Equal )
EXTERNAL NAME
"$INFORMIXDIR/extend/Title/bin/Title.bld(title_eq)"
LANGUAGE C;
```

Listing 5–7. *Example of Functions Overloading a Single Name with Different Signatures*

By contrast, the final pair of UDF declarations are fine. Although they share the same function name, they compare different types for equality.

The ORDBMS figures out which UDF to invoke as it parses query statements. The IDS engine can tell what data types are being passed into each UDF in a query because, as we have seen, all columns in ORDBMS schema tables are strongly typed. Ambiguity, which happens if the ORDBMS finds more than one UDF that matches, generates a parser error.

For example, the query in Listing 5–8 finds all movies with the title "'The Big Sleep." The ORDBMS looks at the data type for the Title column in the Movies table and figures out how it can automatically CAST the string literal 'The Big Sleep' into the Movie_Title type, before invoking the Equal(Movie_Title, Movie_Title) UDF logic.

```
SELECT M.Id,
       M.Title,
       M.Release_Date
  FROM Movies M
 WHERE M.Title = 'The Big Sleep';
```

id ::movie_id	Title::title	Release_date ::DATE
100606	Big Sleep, The	06/01/1946

Listing 5–8. *SQL Query Illustrating How the ORDBMS Uses UDFs*

Note the string in the Title result column in Listing 5–8. It is different from the string literal supplied in the WHERE clause. Conceivably, you might use a SQL-92 type such as VARCHAR to store movie titles. However, real-world movie titles exhibit behavior that does not correspond to the behavior of the built-in VARCHAR data type. Were a movie club member to type the string "'Big Sleep, The'" into our Web site, they would want to see the same movie information. In other words, the movie title "'The Big 'Sleep" is equal to the movie title "'Big Sleep, The', while as simple strings these are entirely different.

We reproduce the behavior of the SQL VARCHAR data type in the query in Listing 5–9 by explicitly casting the Movie.Title column into LVARCHAR. For obvious reasons, this query doesn't find a movie whose title matches the constant string.

```
SELECT M.Id,
       M.Title,
       M.Release_Date
  FROM Movies M
 WHERE M.Title::lvarchar = 'The Big Sleep';


** No matching rows found **
```

Listing 5–9. *SQL Query Illustrating the Power of Overloading SQL Behavior*

The same general idea applies to all data types. Two digitized fingerprint scans may not be bit-wise identical, but they might be considered as equivalent (coming from the same finger), and the ORDBMS allows developers to integrate code that can compare two instances of the data type to find out. Embedding this kind of functionality into the ORDBMS allows OR-SQL developers to reason about the objects in the database even if they have no idea how the behavior of these objects is physically implemented.

We say 'vector of arguments' rather than 'set of arguments' when describing an argument list, because the number *and order* of the arguments can differentiate function signatures. For example, the two UDF signatures in Listing 5–10 are not the same. Although they have the same function name and both take two arguments of the same data types, they can be distinguished by their different argument order.

```
CREATE FUNCTION Some_Function ( First_Type, Second_Type)
. . . ;

CREATE FUNCTION Some_Function ( Second_Type, First_Type )
. . . ;
```

Listing 5–10. *Functions with Same Name and Arguments, Differentiated by Argument Order*

While this kind of difference is an interesting side effect of the function signature mechanism, differentiating functions in this way is poor design. Requiring developers to be mindful of argument order invites confusion and error.

Figuring out which UDF to run based on the name and arguments can get very complicated. If there is a perfect match for the function in the OR-SQL statement, the choice is unambiguous. However, recall that the ORDBMS supports features such as data type inheritance, distinct types, and casting between data types. IDS uses a sophisticated algorithm to determine which function, if any, is the appropriate one to run when no perfect match is found. We revisit the topic of function resolution later in this chapter.

Return Type

UDFs return values of some data type. The return type is specified after the argument list and before any modifiers, and it is preceded by either a RETURNS or RETURNING keyword. Return types can be any of the types the IDS product supports: built-in, OPAQUE TYPE, DISTINCT TYPE, ROW TYPE, or COLLECTION.

Although not strictly part of a function's signature, the return type is important in query processing. For example, the ORDBMS cannot use the Equal() function in Listing 5–11 to substitute for the '=' symbol. The function's signature is correct, but the ORDBMS cannot use it because it does not return a boolean result.

```
CREATE FUNCTION Equal ( Movie_Title, Movie_Title )
RETURNING integer
.
.
```

Listing 5–11. *Example Illustrating Importance of UDF Return Type*

The vast majority of UDFs return a single result calculated from their parameter values. Sometimes a module of embedded logic will return a COLLECTION, but so far as the query processing facilities are concerned this is still a single data object. Certain kinds of UDF can, however, return more than one value. There are two mechanisms for this: *iterator* functions and functions returning *out parameters* for use in queries as *statement local variables*.

- Iterator functions return a sequence of values. They can be thought of as a computed table. The rows returned by an iterator function can be inserted into a table or used to generate a set of values for an IN predicate.

- Out parameters are values returned *by reference*, through the argument list, rather than the singleton result returned by other UDFs. UDFs that need to qualify the values they return use statement local variables. For example, a document search UDF might return true if it determines that two documents meet its criteria for similarity. But it might also calculate a value reflecting the degree of similarity.

We describe both kinds of advanced UDF in a later section of this chapter.

Modifiers

Developers can supply *modifiers* when they declare a new UDF. Modifiers provide the ORDBMS with instructions about how best to handle the function. Such instructions are necessary because UDFs differ in the way they behave with respect to the ORDBMS environment, and these differences affect how they should be treated by the query processor. Modifiers are name/value pairs, and a list of modifiers is preceded by the WITH keyword. They appear between the function's return type and body. Several of the UDF examples in Listings 5-3 and 5-7 illustrate how to supply modifiers with a UDF declaration. In this section we explain what each modifier means so that you can either supply them yourself or answer the DBDK wizard's questions correctly.

VARIANT and NOT VARIANT

Certain kinds of UDFs, even when passed identical argument values, can return different results each time they are called. For example, a function might return a random number (almost certainly different each time) or a person's current age based on their date of birth (run this function twice a year apart and it will yield a different result) or compare two Currency instances for equality (varies with exchange rates). We call such extensions *variant* because their results vary over time.

Variant behavior is particularly important because some OR-SQL query statements are received and parsed by the server some time before they are executed. A statement could be a prepared query, or a query embedded within an SPL routine. NOT VARIANT functions taking constant arguments can be executed at the time the query is initially received by the ORDBMS, and it is the result of this execution that is used by the optimizer and at runtime. In Listing 5–8, for example, illustrates the common situation where the UDF that casts the constant string into a movie title is NOT VARIANT.

By contrast, when a query statement includes a *variant* function, or when a NOT VARIANT function takes argument data from a table's column, the ORDBMS ensures that such functions are invoked at the time the query is executed. This ensures that the query returns the correct answer at the time its results are requested.

To indicate that a function is not variant, you need to supply a modifier with the CREATE FUNCTION statement as shown in Listing 5–12. The ORDBMS assumes that all external UDFs are variant because it can't determine what goes on inside them.

```
CREATE FUNCTION TypeInput(lvarchar)
RETURNS Type
WITH ( NOT VARIANT )
AS EXTERNAL   '$INFORMIXDIR/extend/Type/bin/Type.so'
LANGUAGE C;
```

Listing 5–12. *Example of NOT VARIANT Modifier*

The IDS product enforces certain restrictions on variant functions. For instance, it prevents you from building an index that requires a variant function. A functional index over the variant Age() of a movie club member, or over a column containing Currency values would become inaccurate as time passed and as exchange rates varied. In practice, however, variant functions are fairly rare. For all of these reasons, it is a good idea to always supply the NOT VARIANT modifier for non-variant UDFs.

HANDLESNULL

In Chapter 3, we saw how the ORDBMS uses NULL values to represent missing information. When processing queries involving missing information, the ORDBMS can make a simplifying assumption. It presupposes that any time a NULL argument would be passed into an EXTERNAL UDF, the result would also be NULL. Therefore, as the ORDBM invokes EXTERNAL functions, it first checks to see if any of the arguments is NULL. In such cases, the ORDBMS doesn't actually call the function. Instead, it creates a NULL result value immediately.

In many circumstances this behavior is not what developers want. Instead, they may want to have NULL handled as if it were simply a special data value. In fact the ORDBMS itself includes a built-in function NVL() that lets you substitute another value for NULL. But in practice NVL() is sometimes not enough.

For example, Movies-R-Us Web site marketing might want to determine whether a particular item of merchandise is suitable for a particular movie club member. Some toys are only suitable for children of a certain age, and some apparel is suitable for either men or women. Such a function needs to deal with the occasional NULL date-of-birth or gender argument. And if the date of birth or gender is NULL, the IsSuitable() UDF should return false.

To inform the ORDBMS that an external UDF expects NULL arguments, the ORDBMS supports a HANDLESNULLS modifier. In Listing 5–13 we illustrate how you would declare an IsSuitable UDF with the HANDLESNULLS modifier.

```
CREATE FUNCTION IsSuitable( date, Gender, Merchandise_Type )
RETURNS boolean
WITH (
    NOT VARIANT, HANDLESNULLS
)
AS EXTERNAL NAME
'$INFORMIXDIR/extend/Misc/bin/Misc.bld(MerchIsSuitable)'
LANGUAGE C;
```

Listing 5–13. *Example of HANDLESNULLS Modifier*

Internal UDFs do not behave in the same way. NULL values are always passed into UDFs implemented using SPL. Within SPL code, NULL and three-valued logic operate according to the same rules as they do in OR-SQL queries.

An alternate approach to the whole problem of missing information is for developers to deal with it as part of the data type implementation. For example, in the case of the data type used to store US states, it is inevitable that for some addresses no state value is meaningful. The movie club member might live overseas, for example. In SQL-92 style systems this must be dealt with as a NULL. But this is clearly a different situation than when the member's state is not known or not recorded. And such a distinction might impact the site's operations. Movie club members who do not supply a state cannot receive mail, while overseas club members, even though they do not have a U.S. state, certainly can.

To cope with this, it can make sense for a data type's implementation to include several special statuses for certain situations. Then UDFs that access the type's encapsulated information can react accordingly. Depending on the value, an output function will produce a valid state name string, ""N/A," or a message indicating that the information is missing by using "'Not Known'" or "'Not Available.'""

COMMUTATORs and NEGATORs

Sometimes, reorganizing the data operations implied by a query statement can allow the ORDBMS to arrive at an answer more efficiently. If the IDS product's query processing knows that it can reverse the order of arguments to a function such as Equal(), then it is free to reorder a query's join order. Reversing the order of the parameters passed to an Equal() operation should not change (except in highly unusual, but logically possible circumstances) the function's verdict.

Reversing argument order is called "'commuting'" the arguments. Equal() is a special case. We say that the Equal() operation is *commutative* because reversing its arguments doesn't affect its result. But many operations do not behave in the same way. More usually, reversing argument order changes the function's result. However, if you reverse the argument order *and* replace the function with another, the original result can be preserved. For example, reversing the order of the parameters passed to LessThan() and calling the GreaterThan() function instead, will yield the same result as calling LessThan(). To describe this situation we say that GreaterThan() is the commutator for LessThan(), a situation we illustrate in Listing 5–14.

```
Equal(A::Type,B::Type )  ↔  Equal(B::Type,A::Type);

LessThan(A::Type,B::Type)  ↔
                            GreaterThan(B::Type,A::Type);


NOT ( Equal(A::Type,B::Type )
                        ↔ NotEqual(A::Type,B::Type);

NOT ( LessThan(A::Type,B::Type) )
                        ↔
            GreaterThanOrEqual(A::Type,B::Type);
```

Listing 5–14. *Logical Re-Organization of Certain Mathematical Operators*

Commutators are one example of query re-writing. "Negation" is another. When a query wants all values NOT GreaterThan() some value, if the query planner can, it might choose to rewrite this query as LessThanOrEqual(). Listing 5–14 also illustrates the Negator re-write operation.

By default, the ORDBMS does not make assumptions about what it can and cannot commute and negate. For some objects these rewrite rules do not apply, or else they are unclear. For example, what is the commutator of 'Contains(A,B)'? In general, it is 'Contained(B,A)'.

But this makes an assumption about what functionality a UDF implements based solely on one interpretation of its function name.[2] A type specification holding that although 'A = B', it is not the case that 'B = A', is probably bad design. Never the less, the ORDBMS needs to accommodate it.

In Table 5–2, we list each of the built-in operators and their corresponding commutator and negator functions.

Table 5–2. Table of Commutator and Negator Functions

Function Name	Symbol	Commutator	Negator
LessThan (Type,Type)	<	GreaterThan()	GreaterThanOrEqual()
LessThanOrEqual (Type,Type)	<=	GreaterThan OrEqual()	GreaterThan()
Equal(Type, Type)	=	Equal()	NotEqual()
GreaterThanOrEqual (Type,Type)	>=	LessThanOrEqual()	LessThan()
GreaterThan (Type, Type)	>	LessThanl()	LessThanOrEqual()
NotEqual (Type,Type)	<>, !=	NotEqual()	Equal()
Like(Type, Type)	LIKE	None	None
Matches (Type, Type)	MATCHES	None	None

Table 5–2 illustrates several issues relating to how commutator and negator modifiers are used. What it implies that there is no way to ensure that a UDF is always created before it is named as a commutator or negator. For instance, the negator of Equal is NotEqual, and the negator of NotEqual is Equal, so which should you create first? The ORDBMS does not check that the UDF listed with the modifier exists when you create the function. Inconsistencies produce run-time errors.

Second, only functions returning boolean results can be commuted or negated. For example, one UDF implementing the mathematical operator `Times()` which overloads the SQL '*' symbol is shown in Listing 5–15.

---

2 In the case of Contained() and Contains(), they may not be commutative if the implementation of one includes 'touches' and the implementation of the second does not.

```
CREATE FUNCTION Times ( Arg1 Currency, Arg2 INTEGER )
RETURNING Currency;
      RETURN ROW( Arg1.Quantity * Arg2,
                      Arg1.Denomination )::Currency;
END FUNCTION;
```

Listing 5–15. *Example of Function Overloading Mathematical Operator*

As it processes the first of the queries in Listing 5–16, the ORDBMS succeeds in substituting a UDF with the `Times(Currency, INTEGER)` signature for the '*' symbol. But it generates an error on the second query because the ORDBMS parser is looking for a UDF with a `Times(INTEGER, Currency)` signature. The ORDBMS makes the pessimistic assumption that `Times(Currency, INTEGER)` is not necessarily equivalent to `Times(INTEGER, Currency)`. This is true, for example, of linear algebra operations that multiply matrices.

```
SELECT M.Name,
       M.Price * M.NumberAvailable AS Inventory_Value
   FROM Merchandise M;

SELECT M.Name,
       M.NumberAvailable * M.Price AS Inventory_Value
   FROM Merchandise M;
```

Listing 5–16. *Query Statements Illustrating Non-Commutability of Mathematical Functions*

Unfortunately, there is no way around this issue except to anticipate all of the ways in which a UDF might be called and to ensure that an appropriate declaration exists for that case. In the case of a function such as `Times()`, this means implementing and declaring both the `Times(Currency, INTEGER)` and `Times(INTEGER, Currency)` functions. The additional declaration in Listing 5–17 overcomes the problem.

```
CREATE FUNCTION Times ( Arg1 INTEGER, Arg2 Currency )
RETURNING Currency;
      RETURN TIMES ( Arg2, Arg1 );
END FUNCTION;
```

Listing 5–17. *Commutating an Overloaded SQL Mathematical Operator*

Correctly assigning a commutator and negator modifier helps the ORDBMS query processor. When designing the logic that implements a type's behavior, ask yourself what happens when you swap the argument order to UDFs returning boolean results.

Optimization Information

The ORDBMS uses a technique called cost-based optimization to find the most efficient way to compute the answer for a query. With RDBMS products, the optimizer could afford to make relatively simple assumptions about the CPU cost of SQL-92 expressions in queries. Determining INTEGER equality requires loading two CPU registers and exercising the silicon a little. VARCHAR comparisons are rarely much more costly than this. And RDBMS products could hard code algorithms to estimate how many rows in a table will satisfy a predicate in the WHERE clause.

UDF extensibility invalidates CPU cost assumptions. An individual UDF can be either very computationally expensive, or as simple as a built-in operation. In fact, the time taken to execute a single UDF can represent the majority of time taken to run a query. User-defined types also make it necessary to create new mechanisms to estimate how much data a UDF in the WHERE clause will filter out. Therefore, when creating database extensions developers should provide IDS with information that it can use in query planning.

In this section we briefly review how queries are processed in order to illustrate how the ORDBMS's query optimizer uses UDF information. Then we describe the means by which developers provide this information. Readers should be aware that the following is an extremely simplified description of what actually happens. Nevertheless, the principles described in this section are useful in practice.

Overview of Query Processing

Within the IDS engine, queries are decomposed into a sequence of low-level operations that correspond (roughly) to the relational operators described in Chapter 3. These can be re-arranged, subject to certain rules, without affecting the query's final results. For most of these low-level operations the ORDBMS can choose from among several physical algorithms. Consequently, there are multiple alternate plans that the ORDBMS could use for any given query.

For each data processing step within each alternative plan, IDS tries to estimate factors such as the amount of data involved (row count times column width) and how long any UDFs involved in the operation take to run. Then the ORDBMS calculates each plan's total requirements for physical resources such as disk I/O, memory, and CPU by totaling these estimates. Finally, the ORDBMS selects the "best" of the alternate plans according to some performance goal such as lowest overall hardware cost or fastest response time.

Consider the query in Listing 5–18.

"List Orders placed in the last week by Arizona residents born before January 6th, 1945."

```
SELECT Print ( M.Name ),
       O.OrderedOn,
       Value ( O.Line_Items )
  FROM MovieClubMembers M, Orders O)
 WHERE O.OrderedOn > TODAY - 7
   AND M.Address.State = 'Arizona'
   AND M.DOB < '1945-01-06'
   AND O.Customer = M.Id;
```

Listing 5–18. *Query Illustrating Optimization Strategy*

In Listing 5–19 we present two alternate physical plans for this query

```
1. RESTRICT Orders                          1. RESTRICT Movie_Club_Members
   ( OrderedOn > TODAY - 7 )                    ( ( M.DOB < '1945-01-06' ) AND
2. PROJECT 1.                                     ( M.Address.State = 'Arizona') )
   <Customer, OrderdOn, Value (Order_Line_Items) >  2. PROJECT 1
3. RESTRICT Movie_Club_Members                  < Id, Name >
   ( ( M.DOB < '1945-01-06' ) AND             3. RESTRICT Orders
   ( M.Address.State = 'Arizona') )             ( OrderedOn > TODAY - 7 )
4. PROJECT 4                                   4. PROJECT 3
   < Id, Print(Name) >                            <Customer, OrderdOn, Order_Line_Items)>
5. JOIN [ 2, 4 ]                               5. JOIN [ 2, 4 ]
   ( 2.Customer = 4.Id )                         ( 4.Customer = 2.Id )
6. PROJECT 5                                    6. PROJECT 5
   < 5.Print, 5.OrderedOn, 5.Value >             < Print(5.Name), 5.OrderedOn,
   Efficiency ( 5.OrderdOn, 5. ShippedOn) >       Value(5.Line_Items) >
          Plan A                                        Plan B
```

Listing 5–19. *Two Alternative Query Plans*

How does the ORDBMS decide which of these two is the better plan? Assuming that an index on the `MovieClubMembers.Address.State` column exists, does the ORDBMS use the index or does it simply scan the entire table, checking the restriction for every row in the table?

Also, when should the ORDBMS execute the `Value()` UDF for each result row? The function itself is probably fairly simple and returns a small data value, so it doesn't really matter in this case. But suppose `Value()` is a very complex UDF and takes a long time to run each time it is called (a couple of seconds, perhaps). Then it might make sense to delay running it until the last possible minute on the expectation that some rows from the Orders table will not find matches in the `MovieClubMembers` table. Plan B, which illustrates this approach, minimizes the number of times that the `Value()` UDF is called and might reduce the total time taken to run the query.

There are the two primary kinds of optimizer information that apply to user-defined functions: *selectivity* and *per-function cost*. We introduce both of these in the following section.

Selectivity

To help further understand how the ORDBMS handles selectivity, let us consider the simpler query in Listing 5–20, which is a subset of the one in Listing 5–19.

```
SELECT COUNT(*)
  FROM MovieClubMembers M
 WHERE M.Address.State = 'Arizona'
   AND M.DOB < '1945-01-06';
```

Listing 5–20. *Query Illustrating Importance of Selectivity*

Suppose that both the `Address.State` and `DOB` columns are indexed. The ORDBMS query planner is presented with a dilemma. Which of the two predicates in the `WHERE` clause should it do first, and therefore, which index should it use? Also, in more recent versions of IDS, it is possible to combine two independent indices as part of a single scan.

Consider also that there may be no advantage to using any index. If the query ends up counting most of the rows anyway then the most efficient approach is simply to read every row once, check it, and count the matches. In these circumstances, using the index would incur the additional overhead of reading index data while not significantly reducing the number of data rows read in the base table.

To figure out whether to use an index, the ORDBMS tries to estimate how many rows in the table satisfy each predicate. If the percentage of rows that match falls *below* some threshhold (usually about 10 percent), using the index makes sense. If several predicates fall below the threshhold, the ORDBMS will either choose the most restrictive of them or scan two indices. The key to this scheme is estimating the *selectivity* of each of these predicates: Equals (M.Address.State, 'Arizona') and DOB < '1945-01-06'.

Over the years numerous schemes have been proposed to estimate selectivity. Most commercial RDBMSs estimate selectivity for built-in types fairly accurately. The ORDBMS can use these built-in estimators for the predicate involving the DOB (date) column. Histograms are the most popular mechanism for this. Database administrators regularly run a utility that creates a histogram of the data values in each column. The histogram for the DOB column might look like the one in Figure 5–3.

From this figure you can see how the ORDBMS calculates the selectivity for the date of birth predicate from Listing 5–20. About 21 percent of the population was born before 1945. So the selectivity of the DOB < '01/06/1945' is about 0.21. Therefore, using an index on DOB isn't going to improve the query's performance by much. But what about the second predicate? Is it worth using an index to find Arizona residents?

State_Enum is an OPAQUE TYPE and the Equal() UDF is an EXTERNAL FUNCTION. The IDS product makes naive assumptions about UDFs involving extended types. For example, it assumes that 10 percent of the rows will match an "'=,'" and that 50 percent of rows match other predicates. In other words, the ORDBMS optimizer is biased *against* user-defined extensions, because for all built-in types, sophisticated techniques are used to arrive at (relatively) accurate estimates.

There are two ways for developers to provide selectivity information for UDFs. First, they can specify a constant selectivity estimate as part of the UDF declaration. This is a floating point value between 0.0 and 1.0. Providing a constant selectivity value has the virtue that it is simple, but it is usually useful only in situations where an accurate selectivity estimate follows from the definition of the object and the UDF. Listing 5–21 illustrates how to create a function and to include the specification of selectivity. In this case, there are 52 U.S. states or territories, so you would expect, on average, about 2 percent of them to be returned from an Equal().

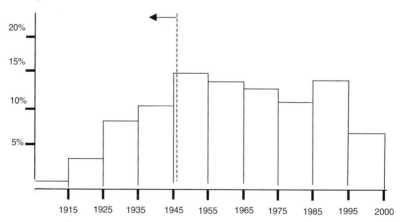

Figure 5–3. *Demographic Histogram of Population Using Dates of Birth*

```
CREATE FUNCTION Equal (State_Enum, State_Enum)
RETURNS BOOLEAN
WITH
(
    NOT VARIANT, PARALLELIZABLE,
    COMMUTATOR = Equal, NEGATOR = NotEqual,
    SELCONST   = 0.02
)
EXTERNAL NAME
"$INFORMIXDIR/extend/State/bin/State.bld(State_EnumEqual)"
LANGUAGE C;
```

Listing 5–21. *User-Defined Function Declaration with Constant Selectivity*

In this case 2 percent falls below the threshhold, and the query optimizer would probably use the State index. But if the state were 'California', which accounts for about 13 percent, then using the index would not be such a good thing. So alternatively, UDF developers can create a support function to *calculate* selectivity for a UDF and instruct the ORDBMS to call that function for an estimate, rather than rely on a constant value. Selectivity support functions need to return a floating-point value between 0.0 and 1.0.

The StateEqualSelectivity UDF in Listing 5–22 calculates the selectivity based on the values it is passed. Internally, it simply looks up the percentage of the U.S. population in the given state from a static array of values and returns it. It is then included as a modifier in the second CREATE FUNCTION statement. This instructs the ORDBMS to call the StateEqualSelectivity function as it processes queries that include the Equal(State_Enum, State_Enum) UDF.

```
CREATE FUNCTION StateEqualSelectivity ( POINTER, POINTER )
RETURNS FLOAT
WITH ( NOT VARIANT )
EXTERNAL NAME
"$INFORMIXDIR/extend/State/bin/State.bld(State_SelEqual)"
LANGUAGE C;
--
CREATE FUNCTION Equal (State_Enum, State_Enum)
RETURNS BOOLEAN
WITH
(
    NOT VARIANT, PARALLELIZABLE,
    COMMUTATOR = Equal, NEGATOR = NotEqual,
    SELFUNC = StateEqualSelectivity
)
```

```
EXTERNAL NAME
"$INFORMIXDIR/extend/State/bin/State.bld(State_EnumEqual)"
LANGUAGE C;
```

Listing 5–22. *User-Defined Function Declaration with Function Calculating Selectivity*

Back to the query in Listing 5–20. Arizona accounts for about 1.9 percent of the U.S. population, so `StateEqualSelectivity` returns 0.019. This indicates that using the `Address.State` index is a good idea for this particular query. Were the query to ask for California, the `StateEqualSelectivity` UDF would tell the optimizer that the selectivity for this operation was 0.13, and that using the index might not be the best plan.

Estimating selectivity is a complex problem. Our `StateEqual-Selectivity` works well only if the data in the address column matches the general population distribution in the U.S. But a database used by an Arizona business will probably find this approximation inaccurate. In another data types, like st_polygon type that records outlines of spatial objects, the problem is more acute. One application may use the type to store national boundaries, while another uses it to record habitat ranges of rodents, and a third to record mold growth in petri dishes. But the type's selectivity estimators need to to figure out how many spatial objects in a column overlap some arbitrary constant value. To accommodate diverse data distributions the ORDBMS provides a *statistics* gathering mechanism that can be used with the *selectivity* function.

It's worth keeping in mind that there is no need to calculate costs *precisely*. Approximate estimates, so long as they accurately reflect the relative costs of different operations, are sufficient. Even in the absence of sophisticated selectivity estimators the ORDBMS can gather quite a lot of information: number of rows, size of rows, presence of primary key and foreign key constraints, and so on.

Function Cost

A second kind of UDF modifier that the IDS product's query processor takes into consideration estimates computational effort whenever the UDF is executed. If you look at the built-in SQL-92 data types and operations over them, you will notice how little hardware resource they require. User-defined functions on the other hand, might include logic that compares images, scans videos, computes complex numerical results, or searches for particular word in a document. These are all examples of *expensive functions*. Executing expensive functions consumes orders of magnitude more hardware resource than built-in functions. For example, consider the query in Listing 5–23.

"Show me cinemas with names something like "'Cinema Royal"'' with a predominant color of blue."

```
SELECT C.Name,
       C.Address
  FROM Cinemas C
 WHERE Soundex(C.Name) MATCHES Soundex('Cinema Royal')
   AND MainColor( C.Photo )= 'blue';
```

Listing 5–23. *Query Illustrating Importance of Per-Call Costing Estimates*

It is unlikely that a convenient index exists for either of these predicates. (In practice the user would be likely to have some other predicate, such as geographic location, on which to restrict the search.) The ORDBMS must check all the records in the Cinemas table to see which ones satisfy both predicates. The order in which you apply these two functions, however, can dramatically affect how long it takes the query to complete.

As you might expect, it takes a lot of CPU and memory to run the MainColors() function. MainColors() needs to read the image from disk into memory—involving I/O from the large object storage—and then step through the image, one pixel at a time, to determine its "main color." On the other hand, by the time the Soundex() and the Matches() function is invoked, all necessary I/O has already been performed, and the CPU overhead for these operations is relatively small. Therefore, the ORDBMS should make sure it evaluates the MATCHES predicate first. It should only go to the trouble of checking the expensive MainColor() function when the names match.

Information about a function's execution cost is provided using the PER_FUNCALL modifier. This modifier is an integer value, and it is important to understand that it does not reflect any absolute measure of cost. Rather, it indicates the cost of the function relative to the cost of other functions. IDS assumes the built-in functions such as Compare (INTEGER, INTEGER) has cost 1. Thus, a function with cost 100 is one hundred times as expensive as a built-in function. In Listing 5–24 we illustrate how this modifier is declared.

```
CREATE FUNCTION MainColor ( image )
RETURNING color
WITH ( NOT VARIANT, PER_FUNCALL = 2500 )
EXTERNAL NAME
"$INFORMIXDIR/extend/Image/bin/Image.bld(MainColor)"
LANGUAGE C;
```

Listing 5–24. *PER_FUNCALL Modifier Example*

The best way to estimate PER_FUNCALL cost is experimentally. Set up a test harness query that can be run with and without the new UDF. Measure the difference and take the multiplier. PER_FUNCALL cost is used by the ORDBMS to order its operations so as to minimize total query costs. When it sees several UDFs ANDed together, the ORDBMS invokes the least expensive functions first. This minimizes the number of times it has to invoke expensive functions.

In many ORDBMS applications, the hardware resources consumed by the UDFs embedded within the engine represent the dominant cost. Financial analysis databases, which evaluate a time series of price and volume data for equity stock prices, may only involve a few thousand rows. But the large object data management and computationally expensive numerical analysis routines mean queries will take a long time. Therefore, it is a very good idea to supply PER_FUNCALL costs when you create an expensive UDF.

Runtime Information for External UDFs

Runtime modifiers provide information to the ORDBMS about an external UDF's runtime requirements. Some UDFs use more memory than typical to store local variables, or the code in the function might call itself recursively. Such atypical functions need extra stack space. Alternatively, because of the way it works, a UDF might need to run in a special location to get around the restrictions that apply when running in the default environment. In this section we provide a list of these runtime modifiers and explain how they should be used.

STACK

This modifier allows developers to specify how much stack space should be allocated to a user-defined function. Stack space is memory used to store arguments, local variables, and bookkeeping information for the database and operating system. By default the ORDBMS ensures that a fairly large block of stack memory is available (typically 32K). But for some user-defined routines—recursive functions, code modules with lots of local variables, or functions that are entry points into other code libraries—this is inadequate.

The STACK modifier tells the ORDBMS to allocate additional space before it calls the UDF. The value supplied with this modifier specifies how many bytes of stack space the ORDBMS should allocate. Listing 5–25 illustrates how to use the STACK modifier to ensure that 128K of space is available to the UDF whenever it is invoked by the ORDBMS.

```
CREATE FUNCTION ImageMerge( Image, Image )
RETURNS Image
WITH ( NOT VARIANT, STACK=128000 )
EXTERNAL NAME
"$INFORMIXDIR/extend/Image/bin/Image.bld(ImageMerge)"
LANGUAGE C;
```

Listing 5–25. *STACK Modifier Example*

Note that memory allocated to the UDF with the ORDBMS's own memory management facilities (mi_alloc(), mi_dalloc(), and so on, see Chapter 10 for details) is *not* taken from the stack. Instead mi_alloc() memory is allocated out of a shared global pool. The difference is important. If your UDF allocates a lot of memory using mi_alloc() there is no reason to conclude that it needs any extra stack space. On the other hand, even if the UDF does not mi_alloc() a lot of memory, it might allocate a large local variable array to hold scratch data from the stack.

How do you know when to use a non-default stack size? In the first place, UDFs that invoke functions in other people's libraries are good candidates. In addition, if your UDF code is recursive or creates a lot of large local variables, you might want to bump up stack size. Ultimately, UDF calls that grow their stack size beyond its allocated limit will generate an error when you test them.

Note that there is also a configuration parameter called STACKSIZE. This parameter has a similar purpose to the STACK modifier, except it modifies the default stack space, which is the amount of memory allocated to every UDF. Some DataBlade™ products require STACKSIZE be set to a higher value.

CLASS

Certain C UDFs need special handling with respect to where they run. For example, they may make direct calls to the operating system, include code from a legacy system that violates one of the rules about writing user-defined extensions, or a UDF might include a *Remote Procedure Call (RPC)* or use sockets to interact with an external process. These UDFs *must* be made to run in a single instance of a special class of *Virtual Processor (VP)*.

To instruct the ORDBMS to switch to this alternative class of VP before it executes the UDF logic, you supply the special class's name with the CLASS modifier. You must also configure the IDS instance to start up this virtual process by adding the necessary entry to the configuration file. Then at runtime, when it needs to invoke this function, the ORDBMS is careful first to switch to the specified VP before loading and running the function's body.

A user-defined function that uses RPC to send a message to another process might be created as shown in Listing 5–26.

```
CREATE FUNCTION RPC_CCValidate (CC_Card , US_Dollars)
RETURNING boolean
WITH ( CLASS = 'RPC_Extent' )
EXTERNAL NAME
"$INFORMIXDIR/RPC_Stuff/CalcRPC/RPCDiscCalc.bld(DC_RPC_Calc)"
LANGUAGE C;
```

Listing 5–26. *Example of UDF Using Non-Default Virtual Processor Class*

UDFs needing this kind of special handling are rare exceptions.

NOMIGRATE

One of the problems encountered by developers writing external UDFs was that sometimes, they are obliged to use libraries of executable logic over which they have limited control. Such library routines violate the rules of good UDF coding practice: they include static variables, are not thread-safe, or are not re-entrant. As long as the library does not use any operating system services, the ORDBMS can be instructed to contain the UDF's execution to a single VP. The NOMIGRATE modifier fulfills this requirement.

There is another means of achieving the same objective. The Data-Blade API includes a call mi_udr_lock(). Calling mi_udr_lock (MI_TRUE) inside an EXTERNAL UDF logic prevents the ORDBMS from migrating the UDF to another VP between calls.

Parallelism and User-Defined Functions

Parallelism is very important to ORDBMS performance and scalability. Parallel query processing techniques break up data processing operations (scan, sort, join, and so on) and allocate pieces of the task to different hardware resources. As a result, IDS can make the best possible use of the hardware resources available to it and minimizes the total time taken to complete a query, as shown in Listing 5–27.

```
SELECT COUNT(*)
  FROM MovieClubMembers M
 WHERE M.CreditCard.Expiry = '03/2001';
```

Listing 5–27. *Example Illustrating Importance of Query Parallelism*

This is not a common query. It is unlikely that a DBA would have created a convenient index. So the ORDBMS must scan every row in the `MovieClubMembers` table and count the matching rows. A large table scan such as this is an example of an operation that can be readily parallelized. The IDS product has been engineered so that it can be reading and checking miltiple rows simultaneously, which dramatically reduces the total time needed for the entire operation.

Suppose the table's data is stored across three disk drives. Breaking the table scan up into three separate scans of table subsets, all of which proceed concurrently, would cut the time required complete the query to a little more than one third of what it would be for the single scan. Internally, this requires that the ORDBMS create multiple threads of execution and invoke the `Equal()` UDF in each thread.

Almost all simple EXTERNAL UDFs can work within a parallelized query plan, but as you might expect, the ORDBMS makes the pessimistic assumption that none can. To indicate that a user-defined function can be used in a parallelized query plan, you need to supply the PARALLELIZABLE modifier as shown in Listing 5–28.

```
CREATE FUNCTION LessThan (State_Enum, State_Enum)
RETURNS boolean
WITH
      (
      NOT VARIANT,
      NEGATOR    = GreaterThan,
      COMMUTATOR = GreaterThanOrEqual,
      SELFUNC    = StateLessThanSelectivity
      PARALLELIZABLE
)
EXTERNAL NAME
"$INFORMIXDIR/extend/State/bin/State.bld(StateEnumLessThan)"
LANGUAGE C;
```

Listing 5–28. *Example of UDF with PARALLELIZABLE Modifier*

UDFs that cannot or should not be parallelized include the following:

- Internal UDFs. Like many interpreted languages, SPL is not designed to be "'re-entrant.'" This means that UDFs written using SPL cannot be parallelized.
- UDFs involving a ROW TYPE or a COLLECTION cannot be parallelized.
- UDFs that must run in special classes of virtual processor. Blocking or unsafe UDFs can suspend the execution of a thread for some period of time, so they are not eligible for parallelism.

- UDFs that include callbacks, or execute OR-SQL queries, cannot be parallelized.
- Certain rarely used DataBlade API calls cannot be called in UDFs that are to be run in parallel. Most particularly, UDFs employing save sets cannot be parallelized.
- Expensive UDFs, such as those performing image processing, consume lots of memory, and should not be parallelized.

These limitations are the consequence of engineering priorities, and do not represent architectural limitations. As the IDS product is developed further they will gradually be lifted.

The phrase, "executing UDFs in parallel" has an alternative interpretation that is quite different from the one given above. Algorithms that transform large blocks of data can usually be broken up into separate threads of execution that are applied to different sub-parts of the problem. For example, should an application need to modify a Video, the preferred approach would be to set separate threads working on subsets of frames and then re-combine the transformed frames in a final step. Within the IDS product such *algorithmic parallelism*—which is to be contrasted to *data parallelism* strategies used by the query processor—is not supported. The ORDBMS uses parallelism to minimize the amount of time taken to complete a large set of small tasks, while algorithmic parallelism is best for a smaller number of larger tasks.

Additional Information

You can supply a variety of additional information with the CREATE FUNCTION statement. Some of this information—such as the language in which an external function is implemented—is used by the ORDBMS to determine how to invoke the UDF. Several CREATE FUNCTION examples in this chapter end with either ' LANGUAGE C ' or ' LANGUAGE Java '. Developers can also provide documentation describing what the UDF does we show in Listing 5–29.

```
CREATE FUNCTION Overlap (Period,Period)
RETURNS boolean
WITH (
    NOT VARIANT, PARALLELIZABLE,
    COMMUTATOR = Overlap
)
EXTERNAL NAME
"$INFORMIXDIR/extend/Period/bin/Period.bld(PeriodOverlap)"
LANGUAGE C
```

```
DOCUMENT "Overlap(Period,Period) returns true iff. one of the",
         "dates in one of the arguments is between the dates ",
         "of the other.   ";
```

Listing 5–29. *Documenting the Functionality of a New UDR*

Documenting the purpose or behavior of your UDFs is very useful. As software development tools to facilitate database design and querying become available, end users will see less and less OR-SQL and more and more "'boxes and arrows'" or "'fill-in-the-forms'" style interfaces.

Function Body

The term *function body* refers to the section of the CREATE FUNCTION statement that specifies either where the logic implementing the new UDF is to be found or the stored procedure language (SPL) code implementing the function itself. The function body is found between the modifiers and the final "additional information" section.

Depending on whether the UDF is internal or external, and if it is external, the language in which it is implemented, function bodies take on different forms.

Internal Functions

With INTERNAL UDFs, the function's body consists of its stored procedure language source code implementation (or the name of a file in which this source code is found). INTERNAL UDFs are compiled into intermediate *pcode* form at the time the CREATE FUNCTION is processed. At the times certain major database events occur, such as when a table mentioned in an SPL function is altered or a data type is modified, the ORDBMS will recompile UDFs that the change may affect.

This pcode is stored in the database's system catalogs. At runtime, the pcode is loaded from disk into the ORDBMS's memory and executed using an interpreter. SPL is simple and robust. It provides most of what you would expect from any programming language: typed variables, conditional branching, looping, and exception handling.

In Table 5–3 we list the syntax features of the language.

Table 5-3. Stored Procedure Language Syntax Keywords

CALL	CONTINUE	DEFINE
EXIT	FOR	FOREACH
IF ELSE	LET	ON EXCEPTION
RAISE EXCEPTION	RETURN	SYSTEM
TRACE	WHILE	END (WHILE IF FOREACH)

Many examples throughout this book illustrate how to use SPL, and in Chapter 6 we explore the language in some detail. In the following listings we present several examples that illustrate the range of ways it can be used.

In Listing 5-30 the example UDF simply takes an integer value that (hopefully) corresponds to a year. It makes a simple data correctness check, and raises an exception if the argument value fails that check. Then it uses the standard algorithm to check whether a year is a leap year. Raising this exception passes an error message back to some end user, and causes the ORDBMS to roll back whatever transaction it is in at the time.

```
CREATE FUNCTION IsLeapYear( Year INTEGER )
RETURNS boolean
    IF NOT Year BETWEEN 0 AND 10000 THEN
        RAISE EXCEPTION -746,
                    "IsLeapYEar: Invalid Year Value";
    END IF;
    IF ( MOD( Year, 4 ) = 0 ) THEN
        IF ( MOD ( Year, 100 )  = 0 ) THEN
            IF ( MOD ( Year, 400 )  = 0 ) THEN
                RETURN 't'
            END IF;
            RETURN 'f'
        END IF;
        RETURN 't'
    END IF;
    RETURN 'f'
END FUNCTION;
```

Listing 5-30. *Example of INTERNAL UDR Body*

Note the use of the (-746) SQL error code in this examples. The (-746) error code is reserved by the system for informational error messages.

Other UDFs—both INTERNAL and EXTERNAL—can be invoked from within an INTERNAL routine. This makes the stored procedure language a kind of extensible procedural language, just as OR-SQL is an extensible query language. The example in Listing 5–31 uses an *iterator function* (seen later in the chapter) called Isplit() implemented in Chapter 10 that breaks a string into a series of words. This UDF simply returns a count of how many words two sentences have in common.

```
CREATE FUNCTION CommonWordCount ( Arg1 LVARCHAR,
                                   Arg2 LVARCHAR )
RETURNS INTEGER
   DEFINE   lvOuterWord, lvInnerWord, lvWordsChecked,
            lvDel, lvInnerString, lvOuterString LVARCHAR;
   DEFINE   nCnt                  INTEGER;
   DEFINE   bWordIsChecked    BOOLEAN;

   LET nCnt = 0;
   LET lvWordsChecked = '';
   LET lvDel = ' ,.-';
   LET lvOuterString = UPPER(Arg1);
   LET lvInnerString = UPPER(Arg2);

   FOREACH EXECUTE FUNCTION ISplit (lvOuterString, lvDel)
           INTO lvOuterWord
     LET bWordIsChecked = 'f';

     FOREACH EXECUTE FUNCTION ISplit (lvWordsChecked, lvDel)
             INTO lvInnerWord
       IF ( lvOuterWord = lvInnerWord ) THEN
         LET bWordIsChecked = 't';
         EXIT FOREACH;
       END IF;
     END FOREACH;

     IF NOT bWordIsChecked THEN

       FOREACH EXECUTE FUNCTION ISplit (lvInnerString, lvDel)
               INTO lvInnerWord
         IF ( lvOuterWord = lvInnerWord ) THEN
           LET nCnt = nCnt + 1;
         END IF;
       END FOREACH;

       LET lvWordsChecked = lvWordsChecked || ' '
                            || lvOuterWord;
```

```
        END IF;

    END FOREACH;
    RETURN nCnt;
END FUNCTION;
```

Listing 5–31. *INTERNAL UDR Using Other User-Defined Routines*

SPL's chief virtue is the ease with which it accommodates OR-SQL. Query statements, procedural logic, and variables declared with a user-defined type, can be commingled with a single internal function body. However, the ORDBMS imposes certain rules on how functions containing OR-SQL statements can be used within other OR-SQL queries.

In programming language terms, you sometimes want a UDF to have some kind of *side effect*. Sometimes it might be useful to include a write query—an INSERT, UPDATE, or DELETE—within an SPL function. When you use such an SPL UDF in another OR-SQL query, however, the ORDBMS generates an error. This limitation is imposed because of the uncertain interaction between the transaction contexts of the outer and inner OR-SQL statements. Read queries inside SPL user-defined functions are usually not a problem.

The simple UDF example in Listing 5–32 illustrates how OR-SQL can be integrated into an SPL function. Another SELECT query uses this routine to find an approximate geographic location for a movie theater or an outlet from which some product may be picked up.[3]

```
CREATE FUNCTION GeoLocate ( ZipCode INTEGER,
                                  State    State_Enum )
RETURNING sp2Pnt
    RETURN ( SELECT Z.Location
                FROM ZipCodes Z
               WHERE Z.ZipCode = ZipCode
                 AND Z.State   = State );
END FUNCTION;
--
SELECT C.Name, Print(M.Name) AS Name
  FROM Cinemas C, MovieClubMembers M
 WHERE Distance ( GeoLocate ( C.Address.ZipCode.Major,
                              C.Address.State),
                  GeoLocate ( M.Address.ZipCode.Major,
                              M.Address.State)
             )  < 0.2;
```

---

[3] State is needed in this query because there are two zip codes whose regions span a state boundary.

Name::Cinemaname	Name::LVARCHAR
Moinahan Mall Theatre	Van Quoc
Moinahan Mall Theatre	Paul Brown
Poignant Point Movie Theatre	George Eliot

Listing 5–32. INTERNAL UDR With Embedded SQL SELECT

While it can be used for general-purpose programming, SPL is not appropriate for many kinds of UDR. SPL is restricted to running within the ORDBMS. A C library can be linked into external programs, and Java's mobility makes it especially powerful. But if you need to develop something quickly, or if your new function needs to use OR-SQL, SPL is the best choice.

External Functions

Different kinds of EXTERNAL functions take different approaches in their function bodies. In all cases the keyword EXTERNAL NAME is used, and the function body part of the CREATE FUNCTION statement indicates where the compiled logic implementing the function is to be found. Different external languages are loaded into the ORDBMS runtime using different linking standards, and, as a result, the way that the compiled objects are managed differs slightly.

C External Functions

C external functions are compiled into a shared library fileand are stored in the computer's file system. The convention is to use the suffix "bld" (for *blade*) to identify them. The function body of an EXTERNAL C UDF declaration identifies this library file; that is, it specifies the library's filename, and optionally, it lists the symbol or entry point within that file. If the symbol is omitted IDS looks for an entry point within the shared library with the same name as the new UDF identifier.

To simplify administration, shared library files can be located relative to an environment variable, usually INFORMIXDIR. In Listing 5–33 we illustrate the range of syntax possible in an EXTERNAL C UDF function body.

```
CREATE FUNCTION GetUnit ( Weight )
RETURNS lvarchar
WITH ( NOT VARIANT, PARALLELIZABLE )
EXTERNAL NAME
```

```
--
-- Use the INFORMIXDIR environment variable and give a
-- relative file name. We also specify the symbolic
-- entry point within the library. Note the use of the
-- $INFORMIXDIR/extend directory. It is the convention
-- to locate all extensions there.
--
"$INFORMIXDIR/extend/Weight/bin/Weight.bld(GetUnit)"
--
-- Locate the runnable file within the file system of
-- the computer on which the ORDBMS is running.
--
"/home/informix/new_blades/bin/Weight.bld(GetUnit)"
--
-- Microsoft NT example. Note that the file naming standard
-- used allows the same UNIX 'file-name' to be applied on
-- Windows platforms when it is expressed relative to the
-- INFORMIXDIR environment variable.
--
"D:\informix\extend\Weight.bld"
LANGUAGE C;
```

Listing 5–33. *Three Legal Alternatives for Specifying an External "C UDR Function Body*

At CREATE FUNCTION time, the library file name and symbol are stored in the ORDBMS's system catalogs. When the C UDF is first invoked, the library file is loaded from its file system location and linked into the ORDBMS engine. All unresolved references within the library are connected to their corresponding symbols within the ORDBMS at that time. If unused for some time, these library files can be unlinked from the DBMS to make room for another. Once loaded, the UDF can be invoked repeatedly with very little overhead.

Library files can be explicitly unlinked by a database administrator, or linked before they are used. The two extremely useful built-in functions that handle this are called ifx_unload_module() and ifx_load_module(). Problems will arise, however, if logic in the library module being unloaded is being referred to from another database object such as a prepared query, a stored procedure, or a function index. A better approach to upgrading an EXTERNAL C UDF is to employ the ALTER FUNCTION statement to modify the function's system catalog reference to the external library file.

Java

Java UDF handling is somewhere between the SPL and C library approach. The examples in Listings 5-3 and 5-4 give you some idea about how it works. Java source code is first compiled into a Java '.class' file. The *pcode* in these files is in Java's universally portable executable format. Several '.class' files can be combined into a Java Archive, or '.jar' file. Regardless of hardware or operating system, Java's *virtual machine* run-time environment can execute the contents of these files.

Unlike the case with C, where the shared library stays in the file system, Java '.jar' files are loaded into the ORDBMS's system catalogs before any UDFs are declared that reference it. A special database procedure called install_jar is used to initiate this load. install_jar takes a URL that locates the '.jar' as its first argument and a string that is to be used to refer to the jar once it is loaded. Example 4 in Listing 5–3 illustrates how this is done. As with C EXTERNAL functions, Java classes are loaded once and can then be executed many times.

Other database procedures remove and replace a loaded Java archive with another, more recent copy. In other words, in contrast with "C libraries, it is not enough to replace the executable file in the file system. For example, Listing 5–34 illustrates how a new Java UDR to compare two PersonName data types might be created.

```
CREATE FUNCTION Compare ( PersonName, PersonName )
RETURNING integer
WITH ( NOT VARIANT, PARALLELIZABLE )
EXTERNAL NAME
'PersonName:PersonName.Compare(PersonName, PersonName)'
LANGUAGE Java;
```

Listing 5–34. *Creating a Compare Function Using a Pre-Loaded .jar File*

In Listing 5–34 the function body specifies that the implementation for the OR-SQL UDF Compare(PersonName, PersonName) is to be found in the '.jar' loaded in Listing 5–3 and known within the database as 'PersonName'. Further, the code implementing the UDF's behavior is found in a Java method called 'Compare ' defined as part of a Java class called 'PersonName' within that '.jar'. Note that the method implementing the logic takes as its arguments two Person-Name object instances. Before it can call the PersonName.Compare() method and pass data from database tables into it, the IDS engine needs to transform the on-disk data into Java objects, a task that is accomplished by the SQL-J SQLData interface described in Tutorial 4.

As part of integrating the Java virtual machine into the ORDBMS, the Java class loader has been modified to look in the ORDBMS's system catalogs for the '.jar' file. Having located the implementation of the UDF, the ORDBMS loads it into the Java runtime environment, and instructs the on-board Java VP to invoke the method within the class.

Loading an external '.bld' or '.jar' file might fail for any number of reasons; if the file is in the wrong place, if its permissions are incorrect, or if the library contains symbols or functions that cannot be resolved at link time. Failure to load the specified file causes the ORDBMS to generate an informative error message. Additional details can be found in the engine's error logs.

Using User-Defined Functions

User-defined functions are the foundation of object-relational database extensibility. The ORDBMS has no understanding of the structure or contents of OPAQUE TYPE data. It merely provides the means to store a byte array reliably and combine that data with UDF using query language expressions.

UDFs are used throughout the ORDBMS engine to add functionality and manipulate data type instances, to perform low-level data management tasks such as indexing, sorting, and client/server communication for OPAQUE TYPE instances, and to implement application-level operations within the ORDBMS. In this section we review the different roles that UDFs play. Then we explain how the ORDBMS chooses which UDF to invoke when a perfect match on the signature is not found.

Kinds of User-Defined Functions

We use the term *User-defined Function (UDF)* to refer to any software module embedded within the IDS product that is called by the engine as it processes an OR-SQL statement. You can classify User-defined Functions into one of three categories based what it does. Regardless of its classification, all functions are developed using the same techniques and handled in the same way by the ORDBMS. In this section we discuss each class of UDF in turn.

OR-SQL Level Functions

OR-SQL level UDFs are characterized by the way that they are typically named in query statements. They tend to be either general-purpose expressions that extend the OR-SQL query language and are applied to built-in data values such as strings or numbers, or they implement behavior for a user-defined data type. OR-SQL level UDFs can appear anywhere in a query, such as in the WHERE clause to specify what data the query is retrieving, in the SELECT clause whenever the query computes some new result based on table data, or in an UPDATE query to modify data values.

Functions implementing behaviors for new data types constitute a distinct subclass of OR-SQL level functions. In ORDBMS development, each new user-defined type corresponds to a class of objects identified in the information system's problem domain. Queries that manipulate these types must use functions defined to work for that type, because these functions are the only way to manipulate instances of the type.

Support Functions

When the ORDBMS invokes a support function, OR-SQL users are rarely aware of it. Support functions perform internal data management tasks, most often for a new OPAQUE TYPE. They are invoked as part of query processing or database administration. These 'invisible' functions perform tasks such as the following:

- Converting query literal values (quoted strings and numbers) into a data type's internal representation. In this role they are often used as conversion functions for a CAST between data types.
- Converting the type's internal representation into a generic format for bulk data unloading, communication with external programs, and backup and recovery. These are UDFs that cast instances of an OPAQUE TYPE into the import/export, send/receive, and import binary/export binary formats.
- Providing the means whereby an access method can be used to create indices on the new data type. Indexing UDFs implement operator class interfaces.
- Providing facilities for certain database operations such as *sorting* and *hashing*. These are most frequently used in join.
- Allowing the ORDBMS to acquire information about the distribution of data in a column to help it with query planning.

OPAQUE TYPE instances require, at a minimum, about ten support functions. If you also consider inessential but useful support functions, there are about fifteen of them in all. Fortunately, the *DataBlade Developer's Kit (DBDK)* generates a list of all of the support functions required when implementing a new OPAQUE TYPE. And in most cases, the tool can even generate the source code for you too.

Support functions are identical to all other UDFs with respect to how the ORDBMS manages them. In fact, they can be invoked directly through OR-SQL like any other UDF, and this is frequently necessary for testing. Because they are performance sensitive, need to deal with byte-level network communication issues, and because they are mostly intended for use with OPAQUE TYPE extensions, support functions are almost always implemented in C or Java.

Additional DBMS Functionality

Up until now, we have focused on OR-SQL functionality, on the techniques used to define an object-relational database schema, and the means by which data in a schema is manipulated. But there are other ways that extensible functions can be used.

Developers familiar with other vendor's DBMS products or other development environments are quick to point out the limits on what they can achieve in the IDS product, and how useful another vendor's ideas are. For example, being able to create and execute a dynamic OR-SQL statement in a database stored procedure, and splitting strings into a set of sub-strings, are both possible in other software systems but not, by default, in the IDS product. Alternatively, in some information systems it would be useful to interpret binary data structures passed into the ORDBMS from external programs.

A third type of UDF extension can be used to achieve these objectives. Such extensions are not typically invoked using OR-SQL. More usually they are deployed within database stored procedures implemented using SPL. In Chapter 10, and in Tutorial 6, we implement two of these three examples.

Invoking Functions Directly

Any UDF can be invoked directly using the EXECUTE FUNCTION statement. This is especially useful when you are developing or debugging a UDF, although this command can be embedded within an external program in the same way an OR-SQL SELECT query can be. Functions return values, so the same client side interfaces used to handle SELECT query results are used to handle function results too. We present several examples of such direct invocation in Listing 5–35.

```
EXECUTE FUNCTION BirthDay ( '02/29/1992' );

EXECUTE FUNCTION Equal ( BirthDay ( '02/29/1992'),
                         BirthDay ( TODAY ));
```

```
EXECUTE FUNCTION Equal ( BirthDay ( '02/29/1992'),
                         BirthDay ( '02/28/1999' ));

EXECUTE FUNCTION BirthDay ((SELECT MAX(Release_Date)
                         FROM Movies ));
```

Listing 5–35. *Invoking a User-Defined Function Directly*

In these examples, the actual invocation of the named functions is not the first thing the ORDBMS does. It first needs to create the objects that are passed as parameters. Creating some of these parameters might involve running other UDFs or even processing a query. And after the named function is invoked, the ORDBMS might call others to transform the named function's results into an appropriate client-side representation.

Function Signatures and Function Resolution

In this section we tackle the difficult question of how the ORDBMS decides which UDF body to run based on what it parses in a OR-SQL query and what it has recorded in its SYSPROCEDURES system catalog table. This is an important topic. In object-relational databases with many interrelated data types and overloaded functions (which will be most of them), being able to figure out which user-defined function is actually being run is frequently useful.

We have seen that functions are distinguished by their *signature*, which is the combination of the function's identifier name and its vector of arguments. In Listing 5–3 we saw an example showing how two routines might share a name, but be distinguished by their argument vector. When an OR-SQL statement invokes a UDF—either directly through EXECUTE FUNCTION, within an OR-SQL query, or indirectly as part of some administrative action—the ORDBMS's parser compares the information in the UDF's signature with what it has stored in the system catalogs. Often, it will find a perfect match. But what if it does not?

Data Type Inheritance, DISTINCT Types, and CASTing Between Data Types

Recall from Chapter 4 how the ORDBMS data model supports the concepts of data type inheritance with the ROW TYPE mechanism and type reuse by creating a DISTINCT TYPE of a built-in type or an OPAQUE TYPE. We also saw how the CAST mechanism could be used to automatically convert an instance of one type into an instance of another. These data model features make it possible to reuse functions created for one data type with others.

When it does not find a perfect match for the function it is looking for, the ORDBMS tries to find another function that it can substitute for the target. The parser's search strategy involves looking for other function signatures that have the same identifying name, but where the other function's argument types are parents—in the case of type inheritance—of the target type, or where the candidate function's argument type can be created using a CAST—in the case of a DISTINCT TYPE.

For the purposes of explaining how function resolution works, we use the following example. In Figure 5–4 we show a set of three interrelated types. For our purposes the exact nature of their relationship doesn't matter. This figure may represent a ROW TYPE hierarchy, two DISTINCT TYPE instances of some built-in type, or two types each with a CAST to a third. On the right, we present a list of functions as they might appear in the SYSPROCEDURES system catalog table. For clarity they are numbered to distinguish them.

The functions listed in the figure can be invoked in several ways. First, they may be explicitly referenced. This happens when the signature of a function in a query expression matches one of the functions in the SYSPROCEDURES table exactly, for example:

```
EXECUTE FUNCTION Function_Name ( 'Literal_String'::A );
```

The ORDBMS uses the following procedure to determine which UDF to invoke.

First, it selects only UDFs with the same function name and the same number of arguments. Then it checks to see that the argument types match perfectly. In this case there is no ambiguity. Only number 1 matches. Therefore, this is the function that the ORDBMS invokes.

Note that this expression causes at least one other UDF to be invoked: the input function to CAST the literal string into an instance of the A data type. As it parses this expression, the ORDBMS realizes that this CAST operation is the first thing it is being asked to do. So it looks up the name of the CAST UDF from the system catalogs and uses

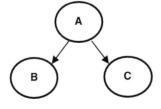

Number	Name	Params
1	Function_Name	A
2	Another_Function	A, A
3	Function_Name	A, A
4	Function_Name	A, X
5	Function_Name	A, A, A
6	Function_Name	C, C

Figure 5–4. *Data Model to Explain UDF Resolution*

the same function resolution algorithm we describe here to figure out what to invoke.

Now consider the following EXECUTE FUNCTION command,

```
EXECUTE FUNCTION Function_Name ('Literal_String'::C,
                                'Literal_String'::A);
```

Based on the function name and argument count, the parser reduces its candidate list to just function' numbers 3, 4, and 6. Function number 2 is eliminated because of its name, and all of the other functions have the wrong number of arguments. But this time, there is no exact match.

UDF Resolution Algorithm

In cases where there is no perfect match, the ORDBMS's strategy is to search through the system catalog information in a systematic way. Whatever matching user-defined function signature it finds first, it runs. In all cases, it only considers candidate functions with the same *name* and the same number of arguments. The procedure examines candidate function's argument vector. Overloading, by definition, is the same function name with alternative arguments.

The UDF begins by looking for candidates whose *first* argument's data type is 'above' the one designated in the expression. By 'above,' we mean those data types from which the known type is inherited, or from where it is CAST. In our example the only type "above" the C data type is the A data type. Therefore, the ORDBMS keeps functions 3 and 4 in its candidate set, and eliminates 6. But examining the *second* argument settles the question. Only function 4 matches on the second argument. So function 4 is the UDF selected.

Now consider another example:

```
EXECUTE FUNCTION Function_Name ('Literal_String'::B,
                                'Literal_String'::B);
```

The candidate set is { 3, 4, 6 }. By checking for close matches on the first argument's type, the parser again eliminates 6. This time, there is no exact match in the second argument, so the parser repeats the exercise, walking back up the list of types until it settles on function 3 as the closest match.

A working definition of the UDF resolution algorithm that the ORDBMS uses to determine which UDF to run looks like this:

1. For each UDF, find all candidate functions for which the user has execution privileges. This means get a list of all functions in the system catalogs that have the same function name and the same number of arguments.
2. Begin with the first (leftmost) argument. One at a time, move right through the argument list. For each argument, try to find functions among the candidate UDFs that have the argument's data type in that location. If a match is found, proceed to the next argument.
3. If no perfect match exists for an argument location, begin to evaluate the candidate list by substituting other data types for the one that wasn't found in that location. Use the following precedence order:

   i. Named ROW TYPE if the supplied type is UNDER any.

   ii. If the supplied type is a DISTINCT TYPE, whatever type(s) it is distinct of.

   iii. Types where a CAST is defined between it and the supplied type.

4. If still no match is found, step *back* to the previous argument, and continue looking above the initial match for alternatives.
5. Continue until all arguments have been satisfied, or all possibilities have been exhausted.

Function resolution can get very convoluted in extreme situations. And things get worse when you consider the quirky cases. In Chapter 4, when we reviewed type inheritance, we saw just how quirky it could get. And the ORDBMS might re-evaluate its decision at runtime if the set of candidates changes, if the UDF takes a variable whose type definition is determined at runtime (generic ROW TYPE arguments), or when an index is created that the planner might use. When any of these events occur, IDS will re-process a query expression that might be affected. Fortunately, although the exact algorithm the parser used is quite complex, you can usually let your intuition guide you.

Advanced User-Defined Functions

In this section we introduce some advanced kinds of UDF. For some tasks a single function that takes some arguments and returns a result is not enough. Therefore the ORDBMS provides facilities to combine several UDFs to achieve a single functionality (aggregates) or more sophisticated kinds of user-defined function (iterators and statement local variables).

User-Defined Aggregates

UDAs are a generalization of the SQL language's standard aggregate functions: `MIN()`, `MAX()`, `AVG()`, and `COUNT()`. The IDS product also includes support for a `VARIANCE()` aggregate that is not part of the SQL-92 standard, but that is very useful.

User-defined aggregates fall into two categories. First, you can over-load the built-in aggregates to work with your new types. For example, it would be useful to have an aggregate function to compute the `SUM()` of a set of Mass data types or Currency. Second, you can create an entirely new kind of UDA. SQL's aggregates are useful, and vendors frequently augment this list with their own. But in many Decision Support Systems (DSSs), more sophisticated analytic routines are frequently useful, and the UDA mechanism is one way to embed them within the data management framework. User-defined aggregates are extensions that analyze a set of objects to compute a single result.

Overloading Built-In Aggregates

Most obviously, it is useful to provide at least built-in aggregates for user-defined types. To understand how this is done, it is necessary to understand how the DBMS handles aggregates. Each aggregate result is computed using an algorithm that steps through multiple rows, tracking some internal state as it goes. Once all rows have been examined, the ORDBMS applies some kind of final computation to the internal state to produce an answer.

Algorithms used to compute each of the built-in aggregates are all quite simple. To compute `AVG()`—or more formally, *arithmetic mean*—the ORDBMS uses the fairly obvious algorithm in Listing 5–36.

```
Value
Mean ( Value pArrayValues[])
{
   int       count = 0;
   value     current_value, running_total;
   while(1)
   {
     current_value := GetValue(pArrayValues, count);
     if ( current_value == NULL )
     {
       break;
     } else {
```

```
            running_total := Plus( running_total, current_value );
            count := count + 1;
        }
    }
    current_value := Divide ( running_total, count );
    return current_value;
}
```

Listing 5–36. *Pseudo-Code for Calculating Arithmetic Mean or AVG()*

As with the SORT algorithm used in Chapter 1 to introduce the concept of extensibility, the function calls we show here in **bold** need to be implemented for a user-defined type to generalize this algorithm. Other aggregates can be generalized in a similar way. In Table 5–4 we present a list of the SQL aggregates and the set of supporting UDFs that must be implemented to use them.

Table 5–4. Required UDFs to Support SQL UDAs for New Data Types (UDTs)

Aggregate Name	Description	List of Needed UDFs
MIN(UDT)	Returns the smallest value.	LessThanOrEqual (UDT, UDT) RETURNS boolean.
MAX(UDT)	Returns the largest value.	GreaterThanOrEqual (UDT, UDT) RETURNS boolean.
SUM(UDT)	Returns the total of the values.	Plus (UDT, UDT) RETURNS UDT.
AVG(UDT)	Returns arithmetic mean.	Plus (UDT, UDT) RETURNS UDT. Divide (UDT, INTEGER) RETURNS UDT.
RANGE(UDT)	Returns difference between largest and smallest values.	LessThanOrEqual (UDT, UDT) RETURNS boolean; GreaterThanOrEqual (UDT, UDT) RETURNS boolean; Minus (UDT, UDT) RETURNS UDT.
STDDEV(UDT)	Standard deviation of the distribution of values.	Times (UDT, INTEGER) RETURNS UDT; Divide (UDT, INTEGER) RETURNS UDT; Plus (UDT, UDT) RETURNS UDT; Minus (UDT, UDT) RETURNS UDT; Sqrt (UDT) RETURNS UDT.
VARIANCE(UDT)	Variance of the distribution (the square of the STDDEV).	Times (UDT, INTEGER) RETURNS UDT; Divide (UDT, INTEGER) RETURNS UDT; Plus (UDT, UDT) RETURNS UDT; Minus (UDT, UDT) RETURNS UDT.

All you need to do to gain the use of a built-in aggregate for your new type is to create all of these UDFs. Once integrated, the ORDBMS can use them to compute aggregate results automatically. Note that aggregates implemented in this way inherit all properties of the built-in functionality. NULL arguments are ignored, for example. And of course, the SQL GROUP BY facilities work together with the new aggregate.

New User-Defined Aggregates

The motivation for including additional decision support or numerical algorithms in the database is to improve data analysis. Statisticians have spent many years developing techniques to estimate things such as the effects of inputs on outputs and how the future is likely to turn out based on the past. SQL's built-in aggregates barely scratch the surface of this rich tradition.

For example, one of the most common techniques involves selecting "outliers," "the top or bottom few values" from a set. This might be useful for managers of our Movies-R-Us site to find orders where the number of items purchased is extremely large, relatively speaking. In Listing 5–37 we illustrate how a user-defined aggregate, TOP_N(), can be used to achieve this. For clarity we include another query that shows you the relevant rows from the table.

"What are the quantities involved in the three largest orders, ranked by quantity?"

```
SELECT TOP_N ( L.NumberBought, 3 )
  FROM Order_Line_Items L;
```

top_n ::SET(integer not null)

SET{4 ,3 }

```
SELECT L.Order, L.NumberBought
  FROM Order_Line_Items L;
```

order ::order_num	numberbought ::quantity
2	1
2	2
3	3
5	4
6	3
7	2
7	1

Listing 5–37. *Example Illustrating Functionality of New User-Defined Aggregate*

Internally, TOP_N() examines each of the NumberBought INTEGER values in turn. As it proceeds, the aggregate keeps a list of the *N* largest NumberBought values it has seen so far, and the number of times it has seen each of them. In this case, it will build a list containing the three largest values in the data set. We illustrate this intermediate result in Table 5–5.

Table 5–5. Intermediate Result Within TOP_N() User-Defined Aggregate

Value	Count
2	2
3	2
4	1

TOP_N() is only interested in the size of orders *ranked* at the top. So in its final step, the aggregate steps down this list in *value* order (4, then 3, and then 2) tracking how many times it saw each value (1 and then 2). When it has accounted for the top *N* counted items (3 in this example), it stops, and returns the set of NumberBought values it has picked off. The effect is the same as if an external program issued a SELECT query with the results ordered by NumberBought, and then examined first *N* rows the query returned.

User-defined aggregates can also be used with a new data type. For example, a Cinema owner might want to find out how widely scattered the people are who bought a particular ticket. To do this, you want to find the geographic locations of a group of movie club members, and compute the *convex hull* of these points. (A convex hull is a minimal perimeter polygon that encloses all of the points. Think of it as a rubber band tightening around a cluster of thumbtacks.) Therefore, the ConvexHull() is an aggregate that takes a set of points and computes a polygon. Such a query would look like Listing 5–38.

```
SELECT ConvexHull ( M.Location )
  FROM Tickets T, Order_Line_Items L,
       Orders O, MovieClubMembers M
 WHERE T.Showing   = 1100704
   AND T.Id        = L.Merchandise
   AND O.Id        - L.Order
   AND O.Customer = M.Id;
```

Listing 5–38. *User-Defined Aggregate as Constructor for Polygon*

`ConvexHull()` calculations are computationally complex but intuitively quite straightforward. One way to think of this particular aggregate is as a constructor. In the example in Listing 5–37, we used an aggregate to populate a COLLECTION of values. Here we use one to build a polygon.

Entirely new user defined aggregates like the ones we introduce above combine four UDFs. This complexity is due partly to the inherent complexity of calculating aggregates, and partly due to the parallel data processing facilities that the IDS product possesses. The four required functions are shown in Table 5–6.

Table 5–6. UDFs Used by a New User-Defined Aggregate

Function	Description
Init	Initialize per-partition scan structures for the aggregate.
Iter	Iterate is called once for each row in the partition. This part of the UDA computes the new intermediate result based on the data.
Combine	Combine the per-partition scan structures (created in Init, adjusted for each row in the Iter function) into a single, global structure.
Final	Compute the final result of the aggregate from the global structure. The return type of this function becomes the return type of the user-defined aggregate.

Four UDFs are necessary because the ORDBMS may break up the aggregation computation into multiple subtasks, each of which iterates over a subset of the data. After every subtask is complete, the ORDBMS combines their intermediate results and performs some additional processing to compute the final result. In Figure 5–5 we represent each subset or partition of the data as a gray circle. For each partition, the ORDBMS calls the INIT UDF once.

Typically, INIT allocates a user data structure that records the state of the scan. Then, for each row in the partition the ORDBMS calls ITER, passing it the row data and a pointer to the state created by the INIT. Once all scans are complete, the ORDBMS calls COMBINE several times to create another intermediate memory structure containing data that is true for the entire scan. Finally, it calls FINAL exactly once and passes its result back as the answer to the query.

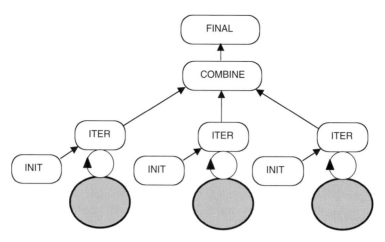

Figure 5–5. *UDFs Used by a New User-Defined Aggregate*

At this time, only a single type instance can be passed into the ITER UDF. In our TOP_N() aggregate introduced in the previous listing, the second value passed into the aggregate is ignored after the ITER UDF returns. Therefore, to implement aggregates that take two values— Linear Regression, for example—you need to use a ROW TYPE with a pair of values.

This script introduces a new concept into the ORDBMS data model: the POINTER data type. POINTER is not strictly a type. It is a reference to memory managed within the ORDBMS engine. UDA processing calls for the state of the scan to be passed among the various UDFs making up the UDA. For convenience, the ORDBMS lets you do this with the POINTER type. Creating an OPAQUE TYPE for this purpose is another way to cope with the same problem. But to the author, that seems like too much work. Examine Listing 5–39.

```
--
--   This script illustrates how to create the support
--   functions for a user-defined aggregate, and how to
--   combine them using the CREATE AGGREGATE command.
--
CREATE FUNCTION top_n_int_init( integer, integer )
RETURNS pointer
WITH ( PARALLELIZABLE , HANDLESNULLS)
EXTERNAL NAME
"$INFORMIXDIR/extend/top_n/bin/top_n.bld(top_n_uda_init)"
LANGUAGE C;
--
CREATE FUNCTION top_n_int_iter(pointer, integer)
```

```
RETURNS pointer
WITH ( PARALLELIZABLE )
EXTERNAL NAME
"$INFORMIXDIR/extend/top_n/bin/top_n.bld(top_n_uda_iter)"
LANGUAGE C;
--
CREATE FUNCTION top_n_int_combine( pointer, pointer)
RETURNS pointer
WITH ( PARALLELIZABLE )
EXTERNAL NAME
"$INFORMIXDIR/extend/top_n/bin/top_n.bld(top_n_uda_comb)"
LANGUAGE C;
--
CREATE FUNCTION top_n_int_final(pointer)
RETURNS SET(integer NOT NULL)
WITH ( PARALLELIZABLE )
EXTERNAL NAME
"$INFORMIXDIR/extend/top_n/bin/top_n.bld(top_n_uda_final)"
LANGUAGE C;
--

CREATE AGGREGATE TOP_N WITH
(
   INIT    = top_n_int_init,
   ITER    = top_n_int_iter,
   COMBINE = top_n_int_combine,
   FINAL   = top_n_int_final
);
```

Listing 5–39. *Creating a New User-Defined Aggregate and Support Functions*

As you might expect, permission to use a UDA and all of its support functions must be granted to users by the DBA. Aggregates may be removed from the ORDBMS with the DROP AGGREGATE command. DROP AGGREGATE removes the references to the user-defined aggregate from the ORDBMS's system catalogs but it does not remove references to the underlying UDFs.

Iterator Functions

Iterator functions are UDFs that return a series or sequence of results. The basic idea is that the ORDBMS calls the same function body multiple times and each time the function computes a new result to return. Iterator functions can be thought of as being like tables in many regards. Values calculated in an iterator function can be inserted into another table, you can define cursors for them, and so on.

There are two ways to create an iterator function. The first uses SPL and creates a function where the RETURN keyword is modified to RETURN WITH RESUME. The second uses an external routine technique. The internal UDF in Listing 5–40 is an example of a simple iterator that takes an INTEGER and returns a sequence of its prime factors.

```
CREATE FUNCTION SPLPrimeFactors ( Arg1 INTEGER )
RETURNS INTEGER
     DEFINE nChecking      INTEGER;
     DEFINE nCurrentState INTEGER;

     LET nChecking = 2;
     LET nCurrentState = Arg1;
     WHILE ( nCurrentState > nChecking )
         IF ( MOD ( nCurrentState, nChecking ) = 0 ) THEN
             LET nCurrentState = nCurrentState / nChecking;
             RETURN nChecking WITH RESUME;
         ELSE
             LET nChecking = nChecking + 1;
         END IF;
     END WHILE;

     IF ( nCurrentState = nChecking ) THEN
         RETURN nChecking;
     END IF;

     RETURN Arg1;
END FUNCTION;

EXECUTE FUNCTION SPLPrimeFactors ( 210 );
```

(expression) ::integer

2
3
5
7

Listing 5–40. *Creating an Iterator UDF*

Earlier, in Listing 5–30, we introduced the ISplit() iterator function. ISplit() is an external UDF. To indicate to the ORDBMS that it is an iterator, you need to use a modifier in the CREATE FUNCTION statement. In Listing 5–41 we illustrate what this modifier looks like.

The external function's implementation uses features of the server's DataBlade API (SAPI), which we describe in detail in Chapter 10.

```
CREATE FUNCTION ISplit ( lvarchar, lvarchar )
RETURNING LVARCHAR
WITH ( NOT VARIANT, ITERATOR )
EXTERNAL NAME
"$INFORMIXDIR/extend/Split/bin/Split.bld(ITerSplitString)"
LANGUAGE C;
```

Listing 5–41. *Creating an External Iterator UDF*

The results of an iterator UDF can be treated much like results of a SELECT query. From a theoretical point of view, it makes sense to view them as calculated relations, which is a set of values calculated based on some argument.

OUT Parameters

Expressions in SQL-92 always return a single result. OUT Parameters are a way to return more than one variable from a function. OUT parameters are used in query expressions by specifying a *statement local variable* (SLV) to hold the additional value. Other parts of the query can use the value in the SLV to perform additional filtering in the WHERE clause, or to return additional values in the SELECT list.

Internally, before it calls the UDF returning the OUT parameter the ORDBMS allocates memory to hold the SLV value. To use language more familiar to C programmers, an OUT parameter returns its value *by reference.*

Listing 5–42 is a simple illustration of how to create a function returning an OUT parameter. Adding the OUT keyword before the fourth argument indicates to the ORDBMS that this is where the value will be returned. In this example, the UDF returns true if the difference between the value of the first argument and the third is less than the value of the second. In addition to computing this boolean result, the function helpfully returns the difference too.

```
CREATE FUNCTION Within_X_of_Y ( Value   INTEGER,
                                X       INTEGER,
                                Y       INTEGER,
                                OUT   retDist INTEGER )
RETURNS boolean
    LET retDist = ABS( Y - Value );
    IF ( retDist < X ) THEN
```

```
            return 't';
        END IF;

        RETURN 'f';
    END FUNCTION;
```

Listing 5–42. *Creating a UDF with an OUT Parameter*

In Listing 5–43 we illustrate how this function might be used in a
query. In lieu of tables, this query gets its data from a pair of COLLEC-
TION instances. Using COLLECTION objects as data sources is explained
in Chapter 3.

```
SELECT 'Value ' || C1.Val || ' is within ' || C1.Delta ||
        ' of ' || C2.Val || ' with distance ' || Calc_Delta
 FROM TABLE(SET{ROW(10,5),ROW(10,3)}) C1 ( Val, Delta ),
        TABLE(SET{8,10,12,14,16}) C2 ( Val )
 WHERE Within_X_of_Y ( C1.Val, C1.Delta, C2.Val,
                        Calc_Delta # INTEGER );
```

(expression) ::CHAR

Value 10 is within 5 of 8 with distance 2
Value 10 is within 5 of 10 with distance 0
Value 10 is within 5 of 12 with distance 2
Value 10 is within 5 of 14 with distance 4
Value 10 is within 3 of 8 with distance 2
Value 10 is within 3 of 10 with distance 0
Value 10 is within 3 of 12 with distance 2

Listing 5–43. *Creating a UDF with an OUT Parameter*

Note that when it looks up a function by using a signature, the
ORDBMS does not check whether a parameter is an OUT parameter. This
makes it possible to include UDFs returning OUT parameters in operator
classes so that they can be used with an index. In the implementation of
the Period data type described in more detail in Chapter 10, we revisit
this idea.

Administering User-Defined Functions

As with other schema objects, an administrator can DROP a user-defined
function and place restrictions on which users can invoke it. In this section we briefly review how this is done.

DROP FUNCTION

A user-defined function can be removed from a database at any time with the DROP FUNCTION command. This removes from the system catalogs all information relating to the nominated UDF. As with all other actions relating to user-defined functions, you need to provide the complete function signature to specify which UDF you want to drop. Examine Listing 5–44.

```
--
-- DROP the function created in Listing 5-43. Note that
-- this signature does not specify that the fourth argument
-- is an OUT parameter.
--
DROP FUNCTION Within_X_of_Y ( INTEGER, INTEGER,
                             INTEGER, INTEGER );

-- DROP function implementing behavior for user-defined
-- types.

DROP FUNCTION Times ( Foo_T, Bar_T )
```

Listing 5–44. *Examples of DROP FUNCTION for UDFs CREATEd in this Chapter*

If you DROP a function, the IDS product does not check to see if there are any dependencies on it. For example, it is possible to drop a function used to build an index or invoked from within another function. Missing functions are detected at run-time. When the ORDBMS cannot find a function referred to from within a prepared query, it will generate an exception and rollback whatever work was in progress.

While clearly problematic for administrators—it means you can DROP functions that an application depends upon—this laissez-faire approach was adopted in response to developer feedback. In the first place, it is impossible to detect every dependency. External UDFs might invoke another UDF, and this fact is buried within the compiled code. Also, it is common to replace a function with a new version of itself. If the ORDBMS prevented an administrator from dropping a function on which something else depended, in the worst case, administrators may find themselves obliged to back out an entire schema.

Security Administration

As with all schema objects, a database administrator must GRANT execution privileges over UDFs to users. This is done using the GRANT command. In its most common usage, you grant execution privileges on a user-defined function as shown in Listing 5–45.

```
GRANT EXECUTE ON FUNCTION LessThan(State_Enum,State_Enum) TO
PUBLIC;
```

Listing 5–45. *Granting Privileges on a New UDR*

Instead of granting execution privileges to everyone, you can limit the use of the function to a specific set of users or to all users who belong to a particular role. Also, it is important that you grant appropriate privileges on all related functions. For example, in Listing 5–45, you should grant the execute privileges on the commutator and negator functions (LessThanOrEqual and GreaterThan). Modifiers associated with a UDF can be changed using ALTER FUNCTION. You revoke execution privileges using the corresponding REVOKE command.

Chapter Summary

User-defined routines, and specifically user-defined functions or UDFs, are the basic building blocks of extensibility. Their principle virtue lies in the way they allow developers to embed modules of procedural programming logic into the ORDBMS and invoke them via the OR-SQL language. In this chapter we have introduced the basic concepts of user-defined functions and explained how they were created, used, and administered.

UDFs are created using the CREATE FUNCTION DDL statement. As part of a function's definition, developers define its *signature*, which is the combination of the function's name and its vector of argument types. A function's signature is important because it is the way the ORDBMS distinguishes functions from each other, and it determines which function to invoke as it processes a query. The CREATE FUNCTION statement includes an extensive set of options that allows you to provide a wide range of information to the ORDBMS to help it optimize and execute queries that include the ORDBMS.

UDFs are used in many ways by the ORDBMS. In fact, one useful way to think about the ORDBMS is as nothing more than a *software back-plan*. Within it, the atomic operations of an information system are integrated and combined. At their simplest, UDFs extend the power of the OR-SQL query language. But they are also used in support roles by the ORDBMS in data management in tasks such as data import, backup, client/server communication, indexing and query processing, and to implement behaviors for user-defined types.

When you implement a set of UDFs, you are in fact creating an interface to a new object class within the ORDBMS. UDFs can be combined together to form other kinds of extensions like user-defined aggregates—which are useful for decision support systems—and access methods. You can even create a kind of function—an iterator—that behaves like a table!

Using Java™ to Create UDTs and UDRs

In addition to C and SPL, developers can use Java to implement user-defined extensions. Certain features of Java—its performance, safety, portability, and the fact it is an open language standard—make it an excellent choice for this kind of work. Once embedded within the IDS product, Java methods can implement user-defined functions used in OR-SQL query statements, or the engine can invoke them to support tasks such as building indices. In fact, by taking a self-contained Java class and surfacing its methods as OR-SQL expressions, it is even possible to create an ORDBMS data type that corresponds to a Java class.

In this tutorial, we explore how Java can be integrated within the IDS product. Writing external Java programs that interact with the ORDBMS is covered in Chapter 7, where we describe the JDBC application programming interface standard. In Chapter 9, where we review implementation alternatives, we investigate the relative performance of the different mechanisms, including Java. In this tutorial the focus is on using Java in the server on user-defined functions and types.

Overview of Java Technology

Java technology consists of two aspects: a *programming language* and *deployment architecture*. When we say that Java can be used to write database extensions, we mean that it is possible to use the Java language to implement the extension logic invoked by OR-SQL queries. Achieving this requires that the ORDBMS embed the Java deployment environment within its run-time engine.

Java is an object-oriented language, which makes it ideal for developing software components such as user-defined types. In object-oriented software development, programs are decomposed into collections of cooperating *classes*, where each class defines the state and behavior of some software concept. Within a Java class, programmers define *attributes*, which represent the state of an instance of the class, and *methods*, which implement the class's behaviors. In Java only environments it is other Java classes that invoke these behaviors. Conceptually, using Java to create an object-relational database extension means deploying a Java class in some context other than another Java program.

In Listing 4–1 we illustrate a very simple Java class: one that implements state and behavior for rational numbers, which are numbers with an integer numerator and a non-zero integer denominator.

```
1  /*
2  **   File:   Rational.java
3  **
4  */
5
6  class Rational {
7
8      private  int   numerator;
9      private int denominator = 1;
10
11     public Rational() {}   // Simple Constructor
12
13     public Rational ( int Arg1 )
14     {
15         numerator = Arg1;
16     }
17
18     public Rational ( int Arg1, int Arg2 )
```

```
19    throws Exception
20    {
21        numerator    = Arg1;
22        if ( Arg2 == 0 )
23        {
24            throw new Exception(
25                   "Rational cannot have denominator == 0");
26        }
27        denominator = Arg2;
28    }
29
30    public int Compare ( Rational Arg2 )
31    {
32        if (( this.denominator * Arg2.numerator ) >
33              ( this.numerator * Arg2.denominator ))
34            return 1;
35        else if (( this.denominator * Arg2.numerator )  <
36                  ( this.numerator * Arg2.denominator ))
37            return -1;
38
39        return 0;
40    }
 . . .
513 }
```

Listing 4–1. *Rational Number Class*

Once developed, this `Rational` Java class can be used in the implementation of other Java programs. Another class might use `Rational` to define variables in its own methods, or elements of its state. It is important to note that the physical techniques—that is, the machine code and memory management algorithms—used to manage Java objects are not accessible by developers. They may even be different from virtual machine to virtual machine. However, there are supported mechanisms for turning any of the data structures found in the ORDBMS into Java object instances.

Java and the ORDBMS

Before it can be deployed, the Java source code—which is stored in a file named `Rational.java`—must be compiled into the platform neutral

Java byte-code format. Compiled Java is stored in files called class_name.class. The code in Listing 4–1 is therefore compiled into a file called Rational.class.

In this byte-code form, compiled Java logic can be moved between different run-time environments, hardware platforms, and operating systems, without being modified. Java's deployment architecture achieves this by using Java Virtual Machines programs that are platform-specific. These interpret the byte-code, performing whatever operations the compiled Java logic specifies.

To invoke a UDF implemented in Java, at least one Java virtual machine (VM) must be executing within the run-time environment of the ORDBMS server. Compiled byte code objects can be loaded by this VM, which then executes the method logic contained within the byte code as it processes an OR-SQL query. Figure 4–1 illustrates this concept.

Over the next few pages, we review the steps involved in implementing a database extension using Java. Later we will review several examples that illustrate how to write the Java source code.

Step 1: Compiling Java Source

Having created a Java source code file, the first step is to compile it. This involves using the standard Java compiler: javac. In Listing 4–2 we illustrate how this is used.

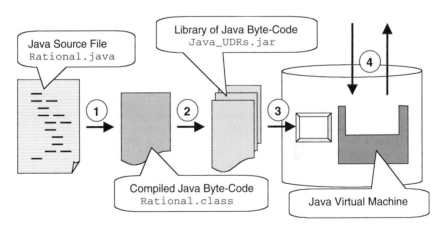

Figure 4–1. Developing Java Extensions for the ORDBMS

```
$ ls
CharUDRs.java CharUDRs.sql
$ javac CharUDRs.java
$ ls
CharUDRs.class        CharUDRs.java        CharUDRs.sql
```

Listing 4–2. *Compiling Java Source Code into Byte-Code Form*

Alternatively, a developer may elect to use a commercial Java development environment to build these classes. Several tools that ship with the ORDBMS, such as the DataBlade Developers Kit and the Object Mapper, can be used to generate Java source.

Step 2: Combine Class Files into a Java Archive (jar) File

For efficiency at runtime, it is a good idea to compress the byte-code into an archive file. Listing 4–3 illustrates how to use the standard Java tool to accomplish this. In this instance, the compiled code in a single file, CharUDRs.class, is compressed and placed into a new file, called CharUDRs.jar. Multiple class files can be compressed and combined into a single archive in this way, and the advantage of this approach stems from the way it makes managing the combined logic more efficient.

```
$ jar cvf CharUDRs.jar CharUDRs.class
added manifest
adding: CharUDRs.class(in = 519) (out= 358)(deflated 31%)
$ ls
CharUDRs.class        CharUDRs.java        CharUDRs.jar
CharUDRs.sql
```

Listing 4–3. *Compress and Combine Byte-Code into a Java Archive*

At this stage, you have a file somewhere in the file system called CharUDRs.jar that contains the compiled byte-code for (at least one) Java class.

Step 3: Load Archive into ORDBMS

The next step is to pull this file into the ORDBMS engine. Rather than rely on the file system to store the embedded logic, the Java facilities within the ORDBMS move a copy of the Java archive into the ORDBMS. In Listing 4–4. We show how this is achieved using an OR-SQL extension that is defined as part of the SQL-J standard.

```
--
--      Install the Java Archive into the ORDBMS Database.
--
EXECUTE PROCEDURE install_jar (
     "file:/tmp/ CharUDRs.jar",      " CharUDRs ");
--
```

Listing 4–4. Installing a Java Archive into ORDBMS and Assigning It a Name

This OR-SQL statement instructs the ORDBMS to load the archive pointed to by the URL in the first argument, and name it using the identifier passed as the second argument. All future references to the archive use this identifier. An important consequence of the way Java extensibility loads the byte-code file is that user-defined function declarations can only refer to Java archives installed in their own database, rather than elsewhere on the server.

Loading the Java archive into the ORDBMS has important implications for administration. With compiled C logic, replacing the shared library in the file system and bouncing the server replaces the library. With extensions written in Java, however, the archive file must be purged and replaced before any changes made to the Java code become apparent in the behavior of any OR-SQL queries that use it.

Step 4: Define User-Defined Functions Using the Archive

The final step in the process involves declaring UDFs where the methods defined within the archive implement the function's behavior. It looks much like any other CREATE FUNCTION statement. Note how the physical location of the external logic is expressed in terms of the

Java archive identifier specified when it was installed, as shown in Listing 4–5.

```
CREATE FUNCTION charAtOffset ( LVARCHAR, INTEGER )
RETURNS CHAR
WITH ( NOT VARIANT, PARALLELIZABLE )
EXTERNAL NAME
'CharUDRs:CharUDRs.charAt( java.lang.String, int )'
LANGUAGE Java
DOCUMENT
"charAtOffset ( LVARCHAR, INTEGER ) returns character     ",
"found at offset [Arg2] within string [Arg1]. If Offset ",
" = 0 this UDF returns first character. Offset =         ",
" LENGTH( Arg1 ) throws an error.       ";
--
GRANT EXECUTE ON charAtOffset ( LVARCHAR, INTEGER )
TO PUBLIC;
```

Listing 4–5. *CREATE FUNCTION Statement Using a Method in the Byte-Code in an Archive*

Once these four steps have been accomplished, the UDF that results is indistinguishable from any other ORDBMS extension.

Java User-Defined Routines

In order to implement a new user-defined routine in the ORDBMS using Java, the source code needs to follow several rules:

- The method implementing the logic must be declared as a `static` Java method, which means that the method behaves more like a C subroutine than a object method. In programming language terms, a static method in Java is *stateless*. It does not have an associated object of the same class of which the method is a part. This is necessary because OR-SQL UDFs may not be called through an object at all.
- The method should be defined with `throws SQLException`. Any errors and exceptions generated by the UDF that are to be passed back to the ORDBMS by throwing a `SQLException` object. The ORDBMS knows about this kind of exception, and it is looking for it to ensure that transaction rollback happens appropriately. Other kinds of exceptions generated within the Java method are handled in the default manner by the VM running within the ORDBMS.

- If the OR-SQL function is to be declared as HANDLESNULL, care must be taken with the types of its arguments. Java has a concept of NULL that is remarkably similar to the SQL concept, but Java nulls are applicable only over Java object classes (java.lang.Integer, java.lang.Float) and not over Java built-in types (int, float). Therefore, if the UDF can accept nulls, its argument types must be classes from the Java libraries.

In Listing 4–6 we illustrate what the Java implementation of the UDF introduced in Listing 4–5 might look like. This is one example from a long list of Java UDFs that bring the potent string handling of the classes java.lang.String and java.lang.StringBuffer into OR-SQL.

```
1    /*
2    **    File: CharUDR.java
3    **
4    **    About:
5    **
6    **    This file implements a large set of String
7    **    manipulation operations absent from SQL. These
8    **    are all implemented using methods defined as
9    **    part of java.lang.String and
10   **    java.lang.StringBuffer classes.
11   **
12   **/
13
14   import java.lang.String;
15   import java.lang.StringBuffer;
16   import java.sql.SQLException;
17
18   public abstract class CharUDRs {
19
20       public static char charAt ( java.lang.String strArg,
21                                    int  offset )
22       throws SQLException
23       {
24           if (( offset < 0 ) ||
25               ( offset >= strArg.length() ))
26           {
27               throw new SQLException (
28                   "ERROR: 0 > Offset >= String.length()");
29           }
30           return strArg.charAt( offset );
31       }
     . . .
```

Listing 4–6. *Java Implementation of charAtOffset() UDF using Java Classes*

All other UDF techniques introduced in Chapter 5 apply to Java UDFs. They may be used for support functions and to overload built-in operators, and Java UDFs can be combined into higher-level extensions such as user-defined aggregates.

Java Environment Inside the ORDBMS

When working with Java code inside the ORDBMS, the server environment provides an interface that gives the Java code access to the context within which it is being called. This interface is known as com.informix.udr.UDRManager. About the only use for this interface is as a means of constructing a com.informix.udr.UDREnv object, which provides the actual information about the ORDBMS.

Information in the com.informix.udr.UDREnv object is approximately equivalent to what is contained in the SAPI MI_FPARAM C structure described in Chapter 10. As shown in Listing 4–7, it can be used to implement iterator UDFs and to cache data between calls to the same UDF in the same query.

```
12   import java.util.GregorianCalendar;
13   import java.sql.Date;
14   import java.sql.SQLException;
15   import com.informix.udr.*;
16
17   public class WorkDaysInRange {
18
19      static GregorianCalendar gc_cur = null;
20      static GregorianCalendar gc_fin = null;
21
22      public static Date WorkDaysInRange (
23              Date   fDate, Date lDate      )
24      throws SQLException
25      {
26   //
27   //   UDRManager is the general interface defined as
28   //   part of com.informix.udr.*. It's primary
29   //   purpose is to serve as a point for retrieving
30   //   other interfaces, like LOG, and the UDR
31   //   execution environment status in UDREnv.
32   //
33          UDREnv iVal = UDRManager.getUDREnv();
34          UDRLog log  = iVal.getLog();
35
36          WorkDaysInRange iState = null;
```

```
37
38        switch( iVal.getSetIterationState() )
39        {
40          case UDREnv.UDR_SET_INIT:
41            iState = new WorkDaysInRange();
42
43            if ( fDate.after(lDate) )
44            {
45              throw new SQLException(
46                "First is after Final");
47            }
48
49            gc_cur = new GregorianCalendar();
50            gc_fin = new GregorianCalendar();
51
52            iState.gc_cur.setTime ( fDate );
53            iState.gc_fin.setTime ( lDate );
54
55            iVal.setUDRState ( iState );
56            iVal.setSetIterationIsDone ( false );
57
58            return null;
59
60          case UDREnv.UDR_SET_RETONE:
61            iState = (WorkDaysInRange)iVal.getUDRState();
62            Date dtRetVal = null;
63
64            walk_loop: while(true)
65            {
66              iState.gc_cur.add( gc_cur.DATE, 1 );
67              if ( iState.gc_cur.after( iState.gc_fin ) )
68              {
69                iVal.setSetIterationIsDone( true );
70                break walk_loop;
71              } else
72              {
73              int DOW =
74              iState.gc_cur.get(gc_cur.DAY_OF_WEEK);
75                if ((DOW != gc_cur.SUNDAY ) &&
76                    (DOW != gc_cur.SATURDAY ))
77                {
78                  log.log("Got One: " + iState.gc_cur );
79                  dtRetVal =
80                new Date(iState.gc_cur.getTime().getTime());
81                  log.log("Got One 2");
```

```
82                    break walk_loop;
83                }
84              }
85            }
86          log.log("Got One 2");
87        return dtRetVal;
88
89        case UDREnv.UDR_SET_END:
90          iVal.setSetIterationIsDone( true );
91          return null;
92
93        default:
94          throw new SQLException("Unknown Iterator Code");
95      }
96    }
97  }
```

Listing 4–7. *Java Implementation of Iterator UDR*

There are several things to note about this example:

- Note the import on line 15. This is a set of interfaces provided by the ORDBMS to access its internal state at the time the UDF is executing.
- The interfaces on lines 33 and 34 construct an object whose state communicates information between the UDF and the ORDBMS, and another interface is used to log debugging messages. Developers are highly advised to remove logging code from the runtime code path in production software.
- The switch() on line 38 indicates which of the three iterator actions the ORDBMS expects the UDF to perform this time around. Initially the UDF creates an instance of an object, which has the same class as this example, for simplicity, and sets its initial state. On other calls, it uses the java.util.GregorianCalendar object to determine the days between the two arguments that are working days.
- Calls to the logging method on lines 77 and 80 write argument messages into a Java logging file maintained in the server's file system.
- Controlling the iteration is handled using another method associated with the com.informix.udr.UDREnv interface. Examples of this can be seen on lines 56, 69, and 89.

Other methods in the com.informix.udr.UDREnv interface can extract information about the argument data types, OUT PARAMETER, and so on.

Embedding Java Classes into the ORDBMS

Standards are rarely created overnight, which makes the rapid materialization of the SQL-J standard quite surprising. SQL-J is intended as a universal mechanism in which objects implemented as Java classes can be embedded within any ORDBMS. Once there, they can be used much like any other UDT: to define table columns, to be variables in stored procedures, or to be arguments to user-defined functions.

The SQL-J Standard, or more properly, SQL-J parts II and III, define a set of interfaces that a developer uses when they write their Java class. More recently these have become part of the JDBC standard.

Table 4-1. Interfaces Used When Embedding Java Class Within ORDBMS

Interface Name	Purpose
SQLData	This provides a set of methods for the ORDBMS to call whenever it needs to construct an instance of the Java class at runtime. Within the ORDBMS, the persistent data is stored in a byte array. At runtime, when a UDF implemented as a Java method is passed an instance of the object, the ORDBMS must first turn the array of bytes into a valid Java object. It does this using the methods in this interface.
SQLInput	This provides the mechanism for managing the array of bytes that the ORDBMS stores on disk. It is used within the Java class to be used to implement a UDT for constructing an instance of the class. The concept is similar to object serialization, except that for these Java "value objects," only data attributes can be read from SQLInput. This mechanism works for any Java class whose state information can be written into a serial form, that is, written into an array of bytes.
SQLOutput	This is the symmetric interface to SQLInput. It writes the object's state to a stream, which the ORDBMS then stores.

There are three methods in the SQLData interface. One of these simply returns the OR-SQL type name that is to be used to characterize an object at runtime. This information need not be written into the byte stream because it is required only after the object has been constructed inside the VM. The other two methods are called, descriptively enough, `readSQL` and `writeSQL`. They are used to transform data between the ORDBMS's byte-oriented storage format and the Java object structure.

`readSQL` is a constructor for the Java class. It takes an instance of the `SQLInput` as one argument and a `String` containing the OR-SQL type name as the second. Within the `readSQL` method, the Java code reads blocks of data from the input stream. `writeSQL` is a symmetric operation to `readSQL`. It takes the data state of the Java object and writes it back to the stream according to the same layout that `readSQL`, or other UDFs, expect to see.

So far we have seen how to write SQL UDFs in Java, and we have been introduced to the Java standards a programmer must follow so that his or her class can become an OR-SQL UDT. But how can the ORDBMS query processor bridge the gap between the database type system and Java? Informing the ORDBMS that a particular OR-SQL data type and a Java class have this kind of relationship involves executing a special user-defined procedure that creates the association in the ORDBMS's system catalogs, as we see in Listing 4–8.

```
--   NOTE: Case is significant here. The first argument must
--         be the ORDBMS data type. It must be in lowercase
--         regardless of how the type was defined in the
--         CREATE TYPE statement because this is how
--         information is stored in the system catalogs.
--
--         The second argument must be the name of the Java
--         class, which is also case-sensitive.
--
EXECUTE PROCEDURE setUDTExtName ( "personname","PersonName");
```

Listing 4–8. *Registering the Association Between a Java Class and a User-Defined Type*

When the ORDBMS detects that it is about to execute a user-defined function implemented as LANGUAGE Java (see Listing 4–5), it consults its system catalogs to determine how to convert any OR-SQL types passed to that UDF into objects that the Java VM can use. It tries to construct an instance of the Java class corresponding to the SQL type using that class's `readSQL` logic.

Note that you need not declare `readSQL()`, `writeSQL()`, or `get-SQLTypeName()` as OR-SQL user-defined functions. Only the ORDBMS calls them, and it does so invisibly.

Design Alternatives for Java Class Storage

There are two basic approaches to storing Java data in the ORDBMS: parse or otherwise manipulate data in a DISTINCT TYPE or access the innards of an OPAQUE TYPE directly.

A DISTINCT TYPE can be used to name the new Java class for the purposes of OR-SQL query processing. Then, in the readSQL constructor, the Java code reads the entire array of bytes holding the DISTINCT TYPE instance's data this data type into a standard Java variable. From there the database data can be parsed to extract the elements of the Java object, or used in its entirety. This approach has the advantage that it is very simple to implement. All support functions that apply to the built-in type for backup, recovery, and client/server communication magically work for the new Java UDT.

In Listing 4–9, consider the PersonName Java class and the way in which we illustrate how parts of it might be defined.

```
 6   public class PersonName implements SQLData
 7   {
 8       private String sql_type = "personname";
 9
10       public String   Family_Name;
11       public String   First_Name;
12       public String   Other_Names;
13       public String   Title;
14
15       private static final int MAX_LEN = 64;
16
17       public PersonName()
18       {
19       }
20
21       public String getSQLTypeName()
22       {
23           return sql_type;
24       }
.  .  .
402       public String toString ()
403       {
404           String strRetVal = Family_Name;
405           strRetVal += ", ";
406
```

```
407          if ( Title != null )
408          {
409              strRetVal += Title;
410              strRetVal += " ";
411          }
412
413          strRetVal += First_Name;
414
415          if ( Other_Names != null )
416          {
417              strRetVal += " ";
418              strRetVal += Other_Names;
419
420          }
421          return strRetVal;
422      }
423
424      public String toString( PersonName Arg1 )
425      throws SQLException
426      {
427          return Arg1.toString();
428      }
```

Listing 4–9. *Definition of Java Class for Use as UDT*

At the OR-SQL level, PersonName can be modeled as a DISTINCT TYPE of VARCHAR, like the one in Listing 4–10, in which we create a UDF that uses one of the methods implemented in Listing 4–9.

```
CREATE DISTINCT TYPE PersonName AS VARCHAR(64);
--
CREATE FUNCTION Print ( PersonName )
RETURNING lvarchar
WITH ( NOT VARIANT, PARALLELIZABLE )
EXTERNAL NAME 'PersonName:PersonName.toString(PersonName)'
LANGUAGE Java;
```

Listing 4–10. *OR-SQL DDL to Create the Type and Define a UDF*

Before it could be used, the setUDTExtName() procedure from Listing 4–8 must be executed. This ensures that the IDS product's query processor calls PersonName.readSQL() to get a valid PersonName-Java object before it calls the other UDF, PersonName.toString (PersonName), to get a string suitable for printing.

Within the 64 bytes of character data, each attribute of the Person-Name class can be combined with special characters used to delineate, and identify, each element. To turn an instance of this DISTINCT TYPE of VARCHAR into an instance of this Java class, the code in read-SQL reads the entire VARCHAR(64) string into a local variable and parses it, picking out each element. In the query in Listing 4–11, we illustrate both what the data looks like as it is stored in a column and the effect of executing the Java UDF introduced in Listing 4–10.

```
SELECT M.Name,
       Print(M.Name) AS Printed
       FROM MovieClubMembers M'
```

Name::PersonName	Printed::String
+Annabel=Wayne/Mr	Annabel, Mr Wayne
+Bezos=Terri/Dr	Bezos, Dr Terri
+Zero=Dulles/Prof	Zero, Prof Dulles
+Edgar=Franchoise*Marie/Ms	Edgar, Ms Franchoise Marie
+Canterville=Ian	Canterville, Ian
+Friend=Emily/Ms	Friend, Ms Emily
+Goi=Lui	Goi, Lui

Listing 4–11. *Sample Table Data for the DISTINCT TYPE and Java UDF*

Listing 4–12 illustrates the first part of the PersonName readSQL() method that would appear in the Java source code from Listing 4–9. For brevity, the actual parsing code is not shown.

```
68      public void readSQL(SQLInput inputstream,
69                       String type)
70      throws SQLException
71      {
72         int nLow = 0, nHigh = 0;
73         char chCur;
74         String strCurrent;
75
76         sql_type = type;
77         String strIn = inputstream.readString();
78
79         while ( nHigh < strIn.length())
80         {
//
//   Parse the contents of the strIn variable and extract
//   from within it each element of the class.
//
110        }
111
```

```
112      if (( Family_Name == null ) ||
113          ( First_Name == null))
114          throw new SQLException(
115             "Format +Family+First*Other/Title. No Family");
116
117    }
```

Listing 4–12. *Implementation of readSQL() Interface Method for SQLData*

On line 77 of Listing 4–12, the content of the byte array stored
within the ORDBMS is read into a local string. Then the rest of the
method logic parses it.

Lines 112 through 115 are included to illustrate how the SQL
Exception mechanism is used to halt processing in the face of an
error condition. In this case, the code enforces a check that all
instances of a PersonName object must have at least a family
name and a first name.

Another example of how SQL expressions are raised can be seen in
Listing 4–13, which implements the symmetric operation to the one in
Listing 4–12. Here, the check ensures that the String to be returned
does not exceed the space allocated for it within the OR-SQL Person-
Name DISTINCT TYPE definition. writeSQL is the final method that
is required by the SQLData interface.

```
119    public void writeSQL(SQLOutput outputstream)
120    throws SQLException
121    {
122
123        String  strOutput = "";
124
125        if ( Family_Name != null )
126            strOutput = strOutput + '+' + Family_Name;
127        if ( First_Name != null )
128            strOutput = strOutput + '=' + First_Name;
129        if ( Other_Names != null )
130            strOutput = strOutput + '*' + Other_Names;
131        if ( Title != null )
132            strOutput = strOutput + '/' + Title;
133
134        if ( strOutput.length() > MAX_LEN)
135        {
136           throw new SQLException (
137            "Total length cannot exceed " +MAX_LEN+ " chars");
138        }
139           outputstream.writeString(strOutput);
140    }
```

Listing 4–13. *Implementation of writeSQL() Interface Method for SQLData*

For some kinds of data this DISTINCT TYPE method could be improved upon. For example, storing large integers as strings is inefficient compared to storing them as four-byte blocks. Because of this, the ORDBMS's Java facilities also permit OPAQUE TYPE data to be used to store the state of a Java class. Instead of reading the entire DISTINCT TYPE in a single operation, several different types of data value can be read from the stream in the same order they are defined in the C structure.

For example, consider a data type that stores measurements. It would encapsulate both a quantity, and a unit.[1] Its C structural definition, and the OR-SQL CREATE TYPE statement, might appear as we illustrate in Listing 4–14. Note that there is no real need for the padding bytes in this structure. They are included to give some richness to the Java code used in this example.

```
typedef struct _PhysicalQuantity
{
        mi_integer                  unit;
        mi_char1                    pad1[4];
        mi_double_precision         value;
} PhysicalQuantity;


--

CREATE OPAQUE TYPE PhysicalQuantity (
        INTERNALLENGTH = 16,
        ALIGNMENT      = 8
);
--
```

Listing 4–14. *C Structure and OR-SQL CREATE OPAQUE TYPE for PhysicalQuantity*

How is the C structure handled in the readSQL method? In Listing 4–15 we present code extracted from the implementation of a Java class that mimics the functionality of the OPAQUE TYPE introduced previously. This example also appears in Chapter 7 to illustrate how to extract data from an OPAQUE TYPE through the JDBC interface.

```
35   import java.sql.*;
36   import com.informix.jdbc.*;
   . . .
```

---

[1] This OPAQUE TYPE, its associated support functions, and a range of mathematical and analytic operations are implemented in the materials accompanying this book.

```
39   public class Length implements SQLData
40   {
41           private double Quantity;
42           private int    Unit;
43           private String strTypeName = "length";
. . .
100    /*
101    ** These three methods are necessary to implement the
102    ** SQLData interface.
103    **/
104
105    public String getSQLTypeName() { return strTypeName; }
106
107    public void readSQL ( SQLInput inpstream,
108                               String    typename )
109    throws SQLException
110    {
111      strTypeName = typename;
112      Unit         = inpstream.readInt(); /* UNIT Integer */
113      byte pad     = inpstream.readByte();/* Then there   */
114      pad          = inpstream.readByte();/* are 4 bytes */
115      pad          = inpstream.readByte();/* of padding.*/
116      pad          = inpstream.readByte();
117      Quantity     = inpstream.readDouble();/* DOUBLE Qty */
118    }
119
120    public void writeSQL ( SQLOutput outstream )
121    throws SQLException
122    {
123        outstream.writeInt( Unit );
124        outstream.writeByte((byte)0);
125        outstream.writeByte((byte)0);
126        outstream.writeByte((byte)0);
127        outstream.writeByte((byte)0);
128        outstream.writeDouble( Quantity );
129    }
```

Listing 4–15. *Java Implementation for SQLData to Work with OPAQUE TYPE*

For the most part, this example is fairly self-explanatory. Lines 107 through 118 implement the `readSQL` method. Within it, the code reads blocks of data from the input stream and uses it to populate the elements of the class. Lines 120 through 128 illustrate the symmetric `writeSQL` operation.

Using Java Classes Within the ORDBMS

Java can be used in two ways. More conventionally, the IDS product permits the embedding of a Java class that includes OR-SQL call-backs to the database schema. Used in this way, the Java extensibility amounts to another flavor of database stored procedure, albeit one with the significant advantage that the procedure's implementation can be moved into or out of the ORDBMS engine as required. Most of the literature describing the use of Java and databases assumes that this is the only model.

In this tutorial, and in Chapter 7 where we review client interfaces, we introduce an alternative approach. The idea is to permit developers using Java to build relational database schema in the same way C or COBOL developers were familiar with. That is, Java programmers should be able to derive the full advantages of the relational model—physical abstraction, rigorous data modeling and ad hoc query language support—without requiring them to render their Java classes down to a list of byte arrays.

For many applications, this set of techniques is ideal for modeling the application specific details of their problem domain. Furthermore, this approach makes it possible to combine high performance software—compiled C code to handle digital imagery, geographic data, for example—with Java classes in a seamless framework.

The ORDBMS
and Data Processing

Data Processing Within Information Systems

Early RDBMS products were simply static repositories for *persistent data*. Developers embedded SQL-92 queries that manipulated this data into programs written using general-purpose languages such as C, COBOL, or a 4GL. Occasionally, they would type queries one at a time into a command line tool, or use a Query By Example (QBE) interface, but large-scale information systems using such methods were uncommon.

General-purpose languages were necessary because SQL was conceived as a declarative interface, and therefore lacked many of the amenities of procedural code. For example, SQL expressions do not have any variable assignment, interquery state, exception handling, or looping and branching. In addition, each SQL write query modifies at most one table. So, for *data processing* operations that included several (optional or alternative) data operations, developers had to use external (or host) language logic to determine what to run, and in what order.

Finally, SQL provided little support for presenting information in ways helpful to end users. Bunches of values arranged in rows and columns are difficult to get your head around. Consequently, developers came to rely on *user-interface (UI) tools*, which were employed to create and manage screens that labeled and displayed data. They also allowed end users to modify data directly or by invoking some data processing logic.

Even today, it is useful to divide information system functionality into these three categories: *persistent storage*, *data processing*, and *user-interface*. For each aspect of the system—storage, processing, and user-interface—a different software technology and development approach is appropriate. We illustrate this arrangement in Figure 6–1.

These functional components can be deployed within several *technical* architectures; that is, you can answer the question "On what machine do these lines of code actually execute?" depending on how you map them to the hardware and server software used as the platform for your information system. In fact, with modern *component-centric* software development, it is possible to write a single module of logic that can be moved between architectural tiers.

Different circumstances call for different approaches. Many systems mix architectures. "Our-size-fits-all" is entertaining marketing, but poor engineering.

Data Processing Logic and the ORDBMS

It often makes sense to embed some of an information system's procedural components within the ORDBMS. Furthermore, by using the distributed database features of the ORDBMS, you can address some of the scalability problems inherent in what would otherwise be a centralized architecture. In this chapter we focus on the set of ORDBMS features that can be used to do the following:

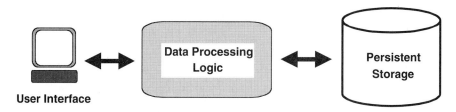

Figure 6–1. *Arrangement of Functional Components of an Information System*

1. Implement procedural data processing aspects of the information system
2. Enforce business rules over any changes made to data in the database
3. Exploit the advantages of distributed computing using the ORDBMS

Many of the technical features described in this chapter will be familiar to readers already acquainted with relational DBMSs. Stored Procedure Language (SPL), `TRIGGER` events, distributed database facilities, gateways, and replications have been a part of DBMS products for some time. The ORDBMS, however, includes some new features that are not part of any previous product. For example, in this chapter we introduce `ON SELECT` triggers and explain the utility of the Virtual Table Interface (VTI).

ORDBMS extensibility can be mixed freely with these traditional RDBMS features. Blending these technologies makes it possible to put information systems together in new ways. Therefore, the larger goal of this chapter is to provide to developers who are building very large systems ideas about how to meet the challenge of scalability without sacrificing too much of the administrative simplicity of a single-box configuration.

Middleware and Distributed Information Systems Architectures

To preempt a possible confusion, it is important to emphasize up front that object-relational extensibility does not obsolete middleware or eliminate the need to write external code. Stored procedures and `TRIGGER` events are part of the ORDBMS. They typically issue OR-SQL queries, in much the same way as external programs. They execute, however, within the DBMS engine, as illustrated in Figure 6–2.
The arguments for embedding data processing logic into the ORDBMS are twofold. First, centralizing common logic simplifies system development. Centralized systems are inherently more manageable than decentralized ones. Modifying a business process in information systems that rely on external programs can involve changing several code modules in several external languages. By contrast, figuring out what to change, and then making the change, is considerably easier where there is only one program to change.

Second, eliminating the need to move data out of the ORDBMS reduces the time taken to complete data processing operations. This is essentially the same technical performance justification motivating *user-defined function (UDF)* and *user-defined type (UDT)* extensibility.

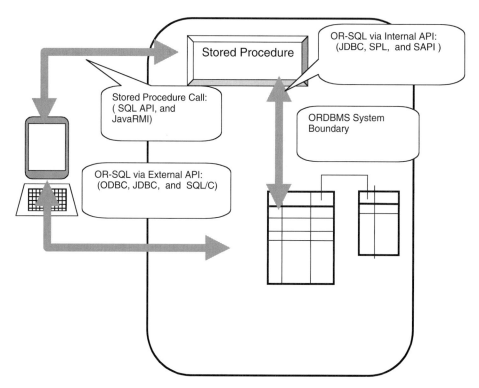

Figure 6–2. *Potential Mapping of UI, Data Processing, and Storage to ORDBMS*

Of course, there are no free lunches. While yielding these benefits, the drawbacks of centralizing data processing has been that it requires the use of proprietary languages, it creates a scalability bottleneck, and it creates a single point of failure. However, distributed ORDBMS technology does provide new ways of mapping information system functionality to underlying hardware resources. In doing so, it blurs the traditional distinction between the static database and flexible middleware.

Over time, we are going to see a blending of persistent storage and data processing frameworks. Unlike current DBMS technologies, these newer approaches will be inherently distributed.

Chapter Overview

This chapter is divided into several sections. The first two describe ORDBMS features: database stored procedures and active database rules. In each section we introduce the feature and illustrate its use. This involves, among other things, a detailed description of what the ORDBMS's *Stored Procedure Language (SPL)* looks like and, coverage of TRIGGER semantics and syntax.

We then move on to describe facilities that are beyond the core DBMS: distributed database functionality, replication, and gateways. These facilities all have a part to play when you are developing *distributed* information systems, which differ from more conventional information systems in that the data and logic managed are partitioned over several computer systems linked by a network. Distributed architectures are increasingly common, as systems are constructed by tying together several pre-existing applications, or because the workload demands of modern Web sites exceeds the capacity of a single box.

The set of distributed data management features described in this chapter are scheduled for release with the next version of the IDS product, due out some time in 2001. Readers should be aware that many of the example in that section will not work on earlier releases.

Stored Procedure Example

In this chapter we develop an example to show how these features might be used in our Movies-R-Us site. The example illustrates how you might build a *shopping-cart*, which is a software product that uses the supermarket experience as its model.

As movie club members purchase items of merchandise through the Web interface, they select the items they want to buy and with a single click of the mouse place them into a "basket." Then, having selected all the goods they want to purchase, members proceed through a "check-out" step that places orders for the items in their basket. The basket metaphor includes concepts such as dumping some or all items from the basket, and so on.

Because the state of the cart may need to endure for some time—minutes or hours—and because shoppers may create a cart and allow the site to "fill" it as goods become available—a process that may take months—we use the database to manage each cart's contents. In Listing 6–1 we present a fairly simple shopping cart database implementation. One table records the cart's existence, and the other table records its contents. For clarity we do not show the set of relevant database constraints. These may be found in the accompanying code.

```
CREATE TABLE Current_Carts (      CREATE TABLE Current_Items (
   Id      SERIAL        NOT NULL,   Cart   INTEGER    NOT NULL,
   Member  Membership_Id NOT NULL,   Item   Part_Code  NOT NULL,
   Start   DATE          NOT NULL,   Qty    Quantity   NOT NULL
   Expires DATE          NOT NULL );
);
```

Listing 6–1. *Object-Relational Tables for Shopping Cart*

As the end user navigates through the Web site's commerce screens, the actions he or she chooses change the state of cart; the end-user actions modify the rows in the tables but do so indirectly by executing stored procedures. The modification is done so that the behavior is consistent with other external interfaces, such as a client/server program or an XML message parser. In Table 6–1 we present the list of the operations that constitute the dynamic behavior of the cart. Some methodologies refer to these individual procedures as *services* provided by a shopping cart *module*.

Each service is invoked procedurally, such as a subroutine using the EXECUTE FUNCTION or EXECUTE PROCEDURE syntax. This assumes that some external program contains a set of state variables to identify the current shopping cart, member, selected item, and so on. Web sites typically work by carrying this information as part of the HTML exchange between the site and the client browser.

Table 6–1. Shopping Cart Services

Service Name and Interface	Description
Initialize_Cart (Membership_Id) -> Cart_Handle	Given a membership Id, this service returns a handle to a shopping cart. The handle is used by other services. If no cart exists for the nominated member, this service creates one. If one exists (that was created within a reasonable period of time we call the 'expired period'), the service returns a handle to that cart.
Reset_Cart (Cart_Handle)	This service removes all items from the nominated cart.
Destroy_Cart Cart_Handle)	This service removes all items from the nominated cart and deletes the cart.
Cart_Status (Cart_Handle) -> ROW (Cnt INTEGER, Value Currency)	This service reports the number of items in the cart and the total value of the items in the cart.
Checkout_Cart (Cart_Handle, Membership_Id, LVARCHAR)	This service takes all items from the nominated cart and inserts them into the Orders tables. It then destroys the cart information. The Membership_Id is used for extra security, and the third argument allows the end user to add extra instructions to the delivery address.
Add_Items (Cart_Handle, SET{ ROW(Item, Number) }|)	This service manages the state of items in the cart. The effect of this service is to change the number of nominated items in the nominated shopping cart by the nominated number. Internally, this is an unexpectedly complex. If the item does not exist in the shopping cart, a new row must be inserted. If one exists, the number must be updated. If this update reduces the number of items to zero or less, the service removes that item record from the cart.

Collectively, these stored procedures provide external programs with a procedural interface to manage shopping carts. As we shall see, some of these operations wrap single OR-SQL queries. Others are more complex.

Database Stored Procedures

Stored procedures are a well-known mechanism for embedding procedural logic into a data management system. They encapsulate each business process behind a kind of subroutine call. External programs invoke stored procedures with the same interfaces used for queries (ESQL/C, JDBC, and Web DataBlade™ markup tags). An external program has no knowledge of how the stored procedure is implemented or even where it actually executes.

In Listing 6–2 we demonstrate what a series of calls to the stored procedures listed in Table 6–1 might look like. This list corresponds to a movie club member's interaction with the Web site: picking a series of items of merchandise, placing them in a cart, and finally checking the cart out. These calls may come to the ORDBMS through different interfaces. They may reflect a Web user clicking through the site's pages or an employee of the site using a client/server interface to record a phone-in order.

```
--
-- First things first. By entering the "on-line store"
-- pages, the member automatically initializes a shopping
-- cart.
--
EXECUTE FUNCTION Initialize_Cart ('brown_p_g');
--
-- To help explain some of the following calls, let us
-- assume that this stored procedure returns the
-- value 101 as a handle to the newly initialized cart.
--
-- Suppose the movie club member decides to buy two
-- tickets to see Casablanca. Through the Web or a JDBC
-- interface, they would invoke the Add_Item stored
-- procedure in the following way.
--
EXECUTE PROCEDURE Add_Item ( 101, 203::Part_Code, 2 );
```

```
--
-- Woah! It's a double date! Better put two more
-- tickets into the shopping cart.
--
EXECUTE PROCEDURE Add_Item ( 101, 203::Part_Code, 2 );
--
-- No. They changed their minds. The Web interface permits
-- members to remove an item from their shopping baskets.
-- To simplify the interface (small and simple are
-- important goals in interface design ), you simply call
-- Add_Item() again with the same basket handle and
-- part_code, only passing in a quantity that is one more
-- than what the HTML page shows to be the current
-- quantity, with a negative sign. Part of the stored
-- procedure's logic removes an item if its quantity
-- falls below zero.
--
EXECUTE PROCEDURE Add_Item ( 101, 203::Part_Code, -5 );
--
-- But as these are on special, pick up a pair of posters
-- instead.
--
EXECUTE PROCEDURE Add_Items ( 101,
                  SET{ ROW(501::Part_Code, 1),
                       ROW(502::Part_Code, 1)
                     }::LIST(Shopping_Cart_Line_Item
                             NOT NULL));
--
--   Finally, check out the cart. Just to be on the safe
-- side, get the member to supply their membership id
-- (and/or password) again. Also, this interface
-- allows the member to provide "special delivery
-- instructions."
--
EXECUTE PROCEDURE Checkout_Cart ( 101, 'brown_p_g',
                                       'Leave on porch' );
```

Listing 6–2. *Invoking Stored Procedures*

Responding to this sequence of six procedural calls requires that the ORDBMS run about thirteen read and write queries, checking several conditions along the way.

Stored Procedures and User-Defined Functions

So far we have talked about *stored procedures*. Notice that this example mixes user-defined FUNCTION and user-defined PROCEDURE. In practice, stored procedure logic can be implemented using the SPL or any of the supported host languages, such as C and Java. In addition, developers can use either a user-defined function or a user-defined procedure mechanism to embed logic into the database.

In practice, what distinguishes stored procedures from the data type specific user-defined functions we introduced in Chapter 5 is that they are used for different purposes. The user-defined FUNCTION in Listing 6–3 contains an INSERT query (and the Current_Cart stored procedure it calls includes a DELETE). UDFs containing OR-SQL write operations should not be used in OR-SQL queries.[1] Only a UDF that performs an encapsulated operation on its data type arguments, while making no change to the underlying database, should be used in this way.

It is best not to get too hung up on the technical approach taken. In practice, it is often useful to implement business logic as a FUNCTION because the business process can then return a value that might be useful in the calling context. To underscore this point we use the term "*stored procedure*" throughout this chapter. For example, in Listing 6–3 we illustrate a user-defined FUNCTION to implement the Initialize_Cart stored procedure.

```
CREATE FUNCTION Initialize_Cart ( Mem_Num Membership_Id )
RETURNS INTEGER

    DEFINE nRetCart INTEGER;
    LET nRetCart = -1;

    WHILE ( nRetCart <= 0 )
       LET nRetCart = Current_Cart ( Mem_Num );

       IF (nRetCart = -1 ) THEN
            INSERT INTO Current_Carts
            ( Member, Start, Expires )
            VALUES
            ( Mem_Num, TODAY, TODAY + 7 );
       END IF;

    END WHILE;
    RETURN nRetCart;
END FUNCTION;
```

Listing 6–3. *SPL Function Implementing a Business Operation*

---

[1] This restriction is due to the fact that allowing write queries to be encapsulated within UDFs within SELECT queries tremendously complicates transaction processing.

We use SPL in this chapter because it is a simple language that makes for clear examples. In addition, a book about INFORMIX's ORDBMS product would be incomplete without some coverage of the language. Nonetheless, all principles illustrated with SPL in this chapter also apply equally to external languages such as Java and C.

Creating Stored Procedures

As we saw in Chapter 5, the IDS server identifies user-defined routines by their *signature*, which is the combination of the routine's name and the data types of its arguments. New stored procedures therefore require a name and an argument list that uniquely identifies them within the database. You can overload stored procedures by creating another with the same name, but with different arguments.

All stored procedure declarations also include the *body* of the procedure. For internal stored procedures, this body is the SPL logic the server executes when the stored procedure is invoked. For external UDRs, it is the location of the executable code to run. Signatures, information about the procedure's body, and any security rules imposed over the new UDR are stored in the ORDBMS's system catalogs.

Internal SPL and Procedures

SPL routines are called *internal* database procedures, just as user-defined functions implemented in SPL are called *internal* functions. Listing 6–4 illustrates the general form used to create a stored procedure using SPL.

```
CREATE PROCEDURE Procedure_Name ( [ Argument Type ]
                                        { ,Argument Type })
BEGIN PROCEDURE

    SPL VARIABLE DEFINITIONS;

    SPL CODE INCLUDING SQL STATEMENTS;

END PROCEDURE;
--
--  This stored procedure deletes the row from the
--  Current_Carts table that records the existence
```

```
--  of a particular cart.
--
CREATE PROCEDURE Destroy_Cart ( Which_Cart   INTEGER )

    DELETE FROM Current_Carts WHERE Id = Which_Cart;

END PROCEDURE;
```

Listing 6–4. *Outline of Stored Procedure Declaration*

At the time that the new routine is created the ORDBMS compiles
the stored procedure logic into a byte-code format called *pcode* and
optimizes all queries within it as best it can. Should something
change—should a table's structure be altered or a new index is created for the table—the ORDBMS will recompile all stored procedures
that involve the altered table.

External Procedures

As with user-defined functions, *external* stored procedures are compiled
using external (non-ORDBMS) tools into an executable library and are
linked to the server executable on demand. Listing 6–5 illustrates what
it looks like to declare a stored procedure that is implemented using
Java. The syntax for creating C stored procedures is identical to the
syntax used for C UDFs.

```
EXECUTE PROCEDURE install_jar(

"file:$INFORMIXDIR/extend/examples/Shopping_Cart.jar",
        "Shopping_Cart", 0);

CREATE FUNCTION Destroy_Cart ( INTEGER )
EXTERNAL NAME
'Shopping_Cart:Shopping_Cart.DestroyCart(java.lang.Integer)'
LANGUAGE Java;
```

Listing 6–5. *Declaring an External Stored Procedure*

Of course, in order to accomplish the same task as the internal
stored procedure in Listing 6–4, the code in this Java UDR would need
to employ the server-side JDBC interface, and a C version of this UDR
would use the DataBlade Interface, also known as the *Server API (SAPI)*.

All rules concerning external UDF logic apply to stored procedures.
For example, C stored procedures must use the server's facilities for

managing memory and file I/O, should not make blocking system calls, and should generally avoid unsafe coding practice. Java has fewer restrictions than C. The Java environment within the ORDBMS permits developers to use facilities provided by the Java language or the Java libraries.

Comparing Stored Procedure Mechanisms

Simple measurements reveal that there is little performance difference between stored procedures implemented using the languages alternatives. The computational cost of running whatever OR-SQL is embedded within a stored procedure is almost always far greater than the cost of the surrounding procedural code. In fact, regardless of the procedural language you employ, you are well advised to push as much processing as you can within the OR-SQL. Set-at-a-time query execution outperforms equivalent row-at-a-time procedural logic.

Some general advice regarding stored procedure implementation is as follows:

1. Use SPL for procedures that you know at design time will only ever be run inside the ORDBMS. If the business process might be part of a middle-ware process or a client, use a host language like Java instead.
2. Data processing logic that might need to be deployed elsewhere—in a middleware server, a client program, or another DBMS—should use Java.
3. If you really think you need C for performance, consider decomposing the C logic into a set of UDFs for its various subroutines, and then using OR-SQL and/or SPL to complete the job. This will result in a far more flexible solution that suffers no performance penalty.
4. Any stored procedure developed using a previous version of the IDS product will work in exactly the same way in the ORDBMS version. SPL itself is similarly unchanged.

Invoking Stored Procedures

Stored procedures are invoked in a very similar fashion to how programs are initiated in a operating system. Syntactically, an external program sends an EXECUTE PROCEDURE or EXECUTE FUNCTION command to the ORDBMS. These statements are just like OR-SQL queries in that they can be invoked through a command-line tool or embedded within an external program and passed into the ORDBMS through an API such as ODBC or JDBC. There is no way to tell, from an external program's perspective, which language is used to implement a particular stored procedure.

EXECUTE PROCEDURE Statement

Listing 6–6 illustrates the general form of the EXECUTE PROCEDURE command.

```
EXECUTE PROCEDURE Procedure_Name (Argument List);
```

Listing 6–6. *OR-SQL Syntax for Executing a Stored Procedure*

If you are using a PROCEDURE to implement the stored procedure logic, the ORDBMS might not return a result. A user-defined function's return results are handled in whatever style the API supports for a single row and a single column query result. For example, in Listing 6–7 we present an ESQL/C fragment illustrating how this is done for a PROCEDURE and a FUNCTION.

```
void
ExecProcedure ( szArgValue )
EXEC SQL BEGIN DECLARE SECTION;
        PARAMETER string * szArgValue;
EXEC SQL END DECLARE SECTION;
{
        EXEC SQL EXECUTE PROCEDURE AddEntityRow (
:szArgValue );
}
. . .
void
ExecuteFunction ( szArgString, pchReturn )
EXEC SQL BEGIN DECLARE SECTION;
        PARAMETER string * szArgString;
EXEC SQL END DECLARE SECTION;
    char * pchReturn;
{
        EXEC SQL  BEGIN DECLARE SECTION;
                string szResult[RES_LENGTH];
        EXEC SQL END DECLARE SECTION;

        EXEC SQL EXECUTE FUNCTION TransExamp( :szArgString )
                INTO :szResult;
        strcpy ( pchReturn, szResult );
}
```

Listing 6–7. *ESQL/C Code Executing PROCEDURE and FUNCTION*

Other APIs, such as JDBC, also employ interface methods intended for SELECT queries to handle FUNCTION return results. Methods exist to determine the return result type of an EXECUTE FUNCTION, and API facilities like prepared queries and binding host language variables to UDF arguments is also supported.

CALL Procedure

Within SPL, you can invoke a user-defined PROCEDURE as shown in Listing 6–8.

```
.
.
CALL Procedure_Name(Argument List);
.
```

Listing 6–8. *Executing a Stored Procedure from Within SPL Logic*

Stored procedures are dispatched dynamically, like all ORDBMS operations. That is, when you write an external program that calls a stored procedure, it is possible to change the logic in the stored procedure without modifying or recompiling the external program. With proper design, it is possible to upgrade the functionality of an entire information system simply by modifying modules in the ORDBMS, rather than by rewriting external programs.

This kind of flexibility is useful because it simplifies ongoing maintenance of the information system. Consider a stored procedure used to add new movies to the site's catalogs. Developers might augment it to add or update rows in additional tables or to send e-mail to movie club members who have expressed an interest in films in which the film's genre is included in their own interests. By dropping the old procedure and creating one with the same signature but with a new body, the external programs need not know about the change.

Stored Procedure Language (SPL)

In this section we review the functionality of SPL. Extensibility makes the object-relational version of SPL more powerful than it was in the RDBMS. Any UDF can be used within SPL as readily as it can be used in OR-SQL.

In many RDBMS-based information systems, a considerable proportion of overall functionality was implemented using SPL. In fact, several commercial development tools are available for the language. This was the consequence of the way that "moving logic to the data" helped performance and reduced maintenance costs.

With stored procedure logic in an extensible DBMS, you are better off thinking of SPL as a kind of scripting language for wrapping OR-SQL statements into transactions. When using an extensible data manager there are often advantages to implementing logic that augments the OR-SQL query language, rather than creating a custom stored procedure each time a question must be answered that is beyond the capacity of SQL-92.

We do not describe the full extent of the SPL language here. Instead, we focus on its most commonly used aspects. All of the features described here can also be used within internal user-defined functions.

Variables and Parameters (DEFINE and LET)

Variables in an SPL routine are declared using the DEFINE keyword. All variable declarations must appear at the top of the procedure body, before any code. Any data types present in the ORDBMS can be used for an SPL variable: a built-in type, a COLLECTION, or any of the extended types. Variable declarations allocate memory resources to contain the variable; they do not assign any initial value. The code fragment in Listing 6–9 illustrates several variable declarations.

```
    .
DEFINE    Count      INTEGER;
DEFINE    Name       PersonName;
DEFINE    Amount     Currency;
DEFINE    Prefers    SET(Genre NOT NULL);
    .
```

Listing 6–9. *Declaring Variables in an SPL Routine*

Values are assigned to SPL variables with the LET keyword. The SPL fragment in Listing 6–10 provides several examples of how to use it.

```
LET  Count    = 7;

LET  Prefers = ( SELECT M.Preferences
                 FROM MovieClubMembers
```

```
                         WHERE Id = 'brown_p_g'  );

    LET  Amount  = Currency( 15000.00, 'CAN');

    LET  Name    = ROW('Davis', 'Willian', 'Mr.', '');
```

Listing 6–10. *Assigning Values to Variables in SPL*

The first two examples assign values to variables from a constant
and a OR-SQL SELECT statement. Readers who have used SPL will be
familiar with this form of assignment, although assigning an entire
COLLECTION variable from a query is novel. The other examples illustrate how the ORDBMS's extensibility works within SPL. Here, we assign
instances of some extended type—created using a UDF constructor or
the general purpose ROW TYPE constructor—to variables.

Parameters can be treated just like variables in almost all respects,
except that you should not assign values to them unless they have
been declared as OUT parameters. You can also define variables to be
GLOBAL, which means that the variable can be accessed in all subroutines called from the procedure in which it is defined.

Control Flow and Branching
(IF-THEN-ELIF-END IF)

SPL supports a basic IF THEN-ELIF-ELSE-END IF syntax for conditional branching. The code fragment in Listing 6–11 illustrates what
conditional branch code looks like in SPL.

```
    .
    IF ( GetUnit( Amount ) != 'USD' ) THEN
    LET Amount = Convert( Amount, 'USD' );
         END IF;

         .
         IF ( Name.Title = 'Mr' ) THEN
              --
         -- SPL Code implementing action taken if
         -- person's Title indicates male.
    --
         ELIF ( Name.Title IN ( 'Ms','Mss','Mrs' ) ) THEN
              --
    -- SPL Code implementing action taken
    -- if person's title indicates female.
    --
```

```
        ELSE
    --
    -- SPL Code implementing action taken when
    -- the person's gender is unknown.
    --
        END IF;
```

Listing 6–11. *Conditional Branching with IF THEN-ELIF-END IF Syntax*

Conditional branching is useful because it is difficult to implement IF logic in OR-SQL. It is especially useful when you are implementing a stored procedure that takes a variety of actions based on the state of the database, such as the one we show in Listing 6–12.

```
CREATE PROCEDURE Add_Item ( Which_Cart_Id INTEGER,
                            Which_Item_Id Part_Code,
                            How_Many        INTEGER )
    DEFINE nCurrrentCount  INTEGER;
--
-- If the cart handle that is passed in does not identify
-- something, raise an exception.
--
    IF NOT (( SELECT 't'::boolean
                FROM Current_Carts
               WHERE Id = Which_Cart_Id )) THEN
        RAISE EXCEPTION -746, 0,
           "Add_Item failed because CART does not exist.";
    END IF;

    LET nCurrrentCount = (SELECT C.Qty::INTEGER
                            FROM Current_Items C
                           WHERE C.Cart = Which_Cart_Id
                             AND C.Item = Which_Item_Id);
--
-- How many of the specified items are in the Cart?
--
    IF ( nCurrrentCount IS NULL ) THEN
--
-- If none (no rows matched, so query result is a NULL),
-- INSERT a new Item.
--
        INSERT INTO Current_Items
        ( Cart, Item, Qty )
        VALUES
```

```
                ( Which_Cart_Id,Which_Item_Id,How_Many::Quantity);
        ELIF (( nCurrrentCount + How_Many ) < 1 ) THEN
        --
        -- To remove a number of items from the cart, this
        -- procedure is called with a negative How_Many value.
        -- If this would remove all
        -- Items, the logic of the stored procedure simply
        -- DELETEs the entire row.
        --
                DELETE FROM Current_Items
                  WHERE Cart = Which_Cart_Id
                    AND Item = Which_Item_Id;
            ELSE
        --
        --  And finally, the default case, where the Quantity of
        --  Items is UPDATEd, adding How_Many.
        --
                UPDATE Current_Items
                    SET Qty = (Qty  + How_Many)
                  WHERE Cart = Which_Cart_Id
                    AND Item = Which_Item_Id;
            END IF;
        END PROCEDURE;
```

Listing 6–12. *Practical Use of Conditional Branching Statements*

This stored procedure manages a shopping cart's contents. A single procedural interface such as this simplifies the information system's non-DBMS logic. In this case the site's Web pages allow end users to add or subtract selected items from their cart, and this procedure is called from the logic that handled the HTML forms returned from a Web browser.

Looping (FOR, FOREACH, and WHILE)

Procedural programming languages usually provide a looping syntax for iterating over a set of data objects until some condition is met. Three sets of SPL statement facilitate looping. Other statements—CONTINUE and EXIT—are used to break out of a looping structure that uses any of these statements. Refer to the next section for more details.

WHILE Looping

In Listing 6–13 we illustrate the general form of the SPL `WHILE-END WHILE` statements. `WHILE-END WHILE` loops execute a block of code until some condition is met.

```
WHILE 0 < ( SELECT COUNT(*)
                FROM Current_Items I
              WHERE I.Cart = Which_Cart_Id )

LET Item_to_Process =(SELECT MIN(Item)
                              FROM Current_Items I
                            WHERE I.Cart=Which_Cart_Id
                      );

  CALL Process_Item ( Which_Cart_Id, Item_to_Process );

END WHILE;
```

Listing 6–13. *Looping in SPL Using WHILE-END WHILE*

This example is not particularly realistic—using a `FOREACH-END FOREACH` loop is preferable because the `WHILE` loop will rerun the SQL `COUNT(*)` query each time it checks the loop condition and the `MIN()` query within each loop iteration—but it does provide another demonstration of how easy it is to embed OR-SQL within SPL.

This code fragment illustrates SPL's modularity; note the use of the `CALL` statement. Having picked an item to process the code calls another database procedure, `Process_Item`, that actually does the work (in order for this loop to ever terminate it must delete the item from the `Current_Items` table). If a subroutine generates an exception, the ORDBMS can pass that exception back to the procedure that called it. Code in the calling procedures can trap both exceptions in its own code and any generated by the subroutines it calls.

FOREACH Looping

`FOREACH-END FOREACH` iterates over a number of rows. `FOREACH` takes a query, or an expression such as an iterator UDR, that produces a number of values that are either scalar values or rows. The `FOREACH-END FOREACH` loop opens a cursor and assigning values from each result row to local variables. For each row, the ORDBMS executes the loop's body using these variables, repeating until there are no more rows to be processed.

FOREACH most typically uses an OR-SQL SELECT query to retrieve the data used within the loop body, as shown in Listing 6–14.

```
CREATE PROCEDURE Add_Items (
        Which_Cart INTEGER,
        Items        LIST(Shopping_Cart_Line_Item NOT NULL)
)

    DEFINE    Which_Item        Part_Code;
    DEFINE    Change_Count      INTEGER;
    DEFINE    nCurrrentCount    INTEGER;

    FOREACH SELECT I.Which_One, I.How_Many
              INTO Which_Item, Change_Count
              FROM TABLE( Items ) I

        CALL Add_Item (Which_Cart,Which_Item,
                         Change_Count);

    END FOREACH;

END PROCEDURE;
```

Listing 6–14. *FOREACH Statement Looping over SELECT Query Results*

Here, the FOREACH mechanism is used to access the contents of a COLLECTION variable. OR-SQL expressions over database tables and views are more typical.

FOR-END FOR

The third looping syntax is useful when you want the body of the loop to be executed a known number of times. Listing 6–15 illustrates how FOR-END FOR can be used.

```
CREATE FUNCTION ReturnEndQMonth ()
RETURNS SET(INTEGER NOT NULL)
        DEFINE setIntRetVal   SET(INTEGER NOT NULL);
        DEFINE nMonthNum                 INTEGER;

        LET setIntRetVal = SET{};
        FOR nMonthNum IN ( 3 TO 12 STEP 3 )
              INSERT INTO TABLE(setIntRetVal)
              VALUES ( nMonthNum );
```

```
            END FOR;

            RETURN setIntRetVal;
    END FUNCTION;
```

Listing 6–15. *FOR Statement Looping over Values*

Here it seems appropriate to make a general point about looping in SPL. The task of writing stored procedures often falls to programmers who are better acquainted with procedural logic than with declarative languages. Consequently, they fall back on the row-at-a-time programming for which they were trained. Given the complexity involved in writing the corresponding SQL-92 this is not surprising.

The result is that you frequently see the pattern in Listing 6–16 in the stored procedures that implement business logic:

```
        DEFINE nIdValue        INTEGER;
        DEFINE nCheckResult    INTEGER;
        DEFINE flIntResult     FLOAT;
        DEFINE vcValue         VARCHAR(12);
        DEFINE dValue          DATE;
        DEFINE decValue        DECIMAL(10,3);

        FOREACH SELECT T.Key, T.VC_Column,
                        T.Date_Column, T.Decimal_Column
                  INTO nIdValue, vcValue, dValue, decValue
                  FROM Table_A T;

            LET nIdValue = Sub_Routine_One(vcValue,decValue);
            IF (nIdValue > Argument_Value ) THEN

            LET flIntResult = Sub_Routine_Two(
                    dValue, decValue);
                    INSERT INTO Table_B VALUES
    ( nIdValue, vcValue, flIntResult );

        END FOREACH;
```

Listing 6–16. *Common and Suboptimal Coding Patterns in SPL Stored Procedures*

Such patterns are quite common. Although using a stored procedure in this way is a better option from a performance and maintainability point of view, it is not as good as it could be. In the ORDBMS, each of the subroutines in this example can be called from OR-SQL, so the procedure in Listing 6–16 can be rewritten as shown in Listing 6–17.

```
INSERT INTO Table_B
SELECT T.Key,
       T.VC_Column,
       Sub_Routine_Two ( T.Date_Column, T.Decimal_Column )
  FROM Table_A T
 WHERE Sub_Routine_One ( T.VC_Column, T.Decimal_Column ) >
                          :Argument_Value;
```

Listing 6–17. *Object-Relational Rewrite of the Example in Listing 6–16*

A relatively simple experiment shows that this second implementation significantly outperforms the first. In addition, if SubRoutineOne() and SubRoutineTwo() were implemented in C or Java, the performance difference would be even greater. Obviously, OR-SQL cannot replace SPL looping in every case. Some subroutines implement entire business processes and therefore include OR-SQL of their own. Nonetheless, in many situations, this query-centric approach results in increased efficiency and takes up fewer programmer cycles.

Breaking Out of a Loop (CONTINUE and EXIT)

CONTINUE and EXIT break out of loops. Both statements immediately jump to the END of whatever loop they are in, but take different paths thereafter. EXIT terminates the entire looping statement and the ORDBMS then proceeds with the first SPL statement after the loop's END. CONTINUE, on the other hand, simply begins the loop body again with the next set of iteration values.

The (slightly silly) SPL example in Listing 6–18 illustrates how to use these statements. It is unrelated to the shopping cart example, but it provides an additional illustration of how COLLECTION objects are handled. Instead of FOREACH–END FOREACH loops getting their values from the COLLECTION arguments, you might get them from queries against database tables.

```
CREATE FUNCTION CommonElemCount (
                First_Set   SET(INTEGER NOT NULL),
                Second_Set  SET(INTEGER NOT NULL),
                Common_Num  INTEGER   )
```

```
RETURNS boolean

    DEFINE i    INTEGER;
    DEFINE j    INTEGER;
    DEFINE nCnt INTEGER;
    LET nCnt = 0;

    FOREACH SELECT F1.Num INTO i
            FROM TABLE(First_Set) F1 (Num)       -- LOOP 1

        FOREACH SELECT F2.Num INTO j
                FROM TABLE(Second_Set) F2 (Num )-- LOOP 2
            IF ( i = j ) THEN
                LET nCnt = nCnt + 1;
                EXIT FOREACH;                    -- EXIT LOOP 2
            END IF;
        END FOREACH;                             --  END LOOP 2

        IF ( nCnt <> Common_Num ) THEN
            CONTINUE FOREACH                     -- NEXT LOOP 1
        ELSE
            CONTINUE FOREACH;                    -- EXIT LOOP 1
        END IF;

    END FOREACH;                                 --  END LOOP 1

    IF ( nCnt = Common_Num) THEN
        RETURN 't'::boolean;
    END IF;

    RETURN 'f'::boolean;
END FUNCTION;
```

Listing 6–18. *EXIT and CONTINUE Statements in FOREACH Loops*

CONTINUE and EXIT break out of the "nearest" named loop (FOREACH, WHILE, and FOR). Another statement that can break out of a loop is RETURN, which not only terminates the loop, but also the routine execution. Regardless of where it appears in the logic, RETURN immediately hands the result of an expression back to whatever invoked the function. Numerous illustrations of RETURN appear in the SPL examples throughout this book.

Exception Handling (RAISE EXCEPTION and ON EXCEPTION)

SPL's exception and error handling is quite sophisticated. In addition, the language includes a set of facilities for accessing status information such as the identity of the current user and the number of rows affected by the last query.

Exceptions can be generated by the ORDBMS when it encounters an error in the SPL code or in an embedded OR-SQL query. Should your code need to raise an exception of its own, it does so using the RAISE EXCEPTION statement as shown in Listing 6–19.

```
RAISE EXCEPTION -746, 0,
        "Error: Hopefully a sensible error message.";
```

Listing 6–19. *RAISE EXCEPTION Example*

Listing 6–19 illustrates the most common way that RAISE EXCEPTION is used in SPL; –746 is a special error number reserved for one off application exceptions. Other error numbers, which are all negative values, correspond to specific conditions. Developers can add their own error numbers, and this is a good idea when the same kind of exception may be raised in several stored procedures. The second number (0) relates to lower-level error information and can generally be ignored. It is mostly of interest to database administrators and technical support staff.

The exception-handling default employed by the IDS product is to halt processing and rollback work in progress whenever an exception is generated. SPL can, however, intercept exceptions and handle them using custom SPL. In Listing 6–20 we illustrate the ON EXCEPTION statement, which is used to intercept an exception raised elsewhere and to indicate how it is to be handled. In this example, if the code that executes after this ON EXCEPTION statement (including any subroutines) raises a –206 error (if it issues a SELECT query against a nonexistent table, for example) the IDS product's SPL interpreter runs the indicated block of code and creates the table.

```
ON EXCEPTION IN ( -206) - This is "No such table"
    CREATE TEMP TABLE Working_Data ( );
END EXCEPTION WITH RESUME;
```

Listing 6–20. *ON EXCEPTION Example*

The question of where the SPL interpreter resumes once it has run the execution handling code is a complex one. In Listing 6-20, the interpreter picks up again at the first SPL statement after the line of code that generated the exception. Without the `WITH RESUME` syntax, execution may continue after the `END EXCEPTION` statement, or behave as though it was a `CONTINUE [LOOP]` command (see Listing 6–18) or it might simply terminate the stored procedure.

`EXTERNAL` procedures can also raise exceptions. The SAPI interface includes a function `mi_db_error_raise ()` that behaves similar to `RAISE EXCEPTION`. Java procedures should throw SQLException. In addition, SAPI allows UDF developers to register callback functions with IDS. Callbacks are special user-defined functions that the ORDBMS invokes automatically whenever it encounters certain conditions; such as the end of a transition or a rollback.

Status Information (DBINFO)

Useful information about the run-time status of the ORDBMS can be retrieved through the `DBINFO` expression. `DBINFO` gives SPL developers a window into the SQL Communication Area (SQLCA), which is an in-memory block of information relating to the current user session. This gives you status information, such as the last `SERIAL` value inserted into a table or the number of rows affected by the most recent query, and access to user and process identity information through the current session ID.

Listing 6–21 illustrates how to use the `DBINFO` expression to get information about the number of rows affected by the last query.

```
--
--   This stored procedure moves the contents of a
--   shopping cart into the Order tables. It illustrates
--   how to use the DBINFO() expression to get information
--   about the number of rows affected by the operation.
--
CREATE PROCEDURE Checkout_Cart (
                        Which_Cart      INTEGER,
                        Membership_Num Membership_Id,
                        Instructions    LVARCHAR )
RETURNS LVARCHAR

    DEFINE nQueryRowCount   INTEGER;
    DEFINE nLastSerialId    INTEGER;

    INSERT INTO Orders
    ( Customer, DeliverTo, OrderedOn )
    SELECT C.Member,
            DeliveryAddress ( M.Address, Instructions ),
```

```
                    TODAY
              FROM MovieClubMembers M, Current_Carts C
            WHERE C.Id = Which_Cart
              AND C.Member = M.Id
              AND C.Member = Membership_Num;
--
-- The first of the following lines of code returns the
-- value of the last SERIAL value assigned.
--
    LET nLastSerialId  = DBINFO('sqlca.sqlerrd1');
    LET nQueryRowCount = DBINFO('sqlca.sqlerrd2');

    IF ( nQueryRowCount = 0 ) THEN
      RAISE EXCEPTION -746, 0,
        "Error: Checkout_Cart() could not find your Cart";
    END IF;

    INSERT INTO Order_Line_Items
    ( Order, Merchandise, Numberbought )
    SELECT nLastSerialId,
           I.Item,
           I.Qty
      FROM Current_Items I
     WHERE I.Cart = Which_Cart;
--
-- This returns the number of ROWs affected by the most
-- recent query.
--
    LET nQueryRowCount = DBINFO('sqlca.sqlerrd2');

    IF ( nQueryRowCount = 0 ) THEN
        RAISE EXCEPTION -746, 0,
          "Error: Checkout_Cart() found the cart empty";
    END IF;

    CALL Destroy_Cart ( Which_Cart );

END PROCEDURE;
```

Listing 6–21. *The Use of the DBINFO Expression*

Other information about the current session can be obtained by using the DBINFO('SessionID') to interrogate the system catalogs and the *System Management Interfaces (SMI)*. It enables you to find out client IP address and other information.

Stored Procedures and Transaction Management

For transaction management purposes, the ORDBMS's treats the OR-SQL operations in a stored procedure exactly as if the same queries were issued from an external program within a set of transaction boundaries (BEGIN WORK / COMMIT WORK). As we mentioned earlier, when a stored procedure generates an exception and the exception is not handled, the ORDBMS rolls back the entire transaction. Thus, by default, a stored procedure either completes or fails without changing anything.

Within a stored procedure, you can issue BEGIN WORK and COMMIT WORK instructions for transaction boundaries, but the conventions of transaction management still apply. The ORDBMS does not support nested transactions: issuing two BEGIN WORK statements without a COMMIT WORK between them will cause the ORDBMS to generate an error.

Administration and Management of Stored Procedures

Like all database objects, IDS product allows administrators to control user access to stored procedures. Further, users executing a stored procedure must have permissions on all database resources used within it. These permissions include appropriate access privileges over any tables and view and usage privileges over user-defined functions and any stored procedures called as subroutines. IDS checks this at runtime, before the procedure is executed.

Permissions

Permissions to execute a procedure can be granted and revoked just like any other schema object. The SQL GRANT EXECUTE command is used to grant the ability to invoke a procedure to a user or group of users. In Listing 6–22 we illustrate how to use this command.

```
GRANT EXECUTE
ON PROCEDURE Add_Movie_Personality (
  PERSONNAME, DATE, DATE, State_Enum, LVARCHAR, LVARCHAR )
TO PUBLIC;
```

```
REVOKE EXECUTE
ON PROCEDURE Add_Movie_Personality (
  PERSONNAME, DATE, DATE, State_Enum, LVARCHAR, LVARCHAR )
TO PUBLIC;
```

Listing 6–22. *GRANT and REVOKE Execution Privileges on a Stored Procedure*

Note that the behavior of databases created as ANSI databases is different from the default behavior. In a mode ANSI database, all database objects are, by default, accessible by all users in the PUBLIC role.

Dropping Procedures

Database procedures can be dropped using the DROP PROCEDURE syntax, as shown in Listing 6–23. This removes any record of the procedure from the ORDBMS system catalogs.

```
DROP PROCEDURE Procedure_Name ( [ Argument Type ]
                                {, Argument Type } );

DROP PROCEDURE Add_Movie_Personality (
                PERSONNAME, DATE, DATE,
                State_Enum, LVARCHAR, LVARCHAR );
```

Listing 6–23. *DROP PROCEDURE Example*

It is possible to drop a stored procedure even when it is being used as a subroutine within another procedure because it simplifies the task of modifying the logic in the database. The ORDBMS generates an error at runtime if it tries to invoke a nonexistent routine.

Documenting Stored Procedures

It is generally a good idea to include with each stored procedure a brief description of what is does, and perhaps a more detailed explanation of its internal processes. This helps developers quickly determine whether there exists a stored procedure that does what they intend. Adding documentation is supported in both the CREATE FUNCTION and CREATE PROCEDURE statements. An example of how to append such a description to a stored procedure can be found in Listing 5-30 of Chapter 5.

Active Database Features

Sometimes you want the ORDBMS to respond automatically whenever some set of circumstances occurs in the database. For example, when a site employee adds a new cinema, it would be useful to verify whether its geographic coordinates place it on dry land. (It is disastrously easy to get the longitude and latitude values wrong.) Alternatively, it might be useful to automatically insert a row into an audit table whenever sensitive information on the site is changed, or perhaps even read.

This kind of functionality can be implemented using the *active database* features of the ORDBMS. In this section we provide a description of the underlying model used to define database rules and the syntax used. Later, we provide some illustrations of how database rules are used and a brief overview of how they are implemented.

Principles of Active Databases

Active database facilities allow the ORDBMS to respond automatically to some event. The alternative to using these facilities is to modify every query, database procedure, and module of external code that might cause the event to occur. Given that the ORDBMS allows for runtime, dynamic queries, it is unreasonable to expect that even exhaustive and perfect code changes would solve the problem.

Database rules watch for a particular kind of data manipulation event: such as UPDATE row in a particular table, for example. When this event happens, the ORDBMS can (optionally) check that the event meets some condition. If it does, the rule instructs the ORDBMS to undertake a specified action, such as executing another query or invoking a database procedure.

We call this concept a *database rule*. Such rules are typically described them in terms of the triple in Listing 6–24.

```
ON    < EVENT >
WHEN  < CONDITION >
DO    < ACTION >;
```

Listing 6–24. *Active Database Rule Triple*

This kind of rule concept is widely applied in computer science. Event based programming—where developers code a series of responses to external events such as function keys or tabbing out of text boxes—is a popular model in 4GL languages.

But it is important to understand that database rules are quite different than expert system rules. Whenever the ORDBMS processes a query, it checks whether a rule is watching for that particular EVENT. When one is, the ORDBMS checks whether the effect of that EVENT meets the CONDITION. If it does meet the CONDITION, the ORDBMS invokes the ACTION. In expert systems, rules are interrelated and compiled into a body of logic that is applied to a set of inputs.

OR-SQL TRIGGER

OR-SQL provides a rules syntax built around the TRIGGER. The database TRIGGER is not a new idea, but the extensibility of the ORDBMS makes it possible to use them in new ways. In addition, the ORDBMS extends the range of triggering events. Traditionally, only INSERT, UPDATE, and DELETE statements could fire a TRIGGER. With an ORDBMS, SELECT queries can fire a TRIGGER as well. In this section we introduce TRIGGER syntax, and illustrate how a TRIGGER is used.

CREATE TRIGGER Statement

In OR-SQL, the three aspects of a database rule are combined into a TRIGGER, which is created as shown in Listing 6–25.

```
CREATE TRIGGER [ TRIGGER_NAME ]
[ QUERY OPERATION ] ON [ TABLE_NAME ]  -- EVENT
[ ACTION CLAUSE ];                      -- CONDITION & ACTION
```

Listing 6–25. *General Form of the CREATE TRIGGER Statement*

Each TRIGGER is given a unique name that is used to identify it for administrative operations such as DROP. EVENTs are always *Data Manipulation Language (DML)* operations: INSERT, UPDATE, DELETE, or SELECT. A TRIGGER can be created for any physical table within the schema, but not for a VIEW or tables that use a VTI interface. Users who create a TRIGGER must have appropriate permissions within the database and over the table.

The ACTION CLAUSE is the most complex part of a TRIGGER definition. It combines the <CONDITION> and <ACTION> aspects of the rule structure introduced in Listing 6–23, and the ORDBMS limits the number of TRIGGER rules you can create per table, which makes it necessary to accommodate multiple database rules within a single TRIGGER.

Listing 6–26 shows a simple CREATE TRIGGER statement.

Whenever an Order_Line_Item is INSERTed, UPDATE Merchandise to reflect the new available stock level.

```
CREATE TRIGGER Keep_Stock_Count_Consistent_On_Orders_INSERT
INSERT ON Order_Line_Items
REFERENCING NEW AS NEW
FOR EACH ROW
( UPDATE Merchandise
    SET NumberAvailable = NumberAvailable - NEW.NumberBought
  WHERE Id = NEW.Merchandise
);
```

Listing 6–26. *Example of the CREATE TRIGGER Statement*

Care is needed when translating business rules like the one in Listing 6–26 into a set of CREATE TRIGGER statements. Enforcing business rules can require several cooperating TRIGGER events because there are three kinds of OR-SQL operations. If only the single TRIGGER in Listing 6–26 were in place, DELETE or UPDATE statements modifying the Order_Line_Items table would cause the Merchandise table to get out of synchronization. In Listing 6–27 we complete the set of CREATE TRIGGER statements that the business rule implies.

```
--
--   Additional TRIGGER 1. Keep the Stock Count consistent
--   on DELETE. When an Order_Line_Item is deleted, add it
--   back to the Merchandise available.
--
CREATE TRIGGER Keep_Stock_Count_Consistent_On_Orders_DELETE
DELETE ON Order_Line_Items
REFERENCING OLD AS OLD
FOR EACH ROW
( UPDATE Merchandise
    SET NumberAvailable = NumberAvailable +
                                        OLD.NumberBought
  WHERE Id = OLD.Merchandise );
--
```

```
--  Additional TRIGGER 2. Keep the Stock Count consistent
--  on UPDATE. If the UPDATE did not affect the Merchandise
--  column, UPDATE the count by whatever change was
--  made (if any) to the Number Bought. If the UPDATE did
--  affect the Merchandise column, add the stock back
--  for the OLD merchandise, and subtract it from the NEW.
--
CREATE TRIGGER Keep_Stock_Count_Consistent_On_Orders_UPDATE
UPDATE ON Order_Line_Items
REFERENCING OLD AS OLD NEW AS NEW
FOR EACH ROW
WHEN
  ( OLD.Merchandise = NEW.Merchandise )
  ( UPDATE Merchandise
       SET NumberAvailable = NumberAvailable +
                              (OLD.NumberBought - NEW.NumberBought)
     WHERE Id = NEW.Merchandise),
WHEN
( OLD.Merchandise <> NEW.Merchandise )
( UPDATE Merchandise
      SET NumberAvailable = NumberAvailable -
                                  NEW.NumberBought
    WHERE Id = NEW.Merchandise,
 UPDATE Merchandise
     SET NumberAvailable = NumberAvailable +
                                 OLD.NumberBought
    WHERE Id = OLD.Merchandise );
```

Listing 6–27. *Examples of the CREATE TRIGGER Statement*

Over the next few pages we go into various aspects of the TRIGGER features in more detail. In keeping with our practice of providing realistic examples, we use this section to illustrate how you would use this feature to implement an audit log of "sensitive" actions in the Movies-R-Us database. The general idea is that rare and possibly nefarious events—such as changing Mailing Addresses or deleting records of shipped Orders—should be tracked for auditing.

We extend our database schema with the table in Listing 6–28, which is used to record these notable events.

```
CREATE TABLE Audit_Of_Sensitive_Actions (
    Table_Name      VARCHAR(32)    NOT NULL,
    When            DATETIME YEAR TO SECOND
                            DEFAULT CURRENT YEAR TO SECOND,
```

```
Who                VARCHAR(128)        NOT NULL,
What               VARCHAR(128)        NOT NULL,
Before             VARCHAR(128),
After              VARCHAR(128)
);
```

Listing 6–28. *Audit Trail Logging Table*

The `TRIGGER` examples in the following subsections of this chapter `INSERT` rows into this table. The idea is to illustrate the diverse range of events and conditions that can fire a `TRIGGER`.

TRIGGER Events

Data in an ORDBMS is always modified with OR-SQL DML queries. Although it is common to encapsulate write operations within stored procedures, the IDS product uses the same facilities to process OR-SQL submitted from either external or internal sources. Identical queries in a database stored procedures, or typed into a command line tool, would both fire the same `TRIGGER` in the same manner.

The full range of query operations that can be `TRIGGER` events is as follows:

1. `INSERT`, `UPDATE`, `DELETE`, or `SELECT` queries over a table
2. `UPDATE` or `SELECT` queries involving a single column in a table

Within a database you can define only one `TRIGGER` for each of these operations; that is, for each table in your database, only one `INSERT` and one `DELETE` `TRIGGER` is permitted, and you can have at most one `UPDATE` and one `SELECT` `TRIGGER` per column. Listing 6–29 presents a range of `CREATE TRIGGER` statements and explains their purposes.

```
-- This listing illustrates a TRIGGER defined on UPDATE of
-- a single column. UPDATES of other columns in this table
-- will not cause this TRIGGER to fire.
--
CREATE TRIGGER Audit_Address_Changes
UPDATE OF Address ON MovieClubMembers
REFERENCING OLD AS OLD NEW AS NEW
FOR EACH ROW
(INSERT INTO Audit_Of_Sensitive_Actions
  ( Table_Name, Who, What, Before, After )
```

```
VALUES
('MovieClubMembers', USER,  'UPDATE of Member Address',
CAST(OLD.Address AS LVARCHAR),CAST(NEW.Address AS LVARCHAR)
));
```

Listing 6–29. *TRIGGER Checking Changes to Movie Club Member Addresses*

In this example the EVENT that the TRIGGER is watching for is a modification to the Address column of the MovieClubMembers table. For each row modified, the TRIGGER stores in the audit log table the name of the modified table, the identity of the user making the change, and the before and after state of the modified column.

In the ORDBMS the range of events that can be used to fire a TRIGGER is extended to include SELECT queries. Sometimes, especially in applications involving large media objects, it is desirable for the ORDBMS to track what objects are retrieved. For example, it might be useful to maintain billing records of what each user downloads. In the example in Listing 6–30, the TRIGGER places a record in the audit log each time a user retrieves a Video_Sample from the database.

```
CREATE TRIGGER Audit_Select_of_Video
SELECT OF Sample ON Video_Samples
REFERENCING OLD AS Row_Read
FOR EACH ROW (
   INSERT INTO Audit_Of_Sensitive_Actions
   ( Table_Name, Who, What, Before, After )
   VALUES
   ( 'Video_Sample', USER,  'SELECT of Video Sample',
      CAST(  Row_Read.Name::LVARCHAR || ' with Id ' ||
            Row_Read.Id::LVARCHAR AS LVARCHAR ),
      NULL
   )
);
```

Listing 6–30. *Example of a SELECT TRIGGER*

There is an important limitation on the functionality of SELECT triggers. Queries that include aggregates, select DISTINCT columns and include certain kinds of joins do not cause the SELECT TRIGGER to fire. They do not fire because the ORDBMS cannot determine the exact row from which the data in the query's result came, and to perform the ACTION CLAUSE, the ORDBMS requires a specific row. This behavior will probably change in future releases.

In addition, you should note that ON SELECT triggers have a significant impact on SELECT query performance. It is generally a good idea to avoid them whenever a performance-sensitive SELECT is involved. For operations involving large objects, however, the cost of the large-object data management is usually much larger than the cost of the trigger.

TRIGGER Conditions

Often you do not want to execute the action for every row affected by an event. Only a subset of the rows modified by a query may be relevant. To accommodate this, the ORDBMS allows you to specify additional *conditions* to check as part of the CREATE TRIGGER. TRIGGER conditions appear after a WHEN keyword in the CREATE TRIGGER.

Each condition must be related to a corresponding action, but you can have multiple WHEN (Conditions)(Action) clauses per TRIGGER. TRIGGER conditions are boolean expressions much like predicates in a WHERE clause. Like WHERE clauses, TRIGGER conditions can include subqueries. Examine Listing 6–31.

```
-- In this case, the EVENT is the DELETE of a row from the
-- Orders table. The condition of the rule checks that
-- we log changes only to those Orders already shipped.
--
CREATE TRIGGER Audit_of_Order_Delete
DELETE ON Orders
REFERENCING OLD AS OLD
FOR EACH ROW
WHEN ( OLD.ShippedOn IS NOT NULL )             -- CONDITION
( INSERT INTO Audit_Of_Sensitive_Actions      -- ACTION
   ( Table_Name, Who, What, Before, After )
  VALUES
  ( 'Orders', USER,  'DELETE of Shipped Order',
      CAST( 'For Customer ' || OLD.Customer ||
            ' Shipped on '  || OLD.ShippedOn AS LVARCHAR ),
      NULL
  )
);
```

Listing 6–31. *TRIGGER Illustrating a Condition Based on Event Data*

Limits on the number of TRIGGER events per table means that several different database rules must be enforced within a single TRIGGER by supplying several, comma-separated WHEN (Condition)(Action) clauses.

We saw this done in the second TRIGGER example in Listing 6–27 and present another example in Listing 6–32. In this listing, we modify the TRIGGER in Listing 6–26.

> *In addition to keeping the stocking numbers synchronized, you will want to create an Audit Log entry every time someone orders more than 100 units of a particular Item of Merchandise.*

```
CREATE TRIGGER Keep_Stock_Count_Consistent_On_Orders_INSERT
INSERT ON Order_Line_Items
REFERENCING NEW AS NEW
FOR EACH ROW
( UPDATE Merchandise
        SET NumberAvailable = NumberAvailable -
                                        NEW.NumberBought
   WHERE Id = NEW.Merchandise
),
WHEN ( NEW.NumberBought > 100 )
( INSERT INTO Audit_Of_Sensitive_Actions
  ( Table_Name, Who, What, Before, After )
  VALUES
  ( 'Order_Line_Items', USER,
    'INSERT of Order for > 100 Items',
    'For Order_Num ' || NEW.Order::LVARCHAR ||
            ' of '  || NEW.Merchandise::LVARCHAR,
    NULL
  )
);
```

Listing 6–32. *Two Conditions in a Single TRIGGER*

Each WHEN (Condition)(Action) clause is independent of the others in the same TRIGGER; that is, the ORDBMS executes all actions where it finds that the condition is true. If the first condition is false but the second is true, the ORDBMS takes only the second action.

In the following subsections, we discuss the kinds of conditions that can be checked in a TRIGGER.

Event-Based Conditions

Some conditions can be checked simply by examining data from the event itself—by examining the data values in rows affected by the firing event. For example, on an INSERT into a table, the TRIGGER can verify whether data values from the newly inserted row meet some condition. With UPDATE queries, both the before and after states of affected rows are available, and a DELETE TRIGGER can access data from the deleted rows.

Rows affected by an event can be accessed within the WHEN (Condition) (Action) clause through the NEW and OLD correlation names. Columns of affected rows are addressed using cascading-dot notation, similar to a query's WHERE clause. You specify the correlation named within the TRIGGER body using the syntax in Listing 6–33.

```
REFERENCING
NEW AS Correlation_Name_One OLD AS Correlation_Name_Two
```

Listing 6–33. *Referencing NEW and OLD Handles to Row Data Associated with Event*

Column values can be addressed as `Correlation_Name_One.Column_Name`, but the generally accepted practice is simply to use NEW and OLD as correlation names, and all of our examples adopted this convention. All UDFs that can be included in OR-SQL queries can appear in WHEN (Condition)(Action) clauses, which makes it possible to check for very complex event conditions.

Schema Conditions

TRIGGER action clauses may examine other data in the database to see if a condition is satisfied. For example, there may be an upper limit on the number of times that a particular value can be present in a table's column, or there may be some kind of check constraint that cannot be expressed as a FOREIGN KEY. You can include an OR-SQL subquery in a condition clause to validate a database rule.

Listing 6–34 illustrates using a subquery to ensure that a newly INSERTed cinema's geographic location is contained by some State boundary.

Perform a data entry check to ensure that new cinemas are always on land and in the correct hemisphere. This can be achieved by checking that a new cinema location is within the geographic boundary of a state.

```
CREATE TRIGGER Check_Cinema_Within_State_Boundaries
INSERT ON Cinemas
REFERENCING NEW AS NEW
FOR EACH ROW
```

```
WHEN ( NOT EXISTS ( SELECT 1
                      FROM States S
                     WHERE Contains ( S.Boundary,
                                        NEW.GeoLocation ) ) )
( EXECUTE PROCEDURE RAISE_EXCEPTION ( -746,
                     "New Cinema not in known State" ) );
```

Listing 6–34. *Checking that Cinema's Geographic Location is Within a State Boundary*

Of course, a `TRIGGER` with a subquery in its conditions can present a performance problem. Each time a new cinema is inserted, the ORDBMS executes the subquery. Thus, it pays to make sure that appropriate indexing strategies are in place. In Listing 6–34 an R-Tree index on the Boundary column would be a good idea.

Environmental Conditions

Environmental factors—such as the current date and time or the current user—can be used in an action clause as well. In Listings 6-28 through 6-32, we saw how the `USER` keyword, which refers to the name of the user whose session submitted the OR-SQL statement that caused the `TRIGGER` to fire, can supply a value for a column in the audit table. In Listing 6–35 we illustrate how to use a `TRIGGER` to limit the times during which new movie club members can be inserted.

```
CREATE TRIGGER Check_MovieClubMembers_INSERT
INSERT ON MovieClubMembers
BEFORE
WHEN ( Outside_Range ( CURRENT::DATETIME HOUR TO MINUTE,
                        Hourly_Range ( 2200, 700 ) ) )
( EXECUTE PROCEDURE
    RAISE_EXCEPTION (
      -746,
     'Locked Out: No new MovieClubMembers at this time')
);
```

Listing 6–35. *A TRIGGER Checking an Environmental Condition (Time Range)*

ORDBMS extensibility means that you can take advantage of the power of user-defined functions in `TRIGGER` conditions. The `TRIGGER` in Listing 6–32 uses a UDF called `Outside_Range()` that returns true if the `DATETIME` value supplied in the first argument is within a moving window created using another UDF as the second argument. OR-SQL's temporal operations are complex and awkward. Using UDFs in this way simplifies development tremendously.

Because the ORDBMS schema can include user-defined routines written in C and Java, and because these routines can reach outside the DBMS, you can use the active database system to integrate the system environment into the database. However, used carelessly, this can lead to performance problems.

TRIGGER Actions

Each TRIGGER instructs the ORDBMS to perform some action when the combination of an event and condition is met. You can use values taken from the rows affected by the event that fired the trigger as parameters to actions in the same way you can access them when you check conditions.

In the following subsections, we discuss the three kinds of actions that a TRIGGER can take.

Execute an OR-SQL Query

The TRIGGER action can specify that an OR-SQL write statement, such as INSERT, UPDATE, or DELETE, should be executed. For example, when a data value in one table changes, it can fire a trigger whose action is to UPDATE a related value in another table. Most of the examples we have introduced in this chapter invoke OR-SQL queries that INSERT or UPDATE rows.

You can also combine several query statements, separated by commas, within a single action, as we illustrated in Listings 6-27.

Execute a Database Procedure

A TRIGGER ACTION clause might execute a stored procedure. For example, adding a new record to a table can TRIGGER a procedure that performs some additional business processing.

Recall the shopping cart module implemented in the first section of this chapter. When an UPDATE to a movie club member's record ends the membership period, it might be a good idea to clean up other tables in the database containing dangling references to the defunct membership. This can be done using the TRIGGER in Listing 6–36.

```
CREATE TRIGGER Cleanup_On_Membership
UPDATE OF Membership_Period ON MovieClubMembers
REFERENCING OLD AS OLD NEW AS NEW
```

```
FOR EACH ROW
WHEN ( NOT Overlap ( NEW.Membership_Period,
                                Period(TODAY - 1, TODAY)))
( EXECUTE PROCEDURE Cleanup_Outstanding_Carts ( OLD.Id ));
```

Listing 6–36. *TRIGGER Executing a User-Defined Procedure as Action*

Each time a movie club member's membership period is updated and the new period of membership does not overlap the current date, the database automatically purges any shopping carts it finds within the system. The purge is handled by a stored procedure.

Raise an Exception

Active database features are useful for enforcing business rules. For example, the management of Movies-R-Us may want to limit the amount of credit extended to each customer. Any time a customer places an order violating this rule, the order should be rejected with an appropriate error message. Such a business rule can be implemented using a TRIGGER. The action clause of a TRIGGER does not support raising exceptions directly. Instead, you need to create a stored procedure as shown in Listing 6–37, and then invoke it in the action.

```
CREATE PROCEDURE RAISE_EXCEPTION ( Arg1 INTEGER,
                                            Arg2 LVARCHAR )
            RAISE EXCEPTION Arg1, 0, Arg2;
END PROCEDURE;
--
GRANT EXECUTE ON PROCEDURE
RAISE_EXCEPTION ( INTEGER, LVARCHAR )
TO PUBLIC;
```

Listing 6–37. *Stored Procedure to Raise Exception in a TRIGGER's Action Clause*

We saw this stored procedure used in Listing 6–34.

Triggered actions can execute at different times, depending on the event causing them to be fired in the first place. The following subsections discuss the different actions that a TRIGGER can cause.

BEFORE the EVENT

Sometimes you want to verify whether an entire operation is allowed. For example, to DELETE a movie club member's record might not be permitted because you might be throwing away information that could be useful in a later marketing campaign. Thus, the correct thing to do is to close the member's membership period, as shown in Listing 6–38.

```
CREATE TRIGGER Prohibit_Delete_of_MovieClubMembers
DELETE ON MovieClubMembers
BEFORE (
EXECUTE PROCEDURE RAISE_EXCEPTION (
   -746
   'DELETE prohibited. Close Membership_Period Instead'
));
```

Listing 6–38. *TRIGGER with Action Executed BEFORE Event*

Checking this condition this on a "FOR EACH ROW" basis can create a performance problem. In contrast, the TRIGGER we show in Listing 6–34 will fire exactly once, and it will roll back whatever transaction initiated the DELETE, regardless of how many rows it would have affected.

FOR EACH ROW Affected by the EVENT

Most examples in this section involve TRIGGER that check each row as it is changed. Although many queries only affect single rows, the TRIGGER mechanism also caters to the general class of set-oriented operations. Even when a single query event affects many rows, only a subset of changes may meet the condition.

Note that if any of the row-level events causes the IDS engine to raise an exception, the entire transaction, of which the individual row event may be but a small part, is rolled back. But unlike the BEFORE and AFTER action semantics, FOR EACH ROW action clauses are run only when actual row data is affected.

AFTER the EVENT

As its name suggests, AFTER is similar to BEFORE, except that the action clause runs once all changes are complete. The difference is that any subqueries in the action clause are applied to the database *after* the event query's changes have been made. This would be the place to implement rules limiting the number of times a value may appear in a table's column.

Special Note on BEFORE
and AFTER TRIGGER Actions

Action clauses specified to execute BEFORE or AFTER a TRIGGER event *are still executed even if no rows are affected by the query.* For example, suppose an application sent the query in Listing 6–39 to the ORDBMS:

```
DELETE FROM MovieClubMembers WHERE Id IS NULL;
```

Listing 6–39. *Query that Cannot Affect any Rows Due to the Definition of the Table*

Under no circumstances can this query ever affect any rows because the Id column is a PRIMARY KEY that cannot have a NULL value. When the ORDBMS tries to process this DELETE, however, it will invoke the action specified in Listing 6–38. That is, this query will cause the ORDBMS to raise the indicated exception, even though the DELETE query would have no effect whatsoever on the MovieClubMembers table.

How TRIGGERs Are Implemented

Understanding how the TRIGGER features are implemented helps to explain their impact on database performance. The IDS product uses a technique called *tuple substitution* to provide TRIGGER functionality. In Figure 6–3 we present an overview of what this looks like.

Whenever a table is opened for some write operation—for example, **Q(t)** in this figure—the IDS product checks for BEFORE conditions on the affected table. If one exists, it takes whatever actions the TRIGGER specifies. Then, each time a row in the table is changed, the ORDBMS verifies whether a TRIGGER has an interest in that change. Finally, just before it closes the table, the ORDBMS checks for any AFTER triggers.

Implementing the TRIGGER feature as we show in Figure 6–3 has at least two practical implications.

- First, whenever OR-SQL is contained in any of the action clauses, whether it is to check for a condition or it is to be executed as part of an action, it runs within the transaction context of the query that fired the TRIGGER in the first place. Thus, extensive use of the TRIGGER facilities can cause the ORDBMS to run a complex sequence of OR-SQL statements when the end user invoked a relatively simple operation. Further, until all of these secondary queries are complete, the ORDBMS will return control to whatever programming context—ultimately the external program—submitted the initial write operation.

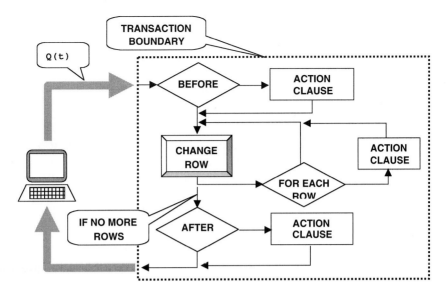

Figure 6–3. *Schematic of Process Flow for ORDBMS Active Database Implementation*

- Second, any queries run as part of the ACTION clause are run once per firing event. In performance-sensitive applications, queries invoked by a TRIGGER should be tuned with great care.

When a TRIGGER fires and executes a query as part of its action, the action query can cause other TRIGGER to fire. When a series of TRIGGER events fire in a chain reaction, we say they are *cascading*. This is a powerful feature, but it can make it difficult to debug database transactions, and it can create an infinite loop. The ORDBMS permits recursive TRIGGER semantics, but when it detects a certain number of cascade levels—by default 61—it will intervene and rollback the entire transaction.

Working with TRIGGERs

In this section we review several OR-SQL features relating to administering each TRIGGER. To create a TRIGGER a user must already have permissions on the table, however, and if they do not have appropriate permissions on a database object included in the EVENT, the IDS engine generates a runtime exception.

Dropping TRIGGERS

A database TRIGGER is dropped using the DROP TRIGGER command. Dropping a trigger deletes the entire trigger from the schema. There is no means by which triggers can be modified. Therefore, to alter a trigger, you must drop and recreate it. In Listing 6–40 we illustrate what the DROP TRIGGER DDL command looks like.

```
DROP TRIGGER Check_MovieClubMembers_INSERT;
DROP TRIGGER Check_Cinema_Within_State_Boundaries;
```

Listing 6–40. *DROP TRIGGER Examples*

Triggers are also dropped if the table for which they are defined is dropped or if you use an ALTER TABLE to remove the column on which the TRIGGER event is defined.

Suspending TRIGGER Actions

An important but rarely mentioned aspect of the ORDBMS's TRIGGER implementation allows database administrators to temporarily suspend TRIGGER actions. By default, TRIGGER conditions are checked on every query operation. Sometimes, when bulk-loading data, for example, checking business rules is unnecessary and time consuming.

The IDS product provides a DDL statement—the SET statement—to modify several kinds of database behavior: In one form it allows you to change the way each database TRIGGER and table CONSTRAINT is handled. In Chapter 2 we saw how to use this facility to disable various kinds of constraints: primary key, foreign key, unique, and CHECK constraints.

For example, to temporarily disable all of the TRIGGER events we created for the Orders_Line_Items and MovieClubMembers tables, you would use the statement in Listing 6–41.

```
SET TRIGGERS FOR Orders_Line_Items DISABLED;
SET TRIGGERS FOR MovieClubMembers DISABLED;
```

Listing 6–41. *Disabling TRIGGERs on a Table*

Later, after some bulk loading for example, the `TRIGGER` events can be enabled again as shown in Listing 6–42.

```
SET TRIGGERS FOR Orders_Line_Items ENABLED;
SET TRIGGERS FOR MovieClubMembers ENABLED;
```

Listing 6–42. Enabling TRIGGERs on a Table

Naturally, if you suspend the mechanisms whereby the ORDBMS is enforcing data integrity, you create the potential for bad data. Care is called for whenever you use this performance tactic in production systems.

Applications of Database Procedures and Triggers

Stored procedures and active database features can be used to implement many aspects of an information system. It isn't immediately obvious, however, when these techniques are better than some alternative such as equivalent logic in a middle-tier or client program. In this section we attempt to give some guidance on the question and provide examples illustrating effective uses for database-centric data processing.

A typical information system provides a variety of services, to a variety of users, who are scattered in many locations. Stored procedures and triggers involve centralizing functionality in the ORDBMS. In general, this strategy works best for those aspects of the information system that are the most widely shared. Recall the functional topology we introduced in Figure 6–1 of this chapter. A more realistic figure might look like Figure 6–4.

This figure illustrates a set of user-interfaces driving a set of data processing modules, which in turn operate over a common database. The thickness of the connecting arrows in Figure 6–4 reflects, very roughly, the volumes of data flows between components.

Data processing can involve large amounts of data; message exchanges with remote user-interfaces is typically constrained by the underlying network (or ether). The challenge is to figure out how to map these functional components to the underlying hardware and software infrastructure. In practical terms, this means deciding where to run the logic.

Whether and how to implement an algorithm is best decided by considering how much data must be moved under each scheme. In this section we describe several application examples and indicate how they may be addressed.

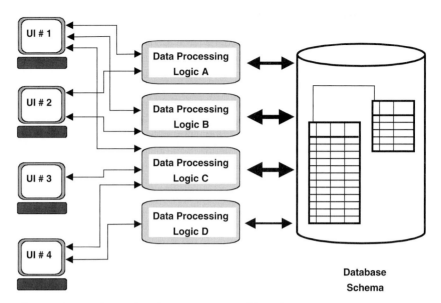

Figure 6–4. *Information System Functional Topology*

Data Integrity

Perhaps the most common use for the database TRIGGER is to enforce data correctness rules that are hard to handle in any other way. Rules spanning several tables or columns, or rules that include the state of an external system, cannot be defined using the table-based techniques we introduced in Chapter 2 (value, role, relational, and referential constraints). We saw several examples of such integrity rules earlier in this chapter.

Software engineers are usually more comfortable using procedural logic to ensure that the system complies with these rules because they are more familiar with procedural programming. The problem with this approach is that data integrity rules must be enforced regardless of the actions performed by any aspect of the system, and in large projects, development teams often work in isolation from each other. By enforcing data integrity centrally, there are obvious advantages to minimizing what each team needs to know.

Ultimately, RDBMSs and ORDBMSs allow data to be modified using ad hoc OR-SQL. Therefore, depending on the correctness of data processing logic will leave you vulnerable to a bug in the data processing module that is generating dynamic SQL or to a fat-fingered DBA. Therefore, it usually best to enforce data integrity rules by using triggers

Business Rules

Another common application for triggers is to enforce complex business rules. In Listings 6-31 and 6-32, we illustrate how to use a `TRIGGER` to limit the period of time during which certain events can occur. As with schema integrity rules, you should enforce a business rule regardless of the mechanism that applied the change.

The difference between data integrity rules and business rules in this context is not always clear, and it is not really important. You should, however, be aware of the following operational distinctions:

- Data integrity rules can usually be checked based on the data in a schema's tables. They are dependent on the structural definition of the schema.
- Business rules tend to be more pliable, and data integrity rules are more strict. Although it might be reasonable to suspend a business rule in a particular situation, any violation of data integrity rules creates an incoherent database.

It is important to distinguish general database rules from rules that are specific to a single end user operation. Pushing every data entry check and process validation into the ORDBMS server results in a slow and inflexible system. For example, although our database schema includes a user-defined type that can be used to store a single US state and that ensures that the data value always contains a valid state, checking the corrections of data entry with a Javascript function in the Web page—or restricting users to choosing from a select box—is still a good idea.

Workflow Management

You can often find in an application a series of events that occur one after the other, with each event dependent on the outcome of a previous. Such situations are often called *workflows*. Listings 6–25 and 6–26 show workflows; new orders, or modifications to old orders, regardless of the source of the change, can be detected and used to drive another business process.

As a means of implementing a generalized workflow system, however, the SQL `TRIGGER` approach has a serious drawback. If you were to implement an entire workflow sequence as a series of cascading triggers, the entire workflow would need to occupy a single transactional context; in other words, it would either succeed completely or fail utterly.

A more immediate practical concern is that in a business, workflow frequently requires human attention. Executives and managers must "OK" or "nay" a decision. Holding technical resources locked while corporate vice-presidents make up their mind would create major log-jams.

Consequently, while workflow systems are implemented using triggers, this is best done using more specialized schema designs and additional software.

Distributed Data Management

When you ask most information system developers to draw a picture explaining how DBMS software is used within a large information system, they usually draw something that looks a lot like Figure 6–5.

All reasonably large information systems distribute their data and procedural logic across a set of interconnected computers (sometimes called *nodes*) because centralizing server software onto one machine creates a bottleneck. In addition, should that server fail—as it always does eventually—the entire information system becomes unusable.

Note that different nodes are specialized for certain tasks. Some of them— traditional database management systems—organize persistent data storage. Others execute logic. As part of runtime operation, the information system moves data between participating computers.

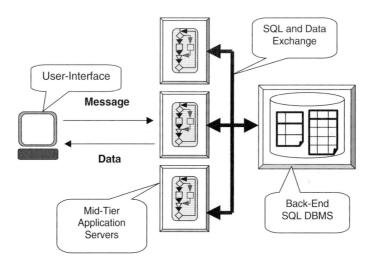

Figure 6–5. *Conventional Topology of Modern Information System*

From the first, DBMS software was conceived of as a large, central data repository. Surrounding the database were the other aspects of the system: clients, transaction processing middleware, and user interfaces. Today, "big DBMS server" approaches are the most common architecture. This is changing, however.

Distributed database technology has been part of commercial DBMS products for some time. SQL-92 queries could address data that was stored within another database on the same machine or even stored on a different computer. Using *replication*, a set of database installations can be configured so that copies of data can be materialized in multiple locations and the synchronization of these copies can be handled automatically.

Figure 6–6 illustrates what such a topology might look like.

In this section we introduce the facilities provided by the ORDBMS for supporting these architectural principles. The fundamental motivation for distributed information systems stems from the observation that the workload that can be sustained using many, self-contained computers is greater than the workload that can be accomplished by a single computer with the same quantity of hardware (disks, CPUs, memory, and so on). The drawback, however, is that using multiple machines complicates development and system administration. Fortunately, distributed ORDBMS facilities can help to achieve the goal of sustaining larger systems, while keeping the associated complexity to a minimum.

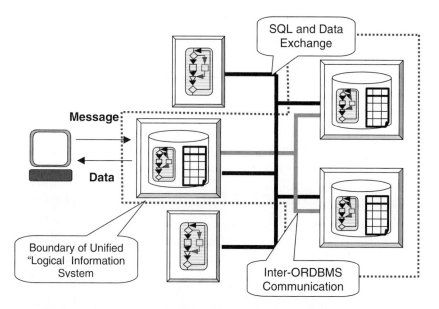

Figure 6–6. *Topology of a Distributed ORDBMS Information System*

The features and functionality described in this section are scheduled for the next release of the IDS product, some time in 2001. Unless stated otherwise, examples in this section will not work on previous releases. The material is included here to ensure that the contents of this book remain current and relevant for some time.

INFORMIX-Star

Like most DBMS products, the distributed database features of the IDS product are called INFORMIX-Star.[2] Distributed ORDBMS technology allows database developers to combine several, reasonably autonomous DBMS installations into a single "logical view" of a collection of data (and logic).

In a perfect distributed database, the physical dispersal is invisible to users and developers. As far as they are concerned, the schema against which they write queries presents the entire database, regardless of where the objects actually reside or execute. This property is known as *location transparency*. Of course, it is the responsibility of DBAs and database designers to maintain the illusion, and in practice, perfect location transparency is hard to achieve.

INFORMIX-Star queries, which are read and write OR-SQL statements, are submitted at one of the databases participating in the distributed system. This site, which we call the *coordinating node*, decomposes the OR-SQL into a set of lower-level operations. Where necessary, some of this work is forwarded from the coordinating node to *remote nodes* where it executes independently of the coordinating node.

Running distributed queries may involve moving data between nodes of the system and performing computational tasks on several of them. The entire answer is ultimately passed back to the external program through the coordinating node.

Fully Qualified Database Identifiers

In several earlier chapters we have explored the notion of schema *identifiers*. An identifier is a string naming a database object, such as a table, a column, an index, a constraint, a data type, or a function. OR-SQL

---

[2] Among the first commercial distributed DBMS offering was INGRES®-Star, which was named after the pioneering System-R *. Subsequent efforts at distributed DBMS technology, while appropriating the name, rarely rival the originals.

queries use identifiers to specify what schema objects are involved in the query. To avoid ambiguity the ORDBMS ensures that identifiers for each kind of database object are unique within a database.[3]

In distributed databases, particularly in circumstances in which several previously independent installations have been combined, local names may not be enough to identify distributed objects. For example, schema in DBMS installations on two machines may both include an Employees table, and each table may contain different data. Thus, when a distributed application needs to use objects in one of these two tables, some mechanism is needed to distinguish Employees in one installation from Employees in the other.

Distributed RDBMS systems provide a SQL syntax that can fully qualify database objects such as tables and views. In Listing 6–43 we illustrate the general form, and a couple of examples, of what we call a *fully qualified database identifier*.

```
--
-- General form of fully qualified database identifier.
-- Note that the [ ] symbols indicate optional elements.
--

    [database_name[@server_name]:]table_identifier

--
-- From another database (on the same server), find the
-- the count of rows in the Movies table, in the book_test
-- database.
--

    SELECT COUNT(*)
       FROM book_test:Movies;

--
-- In another database, on a different server, find out how
-- many of a particular item of merchandise are available.
--

    SELECT COUNT(*)
       FROM warehouse@inventory:items I;
```

Listing 6–43. *General Form and Examples of a Fully Qualified Database Identifier*

In Figure 6–7 we illustrate the simple, three-site distributed database used for examples over the next few pages. Each site contains a different set of tables.

---

[3] Note that user-defined routines are uniquely identified by their *signature*.

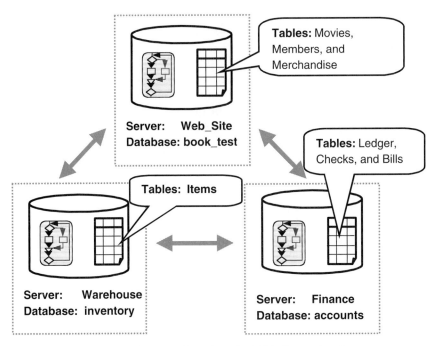

Figure 6–7. *Topology of a Distributed ORDBMS Information System*

From a hardware perspective, these three machines need not use the same make and model of computer (although there are administrative advantages to doing so). Indeed, these nodes may be running different versions of the ORDBMS. Configuring a set of installations for distributed operations requires some administrative effort. Each installation must know how to connect to the others in much the same way a client program needs to know how to connect to a database.

It is important to note that the following discussion assumes that all database instances are initialized with the same *mode* (ANSI or non-ANSI) and the same logging behavior (logged or non-logged). Different operational modes and logging behavior subtly affect the way in which OR-SQL queries are processed, and interactions between instances that have adopted *different* modes and logging are quite complex. It is prudent to choose one standard—logged, ANSI mode, for example—and stick to it.

Object-Relational Extensions

Distributed RDBMS products used fully qualified identifiers for tables and views. In systems that supported stored procedures, this technique was also used to identify them. For example, an SPL procedure created in a remote site can be invoked using the EXECUTE PROCEDURE syntax in Listing 6–44.

```
EXECUTE PROCEDURE
          warehouse@inventory:Change_Item_Count('shoe', 20);
```

Listing 6–44. *EXECUTE PROCEDURE for Remote User-Defined Function*

Suppose this statement was issued by a client program connected to the book_test database in the Web_Server instance. When it receives this command, the ORDBMS checks that the procedure actually exists on the remote site named in the expression. If it does, the statement is forwarded to the named site, and whatever it returns is redirected to the client through the coordinating node (book_test@Web_server).

You should note the following about this operation:

- The "context" within which this procedure executes is the database and server combination listed in the fully qualified identifier. If no database and server are provided, the current database is the one in which the procedure executes. For example, if the body of the procedure in Listing 6–44 includes an OR-SQL query selecting data from a table identified as Items, then in this example, the table is assumed to be the warehouse@inventory:Items table. Should an Items table coincidentally exist in the coordinating node (book_test@Web_server:Items), that table is not used.
- OR-SQL in a stored procedure can refer to tables in multiple databases. The ORDBMS does not care about the source of the query (internal procedure or external client program) when it processes the statement.
- For portability, EXECUTE PROCEDURE statements and table identifiers can name their local database and instance without penalty.

In the ORDBMS, user-defined functions co-opt this naming strategy. For example, consider the query in Listing 6–45.

```
SELECT COUNT(*)
  FROM warehouse@inventory:Spaces S
 WHERE warehouse@inventory:Volume(S.Size) >
                                '100 Cubic Feet';
```

Listing 6–45. *Distributed OR-SQL Query*

In Figure 6–7, regardless of the nodes to which this query is submitted, the way it is executed will always be the same. The query is forwarded to the `warehouse@inventory` site where the table scan of `Spaces` and the execution of the `Volume()` UDF can occur. This technique is called *function shipping*. If the UDF or table is not defined on the named site, the ORDBMS generates an exception.

The way in which this query is executed is less obvious than it might at first appear. The ">" comparison is being applied over an `OPAQUE TYPE`, which means that the ORDBMS is actually executing a UDF named `GreaterThan()`. An unambiguous version of this query would look like Listing 6–46.

```
SELECT COUNT(*)
   FROM warehouse@inventory:Spaces S
  WHERE warehouse@inventory:GreaterThan(
              warehouse@inventory:Volume(S.Size),
              warehouse@inventory:Volume(100, 'Cubic Feet')
        );
```

Listing 6–46. *Unambiguous Distributed OR-SQL Query*

If the query's specification of the UDF includes a location such as database or a server, that is where the ORDBMS schedules the function to run. This rule, however, creates problems of its own. Strictly interpreted, it would mean that the query in Listing 6–45 would run the `GreaterThan()` UDF on the *coordinating node*, not on the node where data resides, which is `warehouse@inventory`. This would happen because in the absence of an explicit location, the parser substitutes the name of the coordinating node's database and server.

Giving the query planner the flexibility to choose where the logic runs can result in more efficient query execution. Sometimes it makes sense to move the UDF to the remote site to reduce the amount of data that is brought back. Other times it makes sense to keep the UDF execution local to the coordinating node.

Enforcing a couple of administrative rules about user-defined types such as `Volumetric_Space` and `Volume`, and the UDFs that apply to them, is necessary to ensure that the planner has the appropriate flexibility:

- UDFs must be marked with a new modifier, called `EXECUTEANY-WHERE`, and should be installed in all participating databases on all participating sites. This does not mean that the same executable object is necessary on all sites; UDFs in this global name space are identified by their signature, and they may be implemented using

SPL, Java, or C. To ensure that queries return consistent answers, however, the UDFs on all sites should be semantically equivalent.

- All UDTs used in the distributed database should be installed everywhere too. This means that all UDFs that support UDTs need to be installed everywhere (and marked as EXECUTEANYWHERE). Further, all of these types need to support one of several mechanisms for moving data between sites either as binaries that can be copied, or by providing support UDFs to move data.

Listing 6–47 illustrates how to use the EXECUTEANYWHERE modifier. The first statement shows how a distributable UDF should be created. The second illustrates how to modify an existing UDF to make it useable in a distributed environment.

```
--
--
CREATE FUNCTION Size ( Volumetric_Space )
RETURNS Volume
WITH ( NOT VARIANT, PARALLELIZABLE, EXECUTEANYWHERE )
EXTERNAL NAME '$INFORMIXDIR/extend/. . . (VS_Size)'
LANGUAGE C;
--
-- Alternatively, if the UDF already exists, the
-- ALTER FUNCTION DDL can be used in the following way.
--
ALTER FUNCTION Size ( Volumetric_Space )
WITH ( ADD EXECUTEANYWHERE );
-
--
```

Listing 6–47. *Use of the EXECUTEANYWHERE Modifier*

Once this has been done, the ORDBMS's distributed query planner is free to move the execution of UDF logic to wherever it makes the most sense. Later in this section, we review distributed query optimization to see how it makes these decisions.

Synonyms

Tables and views, unlike UDFs, cannot be everywhere at once, but writing queries that fully qualify every table and view becomes extremely tedious. Thus, the ORDBMS provides a technique called *synonyms* to provide both brevity and consistency.

A synonym is a short name assigned to a fully qualified database identifier (a table or a view). Each synonym must be unique within a local database, and it must not be a name already used for a table or view within the local database. As it processes an OR-SQL query, the ORDBMS detects when a synonym is used to name a data source, and it substitutes the fully qualified name. The idea is that by coming up with a consistent naming scheme, it is possible to make stored procedure logic more portable.

Synonyms are created using a CREATE SYNONYM statement. This might be issued while connected to the book_test@Web_site database to create in that database the synonym in Listing 6–48.

```
CREATE SYNONYM Spaces FOR warehouse@inventory:Spaces;
```

Listing 6–48. *CREATE SYNONYM Statement*

Synonyms can be chained; that is, a synonym can be created on another synonym, and a synonym can be created on a view. Information about synonyms is stored in system catalogs.

Distributed Query Processing

To compute results for a distributed query, the ORDBMS will probably be required to move data between sites of the distributed system. Before reading further, have another look at Table 1-3 from Chapter 1. It shows that while moving data across a network is actually faster than reading it from local disk, it is still an expensive operation. Thus, the basic goal of distributed query optimization is to minimize the amount of network copying that required to respond to an OR-SQL statement.

While this sounds simple, in practice, minimizing the number of network copies is among the hardest problems in computer science.[4] To simplify the problem, the ORDBMS assumes that it will only need to move blocks of row data *to* the coordinating node. We illustrate the effect of this topological simplification in Figure 6–8.

Further, the ORDBMS's distributed query planner does try to minimize the amount of data that is moved, and it can push individual data objects from the coordinating node to a remote node to identify a subset of data to bring back. For example, consider the three-way join query in Listing 6–49, which arrives on a connection to the Book_test@Web_Server node.

---

[4] It is known as the *file allocation problem*.

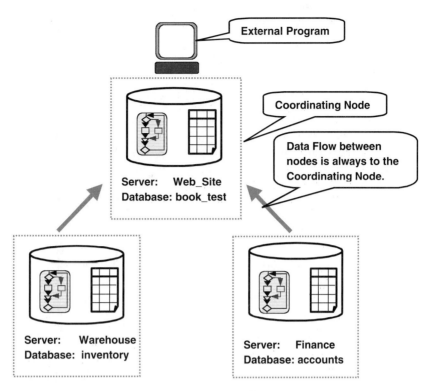

Figure 6–8. *Data Flow Within a Distributed ORDBMS During Query Processing*

```
SELECT B.Amount, I.Part_Code, Description( M )
   FROM accounts@finance:Bills B,
        warehouse@inventory:Items I,
        book_test@Web_server Merchandise M
  WHERE B.Order_Number = I.Order_Number
    AND I.Part_Code    = M.Id
    AND I.Delivery_Date > TODAY - 7 DAYS
    AND B.Vendor = 'T-Shirt Fever';
```

Listing 6–49. *Distributed SELECT Query over Three Sites*

The ORDBMS would probably use the following query plan for this query:

1. Send the following query to `accounts@finance`:

```
"SELECT B.Amount, B.Order_Number
   FROM Bills B
  WHERE B.Vendor = 'T-Shirt Fever'"
```

2. For each row returned from Step 1, send the following query to
`warehouse@inventory`:

```
"SELECT I.Part_Code
    FROM Items I
   WHERE I.Delivery_Date > TODAY - 7 DAYS
     AND I.Order_Number = :B_Order_Number"
```

3. For each row returned by Step 2, perform the local join operation on
`book_test@Web_server`:

```
"SELECT :B_Amount, :I_Part_Code, Description ( M )
    FROM Merchandise M
   WHERE M.Id = :I_Part_Code"
```

The distributed ORDBMS optimizer makes full use of all facilities of
the local optimizer. For example, it would be able to determine approximately how many rows would be identified by the predicate in Step 1
and Step 2, and then estimate how much data would be moved between
servers in each case. Using this two-level strategy means that the
ORDBMS will be able to take advantage of all statistics and selectivity

Large object handling requires special attention. In ORDBMS applications, a small number of large objects can represent the majority of
the bytes recorded in the system. Thus, when it is required to process a
query that includes large-object data types, the ORDBMS will always
try to ship only a large object's handle, rather than the entire byte
array. In addition, UDFs involving large objects are generally shipped
to wherever the large object data is stored.

Each step's queries are shipped to remote nodes, and they can be
optimized there. The application of parallel query processing techniques, and decisions depending on the availability of physical
resources, are all localized. The objective is to leverage the capabilities
of all distributed installations of the IDS product.

Distributed Transactions

So far, we have focused on SELECT queries. But INSERT, UPDATE, and
DELETE are also supported in the distributed environment. Queries submitted at one site can alter data in tables at remote locations. Also,
where he or she has appropriate permissions, a user can issue a CREATE
TABLE on a remote site.

Listing 6–50 presents a sequence of queries that demonstrate how
data in multiple instances can be affected within a single transaction.

```
BEGIN WORK;

CREATE TABLE accounts@finance:Unpacked_Merchandise (
     Merchandise     Part_Code      NOT NULL,
     Number          Quantity       NOT NULL
);

INSERT INTO accounts@finance:Current_Merchandise
SELECT M.Id,
       SUM(I.Quantity)
  FROM warehouse@inventory:Items I,
       book_test@Web_server Merchandise M
 WHERE I.Part_Code    = M.Id
 GROUP BY M.Id;

COMMIT WORK;
```

Listing 6–50. *Distributed INSERT AS SELECT Query over Three Sites*

Distributed databases need to deal with situations in which one site crashes or the network drops out in the middle of a transaction. The technique used to achieve this is called *two-phase commit*. The details are quite complicated, but in practical terms, distributed transactions acquire resources on all systems participating in the transaction as it progresses. Before the distributed transaction commits, the coordinating node polls each participating site in turn to ensure that all remote changes can commit. Only when the coordinating node has assurances from all remote sites does the coordinating node commit the overall transaction.

Potentially the most difficult problem with this arrangement arises in the case of distributed deadlocks. Good transaction design is essential to minimize the possibility of such an event. The only strategy pursued by the ORDBMS, however, is to timeout after some blocked locking interval and to roll back the transaction on all nodes.

Replication

Distributed queries return answers that are logically consistent across the set of physical stores; that is, in a distributed database, every row in every table is located in exactly one place. Sometimes, however, creating a number of *copies* of some data is preferable to forwarding all queries to a single location. Creating and maintaining copies of an entire database, a table, or a set of rows within a table is supported by the replication facilities of the DBMS. These features are known as *Enterprise Replication* (ER) and High-Availability Data Replication or HDR. Other replication facilities exist, though in all cases they follow the same patterns we describe in this section.

Originally, replication was conceived as a solution to problems that arise when an entire computer fails unexpectedly. Overcoming this meant installing a redundant backup machine with an identical hardware configuration. Every change operation on the first machine was forwarded to the second where it was repeated. Another high-availability option called mirroring stores data a second time on separate disks, but these disks are always attached to the same memory and CPU. Mirroring solves local disk availability, but it does not address total site failure or network problems.

Having realized the usefulness of this idea and having figured out the most efficient engineering mechanisms to support it, the next step was fairly obvious: maintain multiple copies of the data on several machines. Replicating data allows more users to access it simultaneously than was possible with a single machine.

In Figure 6–9 we present the basic topology and underlying mechanism used for replication. A single logical table, the Movies table in this figure, resides on the source machine. Runtime operations that UPDATE, DELETE, and INSERT data execute at the source and are recorded in the source database's log file to support transaction rollback. Once the transaction completes, this record of changes can be forwarded to other, remote machines where the same change is made to their local data.

Consequently, there is an interval of time between when the operation commits on the initial node and when the effects of the operation appear on the destination. This interval is called replication latency.

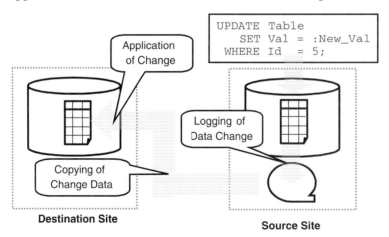

Figure 6–9. *Data Flow Within Distributed ORDBMS*

Replication Goals

Developers should consider using replication in situations in which one or more of the following data management goals are desired.

- High Availability. Replication is still the most viable option for supporting high availability. This requires that the entire database be simultaneously maintained on (at least) two separate computers: a nominal *primary* and a *secondary*. Should the primary machine fail, transactional responsibility is passed to the second machine. This is generally good advice in any consumer-centric Web site application.
- Data Dissemination. Multiple, equivalent copies of the read intensive aspects of the database, for example, the Merchandise and Movies tables of the Movies-R-Us site, can be maintained in their entirety on several computers. Then the SELECT workload can be balanced across these machines. The idea is to improve the application's reliability and response time as shown in Figure 6–10.

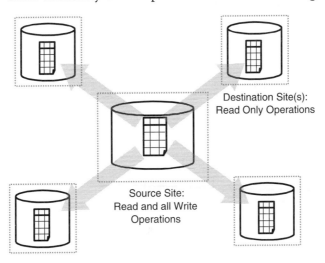

Figure 6–10. *Data Dissemination*

- Workload Partitioning. Databases with large write workloads can be partitioned using replication too. Entire tables still need to be replicated on several machines, but unlike the other replication scenarios, different subsets of rows from the table can be updated on different machines. Such an approach improves reliability and reduces overall response time. However, unlike the read case, keeping the data logically consistent is more difficult because of the way that the logical table is divided over several computers. For example, enforcing table integrity rules like primary keys becomes expensive. Figure 6–11 illustrates what workload partitioning looks like.

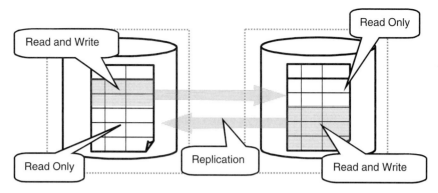

Figure 6–11. *Workload Partitioning*

• Data Consolidation. So far, all replication goals have focused on supporting operational databases that happen to be distributed. In other business circumstances, however, it is desirable to construct an off-line repository to use as a decision support database. Figure 6–12 illustrates how such a system operates.

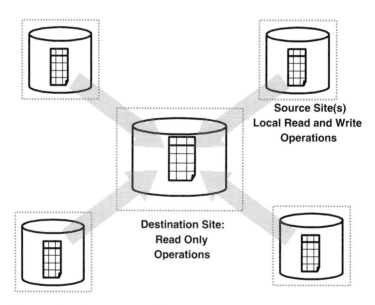

Figure 6–12. *Data Consolidation*

Depending on the operational goal in mind, a different replication strategy may be appropriate. In fact, different tables within the same logical database can be subjected to different replication arrangements.

For example, the various digital content oriented tables within our Movies-R-Us site (`Movies` and `Cinemas`) may be replicated to multiple sites using data dissemination, while the transactional aspects of the system (`Orders`) might be consolidated.

Regardless of the mechanism chosen, it is very important to understand that data in a replicated copy is never guaranteed to be synchronized with its canonical source. It is possible, for example, to use the distributed query mechanism introduced in the previous section to demonstrate that differences exist between replicated tables.

Replication Topologies

Replication can be used in several ways. In its simplest form, to support high availability, two systems can be configured so that every change made on the first is immediately forwarded to the second. Supporting the goals introduced in the previous section, however, requires multiple replication approaches. When all data is changing at one point, these changes must find their way to other places. Sometimes a table's data is being changed in multiple places, and a means must be found to merge these changes.

Primary-Target

In Primary-Target replication, which is also known as master-slave replication, the logically distributed table has a single, canonical location in which all change operations must occur. Once completed, the replication mechanism forwards these changes to the destination sites. This topology is most commonly used to provide data dissemination and sometimes data consolidation (each site's table has a corresponding table at the central database).

Under this arrangement, changes made at the destination site are isolated there. In fact, it is a very good practice to set the permissions on destination data such that only SELECT queries can be issued against them. In fact, with HDR replication this is mandatory. Should the primary site become unavailable, external programs can connect to the second.

Update-Anywhere

Update-anywhere, which is also called peer-to-peer replication, is considerably more complex to administer. The objective is to allow users at several sites both read and write privileges over an entire data set. This introduces a big theoretical problem because a single row of data can be changed by two independent operations, in two different databases. Which change is correct?

Overcoming this problem requires human intervention. Detecting conflicts is something that the replication services can do automatically, but resolving them is beyond its abilities. Consequently, update-anywhere replication is a topology that should be employed with some caution. Nonetheless, it can be used to solve workload partitioning problems, as long as each site is configured in such a way that the possibility of conflict is precluded, or at least minimized.

Synchronous and Asynchronous

In synchronous replication, data changes on the source and destinations are committed all at once; that is, the local transaction does not complete until the remote changes are complete. As with distributed query processing, the two-phase commit protocol ensures consistency and governs behavior in the case of failure. Synchronous replication is necessary to support high availability.

In asynchronous replication, there will be some delay between when the local transaction commits and the change is made at the remote destinations. Asynchronous replication is simply a pragmatic reaction to the fact that in many applications, response time at the source site is more important than timely correctness at the destination sites. Another advantage of asynchronous replication is that the database on either side of the replicate relationship can go down while its counterpart being is able to proceed.

In Table 6–2 we summarize the differences between these synchronous transfer and asynchronous transfer.

Replication has a deserved reputation for complexity, but developers can help themselves a lot by adopting a fairly simply rule when using it: Ensure that every row has exactly one canonical location. Changes to that row should always go first to that site, and from there, the new row can be replicated out to however many locations are needed to meet the workload expectations.

Of course, as with most rules, this one can't be applied in all circumstances, but in general, it is a discipline that will save database administrators hours of wading through conflict reports.

RDBMS Gateways

Ted Codd's relational model spawned a legion of imitators. Some of the most successful of them could not answer even the simplest questions about information management, but the strength of the underlying ideas was such that copycats prospered (aided by an excess of chutzpah and a smattering of gullibility).

Table 6–2. Comparing Synchronous and Asynchronous Replication

Is data logically consistent on both sites?	When can write transactions on the source be committed?	How does the replication mechanism cope with the loss of connection between source and destination sites?	Is data logically consistent on both sites?
Synchronous Transfer	Once the change operation is made on all participating sites.	Replication stops, and the operation of databases at participating sites are impaired.	Yes
Asynchronous Transfer	Once the change operation at the source is complete; changes to destination sites happen after some delay.	Normal operations can continue. The replication mechanism buffers all changes to be made until the connection is reestablished.	No. There is a delay between when a change occurs on the source site and when it appears on the destination. The extent of this delay can be controlled.

Consequently, a great many information systems that have been built using a variety of RDBMS products. Sometimes, developers are called upon to build a system that needs data from several of them. The easiest way to achieve this kind of integration is to use *gateways*. A gateway is a conduit for data that allows a table in a remote database that uses another vendor's DBMS to appear as if it were a table in the local database. Figure 6–13 illustrates how gateways work.

In engineering terms, gateways work in a fashion that is similar to distributed query processing techniques. Tables in the foreign database are addressed using the fully qualified database identifier syntax, read and write queries can access that data, and a two-phase commit strategy is employed to ensure transactional consistency.

Where the techniques are dissimilar in one respect: Most vendor's DBMSs are not as functionally complete as the ORDBMS. For instance, table inheritance and user-defined extensions are not supported to the same degree.

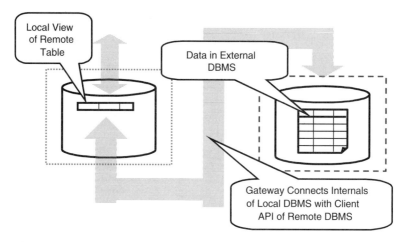

Figure 6–13. *Gateway Architecture*

Architectural Implications

Traditionally, DBMS systems have always been relegated to one edge
of the architecture diagram. The term "mid-tier" suggests a program
that runs between the database on the one hand and the user interface on the other. When building scalable, reliable systems, however, it
can make sense to colocate reliable data repositories with middleware
programs. Distributed ORDBMS technology provides just such a framework, as we illustrate in Figure 6–14.

The purpose of this rather cluttered figure is to illustrate what a
functional, distributed ORDBMS might look like. Within the boundaries of the logical information system, all table data and user-defined
extensions can be addressed using OR-SQL queries. The information
system's schema includes three tables. Table data is physically located
where the table symbol has rows in addition to column definitions.

In some cases, such location transparency is achieved by replicating
a particular table over all participating nodes and using the same
name for it everywhere. Queries against the table with three columns
always resolve locally. For consistency, the only place that data in this
table should be modified is on the central installation. For other data,
the illusion of location transparency is maintained using consistent
synonyms. OR-SQL queries against the tables with two and four
columns are always routed back to the large instance to ensure that
the results of these queries are logically consistent.

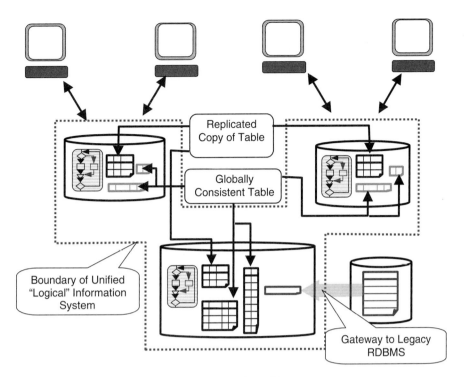

Figure 6–14. *Hybrid Distributed ORDBMS Architecture*

The advantages of such an integrated distributed systems model are as follows.

- Consistent programming model. An ORDBMS can embed components (written in languages such as Java or C) within itself. These components can use open interfaces such as JDBC and high productivity languages such as OR-SQL to interact with the "persistent data" portions of the overall system.
- Administrative simplicity and flexibility. One of the great insights of RDBMS products was the fact that the separation of the logical operations of the system from the physical data management reduced development effort. Modern, multitier information systems development can benefit by adopting similar strategies.
- Scalability. Many hands make light work, and being able to cope with additional workload by adding computers to the set already installed represents the ideal situation for most large systems.

Figure 6–14 is a manifesto for a next-generation data management architecture.

Chapter Summary

In this chapter we have focused on three aspects of ORDBMS functionality that go beyond what is traditionally thought of as core data management functionality. We framed our discussion by describing how the functional components of an information system—user-interface, data processing, and persistent storage—are traditionally arranged. Extensible, or object-relational, DBMS technology does not require that we revisit this description, but it does provide new ways of mapping these functional areas to the hardware underpinning an information system.

First, we examined stored procedures, which are a well-understood technique for introducing procedural logic into the DBMS. In the ORDBMS you can use any of the extension languages, such as SPL, Java, and C, to implement stored procedures. SPL is the easiest language with which to work, and the performance differences among these alternatives are minimal at best. Thus, we spent considerable time describing SPL and exploring how it would be used to implement a shopping-cart module for the Movies-R-Us database.

Second, we introduced the concept of database *rules* and the TRIGGER feature used to implement them. Database rules provide active database functionality. They allow a developer to specify that the ORDBMS is to undertake an automatic response to a particular event when it meets some set of conditions. TRIGGERs are not a new idea, but we illustrate how IDS adds SELECT TRIGGERs to the traditional INSERT, UPDATE, and DELETE and how applying user-defined functions within TRIGGERs extends the power of TRIGGERs into new kinds of applications.

Next we reviewed the ORDBMS's distributed data management functionality. This enables you to partition your database's data and logic across a set of network-connected computers so that your information system's overall goals—availability, response-time, load balancing, and so on—can be met.

In conclusion, we emphasize again that although extensibility makes new deployment models possible, it by no means eliminates the need for external programs. No electronic system is an island. Inevitably, when you build an information system, you will be required to construct interfaces by which other systems—sometimes preexisting, sometimes developed subsequently—communicate with it. In the next chapter we focus on the Application Programming Interfaces (APIs) used to achieve this.

Client Interfaces to ORDBMSs

Client Programs and DBMSs

A database by itself is next to useless. An IDS instance hosts shared data and logic at a central location. User-interface programs are decentralized and scattered geographically, matching the distribution of the user community. Fairly often, the information system's architecture requires a middleware layer of processes for communication with remote clients and other information systems. Simply put, the problem that remains to be addressed is that shared data and logic are located "in here," but are needed "out there."

OR-SQL, the mechanism whereby external programs exchange queries and data with the ORDBMS, is a *data language*. *Graphical User Interfaces (GUIs)*, middleware programs, and the logic implementing user-defined extensions with the database all employ *procedural languages* (also known as *host languages*). Consequently, the IDS product needs to provide host language facilities that allow non-DBMS programs to connect to a database, send query expressions to it, and handle the data and status messages returned from the ORDBMS.

In this chapter we explore several of these external interfaces, which are usually referred to as *client application programming interfaces (client APIs)*.

Client APIs exist for most of the popular host languages: C, C++, COBOL, Java, Standard Generalized Markup Languages (SGML) (HTML, WML, XML), 4GLs such as Powerbuilder and Visual Basic, and even scripting languages such as Perl or Tcl/Tk. We discuss the following ones in this chapter:

- Embedded SQL (ESQL/C). The earliest approach to client interface design was to use explicit directives to embed query expressions within procedural language code. A preprocessor supplied with the IDS client development environment turns the embedded statements into equivalent, but very complex, host language statements before the program is compiled using the external language's regular development tools.
- Java JDBC. One problem with directly embedding a query language into a host language is that embedding requires a two-phase compilation process. A second problem is that programmers working with embedded query languages do not have as much control as they are used to. Therefore, the recent trend has been to provide procedural interfaces. Among these, the Java language's *Java DataBase Connectivity (JDBC)* is fairly representative.
- Markup languages. The exploding popularity of the Web requires yet another interface between the declarative *Hypertext Markup Language (HTML)* and OR-SQL. The Web DataBlade interface takes the form of a set of markup tags that extend the HTML language and ORDBMS extensions that combine these tags with OR-SQL expressions to generate *dynamic* pages. In addition to HTML, there has been tremendous recent interest in the *eXtensible Markup Language (XML)* and the *Wireless Markup Language (WML)*, both of which can be accommodated using the same mechanism as HTML.

Whichever interface is most appropriate is determined by the host language being used, and the choice of host language should reflect the task at hand. Such advice seems obvious, but it is intended as a warning against, for example, spending three months writing an ESQL/C program that achieves the same objective that a Web Blade page could accomplish in ten minutes! When it comes to external interfaces, diversity is a good thing.

Overview of Client API Features

Each client interface includes mechanisms to perform the following:

- Connection handling. Before it can execute any queries, an external program must first open a connection to a database. Other parts of the interface require a connection handle to send OR-SQL messages into the ORDBMS, to get data back, and to act as a context for errors and exceptions. A single external program can open multiple connections to multiple databases and can switch between them at will.
- Manage queries and data. The task of the external program is to create or manage queries that are passed into the database. The ORDBMS responds with data or status messages that must be handled in the external program. With RDBMS technology, the problem of moving data between the database and the client was eased by the fact that the SQL-92 type system was a close equivalent to the type systems of most host languages. Object-relational technology, with its extensible type system, complicates client/server exchange. Understanding how to deal with ORDBMS features using the API is a central topic of this chapter.
- Errors and exceptions. Should the DBMS encounter an error or an exception, such as when a client query violates a security or data integrity rule or when the connection to the remote database is lost, the client program should handle the problem gracefully.

In this chapter we begin by describing the popular architectures or configurations of user interfaces and server processes. Modern information systems frequently need to employ more than one style of interface to support scattered users with diverse requirements. For example, in our Movies-R-Us site, there is an obvious requirement to support a Web interface for public members. However, it's likely that the site's management would need private user interfaces to cater to their own particular needs.

We then provide detailed descriptions of each of the three interfaces. Much of the material in this chapter will be familiar to readers who have used the relational version of the IDS product before, so in particular we focus on how to use these interfaces with extended data types and object-relational schema facilities.

Information System Architectures

Roughly speaking, any line of code in an information system can be categorized based on whether it is implementing some aspect of the following:

- User interface
- Data processing
- Storage management

User-interface code manages the presentation of information to users and invokes data processing logic. Data processing code combines and manipulates persistent data. The storage manager deals with getting data to and from a persistent storage medium efficiently. We illustrate each of these functional components and the relationship between them in Figure 7–1.

This functional division is clearer in some systems than others. For example, in what are known as "three-tier" architectures, the user interface, the data processing logic, and the storage management are implemented in different programs. In contrast, some older systems combined all three into one program, and in widely distributed systems like Napster™, the information organized by the system is scattered to the winds.

Architectural approaches described in this subsection can be categorized according to how the functional components in Figure 7–1 are distributed over the underlying hardware. Depending on the problem, it can make sense to co-locate all of them on a single computer, or partition them over a number of machines.

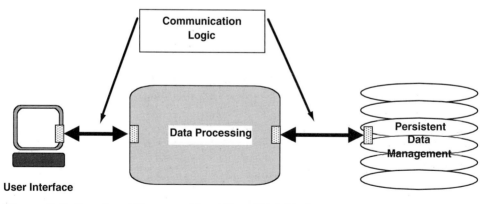

Figure 7–1. *Functional Decomposition of non-Trivial Information System*

Server-Centric Architectures

In server-centric applications, all three functional components are co-located on a single machine. Such architectures were more common when hardware was more expensive and networks were nonexistent. Typically, sever-centric information systems consisted of a single, monolithic program. Server-centric architectures have experienced a popular resurgence recently as the preferred approach for building small to medium-sized data warehousing applications.

ORDBMS technology works well in server-centric architectures because the engine is capable of integrating data processing logic expressed in a host language with the data management facilities of a traditional DBMS. In addition, for warehouse applications requiring complex numerical analysis or incorporating unconventional data, such as spatial decision support, an ORDBMS is really the only solution.

Client/Server Architectures

Client/server architectures distribute the functionality of the information system over two classes of hardware connected by a network. Typically, a client program running on a set of smaller computers is responsible for the user interface and a subset of data processing functionality. The DBMS, which is responsible for the management of shared data and logic, runs on a single, large central computer.

An important performance objective of client/server architectures is to minimize the number of bytes exchanged between the client program and the DBMS. Client computers are usually connected to the server hardware using some kind of network, and networks add significant overhead to communication between the client and the DBMS. To reduce the amount of communication, client-server architectures make extensive use of stored procedures. The idea was to reduce the quantity of query messages going up to the server and result data coming down. Figure 7–2 illustrates the basic topology.

Client/server architectures have the benefit of distributing CPU-intensive activities such as driving the *Graphical User Interface (GUI)* and handling events such as keyboard and mouse interrupts, over a number of machines. Moving user-interface logic closer to the end user improves the responsiveness of the overall system because it reduces communication overhead. RDBMS back end systems and 4GL language front ends proved very effective software tools for building client/server systems, and the ascendancy of personal computers, networking technologies, and cheap server-class hardware made this deployment model cost-effective.

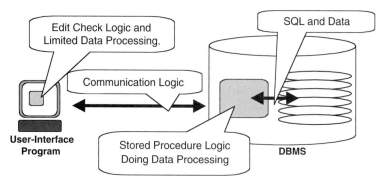

Figure 7–2. *Client/Server Architecture*

The shortcoming of two-tiered client/server architectures is that they concentrate the computational workload onto the central server computer. Information systems with large number of client users, or ones that include lots of logic, require another approach. Today, high-end information systems are typically deployed over several computers, and adopt what is usually referred to as an "*n*-tier" architecture.

Multi-tier Architectures

Multi-tier architectures interpose another process, or set of processes running on several machines, between the data store and the user interface. Client programs exchange messages with the mid-tier program, which in turn communicates with the DBMS. Decentralizing computational load makes the overall system more scalable than configurations relying on a single, central computer.

Figure 7–3 illustrates the basic configuration used in three-tier systems. It represents the participating computers with dotted outlines. Different kinds of software—DBMS installations, middleware servers, and user-interface programs—are shown running on different machines. Large installations can include multiple mid-tier processes using multiple machines. A variety of software tools, from traditional Transaction Processing Monitors (TP Monitors) such as Tuxedo™ or Encina™, queuing products such as MQSeries™, and development tools such as Sun™ Forte™ or any one of several *Object Request Broker (ORB)* vendors, provide this functionality.

Object-relational databases are every bit as effective within n-tier configurations as RDBMS technology, and the innovative features of object-relational products make them an attractive platform for such systems moving ahead. In Figure 7–3 we use gray boxes to represent

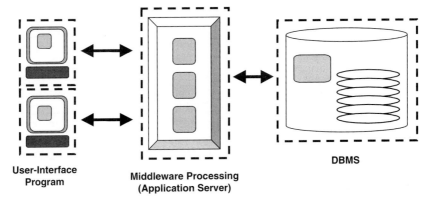

**User-Interface
Program**

**Middleware Processing
(Application Server)**

DBMS

Figure 7–3. N-Tier Client/Server Architectures

modules of business logic deployed at any tier of the system. This kind of "logic anywhere" deployment is made possible when language technologies like Java are combined with the ORDBMS extensible data model.

Web Application Architectures

The World Wide Web, or Web, architectures are the most recent configuration to become popular. Web architectures allow for an even wider geographic distribution of users and better scalability in terms of the number of them who can concurrently access the system. Web architectures are a flavor of multitier architectures in which the communication between the client and the mid-tier is handled using a standard, stateless, message-based protocol, in contrast to client/server or traditional *n*-tier architectures that use stateful connections. The most common of these is HTTP, although there are other, similar technologies, such as the *Wireless Application Protocol (WAP)*.

Wireless architectures envision a generic, lightweight user-interface application that runs on every hardware system. This program—a variety of a *browser*—accepts instructions to display data and simple form-based data entry facilities. Application data and most of the logic is stored and processed on the central server installation. Figure 7–4 illustrates the configuration.

Central to the efficacy of Web architectures is the use of a "markup" language. Messages from the server consist of clear-text ASCII interspersed with special "tags." Browser software processes these messages by interpreting the tags to indicate how the text data is to be formatted

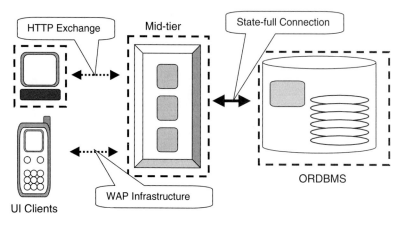

Figure 7–4. *Web and Wireless Application Architectures*

on the screen, or in the case of XML, what the data means. In the earliest Web sites, data was stored in a set of interlinked files, but for dynamic systems such as our Movies-R-Us site, such an approach presents a management challenge. More recently, Web sites have been built to generate the marked-up message data on the fly from data stored in a database.

Advice on Architecture Choices

Before diving into detail, it is useful to give some guidance to information system architects. They face a difficult task, and their decisions are not as clear-cut as an individual programmer's. They must consider the information system's business goals and limits on development costs as part of their decision-making process.

One important consideration is that modern information systems cater to the consumer marketplace, and that individual consumers have the benefit of unprecedented choice. Give them the right information too slowly, or the wrong information just once, and they will seek out your competitors. As a result, if there is a single criteria by which to judge architectural alternatives, it is this: minimize the volume of moving data. Choose whichever approach implies the least volume of data movement, given the "fixed" limitations of the system. In practical terms, the following guidelines are useful:

1. You should minimize the number of copies of volatile data. For example, in an e-commerce site, information about product availability changes, and it often changes quickly. Elaborate caching mechanisms in the middle tier might improve response times

slightly, but consumers are leery of inconsistency and will avoid sites that lie to them. Consequently, caching volatile data implies generating lots of message traffic to keep data consistent. Frequently updating multiple data caches with new information that will not be read before it changes is bad design.

2. On the other hand, if a particular piece of digital content is included on many pages, or a particular item of information is the subject of common queries, caching it in multiple locations can improve performance.

3. You should minimize the total distance between users and where the computational workload they generate is actually executed. Move simple tasks, such as editing checks on user-input, out to the browser, execute more computationally intense work that does not involve shared data, such as image compression and network buffering, on the mid-tier, and centralize only the shared, data, intensive tasks, such as order processing.

4. Another good rule of thumb is to avoid buying software from charlatans proclaiming that there is "one true architecture."

Architecture choice in the Movies-R-Us Web site reflects the reality that different users of the system have different needs. Traditional interfaces, such as ESQL/C, are just as relevant when working with an ORDBMS as they ever have been, because they are the preferred interface to middleware services such as TP monitors. Java and JDBC are a practical necessity when building Web sites because of the way Java "servlets" are emerging as the de facto standard for providing dynamic content. For interfaces that must be developed very rapidly for a widely distributed community of users, few things beat markup languages.

Embedding OR-SQL in C - ESQL/C

Traditionally, the most popular means of integrating OR-SQL and a procedural or host language has been to *embed* the data language into the host language. Embedded SQL extends the host language—C, for example—with data language facilities such as database connections, query expression, management of return results, and exception and error handling. Embedded interfaces provide a means of managing both static queries, which are known at compile time, and dynamic queries, which are generated by the client program's code.

Supporting embedded OR-SQL in an external program written in a host language such as C involes the following:

- A host language *preprocessor* that is typically integrated with a host language compiler. This preprocessor parses the host language code (with data language statements embedded within it) and generates an intermediate file containing only host language code. Any embedded statements are replaced with sub-routine calls to a lower-level client-side API. The intermediate program can then be passed through a compilation phase to produce an object file, which can then be linked into an executable.
- A set of header files that provides a set of useful definitions and macros. Typically, these files provide facilities to manage the DBMS's built-in data types.
- A set of client-side libraries that must be linked into any client executable. These client libraries implement a connectivity layer providing a conduit between the client program and the server, which might be running on a remote machine, for queries and data.
- DataBlade header files, which contain information about the binary definitions of the UDTs added to the server through the extensibility facilities. For example, to make a server-side type, such as a two-dimensional point, useful on the client side, the blade developer needs to provide a header file and a library for external programs.

In this section we briefly explain how to use the embedded OR-SQL statements with the C language. These techniques work in the ORDBMS in largely the same way that they do in the RDBMS product, and similar interfaces exist for other 3GLs such as COBOL. Over time, client-side facilities have been developed considerably and today are quite extensive. For example, client-side libraries are shipped with the IDS product that maps the product's built-in SQL-92 to corresponding C language structures.

Consequently, the focus here is on describing how the client embedding facilities have been changed to use the new server features: extended data types, OO features of the data model, and large-object data values. This description is by no means a complete coverage of everything that is possible. The intention is to provide readers with a background for their own exploration of the topic.

Note that Java also has an embedded interface. Usually referred to as SQL-J Part 0 (zero), this query language embedding standard does for Java what ESQL does for C or COBOL. It is not described in this book.

Introduction to ESQL/C

Like the other external interfaces, ESQL/C contains facilities for the following:

- Managing connections to (multiple) databases.
- Embedding SQL Data Definition Language (DDL) statements and Data Manipulation Language (DML) statements into the host language.
- Passing DDL and DML that was created dynamically by the running client program to a database server.
- Managing the return results from queries, which includes declaring host language variables to contain return results, and, where necessary, facilities to convert these data values into host language variables.
- Detect and handle errors and exceptions.
- Handle large object data values. These can be left on the server and manipulated directly, brought across into the client file system, or read from the server into client-side memory.

We now discuss each of these in turn.

Embedding SQL Directives

OR-SQL statements embedded into client programs are identical to the equivalent statement expressed through a command line interface, except that they are prepended with the EXEC SQL precompiler directive. The directive tells the precompiler that the string following it is an OR-SQL statement, which it can transform into a set of procedural calls in a completely native host language program. As a final step, the intermediate source code generated by the precompiler is compiled into an executable form using a general purpose, host language compiler.

All aspects of the client program relating to database interactions—the declaration of host variables, connection statements, OR-SQL queries, and cursor handling—must be marked up with the EXEC SQL directive. This gives ESQL/C programs their distinctive look, which can be seen in Listing 7–1.

```
1  char * pchGetMemberName ( char * );
2  .
3  main ( int argc, char ** argv )
4  {
5    int              i;
6    char * pchMemberName;
7
8    /*
9    ** Variables that are part of the embedded SQL must
10   ** be declared in a special bracketed section.
```

```
11    */
12    EXEC SQL BEGIN DECLARE SECTION;
13            char            szdbName[48];
14    EXEC SQL END DECLARE SECTION;
15
16    sprintf(szdbName,"%s@%s",
17                            "test_database","wolvi_server");
18    /*
19    ** Open a CONNECTION to the database identified in the
20    ** szdbName char array.
21    */
22    EXEC SQL OPEN CONNECTION :szdbName;
23
24    for(i=1;i<argc;i++)
25    {
26            pchMemberName = pchGetMemberName(argv[i]);
27            printf( "Member : Id is %s: Name is %s \n",
28                    argv[i],
29                    pchMemberName);
30    }
31    /*
32    ** Disconnect
33    */
34    EXEC SQL DISCONNECT CURRENT;
35    return 0;
35 }
```

Listing 7–1. *Embedding SQL and EXEC SQL Directives*

This listing presents a C program with some embedded SQL expressions. It is a simple program designed to retrieve member names for a set of identity numbers supplied at the command line. Later in this chapter we present the pchGetMemberName() subroutine in more detail. In this main() block we see how to declare variables, and how to create and close a connection to a named database.

Declaring Variables

An ESQL/C program can create and use standard C variables as long as the variable is not used in any OR-SQL operations. For example, the variables declared in Lines 5 and 6 of Listing 7–1 fall into this category. Variables used to hold data values retrieved by a query, variables bound to a query before it is executed, connection handles, cursor names, and strings to hold queries are called *host language variables*. These should all be declared in a block of code bounded by EXEC SQL BEGIN DECLARE; and EXEC SQL END DECLARE; embedded statements. In Listing 7–1, Lines 12 to 14 illustrate what this looks like.

Host language variables obey whatever conventions apply in the client language. For example, in C, initial values can be assigned to host language variables at the time they are declared. Also, the usual rules of scope apply. Variables are only accessible within the procedure in which they are defined. Global variables need to be declared outside any procedure body using the appropriate host language syntax (extern in C).

Client Variable Data Structures

As part of the ESQL/C client support, the IDS product provides definitions for structures that can be used to hold instances of each of the server's built-in types. For example, the C program can declare host variables to be char, fixchar, string, varchar, integer, date, interval, decimal, and so on. These structures are defined in the client-side libraries and header files, and the IDS product provides an extensive set of routines to work with these types in the external C code.

For portability, you should use these types wherever possible. When an ESQL/C program is moved to another environment, the product's ESQL/C libraries ensure that equivalent structure definitions exist there as well.

As you would expect, you can also declare arrays of host variables and define structured host variables. As we shall see, when dealing with user-defined OPAQUE and ROW data types, this is very important. One of the challenges of building information systems with ORDBMSs is making the external program as flexible as the server. An ORDBMS stores user-defined objects as byte arrays. All object behavior is implemented within the server using the various UDF mechanisms and is invoked through an extremely simple and flexible interface: the query language.

External programs can send a query to the ORDBMS that returns data values of some user-defined type which typically has no corresponding data type or structure found natively in the host language. For example, there is no "polygon" data type in C (although java.awt.polygon in the Java™ libraries comes close).

Rather than present a set of variable declaration examples here, we include all variable declarations in the code that appears throughout this section. Later in this chapter, we examine issues surrounding client-side support for extended data types in more detail.

Making and Managing Connections

A client program can open (multiple) concurrent connections to several different databases. Once it has established these connections, the external program can switch among them at runtime, or even assign them to different threads if it is a multi-threaded program. It is important to understand that each client connection, from the server's perspective, is completely independent from other connections opened by the same external program. The ORDBMS does not assume that two connections from the same client can share resources such as a transaction context (locks) or memory.

Separate connection contexts means that developers should exercise caution when using multiple connections. Each connection allocates a block of server memory, so each unused connection represents memory that might be put to other uses such as, for example, extra buffer-cache pages. It is a very bad idea to divide the responsibility for executing a single application level operation among multiple connections. Splitting a single business process over multiple connections can cause an external program to arrive at the uncomfortable situation where it is deadlocking on itself!

Making Connections

When a client program connects to a database, it must name the target database explicitly. Typically, clients have a default server (the ORDBMS instance where the database is to be found) configured in their environment, but a connection may name a server explicitly as part of the connection if there are several choices. The server name is resolved into a machine name and interprocess communication service within the client program's environment. Once a connection to the server is established, the named database is opened. A simple connection statement looks like Listing 7–2.

```
EXEC SQL CONNECT TO "test_database@wolvi_server";
```

Listing 7–2. Connecting to a Known Database and Server

In this case, the client program investigates its environment to find the name of the machine on which `wolvi_server` resides and the mode of connection that that server expects.[1] If it succeeds in communicating with the named server, it then tries to open the `test_database`. As part of making the connection, the ORDBMS performs a number of security checks. It ensures that the user running the external program is known on the server machine, that the user has appropriate permissions over the database, and so on. If any of these security checks fail, the IDS product will generate an exception and reject the connection.

Once this connection is established, all subsequent embedded OR-SQL works against the database in that ORDBMS server instance.

Switching Between Connections

When a client program wants to maintain more than one concurrent connection, it must name each connection. To do this, use the syntax in Listing 7–3.

```
EXEC SQL CONNECT TO "test_database@wolvi_Server"
                AS "First_Conn";
```

Listing 7–3. *Naming a Connection to a Known Database and Server*

This creates what is called a *named* connection. A single program can create up to 32 of them. Usually the name of the connection is stored in a host language variable, rather than represented using a literal string. At runtime, you can alternate between them using the SET CONNECTION syntax, as shown in Listing 7–4.

```
EXEC SQL CONNECT TO "test@wolvi" AS "First_Conn";

EXEC SQL CONNECT TO "test2@wolvi" AS "Second_Conn";

EXEC SQL SET CONNECTION "First_Conn";

/*
** Queries with this connection scope are directed
```

---

[1] Server names, computer addresses in a network, and protocol information are stored as client environment variables, in a client-side configuration file, or in a directory registery.

```
**  against the test@wolvi database.
*/
.
EXEC SQL SET CONNECTION "Second_Conn";
.
/*
**  Queries with this connection scope are directed
**  against the test2@wolvi database.
*/
```

Listing 7–4. *Switching Between Named Connections*

Operating in a multi-threaded client environment requires a more complex arrangement. In a multi-threaded client, there can be multiple concurrently running threads, each with its own connection context. However, in an ESQL/C environment, two threads cannot share a single connection because the exchange of queries and data along a connection is handled synchronously, and in this environment, threading models are necessarily asynchronous. If an exception is generated on a connection, working out the thread to which the exception belongs is difficult.

Closing Connections

To close a connection, use the DISCONNECT command. This sends a message from the client to the server that instructs it to terminate the user context within the server. In general, it's a good idea to explicitly close connections, rather than to rely on the server's time-out mechanism to recognize that the client program has terminated. Line 34 in Listing 7–1 illustrates a disconnect.

Embedding Static Queries

The term *static queries* refers to OR-SQL expressions in which the *form* of the query is known at compile time, although the values of any variables used in it might not be known. Static queries are the most common kind of embedded queries because they reflect common application operations.

Listing 7–5 illustrates a complete subroutine that includes an embedded, static OR-SQL query and the code used to handle its return results. Note that Lines 3 through 5 in this example illustrate the standard approach to declaring routine arguments as OR-SQL host variables.

Other techniques, which use standard language sub-routine declarations but assign the argument values to OR-SQL host language variables, are a better approach in C++.

```
1  void
2  MinMaxMerchForMovie ( szMovieName )
3  EXEC SQL BEGIN DECLARE SECTION;
4          PARAMETER string * szMovieName;
5  EXEC SQL END DECLARE SECTION;
6  {
7          EXEC SQL BEGIN DECLARE SECTION;
8              decimal  decMin, decMax;
9          EXEC SQL END DECLARE SECTION;
10         string szMin[RES_LENGTH], szMax[RES_LENGTH];
11
12         printf(" szMovieName is >%s< \n", szMovieName );
13
14         EXEC SQL SELECT MIN(M.Price)::DECIMAL,
15                         MAX(M.Price)::DECIMAL
16                    INTO :decMin,
17                         :decMax
18                    FROM Merchandise M, Movies MO
19                   WHERE M.Movie  = MO.id
20                     AND MO.Title = :szMovieName;
21
22     /*
23     ** Client ESQL facilities operate on instances
24     ** of decimal host language variables.
25     ** Note that this code does not check return
26     ** results from dectoasc() to do error detection,
27     ** which is always a good idea in non-example
28     ** software.
29     */
30         (void)dectoasc( &decMin, szMin, RES_LENGTH, -1 );
31         (void)dectoasc( &decMax, szMax, RES_LENGTH, -1 );
32
33         printf("Retrieved: decMin = >%s<, decMax = >%s<\n",
34                 szMin, szMax);
35  }
```

Listing 7–5. *Embedded Static Query and Result Handling*

At runtime, the client program substitutes the value of the szMovie-Name variable into the query listed in Lines 14 through 20, and then it sends the query to the database on the current connection. The query's results are deposited into the named variables `decMin` and `decMax`. In this case, C logic using the IDS product's client-side facilities converts the results of the query, which has a `decimal` structure, into a null-terminated string, before it can be printed using standard C facilities. This happens on Lines 30 and 31. Of course, this query might also `SELECT` directly into the `szMin` and `szMax` string variables.

Alert readers will note that the `Merchandise.Price` column is in fact, a UDT. Casting specified as part of the query on Lines 14 and 15 converts the more complex `currency` into the more agreeable `decimal`.

Note that you can embed absolutely any OR-SQL statement into a host program, including a DDL statement to create schema objects, DML to change data values in the schema, DML to retrieve results from the schema, as well as database stored procedure calls. In the case of a stored procedure, which by definition does not return values, there is no need to cater for return results. Return values from user-defined functions are handled in a way that is similar to the query case, as the Listing 7–6 illustrates.

```
10  void SetTicketPrice (
11  EXEC SQL BEGIN DECLARE SECTION;
12          PARAMETER integer nCinemaId;
13          PARAMETER integer nMovieId;
14          PARAMETER decimal dNewPrice;
15  EXEC SQL END DECLARE SECTION;
16  )
17  {   EXEC SQL EXECUTE PROCEDURE SetTicketPrice(:nCinemaId,
18                                                :nMovieId,
19                                                :dNewPrice);
20  }
```

Listing 7–6. *Embedded Call to Stored Procedure*

This listing also illustrates how to declare arguments to host language C subroutine as OR-SQL host language variables. A special `EXEC SQL BEGIN/END DECLARE SECTION` is introduced to specify the types being passed into the function.

Pre-Processing Queries with PREPARE

Queries that are to be executed many times should be handled using the `PREPARE` and `EXECUTE` directives. This technique breaks query processing into two phases. In the prepare phase, which happens only once, the query is rendered into an internal format that is stored within the ORDBMS. A reference to it is returned to the external program and this reference can be stored in an ESQL/C variable. As part of preparing a query, the ORDBMS parses it to figure out what tables, columns, and UDFs it involves.

In the execute phase, this preprepared and internalized query format is actually run. This may happen many times throughout the life of the external program. Whenever a prepared query is executed, argument values can be provided to specialize it. The intention of the PREPARED query mechanism is to eliminate the need to pass the query string into the ORDBMS and parse it repeatedly.

Listing 7–7 illustrates the syntax used to prepare and then execute queries.

```
1  EXEC SQL BEGIN DECLARE SECTION;
2    char          szQueryString[1024];
3    decimal        decNewSalary;
4    integer        nEmpId;
5  EXEC SQL END DECLARE SECTION;
6
7    sprintf(szQueryString,
8            "UPDATE Employee SET Salary = ? WHERE Id = ?");
9
10    EXEC SQL PREPARE updStmt FROM  :szQueryString;
11    EXEC SQL EXECUTE updStmt USING :decNewSalary, :nEmpId;
```

Listing 7–7. *PREPAREd Query Syntax*

Note that in the EXECUTE step on Line 11, the code substitutes host language variables into the query string created on Lines 7 and 8 and prepared on Line 10. Lines 7 and 8 illustrate how to use the "?" character to indicate where variables are to be placed in the query statement. Line 10 is the actual prepare, where the query is parsed and the handle (updStmt) is created. Then on line 11, a pair of variables is associated with the prepared query handle, and the query is executed.

Parsing can represent a large percentage of the CPU cost of query processing. Many large or sophisticated application packages use this technique extensively.

Dynamic Queries

In many applications developers cannot anticipate every query at design time. Consequently, they must allow the external program the freedom to extend a basic query statement with additional predicates or to create an entirely new statement from scratch. Such situations require ESQL/C *dynamic SQL* facilities. Dynamic queries are OR-SQL expressions constructed at runtime by an external program that then passes the query to the ORDBMS. Interactive OR-SQL editors and report writers are examples of programs that work almost exclusively with dynamic OR-SQL.

Dynamic write queries are the simplest example. The OR-SQL expression is created as a null-terminated string and passed to the ORDBMS through a CONNECTION. Once the query is complete, host language code can check result status flags to get information about the success or failure of the query and information such as the number of rows it affected.

The simplest way to execute a dynamic query involves the EXECUTE IMMEDIATE directive. To use the EXECUTE IMMEDIATE directive, construct the query as a string within a host variable, and then simply execute it. Examine Listing 7–8.

```
1 EXEC SQL BEGIN DECLARE SECTION;
2   char            szQueryString[1024];
3 EXEC SQL END DECLARE SECTION;
4
5   char            szName[48];
6   integer nEmpId;
 .
10   sprintf(szQueryString,
11             "UPDATE Employee "
12             "   SET Salary = '%s' "
13             " WHERE Id = %d", szName, nEmpId );
 .
16   EXEC SQL EXECUTE IMMEDIATE :szQueryString;
 .
```

Listing 7–8. *Dynamic Write Query*

Line 16 in the external program will block until the query specified in the string has completed. In later sections of this chapter, we review other techniques for issuing dynamic OR-SQL queries that return results from the database.

Managing Result Data

Managing result data is the most complex aspect of an external interface, regardless of the technique used. In all examples introduced so far in this chapter, the OR-SQL queries are write queries or return a single row as their result, and the data types they return have all been built in. Many queries return multiple result rows, and you must decide whether to use ROW TYPE, OPAQUE TYPE, or a COLLECTION to handle the extended data types. In this section we address this issue.

CURSOR Structures

Typical OR-SQL SELECT queries return a set of result rows. Handling result sets in an ESQL/C external program is usually done using a construct called a *cursor*, which is a handle or interface to a set of query results. Queries that might be expected to return a set of row results should be associated with a CURSOR name. Once the query is executed, the client program can loop over the CURSOR, using the ESQL/C FETCH directive to retrieve row data into variables until no more remain. Examine Listing 7–9.

```
      EXEC SQL BEGIN DECLARE SECTION;
          lvarchar          vlResult[25];
      EXEC SQL END DECLARE SECTION;

      ..

      EXEC SQL DECLARE Opaque_Cursor CURSOR FOR
50          SELECT Duration
51             INTO :vlResult
52             FROM Showings
53          WHERE Overlap(Duration,"06/01/2000 to 06/15/2000");
54
55   EXEC SQL OPEN Opaque_Cursor;
56
57  while(1)
58  {
59      EXEC SQL FETCH Opaque_Cursor;
60
61      if (strncmp(SQLSTATE, "02", 2) == 0)
62         break;
63
64      printf("Fetched %s \n", (char *)vlResult)
65  }
66
      EXEC SQL CLOSE Opaque_Cursor;
```

Listing 7–9. *CURSOR Creation and Looping Over a Set of Result Rows*

Listing 7–9 illustrates how a CURSOR is used. Lines 49 through 53 specify the SELECT query and supply a name for the CURSOR. Until

Line 55, the query is not executed, and the code cannot FETCH rows from it. Then Lines 57 through 65 loop over the open cursor, retrieve one row at a time, and place its (single) value into the vlResult variable. Finally, once the rows in the cursors are exhausted, the code at Line 67 closes the cursor. At this time, all resources that the cursor uses are freed.

Line 61 requires additional explanation. Exceptions and status messages from the ORDBMS are communicated through a special block of memory that is created at the time you open a connection to the database. This block of memory is called the SQL Communications Area, or SQLCA. ESQL/C provides special facilities to access it, and we see one of them here.

The code at Line 61 checks one part the SQLCA to control its interaction with the IDS server. In this case the code uses a convenient IDS client C macro labeled SQLSTATE; it checks to see what the effect of the FETCH on Line 59 is. If SQLSTATE is set to "02," it means that the most recent operation resulted in no rows. When this occurs, there are no more rows in the result, so the program breaks out of the loop.

Handling OPAQUE TYPE Values

When a host language program issues a query that returns instances of an OPAQUE data type, the ESQL/C interfaces cannot assume much about its structure or even its length. Further, the client programming language environment may be unable to do much with the data object because it may not know about it at compile time. For example, consider what happens when an OR-SQL query within an ESQL/C client program retrieves an instance of a type created using Java™. The host language may simply be unable to make sense of the format in which the Java object is stored.

ESQL/C provides two ways to manage the passage of OPAQUE data values between the ORDBMS server and an external program using embedded SQL. First, the client program can ask the ORDBMS to return the *literal* or *external* representation of the OPAQUE data object. When it realizes that it must return an OPAQUE TYPE instance to the client, the server can cast the data to an lvarchar type. In the host language code, a local variable is defined that is large enough to hold the query's return value as lvarchar.

Listing 7–9 illustrates the approach. It creates an instance of a host language variable called vlResult of type lvarchar. When the ESQL/C interface realizes that it is being asked to return the OPAQUE type to an lvarchar, it instructs the ORDBMS to call the OPAQUE TYPE output function. Note that as part of the host language variable, you should allocate sufficient room to store the entire object. Even if you don't allocate enough space, the server will still pass you as much data as you have space for. Under these circumstances a warning exception is generated.

The second alternative for handling OPAQUE data types on the client side involves passing data from the server to the client in *binary* format, rather than in character format. In other words, the server can pass data objects to the client in exactly the same format that they are stored on disk, although it does automate some aspects of the problem, such as byte ordering. In certain circumstances, this can yield significant performance benefits.

For example, consider the Period OPAQUE data type. In Listing 7–9 we turn instances of the Period type into strings on the client side. Listing 7–10 reimplements the CURSOR only if it passes the binary form of the type into the local variable.

```
28    EXEC SQL BEGIN DECLARE SECTION;
 .
32        fixed binary "period" Period pPeriodResult;
33    EXEC SQL END DECLARE SECTION;
 .
58    EXEC SQL DECLARE Opaque_Cursor CURSOR FOR
59            SELECT Duration
60                INTO :pPeriodResult
61                FROM Showings
62                WHERE Overlap(Duration,
63                        "06/01/1996 to 06/15/2002");
 .
66    EXEC SQL OPEN Opaque_Cursor;
 .
69    while(1)
70    {
71        EXEC SQL FETCH Opaque_Cursor;
72
73        if (strncmp(SQLSTATE, "02", 2) == 0)
74            break;
75        (void)rdatestr((long)pPeriodResult.start,
76                    pchDateStart);
77        (void)rdatestr((long)pPeriodResult.finish,
78                    pchDateFinish);
79
80        printf("Val: Period( %s -> %s )\n",pchDateStart,
81                                pchDateFinish);
82    }
 .
93    EXEC SQL CLOSE Opaque_Cursor;
```

Listing 7–10. *Passing Binary Data Between ORDBMS and Client*

Periods are composed of a pair of OR-SQL DATE values. The internal representation of a Period requires eight bytes (although in the general case, the size of an OPAQUE TYPE may not be known at compile time, and it may vary at runtime). Line 32 illustrates how to declare a variable to hold the data returned from the server. Compiling this program requires that the structure of the Period (note the capitalization) is known. In practical terms, this means that the source code in Listing 7–10 needs to include a header file containing the definition of the Period C structure.

Lines 75 through 80 extract data from the binary value. Although in this example we address the structural elements of the Period directly, in most cases, you would use a subroutine for this. The calls to rdatestr() on Lines 75 and 77 are used to convert internal date formats to strings.

Variable length OPAQUE data needs a slightly different declaration syntax, which is introduced in Listing 7–11. Handling variable length structures is further complicated by the way the client interface needs to allocate memory to hold them and by the fact that this memory must be freed when it is no longer required. A special memory management interface exists within the ESQL/C interfaces to support this. It uses a variety of ESQL/C directives with labels such as FREE and DEALLOCATE.

```
      EXEC SQL BEGIN DECLARE SECTION;
         .
26           var binary "realmatrix" RealMatrix pMatrixData;
27    EXEC SQL END DECLARE SECTION;
```

Listing 7–11. *Passing Variable Length Binary Data Between ORDBMS and the Client*

In many situations it is difficult to know at the time a client program is being written what the server's data types will look like at runtime. In fact, consequence of the server's flexibility and extensibility is that the types in the server can be changing while the client program is actually running. Later in this chapter, where we review the techniques used to handle the results of dynamic SELECT queries, we examine this topic in more detail.

ROW TYPE Values

The ESQL/C interface provides extensive support for the ROW TYPE mechanism on the client side. ROW TYPE values can be used in many ways. For example, instances of a ROW TYPE might be returned as column values, used as variables in query predicates, or supplied as values for INSERT or UPDATE queries. Indeed, the entire set of columns returned from a query might be converted into an unnamed ROW TYPE when it is passed to the client.

To handle this on the client-side, ESQL/C includes facilities to do the following:

- Declare client-side variables that are of a particular ROW TYPE
- Use the client-side variables in embedded queries
- Extract or modify values from client instances of a ROW TYPE

In Listing 7–12 we present an example illustrating how to create an instance of a client variable that uses a ROW TYPE declaration.

```
20      EXEC SQL BEGIN DECLARE SECTION;
.
23          lvarchar   szFirstName[64];
24          lvarchar   szFamilyName[64];
.
26          row        rPName;
27      EXEC SQL END DECLARE SECTION;
.
48      EXEC SQL ALLOCATE ROW :rPName;
49
50      EXEC SQL DECLARE RowType_Cursor CURSOR FOR
51              SELECT Name
52                  INTO :rPName
53                  FROM MovieClubMembers M
54                  WHERE M.Name.Family_Name = "Brown";
.
59      EXEC SQL OPEN RowType_Cursor;
.
62      while(1)
63  {
64      EXEC SQL FETCH RowType_Cursor;
65
66          if (strncmp(SQLSTATE, "02", 2) == 0)
67              break;
68 EXEC SQL SELECT First_Name,
69                  Family_Name
70              INTO :szFirstName,
71                  :szFamilyName
72                  FROM TABLE(:rPName);
.
```

```
77              printf("Fetched: >%s<, >%s<\n", szFirstName,
78                                                szFamilyName);
79          }
    .

    EXEC SQL DEALLOCATE ROW :rPName;
    EXEC SQL CLOSE RowType_Cursor;
    .
```

Listing 7–12. *ROW TYPEs in ESQL/C*

Listing 7–12 illustrates several features of ROW TYPE use within ESQL/C.

ROW TYPE variables are declared in the SQL DECLARE SECTION. In Listing 7–12, the variable declaration on Line 26 illustrates the simplest of several syntactical forms. If you know the name of the ROW TYPE as the code is written, it can be a better idea to use a more complex form of the declaration syntax. This involves either providing the OR-SQL type name for the row or the actual structure of the ROW TYPE as it is defined in the databases. Providing more details permits ESQL/C to perform more type checking.

Before values can be retrieved into the variable, it must first be initialized. This process is initiated at Line 48 with the ALLOCATE ESQL/C directive. Then at Line 50, the ESQL/C interfaces find out about the structure of the ROW TYPE being retrieved by the CURSOR. Once it knows the ROW TYPE structure, the client can allocate appropriate resources to the host hold variable each time the client program issues a row FETCH.

As far as the CURSOR looping logic is concerned, each ROW TYPE is just another piece of data passed to the client program. Line 64 performs a FETCH of the next row from the cursor and populates memory allocated to hold the variable. All of this makes memory management in the client a more complex problem than it would otherwise be. In Listing 7–12, Line 90 illustrates the DEALLOCATE operation. This frees memory associated with the row variables.

Lines 69 through 73 illustrate how to extract values from an instance of a ROW TYPE variable in an ESQL/C program. Rather than provide a procedural interface—such as the one that the server API provides—the ESQL/C approach is to co-opt OR-SQL embedding. When executing the query on Lines 69 through 73, the client does not communicate with the IDS server: the operation executes entirely within the ESQL/C client program. Beyond retrieving values from within a ROW TYPE variable, this technique can also be used to UPDATE elements within a ROW TYPE variable in the external program.

When the query that retrieves the row value to the client side is run, part of the communication involves the ORDBMS server passing the ROW TYPE definition to the client along with the data. Then the values that are returned to the client are arranged in memory appropriately, and their contents can be interrogated.

Large Object Values

There are two ways to approach the problem of managing the large-object data in an ORDBMS from a client program. The first of these stages the large object in the file system on the client computer, which might be the same as the file system that the ORDBMS installation can see. Facilities within the ORDBMS can copy the entire large object out of the database, depositing the data into a named file. The name of this file, which is the return result of the function that copies the large object to the file, can be used by the client program to open the large object and read its contents.

Listing 7–13 illustrates how to exercise these facilities:

```
EXEC SQL DECLARE LargeObj_Cursor CURSOR FOR
           SELECT LOToFile(M.Photo,
                               "C:/tmp/Img.???",
                               "client")
              INTO   :szFileName
              FROM   MoviePersonalities M
              WHERE  M.Name.Family_Name = "Houston";

EXEC SQL OPEN LargeObj_Cursor;

while(1)
{
    EXEC SQL FETCH LargeObj_Cursor;

    if (strncmp(SQLSTATE, "02", 2) == 0)
      break;

    printf("File Name: >%s<\n", szFileName);
}

EXEC SQL CLOSE LargeObj_Cursor;
```

Listing 7–13. *Extracting Large Objects from the ORDBMS Using ESQL/C*

The chief virtue of this approach is its simplicity. Its major drawback is that the large object's data must be read and written twice. The data goes from the server's disk to the server's memory, over the network to the client's memory, and then to the client's disk. All of this is done before the data can be retrieved into the client program to be used.

Therefore, the IDS product provides a second, more efficient approach that reads the large object data directly into the client program's memory, bypassing the intermediate write to disk. This has a speed advantage, but it is more complex to engineer and requires that the client have enough memory to hold the entire large object.

With smart large object values, or OPAQUE TYPE values constructed using smart large objects, the ORDBMS can return a handle, or reference, to the client program. ESQL/C includes a structure to hold an instance of this handle object and an interface that permits the external program to interrogate it. Part of this interface is a set of calls for opening the large object and for working with its contents within the ORDBMS server. Examine Listing 7–14.

```
10 EXEC SQL INCLUDE locator;
   . . .
17 EXEC SQL BEGIN DECLARE SECTION;
   . . .
21     fixed binary "blob" ifx_lo_t video_handle;
22 EXEC SQL END DECLARE SECTION;
   . . .
57 EXEC SQL SELECT V.Sample
58             INTO :video_handle
59             FROM Video V, Movies M
60             WHERE M.Title = "Casablanca"
61               AND V.Movie = M.Id;
```

Listing 7–14. *Passing a Large Object Handle Between ORDBMS and the ESQL/C Program*

Line 10 in Listing 7–14 is necessary to programs using this large object handling mechanism because these facilities are not part of the default ESQL/C interface libraries or header files. The interface routines that work with the ifx_lo_t data structure are instead defined within these locator facilities. Line 21 illustrates how a variable that holds a large object *handle* structure is declared, and the SELECT query on Lines 57 through 61 retrieves a single handle for a large data object and places it in that variable.

The IDS product implements a two-step mechanism that allows an external program to work with the contents of a large object instance without copying all of the large object data out of the database. Conceptually, an `ifx_lo_t` instance is very similar to a filename in a more conventional C program. Of course, the standard C file I/O calls do not work with this type: it is stored entirely within the ORDBMS's data storage facilities, but the data within it can be read and written just like a file.

A complete list of all the ESQL/C interfaces for working with the `ifx_lo_t` structure is beyond the scope of this book. These calls permit an external program to create a new large object or to interrogate an existing one about its size and where it resides. We reproduce a subset of this interface in Table 7–1.

Table 7–1. ESQL/C Interfaces to ORDBMS Large Object Data

LO Interface	Description

`int ifx_lo_open(`
`    ifx_lo_t * LO_ptr,`
`    int        flags,`
`    int      * error );`
	Given an `ifx_lo_ptr` instance returned by a query, this interface opens the corresponding large object on the server. Note that this function's return value is to be passed into the other functions in this interface as the large object "file descriptor." Large objects can be opened with various permissions (read only, read/write, and append) and these affect the way transactions over the large object data are managed.

`int ifx_lo_close(` `    int    LO_fd );`	This interface closes an open large object.

`int ifx_lo_read(`
`    int LO_fd;`
`    char * buf,`
`    int      nbytes,`
`    int    * error );`
	This interface reads a certain number of bytes of data from an open large object and places it within the memory block passes as the second argument. The data is read from the current offset.

`int ifx_lo_readwithseek(`
`    int      LO_fd,`
`    char * buf,`
`    int      nbytes,`
`    ifx_int8_t * offset,`
`    int      whence,`
`    int    * error );`
	This interface is similar to `ifx_lo_read()`, except that before the read, the offset within the large object is moved to the location indicated by a combination of the whence and offset arguments.

(continued)

Table 7–1. ESQL/C Interfaces to ORDBMS Large Object Data (continued)

LO Interface

Description

```
int ifx_lo_write(
    int     LO_fd,
    char * buf,
    int     nbytes,
    int   * error );
```

This interface writes data to the large object. This call overwrites data at the current offset, or it extends the large object and places the new data at the end.

```
int ifx_lo_writewithseek(
    int      LO_fd,
    char  * buf,
    int      nbytes,
    ifx_int8_t *offset;
    int      whence,
    int    * error );
```

This interface is similar to write, except that before the write, the offset within the large object is moved to the location indicated by a combination of the whence and offset arguments.

```
int ifx_lo_tell(
    int           LO_fd,
    ifx_int8_t * seek_pos );
```

This interface returns the current offset within the large object.

Many readers will be struck by how similar these calls are to the POSIX file I/O interface. This is deliberate. Streaming I/O interfaces are the most common way to model large data objects such as video and digital imagery. The intention is to give developers an interface that is familiar to them.

COLLECTION Values

Queries sent to an ORDBMS can return COLLECTION objects, which contain more than one atomic data value. For convenience, the ESQL/C interface allows external programs to deal with COLLECTION instances as though they were transient tables in the external program. Overall the approach has a similar flavor to the way COLLECTION instances are handled in SPL.

Listing 7–15 illustrates how to declare a client-side variable to hold a COLLECTION.

```
23 EXEC SQL BEGIN DECLARE SECTION;
   . . .
27    CLIENT COLLECTION SET( LVARCHAR NOT NULL )Genre_Set;
   . . .
32 EXEC SQL END DECLARE SECTION;
   . . .
```

Listing 7–15. *ESQL/C Interfaces to COLLECTION Data*

Data within a COLLECTION can be accessed in host language code using an approach similar to the one used with ROW TYPE instances. All OR-SQL operations over COLLECTION instances are supported in the client. Appropriately typed variables can be inserted into a COLLECTION, objects can still be deleted from it, and so on.

Handling Dynamic Query Results

The difficult thing about handling result sets from dynamic queries is that once you let end users submit completely ad hoc queries to the ORDBMS, the external program must cope with completely ad hoc results. At runtime, the host language program may not know the number of columns, their data types, or the size of each data object, or how many rows of data there will be.

ESQL/C includes special facilities for handling dynamic queries. Once a query string has been created, there are certain ESQL/C commands that generate a description of it—any run-time variables it requires and the structure of the rows it will return—and place this description into a client-side data structure. This structure can then be used to prepare host language variables to hold query results. This DESCRIPTION facility is described as part of the SQL-92 language standard, and it needs a little modification to handle features such as extensible data types.

Listing 7–16 contains a code extract from a program accompanying this book. This code extract accepts command-line queries and formats their results into a form suitable for efficient conversion to a table layout for presentation in this text.

```
17  EXEC SQL INCLUDE sqltypes;
18  EXEC SQL INCLUDE locator;

  . . .

29  #define ISSQL92TYPE(X) (!((ISCOMPLEXTYPE(X)) || \
30   (ISUDTTYPE(X)) || ISDISTINCTTYPE(X)))
  . . .

37  EXEC SQL BEGIN DECLARE SECTION;
38     loc_t       lcat_descr;
39     loc_t       lpict;
40     integer     nvl;
41     char        * pchDataArray[128];
42  EXEC SQL END DECLARE SECTION;
43
44  long    getrow();
  . . .

48  int main(
```

```
49              int argc,
50              char *argv[]
51  )
52  {
53     long     ret;
54     short    row_number = 0;
55
56     EXEC SQL BEGIN DECLARE SECTION;
57         char    ans[BUFFSZ], db_name[30];
58         char    name[128];
59         char    typename[128];
60         int     sel_col_cnt, i;
61         short   type;
62         int     nVLCharType = SQLLVARCHAR;
63         char  * pchData;
64     EXEC SQL END DECLARE SECTION;
65
66     EXEC SQL WHENEVER SQLERROR CALL SQL_Error_Check;
67
68     if (argc > 2) /* correct no. of args? */
69     {
70         printf("\nUsage: %s [database]\n",
71                 argv[0]);
72         exit(1);
73     }
74
75     if(argc == 2) strcpy(db_name, argv[1]);
76      else strcpy(db_name, "book_test");
77
78     EXEC SQL connect to :db_name;
79
80     while(1)
81     {
82         /* prompt for SELECT statement */
83         printf("\nEnter a SELECT statement for %s ",
84                 db_name);
85         printf("\n\t(e.g. select * from customer;)\n");
86         printf("\tOR a ";" to terminate program:\n>> ");
87
88         if(!getans(ans, BUFFSZ))
89             continue;
90         if ((ans[0]==";") || (strcmp(ans,"quit")== 0))
91         disconnect();
. . .
102        /* prepare statement id */
```

```
103         EXEC SQL PREPARE query_id FROM :ans;
104
105         /* allocate descriptor area */
106         EXEC SQL ALLOCATE DESCRIPTOR "selcat";
107
108         /* Database server describes the statement */
109         EXEC SQL DESCRIBE query_id
110                 USING SQL DESCRIPTOR "selcat";
111         if (SQLCODE != 0)
112         {
113             printf("** Statement is not a SELECT.\n");
114             free_stuff();
115             disconnect();
116         }
117
118         /* Get the number of Columns in the SELECT */
119         EXEC SQL GET DESCRIPTOR "selcat"
120                     :sel_col_cnt = COUNT;
121         printf("Query has %d Columns \n", sel_col_cnt );
122
123         /* declare cursor */
124         EXEC SQL DECLARE query_curs CURSOR
125                 FOR query_id;
126
127         /* open cursor; process select statement */
128         EXEC SQL OPEN query_curs;
129
130         /*
131         ** The following verifies whether types are UDTs.
132         ** If so, modify descriptor to LVARCHAR. If not,
133         ** the default type will suffice.
134         */
135         nvl=0;
136         for(i = 1; i <= sel_col_cnt; i++)
137         {
138             EXEC SQL GET DESCRIPTOR "selcat" VALUE :i
139                         :type = TYPE,
140                         :name = NAME;
141
142             if (!(ISSQL92TYPE(type)))
143             {
144                 /*
145                 ** Set the UDT column to lvarchar.
146                 */
147                 pchData = pchDataArray[nvl];
```

```
148                        if (pchData != 0 ) {
149                            pchData = (char *)malloc(32768);
150                        }
151
152                        EXEC SQL SET DESCRIPTOR "selcat" VALUE :i
153                                    DATA      = :pchData,
154                                    LENGTH    = 32768,    /* 32K */
155                                    TYPE      = :nVLCharType;
156                    nvl++;
157
158                }
159

. . .
183           row_number = 0;
184           while(ret = getrow("selcat"))
185           {
186               if (ret < 0)
187               {
188                   disconnect();
189                   break;
190               }
191               /*
192               ** Display the data returned in each row.
193               */
194               disp_data(row_number, sel_col_cnt, "selcat");
195

. . .
201               row_number++;
202           }
203
204           if (!row_number)
205               printf("** No matching rows found.\n");
206
207           printf("\n\n");
208
209           free_stuff();
210       }
211   }
212   /*
213   **  Get the next row
214   */
215   long
216   getrow(sysdesc)
217   EXEC SQL BEGIN DECLARE SECTION;
218   PARAMETER char * sysdesc;
```

```
219    EXEC SQL END DECLARE SECTION;
220    {
221        long exp_chk();
222        char statement[128];
223        sprintf(statement, "FETCH %s", sysdesc);
224        EXEC SQL FETCH query_curs
225                 USING SQL DESCRIPTOR :sysdesc;
226        return((exp_chk(statement)) == 100 ? 0 : 1);
227    }
```

Listing 7–16. *ESQL/C DESCRIPTOR Mechanism for Handling Dynamic OR-SQL*

Some details about this example: Lines 17 through 20 illustrate how ESQL/C includes C header files provided as part of the client. Because this example needs to deal with all data types that the ORDBMS provides, the facilities for managing things such as DECIMAL and DATETIME values need to be included. Part of these facilities is a set of C macros that can be used to classify a data type coming back from the server. On Line 29, several of these macros are combined into a single facility that determines whether or not a data type is an SQL-92 built-in type or not. Within this program, the approach to handling UDTs in general is to determine when a query will return a UDT and to ensure that the ORDBMS always casts the UDT into its literal string form.

Lines 102 through 128 illustrate how an ad hoc OR-SQL query is processed. Initially, the query string is passed to the ORDBMS, where it is prepared, parsed, and stored there in an internal form. Because this is a dynamic query, however, the external program needs to determine how it will cope with the returned types. Such a description of the query's return types—and any argument types it accepts—can be represented in the external program using a special structure called a DESCRIPTOR. Lines 105 through 116 illustrate how a new DESCRIPTOR structure is allocated and then populated with information about the prepared query.

Using the GET DESCRIPTOR features of ESQL/C, the external program can determine things such as how many columns are in the return result and the types of each column. Blocks of code on Lines 119 through 120 and 138 through 141 illustrate how this is done. When it is determined that the type being returned is not an SQL-92 type (Line 142), the external program can use the SET DESCRIPTOR mechanism to modify the DESCRIPTOR and tell the ORDBMS what data type ought to be returned.

When the external program issues a FETCH instruction over the data in the subroutine on Lines 224 through 225, it does so using this modified DESCRIPTOR. This instructs the ORDBMS to convert the data type, if it can, to the type specified in the DESCRIPTOR.

Unfortunately, there are some things that the ESQL/C interface—and indeed, most of the standard client interfaces—does not handle well. In an ORDBMS, you can write OR-SQL statements that return *jagged row* results, which means that the structure of the rows within a single result set varies when, for example, a subtable has more columns than its parent. However, a DESCRIPTOR structure applies for the whole query result, rather than for result sets that vary row by row.

Error and Exception Handling

Error and exception handling in an ESQL/C program is a mix of standard approaches and vendor-proprietary specifics. Earlier, we mentioned how ESQL/C uses a data structure called the SQLCA to hold messages from the ORDBMS server. When the server encounters an error, it stops whatever query processing it is performing, and it returns an error status to the client program. On the client-side, the ESQL/C facilities place this error status into SQLCA.

Traditionally, accessing the contents of this data structure was the preferred mechanism for detecting errors. Recently the SQL standards community has moved to provide a standard client-side environment for interrogating this structure. The first piece of the environment is a macro called SQLCODE. Under the covers, this macro refers to an element of the SQLCA data structure, and the value of the SQLCODE reflects the current status of the system. Table 7–2 presents the range of the most common values that the IDS product will place in the SQLCODE after an OR-SQL statement or ESQL/C directive is processed.

Table 7–2. SQLCODE Values and Their Interpretation

SQLCODE Value	Interpretation
0	Success. The previous ESQL/C OR-SQL operation completed successfully. If there was some kind of warning or other status associated with the action, this is recorded in another area of the SQLCA area. This is also the result expected after any Data Definition Language (DDL) statement.
100 SQLNOTFOUND	Success, but no result rows. This is the value to expect after Data Manipulation Language (DML) write queries. Again, any warnings associated with the action are placed in another area of SQLCA.
< 0	This indicates that the ORDBMS encountered a runtime error. The nature of the error is recorded elsewhere in the structure.

Good defensive programming practice requires that the code check for ESQL/C errors and exceptions whenever it sends OR-SQL queries to the ORDBMS or receives data from it. Adding these checks clutters the code, however, and makes programming tedious. An alternative to checking every embedded SQL directive is to use an ESQL/C directive to invoke an error handling subroutine or to undertake some action, such as a `goto`, whenever an error or exception occurs. This approach to handling exceptions is realized using WHENEVER, and Line 66 of Listing 7–16 presents one example of this approach. In Listing 7–17 we include two others.

```
EXEC SQL WHENEVER SQLERROR GOTO Label_Clip;

EXEC SQL WHENEVER SQLERROR CALL Function_Name;
```

Listing 7–17. *Automating Error Handling Using ESQL/C Directives*

The first of these instructs the application logic to jump immediately to a C label in the current scope. The second calls a subroutine instead.

Once an error status is encountered, that is, when the value of SQL-CODE is less than zero, the external program should immediately determine what kind of error has been encountered and what action to take as a result. As ESQL/C has evolved, multiple approaches to performing this diagnosis have been developed. In the most primitive of these, you can access the contents of the SQLCA area directly, but this is not recommended because is not portable between DBMS products. Alternatively, there is a set of function calls that extract the information.

In Listing 7–18 we present a subroutine that is used throughout the ESQL/C examples shipped with this book. It illustrates how to check SQLCODE, and how to extract the error message if an error condition is encountered. This subroutine is called after important SQL operations to check status and report errors.

```
  .
101 void
102 SQL_Error_Check (
103         int nWhich
104 )
105 {
106         char szErr[256];
107         if ( SQLCODE < 0 )
108         {
109             rgetlmsg( SQLCODE, szErr, 257 );
110             printf(" ERROR at %d: ErrNo %d \n Err : %s \n",
111                       nWhich, SQLCODE, szErr );
112                 exit(0);
113         }
}
```

Listing 7–18. *Error Handling Subroutine*

Within the IDS product there is a second level of error detection. Sometimes, several different low-level errors share a single SQLCODE to simplify client programming. This lower level error is referred to as the ISAM error code, and relates to the IDS product's interactions with its operating system and hardware. ISAM errors are rarely of concern to application programmers. They inspire panic in database administrators.

Another important utility in ESQL/C is the macro called SQLSTATE. This is a pointer to a five-character string that encodes status information. In contrast, SQLCODE is an integer. Subsets of characters within this string represent different aspects of the state of the client program's relationship with the server. In Listing 7–19 we present the general structure of a SQLSTATE variable.

```
"@ @ # # #"
```

Listing 7–19. *Structure of the SQLSTATE Variable*

The first two characters are referred to as the status *class code*, and the last three characters are called the *sub-class code*. SQLSTATE is reset whenever an SQL-level exchange takes place between the client program and the server. The correct interpretation of the sub-class characters depends on the class-code value. In Table 7–3 we present a list of the common class and sub-class codes—together with their meanings—to illustrate the kinds of information SQLSTATE contains.

Table 7–3. Interpreting the SQLSTATE Variable

SQLSTATE Class Code	Meanings
00	Success.
01	Success with warning. Sub-class code reflects the kind of warning, such as privilege violations, user-defined warnings, and so on.
02	No data found, or end of data. See cursor code examples presented previously in this section of the chapter.
07	Dynamic SQL error, such as a parameter mismatch.
08	Connection-related error, such as connection closed or refused.
22	Data exception, such as a string truncation or numeric value out of range.

Once an error or exception has been detected, ESQL/C provides a standard mechanism to access diagnostic information. On Line 109 in

Listing 7–18, we extract text associated with the error using an ESQL/C functional interface: `rgetlmsg()`. This is specific to the ORDBMS product's client APIs. The more general mechanism uses the GET DIAGNOSTICS ESQL/C operation. Using this facility gives the code access to additional information about the error, and it deal with multiple, overlapping errors on the same DBMS operation.

Communications Layer

All examples in the previous pages illustrate how to embed OR-SQL into the C host programming language. In addition to these programming language details, developers need to decide another question: By what means does the client program communicate with the ORDBMS server? This decision can be deferred until the client software is deployed, because the client program can be written without knowing how its communication with the server is actually being done.

The choice of communication protocol is decided on when the client program and the ORDBMS's client-side facilities are installed. With ESQL/C, there are two alternative techniques, and under certain circumstances, the performance difference can be significant.

Shared Memory Communication

When the external program and ORDBMS are running on the *same* machine, they can use a *shared memory* mechanism to communicate. To achieve this, the ESQL/C client libraries and the ORDBMS agree to share a segment of their process memory. When the external program needs to send a query to the ORDBMS, it writes this query expression into the shared memory segment and sets a flag to indicate to the ORDBMS that there is work to be done. When the ORDBMS returns data or status messages to the external program, it uses a symmetric channel.

Shared memory connections permit data to be exchanged between the IDS engine and client processes with minimal operating system intervention, which improves the bandwidth of the connection. Consequently, on multi-processor server computers, the shared memory provides the highest possible performance. It is, however, sensitive to factors such as the total number of processes running; too many processes, and the query or data exchange might involve the overhead of operating system context switches.

Although it only allows an external program to have a single database connection, shared memory is the preferred communication mechanism when using middleware such as a transaction monitor, which funnels multiple external programs into a single database connection. In situations in which the information system deploys over several machines, an alternative mechanism is necessary.

TCP/IP Communication

Alternatively, the external program can use TCP/IP communication. This means that the external program and the server process use a network protocol and other operating system facilities to support interprocess communication. When a client program starts up, it interrogates its environment for information about the location of the computer where the database server is located. Then it employs an operating system interface to open a connection to the ORDBMS. Queries and data are exchanged between the external program and the ORDBMS through this connection. While intended primarily for communication over a network, the approach is also possible on a single machine.

The advantage of using TCP/IP communication is its generality. It allows a single ORDBMS server to communicate simultaneously with more external programs than can run concurrently a single machine. Client/server information system architectures work in precisely this way: they achieve a degree of computational load balancing over a number of machines.

When client and ORDBMS processes run on separate machines, there is no alternative to TCP/IP communication. For example, when editors and content management employees on the Movies-R-Us site are all using personal computers to run applications that talk to the ORDBMS, which is a typical client/server configuration, socket-based communication is the only viable alternative. Sometimes—such as when using bulk loading facilities—shared memory based communication offers advantages. The decision is usually fairly easy to make.

Embedded OR-SQL and Application Development

Embedding OR-SQL into a host language such as C has been the most common approach to bringing external programs and databases together. The presentation in this section focused on host-language syntax issues, although we have also touched on issues relating to the low-level mechanisms that ESQL/C employs. Developers experienced with ESQL/C will find that their skill set can be reused with an ORDBMS. User-defined types, and particularly OPAQUE TYPE data with their arbitrary structures, present the biggest complication.

With object-relational technology, the balance between those aspects of the information system's functionality that were handled exclusively in the external program using an RDBMS and those that can now be embedded within the ORDBMS, changes. When designing for performance, a central objective is to minimize the volume of data exchanged between the external program and the ORDBMS. Pushing subroutines written in C within the OR-SQL language helps to achieve this.

ESQL/C-style interfaces have the advantage that handling data type exchanges between client and server can be automated. Other approaches—such as ODBC—require that the programmer deal with such issues. ESQL/C suffers from several drawbacks, however. The most obvious one is that the ESQL/C interface is cumbersome for many developers familiar with procedural languages such as C or Java, while it is a more natural fit for languages like COBOL. Other developers writing utilities for these languages tend to design them as libraries of data structures and function calls. Second, there are several problems with the ESQL/C standard. For example, it leaves things such as the definition of SQLDA and SQLCA areas up to the DBMS vendor, and it defines no standard way to perform useful operations such as schema discovery.

Java Database Connectivity (JDBC)

Java is quickly becoming the preferred language for creating external programs in which modern information systems manage user interfaces or provide middleware services. Java's chief virtue is its ubiquity. Code written using the Java language and deployed using Java's byte-code interpreters, or virtual machines, can be created on one machine architecture and then deployed across a potentially limitless variety of others.

Many widely distributed applications use Java "applets" to manage aspects of the client user-interface. An increasing number of systems use *Enterprise Java Beans (EJB)* as a standard mechanism for implementing component logic. Other developers use *Java Servlet Pages (JSP)* technology to create dynamic Web site content. These mechanisms share a need to communicate with the data repository. Achieving this is what the *Java DataBase Connectivity (JDBC)* interface is all about.

Introduction to JDBC

JDBC differs from ESQL/C in that it is a *procedural* interface. Instead of a precompiler and two-step compilation, JDBC consists of a set of classes and templates whose methods are invoked directly from the host language logic. At runtime, JDBC permits an external program to create a connection to the ORDBMS and to send OR-SQL statements to a database. It also provides a much more general mechanism than SQLDA for working with the data results that a query produces.

JDBC is defined in a manner consistent with other Java library packages: `java.lang`, `java.awt`, or `java.util`. It is a standardized interface, meaning that vendors supporting the Java language have come together and agreed on a document that describes what they should all do. The term *driver* is used to refer to a specific implementation of JDBC, which works against a specific DBMS.[2] The interface is found in the Java class hierarchy under `java.sql`. Line 11 in Listing 7–20 illustrates how it is included in a Java program.

On the plus side, the JDBC standard is considerably ahead of other APIs in its support for ORDBMS features. User-defined types, such as `OPAQUE TYPE` and `DISTINCT TYPE` instances, can be readily mapped into semantically equivalent Java classes. In fact, because of the way the ORDBMS supports the related SQL-J standard (see Tutorial 4), the same Java code can be used to implement an object's behavior both within the database environment and in external programs.

JDBC is also special in one other regard. As we show in Figure 7–5 JDBC is the only standard OR-SQL interface that works both within the ORDBMS—database stored procedures can be written in Java and use JDBC—and in external programs[3]. Here the same Java class library is shown embedded within the ORDBMS, a mid-tier program, and within a client program implementing a user-interface.

Deploying a single Java class across multiple tiers is be a good idea when, for example, the amount of data used in the class's constructor method is much larger than the state information the Java class maintains about itself. Once constructed, the object's state can be moved out of the database and into another tier for better response time.

---

[2] In practice, as with all standards, interpretations of what the words in the document actually mean differ in the details. All standard drivers include all standard calls. It's just that what these calls actually do can be a bit different between drivers.

[3] Most of the Server or DataBlade API (SAPI) can also be used in an external C or C++ program, but SAPI is definitely not a standard interface.

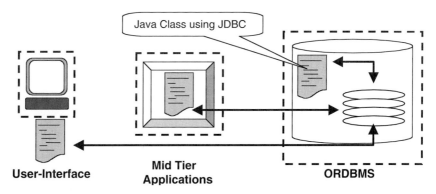

Figure 7–5. Java Class Deployed in Multiple Tiers Showing JDBC
Connectivity

User-Interface   Mid Tier
                  Applications   ORDBMS

Types of JDBC Interface

In a previous section, we discussed the difference between shared memory and network-based communications for ESQL/C. The JDBC standard describes several low-level mechanisms intended to reflect the
variety of environments into which Java applications are deployed. As
with ESQL/C, these differences are not apparent to programmers using
the interface; they are a matter for deployment. Table 7–4 describes
these mechanisms.

Table 7–4. Classifications of JDBC-Driver Implementations

Type of JDBC Driver	Description
Type 1	JDBC calls are turned into "native" ODBC calls. This implies that Java applications using a JDBC Type 1 driver must be deployed with an appropriate ODBC driver. Second, using this type of driver makes it difficult to write a truly "write-once-run-anywhere" application.
Type 2	It is similar to a Type 1 driver, but instead of an ODBC layer between JDBC and the DBMS, the Type 2 driver uses a proprietary API. This kind of driver is designed to operate with higher performance, but experience has shown that the differences are marginal, and it still has all the limitations of a Type 1 implementation.
Type 3	Instead of a direct connection to the DBMS, this kind of driver employs a mid-tier process, which can use any mechanism it likes. This overcomes the deployment problems associated with the Type 1 and Type 2 drivers, but creating an entirely new process layer imposes its own problems.

(continued)

Table 7-4. Classifications of JDBC-Driver Implementations (continued)

Type of JDBC Driver	Description
Type 4	Network communication between a DBMS and an external program involves sending packets of byte data back and forth between the two processes. The Java language is perfectly capable of picking apart byte-level messages, and it can replace the entire set of compiled client libraries making up ESQL/C. This is the insight that guides the development of Type 4 drivers. These use whatever low-level communication is deemed necessary between the external program and the DBMS, but they are implemented in pure Java. This overcomes the deployment problems implied by Type 1, 2, and 3 drivers.

Today, the vast majority of JDBC implementations are in the Type 4 category. Ultimately, in spite of the performance tax Type 4 drivers pay, this mechanism looks likely to become the dominant communication mode for JDBC. It is the simplest to administer and frequently represents the only technically feasible alternative for widely distributed user communities employing diverse client hardware.

Should the application logic use multiple drivers to connect, for example, to several different DBMSs, it is possible to specify which one to load using the Java language facilities for loading class libraries. In Listing 7–20 we present the first part of a simple Java program for connecting to an ORDBMS and issuing a query against it.

```
11   import java.sql.*;
12   import java.util.*;
13
14   public class ConnBasic {
15
16   static String default_url =
17     "jdbc:informix-sqli://host:port/dbnam:INFORMIXSERVER=snam";
18
19      public static void main(String[] args)
20      {
21         String url;
22         if (args.length == 0)
23         {
24            url = default_url;
25         } else
```

```
26          {
27              url = args[0];
28          }
29
30          Connection conn = null;
31          System.out.println("Connect \"" + url + "\"");
32
33          /*
34          ** Load the JDBC Class Driver
35          */
36          try
37          {
38              Class.forName("com.informix.jdbc.IfxDriver");
39          }
40          catch (Exception e)
41          {
42              System.out.println("Failed load JDBC driver.");
43          }
```

Listing 7-20. *Loading a JDBC Driver*

This code illustrates several aspects of JDBC programming. Much of it is discussed in detail in the next subsection.

Within this example, Lines 36 through 43 illustrate how a Java program loads a particular driver instance; in this case, it is the INFORMIX Type 4 JDBC implementation. Making this work smoothly requires that the CLASSPATH environment variable in the external program's environment be configured correctly. It must include a reference to the location where the JDBC implementation is to be found (the ifxjdbc.jar file).

Note also the extensive use of the Java language's exception handling features in this code. Errors in a JDBC driver method generate a java.sql.SQLException, rather than set some globally accessible exception state. Should any of the JDBC methods fail with an error, details about the error can be extracted using standard exception management features of the Java language.

JDBC Connections

The design semantics of JDBC are heavily influenced by WWW protocols. Instead of connecting to a named machine and service, JDBC uses a *Universal Resource Locator (URL)* to locate the target ORDBMS server and database. This is motivated by the fact that Java classes can be deployed as applets in client Web browsers where the Java class logic may be initiated with little environment information. URLs and JDBC permit the applet to connect reliably with a known server.

Lines 16 and 17 of Listing 7–20 illustrate the basic format of the JDBC connection URL. A complete specification for this string is long and rather complex. At a minimum, the URL specifies the name— machine name or IP address—of the computer on which the ORDBMS server runs and a socket number on which the ORDBMS is listening for remote connections.

In the example, we also include a proprietary "name=value" addition to the basic URL to specify the target ORDBMS server instance. This non-standard aspect of the API is driver-specific. Other application information, such as the user name and password, the connection information, and many IDS environment variables can be supplied with the URL in this manner.

In Listing 7–21 we present the remainder of the sample program introduced in Listing 7–20.

```
44
45          /*
46          ** Try to connect using the url
47          */
48          try
49          {
50              conn = DriverManager.getConnection(url);
51          }
52          catch (SQLException e)
53          {
54              System.out.println("Failed to connect");
55          }
56
57          String cmd = "SELECT COUNT(*) FROM Movies";
58
59          try {
60              /*
61              ** Create a Statement object to manage this
62              ** query"s interactions with the ORDBMS.
63              */
64              Statement BasicSelect = conn.createStatement();
65
66              /*
67              ** Execute the supplied query.
68              */
```

```
69              ResultSet BasicResult =
70                          BasicSelect.executeQuery(cmd);
71
72          while(BasicResult.next())
73          {
74              int val = BasicResult.getInt(1);
75              System.out.println(" Got [" + val + "]");
76          }
77
78      } catch (SQLException e)
79      {
80          System.out.println("No on query!");
81      }
82
83      try
84      {
85          conn.close();
86      }
87      catch (SQLException e)
88      {
89          System.out.println("Close connection Failed");
90      }
91    }
92  }
```

Listing 7–21. *Connecting with JDBC and a Simple Query*

On Lines 50 through 55, the code creates a `java.sql.Connection` object, using the URL and the `java.sql.DriverManager` class. Within the JDBC driver implementation, the URL is picked apart and used to open a stateful session within the target ORDBMS; that is, each concurrent user employing JDBC has a block of private memory and a user-level thread allocated for them by IDS. To minimize the overhead of such a stateful connection, the JDBC interface employs a technique called connection pooling, in which several connections in the external program share a physical resource, such as a socket.

A considerable amount of information about the database on the other end of the connection and on the connection itself can be obtained using the interface methods that are part of the class. For example, a transaction mode—READ UNCOMMITTED, READ COMMITTED, REPEATABLE READ, and SERIALIZABLE—is associated with each connection. It can be read and modified using the `getTransactionIsolation()` and `set-TransactionIsolation()` methods.

Information about the state of the connection—autocommit on or off, whether the connection object is open or closed, and commands to perform operations such as beginning, committing, and rolling back transactions—are supported by other method calls on the `java.sql.Connection` class.

JDBC Queries

The principle use of the `java.sql.Connection` class is as a reference point for handling a sequence of OR-SQL statements. In this subsection we review the JDBC classes used to manage OR-SQL within Java host language code, how to bind variables to those statements when they are executed, and how to handle dynamic OR-SQL result sets.

Queries in JDBC are not embedded within the procedural logic in the same manner as they are in ESQL/C. Instead, the query is represented using a `java.lang.String` variable, and JDBC includes a set of object classes that do their work using these strings. What JDBC shares with ESQL/C are the modes in which it works with query statements.

- A query string whose structure is known to the Java programmer can be sent verbatim to the ORDBMS and executed immediately.
- The query is prepared at some point in time and its execution is deferred until later, when, for example, the values of some variables become know.
- A query string created at runtime is subjected to dynamic query management.

One feature that distinguishes JDBC from ESQL/C is the way that JDBC makes a distinction between SELECT and EXECUTE FUNCTION OR-SQL expressions, which return data to the external program, and write queries and DDL statements, which do not. The JDBC classes allow the use of a query string to construct an object that implements the `java.sql.Statement` interface, or one of its subclasses, by calling a constructor method that is part of the `java.sql.Connection` object. Then, depending on the statement type, the Java programmer uses a different method of the `Statement` object to execute the query. Read query methods return a `java.sql.ResultSet` object, while all others simply return a status.

In cases where the program does not know what kind of query is involved—for example, when the query is typed into a query editor or generated—another generic method on `java.sql.Statement` can be used. We describe each of these in turn.

Handling SELECT Queries using JDBC

Lines 57 through 70 of Listing 7–21 illustrate the simplest technique for executing a SELECT query. Using the `Connection.createStatement()` method on Line 64, JDBC creates an object implementing the `Statement` interface. The `statement` class is generic; it can be used for either SELECT queries or write statements. A sequence of `Statement` objects can be created from a single `Connection`, with all of them adhering to the transactional properties of the "parent" connection. If the CONNECTION object has an active (open) transaction at the time that the `Statement` object is created, then the `Statement` becomes part of that transaction.

Executing the SELECT query using `java.sql.Statement.executeQuery()` creates a `java.sql.ResultData` object. Return results from the ORDBMS are retrieved using method calls over this object. Lines 72 through 76 illustrate the simplest possible way that this class is used. In the next section, where we review how JDBC handles return results, we explore the properties of the `ResultData` class in more detail.

Handling INSERT, UPDATE and DELETE Statements and DDL

Write queries and DDL statements are handled somewhat differently from SELECT queries and FUNCTION execution. In Listing 7–22 we present an alternative ending to the program started in Listing 7–20. Instead of a SELECT query, this second example performs an UPDATE.

```
57
58    String cmd = "UPDATE Merchandise SET Price = Price -
      Currency("USD",5) WHERE Id = 104";
59
60    System.out.println("Query ->\n " + cmd);
61
62    try {
63        /*
64        ** Create a Statement object to manage this
65        ** query"s interactions with the ORDBMS.
66        */
67        Statement BasicStatement = conn.createStatement();
```

```
68
69      /*
70      ** Execute the supplied query.
71      */
72      int nRC = BasicStatement.executeUpdate(cmd);
73
74      switch ( nRC )
75      {
76          case 1:
77              System.out.println(" Changed 1 row.");
78          break;
79          default:
80              System.out.println("Changed " +nRC +" rows.");
81          break;
82      }
83
84      } catch (SQLException e)
85      {
86          System.out.println("Query Failed!");
87      }
```

Listing 7–22. *Executing a Write OR-SQL Statement*

On Line 72 of Listing 7–22 the UPDATE statement is executed using
the appropriate method of the JDBC class used to handle such queries:
Statement.executeUpdate(). In contrast to Statement.execute-
Query(), which returns a handle to a set of results, executeUpdate()
returns an integer that reflects the number of rows affected by the statement. Other write queries—DELETE and INSERT—work in a similar way,
as do DDL statements that create schema objects like tables, views, types
and functions.

In Figure 7–6 we present a schematic overview of the basic
sequence of objects and calls necessary to organize the execution of
OR-SQL queries using the set of object classes and interfaces that
make up the bulk of JDBC. Although this is by no means a complete
representation of JDBC, the classes and methods in this figure are the
most commonly used parts of the interface.

Handling Unknown Query Expressions

If, at the time the Java client code is being written, the programmers
do not know whether they are dealing with a read query or a write
query, JDBC provides another combination of interface calls. Code in

Listing 7–23 illustrates how this interface is used. In order to improve the readability of this source, the relationship between line numbers and lines of code has been distorted a little.

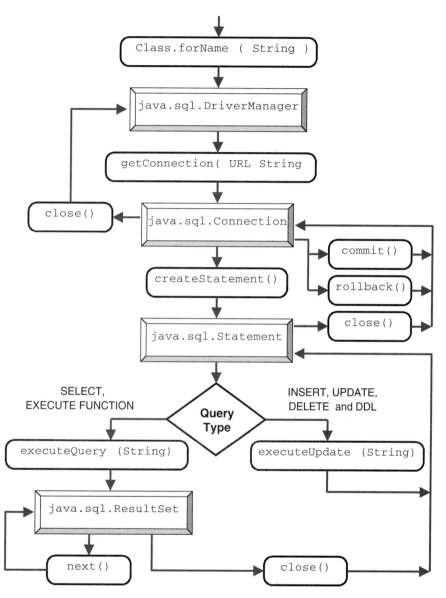

Figure 7–6. *Basic JDBC Connections and Query Handling Classes and Methods*

```
 57   Vector Queries = new Vector(3);
Queries.addElement( new String(
        "SELECT I.Movie, I.Id
           FROM Merchandise I, Movies M
          WHERE M.Title = "Casablanca"
            AND M.Id = I.Movie"));
Queries.addElement( new String(
        "UPDATE Merchandise
            SET Price = Price - Currency("USD",5)
          WHERE Id = 104"));
 60
 61   try
 62   {
 63
 64       Statement BasicStatement = conn.createStatement();
 65
 66       for(int i = 0;i < Queries.size(); i++)
 67       {
 68
 69           String cmd = (String) Queries.elementAt(i);
 70           System.out.println("Query ->\n " + cmd);
 71
 72           try {
 73
 74               if ( BasicStatement.execute(cmd) )
 75               {
 76               /*
 77               ** If this returns a "t", then the query was
 78               ** SELECT or EXECUTE FUNCTION and there is a
 79               ** ResultSet to process.
 80               */
 81                   ResultSet BasicResult =
 82                           BasicStatement.getResultSet();
 83
 84                   while(BasicResult.next())
 85                   {
 86                       int mid  = BasicResult.getInt(1);
 87                       int item = BasicResult.getInt(2);
 88           System.out.println("Movie " +mid+ " Item " +item);
 89                   }
 90
 91               } else
 92               {
 93               /*
 94               ** WRITE query. So all that can be done
 95               ** is to get the count of updated rows.
```

```
96                    */
97                            int nRC = BasicStatement.getUpdateCount();
98                            switch ( nRC )
99                            {
100                              case 1:
101                                  System.out.println("1 row.");
102                                break;
103                              default:
104                                  System.out.println(nRC + " rows.");
105                                break;
106                            }
107                        }
108           } catch ( SQLException e )
109             {
110                   System.out.println(" No on Query " + cmd );
111             }
112         }
113   } catch ( SQLException e )
114   {
115       System.out.println(" No on Statement ");
116   }
```

Listing 7–23. *Using java.sql.Statement.execute() when Query Type is Unknown*

This example introduces another `java.sql.Statement` method called `execute()`, which is the appropriate mechanism to use when the query type is unknown (for example, when it is typed in by an SQL savvy user, or generated by another tool). On Line 74, where it is invoked, this method is shown returning its `boolean` result. When this is "true," it means that the query produced a *result set*. On Lines 81 through 90, the example shows how to get a `java.sql.Result-Data` object and then iterate over it to extract data. If the result of `execute()`is "false," it indicates that the statement did not produce any results. Lines 97 through 107 illustrate an alternative way to extract the number of rows affected by such a query.

Some readers may be wondering which of the two approaches illustrated in Listings 7-21 and 7-22, or in Listing 7–23, is best. There is a considerable degree of overlap between the first approach, where the query type is known, and the second, where it is not. Further, there does not appear to be anything that can be accomplished in one but not the other. In practice, the differences are marginal. Some optimization is possible in the driver if it knows the query type, and slightly less code is needed when the external logic knows that it is dealing with a SELECT instead of an UPDATE. Lacking a perfect memory, the author generally uses the second approach. Smaller interfaces require fewer brain cells.

Handling Prepared Queries

Applications written in Java can derive the same performance benefits as ESQL/C programs by preparing their OR-SQL statements before executing them. JDBC permits a query string to be sent to the IDS product, where it is parsed and stored in an internal format. Then, when the query is to be executed, the Java client supplies literal values for any unknowns in the original expression. Preparing queries provides for more rapid execution than is possible if the entire query statement crosses the wire each time it is executed.

Prepared queries are handled using the `java.sql.Prepared-Statement` class, which implements the `java.sql.Statement` interface (see previous subsection). Over the next few pages, we present an example to illustrate how prepared statements may be used. This example is a little unusual. It employs a database table to store query strings and to load them into an external Java program, which is where they are executed. With the exception of the query that retrieves the query strings from the database this program contains no OR-SQL.

Listing 7–24 illustrates what the table storing the queries looks like and how its queries are formatted. Note the use of the "?" symbol, which indicates that a run-time variable must be substituted in this location.

```
CREATE TABLE Queries (
        Id                  SERIAL          PRIMARY KEY,
        Class               Class_Name      NOT NULL,
        Arg_Count           Quantity        NOT NULL,
        Desc                LVARCHAR        NOT NULL,
        Query               Query_String    NOT NULL
);
—
INSERT INTO Queries ( Class, Arg_Count, Desc, Query )
VALUES
("Employee", 2, "UPDATE_SALARY",
"UPDATE Employees SET Salary = Currency(?,""USD"")\
 WHERE Id = ?");
—
INSERT INTO Queries ( Class, Arg_Count, Desc, Query )
VALUES
("Employee", 1, "GET_EMPLOYEE",
"SELECT Print(Name), DOB, Print(Salary)\
   FROM Employees WHERE Id = ?");
```

Listing 7–24. *OR-SQL Table to Hold*

Before the query strings in this table can be used, we need to develop a new Java class to overcome a significant deficiency in JDBC. As it is currently written, the standard provides no mechanism for determining how many *arguments* a prepared query requires. For simplicity, we simply store this value in the `Queries.Arg_Count` column in Listing 7–24, although in practice it is more likely to be determined at runtime. In Listing 7–25 we present the most important code in this Java class.

```
1   /*
2   **    File:    PrepStmtwArgCnt.java
. . .
13  **      As currently defined, JDBC 2.0 does not
14  **      provide information about the number
15  **      of args in a prepared statement. This
16  **      requires that the number be stored in the
17  **      table along with the query.
18  **/
19  import java.sql.*;
20  import java.lang.String;
21
22  public class PrepStmtwArgCnt
23  {
24      private int                 nArgCount;
25      private PreparedStatement   jinPrepStatement;
26      private String              strQueryString;
27
28      public PrepStmtwArgCnt (
29                              Connection   conn,
30                              String       strQuery,
31                              int          nArgCnt        )
32      throws SQLException
33      {
34          this.strQueryString    = strQuery;
35          this.jinPrepStatement =
36                  conn.prepareStatement( strQuery );
37          this.nArgCount         = nArgCnt;
38      }
39
. . .    getElement() methods for all attributes.
}
```

Listing 7–25. *Class Using* `PreparedStatement`

Lines 35 and 36 illustrate how a query string is prepared. As with the ESQL/C interface, the resulting prepared query must be associated with an active ORDBMS `java.sql.Connection` object. This method returns an object that contains the same information found in the `java.sql.Statement` interface. Other methods in the `java.sql.PreparedStatement` permit the code to set the values of runtime variables before executing the query.

The first thing that the program must accomplish is to load the query strings from the `Queries` table. Achieving this involves revisiting material covered earlier in this section. Listing 7–26 repeats much of Listing 7–21. Lines 138 through 143 create and execute an OR-SQL `SELECT` to retrieve queries from the table introduced in Listing 7–24. Then the loop between Line 144 and 154 iterates over the `java.sql.Result-Set`, populating a vector of prepared query expressions as it does so.

```
14
15   public class PrepQuery
16

. . .

19      private static Vector vecQueries = new Vector(10);
20      private static Connection conn = null;

. . .

132     private static void LoadQueries()
133     {
134        PrepStmtwArgCnt strPrepQ;
135        Statement ST;
136        ResultSet RS;
137
138        try {
139           ST = conn.createStatement();
140           RS = ST.executeQuery(
141              "SELECT Q.Arg_Count, Q.Query " +
142              "  FROM Queries Q " +
143              " WHERE Q.Class = "Employee"" );
144           while(RS.next())
145           {
146              int    nArgCnt  = RS.getInt(1);
147              String strQuery = RS.getString(2);
148
149              strPrepQ = new PrepStmtwArgCnt(conn,
150                                                 strQuery,
151                                                 nArgCnt);
152
153              vecQueries.addElement( strPrepQ );
154           }
```

```
155
156            RS.close();
157
158         } catch (SQLException e )
159         {
160            e.printStackTrace();
161         }
162    }
```

Listing 7–26. SELECT Queries from ORDBMS Table for Use in Java Class

Once all queries from the Queries table have been loaded and prepared, the program can begin to work with them. Before a prepared
query can be executed, any runtime variables it includes must have
real values substituted for them. This is achieved using a series of
methods with the following signature:

```
java.sql.PreparedStatement.setXXX ( int param, Object var );
```

The XXX is a placeholder for the name of a Java class string, INT or
Object.

JDBC provides standard methods for all SQL-92 types. Each call sets
the parameter at offset "param" in the prepared statement object to
value "var." All parameters must have values before the query can be
executed, and the value of all parameters can be cleared with a single
call, as we see at Line 69 in Listing 7–27.

In Listing 7–27 we present the outline of a generic Java dispatch
method that organizes the execution of one of the prepared queries
indexed by the first argument. It takes two arguments: an index to
indicate which prepared query to execute and a Java vector of Object
values to use as arguments. The need for the PrepStmtwArgCnt class
becomes apparent at this point: there is no standard JDBC means of
determining how many parameters a java.sql.PreparedStatement
object requires.

```
54    private static void execIt ( int i, Vector vecArgs )
55    {
56       int j;
57       String strOutLine = "";
58
59       PrepStmtwArgCnt pStmt =
60             (PrepStmtwArgCnt)vecQueries.elementAt(i);
61
62       PreparedStatement cmd=pStmt.getPreparedStatement();
63       /*
64       ** For each element in the Vector, set the
```

```
65      ** parameter in the PreparedStatement.
66      **/
67      try {
68
69         cmd.clearParameters();
70         for(j=0;j < pStmt.getArgCount(); j++)
71         {
72            cmd.setString((j+1),
73                          vecArgs.elementAt(j).toString());
74         }
75
76      } catch ( SQLException e )
77      {
78         e.printStackTrace();
79      }
80
81      try
82      {
83         if ( cmd.execute() )
84         {
85            /*
86            ** If this returns a "t," the query was a
87            ** SELECT or EXECUTE FUNCTION and there is a
88            ** ResultSet to process.
89            */
. . .
. . .    See Listing 7-28
. . .
116        } else
117        {
118           /*
119           ** Query was WRITE. All that can be done
120           ** is to get the count of updated rows.
121           */
.. ..
132        }
133     } catch ( SQLException e )
134     {
135        System.out.println(" No on Query " +
136                           pStmt.getQueryString());
137        e.printStackTrace();
138     }
}
```

Listing 7–27. *Generic Dispatch Method over a Vector of Prepared OR-SQL Statements*

Lines 69 through 74 are the most important part of this example. It illustrates how to set parameters in a prepared query expression. Before setting the parameter values, the code calls the `Prepared-Statement.clearParameters()` method on Line 69, which has the effect of clearing out any variables that had previously been assigned to the query. Then on Lines 72 and 73, the values of data objects stored in the argument vector are substituted into the prepared query. As with ESQL/C, the client interface knows enough to be able to pull these strings into the server for further processing when, for example, the type in the server is an `OPAQUE TYPE`.

Methods to set values of runtime parameters do not care about whether the statement is a read or write query. Later, when we examine how JDBC addresses questions of managing the exchange of data between the Java client and the database, we revisit this topic.

The purpose of this example is to illustrate techniques for handling prepared query statements in a Java program using JDBC. It illustrates how query strings can be retrieved from an ORDBMS and prepared using JDBC some time before variables are assigned to their parameters and the query is actually executed.

Recent editions of the JDBC standard have built upon this basic framework. In JDBC 2.0, it is possible to create a "batch" of queries that are forwarded to the server as a bundle. This reduces the number of round trips between the ORDBMS and the external program. In addition, there exists in the INFORMIX implementation of JDBC a set of extensions that cater to the product's unique capabilities: the `CURSOR STABILITY` isolation level.

Managing Result Data

Handling data exchange between the ORDBMS and an external Java program is slightly simpler with JDBC than it is using ESQL/C. The JDBC standards committee recognized, largely because of overlapping work on the SQL-J standard (see Tutorial 4), that Java objects were finding their way into database tables and query languages. They went to considerable lengths to provide standard mechanisms for determining what the structure of result data should look like and how they should be treated in the client program.

In this section we review these facilities.

ResultSet and ResultSetMetaData Classes

Take another look at Lines 76 through 91 of Listing 7–23. This code iterates over the contents of a `java.sql.ResultSet` object, extracting the data from within it. `java.sql.ResultSet` is a JDBC standard interface for representing the results of a query, and it brings rows to the client "on demand," rather than all at once. Each time the `ResultSet.getNext()` method is called, the interface steps to the "next" row.

If the structure of rows being returned from the ORDBMS—their data types and the order of the columns—is known at the time the Java program is being written, elements within the row can be extracted and placed into external program variables. This is achieved using a set of method calls with the following pattern:

```
Object resObj = java.sql.ResultSet.getXXX(int col_num );

Object resObj = java.sql.ResultSet.getXXX(String col_name );
```

As with the similar `java.sql.PreparedStatement` method calls for setting parameter values, one such method exists for each of the SQL-92 types. These either map column data values to a corresponding Java built-in type—`int`, `char`, `float`—or to a standard library type—`java.lang.String`. In addition, JDBC includes a small set of Java classes for handling SQL-92 types that have no Java equivalent, such as temporal types `java.sql.Timestamp` and `java.sql.Interval`.

For example, look at the code between Lines 140 and 152 of Listing 7–26. This query returns a `java.sql.ResultSet` interface, and each row within it contains an integer and a `java.lang.String`. Successive calls on Lines 146 and 147 extract this data and place it into local variables. This is the simplest mechanism for handling return results. When the external program is dealing with static OR-SQL queries, it is the best approach to follow.

What happens, however, when the query's result format is unknown at compile time? This can occur when the query is constructed by the external program, or perhaps when the data type of a column in a table was changed! JDBC provides another interface, called `java.sql.ResultSetMetaData`, that can be used to determine all the information an external program will ever need about the contents of a `java.sql.ResultSet`. In Listing 7–28 we illustrate how this is used. Note that the code here fills in Listing 7–27 between Lines 89 and 115.

```
90          ResultSet QR              = cmd.getResultSet();
91          ResultSetMetaData MD = QR.getMetaData();
92          int cols = MD.getColumnCount();
93
94          for( j = 1; j <= cols; j++ )
95          {
96              strOutLine = strOutLine + "| " +
97                              MD.getColumnLabel(j) + "::" +
98                              MD.getColumnTypeName(j);
99          }
100         strOutLine += "|";
101         System.out.println( strOutLine );
102         strOutLine = "";
103
104         while(QR.next())
105         {
106             for(j = 1; j <= cols; j++ )
107             {
108                 Object obResData = QR.getObject(j);
109                 strOutLine = strOutLine + "| " +
110                                 obResData.toString();
111             }
112             strOutLine += "|";
113             System.out.println( strOutLine );
114         }
        strOutLine = "";
```

Listing 7–28. *Using* `java.sql.ResultSetMetaData` *to Work with* `ResultSet` *Data*

On Line 91, this code creates a new instance of the `java.sql.`
`ResultSetMetaData` interface using the return results of whatever
query was just executed. `ResultSetMetaData` includes many methods that can be used to get information about the entire result set—
how many columns and which columns are nulls—and information
about individual columns within it: database table name, column
name, column type, and so on. Between Lines 92 and 99, the code
figures out how many columns the return result has and the name
and JDBC type of each column. The code in Listing 7–28 can then
format a header for the column results that are printed on Lines 104
through 114.

The metadata management interfaces of JDBC are intended primarily
to support generalized access to the database. For example, report writer
programs always use them, as do software tools for generating entire

Java components that relate database schema structures to conceptual object definitions. OR-SQL's flexibility means that these interfaces are more important to mainstream Java developers than the SQLDA facilities were in ESQL/C. To avoid runtime errors, such as when an administrative change in the database alters the return type of a UDF, it is a good idea to always check query return types.

JDBC Type Handling

Our examples so far have all dealt with SQL-92 database types, each of which has a Java language equivalent. Java programs using JDBC can get a long way with this kind of approach. User-defined types in an object-relational database use strings or numbers as literal values for constructor functions, and OR-SQL queries can CAST between the built-in and user-defined types. Returning query result data as a string, however, is not always a good option. It means, for example, that code in the Java client must determine what the desired Java class is and how to transform the string or number into an instance of that class.

To help, JDBC provides an enumerated class called java.sql.Types to represent the variety of data types an OR-SQL query can return. Each of the types defined in the XOPEN standard—and by implication, SQL-92—is identified using a unique integer value. java.sql.Types (java.sql.IfxTypes with the JDK 1.1.8 driver) also provides a set of methods for manipulating data type information to get, for example, a type name string. The code in Listing 7–29 illustrates how JDBC supports extracting information about a query result set.

```
169     ResultSet QR          = cmd.getResultSet();
170     ResultSetMetaData MD = QR.getMetaData();
171     int cols              = MD.getColumnCount();
172
173     for( j = 1; j <= cols; j++ )
174     {
175         strOutLine =
176             strOutLine + "| " +
177         MD.getColumnLabel(j) + "::" +
178         MD.getColumnTypeName(j) + "::" +
179         MD.getColumnType(j) + ::" +
180         Types.JDBCTypeToName(MD.getColumnType(j));
181     }
```

Listing 7–29. *Extracting the Column Data Type*

In Listing 7–29, the code on Line 178 retrieves the OR-SQL data type identifier (the 128 byte OR-SQL *name*) of the return result: INTEGER, VARCHAR, ST_POINT or VIDEO. On Lines 179 and 180, the code retrieves the JDBC type identifier (which is an instance of the java.sql.Types class) and its public name. In Table 7–5 we reproduce a list of the valid JDBC type identifiers.

Table 7–5. Valid JDBC Types Standardized in java.sql.Types			
BIGINT	BINARY	BIT	CHAR
DATE	DECIMAL	DOUBLE	FLOAT
INTEGER	LONGVARBINARY	LONGVARCHAR	NULL
NUMERIC	OTHER	REAL	SMALLINT
TIME	TIMESTAMP	TINYINT	VARBINARY
VARCHAR	JAVA_OBJECT	DISTINCT	STRUCT
ARRAY	BLOB	CLOB	REF

This list is the union of all DBMS vendors' individual built-in type mechanisms. Those types shown in gray are newly standardized in JDBC. They correspond to the new kinds of data types introduced in the SQL-3 query language standard.

Mapping Types to Java Classes

What happens when the OR-SQL return type is user-defined? As you can tell from Table 7–5, the standards committee anticipated this in their design, and JDBC provides a powerful mechanism for dealing with such situations. In fact, the JDBC approach to handling the exchange of typed data between the ORDBMS and Java can appear almost seamless.

In Tutorial 4, we saw two ways in which a Java class can be used to implement a UDT. These mechanisms—using the OPAQUE TYPE and the DISTINCT TYPE—rely on another Java standard, which is called SQL-J. Although data is still stored by the ORDBMS as a byte array, the SQL-J standard defines the SQL Data mechanism by which these byte arrays can be used to construct Java objects.

JDBC reuses SQL Data. It automatically converts data from ORDBMS formats into the correct Java object format on the client side before returning them through the ResultsSet.getObject() call. In addition to OPAQUE TYPE and DISTINCT TYPE instances supported within the ORDBMS, JDBC uses a similar technique to convert ROW TYPE instances into Java classes. These client-side Java classes need to implement the Java.sql.SQL Data interface. When an OR-SQL query's results are returned through JDBL, the driver calls the appropriate interfaces in the Java class to transform database data into a Java object.

In the external Java program, a special *type map* is maintained with each connection. This object, which is an instance of the JDK 2.0 `java.util.Map` class, is a hash table that relates OR-SQL database types and Java classes in the client program.

In Listing 7–30, we present an example that illustrates how the `java.util.Map` is used.

```
101    private static void setTypeMap( Connection conn )
102    {
103        Map tmJava_Test;
104
105        try
106        {
107            tmJava_Test = conn.getTypeMap();
108
109            if (tmJava_Test == null)
110            {
111                throw new SQLException (
112                    " Type map is NULL");
113            }
114
115            tmJava_Test.put("physicalquantity",
116                            Class.forName("Length"));
117            tmJava_Test.put("personname",
118                            Class.forName("PersonName"));
119            tmJava_Test.put("mycurrency",
120                            Class.forName("myCurrency"));
121            tmJava_Test.put("name_value",
122                            Class.forName("NameValue"));
123        }
124        catch (ClassNotFoundException e)
125        {
126            e.printStackTrace();
127        }
128        catch (SQLException e)
129        {
130            System.out.println("\nERROR: "+ e.getErrorCode()
131                              + " " + e.getMessage());
132            e.printStackTrace();
133        }
134
135    }
```

Listing 7–30. *Creating and Populating a JDBC Type Map*

setTypeMap () would be called after the `java.sql.Connection` object has been created. On Line 107, a connection is used to create a type mapping structure. Initially, the map can be assumed to be empty.

Lines 115 through 122 provide the actual mapping between the OR-SQL types and the Java classes. They instruct the JDBC interface that the OR-SQL types known as "physicalquantity," "personname," "`mycurrency`," and "name_value," when retrieved through a `Result-Set.getObject()` call, are to be turned into instances of the Length, PersonName, myCurrency, and NameValue Java classes, respectively.[4] Over the next few pages, we will see how these classes are implemented.

OPAQUE TYPE and DISTINCT TYPE Values

Consider OR-SQL schema and query in Listing 7–31. Notice that this table includes columns that use the extended types for which a mapping was defined in Listing 7–30.

```
—
CREATE TABLE Subjects   (
        Id              SERIAL          PRIMARY KEY,
        Name            PersonName      NOT NULL,
        Salary          MyCurrency      NOT NULL,
        DOB             DATE            NOT NULL,
        Size            PhysicalQuantity NOT NULL,
        Report          Name_Value      NOT NULL,
        Conditions      SET( FLOAT NOT NULL ),
        Program         BLOB            NOT NULL
);
—
— SELECT S.DOB, S.Size, S.Name
—    FROM Subjects S
—  WHERE S.Name = PersonName(?,?)
—
```

Listing 7–31. *OR-SQL Schema and Query Illustrating the Type Map*

When the query is executed using the code shown in Listing 7–28, the JDBC interface on Line 108 will attempt to turn the data it received from the ORDBMS into the appropriate Java class. It uses the mapping

---

[4] Note that the Length and PersonName Java Classes are both implemented as part of Tutorial 4.

from Listing 7–30 to determine which Java class is the right one for each column, and therefore, which `readSQL()` implementation to call. In `PreparedStatement.setObject()` calls, JDBC will invoke the `writeSQL()` method of the object being sent to the server to turn the object back into the byte array.

This mechanism is very flexible. Although not supported directly, it is feasible to construct the type mapping by using the information stored within the object-relational database's system catalogs that map Java classes to UDTs. Furthermore, it is possible to overload the default Java class loader mechanism to extract class files from within the database, in addition to the file system and over the Internet. The objective of these techniques is to ensure that the same Java class is used consistently throughout the information system.

Large Object Data Values

JDBC provides support for external Java logic to access large object data stored within the ORDBMS. As with other the host language interfaces, when a query returns a large object result, the ORDBMS does not return the object's data to the client. Instead, it returns a *large object handle*. The different kinds of large objects are identified in the JDBC interface with different type identifiers: `java.sql.Types.BLOB` and `java.sql.Types.CLOB` for the IDS product's `BLOB` and `CLOB` types, respectively.

Java external programs can interact with large object data in the ORDBMS using an interface that is similar in many ways to the interfaces ESQL/C provides. This mechanism keys off the `sql.java.Blob` and `sql.java.Clob` interfaces. In Listing 7–32, we illustrate how these interfaces are used within the JDBC driver implementation.

```
27    private static void processCLOB ( IfxCblob clob,
28                                                int nClobCnt )
29    {
30        int          loOpenFd;
31        long         loSize = 0;
32        IfxLocator   loPtr;
33        IfxSmartBlob   sBlob;
34        try
35        {
36            loPtr    = clob.getLocator();
37            sBlob    = new IfxSmartBlob ( conn );
38            loOpenFd = sBlob.IfxLoOpen(loPtr,
39                                          sBlob.LO_RDONLY );
40            loSize   = sBlob.IfxLoSize( loOpenFd );
```

```
41
42              System.out.println(" LO size :" + loSize );
43
44              sBlob.IfxLoClose( loOpenFd );
45
46          } catch ( SQLException e )
47          {
48              e.printStackTrace();
49              System.exit(1);
50          }
}

.  .  .
187     while(QR.next())
188     {
189         for(j = 1; j <= cols; j++ )
190         {
191             Object obResData =
192                 ((IfxResultSet)QR).getObject(j);
193
194             if ( obResData != null )
195             {
196                 if ( MD.getColumnType(j) ==
197                         java.sql.Types.CLOB )
198                 {
199                     nClobCnt++;
200                     processCLOB((IfxCblob)obResData,
201                             nClobCnt);
202                     strOutLine = strOutLine + "|";
203                 }
204                 else if(MD.getColumnType(j)==
205                         java.sql.Types.BLOB)
.  .  .
217                 } else /* Normal Type */
218                 {
.  .  .
224     }
```

Listing 7–32. *JDBC for Handling Large Object*

The other methods provided with the JDBC driver permit the external Java logic to act on large object data stored remotely as though it were a local file-system file. As with other such interactions, the ORDBMS treats all such operations as though they were part of a single transaction.

When an OPAQUE TYPE contains a large object handle, the Java class that it corresponds to can use similar methods over the SQLInput interface to extract the java.sql.Blob data from within it.

ROW TYPE Values

Although not supported by the ORDBMS's internal Java facilities (yet), ROW TYPE data values can be converted into Java classes within the JDBC interfaces. In JDBC, ROW TYPE instances are referred to as java.sql.Types.STRUCT objects. Overall, the mechanism looks a lot like how an OPAQUE TYPE is handled using the SQLData interface, SQLInput and SQLOutput, and the java.util.Map. In Listing 7–33 we introduce the definition of a ROW TYPE called NameValue.

```
1  /*
2  **    File:   NameValue.java
3  **    About:  Source for a Java class to handle the
4  **            following ROW TYPE through JDBC.
5  **
6  **    CREATE ROW TYPE Name_Value (
7  **        Name   VARCHAR(32),     Value FLOAT );
8  */
9   import java.sql.*;
10
11  public class NameValue implements SQLData
12  {
13      public    String       strName;
14      public    double       dbValue;
15
16      private String sqlTypename = "namevalue";
17
18      public String getSQLTypeName()
19      {
20          return sqlTypename;
21      }
22
23      public void readSQL (SQLInput input,
24                  String type)
25        throws SQLException
26      {
27          sqlTypename = type;
28          strName = input.readString();
29          dbValue = input.readDouble();
30      }
31
32      public void writeSQL (SQLOutput output )
```

```
33         throws SQLException
34         {
35                 output.writeString(strName);
36                 output.writeDouble(dbValue);
37         }
38
39         public    boolean   equals (   Object objArg )
40         {
41            if ((((NameValue)objArg).strName ==
42                 this.strName )  &&
43                 (((NameValue)objArg).dbValue ==
44                 this.dbValue ))
45            {
46               return true;
47            }
48            return false;
49         }
50
51         public String   toString()
52         {
53            return "[ " + strName + " , " + dbValue + " ]";
54         }
55
56 }
```

Listing 7–33. *Java Class Corresponding to ROW TYPE*

Overall, the goal of these techniques is to overcome the impedance mismatch between the external Java language and the database. As far as a programmer using JDBC is concerned, as long as the type mappings are configured appropriately and the OR-SQL UDFs for the UDT match the ones provided in the corresponding Java class, they need not be aware of how the ORDBMS is actually storing the object.

Java, JDBC and ORDBMS Development

Java works very well as part of the ORDBMS extensible data management framework. In Tutorial 4, we saw how Java classes could be used to implement user-defined type logic, and in this chapter, we have seen how external Java programs can interact with an ORDBMS database. Later, in Chapter 9, we review the technical performance and programmer productivity tradeoffs attending different extension mechanisms. Overall, Java yields good—though not the best—performance with much simpler development than is required with C or C++.

For reference, it took the author—who has considerable C experience—two months to create and debug all ESQL/C examples accompanying this book. It required only two weeks to create the Java examples.

In this section, we have seen how the JDBC interface allows Java programs to interact with an object-relational database. Perhaps the most important aspect of JDBC 2.0 is the way it makes the exchange of queries and data between a Java program and such a database practically seamless. If the type mapping mechanism is used correctly, JDBC makes it seem to Java programmers that they are using OR-SQL over Java objects, rather than disassembling Java objects into COBOL records and reassembling them on retrieval. Such a seamless type system reduces the *impedance mismatch* that has traditionally burdened relations between databases and the applications that use them.

Markup Languages

Both API mechanisms introduced so far in this chapter rely on *statefull* connections between the external program and the database. To support statefull connections, the ORDBMS server allocates a block of server memory—about 32K—for each concurrently connected external program. In this memory, the IDS product keeps bookkeeping information, such as user name and connection time, as well as a pool of prepared query plans and results that are being sent back to the external program. By contrast, a stateless protocol requires none of this. Each message exchange from the external program contains enough information that the recipient of the message can figure out what to do.

Stateless protocols have one huge advantage over statefull protocols: they can cope with vastly more external users. When building information systems to be used by the Internet multitudes, stateless protocols are a practical necessity. In this final section of the chapter, we give a brief overview of how the ORDBMS can support Internet deployment using its markup language interfaces.[5]

---

[5] The architecture and techniques described in this section are by no means the *only* way to build scalable dynamic Web sites. A variety of commercial products exist that perform similar tasks, and in many cases, these provide superior performance and scalability when compared to the facilities described here. Most commonly, a middleware application server is placed between the generic Web server and the DBMS. Such a program is indistinguishable, at least from the ORDBMS's perspective, from any other external program. It would make use of either the JDBC or ESQL/C interfaces introduced earlier.

Overview of Markup Languages

A markup language is a mechanism for combining meta-information with data. All markup languages, such as HTML, XML, and WML, are derivatives of a more general standard known as SGML. These standards have become the lingua franca of the Internet, and it looks likely that they will be the standard means of message exchange in wireless and mobile applications too.

In every case, the basic idea is the same: Information is encoded as a message in a (very long) standard ASCII character string. This is done to ensure complete universality; almost all computers and programming languages speak ASCII. Interspersed throughout the message's body are *markup tags*, which convey meta-information about the content. Depending on the markup dialect, the tags may specify how the message should be displayed on a browser (HTML), the semantics and structure of the message (XML), or information relevant to a particular wireless or mobile device (WML).

For readers unfamiliar with the concept (if there are any left), Listing 7–34 illustrates the idea. It presents a very simple HTML document. Pass this to any Web browser, and the browser software will present the encoded information in a standard way.

```
<HTML><HEAD><TITLE> Movies In Your Area</TITLE></HEAD>
<BODY><CENTER>
<H1 ALIGN=CENTER>List of Movies Showing</H1>
<HR>
<H2>This page is a simple example of HTML.</H2>
<P>
<TABLE BORDER=1 CELLPADDING=3>
   <TR>
       <TH>Movie and Cinema:</TH>
       <TH>Description:</TH>
   </TR>
   <TR>
       <TD>Casablanca at Moinahan Mall Theatre</TD>
       <TD>
Humphrey Bogart and Ingrid Bergman star in one of the
greatest movies ever made.
       </TD>
   </TR>
   <TR>
       <TD>The Maltese Falcon at Seven Oaks Theatre</TD>
       <TD>
Humphrey Bogart and Lauren Bacall sizzle in this film noir of
the Dashiell Hammett book.
```

```
      </TD>
     </TR>
  . . .
  </TABLE>
  </BODY></HTML>
```

Listing 7–34. *Illustration of the HTML Flavor of Markup Language*

Listing 7–34 illustrates HTML, but all markup languages use the same pattern. The most significant differences between them are that each flavor uses a different family of tags and that the tags have different purposes. XML tags, for example, define the structure and describe the meaning of the information rather than how it ought to be presented. So long as both the sender and receiver of the message agree on the semantics of the XML tags, communication between quite dissimilar systems is possible.

The Web DataBlade is an SGML compliant interface. All it does is manage mappings between object-relational data and document markup definitions. Where it differs from other approaches is that the mapping is represented using OR-SQL queries and other SGML-compliant tags, rather than procedural logic or a scripting language. One way to describe the difference is to say that the Web DataBlade uses a *declarative* mapping, much as OR-SQL is a declarative language, in contrast to other, procedural approaches. Consequently, the Web DataBlade shares many of the advantages of OR-SQL—rapid development, abstracted programming model—as well as its disadvantages.

Web Site Architectures

In first-generation Web sites, content is stored in a set of interlinked files called *pages*. Each page's location can be specified using a *Universal Resource Locator (URL)*. Internet links (or *hyperlinks*) between pages are achieved by embedding URLs within the page. Hyperlinks permit page creators to include pointers to other pages or resource, located somewhere else on the Internet. For small Web sites focusing on publication of text and pictures content, this approach is extremely effective. It allows the site's creator to present a set of pages linked in ways that allow users to connect from literally anywhere and navigate through the site's pages.

However, for certain kinds of information systems, this is not a viable approach. Consider our Movies-R-Us site. Movie schedules change daily, as does merchandise availability and price. In Web applications with purely commercial purposes, product pricing can be determined on a per-customer basis, and occasionally, on a minute-by-minute basis.

Using a file-system approach to solve this class of problem is a difficult challenge. In addition, the need for security on such sites makes using file-system files doubly problematic.

Consequently, larger Web sites apply database techniques to store information that is served up as *dynamic* content. Although very few sites are completely dynamic—many use a "publish" model that generates static pages from a changing database at regular intervals— incorporating dynamic information into the site and allowing Web users to ask ad hoc questions rather than simply reviewing static pages is an increasingly popular technique. For certain kinds of applications, where Web users are sharing access to constantly changing data, it is the only reasonable approach.

In this section, we describe the simplest approach to building a Web site with dynamic content. It involves using a set of facilities called the *Web DataBlade*. But some caution is called for. As Martin Seigenthaler, the engineer who originally created the product, puts it, "The Web Blade has to be the most over-complicated product I have ever worked on." Martin's point is that the Web Blade has a very simple purpose: format OR-SQL results into a marked-up format. If you find yourself trying to do more with it than this, you're using it inappropriately.[6] Algorithmic logic is best handled with procedural code, rather than an unwieldy combination of markup tags.

Web Blade Architecture

The basic technology of Internet information systems is quite different from the architectures commonly used with ESQL/C and JDBC. The Web is a relative latecomer, and its widespread adoption was made possible by the proliferation of the WAN infrastructure known as the Internet. Before the Internet became dominant, client/server applications relied on LAN technologies in which higher bandwidth and relatively secure wires connected perhaps several hundred computers together.

In Figure 7–7, we present the architecture of a Web site that uses the Web Blade facilities. It illustrates the sequence of events that occur whenever someone uses their browser, which can be a Web browser or a browser embedded within a mobile unit such as a WAP phone, to send a message to a Web site and to receive a response.

---

6   One early adopter succeeded in writing an entire date parser, with edit checks, using Web Blade markup tags. Another constructed a parser to interpret e-mail messages. Such technical heroism should not be copied.

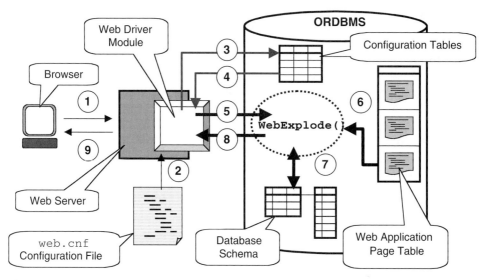

Figure 7–7. *Anatomy of HTTP Request Processing Using the Web Blade Infrastructure*

Over the next few pages, we describe each step in this sequence in detail. Later, we review how to use the Web DataBlade to create dynamic markup content.

Browser and Web Server

The Web is a sprawling landscape. Every computer attached to the Internet is, in some sense, attached to all the others. At any point in time, our Movies-R-Us Web site might have several thousand people concurrently interacting with the site. In addition, each hit on a site is a separate communication, and as we mentioned earlier, no state is maintained between the browser and the server.

Messages from a browser to a server—Step 1—are expressed in the form of a URL. URLs describe the address of the target system, the protocol to use when communicating with it, and any information included with the message. This last part of the URL, the message's state, is what the Web site's software cares about most. Resolving the address into a computer location and determining how to handle the protocol are dealt with by the Internet infrastructure.

Listing 7–35 shows an example URL that requests data from a Web site that used the Web DataBlade on a machine known as "pc415hp" through the CGI.

```
http://pc415hp:443/cgi-bin/webdriver?MIval=first&Id=Paul
```

Listing 7–35. *Universal Resource Locator*

Within this URL, the last two name/value pairs are most relevant to the Web site from a development point of view. They are variables that can be used to represent whatever action the end user has requested. In practice, URLs can be very long and can contain a great deal of information passed in this way. One common practice is to exchange a "session identifier" between the server and the user's browser. A record of the entire session history is maintained on the web server, and a well-engineered web site can use this record to create the illusion of a statefull session.

Web Servers, CGI Modules, and the Web Driver Plug-In

The first program that takes action in response to the URL request is called the *Web server*. Numerous Web server software packages are freely available. They all work by listening to a well known "port" on the host computer; this is port number 443 in the case of `pc415hp`. On receipt of the incoming message, the Web server parses it and decides what to do with it. Often, the appropriate response is to look in the local file system for a file named in the URL. With dynamic content, the usual outcome is to cause another program to run or to invoke a module loaded into the Web server, much like a user-defined function is loaded into the ORDBMS.

On receiving the URL in Listing 7–35, the Web server process determines that it needs to invoke the Web driver, which is shipped as part of the IDS product's Web DataBlade. For each of the common Web server products, there is a plug-in module that embeds within it and registers itself. When this plug-in is invoked, the first thing the Web driver does is check its configuration state to verify the following:

- Which IDS server and database it should route the message to
- How to access the appropriate template page within that database

At this point, it becomes necessary to explain how the Web Blade works and how it differs from more conventional approaches. We illustrate the more conventional approach in Figure 7–8.

In many Web sites, the dynamic content is generated using a *scripting language* (or a Java or C program). Instead of pushing the task of creating the dynamic content into the ORDBMS, this approach embeds the logic into the Web server and uses a standard interface between an interpreter within the Web server and the backend IDS installation. For extremely large sites with large development budgets, this approach has a lot of advantages. The most important advantage is that it distributes the computational load the site needs to accommodate over multiple machines.

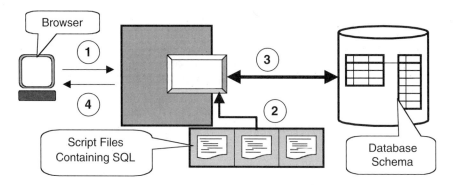

Figure 7–8. *Anatomy of HTTP Request Processing Using Server-Scripting Architecture*

The only drawback to building a Web site this way, and the reason the Web Blade was created in the first place, is that it requires programming effort. In situations in which what is wanted is a small, simple set of dynamic pages that is developed quickly, the Web Blade can't be beat.

Configuration Information

Configuration information is obtained from two sources. First, the Web driver consults an operating system file called web.cnf (Step 2). This configuration file contains enough information for the Web driver to connect to a database server. That is, it contains the server connection information, database name, and user-name. Note that the Web driver actually holds a pool of connections, rather than reconnecting for each request.

web.cnf contains a bare minimum of information. But the set of configuration options supported by the Web DataBlade is quite extensive. In fact, managing all of them is a database problem. So the Web DataBlade uses a set of tables—the most important of which is called WebConfig—for this purpose. The motivation behind using the database to manage configuration data is that many large sites using the Web DataBlade wanted to be able to change the configuration settings without being required to modify multiple external files or to restart Web server processes.

The Web DataBlade can cope with a broad variety of content types, and it can permit these to be stored in a number of different tables. By default, the Web DataBlade's application pages are stored in a table called wbPages, while binary content such as images and audio data are stored in a table called wbBinaries. To simplify the management of these different kinds of objects, the Web DataBlade provides a table called `wdExtensions`, which maps a file extension (".gif", ".avi", ".html", for example) to a column in a table.

All the Web driver does is read this configuration information—Steps 3 and 4 in Figure 7–7—and compose a query of the kind shown in Listing 7–36. All of the variables in this query, such as table name, column, and key column, are configured within the database's tables and they can be overridden by supplying another value for them in the URL.

```
"SELECT WebExplode ( $Micol, < ENV > )
   FROM $Mitab
   WHERE $Minam = $Mival "
```

Listing 7–36. *Basic Query of the Web DataBlade at Runtime*

This is the query that is passed into the ORDBMS during Step 5 in Figure 7–7. All work done by the Web Blade is performed within the `WebExplode()` user-defined function that is shipped as part of the Web DataBlade.

There is a set of other UDF provided with the Web Blade. These perform tasks such as checking the syntax of the Web template (`WebLint`) and returning the Web template's contents to the browser in "raw" form. These are all used to support another useful capability of the Web Blade architecture: Developers working on a Web site's pages can be as remote as end users!

The WebExplode Function and the Web Template Pages

As far as the ORDBMS engine is concerned, `WebExplode()` is just another user-defined function. Internally, however, `WebExplode()` is very sophisticated. It includes a full SGML parser, a dynamic query executor, and page formatting logic. It takes the template pages stored in the database—Step 6—and walks through them, executing any embedded OR-SQL it finds, using the variables supplied with the original URL. As it executes the embedded queries to retrieve data from the application's tables—Step 7—`WebExplode()` formats their results according to the specifications contained in the template.

Finally, the marked-up document produced by `WebExplode()` is passed back to the Web server—Step 8—and from there back to the remote browser—Step 9.

Developing the pages that make up the Web site therefore involves creating Web Application Page Templates. Each of these templates is an instance of a user-defined type that the Web DataBlade adds to the ORDBMS: the HTML data type. Columns named using the Micol configuration parameter must be columns defined using this type.

Web Page App Page Markup Tags

What do Web DataBlade App Pages look like? In short, much like any SGML document. In Listing 7–37, we introduce an example that might be used to generate the page in Listing 7–34, based on the current state of the database.

```
<HTML>
<HEAD>
<TITLE> Movies To Your Taste:<?MIVAR>$genre<?/MIVAR></TITLE>
</HEAD>
<BODY><CENTER>
<H1 ALIGN=CENTER>List of Movies Showing</H1>
<HR>
<H2>This page is a simple example of HTML.</H2>
<P>
<TABLE BORDER=1 CELLPADDING=3>
    <TR>
            <TH>Movie and Cinema:</TH>
            <TH>Description:</TH>
    </TR>
    <?MISQL SQL="SELECT Format ( C.Name, M.Title ),
                       M.Plot
                   FROM Movies M, Cinemas C, Showings S
                  WHERE S.Cinema = C.Id
                    AND S.Movie   = M.Id
                    AND ("$genre") IN M.Genres;">
    <TR><TD>$1</TD><TD>$2</TD></TR>
    <?/MISQL>
</TABLE>
</BODY></HTML>
```

Listing 7–37. *Simple Web Page Template*

This example illustrates several properties of Web Page Templates. First, note the use of the variable "genre" on this page. Variables such as this are passed in as part of the URL. For example, this page might be accessed using a URL of the following form:

```
http://pc415hp:443/cgi-bin/webdriver?MIval=tastes&genre=Noir
```

In this case, "tastes" identifies this page. "genre" might be selected from a select list, or typed into a text field in a form.

Second, note the use of the Web Blade markup tags. These indicate to `Webexplode()` that it needs to pay attention to what comes between the tag pair. In fact, `Webexplode()` completely ignores anything outside the tags it recognizes. It is perfectly reasonable to use techniques such as Javascript on the dynamic content pages that the Web Blade provides. In Table 7–6, we present a list of the most commonly used markup tags and how they are interpreted by `Webexplode()`.

Table 7–6. Common Web Blade Tags

Tag	Description
<?MISQL SQL= "Query String> <?/MISQL>	These tags indicate that what is contained between them is a query `Webexplode()` should execute. For both dynamic and static SELECT queries, the Web Blade provides elaborate techniques for formatting query results. The basic idea is to wrap the query results into regular HTML, XML, or WML tags before sending them back to the end user.
<?MIVAR><?/MIVAR>	Web Blade variables, such as "genre" in Listing 7–37, can be manipulated between these tags. For example, in Listing 7–37, we illustrate how to print the value of a variable.
<?MIERROR> <?/MIERROR>	These tags are used for error handling.
<?MIBLOCK> <?/MIBLOCK>	These tags are used to delineate a block of template. The idea is that sometimes it is useful to be able to specify several alternative template designs and to make `Webexplode()` choose from them, depending on the value of a variable or a query result.

Note that, with the exception of <?MIBLOCK><?/MIBLOCK>, Web Blade tags cannot be nested. Also, sophisticated Web Blade developers can create their own tags.

Because it adheres strictly to ASCII character data, the Web DataBlade does not require complex mechanisms for retrieving user-defined data types from the database. Instead, all OR-SQL statements embedded within application template pages rely on public, literal formats to represent type instances. This required use of literal string values helps explain why it is a good idea to provide a flexible set of UDFs to construct new type instances and to manipulate them. Web applications represent the triumph of slower but universal access over faster but more restrictive interfaces.

Large object data, because it is not textual, requires a slightly different approach. Image data, for example, is embedded within HTML pages using a set of mark-up tags and a URL that refers to where the image data file can be found. Web DataBlade-backed sites can access all of the digital content through the database and a special URL format is used to identify the object. The Web Server then retrieves the large object and passes it back to the browser as though it were just another file-system file.

Other Markup Languages

Although this description of `Webexplode()` and the Web Blade functionality has focused on developing HTML Web pages, it is important to understand that the Web Blade is really an SGML-compliant piece of software. Because it ignores everything outside the tags for which it is looking, the Web Blade is equally adept at building XML generators or providing WML data. It has even been used in a Virtual Reality Markup Language (VRML)-based project!

Chapter Summary

In this chapter, we have reviewed three ways to create client application programs that interact with the IDS product. An important point implicit in this presentation is that the ORDBMS can be used as the logical data store underneath several quite different client applications. Unlike the situation with an object-oriented DBMS, where the database is intimately tied to an application, object-relational database schema can be used in different ways.

In all cases, however, any of the OR-SQL language statements or techniques described elsewhere in this book can be submitted to the ORDBMS through any of these interfaces. This makes it possible for external programs to create OR-SQL statements "on the fly" and manage whatever data the ORDBMS returns to them. Such flexibility is the most useful virtue of relational and object-relational DBMS technology.

The three interfaces covered were the following:

1. Traditional embedded SQL in C or ESQL/C
2. Java connectivity using the JDBC interface
3. Web-based information systems deployment using the Web DataBlade

Developers familiar with how ESQL/C works with an RDBMS should have no trouble using it with an ORDBMS. ESQL/C for the ORDBMS adopts the same syntactical conventions and uses the same connect and query model. In its simplest form, developers can simply drop user-defined function identifiers into their OR-SQL, cast all their input and output types into character arrays, and ignore all questions about how the UDTs and UDFs are actually implemented.

For more sophisticated applications, ESQL/C provides mechanisms for dealing with each kind of UDT. OPAQUE TYPE data can be retrieved in binary form from the ORDBMS and placed into equivalent structures in the memory of the external program. In addition, ESQL/C provides mechanisms for manipulating ROW TYPE and COLLECTION data directly. Finally, the ESQL/C interfaces provided with the ORDBMS include facilities for working with large object data without bringing the entire set of data values into the external program.

JDBC is a more recent API than ESQL/C, and the programming environment it is designed to support is more hospitable to object-relational concepts than is C. The most important innovation JDBC provides is the ability to *map* ORDBMS data types into Java classes and to have the interface automate the transformation at runtime. Achieving this involves using SQL-J interfaces to ensure that the target class implements the methods used to perform the translation. It has the supreme virtue of making the exchange of data between the ORDBMS and the client program seamless.

Finally, we introduced the Web DataBlade facilities. These are intended as a simple and easy-to-use mechanism for turning ORDBMS data into one of several markup language forms. The basic idea is that the ORDBMS becomes the venue for both the application's data and a set of Web Page Templates. Template pages embed OR-SQL queries that are executed at runtime when the template page is accessed. Whatever data these queries produce is processed into a marked-up message, suitable for processing in a Web browser, by an XML parser, or even in a WAP-enabled phone.

Object-Relational Database Development

Introduction to Object-Relational Database Analysis and Design

So far, this book has focused on ORDBMS features and functionality: on data models, query languages, extensible type systems, active database features, host language interfaces, and so on. Starting in this chapter, we turn our attention to describing the best ways to use these features to build a database. We introduce a *development methodology* that begins by analyzing the problem domain from the end user's point of view. It concludes in the next chapter with advice on how to design and implement databases that make optimal use of object-relational technology.

Why is a new methodology necessary? Won't the techniques that worked for relational DBMS products work just as well with an object-relational DBMS? As we shall see, most do; but a fresh look at analysis and design is a good idea. Traditionally, relational DBMSs were viewed as an efficient, reliable, and relatively stupid storage space for business data. Object-relational databases, however, offer developers considerably more.

As an example of what the technology makes possible, consider that one objective of any database is to be able to answer unanticipated business questions quickly. This quickness demands fast software and hardware, but writing the program to answer the question often takes much more time than running it. RDBMS technology was a significant advance on COBOL in this regard, but consider how much effort would be required to answer the question in Listing 8–1 using SQL-92 and C.

"What pairs of Cinemas less than 30 miles apart are screening the same movie on the same day?"

```
SELECT M1.Cinema, M2.Cinema, M1.Movie
  FROM MovieSchedule M1, MovieSchedule M2
 WHERE Distance(M1.Location, M2.Location) < '30 MILES'
   AND Overlaps(M1.Duration, M2.Duration )
   AND M1.Movie    = M2.Movie
   AND M1.Cinema != M2.Cinema;
```

MovieSchedule

Cinema::String	Movie::Movie_Title	Where::Geo_Point	When::Period
. . .	. . .	. . .	. . .
Moinahan Mall Cinema	Casablanca	(-122.217,37.78)	[01/05/2000 to 05/05/2000]
Seven Oaks Theatre	Casablanca	(-99.67,39.378)	[01/05/2000 to 15/05/2000]
Golden Movies	Maltese Falcon, The	(-123.47, 48.234)	[05/10/2000 to 07/10/2000]
Mega-Movie Complex	The Maltese Falcon	(-123.5, 48.23)	[01/05/2000 to FOREVER]
. . .	. . .	. . .	. . .

Listing 8–1. *Object-Relational View and Query*

Object-relational technology lets you create smarter databases. In contrast with traditional data management tools, an extensible DBMS permits developers to combine data and logic within a relational framework. This makes it possible to answer unanticipated, high-level queries like the one in Listing 8–1 without a lot of effort. But how do you go about designing such a database? Where do you begin?

Because the technology allows for something more than representing static data, developers working with ORDBMSs benefit by taking a more holistic approach. Developing an object-relational database application involves the following:

1. You must identify and describe (in terms of both their state and behavior) the multitude of objects that correspond to concepts in the problem domain. These objects would include, for example, Geo_Point, Movie_Title, and Period in Listing 8–1.
2. At the same time that you create this list of objects, you need to arrive at an understanding of the information your database cares about. For example, you should analyze all relevant details about movie schedules and learn how they relate to other real-world phenomena like cinemas, movies, and so on.
3. Finally, you employ features such as user-defined types and functions to implement the objects, OR-SQL tables to store the data, and the OR-SQL language to tie it all together for your end users.

Regardless of the DBMS technology employed, the goal of database development is to construct a data model that is as accurate a representation of the problem domain as feasible. One advantage of object-relational technology is that it helps developers capture more information about the problem domain in this data model. The purpose of this chapter is to explain how.

Chapter Overview

We begin by outlining the overall objectives of information systems analysis and design. We then introduce some useful conceptual background for thinking about database development. Much of this material is nothing new; it covers topics such as the ANSI Three-Tier Model, and the high-level features of various software development methodologies. Experienced readers may omit it.

Then we spend the balance of the chapter going over techniques for analyzing a problem domain for object-relational database development. In subsequent chapters, we will explore implementation issues in more detail. These topics include logical database design, building efficient extensions, and advice on deployment architectures.

Database Development Objectives

The starting point for any *Management Information Systems (MIS)* project is the community of users the system is to support. The project's overriding goal is to meet their needs. We use the term *problem domain* or *Universe of Discourse (UoD)* to refer to the whole set of user requirements. For our purposes, there are some aspects of the overall information system that can be ignored. User-interface issues, while vital to the success of the software project, are of little relevance to the design of the back end.

To meets its obligations to its end users, the information system's database needs to be:

- Complete. The information system must include all relevant details about the problem domain. Another way to say this is that it must be *shareable*. Each user cares about a slightly different subset of the problem domain, and the system must somehow support each aspect of every user's view.
- Correct. The system must be an accurate rendering of the real-world problem domain it models. As with all human undertakings, this reality will change with time, and the system should be capable of adapting to such change.
- Consistent. Ambiguities in the system, such as two contradictory records or inconsistent implementations of the same logic, cause confusion and error in the real world. An information system should be designed to minimize the chance of such problems.
- Flexible. Information systems endure. Over time, an organization must adapt to changes in its competitive environment while maintaining its collective memory. Also, developers should expect that their system will be used in ways that were not anticipated during development.
- Efficient. Developers are required to deliver a system that meets all other design goals in this list within certain rigid restrictions. Efficiency can be measured in several ways—response time to standard queries, throughput if the system is transaction oriented, and overall human costs. In each case there is an acceptable minimum standard or an upper limit that the project team is required to meet.

Of course, while these goals apply to all information systems, projects differ with respect to the weight assigned to each of them. Embedded applications, accessed mainly by other software, place a premium on operational efficiency, but do not need to be particularly flexible. On the other hand, systems supporting managerial decision makers must above all be correct and flexible. Understanding a system's priorities helps when choosing between design alternatives.

Software Life Cycle

As Don Knuth famously observed, programming is modeling the world inside a computer. Models are *abstractions*; they simplify complex phenomena by focusing on their "relevant" aspects while de-emphasizing other details. Modeling is by nature an *iterative* or *cyclic* process. You begin by constructing an initial model. Then you compare what you have built with the reality it is supposed to represent, and then, based on what you learn in this comparison, you modify and evolve the model.

Many software development methodologies, including this one, adopt this iterative approach. Each cycle consists of several subtasks:

- Analyze the problem domain and compare it to the current model. Identify areas in which the model is incomplete (an initial, empty model is by definition incomplete) or incorrect. When there are differences between the model and the problem domain, they are often pointed out by end users—loudly.
- Modify the design according to what you learned in the analysis phase (or come up with an initial design based on the first round of analysis) with the objective of minimizing the potential for inconsistency and maximizing the system's flexibility.
- Implement the modifications (or the initial design). The goal here is technical *efficiency*, which means ensuring that the system performs to the expectations of users.
- Make the system available to end users, which inevitably leads to another cycle of analysis, design, and so on.

The phases of our database development methodology are shown in Figure 8–1.

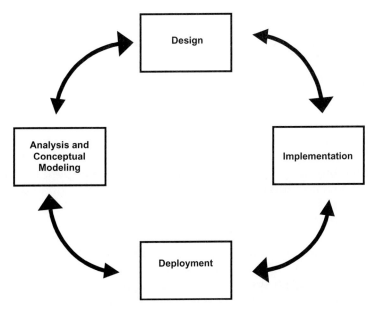

Figure 8–1. *Cyclic or Iterative Lifecycle Model*

Two things complicate this description. First, although the primary input to each phase of the methodology comes from the previous phase, note that the transitions are bidirectional. Lessons learned later in the development cycle feed back into previous stages. In practice, this is frequently necessary. For example, it is relatively common to discover during implementation that a "gotcha" or even a bug in the way the DBMS is implemented leads to inadequate performance. The pragmatic workaround to such problems can be modifying the module's design.

The second complication differentiates this methodology from many others. In Figure 8–1 there is no "maintenance" phase. This is not a waterfall model, nor is it an iterative spiral that concludes when the software leaves the hands of its developers. In fact, it seems to imply that development never ends. A brief digression is necessary to explain why.

Trends in Information System Development

The clearest lesson of the last thirty years of software engineering has been that information system software is not a durable capital investment. Conventional wisdom holds that as little as one-tenth of the cost of a computer program is incurred during its implementation. In contrast, factories, bridges and roads experience almost all their expenditure up front, as they are designed and built. Once completed, they function with minimal maintenance, until finally becoming obsolete.

Managing software projects according to the factory paradigm has proven to be difficult. The lost business opportunities due to the inflexibility of information systems software is probably even more significant, although much harder to measure. Software engineers had little choice; the tools used to develop information systems did not encourage any other approach.

Today, however, information systems software must be more changeable. Never before has there been such a tight dependency between technology and business needs. HTML and scripting languages make modifying an end user's experience on a Web site a trivial task. In addition, business organizations must adapt at Web speed to remain profitable. Thus, today's user-interface (UI) developers and business managers place tremendous pressure on their back-end systems to evolve as rapidly as they do.

This methodology reflects that experience. A better way to think about back-end software is as an *organic* or *evolutionary* system. Unlike factories, information systems are forever works in progress. Rather than upgrade a system in large, infrequent releases, the approach taken here encourages frequent, small changes. In an ORDBMS database, upgrades are minor tasks, such as adding or changing a single function, writing a new query, or altering a table by adding a new column. Testing can be isolated to a single software module, and the change can be deployed without halting the running system.

Over time, the accumulation of many, small changes has the same effect as a smaller number of sweeping rewrites. Incremental changes, however, involve less risk of project overrun or technical failure than major surgery. Taking smaller steps also makes it possible to adapt more rapidly to changing circumstances. The methodology described in this book adopts this "constant improvement" development paradigm.

The ANSI Three-Tier Database Model

ANSI's *Three-Tier DataBase Model* concept is twenty years old, but it is still a useful means of framing discussions about database development. The American National Standards Institute (ANSI) proposed the idea to help in developing and defining requirements for database systems. The model describes three "levels of abstraction," each of which corresponds to how different people involved with the system look at it.

The three tiers of the model are as follows:

- The end user's view, which represents the ways users reason about the problem domain. This is called the *conceptual* or *external* level.
- The database developer's perspective. We call it the *logical* or *internal* level. It is described in terms of the data management tool's features and functionality. In other words, at this level of abstraction, you describe the system in term of tables, columns, queries, types, functions, and procedures.
- The physical structures used to organize data storage and the low-level algorithms used to perform data retrieval and manipulation represent the lowest level of abstraction. Hiding the details of this *physical* level is the primary value-add of a relational or object-relational DBMS.

Figure 8–2 illustrates how these three levels are interrelated.

Each level is more or less a formal description of the problem domain under consideration. Between each tier, we say that there is an *abstraction layer*. The grist of any development methodology is a body of techniques and procedures for representing the model at each level of abstraction and for translating between layers.

Work may proceed in more than one level simultaneously. Separating the subparts of the system—data structure, logic, and data processing

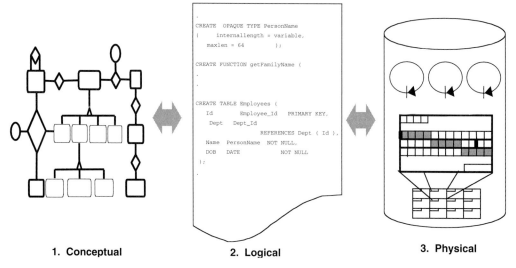

```
CREATE  OPAQUE TYPE PersonName
(      internallength = variable,
    maxlen = 64          );

CREATE FUNCTION getFamilyName (
 .
 .

CREATE TABLE Employees (
   Id          Employee_Id   PRIMARY KEY,
   Dept    Dept_Id
                    REFERENCES Dept ( Id ),
   Name   PersonName  NOT NULL,
   DOB    DATE              NOT NULL
);
 .
 .
```

1. Conceptual   **2. Logical**   **3. Physical**

Figure 8–2. *Three Tiers of the ANSI Database Model*

operations—allows different teams to focus on different aspect of it without too much need for coordination. In most large programming projects, teams periodically synchronize their code before compiling and linking it all. With the ORDBMS, teams can work more independently. Changes to a user-defined type can be designed, developed, and deployed without requiring schema changes or shutting the system down. Of course, this is an idealized description. At this time the IDS product is not so advanced, but it does provide more flexibility than relational DBMS technologies.

Conceptual or External Level

Conceptual models describe the problem domain at the highest level of abstraction. They represent how end users think about their tasks, the objects with which they deal, how these objects are organized, what data processing operations occur, what rules define legal data values and constrain changes, and so on. Working interactively with end users as part of building the conceptual model is very good practice.

Conceptual models are multifaceted. There is likely to be a variety of users in different employment roles or customers with different expectations. Thus, system analysts may need to capture a multitude of conceptual views. In some applications, such as Web sites, "users" are idealized. The site's business architect or marketing department "channels" users and decides what they would like to see, where they would like to see it, and how they want to behave.

Figure 8–3 illustrates why capturing this diversity is necessary. It presents four categories of Movies-R-Us Web site users as circles enclosing the area of the problem domain that they care about. As you can see, these regions overlap, but no user cares about everything. The point is that catering to one conceptual model will optimize for that group of users, but it will not meet the overriding goal of supporting the entire organization.

While a single, enterprise-wide information system is a desirable goal, it is rarely an attainable one. Modern organizations are prohibitively complex. Uncovering subtle or poorly understood interdependencies takes too much time, so to prevent project overruns, it is a very good idea to define the scope of the system clearly and early. One effective way to do this is to limit the set of users the system will support and to focus exclusively on their needs.

Typically, the need for interaction between users of one information system and users of others within the same enterprise is limited. Although it is almost certain that there are additional categories of Movies-R-Us users not shown in Figure 8–3, they can usually be ignored. For example, the company running the Web site is likely to have a group of employees tasked with administrative duties, such as accounting or human resources. Ignoring occasional or possible future users is generally good advice. The ones you have will be trouble enough.[1]

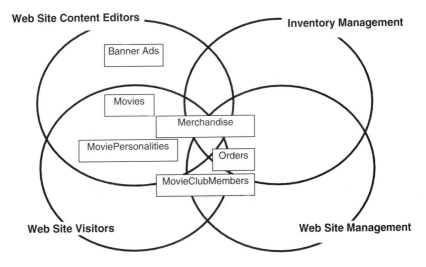

Figure 8–3. *Overlapping Areas of the Problem Domain Falling within Different User's Conceptual Models*

---

[1] Using distributed systems technology to deal with these other systems is almost always more effective than attempting to merge everything into one big database.

Semantic Data Models

Formal computer languages, such as programming code, are meaningless to nontechnical people, but natural language is imprecise. Thus, the best way to document conceptual models is with diagrams. GUIs make drawing complex figures easy, and a number of *semantic data models* exist that standardize the meanings of different figures.

Semantic models are useful because they permit developers and end users to communicate (relatively) clearly about the problem domain and the information system's desired functionality. Pictures really do paint a thousand words.

Some well-known semantic models include the following:

- Extended Entity-Relationship Modeling (E-ER). E-ER extends traditional entity-relationship modeling with notions such as *inheritance* and *abstract data types* (domains or classes of objects). Excellent handbooks for E-ER analysis include Toby Theorey's *Database Modeling and Design* (Morgan Kaufmann) and Fleming and von Halle's *Handbook of Relational Database Design* (Addison Wesley).
- More advanced relational modeling techniques have been recently developed. The best known of these is *Object-Role Modeling,* or ORM. Terry Halpin's *Conceptual Schema and Relational Database Design* (Prentice Hall) is a superb introduction to this technique and to conceptual analysis in general.
- Object-oriented analysis and design have produced several extremely useful diagramming languages. The best known of these is the Universal Modeling Language, or UML. While intended primarily for developers working with object-oriented programming languages, UML can be readily adapted for working with ORDBMSs. Many books and tools describe and use UML.

Numerous *Computer Assisted Software Engineering (CASE)* tools exist that help with conceptual modeling, and using one is highly recommended. Unfortunately, most of them do not, at this time, reflect the full capacities of the ORDBMS. They rarely capture information about the palette of data types that are combined within database tables or the functions implementing the behavior of these objects. These tools will improve over time.

The goal of conceptual modeling is to arrive at a *complete* and *correct* description of the UoD. This description is transformed into a more formal logical or internal model as part of the design phase. Groups of users differ in the way they want their information represented, and even what parts of it mean, but underlying their different conceptual views is a single, global structure. The primary task of conceptual modeling is to document this.

Logical or Internal Level

One of the primary characteristics of any DBMS is its *data model*. This term refers to the style in which the DBMS lets developers organize and manipulate data. Today, the two most important database data models are the *relational* model supported by the various SQL-92 DBMS vendors and the *object-oriented* data model. The *object-relational* data model combines the entire relational model with the best of object-oriented modeling.

An important principle of conceptual modeling is that it is neutral with respect to implementation; that is, conceptual models shape, but do not dictate, how the final system is engineered. Depending on the circumstances, a single conceptual model can drive several different implementations. For example, you might take the conceptual model of the Movies-R-Us Web site to develop either an ORDBMS database or a combination of a SQL-92 database and lots of Java code.

Logical Design and Object-Relational DBMSs

A logical model is a representation of a problem domain using the data modeling facilities of some DBMS. In our methodology we arrive at a logical model by translating the conceptual view, which is neutral with respect to data model, into the ORDBMS's data model, which consists of types, functions, tables, and so on. This translation is referred to as the process of *logical design*.

With ORDBMSs, logical design has three parts.

- First, the various conceptual models for each end user are condensed into a single, minimal model. The final conceptual model is minimal in the sense that it contains the smallest set of database objects that can be used to support the complete set of conceptual views.
- Second, the minimal conceptual model is mapped into an equivalent object-relational representation.
- Third, the data structure or schema is further analyzed using more formal techniques to ensure that it is *consistent*. The idea of this last step is to arrive at a schema that is free from the possibility of error or ambiguity.

The data itself is stored within the ORDBMS, and the internal representation of the data makes up the physical model. Physical abstraction, which is the layer between the physical and logical models, is the primary service provided by the ORDBMS.

Physical Model

The physical model deals with how the system is organized with respect to the hardware on which it runs. As much as possible, the ORDBMS frees developers and end users from needing to know too much about how this works. However, as a practical matter, information systems are required to meet certain performance goals, and runtime efficiency can be improved by paying attention to the ORDBMS's physical organization.

For example, as part of the physical design of any database, you might instruct the ORDBMS to create additional indices, to spread table data out across available disk space, or to combine tables that are frequently accessed together. We call this process *physical design* or *database tuning*.

Of all the steps in the development process, physical design is the least amenable to formal methods. In the first place, physical tuning depends very much on the peculiarities of the ORDBMS and the application, and there are a great many environmental factors to consider. These factors include hardware configuration, performance objectives (throughput, response time, or scalability), and workload. An important effect of using an ORDBMS to separate physical and logical levels is that developers can make changes to their ORDBMS without having to alter any of their program code. For example, you can sometimes slash the time taken to run a query simply by adding an index.

The most effective technique to use in physical tuning is educated trial and error. In this technique, you measure, make a *single* change, measure again, and back out the change if it did not produce any advantage.

ORDBMS Development Methodology Steps

For the remainder of this chapter and into the next, we explore each of the twelve steps listed next in detail. As part of this description, we apply these techniques to the Movies-R-Us database problem domain.

In this chapter we focus on conceptual modeling, which is a technique used to create a semantic model of the problem domain. This involves documenting both the *classes of objects* users care about and the *conceptual schema* within which these objects are arranged. We also present means to catalog the *workload* of business processes and common queries. In Chapter 9, we focus on details of how to implement the extensions, tables, and so on.

The steps of the development methodology detailed in this book are as follows.

Phase 1: Analysis and Conceptual Modeling

1. Use extended entity-relationship modeling techniques to create a high-level data model that catalogs the major entities in the UoD, the relationships between these entities, and any rules that constrain the data each entity can contain.
2. Analyze each entity and decide what *kinds* of data make up its attributes. Then describe each kind of data using a more object-oriented approach. For each database object (entity or attribute type), decide on its state (internal structure) and behavior.
3. Describe the business processes and common queries that the ORDBMS needs to support.
4. Capture any business rules that apply to the overall system.

Phase 2: Logical Design

5. Integrate the various conceptual schema into a single minimal, complete model consisting of the extended ER model, the minimal set of object definitions, and the business processes and rules.
6. Transform the single conceptual model into a "naïve" logical schema.
7. Normalize the logical schema appropriately to ensure consistency and nonredundancy.
8. Write a set of workload queries using both the business processes identified in Step 3 and the typical application query workload.

Phase 3: Implementation and Testing

9. Implement the logical schema. Use the simplest techniques practical to get a working database operational.
10. Load the schema with as much data as you can. Generate synthetic data if necessary.
11. Run the query workload against the loaded database to validate that the database is correct and to identify performance bottlenecks.
12. Apply resources to the problems identified in the previous stage according to the benefits.

Although presented here as a numbered list, each of these tasks is interrelated with the others. In real systems, several independent subprojects may be going on at the same time.

Advice on Upgrading to the ORDBMS

This is a fairly obvious procedure for new software projects. But what about upgrades to existing RDBMS based applications? One way to view upgrading from an RDBMS to an ORDBMS is to say that the upgrade is simply a new cycle of the methodology. Begin by reviewing previous analysis and asking users how well the system meets their current goals. Then, based on this analysis, design and implement necessary changes.

Even small, simple changes can help. For example, you can embed user-defined functions to simplify SQL and improve its performance without changing the database schema at all. One popular approach is to evolve the schema using object-relational design principles but to leave a set of SQL-92 views in place to support existing applications. In addition, by using the DISTINCT TYPE mechanism, you can take advantage of strong typing, thereby improving the amount of semantic information captured in your table schema.

Part 1: Conceptual Modeling

Software engineers frequently complain that users can't make up their minds, or change their minds, and even that they have lost their minds. A common rationalization for project failure is that "management support was inadequate," meaning that the organization's management didn't support the development team when they were exasperated by users' constantly changing demands.

The simple truth, however, is that human beings are far more flexible than computers and are constantly exercising this flexibility. Beginning a software development project mindful of this will save you time and agony. The objective of conceptual analysis is to document a *correct* and *complete* high-level model of the UoD. Having said that, it is very important to understand that *conceptual models change*.

Conceptual models describe the important concepts in the problem domain from the end user's perspective. In keeping with our holistic approach to development, conceptual modeling for an ORDBMS addresses all aspects of the system: data model, object design, business processes, and rules.

These various aspects of the conceptual model are captured in the following ways:

1. Use extended entity-relationship modeling to describe the high-level entities in the problem domain and the relationships between them.
2. Use object-oriented analysis to create a more comprehensive description of each high-level entity and the various kinds of data within them.
3. Apply data flow diagramming (DFD) techniques to represent the business processes in the system and any dependencies between them.
4. Describe the integrity rules users generally agree on.

This is a *top-down* methodology; it begins by examining the higher-level structures in the problem domain before decomposing them into smaller, self-contained objects. An alternative approach, which is called *bottom up*, involves first analyzing the smaller, independent objects and then figuring out how they are combined into higher-level entities. Both approaches have merit, and can even be used together. Deciding between them is a matter of taste and experience.

Entity-Relationship Data Modeling

The first task in our methodology is to create an *Extended Entity-Relationship (E-ER)* model. Like all semantic data models, E-ER diagrams use standardized figures to convey what the problem domain "looks like" to a particular user or group of users.

The choice of E-ER diagrams in this book is somewhat arbitrary. Earlier, we presented a list of other semantic data models. The *Universal Modeling Language (UML)* and *Object-Role Modeling (ORM)* share the relevant benefits of E-ER modeling and provide the means to capture considerably more information. E-ER is, however, a smaller and simpler method, many readers will be at least partially familiar with it, and it works quite well in most cases. Anyone requiring more elaborate techniques is advised to confront the listed reference texts.

Introduction to Extended Entity-Relationship Diagrams

E-ER models describe the UoD in terms of *entities* and the *relationships* between them. A complete picture of the UoD can be conveyed in diagram form. Figure 8–9 illustrates what such a high-level conceptual model looks like.

Entities are principle ideas or "things." Roughly, entities correspond to common nouns that are subjects in a problem domain: people, places, products, or events. An entity is a collective concept; the term *entity instance* refers to an individual example of an entity. Each entity instance reflects the fact that some real-world object exists. In an E-ER diagram, entities are represented as a named box.

For example, establishments like the 'Moinahan Mall Cinema' and 'Seven Oaks Theatre' are all instances of the, Cinemas, entity. In our Movies-R-Us Web site example, Movies, Orders, Merchandise, T-Shirts, Tickets, Cinemas, Personalities, and Movie Club Members are all examples of entities.

E-ER models also record the *relationships* that exist between two or more entities. Relationships are inter entity dependencies or associations. They tend not to be "things" in the same sense that entity instances are. Relationships are rules. They constrain what instances one entity can contain based on what instances exist in another entity. In an E-ER diagram, relationships are represented as lines between entity boxes. Occasionally, when the relationship involves more than two entities, diamond shapes are used.

For example, an analysis of the Movies-R-Us Web site reveals that every Order must have a Movie Club Member who placed it and a reference to an instance of one of the various kinds of Merchandise. Such concepts are modeled as relationships.

Describing the Entities in the Problem Domain

Our first task is to describe the *entities* that correspond to the principle ideas or subjects in the problem domain. The best way to acquire this knowledge is to talk to employees and managers about how they reason about their tasks. For example, because the site's objective is to gain and keep members and to get them to place orders for items of merchandise, MovieClubMembers, Orders, and various kinds of Merchandise are good candidates for modeling as entity types. (In this book, we use the terms "entity type" and "entity" synonymously.) Examine Listing 8–2.

Movies	MovieClubMembers
Cinemas	MoviePersonalities
Tickets	Orders
WebLogAction	Apparel
Toys	etc....

Listing 8–2. Partial List of Entities in Movies-R-Us Web site Problem Domain

As part of E-ER analysis, document each entity's name, the attributes that make it up, and whatever rules differentiate legal and illegal entity instances. The original ER techniques made no more of the entity concept than this. More recently, extended ER models have drawn a distinction between *strong* entities and *weak* entities.

Strong Entities

Instances of strong entities exist independently of everything else in the schema. Cinemas, Movies, and MovieClubMembers are all examples of strong entities. A movie does not depend for its existence on a cinema, and there may be movie club members even if there were no movies and no merchandise. Another way to think about this is to say that the Movie entity might be part of an entirely unrelated problem domain, such as an accounting system for a movie studio or an inventory system for a video store.

Weak Entities

In contrast to strong entities, weak entities have a special, application-specific dependency on (relationship with) at least one other entity. In our UoD, Orders and WebLogActions are examples of weak entities. It is impossible for an Order to exist without there being a related movie club member and item of merchandise. Similarly, you cannot have an instance of a WebLogAction without there being a MovieClubMember who committed the action. Figure 8–4 shows the appropriate diagrams to represent weak and strong entities in ORDBMS modeling.

The first entity representation in Figure 8–4 is in abbreviated form, and the second is in more detail. The distinction between weak and

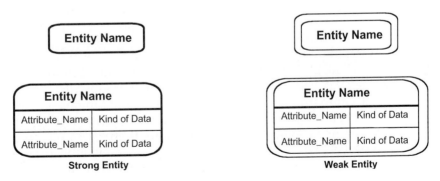

Figure 8–4. *Weak and Strong Entity Figures*

strong entities is useful when it comes time to map the E-ER diagrams into a logical tables schema.

Entity Analysis

Having created a catalog of entities, the next step is to describe each of them in more detail. Each entity has the following characteristics:

- An identifying name. No two entities in the same E-ER model can share a name. Ideally, an entity's name reflects what it is. For example, Movies, Cinemas, Merchandise, and so on are the nouns used by convention.
- A set of *attributes* that collectively define the entity's structure. For each attribute, choose a name that reflects what the attribute contributes to the entity and decide what kind of data the attribute stores. For example, the MovieClubMember entity in our example includes attributes such as the member's Name, which is a PersonName "kind of data," and a HomeAddresses attribute that holds a MailAddress.
- A set of rules that distinguish semantically valid instances of the entity type from incorrect ones. These rules extend the semantic range of the E-ER model by constraining what information an entity can contain. For example, there may be a rule to the effect that budgetary values stored with a Movie entity cannot have negative values or that the Id attribute of a Cinema entity is unique for each entity instance. Some of these rules, such as *keys*, can be indicated on the diagram, but the more complex ones should be written down.

Traditional E-ER analysis would describe the kinds of data in each attribute in terms of the target DBMS's built-in SQL-92 data types. For example, it would be typical with an RDBMS to break the MovieClubMember entity's attributes all the way down into single value attributes such as first name, surname, and area code using VARCHAR and INTEGER types.

ORDBMS development benefits from a more intuitive modeling of each entity's attribute types: an approach closer to object modeling than to traditional E-ER. For example, the Cinema entity contains a set of compound attributes including the cinema's address, phone number, and geographic location. Rather than decomposing these into SQL-92 types, at this level of analysis, simply label the attribute's type to indicate what kind of data it contains. Figure 8–5 illustrates what an E-ER entity diagram for an ORDBMS looks like.

Cinemas	
Attribute_Name	Attribute_Kind
Id	Cinema _Id
Name	CinemaName
Address	MailAddress
Phone	PhoneNumber
Photo	Image
SurroundSound	boolean
DisabledAccess	boolean
ScreenCount	INTEGER
GeoLocation	Geo_Point

Orders	
Attribute_Name	Attribute_Kind
Id	OrderNum
OrderedOn	DATE
ShippedOn	DATE
Basket	SET { Line_Items }

Figure 8–5. *Two Instances of Entities in the Problem Domain*

Later, we pool all of the various kinds of data in attributes and apply object-oriented analysis techniques to analyze them further.

There are several other things to note about entity structural analysis:

- Attributes in different entities will reuse common kinds of data. Movie club members and movie personalities both have names. In all situations, the properties of a person's name ought to be consistent; it is always subject to the same integrity rules and can be manipulated using the same interfaces.
- In the Orders entity, there is an attribute called Line_Items. This contains the set of items that make up the Order. With ORDBMSs, these COLLECTION concepts can be treated somewhat differently from how they were handled in SQL-92. In conventional E-ER modeling, a COLLECTION like this is a cue that another entity is appropriate because the RDBMSs rule states that each entity attribute contain a single value. This restriction is relaxed with the ORDBMS data model, and COLLECTION attributes can be supported directly (although it may or may not make practical sense to do so, as discussed in Chapter 9).

Keys

In addition to naming entities and determining how they are structured, it is equally important to know how to distinguish between instances of the same entity type. For example, how can the database tell the difference between two items of Apparel to prevent the same data from being entered twice by accident? Alternatively, how are items of Apparel identified to other entities in the schema, for example, to record when one is involved in a particular Order? Fortunately, there are two approaches to this problem:

- Entities can be made to include an additional attribute whose system-generated values make the distinction between instances explicit. At the conceptual level, we call this extra attribute the entity's identifier.[2]
- The second approach to instance identity comes from traditional relational modeling. The idea is to find an attribute, or set of attributes, whose values differentiate each entity instance from all others of the same type. In other words, you want to know what properties of the real-world entity instance uniquely set it apart from all others. We call such attribute(s) a *logical key* for the entity.

Over the next few paragraphs we discuss the pros and cons of these two techniques.

System-Generated Entity Identifiers

Entity identifiers are similar to the object-oriented concept of *identity*, which is central to the definition of what "objects" are. They can be supported quite efficiently using facilities provided by the ORDBMS itself. However, system-generated identifiers have several drawbacks in terms of the impact they have on the database's overall effectiveness.

First, system-generated keys are not very helpful for end users. People don't associate Cinemas or Movies with a number; they recognize them by their name, or phone number, or location, or title. In fact, using system-generated keys can *force* developers to write join queries that would otherwise be avoided by carrying the logical key into the foreign table instead of a system-generated value. Having a lot of join queries degrades the overall performance of the database.

Second, system-generated keys do little to prevent accidents. When the values of a subset of an entity's attributes can uniquely identify an entity instance, the system can use this information to detect errors, as when a Movie's information is inserted a second time.

---

[2] We deliberately avoid the term "object identifier" here, because other objects stored by the ORDBMS, such as instances of OPAQUE or DISTINCT types, cannot have meaningful identifiers.

So, system-generated identifiers are not a very good choice for solving the problem of keeping data consistent with the real world.

On the other hand, the ORDBMS can perform data processing operations, such as comparing two system-generated identifier values, very quickly. This makes the system-generated keys very efficient for representing relationships between entities internally. Readers familiar with RDBMSs may know this concept as *surrogate keys*. In the ORDBMS, declaring that a table's column contains a `SERIAL` or `SERIAL8` value indicates that the column is to contain a system-generated value that is guaranteed to be unique within the table (or the hierarchy of tables).

Logical Keys

Logical keys typically reflect some property of the real-world phenomenon being modeled by the entity. They may take many forms. For example, new members of our Movies-R-Us Web site supply their own string of characters to identify themselves, so this membership number attribute is one candidate logical key for the MovieClubMember entity. A single attribute containing a compound object can also be used for, or as part of, a logical key. For example, movie personalities may be uniquely identified using their names, which contain a surname, given name, and so on.

Movies might be uniquely identified by their title, were it not for remakes, sequels, and prequels. In cases in which a movie title is repeated, the different movies can almost always be distinguished by their release dates. Thus, logical keys can span more than one attribute. Combinations of columns are called *composite* logical keys.

Candidate Keys

An entity might possess several alternative logical keys, which are called the *candidate keys* for the entity. For example, the combination of a movie club member's name and phone number is a second candidate key for the MovieClubMembers entity. Capturing the complete list of candidate keys is desirable because each of them expresses an important rule about the data in the entity. Note that a system-generated key is a candidate key too.

Primary Keys

One of the most important decisions in E-ER modeling is choosing which candidate key will be the *primary* key. Primary keys are special because the attributes that compose the primary key are used to record the entity's relationships with other entities. When selecting a primary key from among candidate keys, it is useful to consider the following factors:

- Smaller is better. OR-SQL queries are often required to compute an enormous number of comparisons for primary keys. Integers and other smaller keys consume less CPU and memory than do composite keys or long character column keys. Membership_Num, being shorter than the combination of PersonName and PhoneNumber, for example, makes a better primary key.
- Another characteristic of a good key is immutability. Although a combination of attributes is unique at a particular point in time, if the values are subject to change, their value as an identifier is lessened. For example, a Cinema may be uniquely identified by its name and phone number, but both of these are subject to change when new management is hired or new area codes are assigned. Therefore, although it is a good idea to ensure that these values are UNIQUE within the entity, they are poor choices for a primary key.
- If the logical key is very wide or has the potential to change, using an entity identifier can be a good idea.

Note that we define logical keys in an entity in terms of *equality*. Formally speaking, a set of attributes constitutes a candidate key if there exists no two entity instances in which the values in the key attributes are *equal*. This means that the kinds of data used in key attribute must have an `Equal()` function defined for them. As we saw in our discussion about table `PRIMARY KEY` in Chapter 2, the ORDBMS can use this table to tell when the key constraint is violated. In addition, for efficiency and scalability, data types defining keys (such as MembershipId) need to possess an operator class that lets the ORDBMS create a B-Tree index for the key. Figure 8–6 illustrates two more entity diagrams, along with primary key designations.

Primary keys are represented on an E-ER diagram by underlining the name of the key attribute(s). An example of this appears in Figure 8–6. Other indicators can be used to identify alternative candidate keys. Most CASE tools provide mechanisms to label candidate keys on entity diagrams.

Constraint Rules

Keys are examples of *constraint rules*. Entity constraint rules help distinguish valid entity instances from invalid ones, or they are behavioral rules applied across the entire set of entity instances. In other words,

MovieClubMembers	
Attribute_Name	Attribute_Kind
Id	Membership_Id
Password	Encrypted_String
Name	Person_Name
HomeAddress	Mail_Address
HomePhone	PhoneNumber
LivesAt	Geo_Point
Preferences	SET { Genre }
Photo	Image
CreditCard	CreditCardNum
DOB	DATE

MoviePersonality	
Attribute_Name	Attribute_Kind
Name	PersonName
DOB	DATE
DOD	DATE
Lives_In	State
Biography	Document
Photo	Image

Figure 8–6. *Entities with their Primary Key*

entity constraint rules define what correct data looks like. Documenting them is a good idea because most constraints can be enforced within the database, and doing so improves the quality of the information in the database.

For example, the Movies entity has a budget attribute. The kind of data stored in a budget column is Currency. Movies cannot be made for a negative amount of money (although Currency amounts can certainly have negative values, so this is not a rule about this kind of data in general). Therefore, a good rule to enforce is that movie budget attributes must have positive amounts of Currency (can't be less than "0 USD"). Another hypothetical rule applied to Cinemas might be that no two cinemas can be within 100 feet of each other.

Capturing constraint rules is both difficult and important. Their importance makes it reasonable to spend a significant amount of time on them, but deadlines being what they are, it is also important to move on. Constraints discovered later in the life of the information system are almost always easy to accommodate. Beginning your investigation of the UoD with the goal of describing every constraint rule is a one-way ticket to analysis hell!

Sub-Entities and Inheritance

An inheritance relationship reflects a situation in which each instance of one entity **is_a** instance of some other entity too. For example, an experienced analyst looking at the entities identified in the Movies-R-Us Web site UoD would notice that there are a large number of entities corresponding to the various kinds of merchandise, such as Apparel, Tickets, and so on.

Inheritance

As far as the Movies-R-Us Web site is concerned, Apparel *is_a* kind of Merchandise, and a T-Shirt *is_a* kind of Apparel. (By implication, a T-Shirt *is_a* kind of Merchandise too.) Inheritance support within the ORDBMS data model is one of the biggest differences between the ORDBMS and RDBMS approaches.

Inheritance can be represented directly in extended ER diagrams. Figure 8–7 illustrates two ways to represent *is_a* inheritance relationships with E-ER diagrams.

Dominant entities in inheritance relationships are called the *super-entity* and the others are called the *sub-types* or *sub-entities*. Sub-entities can themselves have sub-entities; inheritance hierarchies with multiple levels are allowed. Sometimes you will find that your problem domain includes entities that are *abstract*; that is, although the entity's existence is implied by the existence of its sub-entities, it has no instances. For example, there is no such thing as a Merchandise item. Every instance *is_a* kind of Merchandise, but they are all different from one another.

Sub-entitie list the attributes added to those inherited from the super-entity's definition. Sub-entities also inherit whatever keys and constraints exist for the super-entity too. For example, the primary key of the Merchandise entity is its product number. All of its sub-entities share this primary key.

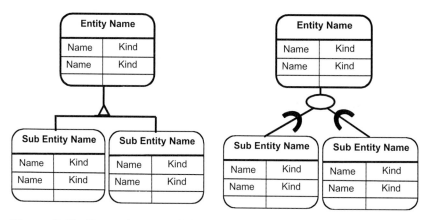

Figure 8–7. *Alternative Extended ER Diagrams for* **is_a** *or Inheritance*

Inheritance is apparently an intoxicating concept. If you squint hard enough, everything can be thought of as being arranged into a gigantic, all-encompassing hierarchy. But modeling the world this way is not a good idea. Philosophically, it somehow fails to capture the world's diversity, and in practical terms, a schema that consists of one, gigantic inheritance hierarchy creates performance problems for OR-SQL.

Describing Relationships Between Entities

The second part of E-ER modeling involves describing the relationships that bind entities together. E-ER diagramming emphasizes entity modeling, but other analytical techniques (object-role modeling, for example) stress the importance of relationships instead.

In addition to *is_a* inheritance, there is another, more common kind of relationship: the *has_a* or *associative* relationship. For example, there is an association or *has_a* relationship associating the strong entities Orders and MovieClubMembers. We say that each Order instance *has_a* MovieClubMember with which it is associated. Most problem domains include many *has_a* relationships between entities. Although relationships do not have a real-world existence in the same way that entity instances have existence, it is convenient to talk about a relationship instance or an occurrence of a relationship.

Representing Relationships

Entities are represented as boxes. The details of an entity's structure, and whatever constraint rules it has, are either written up within the box or with callout labels. Relationships exist between entities, so they are represented by lines connecting entity boxes. Some diagramming techniques place a diamond box in the middle of the line for use as a convenient place to label the relationship, because some relationships involve more than two entities. All example diagrams in this chapter follow this practice.

Others methodologies use a variety of line patterns to represent the various kinds of relationships, but regardless of the representational technique, the fundamental concepts are the same.

In E-ER analysis, relationships are always bidirectional. They correspond to a rule governing legal data in the entities on *both* ends of the line. Figure 8–8 illustrates some examples of relationships among entities in the Movies-R-Us Web site database.

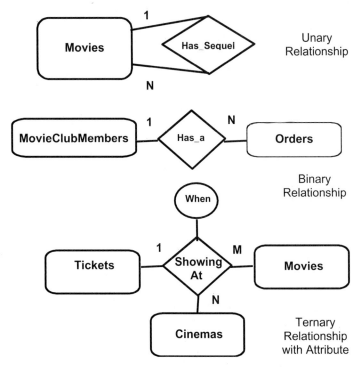

Figure 8–8. *Several Examples of Relationship Diagrams*

While the relationship concept is superficially quite simple, in practice there are a number of decisions to be made about any given relationship. These subtleties become important when mapping the entity-relationship diagram into the logical or model.

Role

The relationship in Figure 8–8 between MovieClubMembers and Orders is about as straightforward as relationships get. But analysts generally use more descriptive terms than **has_a** to label relationships.

This label is sometimes called a *role*. Typically, verb terms taken from the language used to describe the problem domain are used for roles. For example, MoviePersonalities *worked_on* a Movie, and a MovieClubMember *placed* Orders. In the more complex relationship between three entities, the role label indicates that this aspect of the diagram means that each Ticket is for a Movie *showing_at* a Cinema.

Role labels are useful when we map conceptual models to an equivalent logical (i.e., database schema) representation. Occurrences of a relationship can be stored within a table that uses the role name (Showings), or the role name can be used to name a column in a table.

Cardinality

We say that **has_a** relationships are of varying *cardinalities*. The cardinality of a relationship refers to the numbers of instances of each entity that may be present on either side of the relationship. The cardinality of a relationship can be one of the following:

- *One-to-many.* A *one-to-many* relationship from Entity A to Entity B means that any instance of Entity B can correspond to **at most one** instance of Entity A. For example, we say that a one-to-many relationship exists between Merchandise and Movies; each item of Merchandise is related to at most one Movie.
- *Many-to-one.* A *many-to-one* relationship from Entity A to Entity B means that any instance of Entity A can correspond to **at most one** instance of Entity B. The *many-to-one* relationship is simply the corollary of the *one-to-many* relationship, and you can rephrase the one as the other.
- *One-to-one.* A *one-to-one* relationship between Entity A and Entity B means that a *one-to-many* and a *many-to-one* exists between Entity A and Entity B. For example, for every showing of a Movie at a Cinema, there can be at most one Ticket, and each Ticket is good for just one Showing.
- *Many-to-many.* A *many-to-many* relationship exists between two entities that are in neither a *one-to-many* nor a *many-to-one* relationship. For example, a single Order can involve several kinds of Merchandise, and a single kind of Merchandise will be involved in multiple Orders.

In the diagram examples in this book, relationship cardinalities are represented by numbers printed adjacent the corresponding entity. Other diagramming schemes use different line patterns to represent relationship cardinality.

Mandatory or Optional

Mandatory relationships are required relationships. They say that the existence of an entity instance on one end of the relationship requires that an entity instance on the other side of the relationship exist. This is typical of relationships between a strong entity and dependent, weak entities. For example, the many-to-many relationship from Order to MovieClubMember is mandatory. Every Order must have a corresponding MovieClubMember who placed the order. In the same way, each Order must have an item of Merchanside.

Note also that the reverse case is not true: the many-to-many relationship from Merchandise to Orders is *optional*. It is perfectly possible for an item of Merchandise to be an utter failure in the marketplace. Generally, this rule is applied when entity instances are always created in the same business operation. For instance, it is impossible to add a MoviePersonality entity instance by itself: the addition of a MoviePersonality always coincides with the addition of a Movie.

Degrees of Relationships

All relationships we have seen so far involved two different entities. These are called *binary* relationships. However, some relationships can involve just one or more than two entities. Relationships involving a single entity are called *unary* relationships, and relationships involving more than two are called *n-ary* relationships. These terms—unary, binary, and n-ary—are said to refer to the *degree* of the relationship.

For example, it is reasonable to suppose that one of the interesting properties of a movie you might want to record is whether it is a sequel, and if so, the film it is a sequel of. The diagram in our example figures shows a relationship between the Movies entity and itself. This is an unary relationship, and its cardinality indicates that a film may at most have one prequel and potentially many (arguably too many) sequels.

Also, we have several times referred to the cluster of entities and relationships surrounding the screening of a particular film, in a particular movie theater, for which tickets are sold. This is an example of an n-ary relationship. Figure 8–8 illustrates how n-ary relationships are represented.

Attributes of Relationships

Sometimes a relationship between two entities can have an associated attribute recording something about the relationship. For example, each Order involves a quantity of Merchandise items, and each Showing is associated with a range of dates when the movie is to be screened. This kind of attribute is just like an entity attribute; it has a name, data type, and an optional set of constraining rules.

Concepts such as relationship attributes and n-ary relationships tend to blur the difference between relationships and entities. In the end, the distinction can be pretty arbitrary; certain situations can be represented within an E-ER model as either an entity or a relationship with several attributes. However, few things are as unproductive as a two-hour argument about whether something is an entity or a relationship. Besides, they all end up as tables and constraint rules.

Computed Relationships

Another important difference between ORDBMSs and either RDBMSs or OO systems is the way in which the ORDBMS supports what are known as *computed* relationships. In all examples described so far in this chapter, the use of pointers or keys to implement relationships between entity instances is possible. Suppose, however, that the Web site's management decided that they would only accept memberships from people who were within "15 miles" of a cinema, or that each member *has_a* closest cinema?

This relationship is an example of something that can be *computed* efficiently within the ORDBMS. Traditionally, supporting this kind of business rule would have required an external algorithm to determine the closest cinema, which would have been recorded as part of the MovieClubMember's information.

Maintaining such relationships with pointers or references, however, is difficult in operational databases because changes to an attribute on either side of the relationship might cause multiple changes to instances on the other end. For example, what happens when a new cinema opens? Supporting this externally would require that the adding of the new cinema also update all affected MovieClubMembers to show their new closest cinema. Instead, this kind of relationship is better supported using OR-SQL whenever a business operation considers data from entities on both sides of the relationship.

Working an Example

In this section we work an example, using our Movies-R-Us Web site application. The steps involved in creating an extended ER model are as follows:

- Identify the major Entities in the problem domain
- Define Relationships between Entities and categorize each relationship in terms of role, cardinality, and mandatory status
- For each Entity, catalog the entity's attributes and the rules that semantically constrain entity instances
- Determine keys for each entity

Begin with a plain-language description of the site's problem domain. It is possible to infer a great deal of high-level information from such descriptions. Later, when it becomes necessary to dive into detail, having such a document helps maintain your awareness of the forest, in addition to each tree. A verbal description of the Movies-R-Us information system might read like the one below.

> "Our Web site is used as a marketing vehicle for movies. Studios promote movies through the site. They present information such as which movie personalities worked on what movies, where movies can be seen in cinemas, and media for marketing such as still photography, previews and reviews. An important business objective is to sign up as many site members as we can. The 'hook' that brings visitors back again is membership of the site's 'movie club,' which entitles members to discounts and access to the site's comprehensive database of movie information. The site provides B2C e-commerce by selling items of merchandise (toys, apparel, tickets to current releases, and so on). This means that the site's database needs to manage product catalogs and order entry. "

1. Identify Entities.

The first task is to list all principle subjects in the problem domain. Such an entities list appears in Table 8–1.

In practice, identifying entities requires a reasonably good understanding of the problem domain. Such knowledge can be acquired only by a study of the subject area; the business model of an organization, its manufacturing process, or the way an experiment's results are recorded, and so on. Some of the places to look to help build your entities list include the nouns and verbs used in documents describing the problem domain. Other techniques, such as user focus groups or *Joint Application Development (JAD)* sessions, are also very useful.

2. List Relationships among Entities.

In plain language, the relationships among these entities can be expressed as shown in Table 8–2.

We present a total set of entities and the relationships between them in the E-ER diagram in Figure 8–9. Note that at this stage we have not investigated the attributes within the entities, so they are not shown. With large or complex problem domains, it can be difficult to fit all of the details into a single diagram. Also, you may need to create several conceptual models for different user groups. It is therefore a good idea to cluster entities together into related groups with each group on a separate page.

Table 8–1. Principle Subjects in the Problem Domain

Entity Number	Entity Name
E1	Movies
E2	MovieClubMembers
E3	Cinemas
E4	Web_Actions
E5	Orders
E6	Apparel
E7	Toys
E8	Posters
E9	Tickets
E10	Media
E11	Previews
E12	Reviews
E13	Still_Photographs
E14	MoviePersonalities

Table 8–2. Relationships Among Entities in Problem Domain

Relationships among Entities	Cardinality
Movie **promoted_by** Merchandise	One-to-many
Movie **has_sequel**(s) Movie	One-to-many
MoviePersonality **works_on** Movie	Many-to-many
{ Apparel, Toys, Tickets, Media } **is_a** Merchandise	N/A
{ Preview, Review, Still_Photographs } **is_a** Media	N/A
Movie **shown_at** Cinemas **with** Ticket	Many-to-many-to-one
Order **sells** (Quantity_of) Merchandise	Many-to-many
Order **placed_by** MovieClubMember	Many-to-one
MovieClubMember **undertook** Web_Action	One-to-many

This diagram illustrates many of the modeling concepts we discussed in the previous section. Of course, this is not the only reasonable E-ER model for this problem domain. In fact, later in the development cycle, we will see that introducing the concept of MoviePersonalities into the schema changes the design significantly.

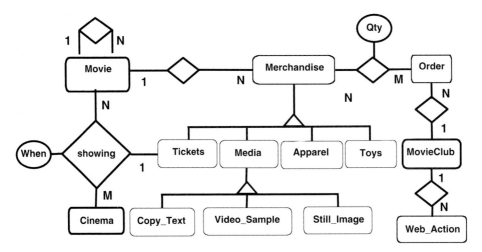

Figure 8–9. *Extended Entity-Relationship Diagram for the Movies-R-Us Web Site*

3. Describe Each Entity's Attributes.

Recall that each attribute consists of a name, the kind of data stored in the attribute, and whatever rules constrain data values the attribute can contain. In Table 8–3 we present a list of the Merchandise entity's attributes.

Table 8–3. Attribute Details of Merchandise Entity

Merchandise Attributes

Name	Kind of Data	Opt/Man	Rules or Constraints
Id	PartNumber	Mandatory	Unique; **Primary Key**
Name	ProductName	Mandatory	
Description	Document	Optional	
Price	Currency	Mandatory	Must be GreaterThan US$0.0
ShippingCost	Currency	Mandatory	Must be GreaterThan US$5.0
NumberAvailable	Quantity	Mandatory	

Each of the various Merchandise sub-entities adds attributes to this set. All inherit the attribute list from Table 8–3, as well as all constraining rules defined for it. For example, all sub-entities have the Id attribute as their primary identifier. Table 8–4 lists the attributes added to the Merchandise definition for some of these sub-entities.

Table 8–4. Attribute Details of Sub-Entities

Apparel Attributes

Name	Kind of Data	Opt/Man	Rules or Constraints
KindofClothing	KindofClothing	Mandatory	
AvailableInSizes	SET{Sizes}	Mandatory	Must be at least one size.
Photo	Image	Optional	

Toys

Name	Kind of Data	Opt/Man	Rules or Constraints
KindofToy	KindofToy	Mandatory	
SuitableFor	Age_Range	Mandatory	No negative age values.
Photo	Image	Optional	

An entity's attribute name cannot be reused in any entity UNDER it in a hierarchy. The various kinds of data that appear in an entity's attributes may, of course, be reused in different attributes as often as necessary. If a similar attribute (similar role in the entity and the same data type) exists in several sub-entities of some given entity, moving this attribute up the hierarchy is often a good idea. A good goal to aim for is to minimize the total number of attributes declared in a set of entities.

4. Determining Keys

At this stage it should be possible to identify the candidate keys for each entity. Sometimes, an entity's keys are obvious, because it is common practice to assign unique identifiers to real-world objects. At other times, the choice of best key is less clear. In some cases, there is absolutely no reasonable key at all. When an entity lacks a candidate key it can indicate that your understanding of the entity is incomplete or inaccurate. But generally, it implies that you should assign that entity a system-generated identifier, pending further analysis.

Analysts differ over the question of the best way to treat keys. Some have a preference for system-generated identifiers, while others avoid the practice. There is no right or wrong answer to the question. So in keeping with this plurality, the E-ER model in our example adopts a mix of techniques. Neither of the Cinemas or Orders entities in Figure 8–5 has an obvious logical key, so we use system-generated keys, but MovieClub-Members and MoviePersonalities both possess workable logical key attributes.

Attributes: Names and Strong Typing

An important difference between the way you use E-ER modeling with an RDBMS and an ORDBMS reflects the way that the ORDBMS model supports *strong typing*; that is, all things in the problem domain that are of a like kind (in relational theory, we say *domain*) should be identified and later analyzed using object-oriented approaches. Cataloging these domains as part of your E-ER model requires paying particular attention to the kind of data each entity's attributes store.

Take a look at Figures 8-5 and 8-6 again. Notice how many different kinds of data there are in these entities. Using RDBMS technology, it would be typical to see only SQL-92 types in the model. You could, for example, use INTEGER or VARCHAR instead of OrderNumber and Cinema_Id. Using the SQL-92 type has the unfortunate consequence that the attribute's name must be used to distinguish different kinds of information. With an ORDBMS, it is easy to create separate types corresponding to each kind of data object and to reserve the attribute's name for its role in the entity.

COLLECTION Attributes

Developers experienced with E-ER techniques learn to preempt some of the procedures used to derive logical models from conceptual models. For example, one tendency is to instinctively produce E-ER models that are very "relational." Keeping the target DBMS tool's facilities and functionality in mind is generally a good habit when working with an ORDBMS, but one place the new and old worlds collide is the question of COLLECTION attributes.

Several of the entities we use as illustrations contain COLLECTION attributes. In Table 8–5 we include an attribute list for the Movies entity, which takes the matter to extremes.

The presence of so many SET attributes in this table is troublesome to experienced data analysts. Consider how regularly films are released in which a single person has multiple roles in the production, for example, as writer and director. Also, consider how many movies a successful Hollywood star will work on during his or her career. This entity's definition implies that the star's name is recorded multiple times—at least once for every film with which the star is associated and occasionally more than once in a single Movie.

What happens if you find out that a movie star's name has been misspelled? You need to find every instance of the misspelled name and change it. What if the problem had been corrected in some places and not others? Further, what if some of the corrections are themselves wrong?

Table 8–5. Attributes of Movies Entity

Movies

Name	Kind of Data	Opt/Man	Rules or Constraints
Title	Movie_Title	Mandatory	First part of primary key
Released_On	Date	Mandatory	Second part of primary key
Directors	SET{MoviePersonality}	Mandatory	
Writers	SET{ MoviePersonality }	Mandatory	
Producers	SET{ MoviePersonality }	Mandatory	
Starring	SET{(MoviePersonality, CharacterName) }	Mandatory	
Awards	SET{Award}	Optional	
Genre	SET{Genres}	Mandatory	
Budget	Currency	Mandatory	GreaterThan "US$0"
Takings	Currency	Optional	
Plot_Summary	Document	Mandatory	
On_Video	Boolean	Mandatory	Default is "t"

On the other hand, consider the Genre and Awards attributes. All difficulties relating to managing movie personalities arise with these attributes, yet the prospect of creating other entities, each containing perhaps 10 rows, and obliging OR-SQL developers to write joins, seems inefficient.

Later in this chapter, when we consider how to map this table into a logical representation, these problems will be revisited. As we shall see, two different schema patterns are employed. The important thing at this level of analysis is not to worry too much about implementation and instead to focus on correctness and completeness.

E-ER Modeling Summary

In this section we have reviewed how to use E-ER techniques to create a high-level, conceptual description of a problem domain. The main differences between how you would perform E-ER analysis for an RDBMS and how you would handle an ORDBMS are as follows:

- Modeling **is_a** relationships between entities is possible using the E-ER techniques, and the ORDBMS data model allows a direct representation of inheritance in a schema.
- With object-relational databases you are better not analyzing each entity's attributes down to atomic data types such as `INTEGER`, `VARCHAR`, and so on. Instead, assign each attribute a domain or data-type name.
- Try to create a strongly typed scheme. Identify attributes in different entities whose values belong to the same domain, such as PersonNames and Geo_Location and ensure that this is reflected in the analysis. Also, if it can be determined that the attribute(s) correspond to an application level class, record that information.
- Using `COLLECTION` attribute types (`SET`, `LIST` and `ARRAY`) is fine.

Readers familiar with E-ER modeling should have little trouble with the techniques described in this section. Later, when we explain how to map your conceptual model into a corresponding logical model, more profound differences emerge. Perhaps the biggest difference between more traditional approaches and the approach advocated in this book is that with an RDBMS, only the data model counts. With ORDBMS databases, the behavior of the schema's objects should also be considered.

In the next two sections we cover the role of object data modeling techniques and data flow analysis, which typically play minor parts in the development of RDBMS-based systems.

Conceptual Object Modeling

In our ORDBMS development methodology, object modeling takes over where E-ER analysis leaves off. E-ER analysis documents the problem domain's high-level components and structure. It also incorporates certain features of object-oriented data models (inheritance and `COLLECTION` attributes), and models data integrity issues such as keys and rules over data values in entity attributes.

However, E-ER modeling does not address other aspects of the problem domain. In relational terms, E-ER modeling helps to understand the database's *relations*, such as the set of facts being recorded, but it does not provide the means to analyze the schema's *domains*, which are the different *kinds* of data used in entity attributes. Also, E-ER modeling does nothing to describe the complex, multistep processes that are characteristic of most information systems.

For example, in the E-ER model for our Movies database, the Movies table included a "Title" attribute storing "movie title" data. It turns out that although movie titles are simply strings of characters, the rules for handling them are more complex than the rules for strings. For example, the strings "Big Sleep, The," and "The Big Sleep" represent equivalent movie titles, although such equivalence does not follow from the way SQL-92 VARCHAR type is defined. Behavior such as this is not captured using traditional E-ER techniques.

In this section we introduce the concepts of object modeling and explain how they are applied in object-relational database analysis. These techniques are useful for several reasons:

- Object modeling clarifies the description of the problem domain by incorporating more semantic information into the model. So far, we have noted the structure of entity types and the existence of attribute types. Object modeling provides the means to examine these in more detail.
- Object-modeling techniques help to minimize the overall development effort. By focusing on the properties of different objects, in addition to the names used to identify them, you can figure out when two things are really the same and when they are actually different.
- Finally, techniques described in this chapter yield results that can be mapped easily into ORDBMS technical features, such as user-defined types and functions. An extremely useful property of object-oriented approaches to software engineering is that analytic features, such as structure and behavior, can be transformed more or less directly into a technical specification.

In this section, we begin with an overview of the subtask relating to OO analysis in our methodology. Then we provide some background information describing the concepts used with OO approaches in general. Finally, we illustrate how to use these techniques to further your analysis of the problem domain.

Overview of Object-Oriented Analysis

The subtasks in conceptual object analysis within this ORDBMS design methodology are as follows:

- Prepare a list of *classes* in the problem domain. Initially, this is simply a list of all of the entities and the kinds of data stored in entity attributes.
- For each *class*, describe the following:

1. The class's public interface (constructors, elements, interface functions, and how instances of the class are manipulated).
2. Algorithms for the class's DBMS interface (export, index, communication with a client program, sorting, and so on).
3. Integrity rules for objects (rules that differentiate valid and invalid instances of the object).

- Classify entity and attribute types into the smallest, complete set of object classes.
- Group like types into hierarchies to facilitate reuse and minimize the development required.

Over the next few pages we review each of these steps in more detail and demonstrate their application in the Movies-R-Us Web site information system.

Background to Object Analysis

Although we use the UML object-class diagrams as a mechanism for documenting object classes, this methodology does not depend on diagrams in the same way that E-ER modeling does. Diagrams are good for "at a glance" overviews of each object's properties, but in practice, the hard work involves determining *how* the object works, in addition to *what* it does.

Figure 8–10 illustrates the basic ideas. The figure is meant to represent a broken clock. To the left of the figure you can see the set of data values—hour, minute, and second—that collectively store the time. To the right is the watch face and the dial used to set the watch's time. Between state and presentation, there are a set of mechanistic algorithms that turn internal state information into hand positions on the dial.

Over the next few pages we introduce some useful background concepts in object modeling. Each of these ideas plays a part in our methodology.

Component Interfaces

The central concept in object analysis is the idea of an object class as a software module *encapsulating* its functionality behind an *interface*. Other software that works with an instance of the object—an end user writing OR-SQL queries and even the ORDBMS itself—is restricted to interacting with it through this interface.

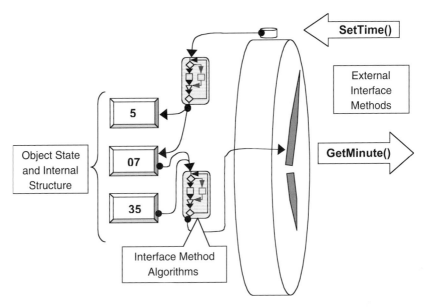

Figure 8–10. *The Broken Watch Model: Structured State and Interface Methods*

Ideally, external logic never directly accesses an object's internals. In practical terms, the ORDBMS enforces this by allowing only those functions explicitly defined for a particular data type to be used in queries over columns of that type. With OPAQUE TYPE and built-in types, there is simply no way (using OR-SQL) to access the bytes recording an object's internal state. Other user-defined type mechanisms, however, are more pragmatic. For instance, ROW TYPE elements can be accessed with cascading-dot notation.

Therefore, an important subtask in ORDBMS development is to analyze all object classes in the problem domain and to identify the set of *interface methods* for each of them. We use the terms *method*, *interface method*, and *interface function* to refer to an operation that may be applied over an object. These operations include getting or setting internal values, calculating derived values based on the object's state, comparing instances, creating new instances of the object, and so on.

Each interface method description consists of the following:

- A name. This is simply a handle with which to refer to the interface method. It becomes the name of the OR-SQL user-defined function.
- The vector of arguments that are supplied when the interface method is invoked. Interface methods are identified by the combination of their name and their arguments.
- An explanation of the interface's semantics. What does the interface method do? How does it do it?

In addition to the interface methods that the object presents to OR-SQL developers, you also need to implement functions that the ORDBMS needs. For example, OR-SQL programmers often need to be able to tell when two objects—say two movie titles—are *equal*.

In order to extract object instances that are equal (to some data value) from a large list of them, the ORDBMS must know how to *compare* two object instances and then to sort and index them. For certain types of objects, you need to specify other *support interfaces*, for things such as communication, backup and recovery, and bulk data loading and unloading.

Component Structure

An object's structural specification describes its internal anatomy. In practical term, it consists of a set of named elements and their types. Collectively these store the object's *state*. The various interface methods operate on the data in these structural elements and on additional values they receive as arguments. Although sometimes a component's structure is obvious from the way it is used, the only requirement is that the structure be sufficient to support all of the object's interfaces. Developers designing objects have considerable scope for creative engineering.

Each structural element consists of the following:

- A name. This identifier has a similar role to a table's column name. It should be unique within the object specification.
- A data type. Elements within objects are objects themselves. This implies that a recursive analytical procedure is a good idea. After each round of analysis, you will arrive at a new set of objects to be given the same treatment. Ultimately the process ends when you get down to built-in types or the specification of an OPAQUE TYPE in terms of C types, or the most basic data structure of all—an array of bytes.
- Data rules. These rules distinguish valid object instances from all possible instances implied by the object's definition. For example, consider an object meant to hold ranges of dates (Begin, End date). Internally the structure consists of a begin and end element, both DATE types or C int types. The semantics of the object, however, dictate that the value in the begin must be less than the value in the end.

Each object class/component is implemented using a combination of user-defined data types and the user-defined routines. Structure drives the type's design, the interface establishes the user-defined functions to be implemented, and the rules governing the type's data and each interface's semantics determine how each function is implemented.

Patterns

Another useful modeling concept is the idea of a *pattern*. Often, as you go about analysis and design, you come across a situation that is similar to one encountered previously. Lessons learned designing and implementing solutions to earlier problems can be referred to when solving the current one. Recurring modeling and analysis designs are called *patterns*.

The advantage of thinking in this way is that once you have decided that the current situation is an instance of a particular pattern, the pattern's description implies a great deal about what the class currently under investigation looks like. Based on a few characteristics, you can determine a complete interface.

For example, consider the attribute data type `Genre` identified in the Movie entity. The genre "kind of data" reflects the style of a film, or its subject matter, or its story. Words like "western", "romance", "documentary", "sports", "art", "non-U.S." and so on are all film genres. In order to be as useful as possible the Movies-R-Us Web site might specify a range of possible genre categories to ensure that employees entering new movies comply with the classification rules.

Based on a few characteristics of this kind of data, we can infer additional things about what the object looks like:

- The total number of genres is relatively small, certainly less than 100.
- Each genre name has a set of synonyms: a "cowboy" movie and a "western" belong to the same genre, for example.
- New genres are rare, and noteworthy.

Taken together, this implies that `Genre` is an instance of a pattern we call *enumeration* after a similar concept in some programming languages. Other examples of the enumeration pattern include days of the week, units of weights and measures, months of the year, star signs, names of U.S. states, countries of the European Union, grades of employee, and so on.

In Table 8–6 we present a few examples of patterns you encounter fairly frequently in object-relational development.

This list is not comprehensive. With time, other patterns will be identified.

UML Object-Class Diagrams

Several diagramming techniques exist that can represent an object class and its interface. In this book, we use the UML object-class diagrams to demonstrate what this kind of modeling creates. Figure 8–11 illustrates two UML object-class diagrams for the Mail_Address and Delivery_Address kinds of data.

Table 8–6. Patterns and Their Descriptions

Pattern Name	Examples	Description
Enumeration	Genres, clothing sizes, U.S. states, and gender	Small set of values (usually less than 100). Often, there exists a set of synonyms for some members.
Quantities	Currencies and physical measurements	Usually a value and unit pair in which you need to apply some kind of mathematical step to convert values to the same unit before comparison, but you still want to maintain original data.
Part Codes	International standard book number and a vehicle identification number	Multipart identifier, usually with information encoded within the representation.
Numbers	Rational numbers, extra-large integers.	Some numeric types are not supported by the SQL-92 language. These include numbers with an integer numerator and denominator. Often, although these data types use mathematical operations (plus, times, and so on), these operations can be complex (such as multiplying two rational numbers).

Mail_Address	
+ Address_Line_One	String
+ Address_Line_Two	String
+ City	String
+ State	String
+ ZipCode	Zip_Code
+ Country	String
+ Mail_Address (String, String, String, Zip_Code)	
+ approximateMatch (Mail_Address, Mail_Address) -> boolean	
+ Label (Mail _Address) -> String	
+ Equal (Mail_Address, Mail_Address) -> boolean	
- Compare (Mail_Address, Mail_Address) -> INTEGER	

Delivery_Address	
+ Address_Line_One	String
+ Address_Line_Two	String
+ City	String
+ State	String
+ ZipCode	Zip_Code
+ Country	String
+ Delivery_Notes	Document
+ Delivery_Address (String, String, String, Zip_Code, Document)	
+ approximateMatch (Delivery_Address, Delivery_Address) -> boolean	
+ Label (Delivery _Address) -> String	
+ Equal (Delivery_Address, Delivery_Address) -> boolean	
- Compare (Delivery_Address, Delivery_Address) -> INTEGER	

Figure 8–11. Examples of UML Object-Class Diagrams

Object-class diagrams consist of a naming label, a section describing the internal structure of the component, and a section that lists the object's interface methods. As with entity diagrams, for each structural element within the object class, you supply a name and the kind of data the element contains. Each interface method is listed with its name, the list of arguments it accepts, and the interface method's return type.

In UML class diagrams, it is common to use a symbol such as "−" or "+" adjacent to each element or interface method. This indicates whether the feature is *public*, which indicates whether it will be made available as part of the SQL interface, or *private*, in which case only the ORDBMS or another interface method can use it. In the diagrams in Figure 8–11, the support interfaces are marked as private.

Of course, you cannot implement the components in Figure 8–11 using just what is shown in an object-class diagram. An understanding of how each interface method works is also required. For example, to compare two MailAddresses to see if they are approximately equivalent (which would result in the same delivery), it is necessary to know how the comparison is performed. The comparison might check for the equivalence of the Zip_Code, State, and City before checking to see if the address's first line has a similar street name and the same number; that is, it can ignore attributes such as whether the strings are in uppercase and the differences between "123 Ajax Avenue" and "123 Ajax Ave."

Also, you will sometimes find that there are data correctness and integrity rules that apply to the object class as a whole. For example, some elements must be supplied with data values, or a relationship between elements must be checked. Such rules must be enforced in the code implementing the object's interface.

Inheritance

An important objective of OO approaches to software design is to minimize development effort by promoting reuse. This means finding classes that are related in such a way that they share significant portions of their functionality. By using the ORDBMS's capacity to model type inheritance, either through ROW TYPE inheritance, the DISTINCT TYPE mechanism, or a CAST, the amount of coding effort is reduced and the quality and logical consistency of the overall system is improved.

For example, it is fairly clear from the UML class diagrams in Figure 8–11 that a Delivery_Address *is_a* subclass of Mail_Address. That is, the various interface methods that operate on the Mail_Address work in similar fashion on the Delivery_Address. There are some differences: Delivery_Address could print a different label (one that includes any delivery instructions) and you would need interface methods that allowed a OR-SQL-level developer to provide delivery instructions when creating an instance of the Delivery_Address object. These differences, however, can be accommodated.

Identifying hierarchies of interdependent data types helps you later on by minimizing the amount of code you need to write.

Object Analysis with an ORDBMS

Two important goals to pursue as part of any software development project are as follows:

- You should minimize the amount of coding effort required to complete the project.
- You should decompose the overall project into modules that can be combined in such a way that upgrades and modifications are localized as much as possible.

In this section, we illustrate how to use object-oriented concepts as part of the analysis and design phase of an ORDBMS database development project. The result of this step in the development cycle is a minimal list of independent low-level data objects from which the database schema is constructed. For each object in this list, we generate a description of its structural elements (state) and interface methods and functions.

In Chapter 9, we take this list and use it to create the database's user-defined types and functions.

Create a List of Different Kinds of Data in the Problem Domain

The first task is the easy one: prepare a list of all kinds of data identified in the problem domain as part of the E-ER phase. This list should include both entity types and the names used to identify the various kinds of data in entity attributes. Although the complete list from our Movies-R-Us Web site is quite extensive, in Table 8–7 we have a representative sample. Grayed names correspond to entities.

Table 8-7. Kinds of Data in the Movies-R-Us Web Site Database

Movies	Movie_Id	Movie_Title	DATE
MoviePersonality	PersonName	Genre	Award
Currency	Document	BOOLEAN	MovieClubMember
MembershipId	MailAddress	PhoneNumber	GeoPoint
Image	CreditCardNumber	Cinema	Cinema_Id
CinemaName	INTEGER	Merchandise	Part_Code
ProductName	Part_Code	Product_Name	LongString
Quantity	Apparel	Clothing_Kind	Size
Toy	Toy_Kind	Age_Range	etc . . .

As you read through this list, you will note that for each entity, the list includes its name and then each of its attribute data types. Because some entities have the same kinds of data in them as others, the number of attribute types shown for each entity decreases as we go down the list. In fact, by the time you get to the last few entities, the list consists of mostly entity names. Almost all later entities' attribute types appear earlier in the list.

Describe Interface Methods for Each of Them

The second step, specifying each object's interface, is an imprecise science. It requires an understanding of how the object being studied works. In his *Meditations*, Roman Emperor Marcus Aurelius, writing in about 100 AD, offers the following sage advice to software developers using object-oriented software development techniques:

"Of each thing ask, what is its essence?"

What Marcus is saying is that in order to understand an object, it is useful to ask questions about what it is, rather than try to anticipate how it will be combined with other objects in your application. In fact, it is counterproductive, at this stage, to anticipate too much *how* your object is to be used. Instead, focus on the ways in which you *reason* about instances of the object. If you perform your analysis correctly, what you implement should be useful in ways you cannot anticipate.

Later, when we describe the workload of common queries, we may need to revisit an object's specification to add new interface methods in response to new information.

Entities as Object Classes

Object-oriented analysis provides insights into entity types. One away to think about this step is to consider that the attributes already defined for each entity are simply a subset of the complete interface to the entity/object. For example, consider the hierarchy of Merchandise entities. In the diagram in Figure 8–12, we present data attributes and a set of interface methods for the root entity of the hierarchy using UML class diagrams.

The goal is to extend entity semantics to include behavior and to minimize the number of entity attributes in the entity by finding out which of them can be calculated "on the fly" rather than stored. As part of analyzing entities, here are some things to look out for:

- How can an entity instance be modified? What data values are required, and how does the modification work algorithmically? For example, setting the price of any item of merchandise requires a new currency value and changes the Price attribute.
- What information can be calculated from an entity instance? How is this calculation done? For example, the `TotalCost()` method adds the item's price attribute to its shipping cost, and the `Print-LineItem()` returns a text string that includes what the item is, its total cost, and so on.
- Can an attribute's value be calculated rather than stored? For example, in the class diagram in Figure 8–12, it is perfectly plausible that an end user might have identified the `TotalPrice()` interface method as an attribute of the entity. Calculating values obviously consumes less storage.

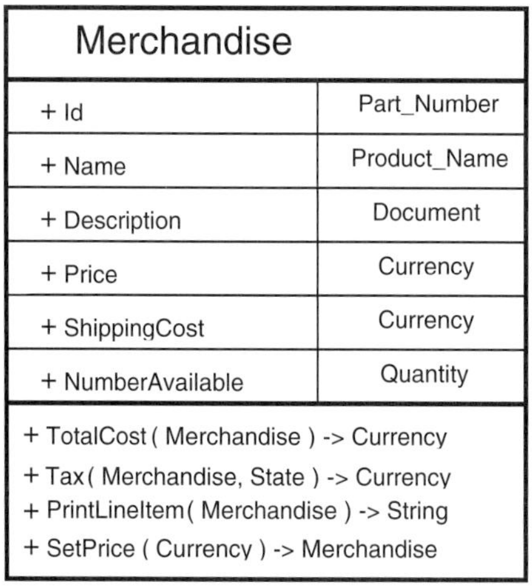

Merchandise	
+ Id	Part_Number
+ Name	Product_Name
+ Description	Document
+ Price	Currency
+ ShippingCost	Currency
+ NumberAvailable	Quantity
+ TotalCost (Merchandise) -> Currency	
+ Tax (Merchandise, State) -> Currency	
+ PrintLineItem (Merchandise) -> String	
+ SetPrice (Currency) -> Merchandise	

Figure 8–12. *Various Kinds of Data in the Movies-R-Us Web Site Database*

There are differences between the approach to object modeling we take with entities and the approach we take with attribute objects. Entities tend to be more structurally complex than the domains. Further, because an entity's structural elements are accessed using OR-SQL (i.e., an entity's structural elements are not encapsulated), they tend to have fewer interface methods.

Attribute Types as Classes

For each of the nonentity objects listed in Figure 8–11, the goal of object analysis is to arrive at a correct and complete description of its structure and behavior. For example, consider the kinds of data we have labeled PersonName and GeoPoint, which appear in several entities. An analysis of these types leads to the kinds of descriptions we see in the UML diagrams in Figure 8–13.

These diagrams help to explain why analysis is a recursive process. For example, in the PersonName type, one of the elements is a Title_Enum. To fully understand what kind of object this is requires more work. What is the full set of name titles? How are they compared or ordered? What are the synonyms for each kind of name title?

Like all recursive operations, this one runs the risk of never ending. Knowing when to stop is something you learn with experience. In the class diagrams in Figure 8–13, there is little point in analyzing the Strings used to represent different subparts of names further. Experienced readers will agree that there is a terrible risk in becoming entangled in

PersonName	
- Family_Name	String
- First_Name	String
- Title	Title_Enum
- OtherNames	String
+ PersonName (String, String, String, String) + PersonName (String, String) + PersonName (String) + getFamilyName (PersonName) -> String, + getFirstName (PersonName) -> String, + getTitleName (PersonName) ->Title_Enum, + String (PersonName) -> String, [Ordinal Operators, B-Tree Support]	

GeoPoint	
- Latitude	FLOAT
- Longitude	FLOAT
+ GeoPoint (String) -> GeoPoint, + GeoPoint(FLOAT, FLOAT) -> GeoPoint, + Latitude (GeoPoint) -> FLOAT, + Longitude (GeoPoint) -> FLOAT, + Distance (GeoPoint, GeoPoint) -> FLOAT + Quadrant (GeoPoint) -> CHAR(2) [Spatial Operators, R-Tree Support, Compare()]	

Figure 8–13. *Two Object-Class Diagrams for Attribute Types*

the analysis process. A little analysis goes a long way, but a lot of analysis leads nowhere.

You will also note how the interface-methods list for the Person-Name object class includes a bracketed pair of labels: Ordinal Operators and B-Tree Support. These stand for a group of interface methods that are typically found together. Ordinal operators determine when instances of an object are less than, less than or equal to, equal to, greater than or equal to, greater than, or not equal to another instance. For efficiency, the ordinal operators are accompanied by the B-Tree support interface, which allows the ORDBMS to index and sort the data type.

Interface Modeling

In an ORDBMS database, the individual methods (user-defined functions) that make up the interface to an object class (user-defined types) can be classified into a number of categories according to the kind of function they perform. Understanding what these are helps to guide analysis. This section lists several of the different ways an object class's interface methods can be used. For each category of interface method, we present an example drawn from our Movies-R-Us Web site and a set of questions to help determine what a new object class needs.

Interface methods fall into the following four categories, depending on how they are used:

- Expressions. Expressions are OR-SQL level operations that involve the object in some way. For example, some expression interface methods change the state of the object, and some compute a result based on inputs from two different types. In Figure 8–13 interface methods like `Latitude()`, `Longitude()` and `Distance()` fall into this category.
- Support functions. Support functions define how the ORDBMS performs its own operations over instances of the type. The support functions perform operations such as casting from public to private representations of the type and interacting with facilities such as backup, recovery, and communication. Support functions usually come in groups. In Figure 8–13 the B-tree support implies a single support function, `Compare()`. R-Tree support implies four functions.
- Operators. Operators are a special subcategory of expressions that return boolean values. WHERE clauses in query expressions combine operators to specify what data is being accessed by the query. The questions you need to answer to define operator functions include

"How are instances of these types compared and contrasted?" In Figure 8–13 Ordinal operators implies six interface methods, while spatial can imply anywhere from four up.

- Aggregators. Aggregators are functions that examine a set of values and return a value that is calculated from the while set. The SQL-92 language includes aggregators such as MIN(), MAX() and COUNT(), and you can create your own new ones for new types. Aggregator functions are used most frequently in report and analysis queries.

Modeling interface methods takes more effort than deciding on an object's structure, because you need to figure out what each interface method does *algorithmically*. This also presents an opportunity. Rigorous analysis and creativity can help you to design objects that allow your database to work in new and very powerful ways.

Constructors

Constructors are methods that create a new instance of the object. In practical terms, they are user-defined functions returning an instance of the new data type. A single object class can have multiple constructors, which can be invoked directly within an OR-SQL query, or they may be used to implement a CAST between one of the ORDBMS's built-in types. The most basic constructor function takes an argument for each element of the object's structure, but these functions come in a wide variety of forms.

The GeoPoint object we introduce in Figure 8–13 has at least two constructors; one of which parses a string, while the other uses two floating-point values to populate the elements of the object. Constructors are good places to implement data integrity and correctness rules. For example, latitude ranges between –90 and +90, while longitude ranges from –180 to +180. Other values are illegal, and they ought to cause an exception.

Questions that help to determine how the set of constructor methods should work include the following:

- How can an instance of an object class be created?
- What data values are required for each constructor, and how are these argument values used to populate the structural elements?
- What rules are used to discriminate legal and illegal data values in the structural elements of the object?
- Is this an example of a "large" object, or will it be relatively small?

For simplicity, assign each constructor class the same name as the object class. For example, the PersonName class in Figure 8–13 possesses three constructor methods, all of which have the same name, but different arguments. Examine Listing 8–3.

```
CREATE FUNCTION PersonName ( lvarchar, lvarchar,
                                 lvarchar, lvarchar )
RETURNING PersonName
WITH ( NOT VARIANT, PARALLELIZABLE )
EXTERNAL NAME
'PersonName:PersonName.PName(java.lang.String,java.lang.String,
                                 java.lang.String,java.lang.String)'
LANGUAGE Java
DOCUMENT
"PersonName ( LastName, FirstName, Title, OtherNames )";
--
CREATE FUNCTION PersonName ( lvarchar, lvarchar,
                                 Lvarchar )
RETURNING PersonName
WITH ( NOT VARIANT, PARALLELIZABLE )
EXTERNAL NAME
'PersonName:PersonName.PName(java.lang.String,java.lang.String,
                                 java.lang.String)'
LANGUAGE Java;
DOCUMENT
"PersonName ( LastName, FirstName, Title)";
--
CREATE FUNCTION PersonName ( lvarchar )
RETURNING PersonName
WITH ( NOT VARIANT, PARALLELIZABLE )
EXTERNAL NAME 'PersonName:PersonName.PName(java.lang.String)'
LANGUAGE Java
DOCUMENT
"This version of the PersonName constructor takes a single ",
"string that contains a formatted name; Johnson, Ray. Mr.  ",
"it is the symmetric operation for String( PersonName ).   ";
--
```

Listing 8–3. *Various Constructor Expressions for PersonName Object From Figure 8–13*

Modifiers and Accessors

Accessors and modifiers are interface methods (they are typically invoked within OR-SQL queries) that get and set state information encapsulated within an object class. Accessors are UDFs that accept an instance of the object as an argument and return another object. Modifiers take an instance of the object, and possibly some other parameters, and return a modified copy of the object. Some object-oriented programming language standards make it compulsory to provide accessors and modifiers as part of the class's implementation.

Figure 8–13 illustrates several examples of accessor and modifier interfaces. Each structural element of the PersonName object class has a corresponding accessor to read its value and a modifier to change it. GeoPoint includes methods to extract longitude and latitude values. As with constructors, you can have multiple interfaces with the same name that take different arguments.

The questions to ask when describing an object's accessors and modifiers include the following:

- What information about an object's state can be accessed? If this information is computed using element data, how should it be done?
- What aspects of an object's state can be modified? What values are needed by the modification logic, and how does the modification affect the object?

Accessor methods can calculate their result value using the internal state of the object. In addtion, a single modifier might imply changes to several elements of the object's structure. Examine Listing 8–4.

```
CREATE FUNCTION  Quadrant ( Arg1 GeoPoint )
RETURNS CHAR(2)
     IF ( Arg1.Longitude <= 0 ) THEN
             IF ( Arg1.Latitude <= 0 ) THEN
                     RETURN 'SW';
             ELSE
                     RETURN 'NW'
             END IF;
     ELSE
             IF ( Arg1.Latitude <= 0 ) THEN
                     RETURN 'SE';
             ELSE
                     RETURN 'NE'
             END IF;
     END IF;
END FUNCTION;
--
CREATE FUNCTION Translate ( Arg1 GeoPoint,
                            Delta_X float,
                            Delta_Y float )
RETURNING GeoPoint
     RETURN GeoPoint ( Arg1.Longitude + Delta_X,
                       Arg1.Latitude  + Delta_Y );
END FUNCTION;
```

Listing 8–4. *Example of Accessor and Modifier Functions*

Most accessors and modifiers are simple and self-contained. What makes them useful is the way they can be nested and combined. Note that modifier UDFs do not, as their name suggests, modify an argument's data value. Instead, they create a new instance of the return type, probably copy the data from an argument into it, and then modify the new object's structure. This is necessary because in OR-SQL queries, a single data value from a table may be used to create multiple new objects. Modifying the original object in place many times within a single query would cause reliability problems.

Other Expressions: Mathematical and Combinatorial

UDTs and UDFs are very powerful. Expressions can return more than one value using the OUT parameter technique, and a single UDF can take arguments of many different types. External user-defined functions implementing byte-level operations over OPAQUE TYPE data objects can be called from within SPL UDFs. In addition to type-centric behavior, UDFs can implement useful tools for built-in types, such as string processing, DATE manipulation, and so on.

Note on Mathematical Operations

User-defined functions that correspond to mathematical symbols such as "+," "*," "SQRT," "||," and so on deserve special attention. Pay close attention to the semantics of the object when you are designing mathematical operators; mathematics is a subtle subject. For example, consider a type like Length, which we introduce in a UML diagram format in Figure 8–14. This is an example of the Quantities pattern, because it includes both a unit and a quantity value. Part of the object's functionality is to automatically convert quantities between different units when instances are compared or added.

What complicates the Length class is the way that certain mathematical operators, for example, Times(), do not work the same way that they do for data such as INTEGER or FLOAT. When you multiply (or divide, but not add or subtract) two Length instances, you get an Area object rather than another instance of a Length. Therefore, there are, strictly speaking, two definitions of Times() as shown in Listing 8–5.

```
CREATE FUNCTION Times ( Arg1 Length, Multiplier FLOAT )
RETURNS Length
      RETURN Length ( Arg1.Quantity * Multiplier,
                       Arg1.Unit );
```

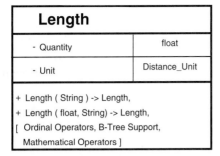

Length	
- Quantity	float
- Unit	Distance_Unit
+ Length (String) -> Length, + Length (float, String) -> Length, [Ordinal Operators, B-Tree Support, Mathematical Operators]	

Figure 8–14. *Length Object-Class Diagram*

```
END FUNCTION; 3

CREATE FUNCTION Times ( Arg1 Length, Arg2 Length )
RETURNS Area
     RETURN Area ( Arg1.Quantity * Arg2.Quantity,
                     Arg1.Unit, Arg2.Unit );
END FUNCTION;
```

Listing 8–5. *Multiplying a Quantity by Another Value*

Unfortunately, the tool used to help implement these types (the Data-Blade Developers Kit or DBDK) generates the more naïve function signature by default. It must be corrected by hand as part of your implementation phase.

Logical Operators

Logical operators are typically used in the WHERE clause of OR-SQL queries. They are UDFs that take two argument data values and produce a boolean (true or false) result.

The relational data model is built upon logical foundations, which makes the logical operators especially important because they are the mechanism for identifying "interesting" data values within a query. Of course, other expressions might be used to calculate intermediate values that are passed into them as arguments. Ultimately, however, it is operator functions that determine which data finds its way into a query's results.

There are basically three categories of operator functions. They differ according to the indexing techniques they use:

---

3 And, as we saw in Chapter 5, you need the commutator function too.

- The first category works for *ordinal* data types and uses B-Tree indices. If you can arrange instances of an object class in ordered fashion along a number line, then the *ordinal* operators are appropriate. Ordinal operators are the ones that can be applied to most numbers, such as `INTEGER` or `DECIMAL` values. Most new types, including the PersonName type introduced in Listing 8–5, will fall into this category. When describing an ordinal data type, the algorithm used to determine ordering—the `Compare()`—is particularly important.
- The second category of logical operators is used for *region* or *multidimensional* data and uses R-Trees. These spatial operators can use the Region Tree or R-Tree indexing method. Data types that are multidimensional, such as a GeoPoint, or that cover a region of some continuum, such as a Period, fall into this category. These logical operators are the `Within()`, `Contains()`, `Overlaps()`, and `Equal()` UDFs
- The third category is simply "all other operators." These tend to be specialized for a particular data type and to use exotic indexing approaches (Documents, for example).

Some of the questions to consider as part of your operator class analysis include the following:

- How can two instances of an object be compared and contrasted? For equality and inequality? For similarity?
- What kind of operator class is appropriate? (Does it behave like a number, or does it have range properties or include more than one dimension?)
- Can it be indexed? What support functions must be provided to help with the indexing?

The fact that instances of a new type can be equal to one another does not, by itself, tell you that it is an ordinal type. Two geographic polygons or boxes might be equal in the sense that they both share the same points in the same order, but boxes and points are not examples of ordinal types. A better test is to ask if one of these objects can be "less than" or "greater than" another. It is reasonable to say that one Length is less than another or that one PersonName comes after another.

For objects such as boxes, polygons, and the T-SQL Period type, comparisons such as LessThan are ambiguous. Does this mean less length, that one ends before the other begins, or that one ends before the other ends? Such types fall into the *spatial* or *region* operator class. The important logical operators for spatial data are `Within()`, `Contains()`, `Overlap()`, and `Equal()`. All of these can be indexed in an R-Tree, rather than a B-Tree. R-Trees are more complex than B-Trees. In the next chapter we explain their use in detail.

However, just because it makes no sense to compare two points to see if one is greater than another doesn't mean you should not do it anyway! Queries that return DISTINCT results or UNION two SELECT queries need to discard duplicate values from the result. Therefore, it may make sense to impose some arbitrary ordering on the objects so that the ORDBMS can sort them. This is why the GeoPoint object class in Figure 8–13 includes the Compare() interface methods.

For example, as shown in Listing 8–6, you might use the Compare() support interface with GeoPoints.

```
CREATE FUNCTION Compare ( Arg1 GeoPoint, Arg2 GeoPoint )
RETURNS INTEGER
     DEFINE nReturnValue INTEGER;
     nReturnValue = Arg1.Longitude - Arg2.Longitude;
     IF ( nReturnValue = 0 ) THEN
             nReturnValue = Arg1.Latitude - Arg2.Latitude;
     END IF;
     RETURN nReturnValue;
END FUNCTION;
```

Listing 8–6. *Semantically Meaningless Compare() for GeoPoints, Supporting Equal*

If, and only if, both instances of the GeoPoint class have identical longitude and latitude values, this function returns zero (0), indicating that they are equal. As a side effect, it also returns a positive or negative value that allows the ORDBMS to "sort" them. In general, supporting the ordinal operators for nonordinal data is a good idea, although you should never create a B-Tree index.

Aggregates

Unlike the other kinds of interfaces introduced above, aggregates work by taking a set of instances and computing a single result from them. For example, one common aggregate involves adding the values in a set of object instances to calculate their SUM() or divides the value by the COUNT() of objects involved to arrive at their AVG() or arithmetic mean.

Different kinds of data require different kinds of aggregates. For instance, it is meaningless to calculate the SUM() of a set of geographic points. A more reasonable thing to calculate from a set of points is their convex hull, or an AVG() that corresponds to the centroid of the points[4]. Of course, in the case of geographic points, you need to pay particular attention to boundary cases, which are sets of points that straddle the International Date Line or one of the Poles. Some questions to ask would include

- What kinds of values can be calculated from a set of object instances?
- What are the appropriate algorithms for calculating these aggregate values?

User-defined aggregates are algorithmically complex. They are made more so by the way the ORDBMS can employ parallelism in their execution. We introduced the technique used to support UDAs in Chapter 5. If the database can use a UDA, the algorithm designer needs to keep in mind the way that the feature is implemented in the IDS product.

Support Functions

Support functions are interfaces that are used by the ORDBMS as part of data management and query processing. The DataBlade Developers Kit (DBDK) can generate appropriate support functions for an OPAQUE TYPE on your behalf, and the ORDBMS can combine the support methods for preexisting types when working with a complex type such as a ROW TYPE or DISTINCT TYPE.

The full list of support functions includes the following:

- Binary Send/Receive interfaces that should be used when the internal format of the object is to be different on the client than it is on the server. Some object-relational databases might be accessed by another program that stores object values in memory differently from how they are stored within the DBMS. For example, an Internet IPV4 address might be stored as an array of four short integers in a C program, but in the DBMS, it might be stored as a string or a single four-byte INTEGER.
- Import/Export interfaces that the engine uses as part of backup/recovery and bulk load/unload of the data. Similar interfaces are necessary when the data type is to be used in a distributed database.
- Insert/Delete notification is in the same vein as the Import/Export interfaces. Sometimes, a data type's data resides outside the DBMS, such as in a file system or on a remote storage facility. Whenever an

---

4 A centroid is the point that minimizes the sum of distances to all other points. It is not necessarily a point constructed from the mean X and mean Y values.

instance of the type is deleted from the database, the ORDBMS can call these interfaces.

- Hash support, for efficient processing of certain types of joins. The basic idea behind a Hash is that it takes an instance of the object and returns an INTEGER value. An important property of the algorithm is that the hash of two types must be identical if the type instances are also Equal(). It is important to note that for types such as floating point, equality is not as obvious as you might expect.[5]
- Statistics support. These interfaces are useful if you can come up with a means of telling the ORDBMS's query planner how to estimate the selectivity of certain operations involving the type.

Large object data types require their own kind of support interfaces. When an instance of the large object data type is created or destroyed, the ORDBMS needs to call the corresponding support functions to manage the actual large object data itself. Why can't it do this automatically? It can't because sometimes the large object data will itself contain handles to additional large objects. The ORDBMS has no idea what is contained within OPAQUE data types. It needs help to sort all of this out.

Working an Example

Our Movies-R-Us Web site database contains many different kinds of data. In this section, we examine two of them in detail. In the Figure 8–15 we present diagrams two object classes; Period and Movie_Title.

It is useful to keep in mind that an attribute type you develop may have widespread uses. There are other kinds of data that share the behavior of movie titles, books, for example, for which using databases to store people's names is very common.

Movie Title

Begin by creating a list of object instances, as we do in Table 8–8.

---

[5] C float and double are defined in such a way that if you take a number and perform a sequence of mathematical transformations on it that should yield the initial value as a result, what you actually get back may not be bit-wise equivalent to the original. For example, POW (POW (X , 2.01), (1 / 2.01)) does not always equal X!

Movie_Title	
- Title	String
+ Movie_Title (String) -> Movie_Title, [Ordinal Operators, B-Tree Support Functions]	

Period	
- Start	DATE
- End	DATE
+ Period (String) -> Period, + Period (DATE , DATE) -> Period, + Start (Period) -> DATE, + End (Period) -> DATE, + Before (Period, Period) -> boolean, + After (Period, Period) -> boolean, + Equal (Period, Period) -> boolean, + NotEqual (Period, Period) -> boolean, [Spatial Operators, R-Tree Support Functions, Compare()]]	

Figure 8–15. Examples of Object-Class Definitions

Table 8–8. Instances of Movie Title Objects

The Best Years of Our Lives	Best Years of Our Lives, The
The Big Sleep	Big Sleep, The
The Bridge on the River Kwai	Bridge on the River Kwai, The
Casablanca	Citizen Kane
The Maltese Falcon	Maltese Falcon, The

Although the Movie_Title object's structure is very simple—it is just a string—and its interface is quite straightforward—ordinal operators and B-Tree support—the way movie titles are handled is actually fairly complex. When you sort a list of movie titles as we do in this list, it is usual to ignore the first word of the title if that word is either a "The" or an "A." When a user types in "The Maltese Falcon" (or "Maltese Falcon, The") the rules governing movie titles dictate that these are equivalent. This is the kind of situation in which the ability to abstract implementation behind an interface is extremely useful.

This analysis suggests two approaches to the design of the object:

1. You make the Input support function (the constructor that casts from the string literal such as "The Maltese Falcon") more sophisticated. To handle the movie title's peculiarities, it parses the input string and stores the title so that a simple string compare does the appropriate thing. You can either do the reverse operation in the

output function or present the title's internal format as a canonical form. Another UDF could format movie titles any way you wanted.

2. You can elect to have the Compare function do the mapping instead of handling it in the input/output functions. (Note that all other logical operators should call the `Compare()` UDF, for consistency.)

Either implementation is quite reasonable. At this stage, simply capture the information. In fact, the Title OPAQUE TYPE implementation in this book opts for the first design based on the observation that the `Compare()` and `Equal()` functions will be used a lot more frequently than the input or output functions.

Period Type

The Period type is part of the Temporal SQL (T-SQL) language standard. It represents a fixed interval in the timeline, in contrast to DATE and DATETIME, which are fixed *points* in the timeline, and the SQL-92 INTERVAL, which is a *floating* or moveable interval. Period has not been implemented in RDBMS products because it was awkward to provide indexing support for the type using B-Trees.

A list of Period instances would include the examples in Table 8–9. In this case, we use only DATE, though of course you might use DATE-TIME instead. Special cases EPOCH and FOREVER represent, respectively, the beginning and the end of time. Another special case might be FORSEEABLY, which corresponds to time intervals that, while not currently scheduled to end, are not expected to continue forever.

Table 8–9. Examples of Period Data Type

A	"01-07-1999 to 31-07-1999"
B	"02-08-1999 to 31-08-1999"
C	"01-09-1999 to 30-09-1999"
D	"15-07-1999 to 15-09-1999"
E	"10-08-1999 to 20-08-1999"
F	"17-09-1999 to 17-11-1999"
G	"01-11-1999 to 31-12-1999"
H	"EPOCH to 17-07-1999"
I	"20-11-1999 to FOREVER"

In Figure 8–16 we illustrate a set of these objects arranged conceptually. The highlighted features in this figure demonstrate how instances of the type interact and help to determine the type's interface.

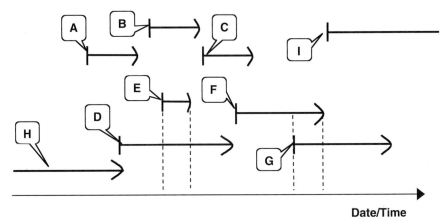

Date/Time

Figure 8–16. *Instances of the Period Type Arranged onto a Timeline*

By looking at the way these examples of the Period are arranged on a timeline, you can establish the interface methods that would be used to reason about them. For example, Period A is *before* B, and B is *before* C. Symmetrically, B is *after* A and C is *after* B. We can also see that D *contains* E (that E is *within* D) and that F *overlaps* G. These relationships mean that the Period type can be categorized as a *region* type, which means it can use the R-Tree access method.

The most important task of the type's constructor method is to parse these strings into the internal format and to check that the initial (begin) date, or datetime, comes before the second (end).

Minimize the Set of Object Classes

The next step is to render the list of object classes down to a minimal, complete set. This is done by identifying pairs of object classes assigned the same name that actually refer to different kinds of data (*antonyms* or *homonyms*) and situations in which the same kind of data is referred to with different names in different places (*synonyms*).

Object-oriented analysis helps to clarify such ambiguities. An object class is defined as an *atomic unit of meaning described in terms of both state and behavior*. Although users may disagree about names, if two objects are sufficiently similar in terms of their *definition*, it is highly likely that they both correspond to a single real-world phenomenon.

Similarly, two kinds of data with the same name but completely different definitions are probably different objects.

Unfortunately, people become very attached to the names they use. In fact, they have been known to fortify the kitchen and take hostages in an effort to defend the virtue of "Customers" over "Buyers." Ultimately, the label selected is technically unimportant. The objective of this analysis is consistency, although clarity and brevity are desirable.

Antonyms

Antonyms are usually fairly easy to spot. For example, we commonly use the term "period of time" to refer to something better modeled using the SQL-92 INTERVAL data type. We refer to the concept of "10 minutes" either as a "period of time" or an "interval of time." In addition, by comparing two intervals of time, we can determine that one is equal to, or greater than, the other. Yet in Figure 8–15 we present an object also called "Period" whose structure consists of two fixed points in a timeline and that responds to logical operations such as `Overlaps()`.

It is clear, based on the structure and behavior of these two objects, that they refer to different things despite having the same name. Another possible antonym pair is movie title, also in Figure 8–15, and person name "'title," which is an enumerated type that is one of a set of options such as "Mr," "Ms," "Mrs," "Dr," and "Rev."

Two objects with different interfaces or internal structures, but with the same name, are almost certainly antonyms. Assign each of them a unique name, and update the E-ER model accordingly.

Synonyms

In a similar fashion, two objects might be synonyms if they have similar structure and behavior, but different names. Synonyms can be handled in one of two ways.

- Recognize that they are synonyms. Pick one name to use and replace all occurrences of the synonym with the canonical form.
- Use the inheritance mechanism to create a differently named version of the same type. This might involve either the DISTINCT TYPE mechanism or the ROW TYPE inheritance mechanism.

For example, Mail_Address and Delivery_Address are candidates for being synonyms. What is clear from the UML Class Diagram in Figure 8–11 is that their definitions are remarkably similar. However, they differ slightly in that instances of a Delivery_Address may include a document giving detailed delivery instructions.

On the other hand, an example of two objects that are more clearly synonyms are PersonName, and MovieCharacter (see the Movies.Starring attribute in Table 8–5). Detailed examination of these two kinds of data would reveal that they are identical for all practical purposes.

Conceptual Modeling for Type System Summary

The analysis techniques introduced in this section help developers arrive at a better understanding of their problem domain. The techniques involve adopting an object-oriented view of the individual elements and the high-level entities identified as part of the extended ER modeling. The purpose of this analysis is to drive the implementation of the object-relational database's type system by documenting what the desired structure and behavior of these problem domain objects ought to be.

Begin by writing down a list of all of the entity types and the names of the different kinds of data found in entity attributes. Then analyze each of them in more detail.

Create a description of the *interface* for each of these objects, and determine whatever internal *structure* is needed to record its state. Interfaces are lists of methods (user-defined functions) for manipulating the object to change its state, to interrogate it, or to compute some result by combining the object's state with other data. An object's structure is a list of named elements and the kind of data stored in each element. This implies a recursive procedure because analyzing an object's structure can add new objects to the list requiring analysis.

Several kinds of interface methods, such as expressions, operators, aggregates, and support methods, are used for different kinds of interaction with the object. Our use of OO analysis differs from other approaches because the objects we describe are deployed within an abstracted, logical framework, rather than compiled into an executable program. This emphasizes the importance of each object's interface over whatever relationships it might have.

Data Processing and Workload Analysis

The last analysis task of this development process examines the database *workload*, which is the set of queries and business processes that the information system performs. Documenting the data processing workload is useful for several reasons:

- It gives developers the basis to create a performance and scalability test harness. One reason that information systems projects fail is that software is not tested under production-like conditions. Consequently, what is delivered does not meet end-user performance expectations. Sometimes project teams can compensate by going over budget on hardware, but often, flawed designs are not noticed until it is too late to do anything about them.
- Workload analysis can indicate that an OR-SQL extension would be useful. For example, employees of the Web site who take phone orders might need to query movie club members or merchandise brand names based on what a name "sounds like." Embedding another user-defined function can solve this problem.
- Development teams often embed portions of an application's data processing within the data manager. Centralizing logic in this way, however, has the potential to create a scalability bottleneck. Thus, an important question to resolve is whether is it best to implement a module of business logic inside or outside the ORDBMS? Analyzing the business process in terms of how widely it is used, and how much data is touched each time it is invoked, helps answer this question.
- Sometimes it is useful to incorporate some aspect of external data processing within the ORDBMS. *Electronic Data Interchange* (EDI) formats are defined as standardized byte arrays with subarrays at various offsets containing the elements of the message. In more recent times, XML based information exchange, which uses self-describing messages, has become a hot topic. Structures such as these are unlikely to be stored in a table's columns, but incorporating them into OR-SQL an OPAQUE TYPES or as UDRs that parse strings make it easier to manage this kind of data.

Traditionally, information systems development methodologies drew a distinction between data modeling, which is the task of building the database schema, and process modeling, which is often undertaken by different teams of software engineers who understood how end users accessed shared data. Business processes used SQL-92 to read table data and to modify it. Simplistic diagramming techniques were enough.

In Figure 8–17 we present one of the more traditional data process modeling approaches. In it, operations are represented as a labeled circle, while input data for the operation is presented in a table. Data processing operations either affect the state of some shared data or invoke other data processing operations. Arrows show these dependencies.

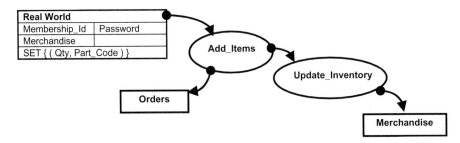

Figure 8–17. *Data Flow Diagram*

Data flow diagrams can be used to define functional specifications and to divide the coding up into discrete, but interrelated, subtasks. Circles, arrows and boxes do not convey much detail, however. Usually data flow diagrams are accompanied by a list of detailed explanations of each operation. As with E-ER diagrams and UML-class diagrams the intention is to document what the information system is intended to do at a conceptual level.

In recent times, however, the fashion has been to apply object-oriented techniques to analyze business processes; that is, instead of conceiving of a business process as a self-contained functional unit of work, modern information systems are decomposed into a group of interrelated object classes reflecting the conceptual views of different kinds of end users. Operations within these application level objects still use SQL, but the way these data manipulation language statements are packaged is very different.

Data Processing Operations

Figure 8–18 illustrates the modern view of data processing. Other programs, such as user interfaces or middleware, can interact with these objects (Shopping_Cart) using message-oriented protocols.

Recall from Chapter 6 the uses of the various methods of the Shopping_Cart class. In each case, the method issues some OR-SQL against the database, either to read its current state or to modify it. Although Chapter 6 demonstrated how these operations might be implemented within the ORDBMS using SPL, they might just as easily be implemented using Java and the Enterprise Java Bean component standard.

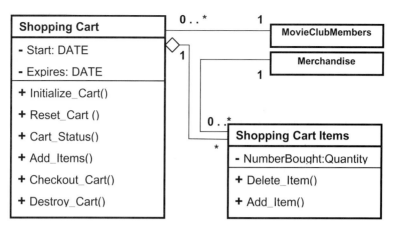

Figure 8–18. *UML Model of Shopping Cart Class*

Depending on the kinds of service provided by the application-level object, the communications protocol will provide different service guarantees. Messages sent to shopping cart objects might or might not be *stateful*; that is, the message exchange assumes that both ends of the communication know about its history so far. In addition, the message might or might not be *transactional*, which means that the entire series of exchanges are subject to ACID guarantees.

What makes up the workload for the database is the set of all of these method operations. The objective of workload analysis is to describe *what* queries are involved in the method logic and *how often* each method is executed.

Individual Data Process

Start with what you expect to be the most common operations, but investigate as many of them as you can. The rule of thumb is that about 10 percent of the application's operations constitute 90 percent of its runtime workload. For example, suppose we anticipate 1,000,000 visitors a day, 5 percent of whom will be buying on average two items. Examine Table 8–10.

If estimating absolute numbers is difficult, at least note the relative frequency of each operation. In practice, the details listed in the Data Operations column of Table 8–10 more properly correspond to a functional specification. What is being advocated here is really just gathering additional information as part of more conventional OO systems analysis. For most application-level objects, estimating how many times each of their methods will be called is unnecessary, but operations involving OR-SQL are a special case.

Table 8–10. Approximate Counts for Data Processing Operations

Operation Name	Data Operations	Daily Count
Initialize_Cart()	Read one row from MovieClubMembers and insert one row into Shopping_Cart.	50,000
Reset_Cart()	Delete average of two rows from Cart_Items.	5000
Cart_Status()	Read two rows from Cart_Items and one row from Shopping_Cart.	50,000
Add_Items()	Read two rows from Merchandise and insert two rows into Cart_Items	100,000
Checkout_Cart	Insert one row into Orders and then update two rows in Merchandise to adjust inventory.	45,000
Destroy_Cart()	Delete two rows from Cart_Items and one row from Shopping_Cart.	5000

Workload Queries

Regardless of how data processing operations are organized, all of them involve OR-SQL queries. Some operations read table data; others modify it. Ultimately, however, the success or failure of the information system will depend on how efficiently these queries are processed, so document as many of them as you can.

At first the lack of a formal schema definition will limit how precisely each query can be specified, but even a rough, natural language description is a start. Later, as the schema design stabilizes, these descriptions can be translated into pseudo-SQL, and finally, into OR-SQL. Although the word "queries" implies a question, and therefore a SELECT statement, it is very important to describe write operations too. This means imperative sentences, in addition to interrogatives.

In Table 8–11 we present many of the query examples that were used to illustrate different aspects of OR-SQL in Chapter 3, together with estimates of what they contribute to the site's overall workload.

These descriptions can be used to validate earlier analysis. Use them to check that the E-ER model and the analysis already performed on the various object classes stored within each entity have enough adequate to respond to the query.

Additional UDTs and UDRs for Workload Queries

One of the experiences of early adopters of ORDBMS technology has been that by introducing logic that was traditionally linked into external

Query Description	Frequency
"Show me the name and a photo of movie club members living in 'some geographic region' who have indicated that they like 'a certain kind of movie.'"	Medium. 1000 per day
"What is the total value (Qty * Price) of all merchandise ordered by either a particular member of the movie club or all movie club members?"	Medium. 1000 per day.
"Get details of movie club member based on their identity string and an encrypted password."	High to extremely high. 100,000 or more per day
"Give me a list of all movie club members who are older than 30 and who live within a 30-mile circle around a particular latitude/ longitude point."	Medium: 1000 per day
"Add a new movie club member."	Low. 100 per day
"Decrement the quantity of a particular item of merchandise by the amount just purchased in an order."	High: 45,000 per day

programs into the ORDBMS, they can improve the performance and flexibility of their overall system. For example, it isn't too much of a stretch to suggest that Movies-R-Us might want to send each of their movie club members a card or note on their birthday.

Supporting an even apparently simple operation such as "Given a date of birth, is today a birthday?" in SQL-92 is impossible because matching birthdays has to take into account the situation of people born on the February 29 during a leap year. During nonleap years, these people must celebrate their birthday on February 28. Ideally, you would like to be able to run the query in Listing 8–7 and have it deal with the complexity of the problem.

```
SELECT E.Name
  FROM Employees E
 WHERE Birthday ( E.Date_of_Birth ) = Birthday ( TODAY );
```

Listing 8–7. Birthday Query

In an external program, it would be obvious to create a "Birthday" class in a language such as C++ or Java. Using it would require that you write a query retrieving the names and dates of birth of everyone born during the current month (about one-twelfth of the total data). Then on the client side, programming logic in the Birthday class would determine matches. Such an object class might look like Figure 8–19.

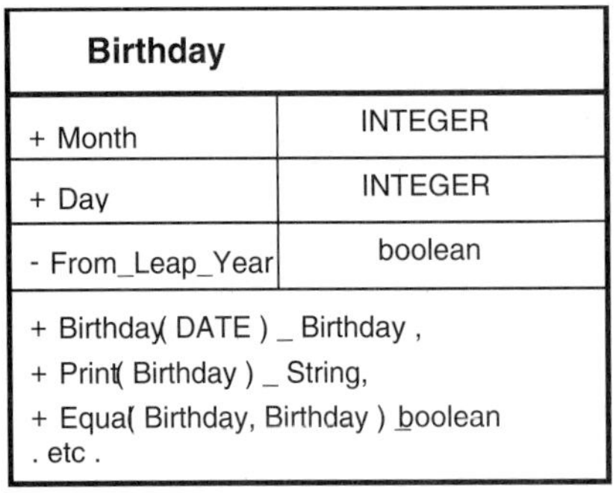

Figure 8–19. *UML Class Diagram for Birthday*

An important principle of the ORDBMS data model is that types like this do not have to be used to define a table's structure or a column. The behavior of this object can be used to implement complex query operations over otherwise conventional data, as we saw in Table 8–1. Also, most object-oriented methodologies acknowledge that sometimes what you want is not really an object, but simply a function or procedure. Readers for whom "object-oriented everything" sounds like babble can take comfort in the fact that it is entirely possible to think about the design of your ORDBMS database in an entirely *functional* or *modular* mode just as easily.

Data Sizing

Of course, for the purposes of estimating the physical resources the information system will require, determining the size of the system is very important. Even the most complex workload does not present any challenge at all with empty tables. Thus, an important aspect of workload analysis involves estimating the sizing and distribution of the data stored on the database's tables.

In this section we present a list of additional information to gather about the database and its contents.

- Size and composition of individual objects. When developing user-defined types, it is necessary to know whether the object is of fixed size, is of variable size but reasonably small, or is variable sized and large. In RDBMS applications the sizes of each built-in type was known when the schema was created. With information systems that includes geography, however, time series or rich media (text, images, and so on) sizing is considerably more complex. As part of this analysis, it is also a good idea to determine how to generate a *random* instance of the object.

- Size of Entity Rows. The sizes of UDT instances may vary, depending on what real-world phenomenon they are storing. Geographic boundaries for U.S. states vary from 70 bytes for Colorado and Wyoming, which is four points, to about 32 Megabytes for Texas. With digital media, object size also varies tremendously.
- Number of Entity Instances. Based on the sizes of the objects in the entity type and the number of entity instances, it is possible to estimate the total amount of data each entity represents.
- Data Distributions. One of the most difficult problems in database design arises when the data stored in a table is skewed; that is, when a range of data values in a table includes more rows that you might expect. Data skew affects physical tuning decisions. For example, an important question in large databases relates to how table data is fragmented across disks. Choosing a fragmentation scheme in which too much data is assigned to too little disk results in poor performance.

Using this information you can estimate how big your database will be and how much computer power it will require.

Business Rules

The term "business rule" is vaguely defined, with broad implications. In some places, the term includes all structural integrity constraints, such as primary keys, foreign keys, and uniqueness rules described earlier in this chapter. Also, some developers advocate using the behavior of the individual object classes within the schema as a framework for describing business rules. These are all good ideas.

In addition to the kind of correctness and consistency rules that can be enforced as part of UDF logic or table constraints, there exists an additional kind of rule we call an *enterprise constraint*. These are higher level rules that are difficult to express as part of the data model. The following list presents some examples of enterprise constraints that might apply in the Movies-R-Us Web site database:

- Whenever someone changes the price of an item of merchandise, record who made the change and what the change was.

- As part of the Movies-R-Us Web site's "family-friendly" policy, whenever a new image is inserted, check to see if it has "objectionable" content, and flag such images for management review.[6]
- If the stock levels of a particular item of merchandise means that a member's order can't be met, reject the order with an apologetic message.

Trying to record every enterprise constraint is futile. In addition to the fact that there are likely to be a great many of them, end users can always be relied upon to come up with more given the chance. Besides, not all of them are general rules, and using the database to enforce application specific procedures is not the best approach to those problems

Chapter Summary

In this chapter we described the first stages of a development methodology for ORDBMS databases. The central ideas of this methodology are that ORDBMSs benefit from adopting a more holistic approach to analysis and design. Therefore in this methodology we consider the problem domain in terms of the objects in it, the facts pertaining to these objects, the processes that make changes to this data, and any rules that are imposed on the system.

We introduced the following subtasks within this methodology:

1. Use E-ER modeling to create a high-level data model of the problem domain. Describe each of the major entities, the relationships between them, and any rules that constrain the data each entity can contain.
2. Decide what kinds of data make up each entity's attributes. Use object-oriented analysis techniques to express the data that describes each kind of data at any point in time and by what mechanisms such an object is modified, interrogated, or otherwise manipulated.
3. Describe the workload of business processes and common queries that the database needs to support.

---

6   See Wang, J, Weiderhold, G, and Firschein, O. "System for Screening Objectionable Images." *Computer Communications Journal* 21(5): 1355–1360. Elsevier Science, 1998. Also, see http://WWW-DB.stanford.edu/IMAGE.

4. Document whatever enterprise integrity rules apply to the overall system.

These various views of the problem are interdependent. The extended ER model we use to express the top-level conceptual structures break the problem domain into smaller units of meaning, which are ideally modeled using object-oriented analysis techniques. Descriptions of the business processes involved often indicate the existence of an object class that, while not stored in any table, is used as part of the query or data processing workload.

One final note: The techniques we describe here are inevitably incomplete. Reality is bewilderingly varied, and no structured set of procedures can address every contingency. Readers are encouraged to abandon any of the hints or words of advice in this chapter should they find that this advice doesn't apply.

Object-Relational Database Design

Design and Implementation of Object-Relational Databases

The result of the procedure described in the previous chapter should be a correct and complete model of what the information system's end-users think they need. Because our development methodology targets an ORDBMS, we use both extended entity-relationship models and object-oriented class diagrams to document the real-world phenomena that must be represented in the finished database.

The conceptual model taken as the starting point in this chapter consists of the following:

- The structure (constituent attribute names and types) of a set of named high-level entities, and the relationships that exist between them.
- A list of object classes (which correspond to relational domains or application-level object) in the problem domain. Each specification describes the class's internal structure and the interface methods by which it is manipulated.

- Business processes and common queries making up the workload of the information system.
- Enterprise rules that can be enforced by constraining what data changes are possible.

Depending on the nature of the system being built, a single conceptual model can be mapped into several, quite different logical models, and each logical model can be implemented using a variety of physical configurations. We touched on this idea in the previous chapter when we pointed out that conceptual models determine how the final product will look, but not how it is deployed. Thus, an important issue in logical database design concerns how you tell a good logical design from one that is not so good.

The way to tell whether one (correct and complete) logical model is superior to another (correct and complete) model is to determine how well it accomplishes the following:

- Ensures that changes made to data in the information system, and the data that is retrieved from it, are always consistent. At any point in time different users should "see" the same data state, and changes should never create ambiguities in this shared data.
- Can cope with the wide range of end-user requirements, some of which were not anticipated at design time. That is, flexible designs are generally better.
- The design is efficient; that is, it makes the best possible use of the available hardware resources and performs to the level of user expectations.

The subject of this chapter is how to design and build object-relational databases with these properties. In addition, we cover two important development related tasks: testing and physical tuning. The importance of testing in software development is self-evident; it is the only way to ensure that a program satisfies its baseline objectives. Because object-relational database development includes embedding *user-defined type (UDT)* and *user-defined function (UDF)* extensions into the DBMS, testing requires more effort than is needed with relational databases. Fortunately, there are ways to use the ORDBMS itself to simplify the task.

Of course, the kinds of requirements developers must meet are so varied that it is extremely difficult to come up with a comprehensive design procedure. Software design decisions tend to be trade-offs among multiple, often conflicting, objectives, and the right choice is heavily dependent on the specifics of the task at hand. Therefore, in addition to the procedures we describe in this chapter, we spend time discussing the tradeoffs involved, describe some useful "rules of thumb," and provide plenty of examples.

Chapter Overview

The steps of the logical design phase of ORDBMS methodology, which also define the structure of this chapter, are as follows:

1. Implement or install UDTs and UDFs that correspond to the various kinds of data domains or object classes identified in the conceptual model:
   - For each UML class diagram, select the appropriate UDT mechanism to represent its structure and a language to implement its interface methods. Deciding which mechanism to use is sometimes difficult. Performance, ease of development, and the kinds of data involved, all affect the decision.
   - In a similar fashion, implement any object classes and standalone functions identified as part of the workload analysis.
   - Generate a set of tests for each of these user-defined types and functions.
2. Apply a set of transformation rules that takes the E-ER data model and generates a corresponding relational schema (a set of tables). The columns of these tables are defined using the types implemented in Step 1.
3. Apply the rules of normalization to eliminate redundancy and inconsistency from the naïve logical model. This may require creating additional data types, breaking up tables, or moving attributes between tables. Some of the techniques used will not be new to readers familiar with RDBMS technology. Certain features of the ORDBMS data model, such as user-defined types, table inheritance, and collection attributes, complicate normalization, although none reduce its importance.
4. Implement a set of workload queries that characterize how the database is to be used. Then populate the database and use this workload to evaluate the design against whatever performance and functionality criteria were identified as part of the analysis phase.

When you recall the continuous improvement philosophy underlying this methodology, arriving at an initial implementation does not mean that the job is done. By the time this system is in production, the demands placed on it by its end users will almost certainly have changed. They will want new business processes, new object behaviors or enhancements to the ones already implemented, and answers to new questions.

In the kind of rapidly evolving application typified by modern Web sites, developers will find themselves working at several levels simultaneously. They may be analyzing new requirements, designing new modules, and implementing and testing modifications—all at the same time. Thus, this chapter is divided into subsections, each of which addresses one of these tasks in more detail.

Implementing the User-Defined Data Types

Chapters 3 and 4 introduced a variety of techniques that you can use to implement the object classes cataloged as part of the conceptual modeling phase. We briefly review these in Table 9–1.

Table 9–1. ORDBMS Type Mechanisms

Mechanism Name	Example
Built-in types	INTEGER, VARCHAR, DATE etc. These are standardized in the SQL-92 language specification.
DISTINCT TYPE	CREATE DISTINCT TYPE String AS VARCHAR(32);
ROW TYPE	CREATE ROW TYPE Address (　　　Add_Line_1　　　String NOT NULL, 　　　Add_Line_2　　　String NOT NULL, 　　　City　　　　　String NOT NULL, 　　　State　　　　　String, 　　　ZipCode　　　　PostCode, 　　　Country　　　　String NOT NULL);
Java classes	A combination of Java UDFs with OPAQUE TYPE or DISTINCT TYPE for storage.
OPAQUE TYPE	CREATE OPAQUE TYPE GeoPoint (　　Internallength = 16);

In theory, you could use any of these extensibility mechanisms to implement any domains/object class identified in the conceptual model. In practice, each technique has different strengths and weaknesses. You might conceivably create a GeoPoint ROW TYPE and use SPL routines to implement its behavior, or you might build an OPAQUE TYPE to store street addresses. Probably, however, these examples do not represent optimal use of development resources.

Trade-Offs Between Different Type Mechanisms

The most important trade-offs among the UDT mechanisms are between the development effort each requires, the flexibility of the mechanism (by which we mean the variety of extensions it can be used to implement), and its runtime performance. In Table 9–2 we list each extensible type mechanism together with its strengths and weaknesses.

Table 9–2. Comparison of Object-Relational Data Type Mechanisms

Type Mechanism	Pros	Cons
Built-in types	They have maturity and high performance because they are compiled into the ORDBMS. They are good as building blocks for other types.	They are inflexible, and because they are byte-level in nature, built-in types contribute little semantic value to the data model.
DISTINCT TYPE	This is the easiest to use of the UDT mechanisms. Each DISTINCT TYPE has the same performance as its underlying type.	It is the least flexible of UDT mechanisms, but it is useful if the new type is similar to an existing one (which is surprisingly often).
ROW TYPE	ROW TYPE objects are reasonably easy to use and mandatory for some object-relational features (inheritance). It supports compound objects (multi-element types) well.	In some situations, ROW TYPE limits the range of OR-SQL features that can be used in queries involving them. They are not as fast as an OPAQUE TYPE equivalent.
Java Classes	It is useful for a wide range of object classes and integrates aspects of external applications into the ORDBMS far more seamlessly than other methods, with reasonably good performance.	It is more complex to develop than a ROW TYPE. Also, the recommended approach requires support functions for an OPAQUE TYPE.
OPAQUE TYPE	It is the fastest UDT mechanism, and the most flexible, and it provides good runtime performance on the broadest range of data types.	It is the most difficult to implement, requiring lots of support UDFs.

Meeting user requirements is always the ultimate goal of any software project, but development teams are almost always subject to time and materials constraints. Consequently, it is often a good idea to validate analysis by developing a quick prototype using the simplest possible methods. Later, if necessary, these initial efforts can be discarded and faster methods used instead. The value of a prototype lies in the way it demonstrates the correctness of the object/domain models and any assumptions that analysts have made.

For example, an application object such as PersonName, and the functions that implement its behavior, can be developed using a ROW TYPE and SPL functions in a matter of hours. This implementation can then be used to create database tables and write whatever queries are described in the workload. This helps developers detect any logical discrepancies. In addition, if users complain about performance, or if the need arises to move a PersonName implementation to other systems, developers can rewrite it as a Java class.

Because it depends on OR-SQL to bind logic to data, an ORDBMS allows you to develop the database's extensions (types and functions) system and its table schema independently of each other. The ability to evolve the information system in this way, even after it has been put into production, is an important difference between how best to use an ORDBMS and traditional development approaches.

Over the next few pages, we examine each UDT mechanism in more detail.

Built-In Data Types

Even in an ORDBMS, built-in types can still be your best option. This is particularly true of the more sophisticated types in SQL-92. For example, our Movies-R-Us Web site database uses the DATE data type for dates of birth, movie release dates, and the dates on which orders are placed and shipped. In addition, date values are used in several of the workload queries and business processes.

The advantages of the built-in types are as follows:

- Maturity. Built-in types are well tested and offer very high levels of performance because they are hard coded into the IDS product core.
- The SQL-92 query language includes a fairly comprehensive set of expressions for handling these types. Finding the average interval of time between when an order is placed and when it ships, or a list of movies released in the year a movie club member was born, can both be handled entirely within standard SQL-92.

- Building user-defined functions to provide additional support for a built-in type is a very straightforward way to take advantage of extensibility. This means that you can upgrade a SQL-92 database and take advantage of the ORDBMS's features without changing your client interfaces or schema definition.

Of course, for some applications, SQL-92's built-in date and time facilities are inadequate. Some Web-based information systems must deal with time zones, for example, but the IDS product does not include support for time zones. Modeling them elegantly in OR-SQL requires a set of new types and functions.

Upgrading Built-In Types to ORDBMS Databases

Developers upgrading from SQL-92 RDBMSs will naturally be starting with lots of built-in types in their schema. Rather than developing entirely new database applications, they will be looking to take advantage of the ORDBMS's features without losing any of the investment they have already made. Fortunately, it is possible to use the ALTER TABLE DDL command to evolve SQL-92 schema into an object-relational schema.

For example, consider the SQL-92 table in Listing 9–1. It includes two attributes that might be better modeled as user-defined types. The idea is that the difference between concepts such as a product's name and its number, which might not even be a number in the SQL-92 sense, can be represented using OR-SQL in ways that aren't possible using SQL-92.

```
--
CREATE TABLE Products (
        Prod_Num        VARCHAR(32)     PRIMARY KEY,
        Name            VARCHAR(32)     NOT NULL,
        Number_Made     INTEGER         NOT NULL
);
--
INSERT INTO Products VALUES ( 'AJAX','Soap Product',100);
--
CREATE DISTINCT TYPE Product_Number AS VARCHAR(32);
DROP CAST ( VARCHAR(32) AS Product_Number );
CREATE IMPLICIT CAST ( VARCHAR(32) AS Product_Number );
GRANT USAGE ON TYPE Product_Number TO PUBLIC;
--
CREATE DISTINCT TYPE Quantity AS INTEGER;
DROP CAST ( INTEGER AS Quantity );
CREATE IMPLICIT CAST ( INTEGER AS Quantity USING Int2Qty );
GRANT USAGE ON TYPE Quantity TO PUBLIC;
--
```

```
ALTER TABLE Products
MODIFY  ( Prod_Num      Product_Number NOT NULL PRIMARY KEY,
          Number_Made Quantity         NOT NULL );
--
--   After these changes the Products table looks as if
--   it were created using the following command;
--
--     CREATE TABLE Products (
--             Prod_Num        Product_Number      PRIMARY KEY,
--             Name            VARCHAR(32)         NOT NULL,
--             Number_Made     Quantity            NOT NULL
--     );
```

Listing 9–1. *Modifying an SQL-92 Schema for Strong Typing*

Note that the type to which a column is being modified must have the same size as the column's original type. To ensure that this is the case, the new type should be a DISTINCT TYPE of the original. The ALTER TABLE commands in Table 9–2 do not change the table's data. They only modify the system catalog entries describing the table. Queries embedded in preexisting applications table will work exactly as they did before.

Naturally, there is a trade-off whenever you undertake such an upgrade. Changes such as the ones shown in Listing 9–1 yield no performance improvement. In addition, more complicated transformations, such as combining several columns into a single ROW TYPE, involve a lot more effort and system downtime. You must create the ROW TYPE, add a new empty column that uses it, update the new column using data from the original columns, and use ALTER TABLE again to remove the old columns. This is already a lot of work, and you still have to rewrite your application's queries!

Such effort might be justified if it lets you take advantage of new indexing methods, such as converting two floating-point columns to a single GeoPoint column or two DATE columns to a Period. These types let you build R-Tree indices over the new columns to accelerate Overlap() queries.

DISTINCT TYPES

Perhaps the best use for built-in types is as building blocks in another UDT, such as a DISTINCT TYPE. A DISTINCT TYPE reuses another data type, such as a built-in INTEGER or VARCHAR, and renames it to distinguish it from other instances of similar objects in the schema. DISTINCT TYPE instances are very easy to create, and the new type inherits all characteristics—and most importantly, the performance—

of the original. At the same time, new UDFs can extend the functionality of a DISTINCT TYPE.

Using DISTINCT TYPE permits the data model to take advantage of strong typing. Although the functionality of the built-in types can get you a long way, there are advantages to being able to distinguish the various kinds of data in the logical schema. The DISTINCT TYPE mechanism lets you model many different kinds of data with similar properties without compromising performance, and without a lot of development effort.

The DISTINCT TYPE mechanism is most useful when the following is true:

* Analysis indicates that the new domain/type is of the same size and structure, and has basically the same behavior, as another type that already exists in the database.
* Some data integrity rules apply over the new type, which distinguish it from other types.
* The new type has a additional behaviors, or uses different logic, to implement a common interface when implementing certain patterns, particularly enumeration. A DISTINCT TYPE of INTEGER is usually sufficient to hold the identifying information, and by overloading the last mechanism, the DISTINCT TYPE can be made to have additional integrity rules and behaviors.

Many of the different kinds of data identified in the Movies-R-Us Web site conceptual model can be implemented as a DISTINCT TYPE. In Listing 9–2 we present several DISTINCT TYPE examples. Note the modifications to the default CAST mechanism in each. This allows OR-SQL programmers to use literal variable values in OR-SQL queries, instead of explicitly casting to the DISTINCT TYPE.

```
CREATE DISTINCT TYPE Geo_Point AS ST_Point;
DROP CAST ( ST_POINT AS Geo_Point );
CREATE IMPLICIT CAST ( ST_POINT AS Geo_Point );
GRANT USAGE ON TYPE Geo_Point TO PUBLIC;

CREATE DISTINCT TYPE Membership_Id AS VARCHAR(32);
DROP CAST ( VARCHAR(32) AS Membership_Id );
CREATE IMPLICIT CAST ( VARCHAR(32) AS Membership_Id );
GRANT USAGE ON TYPE Membership_Id TO PUBLIC;

CREATE DISTINCT TYPE Order_Num AS INTEGER;
GRANT USAGE ON TYPE Order_Num TO PUBLIC;
DROP CAST ( INTEGER AS Order_Num );
CREATE IMPLICIT CAST ( INTEGER AS Order_Num );
```

Listing 9–2. *DISTINCT TYPE Instances in the Movies-R-Us Web Site Database*

As we noted in Chapter 3, were a query to compare an instance of the Quantity from Listing 9–2 with an instance of an Order_Num defined in Listing 9–1, the ORDBMS would generate an error.

Working an Example

Consider the NameTitle_Enum object/data type, which is used to store instances of a known range of data values, such as "Mr.," "Ms.," "Dr.," "Prof.," and so on. The quickest way to implement this is as a DISTINCT TYPE of CHAR(5), as shown in Listing 9–3.

```
CREATE DISTINCT TYPE NameTitle_Enum AS CHAR(5);
GRANT USAGE ON TYPE NameTitle_Enum TO PUBLIC;
```

Listing 9–3. *Examples of DISTINCT TYPEs in the Movies-R-Us Web Site Database*

A basic DISTINCT TYPE does not enforce any data integrity. For example, the way that "Mr." and "MR." are equivalent values of NameTitle_Enum is difficult to model using just CHAR(). A CHECK constraint can ensure that data in a table's column is always correct, but it is clearly a good thing if OR-SQL can figure out that that a query to find a movie club member named "MR. John Wayne" should match on "Mr. John Wayne" too. If nothing else, it saves computational resources if the parser can determine when it is impossible for a query to return any meaningful results because the value supplied for a type is inappropriate.

Integrity constraints such as this are best handled within logic called to CAST literal strings, such as the LVARCHAR type, into the new DISTINCT TYPE. To do this, first drop the casts created automatically by the ORDBMS for the new DISTINCT TYPE. Then you need to redefine the cast, using a function to check the correctness of the value. The example shown in Listing 9–4 illustrates the idea. Of course, in a production system, the validTitle_Enum() and LVAR2Title_Enum() functions are better off implemented in C than in SPL.

```
CREATE FUNCTION validTitle_Enum ( Arg1 LVARCHAR )
RETURNS boolean
    IF ( UPPER(Arg1) IN
            ('','MR','MS','MRS','DR','PROF','REV')) THEN
        RETURN 't'::boolean;
    END IF;
    RETURN 'f'::boolean;
END FUNCTION;
```

```
GRANT EXECUTE ON
FUNCTION validTitle_Enum ( LVARCHAR ) TO PUBLIC;
--
-- Note: You need to be careful CASTing about like this.
-- This function gets its return value by first casting
-- from Arg1{LVARCHAR} to CHAR(5), and only then casting
-- to the Title_Enum. Were I to go directly from LVARCHAR
-- to Title_Enum, I would invoke this CAST function
-- recursively, and without termination.
--
-- What you see here works because OR-SQL interprets
-- everything in quotes as LVARCHAR before it goes to
-- anything else. This is an important subtlety.
--
CREATE FUNCTION LVAR2Title_Enum ( Arg1 LVARCHAR )
RETURNS NameTitle_Enum

    IF ( NOT validTitle_Enum ( Arg1 )) THEN
     RAISE EXCEPTION -746, 0,
       "Unknown Title. Not one of {MR, MS, MRS, DR, PROF}";
    END IF;

    RETURN Arg1::Char(5)::NameTitle_Enum;
END FUNCTION;
GRANT EXECUTE ON FUNCTION LVAR2Title_Enum ( LVARCHAR ) TO
PUBLIC;
--
CREATE IMPLICIT CAST
( LVARCHAR AS Title_Enum WITH LVAR2Title_Enum ); DISTINCT TYPE
```

Listing 9–4. *Enforcing Data Type Integrity Rules with a DISTINCT Type*

Once this mechanism is in place, new NameTitle_Enum instances are limited to the range of values listed in the `validTitle_Enum()` logic.

A complete implementation for this new type requires a new `Compare( NameTitle_Enum, NameTitle_Enum )` user-defined function to cope with case and representational differences. New, overloaded operator functions are also required, which would in turn call the new `Compare()`. Importantly, however, all support functions for tasks such as backup and client–server communication are inherited from the `CHAR(5)` type. This significantly reduces the amount of work involved in implementing the new type while ensuring high levels of performance and reliability.

Using ROW TYPEs

A ROW TYPE is relatively flexible, simple to create, and are well integrated into the OR-SQL query language. Because they are relatively easy for DBMS vendors to implement (as long as they employ only base types in their internal structure), they are the only extensibility mechanism supported by some products. OR-SQL includes cascading dot notation to access the data within an instance of a ROW TYPE, and the ORDBMS combines the support functions defined for the types within the ROW TYPE to manage backup and client–server communication.

The ROW TYPE mechanism is most useful in the following situations:

- When the object class has a compound structure that is unlike any other type in the DBMS; that is, when you cannot use a built-in type or a DISTINCT TYPE.
- Early in the development process, when the goal is to create an implementation of the new object as soon as possible.
- If direct OR-SQL access to the type's innards is desirable.
- For kinds of data that are not persistent, but that are used as part of query processing or in logic that is implementing a business process.
- For object classes derived from entities, particularly if the entities have assessor methods (which will be invoked in queries) or when several entities are arranged in an inheritance hierarchy.
- Where the object's behavior implies the use of complex algorithms, but their performance is not critical.

To implement a new ROW TYPE that corresponds to a UML class diagram, assign an element to the ROW TYPE for each of the class's structural elements. Basic UML class diagrams do not represent it directly, but with the ROW TYPE mechanism, you can specify which elements of the type are compulsory and which are optional using the NOT NULL constraint. At this time, ROW TYPE does not provide a mechanism for distinguishing between public and private elements.

It is also a good idea to implement a set of general constructor functions for the new ROW TYPE. Often, ORDBMS's general ROW TYPE constructor is inappropriate because certain elements of the object may be calculated from a single input argument, and custom constructors help define a more realistic interface to the object.

Working an Example

Consider the BirthDay object class we identified as part of the Movies-R-Us Web site's query workload (see Listing 8-7 in Chapter 8). In Listing 9–5 we illustrate how this kind of domain, and its behavior, might be implemented.

```
--
--   This script illustrates the Birthday Object
-- Class from Chapter 8. This implementation uses the ROW
-- TYPE.
--

   CREATE ROW TYPE Birthday (
   MmDd      SMALLINT        NOT NULL,
   LeapDay BOOLEAN  NOT NULL
   );
 GRANT USAGE ON TYPE BirthDay TO PUBLIC;
--
--    Constructor
--
--   Note that this example uses a combination of built-in
-- SQL-92 expressions { MONTH(), DAY() } and another
-- function whose implementation we do not show here.
--
CREATE FUNCTION BirthDay( Arg1 DATE)
RETURNING BirthDay;
     DEFINE LeapDay BOOLEAN;
     DEFINE Month, Day SMALLINT;
     IF Arg1 IS NULL THEN
             RETURN NULL::BirthDay;
END IF;
     LET Month = MONTH( Arg1 );
     LET Day   = DAY( Arg1 );
     LET LeapDay = 'f';
     IF ( Month = 2 AND Day = 29 ) THEN
         LET LeapDay = 't';
         LET Day = 28;
     END IF;
     RETURN ROW(Month * 100 + Day, LeapDay)::birthday;
END FUNCTION;
GRANT EXECUTE ON FUNCTION BirthDay ( DATE ) TO PUBLIC;
--
--   Compare() support function and another function using
--   it to implement Equal(). Note that the ORDBMS will not
--   use these for sorting or indexing a column of this data
--   type.
--
CREATE FUNCTION Compare( Arg1 BirthDay, Arg2 BirthDay)
RETURNING INTEGER;
     IF Arg1.MmDd < Arg2.MmDd THEN
         RETURN -1;
     ELIF Arg1.MmDd > Arg2.MmDd THEN
```

```
                RETURN 1;
        ELIF Arg1. MmDd != 0228 THEN
                RETURN 0;
        ELIF Arg1.LeapDay = Arg2.LeapDay THEN
                RETURN 0;
        ELIF Arg1. LeapDay THEN
                RETURN 1;
        ELSE
                RETURN -1;
        END IF;
END FUNCTION;
--
CREATE FUNCTION Equal ( Arg1 BirthDay, Arg2 BirthDay )
RETURNING boolean
        DEFINE nIntVal INTEGER;
        LET nIntVal = Compare ( Arg1, Arg2 );

        IF ( nIntVal = 0 ) THEN
            RETURN 't'::boolean;
        END IF;

        RETURN 'f'::boolean;
END FUNCTION;
```

Listing 9–5. *ROW TYPE Implementation of Birthday Object Class*

This example illustrates why prototyping is a very good idea. As you can see, the overall logic is actually more complex than one might think. Because SPL's syntax is so clean, logic errors are easier to find and fix, and modifying an SPL UDF is a simpler task than modifying an equivalent external C or Java function.

The ROW TYPE mechanism's greatest strength is its simplicity. In estimating how long it will take to implement a new type, a good rule of thumb to use is that implementing an equivalent OPAQUE TYPE takes between one and two orders of magnitude more time than implementing an equivalent ROW TYPE. Changing a ROW TYPE is also much simpler. It took about a day to create the BirthDay in the previous listing and to write the user-defined routines for its behavior. Writing and testing the equivalent OPAQUE TYPE took two weeks, mostly because of the time and effort needed to test backup, recovery and communication support functions.

On the other hand, a ROW TYPE consumes more CPU resources for data management than does a C OPAQUE TYPE. This is true because internally, the ORDBMS uses a generic structure to manage each

ROW TYPE. As part of query processing, it must probe this structure to extract element values from within a type instance. On the other hand, implementing a data structure with a lot of elements—say, more than ten—as an encapsulated data object creates other problems. In complex, multi-table queries, there are advantages to being able to extract only relevant data from within a ROW TYPE early in a query, rather than passing an entire object around in memory as part of query execution.

ROW TYPE and Entity Types

A ROW TYPE can also be used to define a table's structure. In fact, creating tables in an inheritance hierarchy requires that you first create a corresponding hierarchy of ROW TYPE instances. Such a ROW TYPE's structure is easily modeled using the entities' structure. For example, the various kinds of merchandise for sale through the site are represented in the E-ER model as a hierarchy. Examine Listing 9–6.

```
--
CREATE ROW TYPE Merchandise_T (
        Id              Part_Code       NOT NULL,
        Name            ProductName     NOT NULL,
        Movie           Movie_Id        NOT NULL,
        Description     lvarchar        NOT NULL,
        Price           Currency        NOT NULL,
        ShippingCost    Currency        NOT NULL,
        NumberAvailable Quantity        NOT NULL
);
--
CREATE ROW TYPE Apparel_Type (
        Kind            Clothing_Enum NOT NULL,
        Sizes           SET(Size_Enum NOT NULL),
        Photo           Image
) UNDER Merchandise_T;
--
CREATE ROW TYPE Toy_Type (
        Kind            ToyKind_Enum    NOT NULL,
        Age_Range       Age_Range       NOT NULL,
        Photo           Image           NOT NULL
) UNDER Merchandise_T;
```

Listing 9–6. *Hierarchy of Types Corresponding to the Merchandise Entity Hierarchy*

When implementing any kind of data type extension, keep in mind that the philosophy of object-oriented development allows for considerable design creativity. Listing 9–5 represents one implementation of the BirthDay type, but there are other ways to achieve the same functional goal.

Sometimes a particular attribute's value can be computed based on the values of other attributes. For example, every item of merchandise has a Brief_Description attribute that appears as a line item on billing statements. Depending on the type of merchandise involved, this string is put together differently. The simplest way to model this is to create an overloaded user-defined function for each type in the Listing 9–6 hierarchy. Modeling read-only attributes as behaviors (implementing them as user-defined functions) saves disk space and can improve performance.

ROW TYPE Limitations

Unfortunately, the ROW TYPE mechanism has significant drawbacks that limit its use in production systems. As at time of writing, you cannot index them, sort them, or use them in UNION queries. It is likely that these limitations will be removed in future versions of the IDS product, but until then, developers should be cautious about how they employ the technique. Java is a better mechanism for indexable types such as PersonName and BirthDay[1].

Nevertheless, a ROW TYPE can be very useful for prototyping new kinds of data and for adding functionality to the OR-SQL query language and SPL database language. They are also useful for implementing application-level objects within the ORDBMS.

Java Classes for Data Types

The ability to implement user-defined types using Java is a relatively recent innovation. Java classes offer many advantages over other type mechanisms, however, particularly when you consider the needs of the overall information system, rather than just the database in isolation. Although Java classes do not offer the absolute best performance, they are generally equivalent to SPL functions, and improves in the comparison as the UDF's logic grows more complex.

---

[1] As a guide to making a judgment about an object's "indexability", consider that the odds someone is born on any given day is 1 in 365.241, and a person's name is even more distinctive. When queries are likely to return less than 1 percent of the data set, indexing helps. This implies that providing useable B-Tree support functions for these types is a good idea.

Java technology's great virtue is its ubiquity. Executable Java code can be moved between different machines and different software environments at runtime without recompilation. As a result, components of an information system can be implemented once as a Java class and then deployed within the ORDBMS, a middleware server, or in a lightweight client applet. Java's host language interface—JDBC—can be used by Java classes running within the IDS product, or within external programs communicating with the database.

Where possible, consider using Java in the following situations:

• Where the new object has a complex, encapsulated internal structure with a set of interface methods implementing its behavior as opposed to a single byte array.
• Whenever instances of the object are to be used both within the ORDBMS and also in external, client, or middleware programs.

Translating UML object-class diagrams into Java classes is a fairly straightforward exercise about which entire books have been written. As we describe in Tutorial 4, embedding a Java class within the ORDBMS requires that the new class implement the standard SQLData interface. Interface methods can be implemented as methods within the class, and these can be used to defined OR-SQL level extensions.

In production systems, Java is the logical way to implement application-specific objects that are to be found in a table's columns. Java classes suffer from none of the limitations that cripple the ROW TYPE. Support methods for data management operations such as sorting and indexing can be implemented as Java methods, and logic implemented in Java can be parallelized. Objects such as PersonName and BirthDate are obvious candidates for such treatment, particularly in light of the fact that a PersonName class may implement other Java interfaces (such as Drawable) and can then be used in Web-client applets.

OPAQUE TYPEs

An OPAQUE TYPE requires more implementation effort than any other kind of UDT. Developers create a C structure that corresponds to the attributes described in the object-class model, and a set of C subroutines implementing the object's behavior. All this code must be compiled into a shared library and extensively tested to ensure its reliability before it can be linked into the ORDBMS engine. Because OPAQUE TYPE extensibility requires custom C code to handle all support tasks, such as backup, client–server communication, and so on, developing one involves a lot of work.

However, the OPAQUE TYPE is the most flexible UDT mechanism. It can be applied to objects ranging from the very small to the extremely large, and even objects whose length varies between these extremes. Also, an OPAQUE TYPE can be used to implement objects that exhibit the kind of complex behavior that can only be handled efficiently in a compiled language such as C. For example, the data structures and logic used for a data type such as a polygon and a function such as Overlaps(Polygon, Polygon) are difficult to implement efficiently using other approaches.

You should consider an OPAQUE TYPE for problem domain objects that have the following characteristics:

- Encapsulated internal structure with complex object behavior that is likely to be used in databases other than the one you are immediately addressing—in other words, potential DataBlades should use the OPAQUE TYPE mechanism.
- Extremely high performance requirements with regard to either the execution of individual interface methods, or indexing support for the type. This is typical whenever the database will be managing a very large number of individual instances of the object, for example.
- Data that is large or extremely variable in terms of its size. OPAQUE TYPE is the best mechanism for dealing with large object data types like digital media and their associated logic.

This combination of performance and flexibility makes OPAQUE TYPE rather specialized. Several kinds of data in our Movie-R-Us Web site database are good candidates for being implemented using this mechanism. These include the Period data type (which is likely to be used in other applications), types that record measurement quantities (such as the size of a movie Poster), and the two-dimensional spatial types. We provide several examples of the OPAQUE TYPE technique throughout this book, focusing on topics related to OPAQUE TYPE development in Chapter 10.

Obvious candidates for OPAQUE TYPE implementation are recorded media data formats, such as digital images, audio, video, and so on, because, in order to be useful, the logic implementing the various behaviors for these data structures must be implemented in a low-level language such as C. To be useful, this logic must be intimately associated with the data itself. When you have very large data objects associated with complex behavior, the OPAQUE TYPE mechanism is the only realistic engineering choice.

Working an Example

For example, in the future, our Movies-R-Us Web site might provide video footage. This makes Video an important kind of data to manage. As far as the data storage facilities of the ORDBMS are concerned, Video objects are simply variable arrays of byte data. They may be small—as compact as a single frame—or large—as extensive as a director's cut of *The French Lieutenant's Woman* with all three alternate endings and Jeremy Irons' hilarious outtakes.

Video formats are quite complex. Each UDF that manipulates video data is required to disentangle the "on disk" format. More sophisticated image processing techniques, such as feature extraction and pattern recognition, involve complex algorithms that must run as close to the silicon as possible for optimal performance.

A Video object class might look like Figure 9–1.

Given the range of potential sizes, the Video object would best be implemented as a multirepresentational type. This requires additional support functions to manage the large object data. Each behavior listed requires a C function that knows the way in which the ORDBMS manages large objects and the internal formats of video data. You should pay considerable attention to how these functions use memory to facilitate parallelism.

Other objects that are good candidates for being implemented using the OPAQUE TYPE mechanism are the Period type (R-Tree indexing), the Mass and Area type (high performance), and all spatial types.

Using DataBlades™

Frequently, data types that are available as a DataBlade™ provide the functionality needed from a data type identified in the analysis phase. In

Video
- Video_Data   Variable Byte Array
+ getLength (Video) -> INTERVAL, + Concat (Video, Video) -> Video, + getFrameCount (Video) -> Quantity, + getFrame (Video) -> Video, + clipFrames (Video, Quantity, Quantity) -> Video, + Video (File_Name) -> Video, + getSceneChanges (Video) -> SET{ Images }, etc.

Figure 9–1. *Universal Modeling Language Object-Class Diagram for Video Data Type*

our example, the Geographic_Point and Document objects are good examples of things that can be bought instead of built. In general, this is a very good idea. When the code in the UDFs is the same that is running in thousands of other databases, and when it was written in the first place by a domain expert in some narrow technical field, it will probably have fewer bugs and will outperform anything that could be customized.

In addition, there are many places on the Web to find so-called "bladelet" extensions. Bladelets are small, useful bundles of extensions written by ORDBMS users, rather than domain experts. For example, all OPAQUE TYPE implementations in this book are available as bladelets. Bladelets are also an excellent mechanism for adding expressions, rather than entire new types, to OR-SQL.

Typically, bladelets come complete with full source code, which makes them easy to modify. They are valuable examples that illustrate more-complex aspects of the DataBlade Application Programming Interface (also known as the Server API or SAPI) and UDT/UDF design. In Table 9–3 we include a partial list of useful Web resources.

Table 9–3. Web Resources for Packaged Extensions and Example Code

URL	Description
http://www.informix.com/idn	Informix Developers Network contains multiple examples and many instructional references on DataBlade development. It is run by the DataBlade Engineering group.
http://examples.informix.com/	Informix By Example hosts self-paced learning guides and lots of examples.
http://www.iiug.org/	Informix's International Users Group hosts a collection of open-source bladelets, each of which implements something small but rather useful.

Readers should feel free to download examples from any of these sites and to look them over. They are also most welcome to submit their own additions.

Final Note on Developing UDTs and Associated UDFs

When developing a new object/data type to be embedded into the ORDBMS, it is helpful keep in mind that you cannot anticipate all the ways in which it will be used. Perhaps the greatest strength of the original relational DBMS products was the way they allowed users to answer ad hoc questions asked at runtime that were not anticipated at design time. In a similar way, it is usually a good idea to implement as much of the behavior of your new type as you think users might need. Focus on implementing each database type and its associated functions one at a time as an autonomous, complete, and self-contained object definition.

Implementing User-Defined Functions

Implementing user-defined functions as part of ORDBMS development takes up a significant portion of time. We devote Chapters 3 and 10 and Tutorial 4 to describing the various UDF mechanisms in detail. Here, we explore the trade-offs between different languages and techniques.

Although in theory any of the UDF mechanisms—internal or SPL UDFs and external UDFs written in Java or C—can be used with any of the different kinds of data type, each mechanism works better with certain types than with others. For example, the database procedure language SPL is able to access the elements of a ROW TYPE using the same cascading-dot notation as an OR-SQL query. On the other hand, SAPI facilities for C make interrogating a ROW TYPE quite cumbersome. As with other extensibility mechanisms, deciding which approach to use in any given situation is a question of balancing trade-offs.

In this section we review approaches to writing UDFs and discuss their strengths and weaknesses. We also provide a set of guidelines to follow when implementing UDFs. For the most part, the task is much like programming in any other environment, but there are a couple of conceptual "gotchas" of which developers should be aware.

SPL Routines

The quickest and easiest way to write a UDF is to use the ORDBMS's Stored Procedure Language, SPL. SPL is a simple language. It supports procedural programming concepts such as variables, branches, loops, and exception handling. OR-SQL embeds into it very naturally. All facilities needed to create an SPL routine are part of the core engine, and the IDS product includes tracing facilities to help developers debug SPL routines. SPL's language features are described in detail in Chapter 6.

All this adds up to a high-productivity development environment, which makes SPL an ideal choice for prototyping user-defined functions and testing the correctness of your design. Earlier we noted that for any new type, it is often a good idea to implement it initially as a ROW TYPE. Correspondingly, you should implement the behavior of such types using SPL.

It is perfectly possible to use SPL to implement routines for the other kinds of data types too. When implementing an SPL routine for a DISTINCT or OPAQUE TYPE, the SPL code will embed external UDFs to access the type's innards. For example, the SPL function in Listing 9–7 takes a Java class (PersonName) and uses a set of interfaces to it to extract information from the argument. Then it returns an XML formatted string that labels the type's values.

```
CREATE FUNCTION XML ( Arg1 PersonName )
RETURNS XML_String
   DEFINE lvcRetVal     LVARCHAR;

   LET lvcRetVal=NewLine() || "<PersonName>" || NewLine();
   LET lvcRetVal=lvcRetVal || " <Family_Name>" ||
                  getFamilyName(Arg1) ||
                  "<\Family_Name>" || NewLine();
   LET lvcRetVal=lvcRetVal || " <First_Name>" ||
                  getFirstName(Arg1) ||
                  "<\First_Name>" || NewLine();
   LET lvcRetVal=lvcRetVal || " <Other_Names>" ||
                  getOtherNames(Arg1) ||
                  "<\Other_Names>" || NewLine();
   LET lvcRetVal=lvcRetVal || "<\PersonName>" || NewLine();

   RETURN lvcRetVal::XML_String;

END FUNCTION;
```

Listing 9–7. *SPL Function Using EXTERNAL Java Routines*

SPL's major drawbacks are its performance characteristics and its proprietary nature. SPL is between one and two orders of magnitude (10–100 times) slower than the equivalent logic written in C. Internally, SPL is implemented as a semi-interpreted language. This means that executing SPL logic requires more CPU cycles than does C. In addition, SPL runs only within the ORDBMS. Routines written in SPL cannot be integrated into other deployment environments such as TP-Monitors, middleware systems, or client-side user interfaces, although they can be *invoked* from these other environments through any standard interface.

External Routines (C and Java)

External routines written in C or Java, although they outperform SPL routines, are not as fast as the equivalent built-in logic would be. However, the most important difference between the SPL and the external routines is that general-purpose programming languages such as C or Java are more powerful than the DBMS stored procedure language. The more complex the interface method's functionality, the better off you are using one of these low-level languages.

External routines are the most suitable technique for OPAQUE TYPE behaviors or for the implementation of new behaviors for a DISTINCT TYPE because low-level logic can access C structures directly or work with an array of bytes that the ORDBMS stores. For large object data, the IDS product's internal API provides the means to handle the contents of the large object as though it were simply a file or byte stream. Instances of each of the built-in types can be passed into and returned from C or Java programming logic. This makes external logic a good choice for fast stand-alone functions.

Bang versus Buck: The Functionality/Performance Trade-off

The most important practical difference between these extension languages is performance. However, performance questions are complicated by the way developers can include OR-SQL callbacks—by which we mean embedded OR-SQL statements—within their logic. The basic rules are as follows:

- If a user-defined function contains an OR-SQL callback (embeds a query within its logic), the cost of running the query is almost always the most computationally expensive aspect of executing the function, regardless of the language used to implement it. This means functions containing OR-SQL callbacks should almost always be created using SPL because it is by far the simplest technique.
- SPL is the easiest language to use, and it represents the fastest way to develop a new function. Java is a more complex language than is SPL, so developing logic in Java takes more time, but the presence of a large library of utilities for Java makes it easier to develop complex extensions. C is the lowest-level programming language, and it is therefore more difficult to use than either Java or SPL.
- Queries that invoke C and Java functions containing no OR-SQL callbacks can be parallelized; others cannot.

- Java code is mobile. A properly implemented Java class can be deployed within the ORDBMS, within a middleware application server, or within an applet running remotely. C and SPL, on the other hand, cannot.

If there is a golden rule to follow with external user-defined functions, it is this: *never embed OR-SQL within any UDF that will be invoked within an OR-SQL query*. Instead, adopt a more object-oriented philosophy. Object-relational analysis is an exercise in identifying the fundamental building blocks of your database; the application's schema and OR-SQL queries are merely the provisional (temporary or interim) way that these objects are arranged. If one of these building blocks needs to know about the schema within it is being run, then it might be a good idea to review the analysis.

Of course, completely eliminating embedded OR-SQL from UDFs is impossible because there will always be situations in which it is required. For example, values of the Currency data type that we develop can be converted between various unit denominations, but the rate at which these conversions are made (exchange rate) varies with time, making it convenient to use a table to record these values.

Measuring the Performance of Alternative Extensible Function Mechanisms

Assessing the runtime performance of the different mechanisms is a complex undertaking. In the following section, we present the result of a simple-minded experiment to address the question.

Runtime costs for UDRs have two components: calling overhead and execution efficiency. Calling UDF logic implemented in C, SPL, and Java involves varying amounts of effort. In theory, C should be the least expensive because it is linked into the IDS product, and because there is no need to transform the representation of data types. C should also have the most efficient execution, but the relative performance characteristics of SPL and Java are less easy to guess.

We measured the calling overhead of SPL, Java, and C by implementing a small UDR in each language that simply returns its argument value immediately. When the ORDBMS calls the Java class, it needs to turn the SQL INTEGER into a java.lang.Integer object. In the case of both the SPL and the Java logic, it needs to initialize the language's interpreter. This UDF is called Pop().

To estimate the runtime performance of the various languages, we implemented another function that determines whether an INTEGER argument is a prime number. This algorithm simply loops through integers in ascending order seeking an integer value that divides the argument value evenly, stopping when it reaches the square root of the argument value. For extra realism, each UDR included a redundant memory allocation and string manipulation step.

The idea is that this UDF—which we call `Prime()`—will consume on average more computational cycles for larger numbers. This is complicated by the fact that the larger the number, the less likely that the number is prime. Nevertheless the experimental results are revealing.

To obtain the measurements we present in Figure 9–2, we exercised these functions over several blocks of numbers for which the count of numbers in each block was identical (10,000), but the size of the numbers varied between 1 and 10,000,010,000. The idea is that it takes more computational resources to determine whether larger numbers are prime. The following figure lists the results of the experiment, which is included in the source code examples accompanying this book.

The conclusion is that the calling overhead of both C and SPL is significantly lower than Java, and C has by far the best runtime performance. However, the superior runtime performance of Java means that once the UDF reaches a certain degree of complexity, Java outperforms SPL. Note that the final value of the SPL Prime Performance was 2401 seconds, which we do not show.

Overview of Schema Design

Eventually, you arrive at the point at which each data type/object class/domain identified in the conceptual analysis phase has a

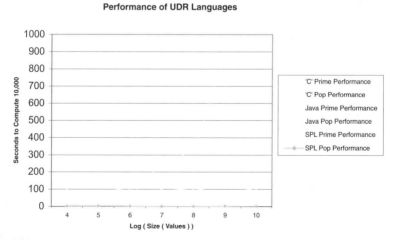

Figure 9–2. *Comparing the Runtime Performance of Three UDR Mechanisms*

corresponding UDT and UDF representation in the database. In addition to the domains in the conceptual data model, it is a good idea to take a look at the set of workload queries and any application-level business processes you have identified. Some types—like the BirthDay ROW TYPE—may never be used in a database table. However, they may still be useful in a query or in business process logic.

The next task is to use these types to create a database schema corresponding to the extended entity-relationship (or high-level object class) model. This process is known as *schema design*. To a degree, schema design can be performed concurrently with the task of type development. In fact, as production systems evolve over time, development will be proceeding at several levels simultaneously.

Schema Design Methodology Overview

The input to the schema design process is the extended ER (or high-level object class) model, and the output is a set of ORDBMS DDL statements. These scripts create the tables and views that support a variety of end-user operations, are structured so that there is no possibility of ambiguity in the database, and possess integrity rules to ensure the correctness of their data. In Chapter 2 we described the extent of the data definition language and the fundamental concepts underlying object-relational database schema.

Recall that an object-relational database schema consists of a set of interrelated tables. Rows within these tables record facts about the problem domain. Some of these facts are concerned with the existence of certain things (a Movie, or a Cinema, or a MovieClubMember), while other facts relate to how these things are interrelated. Because the schema is used to store knowledge shared by all end users, schema design is a central topic in data management.

We divide schema implementation process into several subtasks. Initially, we generate a naïve logical model that is merely a restatement of the conceptual E-ER model as tables rather than E-ER diagrams. Then we apply a set of formal procedures known as *normalization analysis*. Normalization is motivated by a desire to ensure that the database schema is free from even the possibility of error or ambiguity. In a nutshell, the goal of normalization is to ensure that any (relevant) real-world fact is recorded exactly once in the schema.

Finally, in order to ensure that our design is adequate from a performance point of view, we implement the workload of common queries and business processes and investigate how well they run against it. A more detailed description of the steps involved in schema design follows:

1. Converge the several conceptual views into a single canonical conceptual model of the ORDBMS.
2. Transform this integrated conceptual model into a naïve database schema:
   - Using the types created previously, and based on the canonical E-ER model, create a set of tables corresponding to the following:
     - Entities.
     - Certain kinds of Relationships.
3. Apply the rules of normalization to eliminate redundancy and inconsistency from the naive schema.
4. Implement a workload set of queries that describe how the resulting database is to be used:
   - Create the business processes as database functions or procedures.
   - Create an infrastructure to support the most common conceptual views.

Converging Conceptual Views

In Chapter 8, when we introduced the topic of conceptual modeling, we noted that as part of your analysis, you would need to understand how different categories of end users interact with the information system. As a result, you may have produced multiple, overlapping, E-ER models. The first logical design task is to combine these models and create a canonical conceptual view of the ORDBMS. Another way to say this is that you must create a conceptual view that is *shareable* by all end users. From each end user's point of view this canonical model will contain information that is irrelevant to them, but all of the information needed by all end users is represented somewhere.

Generally speaking, smaller, simpler models are better than larger, more complex ones. Rather than simply merging all the E-ER diagrams, as part of this integration you should identify and eliminate as much redundancy as you can. Although this sounds challenging, in practice it is usually fairly easy. For the most part, names are the chief source of disagreement. You should seek to find situations in which two users have different names for the same thing or the same name is used for different things.

In lieu of a lengthy, complex procedure, we explore the issues of conceptual view integration with a list of questions.

1. How do you approach integration? Do you do it in a single step that integrates several of the various user views all at once, or do you do it in a step-wise manner (two views at a time)?

The appropriate strategy depends on the degree of overlap among input views. Some user views have very little in common. For example, the electronic commerce team's problem has very little in common with the problems of maintaining movie information. On the other hand, the group responsible for the site's look and feel and the group responsible for managing movie club member information share a significant interest in the demographic information stored about movie club members.

E-ER models that do not overlap at all are the easiest to merge because there are fewer potential sources of conflict. Therefore, several nonoverlapping user views can be lumped together. As part of this process, it is useful to verify whether you have identified a minimal complete set of the various kinds of data in which you are interested. Conceptual views that do overlap are more difficult. It's a good idea to pair up and integrate views that have significant areas of common interest.

2. What are the sources of conflict and ambiguity?

There are many potential causes of conflict and ambiguity. In one study, researchers determined that any two people working in the same problem domain agree on the name for anything in it only 17 percent of the time. This observation has two implications. First, it means that there is tremendous scope for disagreement about naming issues. Second, it means that the names ultimately chosen are not particularly important. The more important questions relate to structure, relationships, and behavior.

Because of its focus on modeling attribute types as objects, the ORDBMS data model helps in the identification of conflicts and their resolution. Unlike the situation with traditional RDBMS data modeling, an entity's attribute names do not need to reflect both what the attribute contains and what its role is within the table; these are a frequent source of conflict. For example, the attribute name "Id" is used in the Merchandise table and "Merchandise" is used in the Orders table. The fact that they have the same type indicates that these two attributes contain the same kind of information.

Differences that are more difficult to deal with occur in the non-structural aspects of the conceptual model, such as incompatible entity constraint rules or different relationship cardinalities. Frequently these differences are simply a matter of one group having a requirement that another does not, but occasionally, resolving them requires reexamining the original conceptual views.

3. Is the proposed integration still correct and complete?

Having eliminated the ambiguities, it is very important to check that nothing has been lost in the process. Again, ORDBMS techniques can help to solve certain problems. Apparently incompatible entity definition can be integrated by identifying the common attributes and creating an inheritance hierarchy that models incompatible entity types as subtypes of a more general, strong entity. Of course, when one group wants to see the other group's data, they will have to access it through the strong entity. Therefore none of their own attributes will have values. The alternative is to create a single entity with optional attributes.

Transforming the Conceptual Model into a Logical Model

Tables are the basic data storage abstraction used in object-relational database schema. In this section, we outline the procedure for transforming E-ER diagrams into a set of tables, or *logical schema*. The overall approach is very similar to techniques used to map E-ER diagrams into SQL-92 RDBMS tables.

The best way to explain how to transform an E-ER model into a set of relational tables is to describe the two kinds of tables the process produces. Database schema tables are one of the following:

- *Entity tables.* These tables have the same name and a similar structure to their counterpart in the E-ER diagram. In addition to the attributes identified in the entity diagram, entity tables include attributes to manage relationships with other entity tables.
- *Relationship tables.* It is necessary to use a table to manage N:M relationships between two entities and to represent n-ary relationships involving multiple entities.

Of course, there are some important differences between ORDBMS databases and RDBMS databases. First, the types used in the ORDBMS tables must correspond to the object classes identified as part of the conceptual analysis. Second, data modeling features such as the COLLEC-TION and entity inheritance can be represented more or less directly.

Transformation Procedure

In this subsection we present a more systematic description of the transformation procedure. The subtasks in the transformation procedure involve.

Strong_Entity	
Attribute_Name	**Attribute_Kind**
Key_Attribute	**Data_Type_A**
Attribute_One	Data_Type_E
Attribute_Two	Data_Type_C

```
CREATE TABLE Strong_Entity (
  Key_Attribute    Data_Type_A NOT NULL,
  Attribute_One    Data_Type_B NOT NULL,
  Attribute_Two    Data_Type_C NOT NULL
  );
--
ALTER TABLE Strong_Entity
ADD CONSTRAINT
  PRIMARY KEY ( Key_Attribute )
  CONSTRAINT Strong_Entity_PK;
```

Figure 9–3. *Strong Entity to Object-Relational Table*

Strong Entities

For each strong entity in the E-ER model, create a table in which the table's name is the same as the entity name, each entity attribute has a corresponding column in the table, and the kind of data corresponding to each attribute is represented with the corresponding data type.

Figure 9–3 illustrates the simplest kind of mapping: strong entity represented with a single table. Each of the entity's attributes has a corresponding table attribute of the appropriate data type. Mandatory elements are established with NOT NULL column constraints. Strong entities should have at least one candidate key: either a subset of its attributes or a system-generated value to identify the row uniquely. Of course, any other candidate keys should be constrained with a UNIQUE constraint.

Earlier in this chapter we investigated how certain entities may be analyzed in more detail using object-oriented methods. If the entity is found to possess read methods that can be used in a query, the entity is best implemented as follows:

- Use a ROW TYPE to define the table/entity structure.
- Create a table using the ROW TYPE.
- Add whatever constraints have been identified.

Once these steps are complete, the entity read methods can be implemented using UDFs. If these read methods are sufficiently common, such extensions should be implemented in C so that a functional index can be created later.

In Listing 9–8 we illustrate what it would look like to implement the Strong_Entity table using this approach. All other examples in this chapter can be handled in a similar fashion.

```
CREATE ROW TYPE Strong_Entity_Structure (
      Key_Attribute  Data_Type_A    NOT NULL,
      Attribute_One  Data_Type_B    NOT NULL,
      Attribute_Two  Data_Type_C    NOT NULL
```

```
);
--
CREATE FUNCTION Read_Interface_Method
                           ( Argument Strong_Entity_Structure )
RETURNS Result_Type
    RETURN Argument.Key_Attribute::LVARCHAR ||
            ' ' ||  Argument.Attribute_One;
END FUNCTION;
--
CREATE TABLE Strong_Entity
OF TYPE Strong_Entity_Structure;
--
ALTER TABLE Strong_Entity
ADD CONSTRAINT
    PRIMARY KEY ( Key_Attribute )
    CONSTRAINT Strong_Entity_PK;
```

Listing 9–8. *Creating a Table for the Strong Entity using a ROW TYPE*

Again, we emphasize that using a ROW TYPE to define tables complicates the task of altering a table's structure. Consequently, use this approach only when necessary: either when the table is part of an inheritance hierarchy, or when some value can be computed from the table's rows with a user-defined function.

Weak Entities

You rarely encounter a strong entity on its own. More typically, the conceptual model consists of a network of interrelated weak and strong entities. Weak entities are also represented using tables; the table's name is the same as the entity type's name, and it has a set of columns that correspond to the entity type's attributes in much the same way that a strong entity's table does.

When a weak entity is transformed into a table, the columns defining the *primary key* of the related strong entity are added to the columns defining the weak entity's attributes. Sometimes, these extra columns are called *join columns.*

In Figure 9–4, note how the type used in the weak entity's new column is the same data type used in the strong entity's primary key, even though the column's name is different. We use the name of the table, Strong_Entity, as the name for the new column. Using table names to represent relationships is a convenience for developers who write queries; the new column could have any name that makes sense. Sometimes the role label from the relationship is used instead. The constraints added after the tables are created enforce the referential integrity.

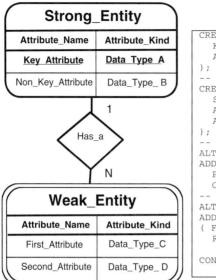

```
CREATE TABLE Strong_Entity (
    Key_Attribute Data_Type_A    NOT NULL,
    Attribute_One Data_Type_B    NOT NULL
);
--
CREATE TABLE Weak_Entity (
    Strong_Entity   Data_Type_A NOT NULL,
    Attribute_One   Data_Type_C NOT NULL,
    Attribute_Two   Data_Type_D NOT NULL
);
--
ALTER TABLE Strong_Entity
ADD CONSTRAINT
    PRIMARY KEY ( Key_Attribute )
    CONSTRAINT Strong_Entity_PK;
--
ALTER TABLE Weak_Entity
ADD CONSTRAINT
( FOREIGN KEY ( Strong_Entity )
    REFERENCES
        Strong_Entity ( Key_Attribute )
CONSTRAINT
        Weak_Entity_FK_to_Strong_Entity
```

Figure 9–4. *Strong Entity and Related Weak Entity*

Depending on whether the relationship is mandatory, you might use a slightly different constraint. If every instance of the weak entity is required to have a corresponding instance of the strong entity, the rule should also delete rows from the Weak_Entity table when the related row in the Strong_Entity table is deleted. This prevents dangling rows from being created. Listing 9–9 illustrates how to declare this kind of constraint rule.

```
ALTER TABLE Weak_Entity
ADD CONSTRAINT
( FOREIGN KEY ( Strong_Entity )
    REFERENCES Strong_Entity ( Key_Attribute )
    ON DELETE CASCADE
    CONSTRAINT Weak_Entity_FK_to_Strong_Entity
);
```

Listing 9–9. *CONSTRAINT that Enforces Mandatory Relationship Rules*

Unary relationships, in which an entity instance has a relationship with another entity instance of the same type, can be modeled in a similar fashion. You need to repeat the columns that make up its primary key in the table. This pattern is often referred to as a *cyclic* or *recursive* constraint. Appropriate constraints ensure the correctness of the data in the table. Note that to insert the first row into the table, you must permit the new foreign key column to contain NULL values. Otherwise, you can never insert a first row. We illustrate this in Figure 9–5.

Cyclic constraints impose several other problems. In practice, they are frequently navigated using iterative or recursive procedures. Without a guarantee that the cyclic relationship terminates, these algorithms are problematic. The ORDBMS itself will halt cascading DELETE operations after a certain number of operations. Consequently, it can be better to adopt a slightly different tactic with this kind of relationship. Refer to Tutorial 6 for another approach to this handling Bill-of-Material problems.

Entities with Inheritance

Entity inheritance hierarchies can be transformed more or less directly into table hierarchies. This requires that you first create a ROW TYPE hierarchy, and then use entity inheritance hierarchies to create a table hierarchy. Earlier in this chapter, we saw how object-oriented modeling techniques can be used to gain a deeper understanding of the structure and properties of entity classes, and by now, you may even have the ROW TYPE already in the database.

In Figure 9–6 we illustrate how a hierarchy of entities may be represented.

Inheritance hierarchies can be either weak or strong entities, so it may be necessary to augment their definition with join columns from another table's primary key and to impose additional constraints. This may require that you revisit the structure of some ROW TYPE instances, but these changes need not alter the code used in functions that implement their behavior.

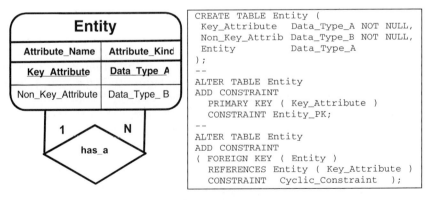

Figure 9–5. Cyclic Constraint: Relationship of Entity with Other Rows Within Itself

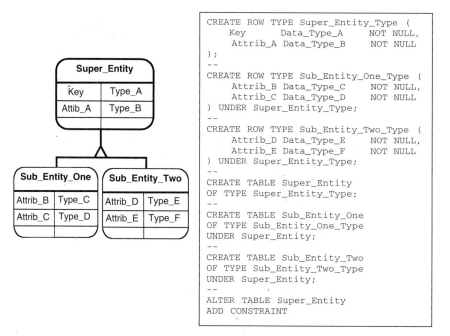

```
CREATE ROW TYPE Super_Entity_Type (
    Key       Data_Type_A   NOT NULL,
    Attrib_A Data_Type_B    NOT NULL
);
--
CREATE ROW TYPE Sub_Entity_One_Type (
    Attrib_B Data_Type_C    NOT NULL,
    Attrib_C Data_Type_D    NOT NULL
) UNDER Super_Entity_Type;
--
CREATE ROW TYPE Sub_Entity_Two_Type (
    Attrib_D Data_Type_E    NOT NULL,
    Attrib_E Data_Type_F    NOT NULL
) UNDER Super_Entity_Type;
--
CREATE TABLE Super_Entity
OF TYPE Super_Entity_Type;
--
CREATE TABLE Sub_Entity_One
OF TYPE Sub_Entity_One_Type
UNDER Super_Entity;
--
CREATE TABLE Sub_Entity_Two
OF TYPE Sub_Entity_Two_Type
UNDER Super_Entity;
--
ALTER TABLE Super_Entity
ADD CONSTRAINT
```

Figure 9–6. *Entity Hierarchy and Matching Table Hierarchy*

Modeling Complex Relationships

So far, all examples we have seen involve converting entities into
tables, but certain kinds of relationships are also represented this way.
For instance, entity relationships that are N:M in their cardinality, or
n-ary relationships involving more than one or two entities, are stored
as rows in a table. The general idea is to create a table that has
columns that are the same as the primary-key columns of the tables
involved in the relationship and rules to ensure the correctness of its
data. We illustrate the idea in Figure 9–7.

You might want to enforce rules over the entire relationship in the
same way you enforce rules over entity tables. For example, in N:M
relationships such as the one in Figure 9–7, it is often desirable to
limit the number of times that a relationship between two instances
can be recorded. For example, in circumstances in which an Employee
may work for multiple Departments, and a single Department will
consequently have many Employees, it may be desirable to ensure
that each relationship between an Employee and a Department is
recorded only once. In other words, the ORDBMS can ensure that a
row of values is not repeated in the relationship table. A primary-key
constraint over the relationship table of the kind shown in Listing
9–10 does exactly this.

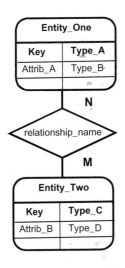

```
CREATE TABLE Entity_One (
     Key          Data_Type_A    NOT NULL,
     Attrib_A    Data_Type_B    NOT NULL
);
--
ALTER TABLE Entity_One
ADD CONSTRAINT
  PRIMARY KEY ( Key )
  CONSTRAINT Entity_One_PK;
--
CREATE TABLE Entity_Two (
     Key          Data_Type_C    NOT NULL,
     Attrib_B Data_Type_D    NOT NULL
);
--
ALTER TABLE Entity_Two
ADD CONSTRAINT PRIMARY KEY( Key )
CONSTRAINT Entity_Two_PK;
--
CREATE TABLE Relationship_Name (
    Entity_One  Data_Type_A   NOT NULL,
    Entity_Two  Data_Type_C   NOT NULL
);
--
ALTER TABLE Relationship_Name
ADD CONSTRAINT (FOREIGN KEY ( Entity_One )
  REFERENCES Entity_One ( Key )
   CONSTRAINT Relationship_Name_FK_Entity_One
);
--
ALTER TABLE Relationship_Name
ADD CONSTRAINT(FOREIGN KEY(Entity_Two)
   REFERENCES Entity_Two ( Key )
```

Figure 9–7. *N:M Relationship Modeled with a Table*

```
ALTER TABLE Relationship_Name
  ADD CONSTRAINT  PRIMARY KEY ( Entity_One, Entity_Two )
  CONSTRAINT Relationship_Name_PK;
```

Listing 9–10. *Adding a Primary Key Constraint to a Relationship Table*

Tables recording relationships are often called *resolution* tables. One advantage of this approach is that it is relatively straightforward to represent more complex kinds of relationships, such as n-ary relationships and relationships with associated attributes. Handling n-ary relationships also calls for creating a table containing key columns of all related tables, and possibly extending it with additional columns to contain any attributes of the relationship. In Figure 9–8 we present an example of how to handle n-ary relationships using a resolution table.

The range of E-ER situations and their corresponding mappings into relational tables is quite extensive. Each example in this section illustrates a common pattern or situation, but almost all practical problems require a developer to employ some variant of these schemes. As with other aspects of data modeling, object-relational technology has little impact on relational techniques.

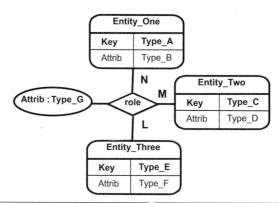

```
CREATE TABLE Entity_One (
  Key          Data_Type_A NOT NULL,
  Attrib       Data_Type_B NOT NULL
);
--
--
CREATE TABLE Entity_Two (
  Key          Data_Type_C NOT NULL,
  Attrib       Data_Type_D NOT NULL
);
--
CREATE TABLE Entity_Three (
  Key          Data_Type_E NOT NULL,
  Attrib       Data_Type_F NOT NULL
);
--
CREATE TABLE Ternary_Role (
  Entity_One   Data_Type_A NOT NULL,
  Entity_Two   Data_Type_C NOT NULL,
  Entity_Three Data_Type_E NOT NULL,
  Attrib       Data_Typc_G NOT NULL
);
--
ALTER TABLE Entity_One
ADD CONSTRAINT PRIMARY KEY ( Key )
  CONSTRAINT Entity_One_PK;
```

```
ALTER TABLE Entity_Two
ADD CONSTRAINT PRIMARY KEY ( Key )
  CONSTRAINT Entity_Two_PK;
--
ALTER TABLE Entity_Three
ADD CONSTRAINT PRIMARY KEY ( Key )
  CONSTRAINT Entity_Three_PK;
--
ALTER TABLE Ternary_Role
ADD CONSTRAINT(
  FOREIGN KEY( Entity_One)
  REFERENCES Entity_One ( Key )
  CONSTRAINT Ternary_FK_Entity_One
),
ADD CONSTRAINT (
  FOREIGN KEY ( Entity_Two )
  REFERENCES Entity_Two ( Key )
  CONSTRAINT Ternary_FK_Entity_Two
),
ADD CONSTRAINT (
  FOREIGN KEY ( Entity_Three )
  REFERENCES Entity_Three ( Key )
  CONSTRAINT Ternary_FK_Entity_Three
);
--
```

Figure 9–8. Tables for a Ternary Relationship with Additional Attributes

General Rules for Table Definitions

There are several "rules of thumb" concerning how attributes are handled. These rules are common to all tables created from E-ER diagrams.

- NULL values in columns complicate query processing and should be avoided. Some of the most notorious and long-running "wrong answer" problems reported to technical support organizations can be traced to an OR-SQL programmer misunderstanding one of the (many) subtle rules governing three-value logic. They should be avoided wherever possible.

- Columns that are included in a table's keys cannot contain NULL values. Columns where there is an obvious default—a type-specific token that means "Unknown" or "Did not respond," a system-generated value such as TODAY, or a generally acceptable value—should insert that value automatically. The only place NULL values are absolutely required is in columns for a FOREIGN KEY that is not mandatory.[2]
- Use CHECK constraints to enforce rules on entity attributes. Some rules on the data in a column will be enforced as part of the data type's implementation, but not all.
- Name all constraints (with the possible exception of the NOT NULL constraints, which should be the de facto standard in the schema). User-defined types provide some control over the values columns can contain. However, when you have identified additional constraints as part of your analysis, it is useful to enforce them. This can lead to a large number of constraint rules per table. Naming constraints simplifies the task of managing them and determines which of them was violated by a particular operation. System-generated constraint names are totally impenetrable.

Working an Example

In this section we apply the rules introduced to the extended entity-relationship model developed for the Movies-R-Us Web site database. To keep this section short, we focus on certain subsections of the schema, although a complete implementation can be found on the CD accompanying this book.

Table 9–4 lists the strong entities identified as part of the extended ER model and provides a more detailed description of each entity's attributes and data integrity rules. Of these, MovieClubMembers is slightly special in that several read-only methods have been identified for it. Thus, it uses the ROW TYPE declaration approach, and we show the definition of the UDF too.

We assume that all data-type building blocks for these tables have already been implemented and that they are available for use in CREATE TABLE statements. Transforming these entities according to our procedure yields the set of OR-SQL CREATE TABLE statements and constraint rules in Listing 9–11. Note that for brevity, we omit the DDL used to grant access to these tables.

---

[2] It is hard to justify ruling out NULL values completely. There will be situations in which three-value logic properties are desirable. Such situations tend to be exceptional, however, and you are wise to avoid them unless you can explain why neither NULL = NULL nor NULL <> NULL is true.

Movie

Attribute	Attribute Type	Optional	Rules or Constraints
Title	Movie_Title	Mandatory	First part of primary key
Released_On	Date	Mandatory	Second part of primary key
Directors	SET{ MoviePersonality}	Mandatory	
Writers	SET{ MoviePersonality }	Mandatory	
Producers	SET{ MoviePersonality}	Mandatory	
Starring	SET{ROW(MoviePersonality, PersonName) }	Mandatory	
Awards	SET{Award}	Optional	
Genre	SET{Genres}	Mandatory	
Budget	Currency	Mandatory	Must exceed U.S. $0
Takings	Currency	Optional	
Plot_Summary	Document	Mandatory	
On_Video	Boolean	Mandatory	Default is "true"

MovieClubMembers

Attribute	Attribute Type	Optional	Rules or Constraints
Id	Membership_Identifier	Mandatory user-defined	Unique; primary identifier;
Password	Encrypted_String	Mandatory	
Name	PersonName	Mandatory	
DOB	date	Mandatory	Must be older than 21 and younger than 125
Address	MailAddress	Mandatory	
HomePhone	PhoneNumber	Mandatory	
'GeoLocation	GeoPoint	Mandatory	
Preferences	SET(Genre)	Optional	
Photo	Image	Optional	
CreditCard	Credit_Card_Number	Optional	

(continued)

Cinemas

Attribute	Attribute Type	Optional	Rules or Constraints
Id	System_Generated	Mandatory	Primary Key
Name	CinemaName	Mandatory	First Part of Unique
Address	MailAddress	Mandatory	Second Part of Unique
HomePhone	PhoneNumber	Mandatory	
Photo	Image	Optional	
SurroundSound	boolean	Mandatory	Default is "false"
DisabledAccess	boolean	Mandatory	Default is "true"
ScreenCount	Quantity	Mandatory	
GeoLocation	Geo_Point	Optional	

```
--
--   Movies:
--
CREATE TABLE Movies (
    Title              Title                       NOT NULL,
    Release_Date       DATE                        NOT NULL,
    Directors          MoviePersonality            NOT NULL,
    Writers            SET(MoviePersonality        NOT NULL),
    Producers          SET(MoviePersonality        NOT NULL),
    Staring            SET(ROW ( Actor   MoviePersonality,
                                 Played PersonName)
                                                    NOT NULL),
    Genre              SET(Genre_Enum              NOT NULL),
    Awards             SET(Award_Enum              NOT NULL),
    Budget             Currency                    NOT NULL
              CHECK ( Budget > Currency(0,'USD')),
    Takings            Currency                    NOT NULL,
              CHECK ( Takings > Currency(0,'USD')),
    Plot_Summary       Doc_Type                    NOT NULL,
    OnVideo            boolean                     DEFAULT 't'
);
--
ALTER TABLE Movies ADD CONSTRAINT
    PRIMARY KEY ( Title, Release_Date )
```

```
        CONSTRAINT Movies_Title_Release_Data_PK;
--
--   Note: To model the Sequel cyclic constraint, you would
--   use the ALTER TABLE command to add a Sequel_Title and
--   Sequel_Release_Date column of the appropriate types.--
-- MovieClubMembers
--
CREATE ROW TYPE MovieClub_Member_Type (
        Id              Membership_Id     NOT NULL,
        PassWord        Encrypted_String  NOT NULL,
        Name            PersonName        NOT NULL,
        DOB             date,
        Address         MailAddress       NOT NULL,
        HomePhone       PhoneNumber       NOT NULL,
        LivesAt         GeoPoint          NOT NULL,
        Preferences     SET(Genre_Enum    NOT NULL),
        Membership_Period Period          NOT NULL,
        Photo           Image,
        CreditCard                        CCDetails
);
--
CREATE FUNCTION Age ( Arg1 Date )
RETURNS INTEGER
    DEFINE rv INTERVAL YEAR(4) TO YEAR;
    LET rv = EXTEND(TODAY, YEAR TO YEAR) -
            EXTEND(Arg1, YEAR TO YEAR);
    IF EXTEND(TODAY, MONTH TO DAY) <
            EXTEND(Arg1, MONTH TO DAY) THEN
        LET rv = rv - 1 UNITS YEAR;
    END IF;
    RETURN rv::LVARCHAR::INTEGER;
END FUNCTION;
--
CREATE TABLE MovieClubMembers
OF TYPE MovieClub_Member_Type;
--
ALTER TABLE MovieClubMembers
ADD CONSTRAINT
( PRIMARY KEY ( Id ) CONSTRAINT MovieClubMembers_Id_PK),
ADD CONSTRAINT
(
   CHECK ( DOB BETWEEN TODAY - 125 YEAR
                 AND TODAY - 21 YEAR )
       CONSTRAINT MovieClubMembers_Age_Range_21_and_Up
```

```
);
--
-- Cinemas:
--
CREATE TABLE Cinemas (
        Id              SERIAL          NOT NULL,
        Name            CinemaName      NOT NULL,
        Address         MailAddress     NOT NULL,
        Phone           PhoneNumber     NOT NULL,
        Photo           Image           NOT NULL,
        SurroundSound   boolean         DEFAULT 'f',
        DisabledAccess  boolean         DEFAULT 't',
        ScreenCount     INTEGER         NOT NULL
    CHECK ( TheatreCount >= 1 )
    CONSTRAINT Cinemas_Must_Have_ScreenCount,
        GeoLocation     GeoPoint        NOT NULL
);
--
GRANT ALL ON Cinemas TO PUBLIC;
--
ALTER TABLE Cinemas
ADD CONSTRAINT
(
    PRIMARY KEY ( Id )
    CONSTRAINT Cinemas_ID_PK
),
ADD CONSTRAINT (
    UNIQUE ( Name, PhoneNumber )
    CONSTRAINT Cinemas_Name_and_Phone_Unique
);
```

Listing 9–11. *Table Definitions for Strong Entities Identified in the E-ER Model*

The E-ER model includes an inheritance hierarchy to represent the various kinds of Merchandise offered for sale. In the Movies-R-Us Web site database, the merchandise hierarchy represents an entire set of weak entities, and every item of merchandise must have a corresponding Movie to which it is related. Also, note the Tickets table, which has a relationship with the Showings table. Its attributes must be augmented with an additional join column.

The complete set of different kinds of merchandise is quite extensive. Tables 8–3 and 8–4 in Chapter 8 present a subset of it. For each item of Merchandise, there is at least one overloaded UDF, called Brief Description(), which was introduced in Chapter 5.

In the Listing 9–12 we present a subset of the DDL used to implement the tables.

```
CREATE ROW TYPE Merchandise_Type (
        Id              Part_Code        NOT NULL,
        Name            ProductName      NOT NULL,
        Movie           Movie_Id         NOT NULL,
        Description     Doc_Type         NOT NULL,
        Price           Currency         NOT NULL,
        ShippingCost    Currency         NOT NULL,
        NumberAvailable Quantity         NOT NULL
);

CREATE TABLE Merchandise
OF TYPE Merchandise_Type;

ALTER TABLE Merchandise
ADD CONSTRAINT
( PRIMARY KEY ( Id ) CONSTRAINT Merchandise_PK),
ADD CONSTRAINT (
  FOREIGN KEY ( Movie )  REFERENCES Movies ( Id ) ON DELETE
CASCADE
  CONSTRAINT Merch_Movies_FK
);

CREATE ROW TYPE Apparel_Type (
        Kind            Clothing_Enum    NOT NULL,
        Sizes           SET(Size_Enum NOT NULL),
        Photo           Image
) UNDER Merchandise_Type;

CREATE TABLE Apparel
OF TYPE Apparel_Type
UNDER Merchandise;

CREATE ROW TYPE Ticket_Type (
        Showing         Showing_Id       NOT NULL
) UNDER Merchandise_Type;

CREATE TABLE Tickets
OF TYPE Ticket_Type
UNDER Merchandise;

ALTER TABLE Tickets
ADD CONSTRAINT (
     FOREIGN KEY ( Showing ) REFERENCES Showings ( Id )
            CONSTRAINT Tickets_Valid_For_Showing
);
```

Listing 9–12. *Table Definitions for Inheritance Hierarchy*

Several complex relationships exist within the Movies-R-Us Web site schema. The most involved of these is the Showing relationship among the Cinemas, Movies, and Tickets. In addition to being a relationship among three entities, it has an additional attribute when it is recording an interval of time. In Listing 9–13 we present the DDL for representing this relationship as a table.

```
CREATE TABLE Showings (
        Id        SERIAL       NOT NULL,
        Cinema    Cinema_Id    NOT NULL,
        Movie     Movie_Id     NOT NULL,
        When      Period       NOT NULL
);
--
ALTER TABLE Showings
ADD CONSTRAINT (
   FOREIGN KEY ( Cinema ) REFERENCES Cinemas ( Id )
   CONSTRAINT Showing_Needs_a_Cinema_FK ),
ADD CONSTRAINT  (
    FOREIGN KEY ( Movie ) REFERENCES Movies ( Id )
    CONSTRAINT Showing_Needs_a_Movie_FK),
ADD CONSTRAINT (
   PRIMARY KEY ( Id )
   CONSTRAINT Showing_Primary_Key
);
```

Listing 9–13. *Tables To Handle a Complex Relationship*

Note that although this example uses a system-generated primary key, it has a logical key, albeit one that is impossible to enforce in OR-SQL. It is impossible that there could be two showings of the same movie, at the same cinema, for *overlapping* periods of time. (Note that we do not break showing up by screen, only by Cinema.) Keys, as we saw in Chapter 8, are defined in terms of equality. Making these tables comply with such a rule would require a TRIGGER.

Logical Schema Modeling

At this point, the conceptual E-ER model has been translated into a correct and complete set of tables. Nonetheless, it is a very good idea to make another pass through this schema and to apply what are known as *logical design* procedures.

Why do we care about logical schema design at all? Why not simply use what we have translated from the conceptual model and be done with it? We care because experience has shown that while there are many syntactically legal ways to represent a conceptual schema, only a few of them represent sound database engineering practice.

Information systems of the kind we are concerned with manage shared data, and this data will be put to uses that cannot entirely be anticipated at design time. As the information system gets new users with new queries and as its functionality is expanded with additional business operations, the core database should make every effort to ensure that the data it manages is always correct and unambiguous. Achieving this objective by requiring all business logic to check for errors has proven difficult to in practice.

DBMSs products based on the principles of the relational model apply logical data analysis to ensure that the database schema is structured in such a way that any possibility of information duplication is removed. Readers familiar with RDBMS technology will know such design principles as *normalization.*

Normalization and ORDBMS Databases

The word "normalization" chills the heart of many database developers. The concept is typically explained as an apparently arbitrary set of complex rules and technical jargon, but at its heart, normalization has a very simple objective: *to ensure that each fact is stored exactly once.* To normalize a database schema is to anneal the initial, naïve design to eliminate the potential for certain *anomalies* to occur.

Normalization is a set of formal techniques that distinguishes database development from other computer programming disciplines. There is no strictly engineering justification, such as improving performance, scalability, or efficiency, for normalization. It is good practice because databases data must first and foremost be *correct*. Running twice as fast in the wrong direction is worse than standing still.

Data Storage Anomalies

The purpose of normalization is to ensure that database schema does not contain any one of a set of bad design patterns known as *anomalies*. Anomalies in a database design occur when a write operation has unexpected or unintended consequences. Because an object-relational database is intended to record facts about objects in the problem domain, these unintended consequences relate to other facts not directly affected by the original action.

In this section we introduce and illustrate three kinds of anomaly that we would like to avoid. The best way to do this is with an example. To avoid any confusion, this example is not taken from the Movies-R-Us Web site database, in which we try at all times to illustrate good practices. Instead, Table 9–5 is a table that stores facts about a bank's customers, its retail branches, and the relationships among them. In this table, the primary key would be the combination of `Cust_Id` and `Branch_Id`.

Table 9–5. Table to Illustrate Anomalies

Cust_Id	Cust_Name	Cust_etc	Branch_Id	Address	Branch_etc
101	"Fred Flintstone"	...	"Sacramento"	"10 F...	...
101	"Fred Flintstone"	...	"Houston"	"2 Gran.	...
103	"Peggy Sue"	...	"Miami"	"8 Del...	...
111	"Laz Artuirez"	...	"San Jose"	"Indus...	...
115	"Sally Lo"	...	"Sacramento"	"10 F...	...
211	"Jamie Petersen"	...	"San Jose"	"Indus...	...

This table's design is appealing from some points of view. It is simple, and it easy to explain. It actually reflects fairly accurately how a lot of "flat file" databases are built. As long as the number of users interacting with this table is limited, it is probably a reasonable solution. It contains, however, the following anomalies that create problems in a shared information system:

1. INSERT Anomaly

   Consider what happens in this table if we were to try to record information about a new Branch. Given this design, adding Branch information requires that we also record information about at least one new Customer, but this information might not be known, so the INSERT could not be completed. This is called an INSERT anomaly.

2. DELETE Anomaly

   Now, consider what happens if our Bank closes the "San Jose" branch. This requires that we delete the corresponding row from this table. However, this has the extremely undesirable side effect of removing the fact about the existence of a Customer! We call this a DELETE anomaly.

3. UPDATE Anomaly

Last, consider what might happen in our Bank if "Fred Flinstone" wrote a letter to his bank in Houston and told them he was changing his address. If the manager in "Houston" made the modification, all of Fred's bills from Houston would go to the right address, but "Sacramento" would have a problem. Fred would be annoyed because, as far as he was concerned, he had given the bank the right information! Changing one row but not the other leads to an inconsistency in the database. We call this an UPDATE anomaly.

Of course, the whole point of this example is that information about branches, customers, and the relationships between should not be modeled in the way shown in Table 9–5. The purpose of normalization is to detect these situations when they arise and then to provide a procedure for modifying the design and eliminating the erroneous situations. Applying the rules of normalization produce a schema such as the one in Figure 9–9.

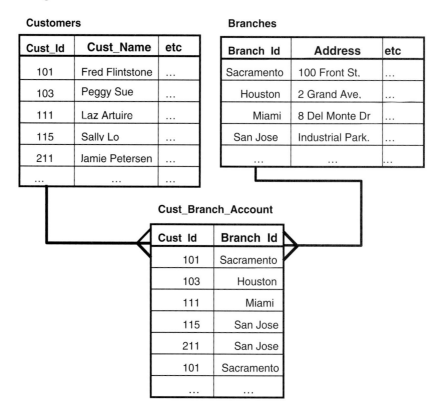

Figure 9–9. *Normalized Version of Table 9–5*

In Figure 9–9, none of the anomalies identified for the situation represented by Table 9–5 are present. In every case, the operation in question, such as `INSERT`, `DELETE`, and `UPDATE`, is required only to adjust a single row.

To give a more practical example, consider our Movies schema, in which we might conceivably use the merchandising type hierarchy to create a separate set of merchandise tables for each movie. This approach might be suggested by the observation that the community of users includes "promotions managers" responsible for different lines of merchandise. The names of the tables created using the same entity type definition could indicate the line to which the merchandising items belong. Thus, the names might be "Sting_Merchandise," "Sting_Apparel," "Sting_Tickets," and so on.

This approach would have the obvious advantage that as long as you knew the movie in which you were interested, merchandise queries would not need to access many rows. Of course, this would be of marginal benefit. It's reasonable to expect that some users will want to formulate queries over all merchandise, that new kinds of merchandise will be added over time (extending the hierarchy), and that the schema will need to cope with a lot of movies. Each of these situations is handled poorly by the set-of-tables-per-movie approach.

This is a fairly coarse example. To most readers familiar with database design, it simply feels wrong. There are, however, more subtle problems that require attention.

Normal Forms

Normal form theory is a formal process to identify and eliminate the opportunity for anomalies, or instances of incorrect or ambiguous data, in the database. Normal Form theory looks at the logical structure of the database and employs a procedure that converts unsafe structures, once identified, into safe ones.

Most recent database development methodologies focus on specifying the conceptual model in such a way that the mapping to logical model produces a well-normalized schema. However, because the ORDBMS data model includes features such as `COLLECTION` attributes that violate the concept of First Normal Form (discussed later in the chapter) and make nested relational schemas possible, normal forms theory is more relevant here.

Note that an individual object or data value may be represented in the database more than once. For example, two movie club members may share an address. Recall, however, how we described the way in which the relational model is a means of structuring facts. By itself, the existence of an address object is not a fact[3]. Only when the object is associated with others in rows of a table does it become a fact. For example, it is fact that "MovieClubMember with the name 'Fred' has a mailing address of '123 Ajax.'"

Informally, the goal of normal forms theory is to arrive at a logical schema design in which *every fact is presented exactly once*.

Functional Dependencies

The concept of the *functional dependency* is central to understanding normalization. Each of the higher normal forms are defined in terms of the relationships between data in a table's columns and data in the table's key.

When the value of one attribute can be used to determine the value of another, we say that the second attribute is *functionally determined* by the first. For example, in the Customer table in Figure 9–9, every customer's name may be different from all others, but it is logically *possible* for people to share a name. Thus, a teller cannot use the name to find out the person's address, or age, or their resume, with absolute certainty. On the other hand, given the Id, all other attributes can be retrieved.

Another way to say it is that in a functionally dependent relationship between values in column A and column B. A functional dependency implies that whenever A changes, B will probably change too. Different normal forms are defined in terms of how many functional dependencies a table has and the kind of functional dependencies these are.

First Normal Form

The First Normal Form (FNF) rules holds that each data value, which is the value in a single column, of a single row, of a single table, is *atomic*; that is, columns cannot contain repeating groups of values (although the value itself may have structure). The FNF rule has more to do with simplicity than data model correctness. Once a column can contain a repeating group of values, it follows that structures such as repeating groups of repeating groups are also possible. In this situation, it is difficult to build indexing support for queries over elements of the set.

To illustrate, consider that in one user's conceptual view of the problem, one attribute of the Branch entity is the set of Customers who have accounts at that branch. One way to model this logically is to use a nested relation with a `SETOF(Employee_Type)` attribute.

---

[3] This is true except in the trivial sense that it is a fact that the object (the address) *exists*.

Non-FNF schema structures have several problems:

- Non-FNF complicates the model. Addressing the contents of a non-FNF attribute would require a substantial grammatical extension to the OR-SQL language. For example, you would have to turn the Branch and Customer structure previously discussed into a single list showing each Customer and his or her Branch.
- Queries over nested relational structures tend to reduce the concurrency of the database. For example, in databases with nested tables the only way to get to Customers is through the Branches table. Consequently, accessing a Customer's details requires that you know their Branch in advance, and a query to find out how many customers in each branch would read in all data relating to Branches.

There are situations, however, in which a COLLECTION attribute is the appropriate solution. The alternative—creating another table to contain each element of the non-FNF attribute—requires that queries recombine the two tables. The query result is in FNF (each data value is singular), so data is moved one row at a time to client programs. Later in this chapter, we provide some guidelines to help determine which of these two alternative approaches is better. For the remainder of this normal forms discussion, we assume a First Normal Form schema.

Second Normal Form (2NF)

If a table is in Second Normal Form (2NF), every attribute in the table (except the key columns) is functionally determined; that is, as long as a value in a row attribute can be addressed by the combination of the table's name, some key column value (or values) and the attribute's name, the table is in 2NF. For example, consider the table definition in Listing 9–14.

```
CREATE TABLE ProductSales (
        Name            Product_Name    NOT NULL,
        Price           Currency        NOT NULL,
        Sale            Sale_Id         NOT NULL,
        Customer        Customer_Name   NOT NULL,
        Customer_Addr   MailAddress     NOT NULL,
        Number          Quantity        NOT NULL,
        When            DATE            NOT NULL
);
```

***Listing 9–14.** Non-2NF Table*

Suppose this table contains all information being recorded about both products and customers and the sales of products to customers. It is clearly in FNF: all values are atomic. It is not, however, in 2NF. Given a product name, it is probable that the product would have a large number of customers. In addition, in terms of anomalies, it is impossible to add a product without adding a customer and a sale.

The two tables in Listing 9–15 represent a reorganized version of the table in Listing 9–14, in which all columns can be determined using a functional dependency within one of the tables. Given a product name, the table provides an unambiguous price. For each product name, there is exactly the one price. For each sale Id, there is only one product, one date, one quantity, and one customer.

```
CREATE TABLE Products (
        Name          Product_Name   NOT NULL PRIMARY KEY,
        Price         Currency       NOT NULL
);


CREATE TABLE CustomerSales (
        Sale          Sale_Id        NOT NULL PRIMARY KEY,
        Product       Product_Name   NOT NULL,
        Customer      Customer_Name  NOT NULL,
        Customer_Addr MailAddress    NOT NULL,
        When          DATE           NOT NULL,
        Number        Quantity       NOT NULL
);
```

Listing 9–15. *2NF Version of Table*

To determine whether a table is in 2NF, compile a list of all of its logical functional dependencies. In addition to knowledge of the problem domain, an analysis of some legacy information is a very effective means of creating this list. Then create a number of tables in which the "arrows" of the functional dependencies point left to right and are chained together to cover every attribute in the table.

Third Normal Form (3NF)

Third Normal Form (3NF) holds that in a 3NF table, each attribute value can be accessed with he key value(s), the whole key, and nothing in addition to the key value. The CustomerSales table in Listing 9–15 is, therefore, not in 3NF, but the Products table is. Suppose each unique customer can be identified using their name, and from the name their other attributes may be inferred from this table. Queries to UPDATE a customer's address would use the customer name in the WHERE clause, not the CustomerSales table's primary key.

When this kind of situation arises, you have *transitive functional dependencies*. In Listing 9–15 the CustomerSales table has a sale Id to uniquely identify each row, and getting to customer addresses involves stepping from the sales Id, to the Customer name, and then to the address. Because of its structure, CustomerSales creates an anomaly. Updating the address of a customer for one sale will not update the address of the customer for other sales.

To get the Listing 9–15 schema into 3NF, the tables needs to be reorganized into the form we show in Listing 9–16.

```
CREATE TABLE Products (
        Name          Product_Name   NOT NULL,
        Price         Currency       NOT NULL
);


CREATE TABLE Customers (
        Customer              Customer_Name  NOT NULL,
        Customer_Addr         MailAddress    NOT NULL
);


CREATE TABLE Sales (
        Sale          Sale_Id          NOT NULL,
        Customer      Customer_Name    NOT NULL,
        Product       Product_Name     NOT NULL,
        When          DATE             NOT NULL,
        Number        Quantity         NOT NULL
);
```

Listing 9–16. *3NF Version of Table*

To convert to 3NF, all arrows defining functional dependencies need to have a single source: some candidate key for the table (in practice almost always the primary key). All other constraint rules, such as UNIQUE columns and so on, still apply, and need to be reflected in the table's design. Of course, a table can have more than one candidate key, but that does not affect the definition of 3NF.

Higher Normal Forms

At this point, the database is in 3NF. It is free of the three kinds of anomalies identified earlier in this chapter. It may have other, more subtle problems, however. There is nothing in ORDBMS technology, however, that has a significant impact on these issues.

There are other, even higher normal forms. In them, the focus is on ensuring that no data is lost through circumstances such as "orphan" rows in tables. Many textbooks and design manuals describe these concepts in detail. To employ these techniques, you must keep in mind the way in which keys are defined in terms of equality. All prescriptions for good database design use examples, such as INTEGER, VARCHAR, and so on, founded on SQL-92 types, but all of these ideas work equally well for user-defined types.

Miscellaneous Design Decisions

The ORDBMS data model adds several structural features to the relational data model in several ways. These additions complicate schema design, because they make it possible to achieve some design objective using several alternative means. In this section we cover a few of the more pressing considerations an ORDBMS developer will encounter.

FNF versus COLLECTION

In an ORDBMS, database table columns can hold a set of values, but in most relational DBMS products, FNF was strictly observed. Earlier, we mentioned that either approach might be appropriate, depending on the circumstances. In this subsection, we explore exactly what these circumstances might be.

Two examples from the Movie-R-Us Web site database motivate our discussion. First, there is the Movies entity and its Genres attribute, which is presented in Table 9–4 of this chapter. Second, there is the Orders entity, which is illustrated in Figure 8–5 of Chapter 8.

There are two ways to model sets of values in an entity's attributes. The first alternative involves normalizing the attribute, which involves creating a second table containing the set's data values and a reference that associates the element with its row in the "parent" table. Figure 9–10 illustrates what this might look like for the Movies table.

With Relational DBMS products, Figure 9–10 shows the only design alternative. Unfortunately, it has several disadvantages:

- First, recreating the set of genres associated with a movie requires a join. When sets are small, the overhead of performing this join can result in a performance problem.

Movies

Title	Released On	etc
Casablanca	06/01/1942	. . .
The Best Years...	06/01/1946	. . .
The Maltese . . .	08/12/1941	. . .
. . .	. . .	. . .

Movie Genres

Title	Released On	Genre
Casablanca	06/01/1942	Drama
Casablanca	06/01/1942	Romance
Casablanca	06/01/1942	War
The Best Years . .	06/01/1946	War
The Best Years . . .	06/01/1946	Drama
The Maltese Falcon	06/01/1941	Mystery
The Maltese Falcon	06/01/1941	Crime

Figure 9–10. *Normalizing Genre Attributes of Movies Table*

- The second problem lies in the way that, in the result set, the join returns an entire instance of the parent row for each of the element values. This means that moving the set from the server to the client program requires moving many times more data than is logically necessary.

The solution to both of these problems is to use COLLECTION attributes. Thus, in Listing 9–11, the Genre attribute is modeled as part of the table.

The more traditional approach, however, works well in other circumstances. For example, when each set is relatively large, the size of the set in-row can increase the size of the table. This slows down queries for other attribute data. Further, the ORDBMS does not provide mechanisms for indexing set elements. Thus, for the Orders entity and its set of line items, the normalized schema presented in Listing 9–17 is more flexible than using a SET, and for a number of common queries, it outperforms the in-row SET approach.

```
CREATE TABLE Orders  (
          Id                  SERIAL              NOT NULL,
          Customer            Membership_Id       NOT NULL,
          DeliverTo           DeliveryAddress     NOT NULL,
          OrderedOn           DATE                NOT NULL,
          ShippedOn           DATE
);
--
ALTER TABLE Orders
ADD CONSTRAINT (
   PRIMARY KEY ( Id ) CONSTRAINT Order_PK );
--
CREATE TABLE Order_Line_Items   (
          Order               Order_Num           NOT NULL,
          Merchandise         Part_Code           NOT NULL,
          NumberBought        Quantity            NOT NULL
);
--
--
ALTER TABLE Order_Line_Items
ADD CONSTRAINT (
     FOREIGN KEY ( Order ) REFERENCES Orders ( Id )
     ON DELETE CASCADE
     CONSTRAINT Order_Line_Items_Orderd_FK
);
```

Listing 9–17. *Normalized Version of the Order Entity*

Here are the general rules of thumb for determining the approach
to take:

- If the number of distinct objects in all of the entity's attribute sets is
  relatively small, use the in-row SET. For example, the number of
  distinct kinds of genres is relatively small, while the number of different items of merchandise is quite large.
- Consider the kinds of queries involved. In the movie genre example,
  queries to find movies of a particular genre are likely to return a
  great many rows, so indexing is of little help. By contrast, queries
  over ordered items are likely to be quite common and indexing
  would help.
- Keep in mind the important objective of recording each fact only
  once. In the movie genre instance, the existence of a particular
  genre is modeled as part of the enumerated type definition, and
  there does not need to be a code table holding all valid genres; the
  existence of various items of merchandise is recorded elsewhere.

One last note: *Do not nest tables!* In earlier data models, it was common to arrange different kinds of data into nested file structures. For some reason, probably because this was the way procedural programmers were taught to structure information, this idea has found its way into some early object-relational database schema. It has almost always resulted in a disaster. Nested table approaches wreak havoc on developer productivity, data integrity, and database performance.

Inheritance and Joins

Adding inheritance to the data models significantly extends its expressive power. Caution is called for, however, when employing it in a schema because of the way queries over inheritance hierarchies are evaluated. Nevertheless, inheritance provides new ways to model certain situations, such as the Movies entity in Table 9–4.

Note that all columns contain sets of MoviePersonality types. This was done because Hollywood being what it is, writers want to act, actors want to direct, and directors get cast in minor roles in their buddy's movies. Recalling our objective of recording each fact only once, this structure implies that each movie personality's details are recorded multiple times, which creates the potential for all kinds of problems.

In Figure 9–11 we present an alternate way of modeling this situation. Instead of repeating the information about movie personalities, this approach normalizes that information out to a separate table. To represent the relationship between the personalities and the movies, the schema uses an inheritance hierarchy constructed over a relationship table. The code in Listing 9–18 implements this model.

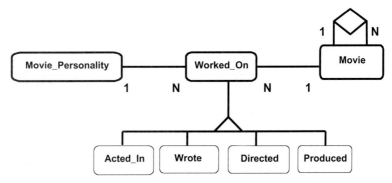

Figure 9–11. Using Hierarchies to Model Complex Relationships

```
CREATE TABLE Movie_Personalities (
        Id              Personality_Id      NOT NULL,
        Name            PersonName          NOT NULL,
        DOB             date                NOT NULL,
        Died            date,
        LivesIn         State_Enum,
        Biography       Doc_Type            NOT NULL,
        Photo           Image               NOT NULL
);
ALTER TABLE Movie_Personalities
ADD CONSTRAINT (
PRIMARY KEY ( Id ) CONSTRAINT Movie_Personalities_PK );
--
CREATE TABLE Movies (
        ID              SERIAL              NOT NULL,
        Title           Title               NOT NULL,
        Release_Date    date                NOT NULL,
        Produced_By     Prod_Company        NOT NULL,
        Genre           SET(Genre_Enum      NOT NULL),
        Awards          SET(Award           NOT NULL),
        Budget          Currency            NOT NULL,
        Takings         Currency            NOT NULL,
        Plot_Summary    Doc_Type            NOT NULL,
        OnVideo         boolean             NOT NULL
);
--
ALTER TABLE Movies
ADD CONSTRAINT (
    PRIMARY KEY ( Id )
    CONSTRAINT Movies_ID_PK
), ADD CONSTRAINT (
    UNIQUE ( Title, Release_Date )
    CONSTRAINT Movies_Title_Release_Date_Unique
);
--
CREATE ROW TYPE WorkedOn_Type (
        Movie           Movie_Id        NOT NULL,
        Person          Personality_Id  NOT NULL
);
--  This table does not have a PRIMARY KEY. A movie
--  personality can work on a film in two roles, such as
--  Actor and Director.
--
CREATE TABLE WorkedOn
OF TYPE WorkedOn_Type;
--
ALTER TABLE WorkedOn
```

```
ADD CONSTRAINT (
 FOREIGN KEY ( Movie )
 REFERENCES Movies (Id)
 CONSTRAINT Worked_On_Movies_FK),
ADD CONSTRAINT (
  FOREIGN KEY ( Person )
  REFERENCES MoviePersonalities (Id)
  CONSTRAINT Worked_on_MoviePersonalities_FK );
--
-- Now, for each of the various roles that a movie
-- personality can play in the creation of a movie, ensure
-- that there is a corresponding table in the hierarchy.
--
CREATE ROW TYPE Directed_Type
UNDER WorkedOn_Type;
--
CREATE TABLE Directed
OF TYPE Directed_Type
UNDER WorkedOn;
--
CREATE ROW TYPE Acted_Type (
        Played          PersonName      NOT NULL
)
UNDER WorkedOn_Type;
--
CREATE TABLE ActedOn
OF TYPE Acted_Type
UNDER WorkedOn;
```

Listing 9–18. *DDL for the WorkedOn Hierarchy*

Rudimentary queries to identify what movies an individual worked on are reduced to a three-table join. Queries about what roles an individual played in a given movie are also three-table joins, but instead of the middle table being the WorkedOn root table in the hierarchy, the various roles are represented in different tables. A "Three Degrees of Kevin Bacon" query (which finds out what movie personalities can be related to the actor Kevin Bacon because of a chain of collaborations) looks like Listing 9–19.

```
SELECT
  'Kevin Bacon in ' || Involvement ( W1 ) || Print(M1.Title),
  Print(MP2.Name)   || Involvement ( W2 ) || Print(M1.Title),
  Print(MP2.Name)   || Involvement ( W3 ) || Print(M2.Title),
  Print(MP3.Name)   || Involvement ( W4 ) || Print(M2.Title),
```

```
        Print(MP3.Name)      || Involvement ( W5 ) || Print(M3.Title),
        Print(MP4.Name)      || Involvement ( W6 ) || Print(M3.Title)

    FROM  MoviePersonalities MP1, WorkedOn W1, Movies M1,
          MoviePersonalities MP2, WorkedOn W2, Movies M2,
          MoviePersonalities MP3, WorkedOn W3, Movies M3,
          MoviePersonalities MP4, WorkedOn W4,
          WorkedOn W5, WorkedOn W6

    WHERE MP1.Name = PersonName('Bacon','Kevin')
      AND MP1.Id   NOT IN ( MP2.Id, MP3.Id, MP4.Id )
      AND MP2.Id   NOT IN ( MP1.Id, MP3.Id, MP4.Id )
      AND MP3.Id   NOT IN ( MP1.Id, MP2.Id, MP4.Id )
      AND MP4.Id   NOT IN ( MP1.Id, MP2.Id, MP3.Id )

      AND MP1.Id = W1.Person AND W1.Movie  = M1.Id
      AND M1.Id  = W2.Movie  AND W2.Person = MP2.Id
      AND MP2.Id = W3.Person AND W3.Movie  = M2.Id
      AND M2.Id  = W4.Movie  AND W4.Person = MP3.Id
      AND MP3.Id = W5.Person AND W5.Movie  = M3.Id
      AND M3.Id  = W6.Movie  AND W5.Person = MP4.Id;
```

Listing 9–19. *The "Kevin Bacon" Query*

For the purposes of query planning, each table in the hierarchy is evaluated separately. For example, in the `WorkedOn` hierarchy in Listing 9–18, the hierarchy splits four ways. Thus, when it creates a plan for this query, the ORDBMS will evaluate all options.

Consider what happens when you write a query that involves a self-join of the worked on hierarchy with itself. Under the hood, this must be evaluated as 16 separate joins. Add a third self join and the optimizer is obliged to consider 64 separate joins, and in each join, the optimizer needs to consider query execution strategies for each join order, the possible index usage, and the several algorithmic alternatives for each operation.

Large table hierarchies cause an explosion in the number of alternate query plans the ORDBMS needs to evaluate. Therefore, prudence is called for. A good principle is to avoid creating table hierarchies too deep or too wide. Performance problems, which are typically queries that involve little data but that take excessive time to complete, might be eased by reducing the depth of the hierarchy. Note that the problem is most evident during the optimization phase. Executions of prepared queries will perform as well as the physical configuration of the database—the indices, the partitioning, and so on—allows.

Surrogate Keys versus Logical Keys

Earlier we described the distinction between logical keys and system-generated surrogate keys. As part of the procedure transforming a conceptual model to a logical model, key columns are repeated in several tables to model relationships between entities. Unfortunately, there is no absolute answer to the question of which technique to use. In this section, we briefly describe the pros and cons of each technique.

Logical Keys

Logical keys are usually identified as part of entity modeling. A logical key is a subset of columns that uniquely identify entity instances. Any data type can be used as part of a logical key as long as an `Equal()`, and ideally an entire B-Tree operator class, is defined for it. This is necessary because the ORDBMS automatically creates indices to enforce the integrity rule efficiently.

Logical keys are effective for the following reasons:

- The keys are reasonably short. Processing join queries using key columns can require many compare operations, and comparing longer keys, or using an index to look them up, consumes more resources.
- They can sometimes avoid joins. Consider the subschema in Listing 9–18, which uses a surrogate key to represent the relationship between `WorkedOn` and `Movies`. Were the `WorkedOn` table to hold the movie's title (and release date) instead of the surrogate key value, there would be no need to join to the `Movies` table at all.
- Logical keys are a more theoretically correct abstraction. Their use encourages correct and consistent data modeling and normalization.

Logical keys are the traditional mechanism for uniquely identifying rows in a table and for managing relationships between tables. In many situations they are a perfectly reasonable way to handle these aspects of the data model.

Surrogate Keys

Surrogate keys are system-generated values that are guaranteed to be unique to the table within which they are used. This means that a table can have at most one column that uses the system's surrogate key type, which is `SERIAL`. Foreign keys are represented in dependent tables using INTEGER types, and the expected referential integrity constraints can be added to the table definition.

Surrogate keys are effective because of the following:

- The logical key is volatile, which means its value is expected to change over time. This is of practical importance because changing a primary-key value means that all equivalent foreign keys in other tables must also be changed. This is frequently difficult to achieve.
- If the logical key is large, then a shorter surrogate key takes up less storage space, and shorter key values require less computational resources when processing join queries.

Some data modeling experts discouraged the use of system generated keys in relational DBMSs because the mechanism was not good at representing relationships as part of the table design. However, with an ORDBMS, the domain of surrogate primary key values for a table can be given additional semantic meaning by using the DISTINCT TYPE mechanism. This makes it possible to ensure, for example, that system-generated values that uniquely identify Movies cannot be compared with the values that identify Orders.

Testing Techniques

"Test early, and test often" is the best possible advice to follow in any kind of software development. Testing helps to identify conceptual errors, design flaws, code bugs, and anything you have overlooked. What is surprising is how often development schedules place testing and validation as the very last task, instead of integrating them into other tasks.

Fortunately, unlike other programming systems in which you need to build elaborate harness code in order to test a module, the environment into which a user-defined function is to be deployed, the object-relational ORDBMS, can also function as a test harness.

Using the DataBlade Developers Kit

The *DataBlade Developers Kit* (DBDK) is a tool shipped with the IDS product to help in writing C and Java extensions. The tool's main value lies in the way it generates much of the code necessary to implement a set of extensions: UDTs, UDFs, and so on. Its use is highly recommended because it dramatically reduces the amount of work required to deploy an ORDBMS extension, and because it ensures that all of the necessary support functions and so on are implemented.

The tools was created as a result of early adopter experience showing that the most difficult aspects of writing extensions are:

- Handling the arguments. External functions must map between OR-SQL built-in types passed as arguments and their SAPI equivalents. DBDK generates C code that handles this mapping automatically. Programmers should not need to change the C or Java function declarations. They should only need to change the body of the function's procedural logic.
- Getting the OR-SQL DML to declare the extensions within the ORDBMS right. DBDK ensures that each OR-SQL level UDF and UDT declaration has all of the relevant modifiers, argument and return types, and so on. Further, for extensibility mechanisms combining multiple functions—like aggregates and operator classes—DBSK gets the function names and signatures right.
- Remembering to implement all of the various support functions for user-defined OPAQUE TYPE instances. There are a great many of them, and some—like the import/export and communication support functions—observe obscure rules.
- Ensuring that the code has appropriate exception management, and defensive programming. The code generated by DBDK is heavily encrusted with logic to check return values and detect error conditions.

As much as possible, DBDK automates the "grunt work" necessary to create ORDBMS extensions.

DBDK itself is a Windows™ based GUI tool. It provides a set of wizards for gathering functional requirements for a new extension. DBDK presents developers with list of the possible kinds of UDT and UDF extensions—types, functions, aggregates etc—and the mechanisms that can be employed for each—external functions, Java, ROW TYPE. Groups of extensions are bundled into projects. For example, in the spatial DataBlade™ products there are perhaps twenty types and four hundred UDFs. All of these reside within a single DBDK project file.

After creating a new project, developers define the extensions contained within it. They describe how a new type is structures—what are its element names and data types—or what the signature of a new user-defined function is to be. Once they are finished, DBDK can generate the '.c' or '.java' files that developers specialize with their own code. Part of this source code is a Makefile used to compile the external code into a shared library.

DBDK also generates a set of OR-SQL related files for defining the new extensions. It provides a mechanism for building and packaging bundles of extensions—UDTs and UDFs—to simplify installing them and upgrading them. Figure 9–12 provides an overview of how DBDK is used.

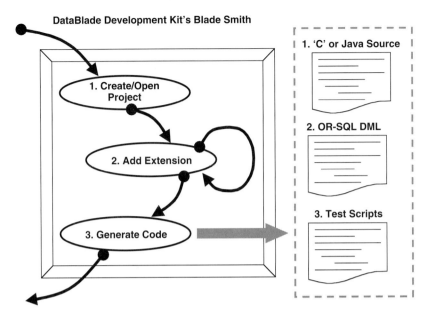

DataBlade Development Kit's Blade Smith

1. 'C' or Java Source

2. OR-SQL DML

3. Test Scripts

1. Create/Open Project

2. Add Extension

3. Generate Code

Figure 9–12. *Using the DataBlade Development Kit*

Extension developers edit the C and Java source to specialize the interfaces generated by DBDK to their particular requirements. The idea is that given a UML Class Diagram, a developer might use a tool like DBDK to generate the outline of the new type. Then they would employ standard development tools to implement the logic within the functions outlined by DBDK.

DBDK has one minor drawback. Changes to the DML scripts, and additions to the source code, cannot be reverse-engineered into the DBDK GUI. Automating this is a very hard problem. But it has the unfortunate consequence that if a developer updates the project file and re-generates the code from DBDK what they will open will be an entirely new file. Changes made to the C or Java source will be lost. Consequently, it is a very good idea to copy the entire directory structure generated by DBDK to a target machine, and to use a tool like UNIX 'diff' to identify the differences and handle the merger.

Testing Individual Types and Functions

Thoroughly tested extensions are essential to the smooth operation of the database. Although the engine's debugging facilities are immature, the nature of the ORDBMS makes both correctness and performance testing relatively easy. Following certain design principles for your user-defined types also helps. For instance, the principles can ensure that the set of behaviors provided for a type are symmetric. An example of symmetry is each constructor function having a corresponding print function.

Rules relating to debugging extensions are the same for external UDTs and UDFs as they are for any other software plug-in. The ORDBMS is informed of most problems only when the operating system becomes aware of them. And when it does, its options are limited. Wherever possible the ORDBMS will handle the exception gracefully: rolling back whatever transaction was in flight when the exception occurred, cleaning up all of the memory allocated to the offending context, and returning a reasonable error to the end user. Tracing external UDF execution is possible but typically provides limited help.

Developers can use a standard symbolic debugger—like the GNU 'gdb' or tools with platform specific names like 'dbx', 'xdb' and even Microsoft's Developer Studio tool—to step through the execution of an external UDF. Keep in mind that the ORDBMS itself is just a set of operating system processes. Debuggers are special programs that use operating system facilities to "attach" to a process, and watch it as it executes. The following figure illustrates a ''dbx' session on a UNIX computer.

```
{tin} 24> onstat -g glo | grep cpu
  class          vps        usercpu    syscpu      total
  cpu            1          3.63       0.32        3.95
  vp     pid         class       usercpu    syscpu      total
  1      26636       cpu         3.63       0.32        3.95
{tin} 25> dbx $INFORMIXDIR/bin/oninit 26636
Reading symbolic information for oninit
Reading symbolic information for rtld /usr/lib/ld.so.1
... etc for multiple libraries linked into oninit ...
Reading symbolic information for libc_psr.so.1
Reading symbolic information for HelloWorld.bld
detected a multithreaded program
Attached to process 26636 with 4 LWPs
t1 (l1) stopped in _semsys at 0xef5364ac
_semsys+0x4:         ta          0x8
(dbx) stop in helloworld
(2) stop in helloworld
(dbx) stop in hellofriend
(3) stop in hellofriend
(dbx) cont
continuing all LWPs
```

(At this point, in a separate window, execute helloworld() UDF in IDS.)

```
(4) stopped in helloworld at line 22 in file "HelloWorld.c"
   22        strcpy(pchBuf, "Hello World");
(dbx) list
   22        strcpy(pchBuf, "Hello World");
   23
   24        return mi_string_to_lvarchar(pchBuf);
   25    }
 (dbx) step
continuing ll
t1 (ll) stopped in helloworld at line 24 in file
"HelloWorld.c"
   24        return mi_string_to_lvarchar(pchBuf);
(dbx) dump
genfParam = 0xbec5a20
pchBuf =  ARRAY
(dbx) print pchBuf
pchBuf = "Hello World"
(dbx) cont
continuing all LWPs
t1 (ll) stopped in hellofriend at line 37 in file
"HelloWorld.c"
   37        nVarLen = mi_get_varlen( plvName );
(dbx) list
   37        nVarLen = mi_get_varlen( plvName );
   38      pchInputData = mi_lvarchar_to_string( plvName );
   39
   40        pchRetData = mi_alloc(6 + nVarLen);
   41        sprintf(pchRetData, "Hello %s", pchInputData);
   42
   43        return mi_string_to_lvarchar( pchRetData );
   44    }
   45
   46
(dbx) step
continuing ll
t1 (ll) stopped in hellofriend at line 38 in "HelloWorld.c"
   38         pchInputData = mi_lvarchar_to_string( plvName );
(dbx) step
continuing ll
t1 (ll) stopped in hellofriend at line 40 in "HelloWorld.c"
   40        pchRetData = mi_alloc(6 + nVarLen);
(dbx) print pchInputData
pchInputData = 0xbed8688 "Paul"
(dbx) print nVarLen
nVarLen = 4
```

```
(dbx) step
continuing 11
t1 (11) stopped in hellofriend at line 41 in "HelloWorld.c"
    41          sprintf(pchRetData, "Hello %s", pchInputData);
(dbx) step
continuing 11
t1 (11) stopped in hellofriend at line 43 in "HelloWorld.c"
    43          return mi_string_to_lvarchar( pchRetData );
(dbx) print pchRetData
pchRetData = 0xbed86a8 "Hello Paul"
(dbx) exit
{tin} 26>
```

Listing 9–20. *Session Using UNIX 'dbx' Tool to Debug an External UDF*

Using this technique a developer can step through the innards of their 'C' UDF as it is executing. To emphasize a point made earlier: keeping each UDF as simple as possible helps in the debugging process. Internals of SAPI calls cannot be stepped through.

For scale testing, which is the running of the extension many times to check for memory leaks and so on, using the DBMS query language's join capacity can is useful. For example, in Listing 9–21, we present the outline of a query to test the GreaterThan(Mass, Mass) user-defined function. This query will cause the construction UDFs to execute 1766 times.

```
SELECT   Mass(Q1.Num,U1.Val) AS Less,
         Mass(Q2.Num,U2.Val) AS More
    FROM
        TABLE(SET{1.0,10.0,100.0,1000.0,10000.0,100000.0
                      }::SET(DECIMAL(10,2) NOT NULL)) Q1 ( Num ),
        TABLE(SET{'G','gram','OUNCE','OZ','Ounce','POUND','LB'
                      }::SET(LVARCHAR NOT NULL)) U1 ( Val ),
        TABLE(SET{1.0,10.0,100.0,1000.0,10000.0,100000.0
                      }::SET(DECIMAL(10,2) NOT NULL)) Q2 ( Num ),
        TABLE(SET{'G','gram','OUNCE','OZ','Ounce','POUND','LB'
                      }::SET(LVARCHAR NOT NULL)) U2 ( Val )

    WHERE  Mass(Q1.Num,U1.Val)  >  Mass(Q2.Num,U2.Val);
```

Listing 9–21. *Query Testing Several UDFs That are Part of the Mass Object*

The idea is that you can use the combinatorial potential of the query language to generate a huge number of individual tests in a single expression. Tests of several user-defined functions can be combined into a single expression. If you keep an eye on the messages the engine prints to its log file, problems such as memory leaks and certain code bugs in the function will be reported.

Negative tests are tests in which you pass arguments into the user-defined functions that make them generate an exception. Tests that are intended to generate exceptions cannot be performed using queries: once the first error is encountered, the entire query halts. Negative testing requires that you create a test set of EXECUTE FUNCTION statements and pass into the function argument values that deliberately provoke an error or exercise the extremes of the range of values each argument can accept. Ensuring that an extension handles exceptional cases is important because it is hard to anticipate how the extension will be deployed.

Generating Data

After you have finalized the schema design, it is an excellent idea to load the database with a set of data that is close to anticipated production volumes. Then you can exercise the database using queries that characterize the anticipated workload. You can use the same technique introduced in Listing 9–20 to create large amounts of data values. For example, Listing 9–22 populates the Products table with a million rows of data.

```
INSERT INTO Products
( Name, Dimensions, Capacity, Available_In, Price )
SELECT MakeString( Random(1000), 24 ),
       Random_Dimensions(),
       Random_Mass(),
       Random_Color_Set(),
       Random_Currency()
  FROM TABLE(SET{0,1,2,3,4,5,6,7,8,9}) N1 ( Num ),
       TABLE(SET{0,1,2,3,4,5,6,7,8,9}) N2 ( Num ),
       TABLE(SET{0,1,2,3,4,5,6,7,8,9}) N3 ( Num ),
       TABLE(SET{0,1,2,3,4,5,6,7,8,9}) N4 ( Num ),
       TABLE(SET{0,1,2,3,4,5,6,7,8,9}) N5 ( Num ),
       TABLE(SET{0,1,2,3,4,5,6,7,8,9}) N6 ( Num );
```

Listing 9–22. *INSERT as SELECT to Populate Products Table*

MakeString(INTEGER, INTEGER), the first user-defined function in this query, creates a randomly distributed string the length of the second argument. Its first argument is a random variable, and its second dictates the length of the string. Each of the other functions behaves similarly.

Based on the results of this testing, you can determine what your next task should be. An underperforming workload query might indicate that you should change the implementation of a user-defined function, create an index, or revisit decisions about how you have organized data storage. Synthetic data is rarely perfect, but it can provide you with valuable and early indications of problems.

Workload Queries

The ORDBMS can also help to manage the workload queries for scalability testing. OR-SQL expressions making up the client workload are just strings. So it is reasonable to create a table that holds them. In Chapter 7, in which we present the details of the JDBC programming interface for Java, we illustrate how certain facilities of the API work by creating a database table to hold queries. When the Java client runs, it reads these queries from the database table and executes them.

A fairly obvious set of modifications can make it possible to change the mix of queries to reflect the anticipated workload.

Scalability Testing

Scale is measured according to several metrics. Two common ones are data volume and number of users. Increasing the volume of data in the schema is achieved by rerunning the kinds of load query in Listing 9–21. Adding to the number of users is also straightforward if the query workload is maintained centrally. It amounts to running the Java client program multiple times, on multiple machines.

Chapter Summary

In this chapter, the second of two that outline a development methodology for object-relational databases, we described a series of techniques for turning pictures into efficient code. This requires a two-step process. First, you need to use the results of previous analysis to design a correct and complete body of code. Second, you need to evaluate this code to ensure that your technical design, and your hardware, meets the system's functionality, performance, and reliability objectives.

Where it falls short, adjust your design or your architecture to meet your goals.

In this second and final installment, we saw a set of techniques for turning these diagrams into working code. First, you develop a set of user-defined types and functions corresponding to the set of domains or objects identified in the conceptual analysis phase. Then you combine these objects into a database schema, which is a set of tables and constraints in which the new types are used in the table's columns. Normalization theory, which seeks to ensure that a database schema does not contain the possibility of error, can be applied in object-relational databases.

Finally, we noted that object-relational DBMS technology represents something quite new. Perhaps the greatest challenge in software development is responding quickly to end users, customers, and consumers. Making these adjustments at Web speed calls for a new approach to server software, one that combines performance, scalability, and reliability with flexibility and an improved ability to model the world. Supporting this kind of organic information system is what object-relational technology is all about.

Several Examples of Interesting Extensions

In this tutorial, we review several interesting examples of ORDBMS extensions. None of these are application specific, although in every case, they were motivated by specific applications. All of them are freely available on the Web and can be downloaded. They come with complete source code. The intention of this tutorial is to give readers some idea of what is made possible when you use extensibility, as well as to provide some documentation on these "open source" bundles.

Node Data Type for Hierarchical Management

Managing hierarchies in relational databases is hard. The Node data type extensions make it easier. Transitive closure, or the "bill of materials" problem, is endemic to many data management applications. The same basic problem is found modeling organizational hierarchies, networks, manufacturing, and process control databases, and the relational model handles the problem quite poorly.

The Node data type provides an unusual solution to this problem. The basic idea is to create a data type and a set of operations over it to model a tree structure. Then this type can be used in ORDBMS tables to represent hierarchies. In this section, we introduce the Node type and provide an example to demonstrate its use.

Hierarchy Example: Managing Personnel

Most readers have been employed at some point in their lives. They will have had a boss, and their boss probably had a boss too. They were organized into the kind of hierarchical chain of command represented in Figure 5–1 .

In this figure, we have added a Node label to each position to illustrate what the data type looks like and how it is used. The external representation of the Node data type is an ordinal number (integer greater than 0), followed by either a ".0" or a sequence of ordinal numbers separated by dots. Examples of valid and invalid Node data elements are presented in Listing 5–1.

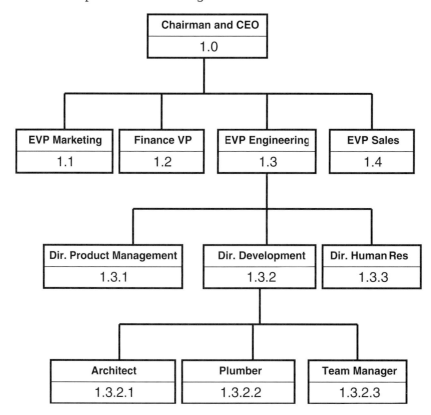

Figure 5–1. *Employment Organization Hierarchy and Node Labeling*

```
Valid Nodes
        { 1.0, 1.1, 1.1.1, 1.2, 1.2.1, 999.0, 999.1.999 }

Invalid Nodes
        { 0, 0.0, 0.1, 1.0.1, 1.1.0, 1.-1.2, 1.A.4 }
```

Listing 5–1. *Valid and Invalid Nodes*

There are several things to note about this data type. First, it can be ordered in a way that conveys information about the hierarchy. For example, suppose we translated the list of nodes in Figure 5–1, and their associated position titles, into Table 5–1. Here, the rows are "ordered by" the node value in ascending order (smallest to largest). In this table, there are several grayed-out lines, which stand for what might be large numbers of rows in a real table. Some of the Node values listed to these rows end in "X.Y.Z," which is meant to convey the idea that a Node can be as long as the hierarchy is deep. In practical applications there will be a great many rows instead of this single place-holder.[1]

Table 5–1. Figure 5–1 Hierarchy Represented as Node Table

Node	Position
1.0	Chairman and CEO
1.1	EVP Marketing
1.1.X.Y.Z	Positions reporting to EVP of Marketing
1.2	Finance VP
1.2.X.Y.Z	Positions reporting to Finance VP
1.3	EVP Engineering
1.3.1	Director of Product Management
1.3.2	Director of Development
1.3.2.1	Architect
1.3.2.2	Plumber
1.3.2.3	Team Manager
1.3.3	Director of HR
1.3.3.X.Y.Z	Positions reporting to Director of HR
1.4	EVP Sales
1.4.X.Y.Z	Positions Reporting to EVP Sales

---

[1] In practice, a hierarchy managed using Node can be 64 levels deep, and 2.1 billion wide at each branching point.

The Node type comes with a `Compare()` UDF that orders Node values as shown in Table 5–1. Consequently the ORDBMS can build a B-Tree index over a Node type column. The usefulness of this sequence is evident when you observe that it can be used to handle "descendant" queries very efficiently. Because of the way the Node type is defined, it is possible to compare two node instances and determine, without having to trace their lineage, whether and how one is related to the other. Node N is a *descendant* of Node M if it comes *after* N in this sequence, but it comes *before* another Node P, which is determined by incrementing the least significant integer in Node N by one. In practical terms Nodes of employees reporting to the EVP of Engineering are under "1.3" because they are greater than "1.3" and less than "1.4".

In Listing 5–2 we present a query that exploits this property. It is important to understand that the two predicates in this query—`GreaterThan()` and `LessThan()`—can use a B-tree index, making the query execution very fast. In very large tables, the problem of finding all descendants of a given node in the tree is reduced to an index scan.

"How many Employees report to the EVP of Engineering?"

```
SELECT N.Position
  FROM Node_Table N
 WHERE N.Node > '1.3'
   AND N.Node < Increment ( '1.3' );
```

Listing 5–2. *Query over Hierarchy*

Note that it isn't enough to treat a Node as a simple string. The ordering of a set of Node objects is not the same as the conventional string ordering of their representations, as we show in Listing 5–3. It is also not possible to define a collation sequence that would result in the correct ordering. This means that it is impossible to use Node in a DBMS that does not support extensible types and generalized indexing.

```
T is the following unordered set of data elements;
    T := { '1.2', '1.0', '1.12' }

T ordered as strings;
    T := < '1.0', '1.12', '1.2'  >

T ordered as Nodes;
    T := < '1.0', '1.2', '1.12' >
```

Listing 5–3. *Sorting Node Instances as Strings and with Correctly Implemented Compare()*

The Node type solves several other, related problems at the same time. It eliminates the possibility of unbound recursion in the table, and it permits OR-SQL developers to write join queries between all rows below a given row and another table.

Finding Ancestors: Querying Up the Hierarchy

Another virtue of the Node type is that in its representation, it contains a complete history of its ancestry. Instead of having to walk the table's rows using join queries, the complete list of Nodes "above" a give Node can be inferred from information it contains. To support this operation, the Node type comes with a user-defined function called Ancestors(), which returns a SET of Node types that are the ancestors of the argument node. Listing 5–4 illustrates how Ancestors() is used.

```
EXECUTE FUNCTION Ancestors ( '1.2.3.4.5.6' );

> SET{ '1.2.3.4.5','1.2.3.4','1.2.3','1.2','1.0' }
```

Listing 5–4. *Finding Ancestors of a Given Node*

This makes it possible to find all rows "above" a given node in a hierarchy using a single query, as we show in Listing 5–5.

"What is the chain of command above the Architect?"

```
SELECT N.Position
  FROM Node_Table N
 WHERE N.Node IN Ancestors ( '1.3.2.1' );
```

Listing 5–5. *Query up the Hierarchy*

In addition, concepts such as the level of the node within its hierarchy can be extracted from the Node instance, as shown in Listing 5–6.

"What is the chain of command two levels above the Architect?"

```
SELECT N.Position
  FROM Node_Table N
 WHERE N.Node IN Ancestors ( '1.3.2.1' )
   AND Level(N.Node) > Level('1.3.2.1') - 2;
```

Listing 5–6. *Query up the Hierarchy*

The queries in Listings 5–5 and 5–6 also use the B-Tree index; however, instead of scanning a subset of rows from it, the B-Tree is used for a series of single row lookups. Another UDF allows developers to create a view of the table that uses the Node type that is identical to the conventional approach. Such a technique is useful in situations in which an existing application is being ported to an ORDBMS. Examine Listing 5–7.

```
CREATE VIEW Usual_Table
AS SELECT T1.Position AS Parent,
          T2.Position AS Child
     FROM Node_Table T1 OUTER JOIN Node_Table T2
    WHERE T1.Id = Parent( T2.Id );
```

Listing 5–7. *VIEW that Maps to Conventional Approach*

Note that the OUTER JOIN query is necessary because the Parent(Node) UDF returns a NULL value if asked to compute the parent of a root node.

Modifying the Hierarchy

Read-only databases aren't very interesting. Being able to modify a hierarchy, add and delete nodes, and even move an entire substructure is more useful and is readily accomplished using the Node type's functions. You should keep in mind, however, that inside the UDFs implementing Node behaviors there are no OR-SQL queries that perform table operations. Node type functions only affect individual Node instances and are invoked—often many times—*within* OR-SQL queries. Readers used to wrestling with SQL-92 to manage hierarchies sometimes become confused about how to use the type most effectively.

For example, to add a new Node to the structure, it is necessary to create a new Node value. This new value cannot already be present among the values stored in the column; it must reflect the new Node's position. Typically, new Nodes are added below a pre-existing nodes. Figuring out what the new Node's value ought to be requires finding the maximum value of those Nodes immediately beneath the parent, and then incrementing that maximum value. Listing 5–8 illustrates how this is done in a single query.

"Calculate a Node value for a new position reporting to the Director of Development."

```
SELECT Increment ( MAX ( N.Id ) )          -- MAX() + 1
   FROM Table_Nodes N
  WHERE  N.Id > '1.3.2'                      -- of the Nodes
    AND N.Id < Increment ( '1.3.2' )        -- under the parent
    AND Level(N.Id) = Level('1.3.2')+1;     -- and 1 level down.
```

Listing 5–8. *Query to Determine Value for New Node Under Another Node*

What happens if there are no Nodes below the one specified as the new Node's parent? Under such circumstances, this query will return a NULL result. This means that an alternative UDF is necessary, which takes an argument Node and returns a new Node value that is equivalent to the old one with a ".1" appended to it. The stored procedure in Listing 5–9 illustrates how to use both techniques in combination.

```
CREATE FUNCTION AddPosition ( ParentNode Node,
                                     Position ShortString,)
RETURNING Node
   DEFINE   nNewNode      NODE;

   LET nNewNode=(SELECT Increment(MAX(T.Id))
                   FROM Node_Table T
                  WHERE T.Id BETWEEN ParentNode
                    AND Increment(ParentNode)
                    AND Length(T.Id) = Length(ParentNode) + 1
                    );

   IF ( nNewNode IS NULL ) THEN
      LET nNewNode =  ( SELECT NewLevel(T.Id)
                          FROM Node_Table T
                         WHERE T.Id  = ParentNode );
      IF ( nNewNode IS NULL ) THEN
            RAISE EXCEPTION -746,0,
                  "ERROR: Invalid Parent Node Id";
      END IF;
   END IF;

   INSERT INTO Node_Table;
   VALUES
   ( nNewNode, Title );

   RETURN nNewNode;
END FUNCTION
```

Listing 5–9. *Stored Procedure to Create a New Node in a Hierarchy*

Node deletion has several curious properties. Although it can remove the parent of (several) other nodes, deletion does not affect "ancestor" or "descendant" relationships because the Node type makes it unnecessary to walk the tree in order to compute these.

Moving subtrees efficiently is another virtue of the Node type. However, although moving subtrees can be achieved in a single query, the mechanism is relatively subtle. It centers on another UDF called Graft(). Moving a subtree requires modifying all of the Nodes 'below' the root of the sub-tree being moved to position them below another Node while retaining the subtree's structure. Consequently, the Graft() UDF takes the following arguments.

- The root node of the subtree being moved
- The root node of the new subtree (*not* the parent node of the new subtree)
- The actual node being moved

In Listing 5–10, we illustrate how the Graft() UDF can be used. This stored procedure moves an entire subtree, which is specified by the first argument, to a new location beneath another node, which is specified by the second argument.

```
CREATE FUNCTION MovePosition ( FromNode Node, ToNode Node )
RETURNING INTEGER

    DEFINE nMoveNodeCount INTEGER;
    DEFINE nNewNode   NODE;

    IF ( IsParent(ToNode, FromNode)  ) THEN
        RAISE EXCEPTION -746, 0,
            "Error: To node is already parent of From Node";
    END IF;
--
-- This UDF is essentially identical to the one in
-- Listing 5-9, except instead of INSERTing the
-- new row into the table, it merely returns it.
--
LET nNewNode = GetNextChild ( ToNode );
--
-- This moves the first node of the "from" subtree to the
-- new location. Note that although the node is now
-- "removed" from the hierarchy, all "descendant"
-- queries continue to work.
--
```

```
    UPDATE Table_Node
        SET HierarchyPosition = nNewNode
    WHERE HierarchyPosition = FromNode;


    --
    -- Because of the limit on correlated queries that
    -- prevents a query from modifying rows in a table
    -- mentioned in the subquery, this operation needs to
    -- use a temporary table.
    --
    SELECT T.HierarchyPosition AS Old,
           Graft (FromNode,
                     nNewNode,
                      T.HierarchyPosition ) AS New
      FROM Table_Node P
     WHERE T.HierarchyPosition > FromNode
       AND T.HierarchyPosition < Increment(FromNode)
       INTO TEMP PositionMoveTemp;


    UPDATE Table_Node
        SET HierarchyPosition =
              ( SELECT New
                  FROM PositionMoveTemp
                 WHERE Old = Table_Node.HierarchyPosition )
      WHERE HierarchyPosition IN (SELECT Old
                                    FROM PositionMoveTemp);
    --
    -- Return the number of rows in the table/nodes in the
    -- hierarchy affected by the operation.
    --
    LET nMoveNodeCount  = DBINFO("sqlca.sqlerrd2");
    RETURN nMoveNodeCount;
END FUNCTION;
```

Listing 5–10. *Stored Procedure to Move Subtrees Within a Hierarchy*

MovePosition() is surprisingly efficient, even for large trees. Each application will require slightly different stored procedures modeled on the pattern in Listing 5–10.

Drawbacks and Limitations

Although the Node type has several advantages over RDBMS alternatives, it does have a couple of drawbacks too:

- Constrained application. The Node type does not address the general problem of transitive closure. It is only suitable for tree structures, which are directed graphs possessing exactly one more node than edge. For example, Node is unsuitable for family trees.
- Growing the tree "up" is expensive. The Node type is designed for maximum efficiency on read operations up and down the hierarchy, and it can perform leaf-level maintenance relatively efficiently.

On the other hand, the Node type and its function do represent an incredibly efficient mechanism for dealing with most common problems in this class. One IDS customer has created an entire application around the idea: their database contains literally tens of thousands of hierarchies corresponding to the way each individual end user classifies a set of shared images.

Ranking User-Defined Aggregates

In Chapter 5, we introduced the concept of user-defined aggregates. In this section of the tutorial, we introduce four user-defined aggregates that are examples of the mechanism and useful extensions in their own right. They are intended to help with *ranking* analysis, which is a variety of data analysis poorly served by SQL-92. Examine Table 5–2, which gives us the beginning data.

With SQL-92, queries asking for the top N students in each class are notoriously hard to write. The problem is compounded when you consider that often it is students *ranked* in the top N that are wanted, rather than students whose scores exceed the nth ranked score. In this subsection, we review several user-defined aggregates that address this problem.

Overview of Aggregates

There are four aggregates in this set. Two of them are described in detail below. There are two symmetric aggregates that extract the lowest ranked values, rather than the highest ranked values.

Given a set of integers (the column in the first argument) the TOP_N(INTEGER, INTEGER) aggregate returns a COLLECTION of the top N' values in that column, where *n* is specified in the second aggregate. Listing 5–11 illustrates how such a user-defined aggregate is used in a query, and what its results look like.

Table 5–2. Data for Illustrating the Use of the Ranking Aggregates

Class_Id	Subject	Student	Score
100	EN 101	Fred	90
100	EN 101	Wendy	65
100	EN 101	Mary	70
100	EN 101	Alan	90
100	EN 101	Ashok	75
100	EN 101	Arin	70
101	CS 101	Tom	45
101	CS 101	Phyllis	65
101	CS 101	Betty	80
101	CS 101	Ling	90
101	CS 101	Errin	75
101	CS 101	Fred	65
102	CS 101	Ben	45
102	CS 101	Mary	95
102	CS 101	Pat	77
102	CS 101	Luc	33
102	CS 101	Ron	65

"Find the top three scores for each class taking CS 101."

```
SELECT C.Class_Id,
       TOP_N( C.Score, 3 )
  FROM Classes C
 WHERE C.Subject = "CS 101"
 GROUP BY C.Class_Id;
```

Class_Id	TOP_N ::SET(INTEGER)
101	SET { 90, 80, 75 }
102	SET { 95, 77, 65 }

Listing 5–11. *Query to Retrieve TOP_N*

The TOP_RANK_N(INTEGER, INTEGER) aggregate is a bit more complex. Often, the application doesn't want the top *n* scores. Rather, the objective is to find the set of scores that are achieved by the top *N* students in the class. In other words, the problem calls for an ordering of all values, stepping down of the list *n* times, and returning of an ordered list of the values in this ranking.

This task is difficult in SQL-92, and it's actually what a lot of statistical techniques that eliminate outliers depend on. The maximum size of the set produced by this query is N, although as you can see from Listing 5–12 that the actual number returned may be less.

"Find the scores of the top three students in EN 101."

```
SELECT TOP_RANK_N ( C.Score, 3 )
  FROM Classes C
 WHERE C.Subject = "EN 101";
```

TOP_RANK_N::SET(INTEGER)

SET { 90, 75 }

Listing 5–12. *Query to Retrieve N Values for Top-Ranked Students*

Although these queries can be useful in some situations, these aggregates are most useful when combined with other query expressions. OR-SQL can access the contents of any COLLECTION variety either by using an IN keyword or by nesting the query within another. These OR-SQL techniques are described in detail in Chapter 3. In Listing 5–13, we illustrate one example.

```
SELECT C.Student
  FROM Classes C,
        TABLE ((SELECT TOP_N (C1.Score, 3)
                  FROM Classes C1
                 WHERE C1.Class_Id = 101 )) C2 ( Score )
 WHERE C.Score = C2.Score
   AND C.Class_Id = 101;
```

Listing 5–13. *Query to Retrieve Top N Students in a Class*

Note how the example in Listing 5–13 uses the nested OR-SQL syntax to convert the SET returned by the TOP_N() aggregate into a set of rows. The derivation of the SQL-92 equivalents of these queries is left as an exercise for more masochistic readers.

These examples are intended to make a broader point. Although user-defined aggregates are a useful technique for statistical analysis and data mining, they can also be used to simplify data manipulation operations in more conventional applications.

Dynamic OR-SQL in the Stored Procedure Language

Often, it is desirable to execute an OR-SQL query that is generated at runtime within the ORDBMS. For example, a developer may not know the name of the temporary table he or she wishes to run the query against, or the developer might want to append predicates to a query. In external programs, this can be accomplished using the ESQL/C SQLCA and DESCRIPTOR facilities.

Unfortunately, the INFORMIX Stored Procedure Language (SPL) does not support dynamic SQL. Queries must be hard-coded into the SPL logic. The objective of the Exec BladeLet is to remedy this. Exec() consists of some user-defined functions that take an OR-SQL query as an argument, execute it, and then return a result (the format of which varies depending on the function and the kind of query). The Exec functions can handle most Data Definition Language (DDL) statements and all Data Manipulation Language (DML) queries.

Design Details

There are three UDRs in the Exec BladeLet. Two of them use the C EXTERNAL FUNCTION technique and internally employ the Server API (SAPI) to process the query. These must be compiled into shared libraries on the target machine, and you need to declare them to the server using CREATE FUNCTION statements (which are shipped as part of the BladeLet). The third UDF is an SPL routine that uses the first two UDFs to do useful things, such as implement a general UDF that returns a MULTISET of rows. It is intended as an sample for your use.

One of the trickiest aspects of developing this blade has been getting the memory management code correct. The iterator function must hold memory allocated within SAPI between calls. This means that most of the code runs at PER_COMMAND memory duration, which makes memory leakage a problem.

List of User-Defined Functions

The EXEC (LVARCHAR) RETURNS LVARCHAR function takes an LVARCHAR that is assumed to be an OR-SQL query. It executes the query and returns a single LVARCHAR result string. Depending on what kind of OR-SQL statement is submitted, Exec() returns a different result format.

If the query is a Data Declaration Language (DDL) expression, `Exec()` either returns a string "OK" or generates an exception.

```
SELECT Exec("
CREATE TABLE Foo ( A Num, B Val, C SET(INTEGER NOT NULL));
") FROM TABLE(SET{1});
```

(expression)::LVARCHAR

OK

Listing 5–14. *EXEC() UDF for a DDL Statement*

For Data Manipulation Language (DML) expressions, the `EXEC()` UDF returns a different result format depending on whether the argument was a SELECT or one of the write queries (`INSERT`, `UPDATE`, or `DELETE`).

Write queries either return a single result string, which indicates how many rows were affected by the query, or generate an SQL error.

```
SELECT Exec(
"INSERT INTO Foo VALUES (1,'Hello',SET{1,2,3});")
 FROM TABLE(SET{1});
```

(expression)::LVARCHAR

1 rows affected

```
SELECT Exec(
"INSERT INTO Foo VALUES (2,'Good-bye',SET{4,5,6}); ")
   FROM  TABLE(SET{1});
```

(expression)::LVARCHAR

1 rows affected

```
SELECT Exec(
"UPDATE Foo SET B = 'Zap!' WHERE A < 4;")
   FROM TABLE(SET{1});
```

(expression)::LVARCHAR

2 rows affected

```
SELECT Exec("
INSERT INTO Foo
```

```
SELECT (T1.Num * 100 + T2.Num * 10 + T3.Num)::Integer::Num,
       ( T1.Val || ',' || T2.Val || ',' || T3.Val )::Val,
       SET{ T1.Num, T2.Num, T3.Num }
    FROM
  TABLE(SET{ROW(0,'Zero'),ROW(1,'One'),ROW(2,'Two'),
            ROW(3,'Three'),ROW(4,'Four'),ROW(5,'Five'),
            ROW(6,'Six'),ROW(7,'Seven'),ROW(8,'Eight'),
            ROW(9,'Nine') }::SET(ROW(Num INTEGER,
                                     Val LVARCHAR) NOT NULL)
      ) T1,
  TABLE(SET{ROW(0,'Zero'),ROW(1,'One'),ROW(2,'Two'),
            ROW(3,'Three'),ROW(4,'Four'),ROW(5,'Five'),
            ROW(6,'Six'),ROW(7,'Seven'),ROW(8,'Eight'),
            ROW(9,'Nine') }::SET(ROW(Num INTEGER,
                                     Val LVARCHAR) NOT NULL)
      ) T2,
  TABLE(SET{ROW(0,'Zero'),ROW(1,'One'),ROW(2,'Two'),
            ROW(3,'Three'),ROW(4,'Four'),ROW(5,'Five'),
            ROW(6,'Six'),ROW(7,'Seven'),ROW(8,'Eight'),
            ROW(9,'Nine') }::SET(ROW(Num INTEGER,
                                     Val LVARCHAR) NOT NULL)
      ) T3;");
```

(expression)::LVARCHAR

1000 rows affected

Listing 5–15. *EXEC() UDF for Write DML Statements*

SELECT queries submitted through Exec return a single LVARCHAR result that is the public format of an unnamed ROW TYPE corresponding to the format of the query's return format. We illustrate how this UDF is used in Listing 5–16.

```
SELECT Exec("SELECT COUNT(*) FROM Foo;")
   FROM TABLE(SET{1});
```

(expression)::LVARCHAR
ROW(1003.00000000)

```
SELECT Exec("SELECT * FROM Foo;")
FROM TABLE(SET{1});
```

(expression)::LVARCHAR
ROW(1,'Zap!',SET{1,2,3})

```
SELECT tabname,
              EXEC('SELECT COUNT(*) FROM ' || tabname || ';')
     FROM systables;
```

Listing 5-16. *EXEC() UDF for Write DML Statements*

There are a few items of note in Listing 5–15. In the second example, the query would return more than one row. But in this context, the `Exec()` UDF can return only one value, so it executes the query, but passes back only the first row result. The third example illustrates how flexible and dynamic the mechanism is. In this single query, all tables in the database are queried to return the number of rows in each of them.

Although `Exec()` returns a `LVARCHAR` result, this can be `CAST` into a named `ROW TYPE` with an equivalent structure. This is likely to be the technique used in most applications of the UDF because it is typically used as a means of passing table and column names as parameters. We illustrate casting an `Exec()` result string into a named `ROW TYPE` in Listing 5–17.

```
CREATE ROW TYPE Named_Row_Type (
     A          INTEGER,
     B          VARCHAR(32),
     C          SET(INTEGER NOT NULL)
);

SELECT Exec(
"SELECT * FROM Foo WHERE A = 3;")::Named_Row_Type
 FROM TABLE(SET{1});
```

(expression)::Named_Row_Type

ROW(1,'Zap!',SET{1,2,3})

Listing 5-17. *Casting EXEC() Results into Named ROW TYPE*

Although the results in Listings 5–16 and 5–17 appear identical, the first is simply an `lvarchar` string, while the second is in fact an instance of the Named_Row_Type `ROW TYPE` (which has been turned back into a string to be printed).

There is only one limit on queries passed into `Exec()`: `DROP` DDL statements are prohibited. Note also that by using this technique, it is possible to circumvent the prohibition on write queries inside UDFs. Doing this will have odd consequences on transaction management, so use this trick with extreme caution!

The `Exec_For_Rows()` UDF is an iterator, which means that it can return more than one result row. Of course, it only does so when it is asked to execute a `SELECT`. Otherwise, it behaves exactly as the `Exec()` UDF.

```
EXECUTE FUNCTION Exec_For_Rows(
"SELECT * FROM Foo WHERE A IN ( 1,2,3,4);") ;
```

(expression)::LVARCHAR

```
ROW(1,'Zap!',SET{1,2,3})
ROW(2,'Zap!',SET{4,5,6})
ROW(3,'Stay Here',SET{7,8,9})
ROW(1,'Zero,Zero,One',SET{0,1})
ROW(2,'Zero,Zero,Two',SET{0,2})
ROW(3,'Zero,Zero,Three',SET{0,3})
ROW(4,'Zero,Zero,Four',SET{0,4})
ROW(1,'Zero,Zero,One',SET{0,1})
ROW(2,'Zero,Zero,Two',SET{0,2})
ROW(3,'Zero,Zero,Three',SET{0,3})
ROW(4,'Zero,Zero,Four',SET{0,4})
```

Listing 5–18. *EXEC_FOR_ROWS() Iterator*

Of course, being an iterator limits the ways in which such a UDF can be used. It can't be used in another OR-SQL query, for example. In fact, about the only place it can be used (at the moment) is inside an SPL routine. Mind you, you can do a lot with it there, and you will soon be able to put Iterators in the `FROM` clause of a query.

`Exec_for_MSet()` is an SPL routine that uses `Exec_For_Rows()`. Instead of returning a set of rows as an iterator, or a single row as the `Exec()` UDF does, this UDF collects the results of the OR-SQL query into a single object: a `MULTISET`. Listing 5–19 illustrates the implementation of this routine.

```
CREATE FUNCTION Exec_for_MSet ( Arg1 lvarchar )
RETURNS MULTISET( LVarchar NOT NULL)

    DEFINE  msLvRetVal  MULTISET( LVARCHAR NOT NULL );
    DEFINE  lvIter      LVARCHAR;

    FOREACH EXECUTE FUNCTION Exec_for_Rows ( Arg1 )
                    INTO lvIter
        INSERT INTO Table(msLvRetVal)
        VALUES ( lvIter );
    END FOREACH;
```

```
        RETURN msLvRetVal;
    END FUNCTION


  EXECUTE FUNCTION Exec_For_Mset (
    " SELECT DISTINCT A FROM Foo WHERE A < 20 AND 7 IN C; " );
```

(expression)::MULTISET(LVARCHAR)

MULTISET{'ROW(3)','ROW(7)','ROW(17)'}

Listing 5–19. *EXEC_FOR_MSET() UDF*

Why is this extension interesting? Well for one thing, it lets you create a new data type called OR-SQL (which is simply a distinct type of LVARCHAR). The results of Exec_For_Mset() run over an SQL query is a "relation" too. This raises all kinds of intriguing design possibilities.

One final note: There is a 32 K limit on the size of LVARCHAR data types in SPL. This limits the size of the queries these dynamic OR-SQL UDFs can handle.

Chapter

10

Forging the Perfect DataBlade

Database Extensibility

We introduced the basics of database extensibility in Chapter 5. In this chapter, Chapter 10, we focus on how to use the C language to create *User-Defined Function (UDF)* extensions. C has the best possible performance of all extensibility techniques. Compiled C code has the lowest calling overhead, its execution is the most efficient, and C has no competitors when it comes to dealing with large or algorithmically sophisticated objects. To support developers with these requirements, the IDS product provides an extensive environment for developing C library components and embedding them.

Recall that developers can modify and extend the ORDBMS through the following mechanisms:

- Creating stand-alone UDF extensions that add expressions to the OR-SQL query language.
- Creating various kinds of new User-Defined data types (UDT) and implementing behavior for them with UDF logic.
- Combining several UDFs to implement more sophisticated extensions: user-defined aggregates, new access methods, and so on.

683

As you can see from this list, UDF extensions are of fundamental importance to ORDBMS development. Object-relational databases typically include a great many UDFs, and the ORDBMS will invoke these extensions many, many times.

Technical Objectives of External UDFs

It is difficult to understate the importance of ensuring that your application's user-defined functions are constructed to the highest possible standards. Almost every aspect of an ORDBMS database depends to some extent on the efficiency of the user-defined extensions running within it.

For example, suppose you create a user-defined OPAQUE TYPE, and implement a Compare () function so that the ORDBMS can build B-Tree indices on it. When the engine builds an index over a table with 10 million rows, it will call this UDF about 70 million times! Obviously, poorly implemented extensions are disastrous. A four-byte memory leak in this Compare() will cause 280 megabytes of memory to be allocated unnecessarily during the index build, and every superfluous line of code in a UDF slows query processing.

The performance of an ORDBMS application depends to a significant degree on how well UDFs perform according to three criteria:

- Speed. The ORDBMS will call UDFs specified in a query's SELECT or WHERE clauses, and UDFs are invoked in performance sensitive-tasks such as sorts, indexing, and joins.
- Efficiency. UDFs execute within a database that will be accessed concurrently by many users. Thus, a second objective of a good UDF is to consume as few hardware resources, such as memory, disk I/O, and CPU, as possible. For example, it is not generally a good idea to write a UDF that uses lots of memory. Even though it might help that individual function execute more quickly, when many queries are issued concurrently, the computer's physical memory may be exhausted, which reduces overall throughput.
- Reliability. Like any other programming project, getting extensions to do the right thing reliably is absolutely necessary to meet the project's goals. Reliability is achieved through good design and rigorous testing.

C is the ORDBMS extension language used by most commercial Data-Blade™ developers, as well as INFORMIX's own engineers and consultants. This is partly due to the language's maturity. C standards, both the programming language and its compiled binary standards, are almost universally adhered to. Over the years, an extensive body of example code and "how-to" manuals have been written. Excellent C language compilers can be had for free (GNU's gcc being the best known).

The biggest advantage of C, however, is performance. C functions execute faster than SPL or Java functions because C functions have extremely low calling overhead relative to other UDF techniques, and C source code is compiled into machine code and executed directly on the computer hardware. When the ORDBMS engine invokes a C UDF, it simply branches to the memory address where the function's machine code is located, and then executes whatever it finds there. In contrast, languages such as SPL and Java need to go through an intermediate setup and interpretation stage. Therefore, performance critical extensions and commercial datablades are typically written in C.[1]

Unfortunately, C is a challenging language with which to work. Its syntax is terse, its grammatical rules obscure, and it lacks the civilizing amenities (such as rigorous type checking) of other languages. Programmers who work in C—unlike programmers who work in interpreted languages such as SPL and Java—also need to cope with physical programming issues such as memory management, writing thread-safe code, and exchanging data with the ORDBMS server.

In general, you are far better off using more hospitable languages for most of your applications, simply because you are more likely to get the job finished on time! Reserve C for those aspects of the application with the very highest performance requirements.

Chapter Overview

In this chapter we set out to explain how to write fast, efficient, and reliable ORDBMS extensions in C. We anticipate that the information here will be of most interest to developers writing DataBlade™ extensions and implementing performance-sensitive UDFs. Other developers, who work at the level of the logical model, simply reuse these extensions within SPL or OR-SQL, without needing to know much about how they work.

We begin by examining how the ORDBMS accomplishes C extensibility. Chapter 3 introduced a range of queries that included UDFs. In this chapter we describe how these query expressions are turned ultimately into calls to UDF code. Understanding how this works is useful when considering your extension's design. It helps to explain several limitations on UDFs and the performance you can expect from various implementation alternatives.

---

[1] Why not C++? The basic problem is the lack of a binary standard. When the ORDBMS links in a C library, it knows how to extract a list of function names and the location of the corresponding code within the library because there is a standard way of doing it. No similar standard exists for C++. Each C++ compiler does something different, making it next to impossible to support C++ universally.

We then move on to explore how to create C UDFs, focusing on issues such as argument handling, memory management, exceptions, return results, and the DataBlade API (also known as the Server API, or SAPI). Finally, we briefly explore issues related to specialized UDFs: large objects, SQL call-backs, and badly-behaved UDFs. We approach the topic by introducing several, increasingly complex examples and then explaining how they work.

How the ORDBMS Uses C UDFs

Perhaps the best way to explain the relationship between user-defined function and the ORDBMS is to compare extensions to mini-programs running within the IDS product, which acts as a kind of operating system. For database procedures, the correspondence is fairly clear. Such procedural logic might just as easily be implemented externally to the DBMS, as an embedded C program for example. But what about functions embedded within OR-SQL?

Part of the answer is that, philosophically, an ORDBMS is a rather unusual operating system. Rather than scattering programs over file-system directories, the ORDBMS maintains a list of all of them in its system catalogs. In contrast to the kinds of programs developers are accustomed to writing, where each program's code knows how to access whatever data the program uses, the ORDBMS 'operating system' performs all data access, passing data into the UDF, one piece at a time, as specified by the query expression.

Consequently, UDF 'mini-programs' rarely includes code that loops over data not passed into the function through its arguments. They tend to look more like sub-routines. The ORDBMS passes data into a UDF through its arguments, and the UDF computes a result that it passes back to the ORDBMS. Multiple UDFs can be combined and nested within a single query expression. One UDF's results can be passed immediately into another.

Simple User-defined Function Example

To co-opt a famous example, let's see how we would write a `Hello-World()` C UDF . Figure 10–1 illustrates the different parts of this task.

The first task is to write the C code implementing the function. Unlike typical C programs, a UDF has no `main()`. In fact, it does not need one. The purpose of `main()` in normal C programs is to tell the operating system where to start the program once it is compiled and linked into an executable binary. The ORDBMS, however, only needs

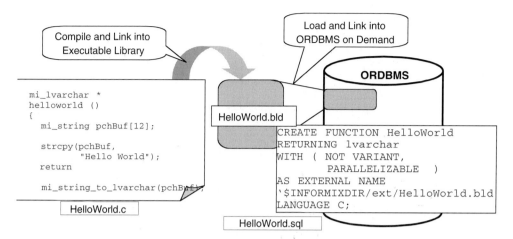

Figure 10–1. *Overview of Creating a C User-Defined Function*

to know where to find the subroutine. This is usually called the *entry point* of the function within the library.

In Listing 10–1 we reproduce the complete C source for the Hello-World() UDF.

```
#include <mi.h>
#include <stdio.h>

mi_lvarchar * helloworld ()
{
    mi_string pchBuf[12];

    strcpy(pchBuff, "Hello World");

    return  mi_string_to_lvarchar(pchBuf);
}
```

Listing 10–1. *Source Code for HelloWorld C UDF*

You should note several things about this source code example:

- It includes two library files (mi.h and stdio.h). These contain specifications for various functions used in the HelloWorld() source code; strcpy() is found in the standard C libraries, and mi_string_to_lvarchar() is implemented as part of the ORDBMS.
- The types used in this code are not native to C. Instead of char, for example, this function uses the ORDBMS environment equivalent, mi_string, and the return type mi_lvarchar has no C equivalent. Using the ORDBMS's types instead of the C native types ensures the portability of your UDF code, while still allowing you to use most standard C functions.

- This code, like every C UDF ever written, does not output its results in the same way C programs generally do (writing to `stdout` using `printf()`, or to an open file). Instead, it creates a return value and passes it back to the ORDBMS.

Having written the UDF, the next step is to compile it into a *shared library*. This is called `helloworld.bld` in our example. The library's name is not important, except that it is registered in the ORDBMS's system catalogs as the place to find the UDF's executable code. Your choice of compiler and development environment determines the syntax used to compile your code and build the library.

The third task is to register the UDF in the ORDBMS. This is done using the CREATE FUNCTION definition language statement introduced in Chapter 5. Listing 10–2 illustrates how `HelloWorld()` is registered with IDS.

```
CREATE FUNCTION HelloWorld()
RETURNS lvarchar
WITH (  NOT VARIANT, PARALLELIZABLE  )
EXTERNAL NAME '$INFORMIXDIR/ext/helloworld.bld(helloworld)'
LANGUAGE C;
```

Listing 10–2. *Declaring the HelloWorld UDF to the ORDBMS*

Now the new UDF can be invoked, or run, either by executing the function explicitly or by including it in a OR-SQL query, as we show in Listing 10–3. As with all OR-SQL identifiers case does not matter. In the EXTERNAL NAME clause of the CREATE FUNCTION, however, case does count because this names an object in the file-system.

```
EXECUTE FUNCTION HelloWorld();

Hello World

SELECT HelloWorld()
   FROM TABLE(SET{1,2,3});

Hello World
Hello World
Hello World
```

Listing 10–3. *Invoking the HelloWorld UDF*

Information about the UDF, such as the name of its shared library file, is recorded in the database's system catalogs. Note that the library file is still stored in the file-system, outside the IDS product. It is not loaded and linked into the ORDBMS engine until it is invoked.

How C UDFs are Executed

At runtime, when instructed to invoke a UDF, the IDS product load and links the function's shared library from the file-system into the server's memory. This process, identified as Step 1 in Figure 10–2, is usually referred to as *dynamic linking* . From the information in its catalogs, the ORDBMS knows the name of the file, and the name of the *entry point* (2) within it, which is where the compiled code begins. This information is placed in a special area of memory maintained by the function manager, as we show in Figure 10–2.

Whenever the ORDBMS needs to execute a UDF, it calls the *function manager*, and passes it references to whatever *argument data* (Step 3) it requires. Data populating this structure might have come from disk or from another function that has just been executed. At this point, control is passed to the *compiled logic* (Step 4) within the shared library. As part of its execution path, this logic might call back into the function manager using the *server API* (Step 5) facilities. These calls allow the logic to perform tasks such as allocating memory, converting data, and even issuing OR-SQL queries.

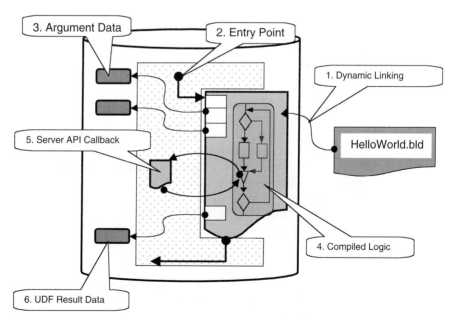

Figure 10–2. *Detailed Design of ORDBMS Function Manager*

Upon completion, the UDF logic returns to the function manager a pointer to its *result data* (Step 6). Then the function manager performs a number of checks to ensure that return values are valid (not NULL pointers), and it frees whatever it can of the memory the UDF allocated to itself as it was executing (unless the UDF's logic marked the memory using special SAPI routines). Finally, the function manager copies the return result to new location before handing control back to the ORDBMS.

The function manager's responsibilities include maintaining memory structures that a UDF uses and checking that the UDF rules are obeyed. For example, the function manager ensures that sufficient stack space is available before executing the function. Just before jumping to the compiled code's memory address, the function manager pushes argument values onto the stack.

Queries and User-Defined Functions

Usually, UDFs are invoked when the ORDBMS processes a OR-SQL expression. Query processing is a complex topic, but a little understanding of it is useful to the UDF developer. We outline the high-level sequence of steps it involves in Figure 10–3.

The whole process is initiated when the ORDBMS receives a query string from somewhere, such as an external program or a stored procedure. First, it parses this string to figure out what the query is intended to do. The parser's task is to establish the tables, columns, data types, and user-defined functions involved in the query. This requires disentangling function overloading and polymorphism and checking user permissions over the various items involved in the query. The result of the parsing phase is a sequence of low-level operations, some of which include calls to user-defined functions.

Next the ORDBMS examines the sequence of operations produced by the parser to see if it can reorder them in some way that minimizes the amount of computer resources required to answer the query.[2] To do this, the ORDBMS uses statistical information about the data involved in the query (how many rows in the various tables and how much data in each row) and weightings for the various UDRs (how many CPU cycles to run a function). This phase is usually referred to as *optimization*.

---

[2] An alternate objective might be to minimize the query's response time. This is generally the most suitable goal for decision support queries because it allows for parallel query processing strategies that might, briefly, consume all available hardware resources.

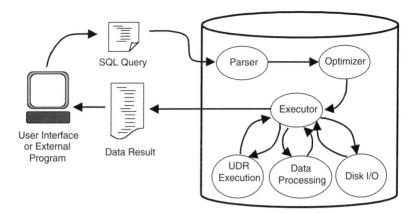

Figure 10–3. *Overview of Query Processing in ORDBMS*

It is important to understand that many queries are not executed at the time they are initially compiled. Rather, the ORDBMS stores a query plan for later use. OR-SQL expressions in stored procedures, and queries that are *prepared*, are handled in this manner. Even before the query is executed, the ORDBMS might be executing UDFs to convert literal representations of constant values into their internal format.

Finally, the ORDBMS actually executes this (hopefully) optimal query plan. In an ORDBMS, query plans are schedules of suboperations such as looping over data, applying user-defined functions to it, and performing tasks such as sorting or counting.

For example, consider the query in Listing 10–4.

```
SELECT User_Defined_Function_1(T.Column_1)
  FROM My_Table T
  WHERE User_Defined_Function_2(T.Column_2) >
                        'Public_Format'::User_Defined_Type
  ORDER BY 1;
```

Listing 10–4. *Query for Illustrating Query Processing*

Suppose the ORDBMS server renders this query into the pseudo-code in Listing 10–5. This plan is relatively simple. In practice, because queries can involve a great many tables and UDFs, their plans are often extraordinarily complicated. Also, an ORDBMS engine has a tremendous number of algorithmic strategies at its disposal, such as various indexing techniques and joins, to make the query more efficient.

```
Query_Constant := CallUDR("CAST_From_Lvarchar",
                          "Public Format");

Initialize( Query_Results );
Begin Scan ( "My_Table" );
while((Row := Read Next Row("My_Table")) != NULL)
{
    Result_1 := CallUDR( "User_Defined_Function_2",
                          Row.Column_2);
    Result_2 := CallUDR("GreaterThan",
                          Result_1, Query_Constant);
    if (Result_2) then
    {
        Return_Value := CallUDR("User_Defined_Function_1",
                                 Row.Column_1);
        Add to Result( Query_Result, Return_Value );
    }
}
End Scan ( "My_Table" );
Sort( Query_Result, 1);
```

Listing 10–5. *Pseudo-Code Plan for Query in Listing 10–4*

Facilities implemented by the ORDBMS are underlined in Figure 10–3. For instance, the ORDBMS knows how to sort a set of query results. You can see from this example why it is that UDF developers do not need to deal with things such as disk storage, transactions, locking, optimization, and so on. These tasks are handled by the ORDBMS, which calls UDFs to handle the semantically interesting aspects of the query.

Binding UDFs and Data

Now let us consider a second example, in Listing 10–6, which is a slight modification on the `HelloWorld()` UDF introduced earlier in this chapter. Our second UDF example does more than return a string; it uses an argument value to compute a new return result.

```
#include <mi.h>
#include <stdio.h>

mi_lvarchar * hello (
mi_lvarchar * plvName,
MI_FPARAM    * Gen_Fparam
)
{
```

```
mi_string    * pchRetBuf;
mi_string    * pchName;

pchName    = mi_lvarchar_to_string ( plvName );
pchRetBuf = (mi_string *)mi_alloc  (strlen(pchName) +
                                    strlen("Hello ") + 1);

sprintf(pchRetBuf, "Hello %s", pchName);

return mi_string_to_lvarchar (pchRetBuf);
}
```

Listing 10–6. *A Slightly More Advanced User-Defined Function Example*

Like `HelloWorld()`, `Hello()` must be compiled into a shared library, declared within the ORDBMS, and linked into the engine before the function manager can invoke it. It might be used as shown in Listing 10–7.

```
SELECT Hello ( Print( M.Name ) )
  FROM MovieClubMembers M;
```

(expression)

Hello Joe Blogs
Hello Mira Freyenbauger

. . .

Listing 10–7. *SQL Example Binding Table Data to Extended Logic*

This query reads row data from the `MovieClubMembers` table. For each row, it extracts the member's name and calls a UDF called `Print()` to format it. Then the engine binds this data to the `Hello()` logic to produce a new string that becomes the query's result. Different name formats, and different greetings, can be achieved by replacing the UDF names in this query, and the same logic can be applied to different data by changing the name of the table (say, `MoviePersonalities`).

Philosophy of UDF Development

Keep each UDF as conceptually simple as possible. Ideally, it should use only its argument data to perform some encapsulated, atomic computation. It should not call too many other routines, and it should not do more than one action. In other words, user-defined functions should be very *internally cohesive*. For many OPAQUE TYPE instances, the behavior implemented in its associated UDFs will require only relatively straightforward algorithms. With complex data types such as video and spatial, however, "conceptually simple" can mean algorithmically complex.

Other developers combine multiple UDFs within an OR-SQL query or an SPL stored procedure. The task confronting a UDF developer is therefore to solve one programming problem well, and to do so almost without regard to how their extension will be used. This maximizes the flexibility of OR-SQL, and it makes is easier for the ORDBMS to break queries up and arrive at efficient plans.

ORDBMS Programming Environment

Operating systems do a lot more than store data and run programs. They also mediate a program's access to hardware resources by allocating and organizing memory, scheduling time on the CPU, managing the communication with other programs, and so on. A programming environment that did not provide these services would be next to useless. Thus, the ORDBMS includes an interface to mimic what more conventional operating systems do. This is known as the DataBlade™ Application Programming Interface. For historical reasons, it is also known as the *Server API*, or SAPI.

SAPI consists of a large library of C subroutines and data structures. As indicated in Figure 10–2, these are actually implemented as part of the ORDBMS engine. When compiling UDF code into a shared library outside the engine, you need to include header files defining the SAPI calls. As the compiled logic executes, however, it calls the SAPI facilities implemented within the ORDBMS.

This helps explain something that happens when developing external UDFs. As the external linker does its job by combining several compiled source code files into a single library, it generates a series of warning messages s about any unresolved symbols it finds. These should all be SAPI calls, which are functions that are to be found the time the shared library is linked into the server. If the IDS product cannot resolve a symbol in the shared library as it links a library, for example, if a SAPI call is misspelled, then the engine generates an error.

SAPI Overview

SAPI consists of a large set of functions and data structures that developers use when writing C extensions. The functions in SAPI perform tasks such as the following:

- managing data values and structures passed by the server as arguments into the UDF
- formatting return results and passing messages about return results to the ORDBMS
- interacting with the server's environment to perform system tasks such as allocating more memory and getting and setting environment variables and file I/O
- handling the server's data types. Each SQL built-in type has a most equivalent, as do most SQL built-in scalar expressions
- dealing with special case data types such as large object and multi-representational data types
- managing connection context issues such as transaction state, query interruption, and server thread preempting
- processing queries in the server; executing queries, iterating through query results, and handling the data values that the server returns in response to queries
- coping with exceptions and errors

In this chapter we describe most SAPI facilities in some detail. `HelloWorld()` and `Hello()` give you the flavor of the interface. `HelloWorld()` uses the `mi_string_to_lvarchar()` SAPI call to take a null terminated string—either a C (`char *`) or a SAPI (`mi_string *`)—and use it to build the `mi_lvarchar` structure the ORDBMS is expecting, and `Hello()` illustrates how a UDF uses SAPI to allocate itself some memory with `mi_alloc()`.

Regrettably, SAPI is a proprietary interface. Although it is consistent between product releases and across all supported platforms, its purpose is unique among data management products. If your C code is required to run in other places, such as in a middle-ware program, it is a good idea to create a layering between the server and the portable code. We illustrate the idea in the source code example in Listing 10–8.

```
/*
** Example of "shim". Creates a CC stub that handles SAPI
** types and calls more portable CC code using native
** CC types.
**/
```

```
mi_lvarchar * UDF_Logic ( mi_lvarchar * plvArg,
                          MI_FPARAM    * pGen_Fparam  )
{
    return mi_string_to_lvarchar  (
                UDF_Logic_in_C (
                    mi_lvarchar_to_string  ( plvArg ) ) );
}
/*
** This is the portable CC. In practice, most logic such as
** this modifies data by reference, rather than by using
** the same mode that UDFs do.
*/
char *  UDF_Logic_in_C ( char * pchArg )
{
/*  Code to implement actual logic. Other SAPI rules apply
**  in this code, which  must still use mi_alloc() and other
**  SAPI calls to get system resources. One good strategy
**  for this is to use CC macros. chRetVal = MALLOC();
*/
}
```

Listing 10–8. *Using Shims to Write Portable C Code*

All examples in this book use SAPI directly. In practice, embedding a body of pre-existing C into the IDS product is a task not to be taken lightly. All server programming rules apply in the "shimmed" code. A pattern such as the one in Listing 10–8 is, however, a useful discipline when doing original development.

SAPI and User-Defined Functions

We proceed in this section by presenting a list of increasingly complex C UDFs and explaining how they work. For the vast majority of readers, the ideas described in this section are all you will need to know about working inside the ORDBMS. More sophisticated developers will probably appreciate the later material in this chapter, which deals with problems of complex UDFs (such as iterators and aggregates) and more sophisticated extensibility mechanisms (such as large objects and OR-SQL call-backs.)

Simple User-Defined Function

For our third UDF example,[3] consider the table in Listing 10–9 that might augment our Movies-R-Us database schema. This example illustrates how UDF logic is also useful in the SELECT list of a query, in addition to the WHERE clause.

```
CREATE DISTINCT TYPE Trans_Type AS LVARCHAR;
CREATE TABLE Transactions (
        Merchandise    Part_Code      NOT NULL,
        Day            DATE           NOT NULL,
        TransType      Trans_Type     NOT NULL,
        Amount         Price          NOT NULL,
        Quantity       Quantity       NOT NULL
);
```

Listing 10–9. *Additional Table to Explain Simple UDF*

This Transactions table stores information about the various cash and inventory changes happening on the Web site. This table is a history of activity; it might be captured using a TRIGGER on other tables.

The small segment of the table in Listing 10–10 records the following:

1. an entry recording the initial cash position
2. three purchases of individual items of merchandise by movie club members
3. two times when the movie club's management bought extra inventory
4. one customer refund
5. one inventory return, when the web site's management was obliged to return inventory to the wholesaler
6. disposal, or dumping, of some inventory

Merchandise	Day	TransType	Amount	Quantity
Cash	1-1-2000	INITIAL	10000.00	1
T-Shirt	1-1-2000	ORDER	12.50	2
Caps	1-1-2000	ORDER	5.00	2
Video	2-12000	ORDER	35.00	1
T-Shirt	2-1-2000	BUY	7.50	1000
Posters	2-5-2000	BUY	6.00	100
T-Shirt	2-7-2000	REFUND	12.50	1
Video	2-27-2000	RETURN	35.00	1
T-Shirts	3-27-2000	DISPOSE	12.50	53

Listing 10–10. *Example Rows for Transactions Audit Log Table*

---

[3] This is a slightly modified version of an actual application running on Wall Street.

The business reason for keeping this data is to be able to compute, on any given day, the amount of cash on hand This calculation is complicated by the fact that this table records trade activity, which indirectly reflects cash changes. Further, you will notice that the Price and Quantity columns contain only positive values. This might be due to accounting standards or to distinguish transactions from reversals (a trade entered in error is never deleted; it is reversed through a compensating record).

Each transaction type has a different impact on cash. INITIAL sets an initial cash amount, ORDERs increase cash, BUYs and REFUNDs reduce cash, RETURNS only increase cash by 87.5 percent of value, and DISPOSAL of inventory has no effect whatsoever.

Traditionally, making sense of this kind of table required procedural logic iterating through the rows and modifying the value of some programming language variable according to the transaction type, quantity, and price. The final value of the programming language variable was revealed as the answer. The biggest problem with this kind of solution was its inflexibility. Adding new transaction types, for example incorporating the DISPOSAL transaction type, involved rewriting every query that touched the table!

A more efficient way to address the problem is to create a UDF called NetCashEffect() that takes three arguments: transtype, price, and quantity. NetCashEffect() returns a value that reflects the net cash change that the transaction caused. Traditionally, such a function (which we illustrate in Listing 10–11) would be a subroutine in a client-side program. Listing 10–11 is not an ideal implementation in some respects. For instance, to keep the example code short and complete, on Line 25 it converts the argument to a double precision value instead of using the decimal arithmetic libraries.

```
1    #include <ctype.h>
2    #include <stdio.h>
3    #include <string.h>
4    #include <stddef.h>
5
6    #include <mi.h>
7    #include <decimal.h>
8
9    #define POS(X)  (((X)<(0))?((-1.0)*(X)):((X)))
10
11   mi_decimal *
12   NetCashEffect (
13                   mi_lvarchar * pvlTransType,
14                   mi_decimal   * pdecPrice,
```

```
15                      mi_integer      nQuantity,
16                      MI_FPARAM     * pGen_FParam
17                      )
18  {
19    mi_string              * pchTransType;
20    mi_decimal             * pdecRetVal;
21    mi_double_precision    dbPrice, dbRetVal;
22    MI_CONNECTION          * pGenCon;
23
24    pchTransType = mi_lvarchar_to_string( pvlTransType );
25    (void)dectodbl( pdecPrice, &(dbPrice) );
26
27    if (strcmp( pchTransType, "INITIAL" ) == 0)          {
28      if (( nQuantity == 0 ) && (POS(dbPrice) < 0.01)) {
29        pGenCon = mi_open(NULL, NULL, NULL);
30        mi_db_error_raise (pGenCon, MI_EXCEPTION,
31          "Invalid INITIAL Transaction in NetCashEffect.");
32        /* not reached */
33      }
34      dbRetVal = dbPrice;
35    }
36    else if(strcmp( pchTransType, "ORDER" ) == 0)            {
37
38     /* Club member's orders */
39      dbRetVal = ( nQuantity * dbPrice );
40    }
41    else if ((strcmp(pchTransType, "BUY") == 0)      ||
42             (strcmp(pchTransType, "RETURN") == 0) ||
43             (strcmp(pchTransType, "REFUND") == 0))          {
44
45  /* "BUY" - purchase merchandise, "RETURN" - Member returns*/
46  /* purchase unopened, "REFUND" - member receives refund   */
47      dbRetVal = -1.0 * ( nQuantity * dbPrice );
48    }
49    else if(strcmp( pchTransType, "DEPOSIT" ) == 0)       {
50
51     /* Cash addition to the inventory account  */
52      dbRetVal = dbPrice;
53    }
54    else if(strcmp( pchTransType, "WITHDRAWAL" ) == 0)   {
55     /* Cash withdrawal from the account */
56      dbRetVal = -1.0 * dbPrice;
57    }
58    else if(strcmp( pchTransType, "DISPOSED" ) == 0)      {
59     /* Unsold inventory returned to supplier */
```

```
60        dbRetVal = -0.875 * dbPrice * nQuantity;
61    }
62    else                                                    {
63      mi_fp_returnisnull(pGen_FParam, 0);
64      return (mi_decimal *)NULL;
65    }
66    pdecRetVal = (mi_decimal *)mi_alloc(sizeof(mi_decimal));
67    (void)deccvdbl( dbRetVal, pdecRetVal);
68
69    return (pdecRetVal);
70  }
```

Listing 10–11. *NetCashEffect() User-Defined Function Written in C*

Once compiled into a shared library, this user-defined function is declared to the IDS product with the OR-SQL DDL command, as shown in Listing 10–12. Note that, although these examples might indicate it, there is no requirement to put each compiled UDF into a separate shared library.

```
CREATE FUNCTION NetCashEffect (Trans_Type, Price, Quantity )
RETURNING Price
WITH ( NOT VARIANT, PARALLELIZABLE)
EXTERNAL NAME "$INFORMIXDIR/extend/NetEffect/bin
             /neteffect.bld(NetCashEffect)"
LANGUAGE C;
--
GRANT EXECUTE ON FUNCTION NetCashEffect( Trans_Type,
                                         Price,
                                         Quantity)
TO PUBLIC;
```

Listing 10–12. *Registering the NetCashEffect() User-Defined Function in ORDBMS*

The obvious use for this kind of UDF is in queries, such as the one in Listing 10–13.

```
SELECT SUM(NetCashEffect(T.TransType,T.Amount,T.Quantity))
  FROM Transactions T
 WHERE T.Day <= '04-06-2000';
```

Listing 10–13. *Using the NetCashEffect() UDF in a Query*

This query selects all rows from the `Transactions` table dated on or before the supplied date, and it runs each of them through the `Net-CashEffect()` function. By adding up these results, you get the amount of cash on hand at the end of the given day. This example illustrates a practical and useful way to bring business logic into the ORDBMS.

In the next section, we briefly explain each section of this code. The idea is to give you a feel for how such extensions work as a total package. Later, we go into more detail about each section by exploring design and implementation alternatives.

Headers and Includes

The first few lines of this program consist of the various header files that include prototypes of the data structures and functions used in this program, as shown in Listing 10–14.

```
1   #include <ctype.h>
2   #include <stdio.h>
3   #include <string.h>
4   #include <stddef.h>
5
6   #include <mi.h>
7   #include <decimal.h>
```

Listing 10–14. *Header Files Included in C Source*

Lines one through four are standard C library header files. You can use the standard C library facilities, with the exception of system calls, in your user-defined functions.

Each of the second pair of header files is INFORMIX ORDBMS specific. The first one, "`mi.h`" includes prototypes for all of the server API functions and data structures. The second is probably more familiar to you if you've used the ESQL/C or CLI client interfaces; "`decimal.h`" belongs to a set of header files for facilities to manage SQL data types in C. In `NetCashEffect()`, one of the arguments is a DISTINCT TYPE of DECIMAL. This needs to be converted into a floating-point value inside the function. Similar files exist for all SQL types: dates, date-times, decimal, interval, and so on.

Passing Arguments

Lines 11 through 17 define the C function's name and the arguments it expects, as well as its return type. Examine Listing 10–15.

```
11   mi_decimal    *
12   NetCashEffect (
13                      mi_lvarchar    * pvlTransType,
14                      mi_decimal     * pdecPrice,
15                      mi_integer       nQuantity,
16                      MI_FPARAM      * pGen_FParam
17                      )
```

Listing 10–15. *Declaration of C UDF*

This declaration specifies the following:

- The function returns a pointer to a decimal data value (Line 11).
  Note that at the OR-SQL level, the UDF appears to return an entire
  Price data type value. Using the decimal works because Price is a
  DISTINCT TYPE of decimal and therefore has the same in-memory
  size. C pointers are used when the data being passed around
  exceeds four bytes, although this mechanism is not visible at the
  OR-SQL level.
- The function is to be referenced by the symbol NetCashEffect
  when it is declared to the ORDBMS (it is in line twelve; note the corresponding declaration in Listing 10–12). If you are using NT, this
  name must appear in the definition file CashEffect.def.
- NetCashEffect() takes three parameters from the OR-SQL (lines
  thirteen through fifteen). As with the return value, one argument
  illustrates how to exchange DISTINCT TYPE data with the UDF.
- There is a final fourth argument that the ORDBMS uses to pass context information into the function's logic (line sixteen).

Different kinds of data values are passed into the C function using
different techniques. Smaller built-in objects, which are those four bytes
or less long, are passed into the function by *value*. Their data value is
placed on the stack, and it is addressed directly within the function. In
NetCashEffect(), the mi_integer argument nQuantity is passed in
by value.

Data objects larger than four bytes in length are always passed into
the UDF by *reference*. Instead of the value itself, the ORDBMS places a
pointer to the data object in the stack. The second and third arguments are mi_decimal and mi_lvarchar types in NetCashEffect()
Both exceed four bytes in length, so pointers to these argument values
are passed into the UDF.

When the ORDBMS calls this function, it will supply arguments in
the order specified in the OR-SQL function declaration. Mismanaging
arguments causes interesting failures. Later, we devote an entire section to describing argument handling in more detail.

Local Variables

You can declare and use local variables within a C UDF. SAPI provides a set of cross-platform data structures corresponding to each of the native C formats. Using SAPI types instead of C types is a good idea because it help make your code portable. For example, instead of char, you should use the mi_string type, which is functionally identical.

SAPI also includes a set of data structures and functions for interacting with the ORDBMS environment. These are frequently used to define local variables, too.

In Listing 10–16, lines nineteen through twenty-two illustrate several local variable declarations.

```
19      mi_string            * pchTransType;
20      mi_decimal           * pdecRetVal;
21      mi_double_precision    dbPrice, dbRetVal;
22      MI_CONNECTION        * pGenCon;
```

Listing 10–16. *Local Variables in C UDF*

The first three variables hold local values for the UDF logic. The last declaration uses a SAPI-specific data type to store a *connection* structure, which is a handle to the database context within which the UDF is executing. Although UDFs typically run within the ORDBMS, an important feature of the extensibility model is that SAPI works on the client side too. Although a UDF can run only inside a single database at a time, client programs can have several concurrent connections at any point in time. Therefore, for consistency, you also find the connection abstraction in C UDF code.

There are differences between native C data types and the formats used for similar data by the ORDBMS SQL. For example, the ORDBMS uses a data structure called mi_lvarchar to store character strings. It does this rather than representing strings as C does (null terminated arrays of character bytes). mi_lvarchar is a particularly important structure, and we go into it in detail later in this chapter.

C cannot operate on SAPI types, such as mi_decimal or mi_lvarchar (and their DISTINCT TYPE instances, which have exactly the same size and structure as their parents) directly. Instead, the code can either convert the data values into a C native type, or it can use the specialist libraries provided for the type. Thus, to use mi_lvarchar data in a C UDF, you need to convert it into a character string first. The next two lines, shown in Listing 10–17, illustrate how to use SAPI or the special libraries on the arguments to convert them into C variables.

```
24          pchTransType = mi_lvarchar_to_string( pvlTransType );
25          (void) dectodbl( pdecPrice, &(dbPrice) );
```

Listing 10–17. *Converting SQL Data to C Structures*

When you create a user-defined OPAQUE TYPE, you typically create a C data structure that the IDS server stores for you. This means that no translation is required; you simply address the contents of the OPAQUE TYPE's structure as if it were any other C structure.

However, the rules for other user-defined types such as DISTINCT TYPE, ROW TYPE, and COLLECTION data are different. A DISTINCT TYPE looks exactly like its parent type does; for example, a DISTINCT TYPE of integer is passed in as a four-byte value. In the NetCash-Effect() example, Price is a DISTINCT TYPE of DECIMAL, so it can be handled using mi_decimal within the C.

ROW TYPE and COLLECTION data, because of their composite nature, require special handling. An entire set of SAPI calls exists to accomplish this. We describe these in more detail in later sections of this chapter.

MI_FPARAM Structure

As you can see from the NetCashEffect() example, when the ORDBMS calls a UDF, it passes into it whatever argument values are specified, and it includes an extra argument that is a pointer to the MI_FPARAM structure. This structure contains information about the context within which the UDF is called. It is the means by which the server passes non-argument information into the UDF, and it also is the means by which the UDF communicates certain information back to the ORDBMS.

The MI_FPARAM structure contains the following:

- A list of the function's arguments and their types.
- A pointer that developers can use to store the location of an area of memory that is cached between calls to the function. This is one of the most useful techniques in UDF development, and we cover it in more detail later in the chapter.
- Information about the return values from the function.
- Facilities to allow the function to act as an iterator function, which returns a set of results.

Accessing data in the MI_FPARAM is achieved using a set of SAPI routines and macros. For example, the two lines in Listing 10–18 use the MI_FPARAM structure to tell the ORDBMS that this time, the function is returning a NULL value.

```
63          mi_fp_returnisnull (pGen_FParam, 0);
64          return (mi_decimal *)NULL;
```

Listing 10–18. *Using MI_FPARAM to Return a NULL Result*

Why not just return a NULL pointer or a NULL value? Well, you don't want to do that because the first thing the ORDBMS does with a return result is copy it elsewhere, and if you try to copy data from a NULL pointer, the operating system will generate a segmentation violation! In addition, it can be difficult to distinguish a C NULL from a legitimate value.

If the same UDR is to be executed multiple times in a query—say, the UDF is included twice in the WHERE clause of query—the ORDBMS creates a separate MI_FPARAM for each invocation context. In addition, when the ORDBMS parallelizes a query, it creates a separate UDF context and separate MI_FPARAM for each separate thread.

Later in this chapter we explore the MI_FPARAM structure and its associated API facilities in more detail.

Function Body

There are few limits on the C code you can write in a UDF. The biggest limits are on the use of system calls, which in normal C programs acquire resources from the operating system. Using the standard C libraries, however, is perfectly reasonable. For example, NetCashEffect() uses the C strcmp() library function to establish which transaction type with which we are dealing.

The most important rules to follow when writing a C UDF are as follows:

- Do not use static variables, or, more precisely, do not *change* the value of a static variable.
- Do not use operating system facilities directly. Library functions like malloc() that enclose system calls, or direct system calls like open(), write() and so on, confuse both the ORDBMS and the operating system.
- Do not modify a UDF argument (unless it is an OUT parameter).
- UDFs should be *re-entrant*; that is, the ORDBMS should be able to run the function many times concurrently without any of them interfering with each other.

Lack of static and global variables raises a troubling question. How do you pass data from one invocation of the UDF to the next? For instance, suppose you wanted to keep a running total of something as you run a set of rows through a UDF. You could do so by using the `MI_FPARAM` structure, which we discuss at length later in the chapter.

Return Value

`NetCashEffect()`, like all UDFs, returns a single data value; in this case, it is a C `mi_decimal`. The value of this decimal is taken from a C double precision variable that the function's logic calculates, and Line 67 illustrates another facility of the SAPI decimal libraries.

Rules that apply to arguments also apply to return values. If the return value is four bytes or less long, it can be returned by *value* (that is, passed back through the stack). Larger data values must be returned by reference (a pointer in the stack), as we show in Listing 10–19.

```
66    pdecRetVal = (mi_decimal *)mi_alloc(sizeof(mi_decimal));
67    (void)deccvdbl( dbRetVal, pdecRetVal);
68
69    return (pdecRetVal);
70 }
```

Listing 10–19. *Formatting Return Values from a UDF*

Returning data by reference requires that you first create a memory block to hold the return result and then return a pointer to that memory. As with other C programming environments, it is a complete no-no to return a pointer to a local variable from a UDF. Therefore, the SAPI provides the means to allocate itself blocks of memory.

In the code in Listing 10–19, line 66 uses SAPI's `mi_alloc()` call to request that the ORDBMS allocate a block of memory big enough to hold an `mi_decimal`. Then, line 67 uses another SAPI function to convert the double precision C variable into the format of a SQL decimal value and place it into the memory block. Finally, the UDF returns a pointer to this memory on line 69. Once the UDF returns, the ORDBMS function manager checks that the return type is not `NULL` and that the pointer returned to it is valid (i.e., refers to a valid memory location).

Memory management inside the ORDBMS is a complex issue. We devote a later section of this chapter to explaining it.

Error Handling

Errors are raised within the ORDBMS using the `mi_db_error_raise()` SAPI routine. It is important to understand that this call is just one aspect of a sophisticated event handling framework within the ORDBMS. Basically, `mi_db_error_raise()` initiates an exception or server message event. By default, this event is handled by the ORDBMS server. It might log a message to a file, push a message back to a client program through the SQL communications area, or terminate an in-flight transaction, but, in any case, you can also register callbacks with the server to undertake actions in response to exceptions.

Listing 10–20 illustrates how to generate an exception within a C UDF.

```
28      if (( nQuantity == 0 ) && (POS(dbPrice) < 0.01)) {
29          pGenCon = mi_open(NULL, NULL, NULL);
30          mi_db_error_raise (pGenCon, MI_EXCEPTION,
31          "Invalid INITIAL Transaction in NetCashEffect.");
32          /* not reached */
```

Listing 10–20. *Exceptions and Error Messages in C UDF*

On line 28, the UDF checks a condition. In this case, it ensures that the data values it is being passed contain valid information. If the data is not valid, the UDF gets a connection handle to the ORDBMS with the `mi_open()` SAPI call, and it immediately raises an `MI_EXCEPTION` with the appropriate error message. `mi_db_error_raise()` takes three arguments:

- A connection handle. By default, in a server UDF, you can supply a `NULL` value to this argument. For completeness on the client side, however, you can specify which of several open connections is the correct one.
- A flag. It indicates whether the exception is a message or an exception flag such as `MI_MESSAGE` or `MI_EXCEPTION`. Messages do not terminate current transactions. Exceptions do.
- A null terminated string. This string becomes the error message.

An important property of the `mi_db_error_raise()` SAPI call is evident when you call it to raise an `MI_EXCEPTION`, and it does not return. At this point, the ORDBMS takes over and aborts your current transaction. On the client side, the program that issued the SQL statement will receive an exception from the server, and the message is returned to the client to explain what happened.

Over the next few pages, we examine each aspect of creating a new UDF in more detail. If anything characterizes what it is like to work with user-defined functions, it is variety. Extensibility was conceived as a means of better addressing complexity, and complexity comes in numerous forms. Thus, we present a series of examples and explain how each works.

Argument Handling

Recall the variety of types, both built in and user defined, supported by the ORDBMS. Any of them can be passed as arguments to a C UDF, and C UDFs can return result values that are instances of any data type. Experience has shown that managing arguments is one of the more conceptually difficult aspects of UDF development. Thus, in this section, we try to cover as many different situations as we can.

As we said earlier, writing C UDFs is a lot such as writing C subroutines. However, what distinguishes working with C inside the IDS engine from working with C in other contexts is that the ORDBMS imposes a lot of rules about how it expects a UDF to behave. These rules are motivated by a desire to make the code as portable as possible between different hardware platforms. Implemented correctly, a C UDF can be moved between operating systems with minimal changes.

Detailed Rules for Passing Arguments

To understand how UDFs manage argument data, it is useful to first give a brief description of how subroutines are called at the lowest possible level within a computer; that is, at the level at which the machine code is executing.

To run a subroutine, the computer branches (jumps) out of a stream of instructions, and begins to execute another sequence at a different location. As part of this branch operation, variable values passed into the subroutine are placed on a runtime stack, where the subroutine's instructions can find them. Once completed, the subroutine also places its return result on the stack before branching (again) back to the next instruction in the original sequence. Each entry on the stack consists of one word—a block of data or an address pointing to where the data can be found.

When the ORDBMS function manager calls a UDF, it wraps each of the UDF's arguments into an MI_DATUM structure and places each on the stack in the appropriate order. An MI_DATUM is an ORDBMS data structure that is always a standard number of bytes in length. For 32-bit architectures, the MI_DATUM is a four-byte block of memory. Data values smaller than four bytes are promoted to four-byte units. Objects larger than four bytes are stored elsewhere in memory, and the four-byte MI_DATUM is used to hold the address of this object (a pointer).

In Figure 10–4 we illustrate what the computer's memory layout looks like when the ORDBMS call the NetCashEffect() UDF.

The detailed rules for argument handling in UDFs are as follows:

- Built-in data types of four bytes or less (except real[4]), and user-defined types of four bytes or less that are declared a PASSEDBY-VALUE (see the following explanation), are passed into the UDF by *value*; that is, the actual data value is placed into the stack. In the NetCashEffect() example, the third argument (nQuantity) is declared to be of mi_integer type, which is four bytes long.
- Data values shorter than four bytes are also passed as an MI_DATUM, even if they are actually shorter than a normal MI_DATUM length. They occupy one or more bytes of the MI_DATUM structure, with the other bytes zeroed out, as shown in the following explanation.
- Data values for types that could be more than four bytes long are passed in by *reference*; that is, the function manager creates a pointer to the actual data, and this pointer is passed to the function. Memory addresses are always the same size as an MI_DATUM. In the NetCash-Effect() function, the first, third, and fourth arguments—pdecPrice, plvTransType and pGen_FParam—are larger than four bytes in length. Thus, in each case, a pointer to the object is placed on the stack.

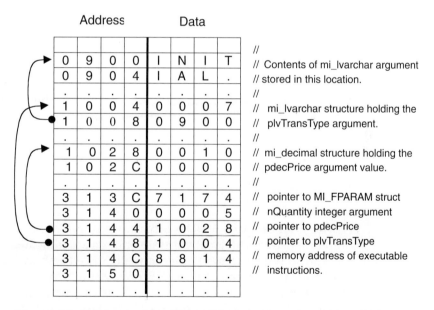

Figure 10–4. *Memory Map Illustrating Arguments Passed into UDF*

---

[4] Reals are a special case because on some machines, they exceed four bytes, but the safer rule can be applied everywhere.

- Meta-information about the arguments, such as each argument's type and whether an argument value is an OR-SQL NULL, is passed in as part of the MI_FPARAM structure. The MI_FPARAM structure is created by the ORDBMS to store information about the context within which the UDF is being invoked. Later in this chapter we describe it in more detail.

Except for certain support functions, and where the argument is declared to be an OUT parameter in the CREATE FUNCTION statement, arguments passed by reference should never be modified by the UDF.

Arguments Passed by Value

Consider a UDF in Listing 10–21. It takes two integer arguments (which are passed by value), adds them, and returns the result to the server. We present this AddEm() function in Listing 10–21.

```
20 mi_integer
21 AddEm (
22          mi_integer    nFirst,
23          mi_integer    nSecond,
24          MI_FPARAM   * genFParam
25          )
26 {
27    mi_integer nRetVal;
28    nRetVal = nFirst + nSecond;
29
30    return (nRetVal);
31 }
```

Listing 10–21. *Passing Arguments into User-Defined Functions by Value*

As you might expect, C UDFs follow all rules of the C language. For example, space for the local variable nRetVal is allocated off the stack, and so it is reclaimed automatically once the function exits. This variable has local scope; that is, it is only visible within the body of the function, but the effect of the return() instruction is to copy the value of nRetVal back onto the stack, and when the logic returns to the ORDBMS, it copies this return value off the stack and into another area of memory.

Arguments are passed by value for convenience. Their value can be accessed directly. Passing arguments by value simplifies UDF coding by allowing you to manage argument values in local variables.

Arguments Passed by Reference

Arguments are passed by reference to minimize the cost of calling the UDF. If the argument data object was very large, it would require significant computational overhead when the ORDBMS allocated stack space for it, copied it into that space, and so on. Accessing arguments passed by reference means reading the value of data in an area of memory pointed to by the argument.

For instance, consider the function implementation in Listing 10–22 taken from the `Period` BladeLet.

```
22
23 typedef struct          /* This is 8 bytes long, so */
24 {                       /* it will not be passable  */
25    mi_date     start;   /* by value. Instead, pass  */
26    mi_date     finish;  /* it by reference.         */
27 } Period;
28
29 mi_boolean DateWithinPeriod (
30 mi_date        Argument1,
31 Period     *   pArgument2,
32 MI_FPARAM *  Gen_fparam     )
33 {
34    mi_boolean Gen_RetVal=MI_FALSE;/* Default return    */
35                                   /*  value.  */
36    if ((pArgument2->start   <= Argument1) &&
37        (pArgument2->finish >= Argument1))
38      Gen_RetVal = MI_TRUE;
39
40    return Gen_RetVal;
41 }
42
```

Listing 10–22. *Passing Arguments into User-Defined Functions by Reference*

In this example, the `mi_date` argument `Argument1`, which is being four bytes long, will be passed by value. On the other hand the `Period`, which is `Argument2`, is eight bytes long, as you can tell from the definition of its structure. Therefore, it is passed by reference. Elements within the `Period` structure (which we show also in Listing 10–22) must be de-referenced using C language mechanisms.

Generally, any OPAQUE type extensions you create will be either larger than four bytes or of variable length. mi_lvarchar structures, and complex types such as ROW TYPE and COLLECTION, data are always passed by reference.

Argument Values Shorter than Four Bytes

The first argument in the function in Listing 10–23 has a single character argument, which is one byte long. We say that arguments of less than four bytes are *promoted* to four-byte data units. Thus, as far as your code is concerned, there is no difference because the compiler handles the transition as shown in Listing 10–23.

```
31 mi_integer
32 CalcQuantity (
33                    mi_char            cArgOne,
34                    mi_integer         nArgTwo,
35                    mi_real      *     prArgThree,
36                    MI_FPARAM    *     genFParam
37                 )
38 {
39    mi_integer         nRetVal;
40
41    switch(cArgOne)
42    {
43        case 'A':
44             nRetVal = nArgTwo;
45           break;
46        case 'B':
47             nRetVal = nArgTwo * (*prArgThree);
48           break;
49        case CC:
50             nRetVal = -nArgTwo;
51           break;
52        default:
53             nRetVal = 10;
54           break;
55    }
56    return (nRetVal);
57 }
```

Listing 10–23. *Arguments Shorter than Four Bytes Are Promoted and Passed by Value*

The place to worry about argument size issues is when you are calculating *stack space* to reserve for the UDF. You must remember to reserve four bytes for each argument and whatever memory is needed to hold local variables. Thus, `NetCashEffect()` reserves 44 bytes (16 for arguments and 28 for local variables), `AddEm()` requires 16 bytes (12 for arguments and 4 for local variables), and `CalcQuantity()` takes 20 (16 for arguments and 4 for local variables).

You should also be aware that the ORDBMS allocates stack space at the time that it calls a UDF. Subsequent calls within the compiled UDF body are invisible to the ORDBMS. Therefore, be careful that any recursive UDFs, or UDFs that call other libraries, do not exceed the stack space allocated for them. Stack space is set to 32K by default, but this can be modified in the `CREATE FUNCTION` statement or at the ORDBMS installation level.

Built-In Data Types

Each standard C data type has a SAPI wrapper to enhance portability, and for each of the built-in SQL data types, the SAPI supports a corresponding C data type or structure. In addition, the facilities used to handle the SQL built-in types in embedded SQL or CLI are available within SAPI. In Table 10–1 we present a list of the built-in SQL types, C primitives, and corresponding SAPI wrappers.

Table 10–1. SAPI Types and Their Corresponding C and SQL Types

SAPI Type	SQL-92 Type	C or ESQL Type	Description
mi_char, mi_char1, mi_int1	CHAR	char	Single-byte character.
mi_wchar		uint2	Unsigned double byte for global language support.
mi_string		char	Single byte that is typically used to declare a pointer to a null-terminated string.
mi_lvarchar	VARCHAR		Structure for variable length arrays of bytes not null terminated.
mi_integer	INTEGER	int, long	Signed integer that is typically four bytes long.
mi_int8	INT8	ifx_int8_t	Ten-byte structure.

(continued)

SAPI Type	SQL-92 Type	C or ESQL Type	Description
mi_smallint	SMALLINT	short	Two-byte integer value.
mi_double_precision	DOUBLE PRECISION	double	Eight-byte, double-precision number.
mi_real	REAL	float	Four-byte floating point number.
mi_interval	INTERVAL	intrvl_t	SQL-92 temporal interval.
mi_date	DATE	int	Date expressed as integer days since 1899/12/31.
mi_datetime	DATETIME	dtime_t	Date time in encapsulated structure.
mi_numeric, mi_decimal, mi_money	DECIMAL, NUMERIC, MONEY	dec_t	Floating point values up to a fixed precision. Note that a large set of macros and functions exists for manipulating this type because it is SQL-language specific.
mi_boolean	BOOLEAN		Boolean "t" or "f" type. A set of appropriate macros are defined for the boolean type.
mi_pointer		void *	A void pointer, used occasionally as arguments to special UDRs.

In earlier chapters we explained how building strongly typed schema (in which each kind of information is represented with a consistent data type) is a useful goal for your object-relational database. This might suggest that the support mechanisms in Table 10–1 are of limited utility. However, many SQL-level data types will be a DISTINCT TYPE of a built-in type. In these circumstances, the new type's C structure and the original type's structure are identical. Thus, these facilities work equally well with the new type.

Further, C structures used to define an OPAQUE TYPE will be composed out of these SAPI types too. For example, the Period OPAQUE TYPE includes two mi_date structures.

Variable Length Data

C-style null-terminated strings are unsuitable for managing variable length data inside the ORDBMS because they create performance problems as they are copied around in memory. The problems occur because the only way to discover the length of such a string is to count characters until you find the null character. They also create problems because variable-length binary data cannot be handled at all using this approach; it will have embedded zero characters.

Thus, SAPI uses a special data structure—called `mi_lvarchar`— together with a set of functions and macros to manage variable length data. `mi_lvarchar` data structures are actually two areas of memory.

Listing 10–24 provides a conceptual illustration of what an `mi_lvarchar` looks like. The actual implementation varies a little from platform to platform, so readers are advised to restrict themselves to using the SAPI facilities when working with such data structures.

```
typedef struct {
    mi_integer    len;
    mi_void     * data;
} mi_lvarchar;
```

Listing 10–24. *Definition of mi_lvarchar Structure*

The first part of an `mi_lvarchar` consists of an integer that stores the length —in bytes—of the data and a pointer referring to a chunk of memory that holds the actual data. Such a container allows variable length structures to be passed around efficiently within the ORDBMS server's memory. The second part of the structure is a pointer to the block of memory where the data object actually resides.

The code snippet in Listing 10–25 illustrates several points about `mi_lvarchar` structures. In it, a simple character array is used to construct an `mi_lvarchar`. Note that the data in the original variable (`pstrBuf`) is unaffected by this operation, and new memory is allocated to hold `pvlRetVal`.

```
mi_lvarchar * pvlRetVal;
    .
mi_string       pstrBuf[20];
    .
    .
strcpy( pstrBuf, "Paul Brown" );
    .
pvlRetVal = mi_string_to_lvarchar( pstrBuf );
    .
```

Listing 10–25. *Code Illustrating Use of mi_lvarchar Structure*

There are several things to note about using the `mi_lvarchar` structure:

- First, data in a `mi_lvarchar` structure, unlike C strings, is not null terminated. This means that you should not use the standard C library string routines (`strlen()`, `strcpy()`, and so on) with `mi_lvarchar` data. Instead, you should use the SAPI routines to transform between `mi_lvarchar` structures to null-terminated strings before using the standard C functions.
- Second, the variable length array is stored in a continuous hunk of memory. Thus, embedding pointers within `mi_lvarchar` data is a very bad idea. When you need to free the memory allocated to an `mi_lvarchar`, or create a new copy of one, the ORDBMS has no understanding of what is contained within the data element. This also explains why it is very important to use the `mi_var_free()` call to free `mi_lvarchar` instances; this call frees both the structure and its associated area of memory.
- Third, notice how general purpose the structure is. The `mi_lvar-char` type is appropriate for strings of characters, or arrays of other data types, and even binary data.

Figure 10–5 illustrates what the situation would be once the `mi_string_to_lvarchar()` function in the code fragment has been executed. The memory map shows how the variables in Listing 10–25 are laid out in memory.

The server's DataBlade API provides a set of functions to work with `mi_lvarchar` objects. These facilities allow you to create new `mi_lvarchar` instances, copy `mi_lvarchar` objects, access the

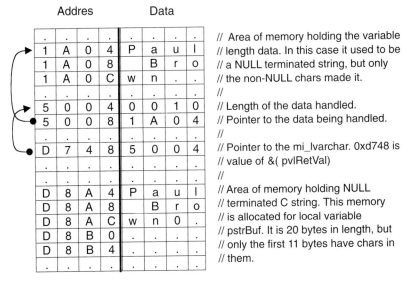

Figure 10–5. *Memory Map of the mi_lvarchar Data Structure from Listing 10–22.*

innards of an `mi_lvarchar`, and transform data between null terminated C strings and `mi_lvarchar` objects. Table 10–2 lists most of the routines and macros provided within SAPI to manipulate `mi_lvarchar` data instances.

Table 10–2. mi_lvarchar Manipulation Facilities

SAPI Function	Description

`mi_string *`
`mi_lvarchar_to_string (`
          `mi_lvarchar * );`
	Places a null-terminated copy of the string in the `mi_lvarchar` argument into a new buffer. Memory to hold the new value is allocated within the SAPI function. Freeing that memory must be handled using `mi_free()`.

`mi_lvarchar *`
`mi_string_to_lvarchar (`
          `mi_string * );`
	Copies the null-terminated string argument into a new `mi_lvarchar` buffer. Memory to hold the new value is allocated within the SAPI function. Freeing that memory must be handled using `mi_var_free()`.

`mi_lvarchar *`
`mi_new_var (`
          `mi_integer n );`
	Creates a new, variable-length array data structure with enough space to hold *n* bytes of data. Memory to hold the new value is allocated within the SAPI function. Freeing that memory must be handled using `mi_var_free()`.

`void mi_var_free (` `mi_lvarchar *);`	Frees the structure created with an mi_new_var(). In fact, this is just a shim for the more general mi_free() SAPI call, but it is provided in the API for symmetry.

`mi_lvarchar *`
`mi_var_copy (`
          `mi_lvarchar * );`
	Creates a complete copy of the data structure passed as the argument. Note that this is *only* a copy of the argument's data. If the data structure being copied includes an MI_LOHANDLE, the large object itself is not copied. This becomes important when you start using multi-representational data types. Memory to hold the new value is allocated within the SAPI function. Freeing that memory must be handled using `mi_var_free()`.

`void`
`mi_lvarchar_to_buffer (`
          `mi_lvarchar *,`
          `mi_char * );`
	This API function takes the contents of the first argument and copies it into the buffer referenced by the second. Of course, there must be enough space in the target buffer to accept the data.

`mi_integer`
`mi_get_varlen (`
          `mi_lvarchar * )`
	Returns the number of bytes of data in the `mi_lvarchar`.

`mi_char *`
`mi_get_vardata (`
          `mi_lvarchar *)`
	Returns a pointer to the start of the data in the `mi_lvarchar` structure.

The code in Listing 10–26 illustrates how these functions are used. Algorithmically, this UDF is not as efficient as it might be because it was written with a secondary intention of illustrating how to use the SAPI calls.

```
102 mi_lvarchar *
103 CConcat (
104           mi_lvarchar    * pvlArgOne,
105           mi_lvarchar    * pvlArgTwo,
106           MI_FPARAM      * genFParam
107 )
108 {   mi_lvarchar  * pvlRetVal;
109     mi_string    * pchRetVal;
110     mi_string    * pchArgOne;
111     mi_string    * pchArgTwo;
112 /*
113 ** Create memory block to hold result. Extra two bytes
114 ** for space and NULL.(varlen is data length only.)
115 */
116     pchRetVal = mi_alloc( mi_get_varlen ( pvlArgOne ) +
117                         mi_get_varlen ( pvlArgTwo ) + 2);
118 /*
119 ** Create a pair of NULL terminated strings that copy
120 ** data carried in the mi_lvarchar arguments. Note
121 ** that these new strings are copies of the argument
122 ** data, and may be modified safely within the UDF.
123 */
124     pchArgOne = mi_lvarchar_to_string ( pvlArgOne );
125     pchArgTwo = mi_lvarchar_to_string ( pvlArgTwo );
126 /*
127 ** Use standard CC string manipulation, to
128 ** concatenate the argument strings.
129 */
130     sprintf(pchRetVal,"%s %s", pchArgOne, pchArgTwo );
131 /*
132 ** Finally, use the following SAPI call to create a
133 ** new mi_lvarchar object containing the same
134 ** characters as the CC string. Then return a pointer
135 **  to it.
136 */
137     pvlRetVal  = mi_string_to_lvarchar ( pchRetVal );
138
139     return pvlRetVal;
140 }
```

Listing 10–26. *Illustrating mi_lvarchar's Support Routines* mi_lvarchar structures also can be used to hold variable length binary data. Because of the diversity of binary data formats, SAPI's mi_lvarchar facilities focus on enabling UDFs to place their binary data within an mi_lvarchar and on getting it out again.

In Listing 10–27 we present a code snippet illustrating how to use binary data in conjunction mi_lvarchar structures. Assume that the BasicObject type is a variable length array of some other structure. This UDF parses the input string (Gen_Param1) and extracts the number of objects—which may be the first number in the string—and then the list of objects within it.

```
66
67 mi_lvarchar *
68 Basic_Variable_Length_Type_Input (
69                    mi_lvarchar * Gen_param1,
70                    MI_FPARAM    * Gen_fparam   )
71 {
    .
86   mi_lvarchar * Gen_RetVal; /* Return pointer       */
87   BasicObject * pvBasicObj; /* Ptr to variable length */
88                             /* array of binary objects*/
89                             /* within Gen_RetVal->data*/
90   mi_integer    nCnt        /* Num of binary objects  */
91                             /* in the array.          */
92   mi_char *     pObject;    /* Ptr to a binary data   */
93                             /* block created from the */
94                             /* second argument (which */
95                             /* is probably a string). */
    .
103 /*  Calculate size of variable length binary object  */
104     Gen_UDTSize = nCnt * sizeof(BasicObject);
    .
115 /* Allocate a new mi_lvarchar to hold return result. */
116     Gen_RetVal = mi_new_var( Gen_UDTSize );
117 /* Get handle to mem allocated for the mi_lvarchar   */
118     pvBasicObj=
119                 (BasicObject *)mi_get_vardata(Gen_RetVal);
    .
128 /* At this point, the code would loop over the data  */
129 /* extracted from the Gen_param1 parameter, and it   */
130 /* would copy that data at the offset into the       */
131 /* mi_lvarchar->data block one object at a time.      */
    .
```

```
153    memcpy ( &pvBasicObj[offset], pObject, nLen);
       .
170 /* But instead of returning pointer to the array of   */
171 /* BasicObject, the UDF returns a pointer to the       */
172 /* mi_lvarchar structure that contains the variable    */
173 /* length array of nCnt BasicObject data objects.       */
174
175     return ( Gen_RetVal );
176 }
```

Listing 10–27. *Using mi_lvarchar to Work with Binary Data*

Many of the code examples shipped with this book illustrate how to
work with variable length binary objects. Consult that source for more
complete examples. `mi_lvarchar` is perhaps the most common SAPI
facility used in C UDF extensions. Whenever a string or a variable
length binary object is passed from a client program, it is handled
within an `mi_lvarchar`.

ROW TYPEs and C UDFs

C UDFs can accept ROW TYPE arguments and return ROW TYPE
instances as results. In addition, the server's facilities for managing
OR-SQL requires that query results be processed as a series of ROW
TYPE instances. Thus, SAPI contains facilities—data structures, functions, and macros—for storing ROW TYPE data objects, prying them
apart, creating new ones, and so on.

When you create an EXTERNAL UDF that takes a named ROW TYPE
argument, you use the ROW TYPE's OR-SQL name to specify the parameter in the CREATE FUNCTION statement. However, when the
ORDBMS invokes the UDF body, it passes into it a pointer to a generic
SAPI data structure, which is called an MI_ROW. The data block pointed
to by the MI_ROW contains the actual values.

Each MI_ROW contains a definition of its structure, in addition to the
actual data values it contains. The composition of the ROW TYPE—
number of elements, element names, data types, and so on—can be
accessed using SAPI facilities. This makes the MI_ROW useful as a general–purpose container for passing data around and as a mechanism
for passing specific ROW TYPE instances.

Consider a Currency ROW TYPE that stores a quantity of money and
the respective currency denomination. Our Movies-R-Us Web site may
use this type to store information about the prices of merchandise
items. Such a type may be defined as shown in Listing 10–28.

```
CREATE ROW TYPE Currency (
    Units           Currency_Unit NOT NULL,
    Quantity        decimal(14,4) NOT NULL
);
```

Listing 10–28. *Currency ROW TYPE Declaration*

A useful routine might extract the Quantity value from an instance of such a ROW TYPE. (Note that using cascading-dot notation would be a simpler way to achieve the same result.) Such a routine is defined in OR-SQL as shown in Listing 10–29.

```
CREATE FUNCTION GetQuantity( Currency )
RETURNS decimal(14,4)
WITH ( NOT VARIANT, PARALLELIZABLE )
EXTERNAL NAME
"$INFORMIXDIR/extend/bin/Currency.bld(CurrencyGetQuantity)"
LANGUAGE C;
```

Listing 10–29. *Creating an EXTERNAL FUNCTION Taking a ROW TYPE Argument*

The C implementation would receive an MI_ROW structure for the argument. MI_ROW objects are always larger than four bytes, so they are always passed by reference. Access to the information contained within a ROW TYPE instance is handled using a set of functions that are part of the SAPI infrastructure. The most important of these is the mi_value() function.

In Listing 10–30 we illustrate how you might implement such a UDF in C.

```
15
16 mi_decimal *
17 CurrencyGetQuantity (
18     MI_ROW     * pRowTCurrency, /* MI_ROW as Argument    */
19     MI_FPARAM  * Gen_FParam
20 )
21 {
22     MI_DATUM    pdatQuantityRowVal;/* Value and size    */
23     mi_integer  nQuantityLength;   /* of MI_ROW data. */
24
25 /*
26 ** Extract the element from within the ROW TYPE
27 ** argument that has the index value '1' (i.e. the
```

```
28  ** second element). Place a reference to it into the
29  ** MI_DATUM structure, and record its length in the
30  **  mi_integer. Use the mi_value() SAPI call to
31  */ accomplish this.
32     if((mi_value(pRowTCurrency,
33                 1,
34            &pdatQuantityRowVal,
35            &nQuantityLength    ))!= MI_NORMAL_VALUE)
36     {
37         mi_db_error_raise((MI_CONNECTION *)NULL,
38                          MI_EXCEPTION,
39   "CurrencyGetQuantity:          Error in mi_value()");
40                                    /* not reached */
41     }
42     return (mi_decimal *)pdatQuantityRowVal;
43 }
```

Listing 10–30. *Implementing an EXTERNAL FUNCTION Taking a ROW TYPE Argument*

Listing 10–30 shows how to use the `mi_value()` SAPI call to extract data from within a ROW TYPE argument. `mi_value()` (or another related function called `mi_value_by_name()`) creates a copy of the data in a specified element of the ROW TYPE , and then returns this copy to the UDF as an MI_DATUM.

In Listing 10–31 we present the definition for these SAPI functions.

```
mi_integer                    mi_integer
mi_value (                    mi_value_by_name (
    MI_ROW *row,                  MI_ROW     * row,
    mi_integer column_no,         char       * column_name,
    MI_DATUM *retbuf,             MI_DATUM   * retbuf,
    mi_integer *retlen);          mi_integer *retlen);
```

Listing 10–31. *SAPI Functions to Extract Values from a MI_ROW Instance*

In both functions in Listing 10–31, the first argument is the ROW TYPE from which the value is being extracted. The second is an index to an element within the ROW TYPE. In Listing 10–30 note how this value is set to 1, although Quantity is the *second* element. The index is an off-set value, so the first element has an index of 0. `mi_value_by_name()` accepts a null-terminated character string (the element name) instead of an index value.

The third argument to mi_value() is a pointer to an MI_DATUM structure. If the mi_value() call is successful, this is where the extracted data element, or a pointer to it, is placed. The final argument to mi_value() is used to communicate the length of the data value retrieved from the ROW TYPE.

Most of the confusion about mi_value() is related to the way in which that data is returned by reference through the third argument. Recall our discussion about MI_DATUM, which is a special type that is used to store either an actual data value (if that value is four bytes or less in size) or a pointer to a data value. In Listing 10–30 mi_decimal data is more than twenty bytes in length, so the value stored in the MI_DATUM *pointed to by the argument* is a reference. Memory to hold the actual data is allocated within mi_value().

Until it is executed, the UDF logic may not know what data type will be found in the ROW TYPE element, and depending on whether the element contains a NULL, a complex type (ROW TYPE or COLLECTION), or a normal UDT, the surrounding code needs to take different action. Thus, the integer returned by these two SAPI routines indicates what has been placed into the MI_DATUM structure. Table 10–3 lists the range of possible return values.

Table 10–3. Return Values from mi_value

Return Value (Macro)	Explanation
MI_NORMAL_VALUE	MI_DATUM contains either the value itself or a pointer to the value. The rules governing what is returned are the same as the rules governing how data is passed into an EXTERNAL UDF.
MI_NULL_VALUE	The element in the ROW TYPE was marked as NULL.
MI_ROW_VALUE	The element was itself a ROW TYPE. Frequently, it can be useful to make the logic extracting elements recursive.
MI_COLLECTION_VALUE	The ROW TYPE element was a COLLECTION.
MI_ERROR	The call encountered an error.

Returning ROW TYPE values from an EXTERNAL C UDF means using another family of SAPI facilities. Before it can be returned, the UDF logic must create a new MI_ROW with the desired structure and populate it with the appropriate data. This means working with a pair of SAPI structures we have not yet introduced: MI_TYPEID and MI_ROW_DESC.

MI_TYPEID is an internal identifier assigned to all types in the ORDBMS (including a previously unseen and unnamed ROW TYPE). An MI_TYPEID can be created in several ways, but the most convenient approach is simply to use a string that either names an existing type or that defines the type's structure. When returning MI_ROW objects from within a C UDF, the MI_TYPEID is used to create a description of the ROW TYPE being returned.

Each MI_ROW carries within it an explanation of its OR-SQL level structure. SAPI uses the MI_ROW_DESC to represent this. MI_ROW_DESC objects can be extracted from an MI_ROW, which was passed into the UDF as an argument, or an MI_ROW_DESC can be created to define the format of a new MI_ROW instance.

The SAPI calls for working with MI_TYPEID and MI_ROW_DESC are listed in Table 10–4. Note that many of them require a connection to the database within which the SAPI call is executing because ROW TYPE structures and identifiers are only unique within a single database. These calls will return a NULL if an error is detected. Errors can occur when, for example, the type string fails to identify a data type or the type ID is not a valid row type.

Table 10–4. SAPI Functions Used for Working With MI_ROW

SAPI Function	Description

MI_TYPEID *
mi_typename_to_id (
     MI_CONNECTION *conn,
     mi_lvarchar *name)
	Given a type's name formatted as an mi_lvarchar, it returns a pointer to an ID.

MI_TYPEID *
mi_typestring_to_id (
     MI_CONNECTION *conn,
     mi_string *name   )
	Given a type's name formatted as a NULL-terminated C string, it returns a pointer to an ID.

MI_ROW_DESC * mi_row_desc_create (MI_TYPEID *type_id)	Given a TYPEID, it returns the MI_ROW_DESC structure.
void mi_row_desc_free (MI_ROW_DESC *rowdesc)	This frees the memory associated with the MI_ROW_DESC and all other memory referred to from within it. Do not use mi_free() on any of these structures.

MI_ROW *
mi_row_create (
   MI_CONNECTION *conn,
   MI_ROW_DESC   *rowdesc,
   MI_DATUM   coldata[],
   Mi_boolean colisnull[]
	Given a description of the row (MI_ROW_DESC), and two arrays containing i. the data elements for the array (coldata), and ii. whether or not the element is NULL (colisnull), this call returns a well-formed MI_ROW instance.

mi_integer mi_row_free (MI_ROW *row)	If at any time some code needs to free an MI_ROW, it should use this call. Do not mi_free() MI_ROW instances.

The code snippet in Listing 10–32 illustrates how these SAPI calls are used. CurrencyConvert() takes an instance of the Currency ROW TYPE introduced in Listing 10–28, and a second argument which is the denomination of the currency—US Dollars, British Pounds, Zambian Kwacha—that the value in the first argument is to be converted to. Achieving this requires that the UDF extract data from the argument and create a new MI_ROW to return.

```
281  MI_ROW *
282  CurrencyConvert (
283  MI_ROW         *  pRowCurrency,
284  mi_integer        nArgToUnit,
285  MI_FPARAM      *  Gen_FParam
286  )
287  {
  .
293      MI_ROW                  * prowRetVal;
294      MI_ROW_DESC             * pOutRowDesc;
295      MI_CONNECTION           * Gen_Conn;
296      MI_DATUM                  arDatums[2];
297      mi_boolean                arIsNull[2];
298

  .
 /* Missing code would use mi_value() to extract elements
 ** from the arguments, look-up the conversion rate, do
 ** the conversion and place the new quantity into
 ** decOutQuantity local variable.
 */

  .
329 /*
330 **  Now you need to create an MI_ROW for the return
331 ** value. To do this, you need a description of the
332 ** 'Currency'TYPE and a pair of arrays containing the
333 ** data values, and whether any of the values are NULL.
334 ** In this case, the ROW TYPE doesn't take NULLs so
335 */ this is redundant.
336      Gen_Conn = mi_open(NULL, NULL, NULL);
337      pOutRowDesc = mi_row_desc_create(
338                     mi_typestring_to_id(Gen_Conn,
339                                            "currency"));
340
341      arDatums[0]=(MI_DATUM)nArgToUnit;
342      arIsNull[0]= MI_FALSE;
343      arDatums[1]=(MI_DATUM)&decOutQuantity;
```

```
344      arIsNull[1]=MI_FALSE;
345
346      if ((prowRetVal = mi_row_create(Gen_Conn,
347                                          pOutRowDesc,
348                                          arDatums,
349                                          arIsNull)) == NULL)
350          mi_db_error_raise(Gen_Conn, MI_EXCEPTION,
351                                  "Failed to create row.");
352
353      mi_close(Gen_Conn);
354
355      return prowRetVal;
356  }
```

Listing 10–32. C UDF Example Returning ROW TYPE Result

Before leaving this subject, a word of practical advice is in order:
Using SPL to access named ROW TYPE innards is only a little less efficient than using C, and it is a lot easier because packing and unpack-
ing ROW TYPE instances is relatively expensive and tends to dominate
the cost of running the UDF. However, there are things that can be
done using C, such as passing unnamed ROW TYPE arguments, which
are impossible in SPL.

COLLECTION Types and C UDFs

COLLECTION objects can be passed into UDFs as arguments and
returned as results. SAPI provides a set of routines for extracting data
elements from a COLLECTION, creating new COLLECTION instances,
and modifying the contents of a COLLECTION. However, it is difficult to
write general purpose UDFs that cater to COLLECTION data in general,
such as when a UDF returns a COLLECTION that is the intersection of
two or more COLLECTION instances. Functions performing actions over
specifically defined COLLECTION, a SET of LVARCHAR, for example, is
more common.

SAPI facilities for handling collections include two data structures:
MI_COLLECTION and MI_COLL_DESC. The first of these holds informa-
tion about a COLLECTION instance. The second is a handle to an open
COLLECTION and is used whenever your code accesses data within a
COLLECTION. In Table 10–5 we list a subset of the routines SAPI pro-
vides to work with COLLECTION data in C.

Table 10–5. SAPI Facilities for Managing COLLECTION Data Structures

SAPI Function	Description
| ```
MI_COLLECTION *
mi_collection_create (
    MI_CONNECTION *,
    MI_TYPEID    * );
``` | It creates internal memory structures for storing metadata about a COLLECTION and for storing data in the COLLECTION. The MI_TYPEID, for example, comes from mi_typestring_to_id(). |
| ```
MI_COLL_DESC *
mi_collection_open (
    MI_CONNECTION *,
    MI_COLLECTION * );
``` | It opens a COLLECTION in preparation for inserting new elements into it or reading elements from it. The structure referenced by this SAPI routine's return result is used to mediate read and write operations over the COLLECTION. |
| ```
mi_integerG
mi_collection_insert (
    MI_CONNECTION *,
    MI_COLL_DESC  *,
    MI_DATUM,
    MI_CURSOR_ACTION,
    mi_integer );
``` | Given an open COLLECTION ( MI_COLL_DESC from mi_collection_open() ), this SAPI routine inserts the object in the third MI_DATUM argument into it. Depending on the value supplied to the fourth and fifth argument, the object will be inserted at different offset locations within the COLLECTION. As with all the other write operations on COLLECTION instances, this SAPI routine enforces the rules for the COLLECTION. |
| ```
mi_integer
mi_collection_fetch (
    MI_CONNECTION *,
    MI_COLL_DESC  *,
    MI_CURSOR_ACTION,
    mi_integer,
    MI_DATUM *,
    mi_integer * );
``` | It fetches an element from COLLECTION. The element fetched is determined by what is in the third and fourth argument. Fetched data is placed into locations specified by the fifth and sixth arguments, which behave exactly like their counterparts in the mi_value() SAPI routines. The return result indicates success or failure. |
| ```
MI_COLLECTION *
mi_collection_copy (
    MI_CONNECTION *,
    MI_COLLECTION *);
``` | It creates a complete copy of COLLECTION passed as the second argument. |
| ```
mi_integer
mi_collection_close (
    MI_CONNECTION *,
    MI_COLL_DESC  *) ;
``` | It closes an open COLLECTION. The symmetric operation is mi_collection_open(). |
| ```
Mi_integer
mi_collection_free (
    MI_CONNECTION *,
    MI_COLLECTION * );
``` | It frees memory and data structures associated with the COLLECTION argument. The symmetric operation is mi_collection_create(). In case it needs re-stating, do not use mi_free() with a COLLECTION. |
```

One kind of COLLECTION, a set of mi_lvarchar objects, provides the grist of the example in Listing 10–33. This listing was taken from the Split() code accompanying this book. This UDF takes a string argument and returns a new COLLECTION that contains a set of elements, one for each word in the argument string. It literally splits the first argument into separate words. Split() takes a second argument that contains a set of potential delimiter characters.

```
10 /*
11 **   OR-SQL to install this UDF.
12 **
13 **   CREATE FUNCTION SPLIT ( lvarchar, lvarchar )
14 **   RETURNING LIST( lvarchar NOT NULL )
15 **   WITH ( NOT VARIANT )
16 **   EXTERNAL NAME
17 **   "$INFORMIXDIR/extend. . .(StringSplit)"
18 **   LANGUAGE C;
19 **/
  .
23
24   MI_COLLECTION *
25   StringSplit (
26   mi_lvarchar * pvlArg,
27   mi_lvarchar * pvlSplitDelim,
28   MI_FPARAM    * Gen_Fparam     /* Standard - DBDK docs.  */
29   )
30   {
31      MI_CONNECTION * Gen_Con;       /* Connectn handle   */
32      MI_TYPEID     * Gen_TypeId;    /* Collectn typeID   */
33      MI_COLLECTION * Gen_RetVal;    /* Return value      */
34      MI_COLL_DESC  * Gen_OutCollDesc;/* Collectn descr   */
35      mi_integer      Gen_Result;    /* INSERT return val */
36      mi_string     * pchSplitDelim; /* Delim string      */
37
38      mi_lvarchar   * pvlLVToInput;  /* Word to INSERT    */
39      mi_string     * pchInputStr;   /* String for word   */
40      mi_string     * pchPrev;       /* Pointers to walk  */
41      mi_string     * pchCurr;       /* argument data     */
42      mi_integer      i;             /* loop counter      */
43
44      /* Get MI_CONNECTION. Used by SAPI routines.      */
45      Gen_Con = mi_open( NULL, NULL, NULL );
46
47      /* Get the MI_TYPEID for the new COLLECTION       */
```

```
48      Gen_TypeId = mi_typestring_to_id(
49                              Gen_Con,
50                              "list(lvarchar not null)");
51
52      /* Create COLLECTION to insert return results into*/
53      Gen_RetVal = mi_collection_create ( Gen_Con,
54                                      Gen_TypeId );
55
56      /* Open collection for use and get handle.        */
57      Gen_OutCollDesc = mi_collection_open(Gen_Con,
58                                      Gen_RetVal);
59      /*
60      **  Now, loop through Input String, clipping as I
61      **  go. Break it into little words, all in a row.
62      **/
63
64      pchSplitDelim= mi_lvarchar_to_string (pvlSplitDelim);
65      pchInputStr  = mi_lvarchar_to_string ( pvlArg );
66
67      /* Step over prefixed delimiters                   */
68      while( strspn( pchInputStr, pchSplitDelim) > 0)
69          pchInputStr++;
70
71      pchPrev = pchCurr = pchInputStr;
72
73      i=0;
74      while (i!=1)
75      {
76          if ((strspn(pchCurr,pchSplitDelim)!=0)||
77                  (*pchCurr == '\0'))
78          {
79              if (strspn(pchCurr,pchSplitDelim)!=0)
80                  *pchCurr = '\0';
81              else
82                  i = 1;
83
84              pvlLVToInput = mi_string_to_lvarchar (pchPrev);
85
86              /* INSERT mi_lvarchar into the COLLECTION */
87              Gen_Result    = mi_collection_insert(Gen_Con,
88                                      Gen_OutCollDesc,
89                                      pvlLVToInput,
90                                      MI_CURSOR_LAST,
91                                      0);
92              pchPrev = pchCurr + 1;
```

```
93           }
94          pchCurr++;
95      }
96
97      /* Close the open COLLECTION                    */
98      mi_collection_close( Gen_Con, Gen_OutCollDesc );
99
100     /* Close this for perfection.                    */
101     mi_close ( Gen_Con );
102
103     return Gen_RetVal;
104  }
105
```

Listing 10–33. *Split() Takes Word String and Delimiters and Returns* COLLECTION

As you can no doubt tell from the amount of code here, stored pro-cedure language is generally a better choice for working with COLLEC-TION data. Most of the overhead in managing a COLLECTION in SAPI is incurred within the COLLECTION management module itself (the mi_collection_ interface in SAPI), so your choice of mechanism for implementing the rest of the UDF is less important than for other kinds of UDF.

OUT Parameters

Chapter 5 introduced the concept of OUT Parameters. This is a mecha-nism in which a data object may be passed into a UDF by reference and modified within the UDF. OUT parameters are closely associated with the concept of statement local variables (SLV). In brief, when the ORDBMS sees a SLV in a query, it allocates memory to hold it. Then, as it processes data as part of the query execution, it passes pointers to the SLV memory into each UDF in turn.

In Listing 10–34 we illustrate how OUT Parameters work with C UDFs.

```
585  /*
586  **   PeriodOverlapRetVal
587  **
588  **   Takes two Period arguments, and a third INTEGER
589  **   OUT parameter. If the two Period arguments
590  **   overlap, it returns MI_TRUE as a result, and into
591  **   the OUT parameter it places the number of days
592  **   that the two Overlap. If the two Periods do not
593  **   Overlap, the UDF returns FALSE, and the OUT
594  **   Parameter will hold a NULL.
595  **
```

```
596  **  This UDF is declared as follows:
597  **
598  CREATE FUNCTION Overlap (Period,Period, OUT INTEGER)
599  RETURNS boolean
600  WITH ( NOT VARIANT, PARALLELIZABLE )
601  EXTERNAL NAME
602  "$INFORMIXDIR/extend/. . .(PeriodOverlapRetVal)"
603  LANGUAGE C;
604  **
605  **  It would be used to calculate the
606  ** total number of days that Reservations overlapped
607  ** Conferences within some period of time.
608  **  SELECT  C.Conf_Name,
609  **           SUM(Calc_Days)
610  **    FROM Conferences C, Reservations R
611  **    WHERE Overlap(C.Duration,
612  **                    '01/01/2000 to 03/31/2000')
613  **      AND Overlap(C.Duration,R.Reservation,
614  **                    Calc_Days # INTEGER )
615  **    GROUP BY C.Conf_Name;
616  **
617  **/
618  mi_integer
619  PeriodOverlapRetVal
620  (
621  Period *     Argument1,
622  Period *     Argument2,
623  mi_integer  * nRetInterval,
624  MI_FPARAM      *    gen_fParam
625  )
626  {
627      mi_integer  Gen_RetVal;
628      mi_fp_setargisnull(gen_fParam, 2, MI_TRUE);
629
630      if (( Gen_RetVal = PeriodOverlap ( Argument1,
631                                          Argument2,
632                                          gen_fParam ))
633          == MI_TRUE )
634      {
635          mi_fp_setargisnull(gen_fParam, 2, MI_FALSE);
636
637          *nRetInterval = ((MIN( Argument1->finish,
638                              Argument2->finish )) -
639                          (MAX( Argument1->start,
640                              Argument2->start))));
641      }
642      return Gen_RetVal;
643 }
```

Listing 10–34. *External UDF that Includes an OUT PARAMETER*

Note in this listing that although the OUT PARAMETER is an INTE-
GER, it is passed into this UDF by reference, rather than by value. Passing by reference is always the strategy used for an OUT PARAMETER
because the memory to hold the corresponding statement local variable is maintained by the ORDBMS.

MI_TYPEID and MI_TYPEDESC

Sometimes it is useful for a UDF to know something about the types of
the arguments it is passed. Recall that data type inheritance, and the
CAST mechanism, mean that a UDF defined with one data type might
be used over a completely different kind of type in an OR-SQL query.

Additional information about the types being passed into a UDF
can be retrieved using information in the MI_FPARAM structure. SAPI
provides two structures for representing type information: MI_TYPEID
(which was introduced earlier) and MI_TYPE_DESC. The chief use for
MI_TYPEID is to get an MI_TYPE_DESC structure containing descriptive
information about the type; the type's name, its length, its owner (or
creator), and so on.

The UDF example in Listing 10–35 illustrates how to use the various
SAPI calls you would use to access this information. It also illustrates
several other SAPI routines for answering questions about the context
within which the UDF is called—such as whether or not an argument
is NULL—and it is used to indicate that a UDF return value is NULL.

In the code, we make use of the mi_type_name() SAPI call to get
the type's name from its descriptor. There are other SAPI calls to
extract information about the type instance. This information includes
its length or its precision (if it is a decimal type). You can also extract
information about the type in general.

```
163   /*
164   **    Function: WhatIsTypeName
165   **
166   **    About:
167   **
168   **      This illustrates how to use MI_TYPEID and
169   **    MI_TYPE_DESC structures (and their functions) to
170   **    extract argument type information.
171   **
172   **
173   **      This function takes three arguments. The
174   **    first two are INTEGER and LVARCHAR. The last
175   **    is an INTEGER that is either a 1 or 2. The
```

```
176  **  function returns the name of the data type passed
177  **  in as the nth argument, where n is the final
178  **  argument value.
179  **    This is defined in the following way.
180  **
181  CREATE FUNCTION WhatIsTypeName ( INTEGER, LVARCHAR,
182                                          INTEGER )
183  RETURNS LVARCHAR
184  WITH ( HANDLESNULLS, NOT VARIANT )
185  EXTERNAL NAME
186  '$INFORMIXDIR/extend/bin/ArgsExmp.bld(WhatIsTypeName)'
187  LANGUAGE C;
188  **
189  **/
190  mi_lvarchar *
191  WhatIsTypeName (
192  mi_integer  nIntegerArg,
193  mi_lvarchar  *  plvSecondArg,
194  mi_integer  nThirdArg,
195  MI_FPARAM      * genFParam
196  )
197  {
198      mi_integer i, nVal,nBest, nCounted = 0;
199      mi_lvarchar * plvRetVal;
200      mi_string    * pstrTypeName;
201
202      MI_TYPEID    * pTypeId;
203      MI_TYPE_DESC * ptypeDesc;
204
205      if (((mi_fp_argisnull(genFParam,2)) == MI_TRUE) ||
206          ((nThirdArg < 1) || (nThirdArg > 2)))
207          mi_db_error_raise( (MI_CONNECTION *)NULL,
208                  MI_EXCEPTION,
209  "Error: WhatIsType third arg not 1,2,3");
210      if ((mi_fp_argisnull(genFParam,(nThirdArg-1)))
211
212          == MI_TRUE)
213      {
214          mi_fp_setreturnisnull(genFParam,0,MI_TRUE);
215          plvRetVal = (mi_lvarchar *)NULL;
216      } else {
217          ptypeDesc = mi_type_typedesc(
218                  (MI_CONNECTION *)NULL,
```

```
219                    mi_fp_argtype(genFParam,(nThirdArg-1))
220                         );
221
222          pstrTypeName = mi_type_full_name(ptypeDesc);
223          plvRetVal   = mi_string_to_lvarchar(pstrTypeName);
224     }
225
226     return plvRetVal;
227 }
```

Listing 10–35. UDF Illustrating Use of SAPI to Access Data Type
Information

The information that the IDS engine passes to the UDF refers to the
data type passed into the function at the OR-SQL level. This means
that if the argument's data type is a DISTINCT TYPE, or a ROW TYPE
created under another ROW TYPE in an inheritance hierarchy, the
name in the pstrTypeName string is the name of the actual type.

The OR-SQL statements in Listing 10–36 illustrate what this looks
like. These statements show the WhatIsTypeName() function being
called several times with different arguments and different results.

```
EXECUTE FUNCTION WhatIsTypeName(1,'Foo',1);

integer

EXECUTE FUNCTION WhatIsTypeName(1,'Foo',2);

lvarchar

CREATE DISTINCT TYPE ShortString AS LVARCHAR;

EXECUTE FUNCTION WhatIsTypeName(1,'Foo'::ShortString,2);

Shortstring
```

Listing 10–36. Executing the WhatIsTypeName() User-Defined Function

You rarely need these SAPI facilities in UDFs written to support new
data types. Certain kinds of generic extensions are, however, required
to be able to determine type information at runt-time.

MI_FPARAM Argument: Structure and Uses

The `MI_FPARAM` argument is a reference to a data structure created by the ORDBMS to hold information about the query context within which the UDF is being called. Before it executes a query, the ORDBMS allocates a block of memory for each UDF mentioned in the query. (In fact, when it is employing parallel query processing, the ORDBMS allocates one such structure per UDF *per thread*.) It passes a pointer to this memory into the UDF each time it calls the function.

If the UDF is called multiple times as the query executes, the ORDBMS will pass the same reference each time; that is, the `MI_FPARAM` structure remains in place for the duration of the entire query, although its values can be read and changed by UDF logic each time the ORDBMS calls the UDF.

The `MI_FPARAM` structure contains the following:

- A list of the function's arguments, their types, and whether the data value being passed in is NULL
- A pointer that you can use to store the location of an area of memory that is useful to cache data between calls to the function
- Places to store information about the return values from the function
- Facilities to allow the function to act as an iterator function that returns a set of results

SAPI includes functions and data structure definitions allowing you to get this information out of the `MI_FPARAM` structure and to modify the information in it. We review these facilities over the next few pages.

Argument Information

In Table 10–6 we present the SAPI functions used to interrogate the `MI_FPARAM` structure and extract information about the arguments passed into a UDF. It also illustrates the general pattern SAPI follows for all `MI_FPARAM` interfaces: SAPI provides interface routines to extract information from the `MI_FPARAM` and symmetric functions to set it.

UDFs can have multiple arguments, so SAPI routines for getting and setting `MI_FPARAM` information use an integer argument to specify the argument. Argument information is stored in a C array, so the first argument corresponds to the 0 element.

SAPI Function	Description
mi_integer mi_fp_nargs (MI_FPARAM *);	Returns the number of arguments being passed into the function.

MI_TYPEID *
mi_fp_argtype (
    MI_FPARAM *,
    mi_integer);
	Returns the data type of the nth argument (indicated by the second argument). The return value is a pointer to an array element in the MI_FPARAM structure. You can use this reference with other SAPI calls to extract more information about the type.

mi_boolean
mi_fp_argisnull (
    MI_FPARAM *,
    mi_integer);
	Returns MI_TRUE if the nth argument is NULL. Otherwise, the function returns MI_FALSE.

Note that these routines also are used to indicate when, for example, an OUT Parameter value is NULL.

NULL Arguments

NULL values require special handling. In Chapter 5, we described how, by default, the IDS product will not call a UDF if it would have to pass a NULL into it. Instead, it automatically substitutes a NULL result. Only by marking a UDF as being one that handles NULL values can you get the ORDBMS to pass it a NULL. NULL arguments present a problem, however, because attempts to represent NULL with special values for each data type would make it difficult to distinguish actual values from a NULL.

Therefore, the ORDBMS indicates through the MI_FPARAM structure when an argument is NULL. The SAPI function mi_fp_argisnull(), which was introduced in Table 10–6, provides this information. If a UDF accepts OR-SQL NULL arguments, its code must check for them because the typical pattern is to pass each NULL as a pointer. Seen from another point of view, creating UDFs that accept NULL values requires a lot of work. Avoiding NULL values, and relying instead on a combination of the standard behavior and a few SQL expressions specifically intended to cope with NULL, is generally a good idea.

Handling NULL Return Results from EXTERNAL C UDFs

Occasionally, having a UDF return a NULL result can be useful. To do this, you inform the server that the result is NULL using the MI_FPARAMS structure and set the variable you return to NULL (or zero). The ORDBMS notification is achieved using the SAPI function mi_fp_setreturn-null(). The idea is that, when a UDF returns, one of the things that the ORDBMS does is check the status in the MI_FPARAM structure as well as the value of the return type.

The code in lines 63 and 64 of Listing 10–9 illustrates how this SAPI function is used.

UDF Inter-Call Memory Cache

Sometimes, it is desirable to cache an intermediate data between calls to the UDF. For example, routines that generate a series of random numbers need to maintain a "seed" value between calls. The C library seed() and rand() calls work in this way; the seed() call places a value in an area of global memory that the rand() call manipulates.

It is generally a good idea to minimize the number of memory allocation calls that a UDF makes. Each memory allocation call is not terribly expensive. But with a lightweight UDF, such as one that requires only a few hundred machine code instructions or one that often is called in a single query, there are significant benefits to avoiding allocating temporary space each time.

Thus, the MI_FPARAM structure includes an MI_DATUM element in which UDF logic can save a pointer to an area of memory that is used by several calls to the same UDF. SAPI provides two calls to get and set this pointer which we list in Table 10–7.

Table 10-7. SAPI Routines to Access MI_FPARAM Information About Arguments

SAPI Function	Description
void * mi_fp_funcstate (MI_FPARAM *fparamPtr)	Given the MI_FPARAM structure passed into the UDF, this call extracts the pointer from it. This call returns a pointer to the inter-call cache. If no inter-call cache has been allocated, it returns a NULL pointer.

void
 mi_fp_setfuncstate (
    MI_FPARAM *fparamPtr,
      void *value   )
	Given the MI_FPARAM structure passed into the UDF and a pointer to an area of memory that the code wants preserved between calls, this call sets the pointer in the MI_FPARAM.

In describing how this works, we touch upon the extremely important topic of *memory durations*, which are explained in some detail later in this chapter. At this time it is enough to note that memory to be preserved between calls to the UDF requires special treatment. By default, the ORDBMS will attempt to free all memory allocated within a UDF at the time the UDF returns control to the ORDBMS. Memory passed between calls to the UDF, however, cannot be freed so aggressively.

```
1   /*
2   **   Increment
3   **
4   **     Very simple little function that returns a
5   **     different INTEGER each time it is called in
6   **     a query. It takes the initial value, which
7   **     it keeps in the Inter-Call cache. Each time
8   **     it is called, it returns this cached value,
9   **     and increases it by one.
10  **
11  **     This is a simple illustration of
12  **     how to use the inter-call MI_FPARAMS stuff.
13  **
14  **     CREATE FUNCTION Incr ( integer )
15  **     RETURNING integer
16  **     EXTERNAL NAME
17  **     "$INFORMIXDIR\Incr\bin\Incr.bld(_Increment)"
18  **     LANGUAGE C;
19  **
20  **/
21  #include <mi.h>
22
23  mi_integer
24  _Increment (
25  mi_integer nArgVal,
26  MI_FPARAM * pFParam
27  )
28  {
29      mi_integer * pnFArg;
30      mi_integer nRetVal;
31
32      if ((pnFArg = mi_fp_funcstate(pFParam)) == NULL)
33      {
34  pnFArg = (mi_integer *)
35                  mi_dalloc(sizeof(mi_integer),
```

```
36                                          PER_COMMAND);
37          *pnFArg = nArgVal;
38          mi_fp_setfuncstate(pFParam, (void *)pnFArg);
39      }
40
41      nRetVal = *pnFArg;
42      *pnFArg+=1;
43
44   return (nRetVal);
45   }
```

Listing 10–37. *Increment Example of Inter-Call Cache in MI_FPARAMs*

On line 32, this code probes the MI_FPARAM to see if the inter-call
cache has been established. Of course, the first time the function is
called, the cache will never be there. Consequently this UDF only executes the code on lines 33 through 38 the first time. Note the way in
which the memory on line 34 is allocated using a PER_COMMAND flag.
This tells the ORDBMS that this piece of memory should not be cleaned
up until the current command, which is a read OR-SQL query, completes.

During subsequent calls to this UDF, the probe on line 32 returns a
valid pointer for each row in a table. The INTEGER value being
pointed to is then accessed and incremented on lines 40 and 41.

Passing blocks of memory between invocations of a UDF within a
query is a very useful technique. Other examples of the technique
include the Random() UDF and the Currency type, the latter of which
caches all current conversion rates the first time it is called. Caching the
conversion rates avoids reselecting them on subsequent invocations.

Iterator Function Controls

Iterator functions are UDFs that return a series of values. We introduced
the concept in Chapter 5 and illustrated how to implement an Iterator
using the Stored Procedure Language's RETURN WITH RESUME syntax.

EXTERNAL UDFs also can be used to define iterators. When executing an iterator UDF, the IDS product calls it repeatedly. The first
time it is called, the iterator UDF logic can initialize some state that
the ORDBMS will pass into it again on subsequent invocations.
Return results from the UDF from this initialization call are ignored.
Then IDS calls the UDF repeatedly, and the UDF returns one result
each time, until there are no more results to be had. Then finally,
the ORDBMS calls the iterator once more to clean up any state left
laying about.

Different modes of calls to an iterator UDF are indicated through the MI_FPARAM argument. Figure 10–6 illustrates the logic flow within an iterator UDF.

The user-defined function example in Listing 10–38 illustrates several things about using the MI_FPARAM argument to implement an iterator. This function returns a set of strings, each of which is a word extracted from the first argument, which is split into segments defined by any of the delimiter characters in the second argument string.

```
 1   /*
 2   **    Function:   IterSplitString()
 3   **
 4   **       About:
 5   **
 6   **    This is the EXTERNAL FUNCTION implementation of
 7   ** the Split Iterator. The function takes two string
 8   ** arguments. The first is the string to be split into
 9   ** words. The second arg is a string that include a
10   **  set of potential delimiter characters.
```

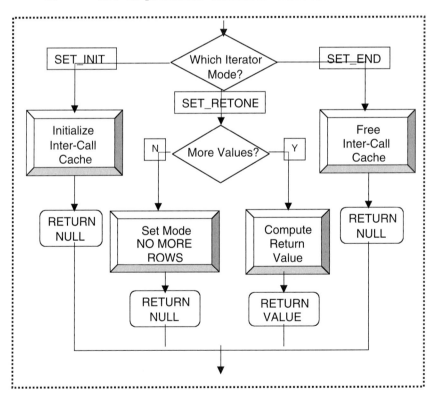

Figure 10–6. *Schematic of Internal Design for EXTERNAL Iterator UDF*

```
11  **
12  **    IterSplitString() walks through the first string,
13  ** looking for characters that are in the second.
14  **
15  **    Each time it finds a word, the function returns
16  ** it as an LVARCHAR result.
17  **
18  **    On the first call to the UDF, it allocates a
19  ** block of memory to hold the following structure. At
20  ** each call, the UDF logic walks pchWhere pointer
21  ** along the pchInterChar string, extracting as it
22  **  goes.This structure is the Inter-Call cache.
23  **
24  ** typedef struct {
25  **            mi_string  *  pchInterChar;
26  **            mi_string  *  pchWhere;
27  **            mi_string  *  pchDelim;
28  **  } Split_Inter;
29  **
30  */
31  mi_lvarchar *
32  IterSplitString (
33                    mi_lvarchar *  pvlArg,
34                    mi_lvarchar *  pvlSplitDelim,
35                    MI_FPARAM   *  Gen_Fparam
36  )
37  {
38    Split_Inter * pIterSt;   /*Struct pass between calls*/
39    mi_string   * pchWhere; /*Pointer to location      */
40    mi_lvarchar * pvlRetVal;/*Pointer to return mem.   */
41
42  /*
43  **   The behavior of this UDF varies, depending on the
44  ** mode in which it is called. Iterator mode is passed
45  ** into the UDF through the MI_FPARAM, and it is
46  ** determined here. This switch() corresponds to the
47  ** Check Iterator Mode branch in Table 10-7.
48  */
49
50    switch(mi_fp_request(Gen_Fparam))
51    {
52      case SET_INIT:
53  /*
54  **   The first time this UDF is called, allocate memory
55  ** to hold the state passed between UDF calls.
```

```
56  */
57          mi_switch_mem_duration(PER_COMMAND);
58  if((pIterSt=(Split_Inter *)
59                  mi_alloc( sizeof(Split_Inter)) )
60          mi_db_error_raise ((MI_CONNECTION * )NULL,
61                                  MI_EXCEPTION,
62                                  "ISplit: alloc failed" );
63
64      pIterSt->pchInterChar =
65                          mi_lvarchar_to_string(pvlArg);
66      pIterSt->pchDelim =
67                      mi_lvarchar_to_string(pvlSplitDelim);
68      mi_switch_mem_duration(PER_FUNCTION);
69
70      pIterSt->pchWhere=pIterSt->pchInterChar;
71      mi_fp_setfuncstate(Gen_Fparam,pIterSt);
72     break;
73
74    case SET_RETONE:
75      pIterSt= (Split_Inter *)
76                          mi_fp_funcstate(Gen_Fparam);
77
78      while((strspn(pIterSt->pchWhere,
79                      pIterSt->pchDelim) > 0 ) &&
80          (*(pIterSt->pchWhere) != '\0') )
81        pIterSt->pchWhere++;
82
83      pchWhere = pIterSt->pchWhere;
84
85      if (*pchWhere == '\0' )
86      {
87        mi_fp_setisdone(Gen_Fparam,MI_TRUE);
88        return mi_string_to_lvarchar("Ignored");
89      } else {
90        while((strspn(pIterSt->pchWhere,
91                      pIterSt->pchDelim) == 0 ) &&
92            (*(pIterSt->pchWhere) != '\0') )
93          pIterSt->pchWhere++;
94
95        if ( *pIterSt->pchWhere == '\0' )
96        {
97          pvlRetVal = mi_string_to_lvarchar(pchWhere);
98        } else {
99          *pIterSt->pchWhere = '\0';
```

```
100                    pvlRetVal = mi_string_to_lvarchar(pchWhere);
101                    pIterSt->pchWhere++;
102                }
103                 return pvlRetVal;
104              }
105          break;
106
107      case SET_END:
108          pIterSt=(Split_Inter *)
109                       mi_fp_funcstate(Gen_Fparam);
110          mi_free( pIterSt->pchInterChar );
111          mi_free( pIterSt->pchDelim );
112          mi_free( pIterSt );
113          break;
114      }
115     return (mi_lvarchar *)NULL;
116  }
117
```

Listing 10–38. ISplit() Iterator Implemented as EXTERNAL FUNCTION

All iterator UDFs follow this pattern. Code examples on the accompanying CD include a dynamic SQL in SPL iterator described in Tutorial 6.

Coding Guidelines for EXTERNAL UDFs

For the most part, working with C inside the IDS product presents much the same challenge as working with C in any other programming context, but it has its own quirks too. In this section we cover some of the more obvious ones.

Connections

Many SAPI calls need to know the database context within which they are running. They need access to the system catalogs to get data type information, or the UDF needs to know where to send change of status messages or to report errors. Context information is represented using a MI_CONNECTION structure. In Table 10–8 we list the SAPI routines that work with MI_CONNECTION data structures.

Table 10–8. SAPI Commands for Handling Database Connections

SAPI Function	Description

```MI_CONNECTION *```
``` mi_open (```
```   char * db_name,```
```   char * user_name,```
```   char * user_passwd)```
	This call opens a connection to the named database as the named user. In situations in which a password is required, the call accepts one as the third argument.

```mi_integer```
``` mi_close   (```
```   MI_CONNECTION * conn)```
	This call closes an open connection.

Open connections can be interrogated for information such as the current database name, user name, and so on. Several earlier code examples illustrate how to use these SAPI functions; check line 28 of Listing 10–11 and lines 336 and 353 of Listing 10–32. In these examples, open connections are necessary to handle an error and to get data type information.

Why do we need the MI_CONNECTION handle? Invoking a user-defined function requires a database connection in the first place, so why open another? MI_CONNECTION handles in the server are a little redundant, but the DataBlade API is also used on the client side where code may open multiple connections. By far the most common way that C logic uses the mi_open() SAPI call is to pass it three NULL values and have it return a default connection to the local database.

Memory Management

How memory is handled within the server is an important UDF development topic. UDFs typically use memory to hold intermediate or partial results. This implies that, in general, memory allocated to a UDF can be reclaimed when the UDF returns control to the ORDBMS. There are occasions, however, such as with inter-call cache (discussed previously), when memory needs to be preserved for longer periods.

Reclaiming memory while a query is running turns out to be necessary. Suppose you develop a UDF that allocates a mere eight bytes of data, but doesn't reclaim it. (This might be deferred until after the entire OR-SQL command is finished.) Now consider what happens when you write a query that joins two 10,000 record tables and uses the eight-byte function to check for a join. If the join algorithm is a nest-loop, the UDF will be called 10,000 x 10,000 (100,000,000) times. Thus, this UDF would end up allocating 800 megabytes of memory, eight bytes at a time!

The ORDBMS manages memory on behalf of all users and all UDFs. EXTERNAL UDF's can allocate and free memory using a family of SAPI functions, and the SAPI calls used to arrange these are modeled on the standard C library calls for memory allocation. These calls are reproduced in Table 10–9.

Table 10–9. SAPI Commands for Handling Memory

SAPI Function	Description

`mi_char *`
`mi_alloc (`
    `mi_integer len )`
	Allocates a memory area of length-size bytes. This memory is allocated in the current memory context, which is, by default, PER_ROUTINE (see the discussion below).

`mi_char *`
`mi_dalloc (`
  `mi_integer      len,`
  `MI_MEM_DURATION duration`
      `)`
	Allocates a memory area of length-size bytes. This memory is allocated in the memory context supplied in the second argument (see the discussion below).

`mi_char *`
  `mi_zalloc (`
    `mi_integer len )`
	Same as `mi_alloc()`. The only difference is that the memory allocated by `mi_zalloc()` contains all zero-byte values.

`MI_MEMORY_DURATION`
`mi_switch_mem_duration (`
`MI_MEMORY_DURATION durat )`
	Sets the default memory duration, which is the one used by mi_alloc, `mi_zalloc()`, and the SAPI functions creating `mi_lvarchar` objects, to the duration supplied as argument. The return value of this SAPI function is the memory duration before the switch.

`void`
  `mi_free (`
    `mi_char * mem )`
	Frees the area of memory pointed to by the argument for use by other UDFs and ORDBMS's other facilities.

Memory can always be explicitly freed, regardless of its memory context, using the `mi_free()` API call. In general it is a very good idea to free memory wherever it makes sense to do so. This helps minimize the potential for memory leaks and other performance problems. It is important also **never** to use `mi_free()` on `mi_lvarchar` structures.

There is one big difference between how an operating system allocates memory, and how IDS handles memory allocated by an EXTERNAL C UDF. When a UDF asks the ORDBMS to allocate an area of memory for the UDF to use, that memory is marked as having a particular *memory duration*.

We have seem that sometimes, memory needs to remain allocated for a longer period than a single UDF execution. Most often the memory is allocated one time, the first time the UDF is called within a query, and references to that memory are passed between invocations of the UDF.

Thus, memory that is used by many *different* functions over the life of the server must be allocated once and never can be reclaimed.

In Table 10–10 we list the two most commonly used memory durations that can be assigned to a newly allocated block of memory. These C macros are supplied as the second argument to `mi_dalloc()` (see the previous discussion), or they are used when switching between default memory durations (which is what `mi_alloc()` and the SAPI functions creating new `mi_lvarchar` structures use).

Table 10–10. Memory Durations

Duration Name	Description
PER_ROUTINE	Memory is reclaimed when the function returns its results to the server; that is, memory is freed once the row being scanned is done. This is the default memory duration, and it should be used when allocating memory that is used within the function. This memory might, for example, hold return results. The server handles return results appropriately. It copies the memory to another location and only then free the return result memory.
PER_COMMAND	Memory is reclaimed when the subquery within which it is allocated completes. This is generally a good choice for the inter-call cache and in user-defined aggregates.

A quick check of the product documentation will reveal a number of other memory durations. These have special uses. For example, it is possible to allocate memory blocks that endure for the entire transaction or for the life of the plan generated by a PREPARE (see Chapter 7). In this section we focus on the simplest cases.

Allocating Memory Off the Stack

Each `mi_alloc()` call has some overhead, and when the UDF completes, freeing the memory requires computational effort. Thus, it is good practice to avoid calling `mi_alloc()` wherever it is reasonable to take another approach. In C programming, it is quite acceptable to allocate storage space from the *stack*, which is memory allocated at compile time to hold local variables, rather than from the IDS product's virtual memory pools, which is from where memory allocated using `mi_alloc()` comes.

To do this, simply define an appropriately sized local variable within the function. When the UDF is called by the server, space for these variables is allocated from memory on the per-thread stack.

When the function returns, the ORDBMS merely lowers the stack reference to reclaim the space automatically. Examine Listing 10–39.

```
57 mi_lvarchar *                     /* Output for enumerated type */
58 StateOutput (
59      StateCode  * pArg1,
60      MI_FPARAM   * pFParam
61 )
62 {
63      mi_char        pBuf[32]; /* Allocate space from    */
64      mi_lvarchar * pRetVal;   /* stack for intermediate*/
65                               /* data.                 */
66
67          switch(*pArg1)
68          {
69              case 0:
70                      strcpy(pBuf,  "ALABAMA");
71                  break;
72              case 1:
73                      strcpy(pBuf,  "ALASKA");
74                  break;
75              case 2:
76                      strcpy(pBuf,  "ARKANSAS");
77                  break;
   .
173              default:
174                  break;
175          }
176
177          pRetVal = mi_string_to_lvarchar(pBuf);
178
179          return (pRetVal);
180 }
```

Listing 10–39. *Using the Stack to Allocate Memory[5]*

Although this may seem obvious, for some reason many first time developers writing C UDFs make excessive use of mi_alloc(). An important lesson is that good programming practice in C is usually good programming practice in C UDFs. There are obvious limits to this. At most, the server can handle 32K of stack memory. Consequently, it is not a good idea to allocate large chunks of memory in this manner.

---

[5] The author is well aware of the advantages of an array of constant values over this approach, but feels that would complicate the example code.

Allocating and Freeing Memory

Many examples in this chapter illustrate how to use the memory allocation functions. Because UDFs need to allocate memory to hold return results, almost all include some kind of memory allocation call, even if the memory is allocated within an `mi_string_to_lvarchar()` SAPI call.

Lines 66 through 70 from Listing 10–11 illustrate this in Listing 10–40.

```
20    mi_decimal            * pdecRetVal;
21    mi_double_precision    dbPrice, dbRetVal;
.
66    pdecRetVal = (mi_decimal *)mi_alloc(sizeof(mi_decimal));
67    (void)deccvdbl( dbRetVal, pdecRetVal);
68
69    return (pdecRetVal);
70 }
```

Listing 10–40. *Using mi_alloc() to Allocate Memory to Hold Return Value*

As with any programming environment, it is a good idea to free memory once it is determined that the code will not need it. This is good discipline even in UDF logic because one UDF might call another directly, without doing so through the OR-SQL function manager.

Sometimes, when using the inter-call cache technique, it is necessary to re-allocate space occasionally to hold a newer, larger value. Simply replacing the pointer does not free the memory to which it was pointing. The code in Listing 10–41 should be used instead.

```
29    mi_char * pchFArg;
.
32    if ((pchFArg = mi_fp_funcstate(pFParam)) == NULL)
33                                                    {
34                                pchFArg = (mi_char *)
35                                    mi_dalloc(64,
36                                PER_COMMAND);
37        memcpy( pchFArg, pchInitialValue);
38        mi_fp_setfuncstate(pFParam, (void *)pchFArg);
39    }
.
50 /*
51 ** Need to replace the mi_fp_funcstate inter-call
52 ** cache with a bigger one. Free old, allocate new.
53 **/
54    mi_free( pchFarg );
```

```
55     pchFArg = (mi_char *) mi_dalloc ( 128,
56                                         PER_COMMAND );
57    memcpy( pchFarg, pchNewValue );
.
```

Listing 10–41. *Freeing Memory Used in an Inter-Call Cache*

Freed memory is immediately reclaimed by the ORDBMS, regardless
of its duration.

Switching Memory Contexts

While the `mi_dalloc` () API call permits the developer to control
memory duration, no corresponding call exists for the API calls that
allocate variable length structures. Therefore, the API includes functions to change the current memory context to another duration. This
is done using the `mi_switch_mem_duration()` API call.

For example, if the inter-call cache structure was to be an `mi_lvar-`
`char`, the code in Listing 10–42 must be used.

```
58 OldMemDev = mi_switch_mem_duration(PER_COMMAND);
59
60 if((pIterSt=(Split_Inter *)
61              mi_alloc( sizeof(Split_Inter)) )
60         mi_db_error_raise ((MI_CONNECTION * )NULL,
61                              MI_EXCEPTION,
62                              "ISplit: alloc failed" );
63
64    pIterSt->pchInterChar =
65                          mi_lvarchar_to_string(pvlArg);
66    pIterSt->pchDelim =
67                       mi_lvarchar_to_string(pvlSplitDelim);
68
69    mi_switch_mem_duration( OldMemDev );
70
71    pIterSt->pchWhere=pIterSt->pchInterChar;
72    mi_fp_setfuncstate(Gen_Fparam,pIterSt);
```

Listing 10–42. *Switching the Default Memory Duration*

On line 58, this code switches the default memory duration to
PER_COMMAND. After this change, all memory allocated within the code
will endure until the current query (or subquery) completes. Therefore,

the memory allocated within the `mi_lvarchar_to_string()` calls on lines 64 and 66 can be safely passed around using the inter-call cache.

As an aside, many SAPI calls allocate memory. For example, before a new type or row descriptor can be created, the server must allocate memory for it. Thus, if the code is passing one of these SAPI objects around, it needs to ensure that the memory is created in an appropriate duration.

Large Objects

The OPAQUE TYPE mechanism is intended for handling large data objects (LOs) like digital media images, text, or big arrays of data. For efficiency, the ID product stores large object data separately from table data. For example, if you have a table that contains a large object column—such as an employee's resume—then the ORDBMS only places a handle or reference to the large object within the table's column. It actually stores the LO data separately, in what are known as blob spaces, or smart blob spaces.

This approach is used so that when queries scan a table with a large object type in a column, the entire large object is not read into memory with each row. However, as with other extended data types, the ORDBMS does more than just store this data. It also lets user-defined functions operate on the data in these large-objects to compute new data values, or compare them.

The ORDBMS provides facilities to perform random access to data in the large object in a manner very similar to the way that you access data in a file-system. In fact, the facilities the ORDBMS provides to handle large objects is very like the standard POSIX file interfaces. There are two reasons for this. First, these objects are likely to be too large to fit entirely into main memory. Conceivably the ORDBMS might read the entire array of bytes into memory and pass a pointer to this memory to the UDF. But if the UDF simply wants to check information in the header of the large object, this would not be very efficient. Currently these objects can be up to 4 terabytes in size.

Second, this mode of streaming file-access is fairly well understood by programmers.

Large Object Storage

The objective of the architecture is to permit maximum flexibility in the handling of large object data—no limits on data sizes or on the ways in which the large object data can be used—while providing the usual DBMS guarantees of transactions and security. Also, any handling of large object data needs to address the question of how to handle large volumes of data, when to reclaim unused space, and how to minimize the space used.

The ORDBMS stores the large object data separately from the rest of the table data. These large object storage spaces are called *smart large-object spaces*. Smart large-object spaces are simply a different kind of data space: they are just like table spaces for BLOBS. When a column in a table is defined to contain a BLOB type (or a multi-representational data type) the column only contains a *large object handle*. This handle contains information that points to the location of the actual large object data, stored separately in a BLOB space.

Designing Large Object Data Types

An OPAQUE TYPE that contains a large object must be defined, as we illustrate in Listing 10–43.

```
typedef struct
{
        MI_LO_HANDLE                    data;
}  Video;
```

Listing 10–43. *C Structure Definition for Large Object Type*

An `MI_LO_HANDLE` is 72 byte of data that the IDS engine can use to locate the actual large object data in its storage space. Most large object types have C structures that include an `MI_LO_HANDLE` that refers to the actual data, but a useful summary of the large object data—a boundary box, or a feature vector—is include in the structure. Summary data is created when the large object is loaded into the ORDBMS.

Accessing Large Object Data

User-defined functions that accept large object data types as arguments are actually passed large object handles. Within the UDF source code, SAPI calls are required to open, access and close large object data objects. In Table 10–11 we present a summary of the most commonly used of these calls.

Table 10–11. SAPI Functions to Access Large Object Data

SAPI Function	Description

``MI_LO_FD mi_lo_open(
    MI_CONNECTION *,
    MI_LO_HANDLE *,
    mi_integer);```
	Given a connection handle to a database, and an instance of an `MI_LO_HANDLE`, open the large object data according to a mask supplied as the third argument. `mi_lo_open()` returns a handle to the open large object used by other SAPI large object interface functions.

``mi_integer mi_lo_seek(
    MI_CONNECTION *,
    MI_LO_FD,
    mi_int8 *,
    mi_integer,
    mi_int8 *);```
	Given an open large object, this SAPI call seeks into the large object data. `mi_lo_seek()` is the equivalent of the POSIX `seek()` operation over files. It positions the current file location to some byte offset within the large object data.

``mi_integer mi_lo_read(
    MI_CONNECTION *,
    MI_LO_FD,
    char *,
    mi_integer);```
	Given an open large object, read some number of bytes from that large object into the block of memory passed in at the third argument. `mi_lo_read()` is the SAPI equivalent of the POSIX `read()` operation.

``mi_integer mi_lo_write(
    MI_CONNECTION *,
    MI_LO_FD,
    const char *,
    mi_integer);```
	Given an open large object, write data from the block of memory passed in at the third argument into it at its current offset. `mi_lo_write()` is the SAPI equivalent of POSIX `write()`.

``mi_integer mi_lo_close(
    MI_CONNECTION *,
    MI_LO_FD);```
	Closes an open large object. Equivalent of the POSIX `close()`.

``MI_LO_FD mi_lo_copy (
    MI_CONNECTION *,
    MI_LO_HANDLE *,
    MI_LO_SPEC *,
    mi_integer,
    MI_LO_HANDLE **)```
	In a single operation, this SAPI call creates a complete copy of a large object, and opens it.

``MI_LO_FD mi_lo_create(
    MI_CONNECTION *,
    MI_LO_SPEC *,
    mi_integer,
    MI_LO_HANDLE **);```
	Creates and opens a new large object.

A complete description of the extent of SAPI's facilities would constitute a complete chapter unto itself.

Top Six Rules for Writing External User-Defined Functions

By now we have covered the most common facilities used to create external UDFs. In this section we briefly summarize several rules to follow when using C to implement UDFs.

Smaller and Simpler is Safer

One of the most common mistakes made by early adopters of Object-Relational DBMS technology was to attempt to implement entire applications within their user-defined extensions. Part of the problem was the belief was that C promised higher performance, but the bigger misunderstanding was about how their extensions would be used.

When writing a user-defined extension that will be invoked within OR-SQL statements, strive to keep it as conceptually simple and as self-contained as possible. Algorithmically, a UDF can be quite complex, and a user-defined type can encapsulate complex file-formats, but the behavior implemented by the extension logic should be conceptually obvious to end users.

Write thread-safe code

Recall the description of how the IDS product works as a set of processes cooperatively executing a workload that is broken up into a set of user level threads. As a consequence of this architecture an embedded UDF may find itself running within several operating system level processes as part of a single query.

In practical terms, avoid variables defined with the C `static` modifier, and avoid any kind of global variable (which are usually identified by an `extern` modifier on the local variable declaration).

Be mindful of the difference between C strings and mi_lvarchar

Many readers will be familiar with C null-terminated strings and the standard library of routines provided to work with them. However, null terminated strings have several disadvantages as a mechanism for storing variable length data, so the ORDBMS provides its own structure, called the mi_lvarchar, for storing variable length data and passing it around within the server.

System calls are way out

If code embedded within a CPU virtual processor makes a call to the operating system environment on which it is running, confusion and havoc will follow shortly thereafter. System calls can be embedded within the ORDBMS, but they must be executed in their own, specially reserved virtual processor.

Always free mi_lvarchar data with mi_var_free(), never mi_free()

Each `mi_lvarchar` is an eight byte structure. But its second element can be a pointer to a 2 gigabyte object. The `mi_var_free()` SAPI call knows this, and does the right thing with the embedded pointer. But the SAPI `mi_free()` call does exactly what it says on the tin: It frees the `mi_lvarchar`. Leaving orphaned large objects lingering in memory quickly creates severe problems for the ORDBMS.

In general, memory leaks are fairly easy to detect. While running a test query that deliberately executes the UDF a tremendous number of times, look for the allocation of additional virtual segments in the IDS product's log file.

Avoid OR-SQL Callbacks unless absolutely necessary

This is a similar rule to one expressed earlier. UDF logic that is to be invoked within an OR-SQL query should rarely include any OR-SQL itself. There is rarely any performance advantage to doing so, and the design does not make the best use of ORDBMS technology.

Chapter Summary

In this chapter we have seen how external C user-defined functions work in the ORDBMS. You can think of a UDFs as a little program—more like a subroutine than a complete program—that executes in the context of the ORDBMS mini-operating system. Unlike more conventional programs and operating systems, user-defined functions are bound to data in the database using a declarative query expression.

The nature of the IDS product architecture implies certain constraints (such as strictly re-entrant or no use of real operating system resources) over what you can do in these programs. The highly concurrent query processing framework of the ORDBMS implies certain design objectives (such as using simple, small, self contained routines that use as little memory resource as possible). This said, the ORDBMS environment makes it possible to specify entire business processes as a single query combining complex data with many user-defined functions, and this query expression will be optimized by the ORDBMS and made to run in parallel.

Then we moved on to show what a simple UDF looks like and to explain how it works, before turning to a more detailed explanation of various aspects of the server application programming interface. In this section we saw how to specify a UDF, how the ORDBMS passes data values into the function, and how to convert between the server's data formats and C structures. Collectively, these features make up the server's DataBlade API, SAPI.

SAPI provides facilities to handle built-in SQL-92 type arguments, and these provide the foundation for dealing with DISTINCT TYPE and ROW TYPE values passed into a C UDF. SAPI provides other functions to extract elements from within the complex types, and to format complex return results.

Several complex areas of C extension development were discussed: memory management, inter-call data cache, and handling OR-SQL NULL data. And we concluded with a series of observations about what works in C external function development and what does not.

Virtual Table Interface

The *Virtual Table Interface (VTI)* is an innovative feature of the IDS product. It implements what is known as an *open storage manager*, which allows database developers to integrate a variety of non-DBMS data, such as data on tertiary storage devices, flat file data, and even entire external information systems, into an object-relational database schema. We introduced the concept in Chapter 1, and the accompanying CD material includes implementations of two (hopefully useful) VTI access methods.

Overview of Tutorial

In this tutorial we review what VTI is, how it works, and how to implement simple access methods with it. We begin by explaining how VTI fits into the architecture of the ORDBMS. User-defined access methods give OR-SQL developers real-time access to non-DBMS data. The external data is not loaded into an ORDBMS table: it remains wherever it was stored originally, and it is accessed in place using query language statements. Then we move on to illustrate the programming steps required to implement a new access method. Finally, we give a brief description of how some early adopters have successfully employed the technology.

It is important to note that using the virtual table interface should be viewed as something of a last resort. Other mechanisms—such as the *Enterprise Gateways Manager (EGM)* and the distributed query capabilities (see Chapter 6)—are commercially supported mechanisms to access external relational data. But in situations where there is simply no alternative—for example, when the external structure of the data is such that it requires transforming before being presented in table form, or where there the data is generated by another program rather than stored—VTI is the only viable approach.

How VTI Works

The internal architecture of a *DataBase Management System (DBMS)* has traditionally seen it divided between an upper half—responsible for communication with external programs, query parsing, optimization, and execution—and a lower half that is responsible for disk management, locking, logging, and so on. The idea is that, as it processes OR-SQL statements, the upper half of the ORDBMS—the *query engine*—makes requests of the lower half—the *storage manager*—to perform all low level data management tasks. We illustrate the idea in Figure 6–1.

This division simplifies the task of DBMS engineering. Within INFORMIX, engineers are organized into two teams with each team working on one half of the product. The storage manager team

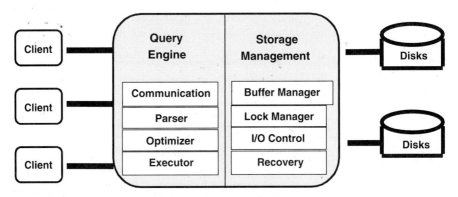

Figure 6–1. *Internal Architecture of DBMS Engine*

concentrates on efficient data management, while the query engine team focuses on the problem of turning query language statements into a minimum number of calls to the storage manager.

The Virtual Table Interface makes it possible for developers to embed storage management code into the ORDBMS in much the same way that they embed business logic into the OR-SQL query language. Then the upper half of the ORDBMS calls the user-supplied routines, rather than the built-in ones, as it executes queries. To do this, the ORDBMS opens up the interfaces between the query processor and the storage manager. We illustrate the architecture in Figure 6–2.

Rather than providing a procedural interface as part of a middleware facility the intention is to allow developers to use OR-SQL when accessing the data. As with the distributed query processing facilities of the ORDBMS, it is possible for OR-SQL developers to be using an external interface without being aware of it. The overall flexibility of the final information system is increased when declarative queries can be applied everywhere. And as we shall see, the effort to implement an interface using VTI is not all that different, either in design or in performance characteristics, from a hand-coded library.

How the ORDBMS Uses VTI Interfaces

To implement a new virtual access method, developers write a set of User-defined Function (UDF) modules that can substitute for the built-in storage management routines implemented by the ORDBMS.

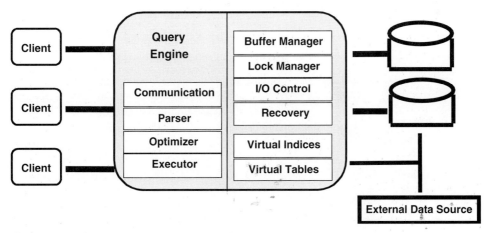

Figure 6–2. *External Data Access Architecture*

To understand what we mean by this, let us examine how an ORDBMS works by default.

Within the ORDBMS, OR-SQL queries are decomposed into a schedule of operations called a *query plan*. Query plans typically include operations that scan records in a table and hand each record, one at a time, to another part of the query plan, perhaps after discarding some records or reducing the number of columns. For example, when a query such as the one in Listing 6–1 is passed into the ORDBMS its query processing facilities create a plan that implements a particular algorithm to scan and filter data.

```
SELECT M.Title, M.Budget
  FROM Movies
 WHERE M.Release_Date < '01/02/1950';
```

Listing 6–1. *Simple Query to Illustrate Data Processing within ORDBMS*

The pseudo-code in Listing 6–2 illustrates what such an algorithm may look like. Functions printed in **bold** type are part of the interface that the query processing upper-half of the ORDBMS uses to invoke facilities within the storage manager.

```
TABLE_DESCRIPTION   *     Table;
SCAN_DESCRIPTION    *     Scan;
ROW                 *     Scan_Record,
                    *       Result_Record;

 .

 .

Table   :=  OpenTable(Movies);
Scan    :=  BeginScan(Table,
                    'Release_Date < 01/01/1950');
while (( Scan_Record := GetNext(Scan)) != END_OF_SCAN)
{
     Result_Record := PROJECT ( Scan_Record,
                                  'Title, Budget' );
/*
** Within this loop the next task is to deal with
** Result_Record appropriately. It might be handed
** to some other aspect of query processing: perhaps
** the client communications facilities, or another
** algorithm like a JOIN.
*/

 .

}
EndScan(Scan);
CloseTable(Table);
```

Listing 6–2. *Pseudo-code for Listing 6–1 Query Plan*

Within the ORDBMS the functions shown in bold in Listing 6–2 perform particular *interface roles*. Implementing a new access method requires that developers write their own versions of these highlighted operations, and then combine them together into an *access method* that allows the ORDBMS to substitute the user-defined logic for its built-in ones. Within the database schema an administrator can create tables that use the new access method. OR-SQL treats all tables, built-in or VTI based, equally. Note that the underlined functions are part of the ORDBMS's run-time operations. In theory these could be opened up in the same way that the storage management layer has been, but at this time this has not been done.

The ORDBMS's built-in versions of these operations are very sophisticated. They interact with the locking system to guarantee transaction isolation. They understand how to make the best use of the memory cache and chunk I/O for optimal efficiency. User defined access methods—written by applications developers rather than ORDBMS engineers—are usually much simpler than the built-in storage manager functions because their functionality is more specialized. When you write a new read-only VTI access method there is rarely any need to implement a locking or logging system.[1]

To support INSERT, UPDATE, and DELETE queries over a data source you must implement several additional functions to *insert, update,* and *delete* data records. Further, there are facilities within VTI that allow you to perform functions such as gathering statistics, checking the data integrity of the ORDBMS schema, and so on. Because the results of these operations can be used in other data management processes such as sorts, aggregation, and joins, there is a requirement that scan positions can be marked and that the scan operation can skip back or forward. This means that a query processing plan can ask for a ReScan of the data, rather than simply calling a combination of the End-Scan and another BeginScan.

Implementing a New VTI Storage Manager

To explain how a new VTI access method is implemented we walk through a simple example. Often it is desirable for a data-centric information system to incorporate data stored in a file-system file. For example, on UNIX™ systems information about user accounts

---

[1] If you really feel the need to do so the author suggests you buy Gray and Reuter's 600 page masterpiece *Transaction Processing: Concepts and Techniques* and study it until you know it all by heart. Then apply for a job at a database company. They will hire you in a second.

and the network is stored in configuration files, and sometimes data can be transferred to the server as a large regular file that uses special characters to delimit fields. The access method developed in this tutorial allows an OR-SQL developer to create a "table" that can present data from such a file as a set of query-able rows.

For example, suppose the Movies-R-Us web site receives a file like the one shown in Listing 6–3 once a week from companies that book movies into `Cinemas`. (Similar files may be sent by companies providing `Merchandise` or studios providing information about new `Movies`.) For administrative reasons, it may be awkward to use the ORDBMS's bulk load utilities to accomplish this: for example, the files may arrive at irregular intervals.

```
Casablanca|1942|Moinahan Mall Cinema|01/15/2001|02/20/2001
Casablanca|1942|Seven Oaks Theatre|01/15/2001|02/20/2001
Casablanca|1942|Seven Oaks Theatre|01/15/2001|02/20/2001
```

Listing 6–3. *Sample Data Detailing Upcoming Movie Scheduling*

Making the contents of such a file available as a query-able table requires an access method that can open a file, parse its contents, and form this data into IDS row structures. Rather than building a single VTI specialized for one file format it is generally better to design something more general. The implementation in this tutorial uses an OR-SQL table's structure—its set of columns—to format the delimitered rows of file data. A single VTI access method implementation can be used in multiple tables and a parameter value—called am_param—can be supplied to differentiate among them. In our example table, am_param specifies the name of the external file, and possibly its delimiter character(s).

The following steps are necessary to create a new primary access method using the virtual table interface:

1. Create a set of external user-defined functions implementing the various aspects of the interface. These should be compiled and installed within the ORDBMS like any other external UDF.
2. Combine these functions into an *access method* using the CREATE ACCESS METHOD statement.
3. Create tables that use the new access method.

When the query processor encounters a table in a query it looks up the system catalogs to see whether that table uses the built-in storage mechanisms, or if it is created using a user-defined access method. If the table employs a VTI based access method the ORDBMS creates a query plan that calls the user defined functions associated with that access method in place of the built-in functions. Then it executes the query exactly as before.

We now examine each of these steps in more detail. Along the way, we present code examples from a VTI implementation that makes data in an external file look like a table in the ORDBMS.

VTI User-Defined Functions

Implementing an access method using VTI means first creating a set of user-defined functions, each of which has a particular signature and accepts a predefined set of data types. These UDFs are assigned to specific roles in the access method. A nearly complete list of VTI interfaces roles is presented in Table 6–1. New access methods must supply a UDF for the am_getnext role at minimum. When am_getnext is the only interface role assigned a UDF, the ORDBMS calls that UDF repeatedly until it returns a result indicating that it can return no more ROW TYPE values.

Other roles may or may not have functions assigned to them, and the ORDBMS accommodates "missing" UDFs. For example, when as part of query processing the server needs to rescan a user-defined access method it tries to call whatever UDF is assigned to the am_rescan role. If an am_rescan UDF is not defined the ORDBMS instead calls am_endscan (if it exists) and then am_beginscan (if it exists) before starting again calling am_getnext. For any reasonably sophisticated VTI implementation it is a good idea to supply as many interface functions as possible.

Table 6–1. Partial List of User-Defined Functions Used by the Virtual Table Interface

VTI Role	Description
am_create	The ORDBMS calls this function whenever a CREATE TABLE is executed that involves the user-defined access method. This is a good place to perform whatever checks are necessary over the definition of the table: the am_param, the table's structure, and so on. Listing 6–4 is an example of an am_create UDF. In our example am_create would check that the external file exists and that the ORDBMS can open it for reading (and writing).

(continued)

VTI Role	Description
am_open	The server calls this function whenever an operation that involves the table—a SELECT query or an oncheck, scan for example—is initiated. The purpose of this function is to perform any processing that must be done before the data management task can be initiated. As part of its logic this process can create a block of memory that is passed into other functions making up the interface. In our example am_open would open the external file, and it would create a block of memory to hold a "chunk" of data from it.
am_beginscan	This function is called whenever a scan of the external data is initiated. Often, scans must be performed multiple times in the context of a query. The VTI table may be on the inner of a nested loop join, for example. When this function returns, the scan position should be reset to the first record that the scan will produce. In our example am_beginscan would set the file pointer to the beginning of the file.
am_getnext	At the innermost part of the scan this function simply reads the next record in the scan and returns, by reference, a correctly formatted MI_ROW type. The return status of this function tells the server what the status of the scan is. Code in the Listing 6–6 outlines what an am_getnext UDF needs to do. In our example, the am_getnext UDF would parse the next row (performing a buffer read operation if necessary) and format it into an MI_ROW before returning it. Or if there no more data were available it would return a result indicating the end of the scan.
am_endscan	When a scan pass is completed the ORDBMS calls this function to perform any end of scan processing. The code in this function should free up any memory and reset any scan state. In our example am_endscan has little to do.
am_close	When the query is complete, the server calls this function and it is its responsibility to perform any end of query processing, clean up any remaining memory, close the connection to the external data source, and so on. In our example am_close would close the file and free the buffer memory.
am_rescan	When a data source is scanned multiple times in a single query—for example, it is used in the inner loop of a join—it is more efficient simply to reset a counter than to call the am_endscan and then am_beginscan once again. am_rescan in our example would empty the buffer and reset the file pointer to the beginning of the file. For coding efficiency in our example the last thing the am_beginscan does it is to call the am_rescan UDF.
am_insert	A new record can be inserted to the external data store using this call. Alternatively, this might be interpreted as a message to an external system to turn something on.

(continued)

VTI Role	*Description*
am_update	Records can be updated to new values. This requires that the record is retrieved before it is modified.
am_delete	Record is removed from the external store. This might also be interpreted as a message to shut down an external process.
am_drop	This UDF is called when the external store is dropped. It might include logic to clean up any resources, such as a file, or a set of files, that contains data being accessed.
am_check	This routine is called in the oncheck utility. It can contain some kind of integrity check for a specific table passed in the first argument. Because the oncheck utility can be called with many options, the am_check function takes a second argument that passes this command into the function.

Traditionally 'C' has been the language of choice for implementing the UDFs used by a VTI access method. This was because 'C' provided the highest performance, and SAPI had the kind of low-level data management operations VTI requires. More recently, though an interface named 'J-VTI', the Java language can be used to implement user-defined access methods as well.

VTI Memory Structures

When the server initiates an operation using an access method—say, a scan of a set of remote data—it creates a couple of memory structures to store information relevant to the operation. References to these memory structures are passed between the various UDFs of the interface. Each function can use this information to make decisions about its own processing.

In addition to data elements that the server creates and populates, each of these structures has an element used to hold a pointer to a memory block that the access method UDFs define and use. This is similar in concept to the user-area in the MI_FPARAM structure, but it is slightly different in that user data can be passed between *different* UDFs. That is, a block of memory can be allocated in the am_beginscan that is subsequently passed into each call to the am_getnext function. This user-data area can be used to hold things like connection handles, buffers, position information, and so on. It may be read and modified by other UDFs later in the scan process and therefore needs to be allocated out of PER_COMMAND memory.

The MI_AM_TABLE_DESC structure is passed in as the only argument to almost all VTI functions. The exception is those functions dealing with the scan operation, which get the MI_AM_SCAN_DESC structure. And this contains a pointer to an appropriate MI_AM_TABLE_DESC in any case.

Several tables in the same schema can use the same user defined access method. Consequently, the information in the MI_AM_TABLE_DESC structure is specific to one table rather than one access method. An instance of this structure is created for each data operation such as CREATE, SCAN, INSERT, and so on. In Table 6–2, we present a list of this structure's most important elements and the VTI mechanisms used to interact with it.

Table 6–2. Elements and Attributes of MI_AM_TABLE_DESC Structure

Type and Name	Server API Calls Accessing the Element
mi_string * tableName	This string contains the name of the table defined to use the new primary access method. It is retrieved using the server API call: ```string *\nmi_tab_setname(MI_AM_TABLE_DESC * table).```
MI_ROW_DESC * rowDesc	This is a pointer to a descriptor for the ROW TYPE that the table has been created with. This row descriptor is used to correctly format a return value in the am_getnext function: ```MI_ROW_DESC *\nmi_tab_rowdesc (MI_AM_TABLE_DESC * table);.```
mi_string * amParam	This element contains the parameter that can be supplied when a table is created that uses the new access method. This is simply an unprocessed string so this is unsuitable for storing connection handles and so on. Rather, this structure is ideal for things such as the names of files, servers, databases, and tables that can be used by the VTI functions. This string is retrieved using this function: ```mi_string *\nmi_tab_am_param (\nMI_AM_TABLE_DESC * table).```

void * userData	This is a pointer to a block of memory that can be initialized when the table is opened in am_open. The userData element can be set using this function:
	```void\nmi_tab_setuserdata(MI_AM_TABLE_DESC *,\n void *);```
	and the reference can be got again using;
	```void *\nmi_tab_userdata(MI_AM_TABLE_DESC *);.```

The first UDFs in a VTI primary access method that gets called is the one assigned to the `am_create` role, which is called when a table is created. This is an opportunity for some "sanity checks" to ensure that the table has the right structure or that the external resource exists. Listing 6–4 illustrates what this UDF looks like for our File Access example. In it, the C code extracts from the structure passed in as the only argument a set of information that it checks.

```
21  /*
22  **    am_create <-> FA_create(MI_AM_TABLE_DESC *)
23  **
24  **      Called when ever a table is created, before
25  **      any queries can be run. am_create is a good
26  **      place to make checks to ensure that the setup
27  **      will not cause run-time errors.
28  **/
29  mi_integer
30  FA_create (
31  MI_AM_TABLE_DESC * tableDesc
32  )
33  {
34      MI_ROW_DESC           *    pRowDesc;
35      MI_TYPE_DESC          *    typeDesc;
36      mi_string             *    pchTypeName,
37                            *    pAmParam;
38      mi_integer               i, nFileHandle, nColCount;
39
40      /*
41      **  Get the table's am_param, and an MI_ROW_DESC
42      ** that describes the structure of the table.
43      **/
44      pAmParam=mi_tab_amparam(tableDesc);
45      pRowDesc=mi_tab_rowdesc(tableDesc);
46
47      /*
48      ** 1. Check that an am_params has been provided, and
49      **      check that the file to which it points can be
50      **      openned for the kinds of operations than VTI
51      **      wants to perform.
52      */
53      nFileHandle = FA_open_file ( pAmParam );
54      mi_file_close( nFileHandle );
55
56      /*
```

```
57      **  2.  Check that the types in the table are OK.  The
58      **      interface supports the built-in types, and
59      **      lvarchar.
60      */
61      nColCount = mi_column_count ( pRowDesc );
62      for(i=0;i<nColCount;i++)
63      {
64          typeDesc     = mi_column_typedesc(pRowDesc,i);
65          pchTypeName = mi_type_typename(typeDesc);
66          (void)FA_GetTypeNumber(pchTypeName);
67      }
68
69      return (MI_OK);
70      /* not reached */
71  }
```

Listing 6–4. *am_create Element of VTI Implementation*

On line 44 of Listing 6–4 the `am_param` specified as part of the CRE-
ATE TABLE statement is extracted from the `MI_AM_TABLE_DESC` structure. Later we will see how the table's creator specifies this parameter
value. Then on line 45 the structure of the table that has been created
using this access method is extracted. The two checks in this code illustrate how to use these structures.

Once a table has been opened and a scan over its data initiated the
server allocates a second memory structure that contains information relevant to the scan. This structure, called `MI_AM_SCAN_DESC`, is more complex than `MI_AM_TABLE_DESC`. It is passed into the VTI functions that
implement scan operations: `am_beginscan`, `am_getnext` and `am_end-
scan`. Listing 6–5 presents the implementation of an `am_beginscan` UDF
that extracts and uses data from the `MI_AM_SCAN_DESC` data structure.

```
123  /*
124  **  am_beginscan -> FA_beginscan(MI_AM_SCAN_DESC   *)
125  **
126  **  Having called the am_open function, VTI next
127  **  calls the am_beginscan function.
128  **
129  **  This is a symmetric operation to the am_endscan
130  **  call. Any resources that am_beginscan allocates,
131  **  am_endscan should free.
132  **
133  **  Also note the call to FA_rescan. FA_rescan may be
```

```
134   **   called multiple times in a query, when the data
135   **   being scanned is on the inner of the loop.
136   **
137   **/
138   mi_integer
139   FA_beginscan       (
140   MI_AM_SCAN_DESC    * scanDesc
141   )
142   {
143       MI_AM_TABLE_DESC      *    tableDesc;
144       FA_data_t             *    pScanData;
145
146       tableDesc=mi_scan_table(scanDesc);
147
148       pScanData=(FA_data_t *)mi_dalloc(sizeof(FA_data_t),
149                                           PER_COMMAND);
150
151       mi_scan_setuserdata(scanDesc, pScanData);
152
153       pScanData->nFileHandle=
154             FA_open_file( mi_tab_amparam(tableDesc));
155
156       pScanData->pConn = mi_open(NULL,NULL,NULL);
157       pScanData->pchScratch=mi_dalloc(FA_BLOCK_SIZE,,
158                                           PER_COMMAND);
159
160       return FA_rescan ( scanDesc );
161
162   }
```

Listing 6–5. *am_beginscan Element of VTI Implementation*

The UDF implementing the am_beginscan receives an
MI_AM_SCAN_DESC structure. MI_AM_SCAN_DESC contains a reference
to the MI_AM_TABLE_DESC created for the table operation, a reference
to a block of user data, and a special structure known as a *qualifier*.
Line 146 of Listing 6–5 illustrates how the MI_AM_TABLE_DESC structure is extracted from the argument. Line 147 allocates memory to
hold data being processed as part of the scan. On line 157 a larger,
unstructured block of memory is allocated. This is used to cache external data rather than read it into the ORDBMS one row at a time. The
open storage manager interface includes a number of functions, which
are described in Table 6–3, that get and set the contents of
MI_AM_SCAN_DESC.

Table 6-3. Elements of MI_AM_SCAN_DESC Structure

Element type and Name	Server API Calls Accessing the Element
MI_AM_QUAL_DESC * qual	This structure encapsulates all the information about the qualification passed into the scan from the query context. It is retrieved from the MI_AM_SCAN_DESC structure using ```\nMI_AM_QUAL_DESC *\nmi_scan_quals(\nMI_AM_SCAN_DESC * scanDesc).\n```
MI_AM_TABLE_DESC * tableScan	This is a data structure that contains information about the table that is being scanned. The userdata allocated in the am_open function can be accessed here. This structure is accessed using the call ```\nMI_AM_TABLE_DESC *\nmi_scan_table (\nMI_AM_SCAN_DESC * scanDesc).\n```
void * userData	This is a pointer to a block of memory that can be initialized when the scan is initiated in am_beginscan. The userData element can be set using the following VTI functions. ```\nvoid\n\nmi_scan_setuserdata(\n MI_AM_SCAN_DESC *,\n void *);,\n\n\nvoid *\nmi_scan_userdata(MI_AM_SCAN_DESC *);.\n```

The MI_AM_QUAL_DESC is the final structure VTI structure we describe in this tutorial. It is derived from the query context within which the scan operation was initiated, and all records that the scan returns need to "satisfy" this qualification. To see how MI_AM_QUAL_DESC works we turn to the last and usually most complex function in the access method: am_getnext. All of the rows returned by the VTI scan are returned by separate calls to this UDF, and this data must be returned as an MI_ROW structure that maps to the definition of the table.

am_getnext takes three arguments. The first of these is a pointer to the current scan's MI_AM_SCAN_DESC structure. The second is an MI_ROW pointer, and the function's return results are passed back to the ORDBMS by reference using this argument. That is, the UDF needs to construct a new MI_ROW instance based on the external data, and make this argument point to that newly assigned data structure before returning. Recall that an access method is used to define the "plumbing" that supports a table. The table's column structure needs to be reflected in the MI_ROW instance returned from am_getnext.

The final argument is used by other VTI calls. It identifies, again by reference, a "location" or an "address" where the data in the ROW TYPE can be found in the external source. For example, it might be a record number or a byte offset within an external file. If the OR-SQL query is an UPDATE or a DELETE the ORDBMS first scans the table and for each matching row calls the am_update or am_delete UDF to make the change, passing this address value into the UDF as the argument. Also, tables created with a user-defined access method can have conventional database indices built for them, and this identifier is the link between the internal index and its corresponding external data.

Listing 6–6 outlines what an am_getnext UDF might look like.

```
163   /*
164   **  am_getnext -> FA_getnext ( MI_AM_SCAN_DESC * ,
165   **                               MI_ROW *,
166   **                               mi_integer * )
167   **
168   **/
169   mi_integer
170   FA_getnext   (
171   MI_AM_SCAN_DESC  * scanDesc,
172   MI_ROW            ** retRow,
173   mi_integer          * retRowID
174   )
175   {
.  .  .
198   /*
199   ** Get the structures passed around between UDFs as
200   ** part of the VTI scan.
201   */
202
203   pScanData = mi_scan_userdata(scanDesc);
204   tableDesc = mi_scan_table(scanDesc);
205   qualDesc  = mi_scan_quals(scanDesc);
206
207   pRowDesc  = mi_tab_rowdesc(tableDesc);
208   nColumn   = mi_column_count(pRowDesc);
209
210   /* The Server API provides a set of interfaces for
211   ** building ROW TYPE instances from a vector of data
212   ** values. These two arrays -- which contain a set of
```

```
213   ** pointers to data and boolean values indicating
214   ** whether or not the attribute is NULL -- are used in
215   ** conjunction with an MI_ROW_DESC structure to create
216   ** the ROW TYPE being returned.
217   */
218   pDatum = mi_alloc(nColumn * sizeof(MI_DATUM));
219   pNulls = mi_alloc(nColumn * sizeof(mi_boolean));
220
. . .
234   while( STILL_HAVE_DATA )
235   {
236       /*
237       **  For each column in the ROW TYPE, get data from
238       ** the external source. In this example code I am
239       ** reading the data one byte at a time because of
240       ** the need to cope with caching data from the
241       ** external source.
242       */
243       for(j=0;j<nColumn;j++)
244       {
245         typeDesc    = mi_column_typedesc(pRowDesc,j);
246         pchTypeName = mi_type_typename(typeDesc);
247
248         pchBuffer = pchBufStart;
248         pchBuffer = pchBufStart;
. . .
          /*
          ** Read bytes of data from the external source
          ** into the pchBuffer, until you get to a
          ** delimiter.
          */
. . .
275       /*
276       ** Having gotten one column's data, use it to
277       ** figure out whether or not the value is NULL,
278       ** and construct a valid instance of the type
279       ** to fit into the ROW TYPE column's type.
280       */
281
282         *pchBuffer='\0';
283         if ( strlen(pchBuf) == 0)
284           pNulls[j] = MI_TRUE;
285         else
286           pNulls[j] = MI_FALSE;
287
```

```
288            switch(FA_GetTypeNumber(pchTypeName))
289            {
290              case LVARCHAR: /* lvarchar */
291              case VARCHAR:  /* varchar  */
292                pDatum[j] = mi_string_to_lvarchar(pchBuf);
293               break;
294              case MI_INT:   /* integer  */
295                pDatum[j] = atoi(pchBufStart);
296               break;
297              case MI_DEC:   /* decimal  */
298              {
299                pdecValue = mi_alloc(sizeof(dec_t));
300                if (deccvasc(pchBufStart,
301                             strlen(pchBufStart),
302                             pdecValue) != 0)
303                {
304                  mi_db_error_raise(NULL, MI_EXCEPTION,
305                       "Error: Bad decimal conversion.");
306                }
307                pDatum[j]=pdecValue;
308              }
309             break;
318           }
. . .
. . .      /*
. . .      ** Repeat for each required OR-SQL type.
. . .      */
333        }
. . .
. . .
339        /*
340        ** Having built the array of pointers to the data
341        ** in the row and an array of information about
342        ** about NULL status, create return ROW TYPE.
343        */
344        plocalRow = mi_row_create(pScanData->pConn,
345                                  pRowDesc,
346                                  pDatum,
347                                  pNulls);
348
349        /*
350        ** Finally, check the qualification against the
351        ** ROW TYPE. If the check determines that the
352        ** row does not match the qualification then
353        ** loop back to try the next row.
```

```
354        */
355        if ((qualDesc == NULL) ||
356          ((qualDesc != NULL) &&
357           (mi_eval_am_qual(plocalRow,qualDesc)==MI_TRUE)
358          ))
359        {
360           (*retRow) = plocalRow;
361           (*retRowID) = pScanData->nRowCount++;
362
363            return MI_ROWS;
364        }

    . . .

368     }
369  return MI_NO_MORE_RESULTS;
    }
```

Listing 6–6. *Skeleton of am_getnext Element of VTI Implementation*

There are three possible return values from this UDF:

- MI_ROWS. This means that the MI_ROW instance returned by the UDF is valid and correct. If the ORDBMS sees this return value, it merely calls the same UDF again to get the next row.
- MI_NO_MORE_RESULTS. This means that the scan is at its end. If the server sees this return result, it concludes that the scan is over and moves on to its next task (calling the am_endscan UDF or the am_close UDF).
- MI_ERROR. This return value indicates that an error was encountered. This causes the ORDBMS to abort the scan. However, the better way to do this is to use the mi_db_error_raise() SAPI call.

Caching data between invocations of each call to am_getnext is a useful technique when creating an efficient VTI interface. Reading remote data is a very expensive operation although this cost can be attributed more to the overhead of exchanging messages with the operating system than moving the data. By bringing in data a chunk at a time, caching it in memory between calls to am_getnext (line 203 of Listing 6–6 illustrates this), and then reading rows from the cached chunk, the overall scan can be made more efficient. This technique is used in the VTI example that accompanies this book.

Qualifications should be checked in am_getnext routine against a correctly formatted MI_ROW structure before it is returned. If the row does not satisfy the qualification, the row should not be returned.

Instead, the `am_getnext` should simply repeat its functionality getting the next candidate row, performing the qualification check, and so on. Only rows satisfying the predicate should be returned by `am_getnext`. Lines 355 through 357 of Listing 6–6 illustrate how to check the qualification against the `MI_ROW` before it is returned.

Sometimes the most run-time efficient way for a new access method to handle a qualifier is to pass it to the remote data source and deal with in the remote system, thereby minimizing the number of rows read into the ORDBMS. This technique is sometimes called "pushing" the predicate. However, if the predicate includes UDFs that are defined in the ORDBMS, then it is unlikely that they can be pushed to the external system. Refer to the IDS product documentation for more details.

Creating VTI User-Defined Functions

Although each of the functions has a specific argument list and a defined range of results is expected of it, the data structures involved are not part of the ORDBMS type system. To get around this, the ORDBMS allows functions to be declared with a generic `pointer` argument. Thus Listing 6–7 illustrates the correct `CREATE FUNCTION` syntax for the `am_create` and the `am_getnext` UDF.

```
--
CREATE FUNCTION FA_create( informix.pointer )
RETURNING INTEGER
WITH ( NOT VARIANT )
EXTERNAL NAME
"$INFORMIXDIR/extend/F_A/FileAccess.bld(FA_create)"
LANGUAGE C;
--
CREATE FUNCTION FA_getnext(informix.pointer,
                           informix.pointer,
                           OUT int)
RETURNING INTEGER
WITH ( NOT VARIANT )
EXTERNAL NAME
"$INFORMIXDIR/extend/F_A/FileAccess.bld(FA_getnext)"
LANGUAGE C;
```

Listing 6–7. *CREATE FUNCTION for VTI UDFs*

For `pointer` arguments the ORDBMS passes a pointer to a memory structure into the UDF. This only works because the rigid definition of VTI means that the ORDBMS knows what structures to pass into the UDF, and because each UDF understands what needs to be done with the structure passed to it. `pointer` arguments are a practice to be generally avoided.

Creating a New Access Method

These UDFs must be combined to create a new Access Method using the CREATE ACCESS METHOD data definition statement. In this statement developers can associate one of the VTI interface functions listed in Listing 6–2 with a UDF. In addition, a number of modifiers can be supplied which affect the way tables created using the new access method are handled by the ORDBMS. Listing 6–8 illustrates what the CREATE ACCESS METHOD statement looks like for a read only VTI implementation.

```
CREATE PRIMARY ACCESS_METHOD FileAccess(
        am_create      = FA_create,
        am_open        = FA_open,
        am_close       = FA_close,
        am_beginscan   = FA_beginscan,
        am_endscan     = FA_endscan,
        am_getnext     = FA_getnext,
        am_sptype      = "A"
);
```

Listing 6–8. *Creating a Primary Access Method Using the UDFs*

Primary access methods are data repositories. Secondary access methods are used to create indices. A secondary access method is implemented using VII. Access methods can be dropped using the DROP ACCESS METHOD command, as illustrated in Listing 6–9.

```
DROP ACCESS METHOD MyAccessMethod RESTRICT;
```

Listing 6–9. *Dropping a Primary Access Method*

Of course, if there are any tables in the database that employ the access method, the ORDBMS will generate an error, rather than allow the access method to be dropped. Lastly, access method definitions can be altered using an ALTER ACCESS METHOD statement.

Creating a Table Using the New Access Method

As part of the ORDBMS's CREATE TABLE syntax, a developer can specify that it uses a user-defined access method rather than the server's built-in storage manager. Tables created to use an extended access method can be partitioned, just as tables that use the default storage manager can. As part of the table's creation, the creator can supply a parameter that gets passed into the access method functions as part of the MI_AM_TABLE_DESC structure.

The variations on the CREATE TABLE syntax that allows a table to use a user-defined access method are illustrated in Listing 6–10. This table mimics the structure of the data file introduced in Listing 6–3.

```
CREATE TABLE Upcoming_Shows (
        Movie_Title     LVARCHAR       NOT NULL,
        Release_Year    INTEGER        NOT NULL,
        Cinema_Name     VARCHAR(32)    NOT NULL,
        Opens           DATE           NOT NULL,
        Closes          DATE           NOT NULL
) USING FileAccess (file="D:\tmp\Shows.unl");
```

Listing 6–10. *Creating a Table using a User-defined Primary Access Method.*

A table created in this way can be DROPPed and modified like any other table. However, if the table is to be ALTERed, the access method should be very careful to ensure that the return result from the am_get-next uses the mi_row_create call correctly. In general, ALTERing a table using a user defined access method is not a good idea.

The point of such an interface is that it allows developers to write OR-SQL queries like the one in Listing 6–11, which illustrates a check that can be performed on the load file before it is used to modify the contents of the Movies-R-Us database.

> *"Show me Upcoming_Shows for which there is no unambiguous Movie and unambiguous Cinema. This checks the integrity of the data."*

```
       SELECT *
         FROM Upcoming_Shows U
        WHERE NOT EXISTS ( SELECT M.Title, M.Release, COUNT(*)
                             FROM Movies M
                            WHERE M.Title = U.Movie::Title
                              AND YEAR(M.Release) = U.Release_Yr
                            GROUP BY M.Title, M.Release
                           HAVING COUNT(*) = 1 )
           OR NOT EXISTS (SELECT C.Name, COUNT(*)
                            FROM Cinemas C
                           WHERE M.Name = U.Cimema::Cinema_Name
        GROUP BY M.Title, M.Release
                          HAVING COUNT(*) = 1 );
```

Listing 6–11. *OR-SQL Query Over Table Created with User-Defined Access Method*

So far as the rest of OR-SQL is concerned there is no difference between data stored in an external location and accessed through a user-defined access method, and data stored within the ORDMS's own storage system. Of course, there will be performance differences. Internal data is subjected to transactional controls, and the ORDBMS's own algorithms are extremely efficient.

Writeable VTI Interfaces

VTI interfaces can write data too. Developing read/write access methods is, however, much more complex than read only interfaces, particularly where UPDATE and DELETE operations are desired. Listing 6–12 illustrates how the simplest of the write operations, am_insert, could be implemented.

```
404   /*
405   **  am_insert - FA_Insert ( MI_AM_TABLE_DESC * ,
406   **                            MI_ROW              * )
407   **
408   **    This function is called whenever a ROW is
409   **  inserted into the table. The function needs to
410   **  unravel the MI_ROW and add its data to the
411   **  non-DBMS Storage in whatever form that external
412   **  storage manager uses.
```

```
413   */
414   mi_integer
415   FA_insert (
416   MI_AM_TABLE_DESC * pTabDesc,
417   MI_ROW            * pRowData,
418   mi_integer        * nnewRowId
419   )
420   {
421      MI_ROW_DESC    *    pRowDesc;
422      MI_TYPE_DESC   *    pTypeDesc;
423      MI_DATUM       *    pDatum;
424      mi_string      *    pchTypeName,
425                     *    pchScratch;
426      mi_integer     i, nFileHandle, nColCount,
427                        nLen, nValue, nWriteLen;
428
429      pRowDesc = mi_tab_rowdesc(pTabDesc);
430
431      nFileHandle= FA_open_file(mi_tab_amparam(pTabDesc));
432      pchScratch  = mi_alloc( FA_PRINTSIZE );
433      (void) mi_file_seek(nFileHandle,0,MI_LO_SEEK_END);
434
435      nColCount = mi_column_count ( pRowDesc );
436      for(i=0;i<nColCount;i++)
437      {
438         pTypeDesc    = mi_column_typedesc(pRowDesc,i);
439         pchTypeName  = mi_type_typename(pTypeDesc);
440
441         switch(FA_GetTypeNumber(pchTypeName))
442         {
. . .
457            case 1: /* integer */
458               mi_value ( pRowData, i, &nValue, &nLen );
459               sprintf(pchScratch, "%d", nValue );
460             break;
. . .
. . .         /*
. . .         ** Symmetric logic in Listing 6-6 handles the
. . .         ** transformation of external data into ORDBMS
. . .         ** data type structures.
. . .         */
. . .
476         }
477         if ( i < (nColCount - 1))
478            strcat( pchScratch, "|" );
```

```
479
480         nWriteLen=strlen ( pchScratch);
481         if ((nLen=mi_file_write(nFileHandle,
482                                     pchScratch,
483                                     nWriteLen)
) != nWriteLen)
485           {
486             mi_db_error_raise(NULL, MI_EXCEPTION,
487                                 "Bad Write");
488             /* not reached */
489           }
490       }
491       mi_file_write ( nFileHandle, "\n",1);
492       mi_file_close ( nFileHandle );
493
494       return MI_OK;
}
```

Listing 6–12. am_insert Element of VTI Implementation

Readers familiar with OR-SQL usage will immediately detect that this is not a very efficient algorithm for sets of INSERT operations. It's implementation means that for each row added into the table the external file is opened and the new data appended. For correlated INSERT queries this implies significant overhead. Unfortunately there is no MI_AM_SCAN_DESC equivalent for insert operations. Single row inserts, however, work as efficiently as can be expected. Note also the complete lack of isolation logic in this example. Were two OR-SQL queries to simultaneously insert rows the outcome would be unpredictable.

In addition to providing the am_insert VTI interface UDF an additional line must be added to the CREATE ACCESS METHOD statement. This instructs the ORDBMS that INSERT, UPDATE and DELETE OR-SQL statements will be executed over tables using the new access method. Internally, the ORDBMS takes this as its cue to keep track of the integer row identifiers returned by the am_getnext for use in calls to am_update and am_delete. Listing 6–13 illustrates what this modified version of the CREATE ACCESS METHOD command looks like.

```
CREATE PRIMARY ACCESS_METHOD FileAccess(
    am_create       = FA_create,
    am_open         = FA_open,
    am_close        = FA_close,
```

```
am_beginscan   = FA_beginscan,
am_endscan     = FA_endscan,
am_rescan      = FA_rescan,
am_getnext     = FA_getnext,
                 AM_READWRITE,
am_insert      = FA_insert,
am_sptype      = "A"
);
```

Listing 6–13. *am_insert Element of VTI Implementation*

Alternatively, an ALTER ACCESS METHOD statement can accomplish the same objective.

Applications of VTI

The open storage manager changes the nature of how a DBMS can be used. Traditionally, it was always implicit in any discussion of DBMS functionality that the DBMS first and foremost provided data storage services. Developers created a table schema, loaded data into these tables, and used SQL to read and write the data. Everything that the DBMS could touch was stored within it, under its complete control.

For the most part, this is also the model that will be pursued by ORDBMSs too. But VTI subverts these assumptions because it requires developers to write queries that involve data that are not "stored" within the DBMS at all. In this section, we review some of the possibilities this presents.

Value Tables

A value table is simply a table of fixed values. Example of value tables might be tables that contain all the integers, or the results of some function. For example, one of the most useful VTI extensions is a table that contains all of the integers in a certain range. Such a table permits you to write loops in SQL or to rapidly populate tables with test data.

Custom Gateways

One of the biggest MIS challenges of the next few years will be the problem of legacy information systems. Put bluntly, the year 2000 crisis, as challenging as it was, is just one of a series of much more pernicious problems. For four decades, MIS shops have been busily building systems to meet expanding corporate demands for information management. As a result, the MIS landscape has become strewn with such "stove-pipe" systems. Typically, these systems have the following properties:

- They were implemented on hardware technology that is either no longer supported by the original vendor, or that is incredibly expensive to maintain.
- They were implemented with software technology that makes adapting the system to changing business circumstances very difficult. For example, it is frequently very difficult to separate the data from the application in such systems. The only thing that understands the way the data files are structured is the half-million lines of COBOL.
- They were implemented by programmers who are by now retired, dead, or in management.
- These systems are still mission critical. Upper management, quite reasonably, has zero tolerance for down-time and a terror of the risk associated with migration.

However, as we noted earlier, it is almost always good advice to use a packaged product rather than to try and build one. There are existing gateways to a wide range of legacy relational and mainframe systems. And often, live data exchange between the ORDBMS and the external data is unnecessary, so other technical strategies make more sense.

Summary

In this tutorial we have introduced the ORDBMS's open storage manager, also known as the Virtual Table Interface or VTI. The motivation for the open storage manager is to allow developers to extend the ORDBMS's data storage model with new access methods and data storage interfaces. Once implemented, these new interfaces can fulfill several functions. Most importantly they allow an external data source to be presented within the ORDBMS as a table that can be used in OR-SQL statements.

Glossary

Active Database Features: These are features of the ORDBMS, such as `TRIGGERS`, that allow you to specify automatic actions taken in response to certain actions, such as `INSERTS`, `UPDATES`, `DELETES`, and `SELECTs`, over schema objects.

Aggregate: An aggregate is a facility of the SQL query language that lets you compute a value from a set of values. For example, SQL supports aggregates such as `MIN()`, `MAX()`, and `AVG()`. In an ORDBMS, you can specify your own user-defined aggregates.

Applications: An application is an interrelated set of data-centric operations. An individual operation might be found in several applications. Usually the set of operations in an application corresponds to the tasks performed by a particular class of employee. Several applications address themselves to a central database.

BladeManager: This is a set of client tools that simplify the task of installing and managing bundles of related extensions from a commercial provider or from your own efforts as you develop your application.

Callbacks: This term can refer to SQL statements issued from within a user-defined routine extension. Callbacks use features of the SAPI to acquire connections to the database, to submit queries, and to manage return results.

Term used to refer to a style of error handling, in which you register a function to call back whenever the ORDBMS encounters a certain exception or error.

COLLECTION: COLLECTION is the name given to a group of non-first normal form column values, which are SET, MULTISET and LIST. A COLLECTION contains a collection of instances of a specified data type. Each kind of COLLECTION is distinguished by the rules it imposes on data values.

Database: A database in the context of ORDBMS technology is the set of shared resources (data, schema structure, integrity rules, object definitions, and common data processing operations) that represent a particular problem domain.

Database Identifier (Identifier): This is a string composed of ASCII characters ("a" to "Z"), digits ("0" to "9"), or the underscore character ("_"). Identifiers are used to name database objects such as types, functions, tables, columns, indices, databases, and so on. Note that an identifier cannot begin with a digit. In the 9.14 release of the ORDBMS, identifiers must be eight characters or less. In the IDS 2000 release, this restriction is removed and identifiers can be up to 128 characters.

DataBlade: "DataBlade" is a term with two, overlapping meanings. First, the term can refer to a commercial product, such as a bundle of software, documentation, and support for which a development organization pays. In other words, this is something you purchase. Alternatively, a DataBlade can be a group of semantically related extensions to the ORDBMS that are written to a specialist definition. In this sense, a DataBlade can encompass the specifics of a particular problem domain. Both meanings share the notion of a component-oriented software module that plugs into the ORDBMS and that is used to define schemas in queries, to enable communication, and so on. In other words, this is something you build. Both kinds must be installed into the ORDBMS to be useful.

DBDK: This acronym stands for DataBlade Developers Kit, which is a software package that uses a wizard-driven approach to generate code stubs for developers implementing extensions. DBDK generates C, Java, or COM source code outlines. SQL is used to create and test the new types, and scripts used by the Blade Manager infrastructure manage extensions within the ORDBMS.

DBMS: This acronym stands for DataBase Management System. A DBMS is a server software platform developers use to implement databases. Traditionally, RDBMS products provided transactional storage management facilities and a flexible data model for structuring and manipulating business data types. To this, an ORDBMS adds the ability to embed new object definitions within the relational schema framework.

Federated Database: In a federated database, access to data at several different sites is made available through a single system. The ORDBMS has several features that make access to extremely exotic data sources possible. (*See* VTI).

Gateway: Gateways are a form of DBMS middleware. They allow one DBMS instance to connect to another and to make the data in this second instance available within the first system as though it were local. Gateways are useful with an ORDBMS because they allow you to implement some aspects of a federated DBMS.

GIS: This acronym stands for Geographic Information Systems, which handles data related to mapping (cartography) and geography.

Host Language: This is a procedural language used to implement external programs. The most popular host languages today are C, C++, Java, and various 4GLs (fourth generation languages) such as Visual Basic and Powerbuilder. An important difference between an ORDBMS and traditional RDBMSs is that you can integrate procedural code written in a procedural host language into the ORDBMS. (*See* UDR)

IDS: This acronym stands for INFORMIX Dynamic Server. This is the name used thoughout this book to refer to the current release of the INFORMIX ORDBMS.

Integrity: Issues of data integrity focus on the data correctness in the ORDBMS schema. Correctness in an ORDBMS schema is the result of good table design (normalization), which is enhanced by declaring table and column constraints.

ITERATOR Function: This is a UDF returning a sequence of values. An iterator function can be thought of as a table whose records are calculated rather than stored.

Keys: A key is a column or set of columns that can be used to uniquely identify a row in a table. Often several such column sets, or candidate keys, exist for a table. Sometime, you can create an artificial, single column key called a surrogate key. One candidate key is selected to be the primary key for the table. Primary keys values are carried into other tables where they are used as foreign keys that refer (several) rows back to a single row in the original table.

LIST: A `LIST` is a `COLLECTION` in which each element of the list is numbered, such as in an array.

Location transparency: The idea behind location transparency is that in a distributed system, users issuing queries are unaware of how or where their query is actually processed. For example, in a distributed database of three nodes, a query submitted through a connection to just one node may be passed to another node, executed there, and the query result communicated back to the end user through the initial node's connection.

LVARCHAR: This structure is used to store variable length arrays of characters. The first four bytes of an lvarchar contain an integer number of bytes of data follow. You can store variable length arrays of binary data (which may contain zero bytes) in an lvarchar.

MULTISET: A `MULTISET` is an unrestricted `COLLECTION`. It can contain duplicates, and its members are not numbered.

MULTI-REPRESENTATIONAL Type: This is a kind of `OPAQUE type` that can be stored either on a page or in large object storage, depending on its size.

OPAQUE Type: An `OPAQUE TYPE` is an arbitrary C structures stored in the database. `OPAQUE TYPE` can be fixed length, variable length, large object, or multi-representational.

OR-SQL: This acronym stands for Object-Relational SQL. This is the version of SQL supported by the IDS product. It is a superset of SQL-92, and it implements most of the features described in SQL-3. However, it goes beyond these standards in several important respects. For instance, OR-SQL is less a complete language and more a set of structural rules. It is anticipated that each OR-SQL query will invoke user-defined extensions to accomplish some high-level data processing task.

OUT Parameter: This is the value returned by reference from a UDF. In addition to computing a return result, a UDF can compute other values and pass them back into the query by using an OUT parameter. These values are handled in the query as Statement of Local Variables (SLV).

Overloading: Overloading is a SQL feature in which several different functions might have the same name or SQL identifier. Overloaded functions are distinguished based on their entire signature, which is the combination of the function's name and its argument vector.

Parallelism: This is the techniques in which the ORDBMS decomposes a query into multiple internal subtasks, all of which execute simultaneously. This is useful for reducing response time for queries involving large data volumes.

Partitioning: This is the name given to techniques for scheduling the distribution of rows over different physical storage units. These techniques are needed to cope with large amounts of data and to enable query parallelism.

Polymorphism: This term is used when describing the behavior of queries involving table hierarchies. The term describes the way that different user-defined functions (which have the same name) can be applied over different tables in a hierarchy.

Privileges: Privileges relate to user permissions to perform various database operations, such as creating schema objects, queries over tables, and so on. Privileges are managed with the GRANT and REVOKE statements.

Problem Domain: This term refers to the real-world subject area addressed by an information system. (*See* UoD)

Relational Operators: These are procedures described as part of the theoretical relational model. Each operator takes one or two relations (tables, views, or `SELECT` queries) as input and then produces a relation as output.

ROW Type: A `ROW TYPE` is a kind of extended type. It is similar to a table in that it consists of a set of named, typed elements. Unlike other extended types, `ROW TYPES` can be used to define a table structure.

SBLOB: This acronym stands for Smart Binary Large OBject. Data objects too large to fit conveniently within a table's record length—32K—are handled using the SBLOB facilities. This involves storing the data in reserved locations and storing a handle or identifier in the table row. Within SAPI is a set of routines for opening SBLOB instances and accessing their contents.

Schema: This is a set of database objects, such as types, functions, tables, views, indices, and so on, that collectively describes the structure of the problem domain. A logical schema refers to the permanent or base tables and the views that rely on them.

Selectivity: This is the estimate of the proportion of rows in a table that match a certain predicate. These estimates are used in query planning. They are arrived at by gathering statistics on data in a column and then invoking a function to calculate the selectivity that is associated with the relevant user-defined function.

SET: A `SET` is a `COLLECTION` in which no two elements of the set can have the same value.

Signature: A user-defined function's signature consists of a combination of its name and its vector of arguments. By including the function's arguments as part of its semantic definition, the ORDBMS provides support for features such as overloading and polymorphism.

SQL: This acronym stands for Structured Query Language. SQL is "intergalactic database speak," which is the standard declarative data language used by generations of RDBMS products.

SQL-92: This acronym stands for the SQL language as standardized in 1992. This was the second major version of SQL; the first was SQL-86. SQL-92 has recently been superseded by SQL-3, which is also known as SQL-99.

SLV: This acronym stands for Statement of Local Variable, which is a technique used to cope with UDFs that return a value using an OUT parameter. The ORDBMS query processor allocates memory to hold the value to be returned "by reference" from the UDF and then it gives this variable a name that can be used to address the SLV in other parts of the query.

Statistics: Statistics, in the ORDBMS context, refers to information stored in the ORDBMS's system catalogs that reflects the distribution of data in a particular table's column. Statistics are combined with selectivity functions to estimate costs as part of query planning.

String: A string is a NULL (zero byte) terminated array of character bytes. By convention, C character arrays are always NULL terminated, and the C standard library calls (strlen, sprintf, and so on). Strings should be contrasted with lvarchar structures, which are also used to handle variable length arrays of bytes.

Strong Typing: This refers to the ORDBMS data model. In RDBMSs, the query interface supported a small set of data types, so the query language had to be weakly typed. Columns of different object types or problem domains had to be modeled with a simple type, which made it syntactically possible to ask semantically nonsensical questions. Because of its extensible data model, the ORDBMS enforces strong typing, which means that the syntax and semantics of queries are tied more closely.

Surrogate Key: This is the artificial primary key. It is useful when the candidate keys are long or too volatile and is implemented in the IDS product using the `SERIAL` and `SERIAL8` data types.

System Catalogs: This is a schema of tables maintained by the ORDBMS that contains information about user database objects. The ORDBMS populates system catalogs from information in `CREATE` statements that define the schema.

Transaction: The transaction concept refers to certain quality assurance guarantees supplied by the ORDBMS. The transaction guarantee ensures that every interaction with the ORDBMS complies with what are known as the ACID properties: Atomicity, Consistency, Isolation, and Durability.

UoD: This acronym stands for Universe of Discourse, which refers to the subject area modeled by an information system. In our example, the Movies-R-Us Web site is our UoD. All activities that relate to the site are said to be part of the UoD. (*See* Problem Domain)

URL: This acronym stands for Universal Resource Locator, which is the address or handle to a file or resource located on an intranet or on the Internet.

UDR: This acronym stands for User Defined Routine, which is a fragment of a procedural program, such as a C function, a Java method, or an SPL routine, that is integrated into the server. UDRs represent the fundamental unit of database extensibility.

VTI: This acronym stands for Virtual Table Interface, which allows developers to make data stored externally to the DBMS available as though it were an internal table. To use VTI, you combine several user-defined routines into a new access method. Then you can create tables using this access method. When you create tables in this manner, queries over these tables use the VTI routines, instead of the ORDBMS's storage manager, to get the data.

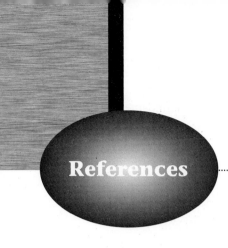

References

Abiteboul, Serge, Richard Hull, and Victor Vianu. *Foundations of Databases*. Menlo Park, California: Addison-Wesley, 1995.

Adriaans, Pieter, and Dolf Zantinge. *Data Mining*. Menlo Park, California: Addison-Wesley, 1996.

Blaser, A., ed. *Database Systems of the 90s*. Berlin: Springer-Verlag, 1990.

Brodie, M., and M. Stonebraker. *Migrating Legacy Systems*. San Francisco, California: Morgan Kaufmann, 1995.

Camps, R. "Domains, relations and religious wars." *Proceedings on Database Systems*. Association of Computer Machinery, 1997.

Carey, Michael J., and David J. DeWitt. "Of objects and databases: A decade of turmoil." In *Proceedings of the 22nd International Conference on Very Large Databases*. Mumbia (Bombay), India: 1996.

Cattrell, R. G. G., ed. *The Object Database Standard ODMG-93*. San Francisco, California: Morgan Kauffmann, 1993.

Chamberlain, Don. *Using the New DB2*. San Francisco, California: Morgan Kaufmann, 1996.

Chandler, David M. *Running a Perfect Web Site*. Que Corporation, 1995.

Chen, P. P. "The entity-relationship model: towards a unified view of data." *ACM Transactions on Database Systems* 1:1 (1977): 9–36.

Connolly, Thomas, Carolyn Begg, and Anne Strachan. *Database Systems A Practical Approach to Design, Implementation and Management*. Menlo Park, California: Addison-Wesley, 1996.

Coad, Peter, and Edward Yourdon. *Object-Oriented Analysis, Second Edition*. Englewood Cliffs, New Jersey: Prentice Hall, 1991.

Coad, Peter, and Edward Yourdon. *Object-Oriented Design*. Englewood Cliffs, New Jersey: Prentice Hall Inc., 1991.

Cortada, James W. *TQM for Information Systems Management*. San Francisco, California: McGraw-Hill, 1995.

Date, C. J. *Relational Database Writings 1991–7911994*. Menlo Park, California: Addison-Wesley, 1995.

Date, C. J., and Hugh Darwen. *Foundations for Object/Relational Databases: The Third Manifesto*. Menlo Park, California: Addison-Wesley, 1998.

Date, C. J., and Hugh Darwen. *A Guide to the SQL Standard Third Edition*. Menlo Park, California: Addison-Wesley, 1994.

Date, C. J., and Hugh Darwen. *Relational Database Writings 1989–1991*. Menlo Park, California: Addison-Wesley, 1992.

Derr, Kurt W. *Applying OMT: A Practical Guide to Using the Object Modeling Technique*. New York: SIGS Books, 1995.

Fleming, Candace C., and Barbara von Halle. *Handbook of Relational Database Design*. Menlo Park, California: Addison-Wesley, 1989.

Freytag, Johann Christoph, David Maier, and Gottfried Vossen. *Query Processing for Advanced Database Systems*. San Mateo, California: Morgan Kaufmann, 1994.

Gray, Jim et al., "Data cube: A relational aggregation operator generalizing group-by, cross-tab and sub-totals." *Microsoft Technical Report MSR-TR-95-22*. Redmond, Washington: Microsoft Research, 1995.

Gose, Earl, Richard Johnsonbaugh, and Steve Jost. *Pattern Recognition and Image Analysis*. Upper Saddle River, New Jersey: Prentice Hall, 1996.

Haderle, Donald J. "Database role in information systens: The evolution of database technology and its impact on the enterprise information system." Reprinted in Blaser, A., ed. *Database Systems of the 90s*. New York: Springer-Verlag, 1991.

Hahn, Harley, and Rick Stout. *The Internet Complete Reference*. Berkeley, California: Osborne McGraw-Hill, 1994.

Haplin, Terry. *Conceptual Schema and Relational Database Design: Second Edition*. Sydney, Australia: Prentice Hall Australia, 1995.

Heller, Philip, Simon Roberts, Peter Seymour, and Tom McGinn. *Java 1.1 Developer's Handbook*. Alameda, California: Sybex Inc., 1998.

Kent, William. "A simple guide to five normal forms in relational database theory." *Communications of the ACM* 26:2 (1983).

Kim, Won. "Bringing object-relational down to earth." In *Database Programming and Design.* July 1997.

Kim, Won, ed. *Modern Database Systems: The Object Model, Interoperability and Beyond.* Menlo Park, California: Addison-Wesley, 1995.

Knuth, Don. *The Art of Computer Programming, Volume 3: Searching and Sorting.* Menlo Park, California: Addison-Wesley, 1973.

van Leeuwen, J. *Handbook of Theoretical of Computer Science.* Cambridge, Massachusetts: The MIT Press, 1994.

Loomis, Mary. *Object Databases: The Essentials.* Menlo Park, California: Addison-Wesley, 1995.

Lu, Hongjun, Beng-Chin Ooi, and Kian-Lee Tan, eds. *Query Processing in Parallel Relational Database Systems.* Los Alamitos, California: IEEE Computer Society Press, 1994.

Mannila, Heikki, and Raiha Kari-Jouko. *The Design of Relational Databases.* Menlo Park, California: Addison-Wesley, 1992.

Muller, Pierre-Alain. *Instant UML.* Birmingham, UK: Wrox Press Ltd., 1997.

Rao, Bindu R. *Object-Oriented Databases: Technology, Applications and Products.* San Francisco, California: McGraw-Hill, 1994.

Russell, Bertrand. *Introduction to Mathematical Philosophy.* London: Macmillan, 1919.

Ryan, Nick, and Dan Smith. *Database Systems Engineering.* Belmont, California: Thomson Computer Press, 1995.

Silberschatz, Avi et al. "Database research: Achievements and opportunities into the 21st century." In *Proceedings on Database Systems* (Sept 1996).

Simon, Alan R. *Strategic Database Technology: Management for the Year 2000.* San Francisco, California: Morgan Kaufmann, 1995.

Stonebraker, M. *Object-Relational DBMSs: The Next Great Wave.* San Francisco, California: Morgan Kaufmann, 1995.

Strassmann, Paul A. *The Politics of Information Management.* New Canaan, Connecticut: The Information Economics Press, 1995.

Subrahmanian, V. S., and Sushil Jajodia, eds. *Multimedia Database Systems: Issues and Research Directions*. Berlin: Springer-Verlag, 1996.

Taylor, David. *Object-Oriented Technology: A Manager's Guide*. Menlo Park, California: Addison-Wesley, 1990.

Teorey, Toby. J. *Database Modeling and Design: The Fundamental Principles*. San Francisco, California: Morgan Kaufmann, 1990.

Ullman, Jeffrey. *Principles of Database and Knowledge-Base Systems*. Rockville, Maryland: Computer Science Press, 1988.

Vinoski, Steve. "CORBA: Integrating diverse applications within distributed heterogeneous environments." New York: IEEE, 1996.

Widon, Jennifer, and Stefano Ceri, eds. *Active Database Systems: Triggers and Rules for Advanced Database Processing*. San Francisco, California: Morgan Kaufmann, 1996.

Zaniolo, Carlo et al., *Advanced Database Systems*. San Francisco, California: Morgan Kaufmann, 1997.

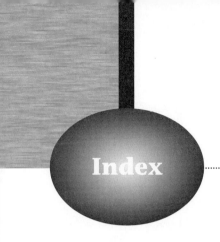

Index

Client Application Programming
Interfaces 26, 443–446
Client/Server Architectures 447
CLOB 217
COLLECTION 16, 49, 59–61,
224–231, 269
and Bulk Data Loading 267
and Data Modeling 560,
644–645
and LIST 225
and MULTISET 168
and SET 225
as data source in OR-SQL
SELECT 126, 141,
164–168, 350
as result of User-Defined
Aggregate 344–345, 674
ESQL/C and client
representation
examples of 58, 171, 228
in 'C' User-Defined Function
704, 712, 726–730
versus normalization
648–650
Columns 48
COMMIT WORK 196
COMMUTATOR 312–315
compare(). *See* Support
Functions, compare()
Completeness (of information
system) 528
Components. *See* object–oriented data modeling
Conceptual Model 531–533, 537
merging conceptual views
623–625
transform to logical model
625–639
Consistency of information
system 528
Constraints Administering 80
Constraints 72–84, 546–547
CHECK 74, 87
DEFAULT 74
NOT NULL 73
PRIMARY KEY 77–78,
545–546, 626–627
Referential Integrity. *See*
Referential Integrity

TABLE Constraints and ROW
TYPE 75
UNIQUE 78, 545
Constructor Functions for ROW
TYPE 249
Constructor Functions 573. *See
also* ROW TYPE, user-
defined functions
CONTINUE 328, 396
convex hull 344
Correctness (of information
system) 528
Correlated Queries 173, 178,
180–182
CREATE ACCESS METHOD 762,
776, 780–781
CREATE AGGREGATE 347
CREATE FUNCTION examples of
19, 209, 228–230, 242, 250,
252–253, 281, 300
CREATE FUNCTION 299–314
CREATE ROW TYPE 246
CREATE SYNONYM 430
CREATE TABLE 66–70
and Virtual Table Interface
768, 777
examples of 5, 6, 9, 30, 32,
67–69, 72–79, 82, 83, 88,
103–104, 201, 216, 244,
274, 281, 283
schema guidelines 632–633
Temporary Tables 71–72
CREATE TRIGGER 404–417
CREATE TYPE examples of 19,
237–238, 247, 257–258
CURSOR 140, 463–464
CURSOR STABILITY 195

D

Data Definition Language 65
Data Flow Diagrams 588
Data Loading 174
and User-Defined Types 266
Data Manipulation Language
using DML 138–140
Data Manipulation Language
65, 123

Data Model
general definition of 535
data pages 111
Data Sizing 592–593
Data Source(s) 141, 150,
164–168
and Other SELECT Queries
167, 676
and Table Aliases 145
and Table Inheritance
161–162
Data Types
Built-in Data Types 215–223
choosing between
mechanisms 601
COLLECTION. *See*
COLLECTION
DISTINCT. *See* DISTINCT TYPE
extensibility 7
OPAQUE. *See* OPAQUE TYPE
overview of different types
214, 600
ROW. *See* ROW TYPE
User-Defined. *See also* User-
Defined Types
data warehousing 157
Database Business Rules 420
DataBase Management Systems
(DBMS) 2
Database Security 105–108
DataBase Stored Procedure. *See*
Stored Procedure
Database Tuning 536
DataBlade Developers Kit 300,
335, 359
DataBlade Developers Kit and
testing type extensions
656–658
DataBlades 17, 213, 271–288
DataBlades 'C' header files for
Client Programs 452
DataBlades in OR analysis and
design 615–616
DATE (SQL–92 Type) examples
of 142
DATE and DATETIME 217
DBINFO() 399–400
Deadlocks 198–199
DECIMAL 216

DEFAULT Constraint. *See*
    Constraints, DEFAULT
DEFINE SPL Keyword 389
DELETE Query 179–181
DELETE Query examples of 25
DESCRIPTOR 477
Digital Asset Management
    273–280
DISTINCT (in SELECT Queries)
    127, 148, 579
DISTINCT TYPE 68, 239–245,
    269, 600, 601, 604–607
    and User-Defined Function
        resolution 337–338
    argument to 'C' User-Defined
        Function 703
    for Java class 368
Distributed Database
    Functionality AKA:
    INFORMIX Star 422–431
Divide (Type, INTEGER) 314
Documentation for User-Defined
    Functions 326–328
Domain 52, 158, 203, 558, 560
DOUBLE PRECISION 216
DROP ACCESS METHOD 776
DROP FUNCTION 351
DROP PROCEDURE 402
DROP TABLE 93
DROP TRIGGER 418
DROP TYPE 238
Dyadic Operators (LessThan,
    Equal, etc.) 313, 301, 303,
    306, 308, 312–316
    dynamic content 515
    dynamic linking 689
    efficiency of information sys-
        tem 528
Embedded SQL in C. *See* ESQL/C
    encapsulation 207, 562
Entity 539–541
    describing an entity 542,
        554, 626, 628, 629–632
    diagram examples 543, 547
    strong and weak entities 541
    transform to tables 626–639

using UML Class Diagrams
    570–571
Entity–Relationship Model
    example of derivation
    553–560
Entity–Relationship Model 534,
    539–560
enumeration pattern of user-
    defined type 565
Equal. *See* dyadic operators
    equi–join 132
ESQL/C 444, 451–483
    ALLOCATE and DEALLO-
        CATE 467–468
    communication layer 481
    database connections
        456–458
    dynamic query management
        473–478
    embedding directives
        453–454
    embedding SQL statements
        458–460
    error and exception han-
        dling 478–481
    examples of 30–31, 197, 387,
        453, 459, 463, 465–480
    return results 462–478
EXCEPTION 328
EXEC SQL ESQL/C Directive 453
EXECUTE FUNCTION and PRO-
    CEDURE 139, 336–340,
    380–383, 386–388
EXECUTEANYWHERE 429
EXISTS, and NOT EXISTS 187
EXIT 328, 397
    expensive functions. *See*
        User-Defined Functions,
        expensive functions
    expressions OR-SQL
        extensions 572
    eXtensible Markup Language
        444, 513
    extents 112
    external symbol name 302

F

FETCH 463
FileToLO. *See* Large Object Data
    Management
First Normal Form 644–645
    flexibility (of information
        system) 528
FLOAT 216
FOREACH–END FOREACH
    328–330, 393–394
FOREIGN KEY. *See* Referential
    Integrity Constraints
FOR–END FOR 328, 394–396
Function Dependencies 644
Function Manager 297–298
FUNCTION verses PROCEDURE
    291–292
Functional Indices 100–101

G

Gateways 438–441, 758
    generating random data
        592, 662–663
Geographic Information
    Systems 204, 283–284
GET DIAGNOSTICS 481
GRANT (and REVOKE) 106–108,
    266, 351, 401–402
GROUP BY. *See* AGGREGATE
    and GROUP BY

H

HANDLESNULL 310–311, 362
    has_a relationships. *See*
        Relationships
HelloWorld() User-defined
    function 686–687
High Availability 435
Higher Normal Forms 648
Histograms 318
    host language 139, 443
HTML 444, 513–514
    hyperlinks 514

identifiers and Distributed
Database Identifiers 424
HTML data type 520

I

Identity and PRIMARY KEY/
FOREIGN KEY 84
Identity and Reference 61
Identity object–identity
212–213, 544
IDS Architecture 293–299
IF–THEN–ELIF–ELSE 328,
390–392
ifx_lo_t 470–471
ifx_load_module() and
ifx_unload_module() 332
impedance mismatch 512
IMPLICIT and EXPLICIT
Casts 234
Index. *See* Indices
Indices 98–101, 287
Information System Architectures
440–441, 446–451
Inheritance
and type inheritance
567–568
and User-defined Functions
252–255
Inheritance Entity Modeling
547–549
Inheritance ROW TYPE
Inheritance 210–212,
250–251
Inheritance Table Inheritance
15, 62, 85–88, 163,
629–630
and INSERT, UPDATE,
DELETE 162
and SELECT queries 159
examples 86
Inheritance transforming inher-
iting entities to tables
629–630
INSERT Query, examples of 11,
17, 26, 172–174, 220, 262,
276, 286
INSERT Query 14, 170–175
install_jar() 301, 33, 360

INTEGER and INT8 216
Interfaces (interface methods)
and object–modeling
562–563, 569, 572–573
Interfaces (interface methods)
public and private 567
INTERVAL 217
is_a relationships. *See*
Inheritance
Isolation Levels defined 194–195
Iterators. *See* User-Defined
Function, Iterators

J

'jar' file. *See* Java
Java and User-Defined
Functions 291, 297, 301,
326, 333–334, 361–374
Java and User-Defined Types 19,
600, 601, 612–613
Java developing Java extensions
355–361
Java DataBase Connectivity API
355, 388, 444, 483–512
Java DataBase Connectivity API
connections
java.sql.Connection 487–490
Java DataBase Connectivity API
data type management
java.sql.Types 504–511
Java DataBase Connectivity API
diagrammatic overview 493
Java DataBase Connectivity API
dynamic queries
java.sql.ResultSetMetaData
492–493
Java DataBase Connectivity API
examples of 486, 488–489,
496–500
Java DataBase Connectivity API
handling query results
java.sql.ResultSet 491,
501–504
Java DataBase Connectivity API
prepared queries
java.sql.PreparedStatement
496–498
Java DataBase Connectivity API
queries

sql.java.Statement 490–501
Java DataBase Connectivity API
setting transaction state
489–490
Java DataBase Connectivity API
types of JDBC driver
485–486
JDBC. *See* Java DataBase
Connectivity API
join 130–135, 182–184

K

Keys entity to table 626–627
Keys in entity diagrams
543–544, 557–558
Keys 48

L

Large Object Data Management
41, 103, 201–202
and Bulk Data Load 267
and 'C' User-Defined
Functions 750–752
and ESQL/C 469–472
and JDBC 508–510
client 'C' API for accessing
471–472
Large Object Handles 41,
261–263
LessThan. *See* dyadic operators
LET SPL Keyword
linking external libraries
297–298, 332
LIST. *See* COLLECTION, LIST
location transparency 424
Lock Mode and SET LOCK
MODE 195–196
locking 199–200
LOCopy. *See* Large Object Data
Management
LOFromFile. *See* Large Object
Data Management
logging 199
Logical Design 535, 639–656
Logical Expressions 572,
577–579
Logical Key 544, 545

LICENSE AGREEMENT AND LIMITED WARRANTY

READ THE FOLLOWING TERMS AND CONDITIONS CAREFULLY BEFORE OPENING THIS SOFTWARE MEDIA PACKAGE. THIS LEGAL DOCUMENT IS AN AGREEMENT BETWEEN YOU AND PRENTICE-HALL, INC. (THE "COMPANY"). BY OPENING THIS SEALED SOFTWARE MEDIA PACKAGE, YOU ARE AGREEING TO BE BOUND BY THESE TERMS AND CONDITIONS. IF YOU DO NOT AGREE WITH THESE TERMS AND CONDITIONS, DO NOT OPEN THE SOFT- WARE MEDIA PACKAGE. PROMPTLY RETURN THE UNOPENED SOFTWARE MEDIA PACKAGE AND ALL ACCOMPANYING ITEMS TO THE PLACE YOU OBTAINED THEM FOR A FULL REFUND OF ANY SUMS YOU HAVE PAID.

1. **GRANT OF LICENSE:** In consideration of your payment of the license fee, which is part of the price you paid for this product, and your agreement to abide by the terms and conditions of this Agreement, the Company grants to you a nonexclusive right to use and display the copy of the enclosed software program (hereinafter the "SOFTWARE") on a single computer (i.e., with a single CPU) at a single location so long as you comply with the terms of this Agreement. The Company reserves all rights not expressly granted to you under this Agreement.

2. **OWNERSHIP OF SOFTWARE:** You own only the magnetic or physical media (the enclosed software media) on which the SOFTWARE is recorded or fixed, but the Company retains all the rights, title, and ownership to the SOFTWARE recorded on the original software media copy(ies) and all subsequent copies of the SOFTWARE, regardless of the form or media on which the original or other copies may exist. This license is not a sale of the original SOFTWARE or any copy to you.

3. **COPY RESTRICTIONS:** This SOFTWARE and the accompanying printed materials and user manual (the "Documentation") are the subject of copyright. You may not copy the Documentation or the SOFTWARE, except that you may make a single copy of the SOFTWARE for backup or archival purposes only. You may be held legally responsible for any copying or copyright infringement which is caused or encouraged by your failure to abide by the terms of this restriction.

4. **USE RESTRICTIONS:** You may not network the SOFTWARE or otherwise use it on more than one computer or computer terminal at the same time. You may physically transfer the SOFTWARE from one computer to another provided that the SOFTWARE is used on only one computer at a time. You may not distribute copies of the SOFTWARE or Documentation to others. You may not reverse engineer, disassemble, decompile, modify, adapt, translate, or create derivative works based on the SOFTWARE or the Documentation without the prior written consent of the Company.

5. **TRANSFER RESTRICTIONS:** The enclosed SOFTWARE is licensed only to you and may not be transferred to any one else without the prior written consent of the Company. Any unauthorized transfer of the SOFTWARE shall result in the immediate termination of this Agreement.

6. **TERMINATION:** This license is effective until terminated. This license will terminate automatically without notice from the Company and become null and void if you fail to comply with any provisions or limitations of this license. Upon termination, you shall destroy the Documentation and all copies of the SOFTWARE. All provisions of this Agreement as to warranties, limitation of liability, remedies or damages, and our ownership rights shall survive termination.

7. **MISCELLANEOUS:** This Agreement shall be construed in accordance with the laws of the United States of America and the State of New York and shall benefit the Company, its affiliates, and assignees.

8. **LIMITED WARRANTY AND DISCLAIMER OF WARRANTY:** The Company warrants that the SOFTWARE, when properly used in accordance with the Documentation, will operate in substantial conformity with the description of the SOFTWARE set forth in the Documentation. The Company does not

warrant that the SOFTWARE will meet your requirements or that the operation of the SOFTWARE w
uninterrupted or error-free. The Company warrants that the media on which the SOFTWARE is deliv
shall be free from defects in materials and workmanship under normal use for a period of thirty (30) da
from the date of your purchase. Your only remedy and the Company's only obligation under these limite
warranties is, at the Company's option, return of the warranted item for a refund of any amounts paid by you
or replacement of the item. Any replacement of SOFTWARE or media under the warranties shall not extend
the original warranty period. The limited warranty set forth above shall not apply to any SOFTWARE which
the Company determines in good faith has been subject to misuse, neglect, improper installation, repair,
alteration, or damage by you. EXCEPT FOR THE EXPRESSED WARRANTIES SET FORTH ABOVE,
THE COMPANY DISCLAIMS ALL WARRANTIES, EXPRESS OR IMPLIED, INCLUDING WITHOUT
LIMITATION, THE IMPLIED WARRANTIES OF MERCHANTABILITY AND FITNESS FOR A PAR-
TICULAR PURPOSE. EXCEPT FOR THE EXPRESS WARRANTY SET FORTH ABOVE, THE COM-
PANY DOES NOT WARRANT, GUARANTEE, OR MAKE ANY REPRESENTATION REGARDING
THE USE OR THE RESULTS OF THE USE OF THE SOFTWARE IN TERMS OF ITS CORRECTNESS,
ACCURACY, RELIABILITY, CURRENTNESS, OR OTHERWISE.

IN NO EVENT, SHALL THE COMPANY OR ITS EMPLOYEES, AGENTS, SUPPLIERS,
OR CONTRACTORS BE LIABLE FOR ANY INCIDENTAL, INDIRECT, SPECIAL, OR CONSEQUEN-
TIAL DAMAGES ARISING OUT OF OR IN CONNECTION WITH THE LICENSE GRANTED UNDER
THIS AGREEMENT, OR FOR LOSS OF USE, LOSS OF DATA, LOSS OF INCOME OR PROFIT, OR
OTHER LOSSES, SUSTAINED AS A RESULT OF INJURY TO ANY PERSON, OR LOSS OF OR DAM-
AGE TO PROPERTY, OR CLAIMS OF THIRD PARTIES, EVEN IF THE COMPANY OR AN AUTHO-
RIZED REPRESENTATIVE OF THE COMPANY HAS BEEN ADVISED OF THE POSSIBILITY OF
SUCH DAMAGES. IN NO EVENT SHALL LIABILITY OF THE COMPANY FOR DAMAGES WITH
RESPECT TO THE SOFTWARE EXCEED THE AMOUNTS ACTUALLY PAID BY YOU, IF ANY, FOR
THE SOFTWARE.

SOME JURISDICTIONS DO NOT ALLOW THE LIMITATION OF IMPLIED WARRAN-
TIES OR LIABILITY FOR INCIDENTAL, INDIRECT, SPECIAL, OR CONSEQUENTIAL DAMAGES,
SO THE ABOVE LIMITATIONS MAY NOT ALWAYS APPLY. THE WARRANTIES IN THIS AGREE-
MENT GIVE YOU SPECIFIC LEGAL RIGHTS AND YOU MAY ALSO HAVE OTHER RIGHTS
WHICH VARY IN ACCORDANCE WITH LOCAL LAW.

ACKNOWLEDGMENT

YOU ACKNOWLEDGE THAT YOU HAVE READ THIS AGREEMENT, UNDERSTAND IT,
AND AGREE TO BE BOUND BY ITS TERMS AND CONDITIONS. YOU ALSO AGREE THAT THIS
AGREEMENT IS THE COMPLETE AND EXCLUSIVE STATEMENT OF THE AGREEMENT
BETWEEN YOU AND THE COMPANY AND SUPERSEDES ALL PROPOSALS OR PRIOR AGREE-
MENTS, ORAL, OR WRITTEN, AND ANY OTHER COMMUNICATIONS BETWEEN YOU AND THE
COMPANY OR ANY REPRESENTATIVE OF THE COMPANY RELATING TO THE SUBJECT MAT-
TER OF THIS AGREEMENT.

Should you have any questions concerning this Agreement or if you wish to contact the Company for any reason, please contact in writing at the address below.

Robin Short
Prentice Hall PTR
One Lake Street
Upper Saddle River, New Jersey 07458

About the CD

This CD contains a large body of implementation examples used to illustrate different aspects of ORDBMS technology in the book. The purpose of this CD is to give readers a body of sample code to read and use as a foundation for their own development. Further details regarding setup and installation are located on the README file on the CD.

Directory Contents

./Source This directory contains the OR-SQL source scripts to create the Movies-R-Us database schema.

./Examples In each of the book's chapters, there is a list of example OR-SQL or host language code. Listings are broken out by Chapter or Tutorial.

./extend In this directory there is a large set of "BladeLet" implementations.

System Requirements

This CD was created on the Microsoft Windows NT® operation system. It's contents, however, are useful across any of the operating systems on which the INFORMIX IDS ORDBMS product can be installed.

Technical Support

Prentice Hall does not offer technical support for this CD-ROM. However, if there is a problem with the media, you may obtain a replacement copy by emailing us with your problem at:

disc_exchange@prenhall.com